MODERN HUMAN RELATIONS AT WORK

FOURTH EDITION

MODERN HUMAN RELATIONS AT WORK

FOURTH EDITION

RICHARD M. HODGETTS
FLORIDA INTERNATIONAL UNIVERSITY

THE DRYDEN PRESS

CHICAGO   FORT WORTH   SAN FRANCISCO   PHILADELPHIA
MONTREAL   TORONTO   LONDON   SYDNEY   TOKYO

ACQUISITIONS EDITOR: ROBERT GEMIN
DEVELOPMENTAL EDITOR: PENNY GAFFNEY
PROJECT EDITOR: PAULA DEMPSEY
ART AND DESIGN MANAGER: JEANNE CALABRESE
PRODUCTION MANAGER: BARB BAHNSEN
DIRECTOR OF EDITING, DESIGN, AND PRODUCTION: JANE PERKINS

TEXT AND COVER DESIGNER: NANCY JOHNSON
COPY EDITOR: HOLLY CRAWFORD
COMPOSITOR: G&S TYPESETTERS, INC.
TEXT TYPE: 10/12 NEW BASKERVILLE

LIBRARY OF CONGRESS CATALOGING-IN-PUBLICATION DATA

HODGETTS, RICHARD.
    MODERN HUMAN RELATIONS AT WORK / RICHARD M. HODGETTS—4TH ED.
        P. CM.
    INCLUDES BIBLIOGRAPHICAL REFERENCES AND INDEX.
    ISBN 0-03-030692-2
        1. PERSONNEL MANAGEMENT. 2. ORGANIZATIONAL BEHAVIOR. I. TITLE.
HF5549.H519 1990
658.4—DC20   89-1424
                                                                                    CIP

PRINTED IN THE UNITED STATES OF AMERICA
 01-016-98765432
COPYRIGHT © 1990, 1987, 1984, 1980 BY THE DRYDEN PRESS, A DIVISION OF
HOLT, RINEHART AND WINSTON, INC.

ADDRESS ORDERS:
THE DRYDEN PRESS
ORLANDO, FLORIDA 32887

ADDRESS EDITORIAL CORRESPONDENCE:
THE DRYDEN PRESS
908 N. ELM ST.
HINSDALE, IL 60521

THE DRYDEN PRESS
HOLT, RINEHART AND WINSTON
SAUNDERS COLLEGE PUBLISHING

COVER PHOTO: © 1989 CHARLES BECK, BIRMINGHAM, ALABAMA.

BACKGROUND IMAGE SOURCE: KOHN PEDERSEN FOX/PERKINS & WILL, ASSOCIATED
ARCHITECTS.

THE PALMER GROUP LTD., DEVELOPERS.

TO SARA AND EMILIO

THE DRYDEN PRESS SERIES IN MANAGEMENT

PREFACE

In writing the fourth edition of *Modern Human Relations at Work,* I have attempted to capture the dynamic elements of human relations by incorporating the most significant developments that have occurred during the last several years. At the same time, I have tried to remain faithful to my initial objective in writing the book, namely to provide an up-to-date text geared toward readers who are novices in the area of human relations or practitioners with little formal training in the subject.

MAJOR REVISIONS

This edition contains approximately 30 percent new material and incorporates some of the most interesting human relations developments of the 1980s. Many of these, not found in most other human relations texts, relate to topics and issues discussed in today's newspapers and magazines. Examples include changing work values, left-brain–right-brain thinking, office politics, creative decision making, value profiles of successful men and women, the value of cafeteria-style incentive plans, productivity and the quality improvement challenge, the impact of smoking in the work place, effective speaking skills, intrapreneurship, parental leave, and international human relations challenges. The purpose of including these topics is to bridge the gap between human relations theory and human relations practices. Theory helps explain why things are done the way they are; practice describes what is being done. No study of human relations can be effective without consideration of both areas.

In addition, a newly written case opens each chapter and serves to tie all of the material together using new "STOP!" exercises. Students are asked periodically to stop and apply concepts learned throughout the chapter to material presented in the opening case. Over half of the end-of-the-chapter cases and half of the experiential exercises have been written for this edition.

DISTINGUISHING FEATURES

The field of human relations is a very broad one. To provide students with a comprehensive picture of the subject, I have concentrated on the most important topics and concepts. The material is organized in a logical progression, beginning with the human element, moving on to the environment in which people work, and then examining the ways to achieve an effective fit between people and the organizational system. The last section of the book addresses ways in which readers can use these ideas to help manage their careers.

ORGANIZATION

The text is divided into six parts. Part 1 examines the foundation of human relations. Subsequent parts focus on the social system (individuals, groups, and the informal organization), the technical system (technology, productivity and quality improvement, job enrichment, and job design), the administrative system (leadership, appraisal, and rewards), and organizational effectiveness (communication and the management of change). The last part of the book focuses on future human relations challenges and the ways in which the information in this book can be of value to the reader.

EXHIBITS

Modern Human Relations at Work, fourth edition, uses numerous charts, tables, and figures that highlight important concepts. These visuals are designed for maximum clarity.

HUMAN RELATIONS IN ACTION

Each chapter contains a "Human Relations in Action" box that illustrates the practical application of chapter concepts. These examples stimulate the reader to think practically about the theories presented. Subjects include how to increase personal achievement drive, keep quality circles alive, make accurate self-appraisals, deal with sexual harassment, use active listening, and ask the right questions during a job interview. These examples help students gain familiarity with the topics they will face in the business world.

SELF-EXAMINATION EXERCISES

Each chapter includes a "Time Out" self-examination exercise designed to provide readers with personal insights by encouraging participation. These exercises complement the material in each chapter and help readers think more deeply about key concepts.

CASES

All too often, students learn theories without ever understanding their practical application. For this reason, I have included three cases in every chapter. The first is an opening case that contains issues related to the main topics in the chapter. The reader is then provided a series of questions from which to make a preliminary analysis of the case. These questions are revisited in the chapter and recommended answers are provided so that the reader can compare his or her responses and evaluate personal progress.

In addition, two short cases are presented at the end of each chapter. These cases provide an opportunity for readers to resolve human relations problems by applying information that has just been learned. Instructors may want to use these cases as lecture supplements, in-class exercises, or take-home assignments.

EXPERIENTIAL EXERCISES

Every chapter contains one or more experiential exercises. These exercises are group projects designed to highlight one or more of the important concepts presented in each chapter and to allow students to interact with their peers in discussing concepts, setting forth answers, resolving problems, and discussing the impact of the concepts on the way in which people behave. The exercises are designed to help readers "experience" a real-life situation and analyze how it can be addressed. Many modern organizations make use of these types of experiential assignments in providing their personnel with human relations training.

GLOSSARY OF TERMS

A comprehensive glossary of terms, which appears at the end of the text, identifies and describes many of the key concepts used in the book. Students will find this glossary to be a valuable aid for both study and review.

PHOTOS

A series of photos has been integrated throughout this new edition. These photos are designed to increase reader interest and provide real-life examples of concepts that are discussed in the chapter.

INSTRUCTOR SUPPORT

A comprehensive instructor's support package in the form of a combined *Instructor's Manual/Test Bank* has been prepared for *Modern Human Relations at Work,* Fourth Edition. The *Instructor's Manual* provides suggested class schedules and assignments for both 15-week semesters and 10-week quarters. For each chapter, the manual includes a chapter outline, chapter summary, teaching suggestions, answers to end-of-chapter review and study questions, answers to the experiential exercise at the end of the chapter, teaching notes for the cases at the end of the chapter, additional questions and answers for each case, two additional experiential exercises, two additional cases, and a list of suggested chapter readings. Forty transparency masters are also provided for use in supplementing lecture presentation.

The *Test Bank* contains 25 true/false and 50 multiple choice questions for each chapter. This test bank has been substantially rewritten and includes approximately 30 percent new material. A key for each question indicates the answer to each question, the learning objective to which it relates, the text page where each question is discussed, and the question's level of difficulty. For each chapter there is also a matching quiz and three essay questions that can be used to further test student comprehension.

STUDENT STUDY GUIDE/EXERCISE MANUAL

A student *Study Guide/Exercise Manual* is new to this edition. It provides excellent supplementary material to the basic text. The *Study Guide/Exercise Manual* contains chapter outlines, chapter summaries, key term reviews, self-help tests (both true/false and multiple choice), mini-cases, and experiential exercises. Answers for all objective material are provided at the end of the guide, making it an extremely useful complement to students' classroom learning.

ACKNOWLEDGMENTS

Many individuals have played a decisive role in helping me write this book, although I accept full responsibility for any errors of omission or commission. In particular I would like to thank Dr. Fred Luthans of the University of Nebraska, Lincoln, Dr. Jane Gibson of Nova University, Dr. Steven Altman of the University of Central Florida, Dr. Charles Nickerson and Dr. Enzo Valenzi, both of Florida International University, and Dr. Ronald Greenwood of GMI, who provided continued encouragement in this effort.

I would also like to thank those who read, reviewed, and commented on portions of this text, including John Adamski II, Indiana Vocational Technical College Northwest; Dennis G. Allen, Grand Rapids Junior College; Joy D. Andrews, Indiana Vocational Technical College; Stephen C. Branz, Triton College; J. E. Cantrell, De Anza College; Renee L. Cohen, Southwestern Community College; Lorene B. Holmes, Jarvis Christian College; Marilyn A. Hommertzheim, Seward County Community College; James R. Hostetter, Illinois Valley Community College; Steven Jennings, Highland Community College; Miles LaRowe, Laramie County Community College; Gary D. Law, Cuyahoga Community College; Peter J. Moutsatson, Montcalm Community College; Robert O. Nixon, Pima Community College; William S. Pangle, Metro Community College; and Gary W. Piggrem, DeVry-Columbus.

Thanks also go to the staff at The Dryden Press who provided assistance and guidance, including Butch Gemin, Penny Gaffney, Paula Dempsey, Jane Perkins, Jeanne Calabrese, Nancy Johnson, Barb Bahnsen, and Doris Milligan.

Richard M. Hodgetts
Coral Gables, Florida

ABOUT THE AUTHOR

Richard M. Hodgetts, Ph.D. (University of Oklahoma), is a professor of business administration at Florida International University (FIU). Dr. Hodgetts was a professor of management at the University of Nebraska, Lincoln, for ten years before joining the faculty at FIU in 1976. He has been named an outstanding teacher of the year twice at the University of Nebraska and twice at FIU, most recently in 1988. Dr. Hodgetts teaches in the general management area with specific emphasis on management principles, small business and entrepreneurship, and business policy.

Dr. Hodgetts has written numerous articles, some of which have appeared in the *Academy of Management Journal, Personnel Journal, Personnel Management, Simulation, Simulation and Games,* and *Management Advisor.* He is also the author or coauthor of 30 books including *Business, Entrepreneurship: A Contemporary Approach,* and *Real Managers.* The latter has been acclaimed as the most comprehensive study on how successful and effective managers spend their time.

Dr. Hodgetts is active in training and consulting in industry, both in the United States and in South America, and has been particularly active in Wal-Mart's management training program where he teaches situational leadership. Dr. Hodgetts is a Fellow in the Academy of Management, and serves on the review boards of five academic journals. He also writes a weekly business column entitled "Minding Your Business" in the *Fort Lauderdale News & Sun Sentinel,* and he is currently engaged in research among managers in overseas operations.

CONTENTS IN BRIEF

CONTENTS

PART 1

INTRODUCTION

■ ■ ■ ■ ■ ■ ■ ■ ■ ■ ■ ■ ■ ■ ▬

The overall goal of this part of the book is to introduce you to the area of human relations. We do so by first examining the nature of human relations. In Chapter 1, we define the term *human relations* and trace the evolution of human relations thinking from industrialism through scientific management up to the current day. In our historical analysis, we examine some of the important human relations studies that have been conducted during the last five decades. We also compare and contrast the classical model of the workers with the modern human resources model. Finally, we identify the steps in the scientific method and discuss the role of behavioral science in human relations. When you are finished reading Chapter 1, you will know where modern human relations is today, who the people are who study and investigate human relations problems, and how they go about conducting their investigations.

In Chapter 2, our attention is directed to one of the overriding questions in human relations today: "How do you get people to do things?" In answering this question, we study the fundamentals of motivation. We begin by describing the two sides of motivation, movement and motive, and then we move on to identify the five basic needs that all people have and to explain each of these needs and its importance in the motivation process. We then study the now-famous two-factor theory of motivation and its relevance for the practicing manager. In the last part of the chapter, we deal with a recent theory in motivation—expectancy theory—and explain how this theory can help you understand the fundamentals of motivation. Finally, we discuss the practical side of rewards and their relevance to motivation.

When you have finished reading this part of the book, you should have a solid understanding of the nature of human relations. You should also know a great deal about motivation and its role in directing, influencing, and channeling behavior at work.

CHAPTER

1

THE NATURE OF HUMAN RELATIONS

GOALS OF THE CHAPTER

The initial goal of this chapter is to explain what is meant by the term *human relations*. We address both what human relations is and what it is not.

Our second goal is to trace the evolution of human relations from the emergence of industrialism up to the present day. We review the behavioral challenges that confronted management and the progress that was made in meeting them. Particular attention is given to current thinking in human relations.

Our third goal is to examine the impact of behavioral science on human relations. A great deal of human relations training and practice in successful modern organizations is based on empirical findings. Less reliance is now being placed on intuition and "gut feeling," and more attention is being given to the systematic observation and analysis of behavior at work. The scientific method is replacing seat-of-the-pants theory.

Our fourth goal is to review some of the emerging challenges in the human relations area. These include women and minorities.

When you have finished reading this chapter you should be able to:

1.   Trace the evolution of human relations thinking from industrialism through scientific management up to the current day.

2.   Compare and contrast the classical model of the worker with the modern human resources model.

3.   Discuss the role of behavioral science in human relations.

4.   Describe some of the emerging challenges in the human relations area.

5.   Explain how this book can be of value to you.

OPENING CASE

A 10 A.M. START

When Frank O'Keefe's company bid on a government project last year, management never expected to win the competition. However, the firm believed that the experience would be important in learning how to compete effectively for government projects. To its surprise, six months ago Frank's company landed a $3.5 million job. Last year, when business was poor, the company had cut everyone back to six hours a day in order to preserve jobs. Now the company has gone in the opposite direction. In order to avoid having to hire temporary employees to help meet the contract, the firm has extended everyone's hours from 9 A.M.–5 P.M. to 7 A.M.–5 P.M. and requires all personnel to work at least every other weekend.

At first, this new arrangement worked well and everyone was pleased with their increased salary. However, over the past six weeks Frank has noticed a dramatic increase in tardiness. Most of the people who are scheduled to work on weekends do not show up before 9 A.M. either day, and during the week the percentage of tardy workers has increased from 22 percent three weeks ago to 64 percent last week. This is having an effect on output and, if it continues, will result in the firm's failing to meet its contract deadline.

Frank is puzzled about why so many people are showing up late. In an effort to determine the cause, he has talked to a couple of the workers. One told him, "I just don't need the extra work. I'm making more than enough money now." Another said, "My wife and kids want me home more often. Working every other weekend is tough. It takes a lot away from my family."

In an effort to deal with the problem, Frank has decided to call a meeting of the workers and discuss the situation. "I don't intend to fire people or discipline them, unless it's absolutely necessary," he told his assistant. "That's not the way to manage people. However, we can't come in late on our first government contract. We'll never get another, and this is very lucrative work for us. We need these opportunities in the future. During this meeting, we have to find out the reason for the problem and see if we can jointly figure out a solution."

1.   Does Frank use a traditional or a human resources approach in managing his people?

2.   Does Frank believe in the work ethic? Do the employees?

3.   In addition to calling a meeting, how else could Frank gather data on the cause of the tardiness problem?

Write down your answers to these questions and put them aside. We will return to them later. ■

WHAT IS HUMAN RELATIONS?

The process by which management brings workers into contact with the organization in such a way that the objectives of both groups are achieved is **human relations**. The organization is concerned with such objectives as survival, growth, and profit. The worker is concerned with such objectives as good pay, adequate working conditions, a chance to interact with the other personnel, and the opportunity to do interesting and meaningful work. Human relations, then, is concerned with four major areas: the individual worker, the group, the environment in which the work is performed, and the leader responsible for seeing that everything is done properly. In this book we study human relations from the standpoint of the leader or manager who must influence, direct, and respond to both the people and the work environment. Before we begin our study of human relations, however, two points merit attention.

■ ■ ■ ■ ■ ■ ■ ■ ■ ■ ■ ■ ■
HUMAN RELATIONS BRINGS MANAGEMENT AND THE WORKERS TOGETHER IN A HARMONIOUS WAY.

First, human relations implies a concern for the people, but the effective manager never loses sight of the organization's overall objectives. He or she must be interested in the people, the work, *and* the achievement of assigned objectives. Some managers are so interested in pleasing their people that they never get the work done. Others are overly concerned with the work and spend very little time trying to understand the psychological and sociological aspects of the job. The effective manager balances concerns for people and work. In addition, he or she draws upon experience and training in deciding how to use many of the ideas presented in this book. Second, the effective manager realizes that human relations is important at all levels of the organization but that the way the ideas are applied is *not* always the same. The situation dictates the right way to use human relations ideas.

Much of what we know about people in organizations is a result of careful study. If we were to trace the development of human relations in industry, we would see that 200 years ago managers knew very little about how to manage their human assets. The next section of the chapter examines the evolution of modern human relations and sets the stage for our study of this area. Before going on, however, take the true-false quiz in the accompanying Time Out box and see how much you already know about human relations.

TIME OUT

HUMAN RELATIONS IN ORGANIZATIONS

The following 10 true-false questions are designed to give you some initial insights regarding your current knowledge of human relations in modern organizations. Read each statement carefully and then choose the correct answer. The key, along with explanations, is provided at the end of the chapter.

T   F-   1. When asked what motivates them, most workers put money at the top of their list.

T - F   2. In the long run, a work group with high morale and a basic understanding of job requirements will always outperform a work group with moderate morale and a basic understanding of its job requirements.

- T - F   3. While in physics it is true that opposites attract, in human relations just the reverse occurs, i.e., people tend to associate with others who do the same jobs, have the same training, or work in the same unit.

T   F-   4. The most efficient employees report that they do their best work when placed under high stress.

- T   F   5. When it comes to getting and giving information along informal lines, managers tend to use the grapevine more than workers.

T   F-   6. Most top managers are not very intelligent, but they have terrific personalities.

T   F-   7. The reason why many managers do not get all of their daily work done is that the boss overloads them with assignments.

T - F   8. The higher up the organization you go, the greater the amount of job-related stress you will encounter.

T   F-   9. The major reason why workers do not have high productivity is that they are lazy.

- T   F   10. Most managers say that they are very effective two-way communicators, but their subordinates report that the managers seldom listen and are usually interested in only one form of communication—downward.

THE EVOLUTION OF HUMAN RELATIONS

In industry today it is common to hear a great deal of talk about human relations and its importance to management. However, a concern for human relations is largely a modern development. This should become clearer as we discuss the three major stages through which business has progressed on its way to developing a philosophy for managing human assets: (1) the emergence of industrialism, (2) the scientific management movement, and (3) the behavioral management movement.

KNOW

THE EMERGENCE OF INDUSTRIALISM

Industrialism emerged in England in the latter half of the eighteenth century. New inventions enabled wealthy proprietors of this period to invest their money in efficient machinery that could far outpace people doing similar work by hand. For example, no weaver could hope to match the speed and accuracy of the power loom. The age of machine-made goods had begun. These machines were placed in factories, and a work force was hired to run the equipment. The same pattern emerged as industrialism spread to the United States.

FIGURE 1.1   **THESE RULES WERE POSTED IN 1872 BY THE OWNER OF A CARRIAGE AND WAGON WORKS**

STARTING THE NEW YEAR RIGHT

1. Office employees will sweep the floors and dust the furniture, shelves, and showcases every day.
2. Each clerk will bring a bucket of water and a scuttle of coal for the day's business.
3. Clerks will fill the lamps, clean the chimneys, and trim the wicks every day and wash the windows once a week.
4. Make your pens carefully. You may whittle the nibs to your own individual taste.
5. This office will open at 7 a.m. and close at 8 p.m. daily, except on the Sabbath, when it will remain closed.
6. Male employees will be given an evening off each week for courting purposes, or two evenings a week if they attend church regularly.
7. Every employee should put aside some of his pay so as to provide for himself in later years and prevent becoming a burden on others.
8. Any employee who smokes Spanish cigars, uses liquor, gets shaved at a barber shop, or frequents pool or public halls will give the employer good reason to suspect his worth, integrity, and honesty.
9. Any employee who has performed his labors faithfully for a period of five years, has been thrifty, attentive to religious duties, and is looked upon by his fellow workers as a substantial and law-abiding citizen, will be given an increase of 5¢ per day in his pay, providing profits allow it.

The primary concern of the factory owners was increased output. However, there was a great deal the owner-managers did not understand about this new work environment. For example, they knew very little about machine feed and speed, plant layout, and inventory control. Nor were they very knowledgeable about the management of people. Some tended to use a paternalistic style, in which they told the workers what was expected of them and rewarded those who "toed the line" by giving them more money than their less cooperative counterparts. Others simply exploited their people in the name of efficiency and profit.

■ ■ ■ ■ ■ ■ ■ ■ ■ ■ ■ ■ ■
EARLY FACTORY OWNERS USED A
PATERNALISTIC STYLE.

In the United States the people who helped the factories and industrial establishments develop more efficient work measures for increasing output brought about what is known as the scientific management movement. Today, of course, we can fault them as being shortsighted. However, they simply did not understand how to manage a factory, so they sought to solve the technical (work) problems facing them, which are simpler to resolve than the human (people) problems.

SCIENTIFIC MANAGEMENT MOVEMENT

■ ■ ■ ■ ■ ■ ■ ■ ■ ■ ■ ■ ■ *Know*
SCIENTIFIC MANAGEMENT SOUGHT
TO MERGE THE PEOPLE AND THE
WORK.

The **scientific management** movement in America had its genesis in the post–Civil War era. The scientific managers were, for the most part, mechanical engineers. Applying their technical expertise in factories and industrial settings, they tried to *scientifically* merge the people and the work environment so as to achieve the greatest amount of productivity.

The interest of these managers in people involved identifying the "one best man" for each job. For example, in a task requiring heavy lifting, they would select that person who had the best combination of strength and endurance. If a machinist was needed to feed parts into a machine, a scientific manager would choose that person with the best hand-eye coordination and the fastest reflexes. If someone lacked the requisite physical skills for a job, he would be scientifically screened out.

■ ■ ■ ■ ■ ■ ■ ■ ■ ■ ■ ■
SCIENTIFIC MANAGERS TRIED TO
INCREASE EFFICIENCY.

The scientific managers sought to increase work efficiency by employing such measures as plant design, plant layout, time study, and motion study. By placing the machinery and materials at strategically determined points on the shop floor, they sought to reduce the amount of time needed to move goods from the raw materials stage to the finished products stage. By studying the rate at which the machines were run and the way in which material was fed in, they attempted to achieve optimum machine speeds while eliminating excessive time taken and motion used by the machinists.

Yet scientific management had its problems. Primarily, they stemmed from the tendency to view all workers as factors of production rather than as human beings. Many of the scientific managers saw the hired help as mere adjuncts of the machinery, who were to be carefully instructed in how to do the job and then offered more money for productivity increases. Quite obviously, this behavioral philosophy is shallow. While scientific managers may have known a lot about machinery and equipment, they knew very little about human relations in a work setting.

BEHAVIORAL MANAGEMENT MOVEMENT

If business and industrial organizations were to continue expanding, investigations of individual and group behavior were imperative. It was obvious that management knew a great deal more about its production facilities than it did about the people staffing them. By the 1920s, breakthroughs began to occur.

As scientific management moved into its heyday, an interest in the behavioral side of management started to grow. It was becoming obvious that concern for production brought about people-related problems and that the effective manager had to be interested in *both* the personnel and the work.

Many people believe that modern behavioral management had its genesis in the Hawthorne studies. These studies were started as scientific management experiments designed to measure the effect of illumination on output and wound up lighting the way for much of the behavioral research that was to follow.

The second phase of the Hawthorne studies utilized a specially constructed relay assembly room to test the relationship between working conditions and worker productivity.

THE HAWTHORNE STUDIES   The **Hawthorne studies** were begun late in 1924 at the Hawthorne plant of Western Electric, located near Cicero, Illinois. In all, there were four phases to these studies.

PHASE 1   The researchers first sought to examine the relationship between illumination and output. Was there an ideal amount of lighting under which workers would maximize their productivity? The researchers sought to answer this question by subjecting some employees to varying amounts of illumination (the test group) while others kept on working under the original level of illumination (the control group). To the surprise of the researchers, the results of these experiments were inconclusive, because output increased in *both* the test group and the control group. They concluded that variables other than illumination were responsible for the increases. At this point, Elton Mayo and a number of other Harvard University researchers took an interest in the problem.

THE RELATIONSHIP BETWEEN ILLUMINATION AND OUTPUT WAS STUDIED.

PHASE 2   In order to obtain more control over the factors affecting work performance, the researchers isolated a small group of female workers from the regular work force and began to study them. The women were told to keep working at their regular pace because the pur-

A SMALL GROUP OF WORKERS WAS ISOLATED AND STUDIED.

pose of the experiment was not to boost production but to study various types of working conditions in order to identify the most suitable environment. During this period the researchers placed an observer in the test room. This observer was chiefly concerned with creating a friendly atmosphere with the operators so as to ensure their cooperation. He also took over some of the supervision, conversed informally with the women each day, and tried to dispel any apprehensions they might have about the experiment. In turn, the women began to talk more freely among themselves and formed much closer relationships with one another than they had in the regular factory setting. The researchers then began introducing rest breaks to see what effect they would have on output. As productivity increased, the researchers believed that these work pauses were reducing fatigue and thereby improving output. Shorter work days and work weeks were instituted, and output again went up. However, when the original conditions were restored, output still remained high. This proved that the change in physical conditions could not have been the only reason for the increases in output. After analyzing the possible cause of the results, the researchers decided that the changes in the method of supervision might have brought about improved attitudes and increased output.

PHASE 3   At this point the investigators began to focus on human relations. Over 20,000 interviews were conducted, in which the interviewers were primarily interested in gathering information about the effect of supervision on the work environment. Although the interviewers told their subjects that everything would be kept in strict confidence, the workers often gave guarded, stereotypical responses. This led the inter-

■ ■ ■ ■ ■ ■ ■ ■ ■ ■ ■ ■ ■ ■
THE INTERVIEWERS USED INDIRECT
QUESTIONING.

viewers to change from direct to *indirect* questioning, allowing the employee to choose his or her own topic. The result was a wealth of information about employee attitudes. The researchers started to realize that an individual's performance, position, and status in the organization were determined by both the person and the group members. In order to study this impact more systematically, another test group was chosen.

PHASE 4   In the fourth phase of the studies, the investigators decided to examine a small group engaged in one type of work. They chose the bank wiring room, in which the workers were wiring and soldering bank terminals. No changes in their working conditions were made, although an observer was stationed in the test room to record employee interactions and conversations. During these observations, several behaviors were noted. First, the group had an informal production norm that re-

■ ■ ■ ■ ■ ■ ■ ■ ■ ■ ■ ■ ■ ■
NORMS OF GROUP BEHAVIOR WERE
DISCOVERED.

stricted output. Second, there were two informal groups or cliques in the room, and individual behavior was partially dictated by the norms of the groups. Third, to be accepted by the group one had to observe informal rules such as not doing too much work, not doing too little work, and never telling a superior anything that might be detrimental to an associate.

RESULTS OF THE HAWTHORNE STUDIES   From their work the researchers were able to arrive at some conclusions about human behavior in organizations. However, it should be noted that some of their findings were not developed until years later because more information was needed, while other conclusions were only partially accurate. Some of the major conclusions were the following:

1.   Organizations were not just formal structures in which subordinates reported to superiors; they were **social networks** in which people interacted, sought acceptance from and gave approval to fellow workers, and found enjoyment in the work and in the social exchange that occurred while doing the work.

■ ■ ■ ■ ■ ■ ■ ■ ■ ■ ■ ■ ■

SOME CONCLUSIONS FROM HAWTHORNE.

2.   People will act differently when they know they are being observed.

3.   Quality of supervision has an effect on the quality and quantity of work output.

REFINEMENT OF HUMAN RELATIONS THEORY   The Hawthorne research generated a great deal of interest in human relations. However, some misunderstandings also arose from the findings of both these studies and subsequent research.

HAPPINESS AND PRODUCTIVITY   Many behaviorists have attacked some of the Hawthorne findings, calling them naive and, in certain cases, erroneous. One of the most vigorous attacks has been made against the supposedly Hawthorne-generated finding that happy workers will be productive workers. This stinging attack has so stigmatized human relations that in many colleges of business the term is no longer used because it carries the connotation that "happiness automatically leads to productivity"; the term *organizational behavior* is used instead.

■ ■ ■ ■ ■ ■ ■ ■ ■ ■ ■ ■ ■

HAPPY WORKERS ARE NOT NECESSARILY PRODUCTIVE WORKERS.

THE ROLE OF PARTICIPATION   A second misunderstanding revolved around the role of participation. For many of the post-Hawthorne human relationists, participation was viewed as a lubricant that would reduce resistance to company directives and would ensure greater cooperation.

Over the past 50 years this view has changed. Human relationists realize that it is important to allow people to participate, feel important, "belong" as members of a group, be informed, be listened to, and exercise some self-direction and self-control. However, this is not enough. All these things ensure that the workers will be treated well, but modern human relationists now realize that the personnel do not want only to be treated well, they want to be *used well*. A good example is found in the currently popular use of job autonomy in which people are given a task and then allowed to do it without interference or unnecessary direction on the part of the manager. The very subtle yet important difference between these two philosophies is that the latter views people as vital human resources who *want* to contribute to organizational goals and, under the proper conditions, will do so. This is why it has been said that human relations is in a "human resources" era. (See Human Relations in Action.)

MODERN WORKERS WANT TO BE USED WELL.

HUMAN RESOURCES ERA

The scientific managers had a philosophy of management. Its basic ideas constitute a **traditional model**. Today this philosophy has given way to a **human resources model** that, in essence, sees the personnel as untapped resources containing unlimited potential. Through the effective application of human relations ideas, these resources can be released and used for the overall good of both the organization and the personnel. Table 1.1 on page 14 provides a summary of the points of contrast between the traditional (scientific management) and human resources models.

THE HUMAN RESOURCES MODEL VIEWS PEOPLE AS HAVING UNTAPPED POTENTIAL.

KNOW

How can the human resources model be used by modern managers? An answer can be found through an analysis of Rensis Likert's four systems of management, which extend from exploitive autocratic (System 1) to participative democratic (System 4). A brief description of each is provided below.

System 1: Exploitive autocratic. Management has little confidence in the subordinates, as seen by the fact that they are seldom involved in decision making. Management makes most of the decisions and passes them down the line, using threats and coercion when necessary to get things done. Superiors and subordinates deal with each other in an environment of distrust. If an informal organization develops, it usually opposes the goals of the formal organization.

System 2: Benevolent autocratic. Management acts in a condescending manner toward the subordinates. Although there is some decision making at the low levels, it occurs within a prescribed framework. Rewards and some actual punishment are used to motivate the personnel. In superior-subordinate interaction, the management is condescending and the subordinates appear cautious and fearful. Although an informal organization usually develops, it does not always oppose the goals of the formal organization.

System 3: Consultative democratic. Management has quite a bit of confidence and trust in the subordinates. Although

HUMAN RELATIONS IN ACTION
THE CONTINUING SEARCH FOR EXCELLENCE

Many organizations are finding that getting ahead of the competition is easy; staying ahead is difficult. How do they do it? Supported by recent research, management experts such as Robert H. Waterman, of *In Search of Excellence* fame, report eight major, widely used themes. All of them rely heavily on human relations. They are the following:

1.   *Information Gathering.* Effective managers treat information as an important weapon. They are continually searching for new ways of doing things. They know that one of the primary means of learning these new ways is by gathering information from subordinates, colleagues, superiors, and anyone else who has something to contribute.

2.   *Decentralized Control.* Good managers give their people jobs to do, set limits on this authority, and then stay out of the way. As long as subordinates operate within the established boundaries, they are given a free hand.

3.   *Friendly Facts.* Effective leaders make sure their people know what is going on; they provide information to help their subordinates to do a better job. Cumbersome controls are abandoned and replaced by ones that encourage productive activity.

4.   *Openness and Inquisitiveness.* Successful managers listen to their people, ask questions, and find out what is going on. They stay in touch with their people by giving and getting information.

5.   *Teamwork.* Effective leaders encourage and develop teamwork. They share the goals and values of the enterprise with their people and get the latter to buy in. They trust their people, treat them well, and in the process, create strong bonds of loyalty.

6.   *Stability.* Good managers know that change is inevitable. At the same time, they protect the stability of the organization by not letting change go too far. For example, many enterprises reorganize every 2 or 3 years in order to streamline their operations and to prevent bureaucracy from setting in while still maintaining the basic goals and values of the organization.

7.   *Attention.* Successful leaders listen to their people. They let their subordinates know that new ideas are important and they reward people for these contributions. They also practice "management by walking around," letting their people know that they are vital to human assets and that management is aware of what they are doing.

8.   *Commitment.* Effective managers identify causes and get their people committed to them. In recent years, one of the main targets has been product and service quality. By getting the workers to commit time and effort to improving quality, many American firms are reestablishing themselves as the leaders in their industries.

Source: Robert H. Waterman, *The Renewal Factor: How the Best Get and Keep the Competitive Edge* (New York: Bantam Books, Inc., 1987); and John A. Byrne, "How the Best Get Better," *Business Week*, September 14, 1987, pp. 98–99.

TABLE 1.1   **THE TRADITIONAL AND HUMAN RESOURCES MODELS**

Traditional Model (Theory X)	**Human Resources Model** (Theory Y)
Assumptions	***Assumptions***
1. Work is inherently distasteful to most people.	1. Work is not inherently distasteful. People want to contribute to meaningful goals which they have helped establish.
2. What workers do is less important than what they earn for doing it.	
3. Few want or can handle work which requires creativity, self-direction, or self-control.	2. Most people can exercise far more creative, responsible self-direction and self-control than their present jobs demand.
Policies	***Policies***
1. The manager's basic task is to closely supervise and control his subordinates.	1. The manager's basic task is to make use of his "untapped" human resources.
2. He must break tasks down into simple, repetitive, easily learned operations.	2. He must create an environment in which all members may contribute to the limits of their ability.
3. He must establish detailed work routines and procedures and enforce these firmly but fairly.	3. He must encourage full participation on important matters, continually broadening subordinate self-direction and control.
Expectations	***Expectations***
1. People can tolerate work if the pay is decent and the boss is fair.	1. Expanding subordinate influence, self-direction, and self-control will lead to direct improvements in operating efficiency.
2. If tasks are simple enough and people are closely controlled, they will produce up to standard.	2. Work satisfaction may improve as a "byproduct" of subordinates making full use of their resources.

Source: From Raymond E. Miles, *Theories of Management* (New York: McGraw–Hill Book Company, 1975). Copyright © 1975 by McGraw–Hill Book Company. Used with the permission of McGraw–Hill Book Company.

When a participative democratic style is the norm, communication at all levels of the organization is encouraged. These Commercial Credit Company employees are discussing new marketing materials.

important decisions are made at the top of the organization, the subordinates make specific decisions at the lower levels. Two-way communication is evident, and there is some confidence and trust between superiors and subordinates. If an informal organization develops, it either gives support or offers only slight resistance to the goals of the formal organization.

System 4: Participative democratic.   Management has complete confidence and trust in the subordinates. Decision making is highly decentralized. Communication flows not only up and down the organization but among peers as well. Superior-subordinate interaction takes place in a friendly environment and is characterized by mutual confidence and trust. The formal and the informal organization are often one and the same.[1]

■ ■ ■ ■ ■ ■ ■

[1] Adapted from Rensis Likert, *The Human Organization* (New York: McGraw–Hill Book Company, 1967), pp. 4–10.

The use of these four systems in an organization can be identified with a Likert questionnaire. A partial example of this inducement is provided in Figure 1.2. After subordinates fill out the questionnaire, the organization is able to determine under which system (1, 2, 3, or 4) it is operating.

Likert has found that the most effective organizations have System 4 characteristics and the least effective organizations have System 1 and System 2 characteristics. A number of organizations have converted to System 4 with very good results. For example, a comprehensive organizational change project involving the Weldon Company, a sleepwear manufacturing firm, has been well documented.[2] In this project, substantial changes were made in the organization's work flow, training programs, leadership styles, incentive and reward systems, and use of employees as a source of expertise. The results were impressive. There were improvements in all aspects of the organization's functioning that were maintained over an extended period.

■ ■ ■ ■ ■ ■ ■ ■ ■ ■ ■ ■
MANY ORGANIZATIONS USE SYSTEM 4.

System 4 management has also been used in a General Motors assembly plant. Dowling has reported that training sessions on Likert's theory, team-building sessions starting at the top of the organization and moving to lower levels, improved information and communication flows to the hourly employees, changes in the job of the first-line foremen, increased participation of hourly employees in job changes, and new approaches to goal setting were all used in this program. The results were improved operating efficiency and decreases in grievances and waste.[3]

■ ■ ■ ■ ■ ■ ■ ■ ■ ■ ■ ■
SYSTEM 4 IS OFTEN BETTER.

Quite obviously, System 1 represents the traditional model, while System 4 represents the human resources model. At the present time there appears to be a decided swing toward the use of Systems 3 and 4. Modern managers are realizing that the way to handle personnel has changed dramatically since the heyday of the scientific managers. One reason is because today's employee has a much different view of work than the employee of the past. The very meaning of work is changing.

STOP!

Review your answer to the first question and make any changes you would like. Then compare your answer to the one below.

1.   Does Frank use a traditional or a human resources approach in managing his people?

■ ■ ■ ■ ■ ■ ■

[2] For a complete account of the program see Alfred J. Marrow, David G. Bowers, and Stanley E. Seashore, *Management by Participation* (New York: Harper & Row, 1967).

[3] William F. Dowling, "At G.M.: 'System 4' Builds Performance and Profits," *Organizational Dynamics*, Winter 1975, pp. 23–28.

FIGURE 1.2　THE SYSTEM 4 APPROACH

	SYSTEM 1	SYSTEM 2	SYSTEM 3	SYSTEM 4
Extent to which subordinates have confidence and trust in the superior	Have no confidence and trust in the superior	Have subservient confidence and trust, such as a servant has to the master	Substantial but not complete confidence	Complete confidence and trust
Extent to which superiors behave so that subordinates feel free to discuss important things about their jobs with their immediate superior	Subordinates do not feel at all free to discuss things about the job with their superior	Subordinates do not feel free to discuss things about the job with their superior	Subordinates feel rather free to discuss things about the job with their superior	Subordinates feel completely free to discuss things about the job with their superior
Attitudes toward other members of the organization	Subservient attitudes toward superiors coupled with hostility; hostility toward peers and contempt for subordinates; distrust is widespread	Subservient attitudes toward superiors; competition for status resulting in hostility toward peers; condescension toward subordinates	Cooperative, reasonably favorable attitudes toward others in the organization; there may be some competition between peers with resulting hostility and some condescension toward subordinates	Favorable, cooperative attitudes throughout the organization with mutual trust and confidence
Satisfaction derived	Usually dissatisfaction with membership in the organization, with supervision, and with one's own achievements	Dissatisfaction to moderate satisfaction in regard to membership in the organization, supervision, and one's own achievements	Some dissatisfaction to moderately high satisfaction in regard to membership in the organization, supervision, and one's own achievements	Relatively high satisfaction throughout the organization in regard to membership in the organization, supervision, and one's own achievements
Amount of cooperative teamwork that is present	None	Relatively little	A moderate amount	Very substantial amount throughout the entire organization
Are there forces to accept, resist, or reject goals?	Goals are overtly accepted, but covertly they are resisted strongly	Goals are overtly accepted but often covertly resisted to at least some degree	Goals are overtly accepted but at times with some covert resistance	Goals are fully accepted both overtly and covertly
Extent to which there is an informal organization present and supporting or opposing goals of the formal organization	Informal organization is present and opposing the goals of the formal organization	Informal organization is usually present and partially resisting formal goals	Informal organization may be present and may either support or partially resist the goals of the formal organization	Informal and formal organization are one and the same; all social forces support efforts to achieve organization's goals

Frank uses a human resources approach. Notice that in dealing with the tardiness problem, he does not resort to firing or disciplining the employees. His first approach is to find out the reason for the problem and to work with the employees in resolving it. ■

THE MEANING OF WORK

Work is the use of physical and/or mental effort that is directed toward the production or accomplishment of something. Do people today work as hard as they used to work? Some individuals say no, arguing that many workers do just enough to get by. Others challenge this contention, pointing out that the American work ethic is alive and well in many organizations. Both groups are partially right and partially wrong. This can be seen by examining the meaning of work along a continuum ranging from those who regard work as highly desirable to those who see it as highly undesirable. The most extreme example of the individual who sees work as a "good thing" is the workaholic; the most common example of the individual who sees work as a "bad thing" is the person who subscribes to the leisure ethic.[4]

WORK IS PHYSICAL OR MENTAL EFFORT DIRECTED TOWARD ACCOMPLISHING AN OBJECTIVE.

THE WORKAHOLIC

The **workaholic** obtains satisfaction from continual work. This individual enjoys having something to do at all times. Many people confuse the workaholic with the efficient worker. Actually there is quite a difference between the two. In particular, a workaholic has an uncontrollable compulsion to work. He or she obtains enjoyment from being busy at all times; if there were no more work to do, the individual would feel nervous or guilty.

WORKAHOLICS OBTAIN SATISFACTION FROM CONTINUAL WORK.

Research reveals that many people are workaholics. A recent survey by *Venture* magazine asked readers to relate how many hours a week they worked and how many they spent with their spouses on workdays.[5] Figures 1.3 and 1.4 present the findings. *Venture* also found that of the more than 1,000 readers who responded to the survey, one-third said that when work and family commitments were incompatible, the work came

▪▪▪▪▪▪▪

[4] For an excellent in-depth discussion of the work ethic and the meaning of work, see: David J. Cherrington, *The Work Ethic* (New York: American Management Association, 1980).

[5] Barbara Presley Noble, "Striking a Balance Between Work and Family," *Venture*, January 1985, p. 24.

■ ■ ■ ■ ■ ■ ■ ■ ■ ■ ■ ■ ■ ■
MANY PEOPLE WORK VERY HARD.

first. Additionally, only 13 percent said that they would neglect work in favor of their families. Another interesting finding is that 460 of the respondents reported that they had not taken a vacation in three years, and some of them had not had one in more than 25 years! Clearly, many of these people have a tendency toward workaholism.

On the other hand, most respondents to the survey did not report workaholism tendencies. A close look at Figure 1.3 shows that those working fewer than 70 hours a week put their family ahead of work. Figure 1.4 reveals that most of these people spend 7 or more hours a week with their spouse. *Venture* also found that 28 percent of the respondents had taken a vacation within the last 90 days. Additionally, of those who did work more than 80 hours a week, only 5 percent were married in contrast to 68 percent for the respondents as a whole. So while there are workaholics in our society, they do not constitute a significant percentage of the work force.

When examined from a human relations standpoint, the workaholic presents a major challenge to the manager. Unless this worker can be made to see that his or her meaning and purpose of work is distorted, the individual is highly likely eventually to suffer a heart attack, high blood

FIGURE 1.3   FOR WORKAHOLICS, WORK COMES BEFORE FAMILY

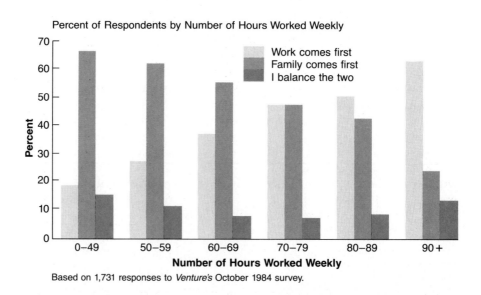

Percent of Respondents by Number of Hours Worked Weekly

Work comes first
Family comes first
I balance the two

Based on 1,731 responses to *Venture's* October 1984 survey.

Source: Reprinted from the January 1985 issue of VENTURE, The Magazine for Entrepreneurs, by special permission. © 1985, Venture Magazine, Inc., 521 Fifth Avenue, New York, NY 10175.

FIGURE 1.4   **KEEPING THE HOME FIRES BURNING**

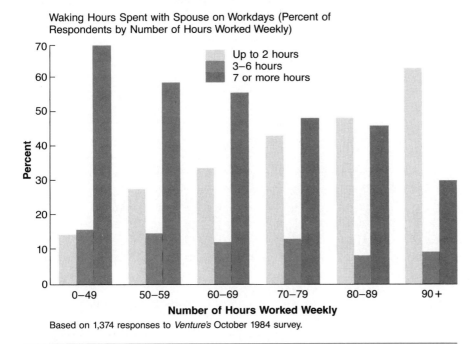

Waking Hours Spent with Spouse on Workdays (Percent of Respondents by Number of Hours Worked Weekly)

Legend:
- Up to 2 hours
- 3–6 hours
- 7 or more hours

Y-axis: Percent

X-axis: **Number of Hours Worked Weekly**
0–49   50–59   60–69   70–79   80–89   90+

Based on 1,374 responses to *Venture's* October 1984 survey.

Source: Reprinted from the January 1985 issue of VENTURE, The Magazine for Entrepreneurs, by special permission. © 1985, Venture Magazine, Inc., 521 Fifth Avenue, New York, NY 10175.

pressure, and/or job burnout. While more will be said about workaholics later in the book, it is important to remember that the development of workaholic practices is bad for the worker and should be discouraged by the manager.

WORKAHOLISM SHOULD BE DISCOURAGED.

THE WORK ETHIC

The **work ethic** holds that work is a desirable activity. Those who subscribe to this ethic believe that:

THE WORK ETHIC VIEWS WORK AS A DESIRABLE ACTIVITY.

1.   It is acceptable to work long and hard every day.

2.   One should strive to be highly productive on the job.

3.   People should take pride in their work.

4.   Commitment and loyalty to one's profession, organization, and work group are to be encouraged.

FIGURE 1.5   WHO HAS THE WORK ETHIC?

The percentage of workers with a strong work ethic varies widely from occupation to occupation. There also are interesting differences in the work ethic levels of men and women who feel that their jobs have good pay and give them a say in important decisions. The dotted line indicates the percentage of the survey as a whole that subscribes to the work ethic.

Who has the work ethic?   "I have an inner need to do the very best I can regardless of pay"

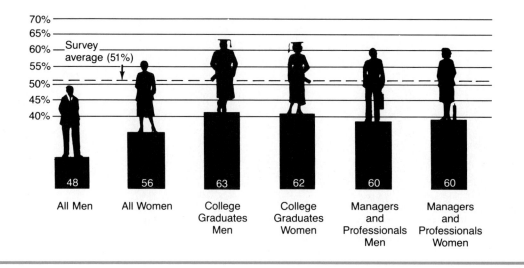

5.   People should be achievement-oriented and constantly striving for advancement and promotion.

Many successful people believe in the work ethic. In large part, they feel that this philosophy has helped them to succeed in life.

When examined from a human relations standpoint, the manager has to keep in mind that not everyone subscribes to the work ethic. Many people work hard but do not attach extreme importance to the job. In managing these individuals the manager has to be careful not to foist his or her work values on them. If the workers are doing an acceptable job, this may be all the manager can expect. On the other hand, it is erroneous to believe that the work ethic in America is dead. A survey by *Working Woman* found that over half of the work force has the work ethic, and more women have it than men (see Figure 1.5). Additionally, while many Americans believe that Japanese and Germans are much more work

FIGURE 1.5   *(Continued)*

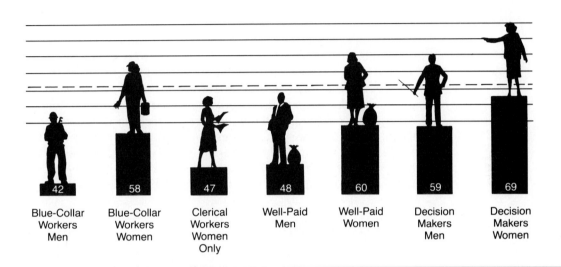

Blue-Collar Workers Men	Blue-Collar Workers Women	Clerical Workers Women Only	Well-Paid Men	Well-Paid Women	Decision Makers Men	Decision Makers Women
42	58	47	48	60	59	69

Source: Julia Kagan, "Survey: Work in the 1980s and 1990s," *Working Woman*, May 1983, p. 24. Reprinted with permission from *Working Woman* Magazine. Copyright © 1985 by HAL Publications, Inc.

ethic oriented than they are, overseas managers disagree. They feel the Americans are very strong work ethic people.[6]

THE WORTH ETHIC

The **worth ethic** is held by those who work because they want to achieve something of worth or value. These people fall into one of two groups. The first group works because their jobs give them feelings of competence and job mastery. They like what they do because they feel in command of the situation. They also have feelings of self-esteem as reflected in their belief that they do a good job. These beliefs are often shown by

■ ■ ■ ■ ■ ■ ■ ■ ■ ■ ■ ■ ■ ■
SELF-ESTEEM IS IMPORTANT.

■ ■ ■ ■ ■ ■ ■
[6]Charles A. Burden and Milton S. Hochmuth, "Why Foreign Firms Like American Workers," *Business Horizons*, September–October 1983, pp. 10–15.

such statements as: "I am a very competent worker," "I am a valuable member of this organization," or "I can really get things done around here." These people like to work because of the psychological satisfaction it provides to them.

SO ARE PERSONAL, TANGIBLE
REWARDS.

The second group of people that subscribes to the worth ethic does so because of the personal, tangible rewards. The rewards come in such forms as money, status, recognition, and/or promotion, and they help the individual meet the desire for tangible rewards. The worker who can point to a new car, a house, a boat, a large office, or a key to the executive washroom falls into this second group of individuals.

Both of the rewards discussed above (self-esteem and personal, tangible rewards) can be successful motivators. The important thing for the manager to remember is that in many cases he or she has no authority to give out additional money or provide special promotions. The manager can merely encourage the personnel to work hard and try to provide them with feelings of self-esteem by giving them continuous positive feedback. In this case, those seeking personal, tangible rewards will not be as satisfied as those desiring self-esteem. Yet this is all the manager can do. It is a problem with which the organization must live.

THE LEISURE ETHIC

SOME PEOPLE SEE WORK AS AN
UNFORTUNATE OBLIGATION.

Many workers today subscribe to the **leisure ethic**. These people fall into one of two groups. The first group sees work as an unfortunate obligation. However, they are willing to work because they know that it is the only way for them to maintain a desirable lifestyle. These individuals cannot be counted on to do much more than the minimum needed to keep their job. If they do work hard in an effort to earn a promotion or advancement, it is only because they want to use the money to pursue nonwork activities.

OTHER PEOPLE SIMPLY HATE
WORK.

The other group which subscribes to the leisure ethic believes that work is totally undesirable and punishing. There are no rewards associated with it. An individual who fits into this category was well described by Studs Terkel in his book *Working,* when he reported the comments of a steelworker.

> The first thing happens at work: When the arms start moving, the brain stops. I punch in about ten minutes to seven in the morning . . . at seven it starts. My arms get tired about the first half-hour. After that they don't get tired any more until maybe the last half-hour at the end of the day. I work from seven to three-thirty. My arms are tired at seven-thirty and they're tired at three o'clock. I hope to God that I never get broke in, because I always want my arms to be tired at seven-thirty and three o'clock (laughs). 'Cause that's when I know there's a beginning and

there's an end. That I'm not brainwashed. In between, I don't even try to think. . . . Unless a guy's a nut, he never thinks about work or talks about it. . . . I'd say one out of a hundred will actually get excited about work.[7]

The challenge presented to the manager by individuals who believe in the leisure ethic is the most difficult to meet. However, it is not an impossible task. One of the most effective approaches, used in many jobs, is to redesign the work so that it becomes more challenging and meaningful. This can help greatly. Of course, if the workers do not like challenge and meaningful work, the redesign effort is a waste of time. A second, and often complementary, approach is to develop a system of positive reinforcement designed to encourage work output and discourage loafing. If used for an extended period of time, it is possible to turn some of these leisure ethic people around and move them into the category of worth ethic. This book examines some of the ways that this can be done.

■ ■ ■ ■ ■ ■ ■ ■ ■ ■ ■ ■ ■ ■
BUT THERE ARE WAYS OF DEALING WITH THESE PEOPLE.

Before we begin our study of how this is possible, however, there is one final point that merits consideration. It relates to human relations and the scientific method. Much of what we now know about people in organizations is based on systematic analysis. Although the study of human relations is not a true science, it is far less an art than it was 50 years ago. Much of this progress can be attributed to the rigorous application of scientific measures in answering the question: "Why do people behave as they do?"

STOP!

Review your answer to the second question and make any changes you would like. Then compare your answer to the one below.

2.   Does Frank believe in the work ethic? Do the employees?

He certainly does believe in the work ethic. Notice that he expects the employees to work 10 hours a day and at least one full weekend out of two. The employees also believe in the work ethic. They have been working this schedule for quite a while and, even though many of them are beginning to show up late, they are still putting in a very large number of hours every week. Prior to the government contract, they were working 40 hours a week. Now they are working 50 hours a week and an extra 20

■ ■ ■ ■ ■ ■ ■
[7] Studs Terkel, *Working* (New York: Avon Books, 1972), p. 5.

hours every other weekend. So their average workweek has increased from 40 to 60 hours. They certainly do believe in the work ethic! ■

BEHAVIORAL SCIENCE AND HUMAN RELATIONS

A great deal of what people know about human relations is a direct outgrowth of what they have heard, read, or experienced. Many try to classify this information into the form of rules or principles of behavior. For example, just about everyone knows Murphy's first law: "If anything can go wrong, it will." Another commonly cited behavioral adage comes from Parkinson, who holds, "The time spent on the discussion of any agenda item is in inverse proportion to the sum involved."[8]

Are these laws scientific or are they generalizations that make for an interesting discussion but little else? Human relations experts opt for the latter view, noting that such rules are too broad in coverage to provide much operational assistance. Furthermore, since nothing is more dangerous than generalizing behavioral findings from one situation to another without systematically studying the facts, modern human relationists prefer to use the scientific method in developing their theories and rules about human relations.

THE SCIENTIFIC METHOD

The greatest barrier to our understanding of human relations can be found within ourselves. Biases, personal opinions, inaccurate perceptions, and errors of judgment all combine to give us our own views of the world. Sometimes these factors lead us to see things as we would like them to be rather than as they really are. For example, a manager who dislikes the union may easily regard the shop steward as a mouthpiece for union dissension and may discount anything the steward says as mere "union rhetoric."

Practitioners of modern human relations know that they must step outside themselves and try to study human behavior in the work place from an *objective* standpoint. In analyzing behavioral problems, for example, they must rely on the scientific method, because, as Kerlinger has noted:

> The **scientific method** has one characteristic that no other method of attaining knowledge has: self-direction. There are built-in checks all along the way to scientific knowledge. These checks are so conceived and used that they control and verify the

....

[8]C. Northcote Parkinson, *Parkinson's Law* (Boston: Houghton Mifflin Company, 1957), p. 24.

scientist's activities and conclusions to the end of attaining dependable knowledge outside himself.[9]

The following are generally regarded as the basic steps in the scientific method:

■   Identify the problem. What exactly is the objective of the entire investigation?

■   Obtain background information. Gather as much data as possible about the problem under study.

■   Pose a tentative solution to the problem. State a hypothesis that can be proved to be either right or wrong and that is most likely to solve the problem.

■   Investigate the problem area. Using available data, as well as any information gathered through experimentation, examine the problem in its entirety.

■   Classify the information. Take all the data and classify them in a way that expedites their use and helps establish a relationship with the hypothesis.

■   State a tentative answer to the problem. Draw a conclusion regarding the right answer to the problem.

■   Test the answer. Implement the solution. If it works, the problem is solved. If not, develop another hypothesis and repeat the process.

STEPS IN THE SCIENTIFIC METHOD.

STOP!

Review your answer to the third question and make any changes you would like. Then compare your answer to the one below.

3.   In addition to calling a meeting, how else could Frank gather data on the cause of the tardiness problem?

Frank could personally interview a cross section of the workers to find out the reason for the problem. He has already talked to two workers, but these individuals may not be representative of the entire work force. Frank could also keep records on who is late and find out if there are any particular departments or groups that have a higher tardiness rate than all of the others. The problem may be restricted to certain employees or jobs and not the company at large. This analysis would help him better determine the reason for the tardiness. ■

[9] Fred N. Kerlinger, *Foundations of Behavioral Research*, 2nd ed. (New York: Holt, Rinehart and Winston, 1973), p. 6.

BEHAVIORAL RESEARCH IN HUMAN RELATIONS

It is quite obvious that practitioners of human relations do not have time to make a systematic study of human behavior at work. They are too busy being operating managers. However, there are people in academia and industry who do have time for scientific, behavioral research, including psychologists, who are interested in individual behavior, and sociologists, who are most concerned with group behavior. These highly skilled people are known as **behavioral scientists,** and they are responsible for a great deal of what we know about human relations in industry.

How is the scientific method applied in the study of human relations? There are numerous ways: One is to set up **test** and **control groups.** A test group is a group that is given some form of "treatment" such as a training course. A control group is a group that is not given any treatment. For example, a company is considering the value of customer-service training for store personnel. Will this training be useful? One way of answering this question is by giving the training to some of the personnel and then evaluating the results. The group that is chosen would be randomly selected. This means that each one of the personnel would have an equal chance of being picked for the training; the company would not send the best or poorest workers even if it felt these individuals would profit most from the training. Then the training would be provided and the results would be analyzed. If those with the training were found to be more effective in providing customer service, the behavioral scientist would conclude that the training accounted for these results. If the group members were no more effective than the other personnel in providing customer service, the behavioral scientist would conclude that the training was of no substantive value.

Behavioral scientists also use their knowledge to help managers motivate and lead people. For example, in recent years many managers have been taught how to use effective reinforcement to encourage desired behaviors and to discourage undesired behaviors. Through the effective use of rewards, personnel are motivated to perform their duties quickly and efficiently. Conversely, by withholding rewards, personnel are motivated to modify their behaviors and stop doing things (coming in late, filing incomplete reports, failing to get work done on time) that are nonproductive.[10]

Behavioral scientists also obtain important human relations information through the use of formal questionnaires; **structured interviews,** in which specific questions are asked in a predetermined order; and **unstructured interviews,** in which the interviewer has questions to be asked but follows no set format, allowing the interview to develop on its own.

■ ■ ■ ■ ■ ■ ■ ■ ■ ■ ■ ■ ■
BEHAVIORAL SCIENTISTS ARE INDIVIDUALS WHO APPLY THEIR TRAINING TO THE STUDY OF BEHAVIOR IN ORGANIZATIONS.

■ ■ ■ ■ ■ ■ ■ ■ ■ ■ ■ ■
BEHAVIORAL RESEARCH IN INDUSTRY USES THE SCIENTIFIC METHOD.

■ ■ ■ ■ ■ ■ ■ ■ ■ ■ ■ ■ ■
STRUCTURED INTERVIEWS USE SPECIFIC QUESTIONS ASKED IN A PREDETERMINED MANNER.

■ ■ ■ ■ ■ ■

[10] For more on this, see B. F. Skinner, *Contingencies of Reinforcement* (New York: Appleton-Century-Crofts, 1969); and Fred Luthans, *Organizational Behavior* (New York: McGraw-Hill Book Company, 1989), Chapter 7.

All these approaches are designed to gather data about workers and working conditions. Through analysis of this information and study of the environment in which the subjects work, it is often possible to draw conclusions about factors that affect communication, attitudes, and work habits.

■ ■ ■ ■ ■ ■ ■ ■ ■ ■ ■
UNSTRUCTURED INTERVIEWS HAVE GENERAL DIRECTION BUT NO RIGIDLY SET FORMAT.

It is important to remember that modern human relations is based, not on generalizations, hunches, opinions, and "gut feeling," but on empirical information that is systematically gathered and analyzed by trained scientists. Much of what you will study in this book is a direct result of their investigations.

Very Imp.

EMERGING CHALLENGES

Over the last decade human relations concerns have not remained static. New challenges have emerged, making it even more important for one to have a basic understanding of human relations at work. Three of the major challenges are coming from women, minority groups, and international operations.

WOMEN

In 1960 women made up approximately one-third of the civilian work force. Today they constitute approximately 48 percent of this work group and by the early 1990s this figure will be around 50 percent. No effective manager can afford to overlook the human relations implications of a sizable female labor force.

There are three specific areas that warrant attention. The first is salaries. Despite the fact that their numbers are growing, employed women on average earn only about 70 percent as much as men.[11] Part of this is accounted for by the fact that a greater percentage of women work at the lowest paying jobs. Another contributing factor is that many women have entered the work force only in the last decade and it will take time for them to move up the ranks to higher paying jobs. A third factor is discrimination. In some organizations women are not paid the same salaries as men doing similar work under similar working conditions. A fourth factor is that older women tend to be more subject to wage discrimination than are younger women as shown by the latest wage statistics based on age as shown by the following data:

■ ■ ■ ■ ■ ■ ■ ■ ■ ■ ■
WOMEN ARE PAID LESS THAN MEN.

■ ■ ■ ■ ■ ■ ■
[11] Judy Mann and Basia Hellwig, "The Truth about the Salary Gap(s)," *Working Woman*, January 1988, p. 61.

■ **WOMEN'S EARNINGS AS A PERCENTAGE OF MEN'S** [a]

AGE	1975	1986
18–24	76	86
25–34	65	74
35–44	52	60
45–54	53	54
55–64	55	54

---

[a] Annual average.
Source: U.S. Census Bureau.

At the same time, there are many areas where the gap between women's and men's earnings has begun to close. (See Table 1.2.) One reason is the rising number of professionals. For example, in 1972 women received 4 percent of all MBAs and held 25 percent of all management and administrative jobs. In 1987 women received 33 percent of all MBAs and 37 percent of all management and administrative jobs.[12] Today they also account for 45 percent of all accountants and auditors, 30 percent of computer systems analysts, 30 percent of scientists, and 15 percent of lawyers.[13] Yet wage discrimination continues to be a human relations challenge.

A second area is promotions. In some enterprises the highest level jobs are held by men. This lack of representation is true even at the board level where in 1987 there were only 4 or 5 women on the boards of the top 1,000 companies in the United States.[14] Whether or not this practice is a conscious effort to discriminate, it is a human relations challenge that must be confronted and overcome. Women are too important an organizational resource to be underutilized.[15]

A third area is sexual harassment. The term has been defined in many different ways, depending on the specific organization. One major university defined it this way: "Sexual harassment is the unwelcome verbal or physical conduct which: (1) is aimed at coercing an unwilling person into a sexual relationship; or (2) makes submission or rejection of such conduct the basis for decisions affecting the individual; or (3) un-

■ ■ ■ ■ ■ ■ ■

[12] *Business Week*, May 9, 1988, p. 36.

[13] *Working Woman*, January 1988, p. 61.

[14] "The $179-an-Hour Job That Nobody Wants," *Working Woman*, January 1988, p. 60.

[15] Julia Kagan, "Work in the 1980s and 1990s," *Working Woman*, December 1983, p. 16.

TABLE 1.2   WHAT JOB PAYS THE MOST NEARLY EQUAL WAGES?

	WOMEN'S EARNINGS AS A PERCENTAGE OF MEN'S	
	1979	1986
Teachers, elementary school	82	95
Computer systems analysts and scientists	79	83
Computer programmers	80	81
Sales of business services	58	79
Public administrators	67	76
Accountants and auditors	60	72
Lawyers	55	63
Managers in marketing, advertising, and public relations	55	60

Source: US Census Bureau.

reasonably interferes with the individual's work or school performance by creating an intimidating, hostile or offensive environment."[16] This harassment can take a number of different forms. Some of the most common include physical assault; the requesting of sexual favors accompanied by implied or overt threats concerning one's job or position in the organization; verbal harassment or abuse; physical contact such as patting, pinching, or unnecessary touching; subtle pressure for sexual activity; or sexist remarks or gestures regarding a person's body, clothing, or sexual activities.[17] Under Equal Employment Opportunity Commission guidelines, sexual harassment is illegal and those found guilty of it can be reprimanded and/or fired. Managers must be aware of the effect of sexual harassment on the personnel (attitude, motivation) and on the organization (lawsuits).[18]

∎∎∎∎∎∎∎

[16] "Policy to Prohibit Sexual Harassment," Division of Human Resources, Florida International University, 1984.

[17] Ibid.

[18] For more on this topic, see "You've Come a Long Way Baby . . . But Not as Far as You Thought," *Business Week*, October 1, 1984, pp. 126–131; Diane St. James, "Coping with Sexual Harassment," *Supervisory Management*, October 1983, pp. 4–9; Jacqueline F. Strayer and Sandra E. Rapoport, "Sexual Harassment, 2: Limiting Corporate Liability," *Personnel*, April 1986, pp. 26–33; and David E. Terpstra and Douglas D. Baker, "Outcomes of Sexual Harassment Charges," *Academy of Management Journal*, March 1988, pp. 185–193.

MINORITIES

■ ■ ■ ■ ■ ■ ■ ■ ■ ■ ■ ■ ■ ■
MINORITY GROUPS ARE PAID LESS
THAN WHITE MEN.

There are many minority groups in the work force. The largest group is blacks. Next in size is Hispanics. Like women, these groups are paid less than the average worker and are underrepresented in upper management ranks. For example, the latest statistics show that the median income for white families is $26,175. The median income for blacks and Hispanics is $15,080 and $18,352, respectively.[19] Also, although blacks and Hispanics can be found in every sector of the economy, more of them are in blue-collar jobs than in executive, administrative, or managerial positions. The federal government's latest reports show that only 6.6 percent of all individuals employed in executive, administrative, or managerial positions are Hispanics, and only 9.9 percent of these jobs are held by blacks.[20] Like women, many of these minorities are untapped organizational potential. However, if the enterprise can attract, train, and retain these people through effective human relations, its productivity and efficiency will increase.

Bell Atlantic believes that international markets offer great opportunities for the firm. Bell Atlantic International markets telecommunications software and systems support and provides consulting services to foreign telephone companies.

INTERNATIONAL OPERATIONS

The devaluation of the dollar, the international trade deficit, and the growing impetus toward improved productivity and service quality are leading to an increase in international operations for many firms. Companies that never sold a unit overseas are now discovering attractive international markets for their outputs. They are also finding foreign firms coming to the states in search of suppliers and producers. These developments illustrate an inevitable fact: More and more American business will be done overseas and/or with foreign firms.[21] In turn, this will mean that managers will have to be sensitive to foreign cultures and learn how to interact effectively with these people. Many of the human relations ideas used here in the states will have to be adapted for international operations.

HOW THIS BOOK WILL HELP YOU

Having discussed the nature of human relations, let us now examine the way in which this text can be of help to you. The primary objective of the book is to familiarize you with the field of human relations, pointing out

■ ■ ■ ■ ■ ■ ■

[19] *Statistical Abstract of the United States, 1988* (Washington, D.C.: Department of Commerce, 1988), p. 422.

[20] Ibid., p. 376.

[21] *Business Week*, May 9, 1988, p. 36.

ways in which this information can be of personal value. For the most part the text is written from the standpoint of human relations in organizations, since this is where most adults have the greatest need for this information. However, much of the material is also applicable in your own life. In particular, there are four major benefits that this book will provide to you.

1. *Fact Not Intuition.* The information in this book is based on fact. Research studies and reports from industry, government, and other major organizations have been drawn upon in gathering together the material in each chapter. While the art of human relations is not overlooked, it is not allowed to get in the way of proven, scientific findings.

SCIENTIFIC FINDINGS WILL BE REPORTED.

2. *Comprehensiveness.* This book is thorough in its coverage of the field of human relations. All of the major areas of concern to the modern manager, as well as many minor ones, are addressed. This edition has also been thoroughly updated and revised so as to contain the very latest available human relations material.

THOROUGH COVERAGE WILL BE EMPLOYED.

3. *Applicability.* Information that is too theoretical has limited value for practicing managers and others who are interested in learning about human relations. In this book, every effort has been made to show how the information can be applied.

THERE WILL BE AN EMPHASIS ON PRACTICALITY.

4. *Personal Insights.* In all of the chapters there are short quizzes and workshop projects assigned to provide feedback on your own personal human relations style or philosophy. The purpose of these projects is to supplement the text material and get you involved in further analysis of the concepts under discussion, thereby increasing your personal insights.

PERSONAL INSIGHTS WILL BE INCREASED.

Some of the information we will be studying will be of value to you almost immediately, as in the case of material related to communication effectiveness. Some of the material may be of more value to you a little bit later in your career, as in the case of the material related to performance evaluation and appraisal. Yet, regardless of where your career path takes you, the material in this book is designed to help you meet the human relations challenges you will face in the world around you.

SUMMARY

Human relations is a process by which management brings workers into contact with the organization in such a way that the objectives of both groups are achieved. Human relations is people-oriented, work-oriented, effectiveness-oriented, based on empirical experience as opposed to relying solely on intuition and common sense, and useful at all levels of the work hierarchy.

The modern manager has to be concerned with human relations if he or she hopes to be effective. When industrialism emerged in the latter half of the eighteenth century, however, the owner-managers were more interested in efficient production than in their employees. This concern for efficiency continued through the nineteenth century and was vigorously promoted by the scientific managers. Employing their engineering skills in a work setting, these managers studied plant design, plant layout, machine feed and speed, and a host of other factors that could bring about increases in productivity. The greatest weakness of the scientific managers, however, was that they knew very little about the management of people.

As the scientific management movement progressed, an interest in the behavioral side of management started to grow. It was becoming obvious that concern for production brought about people-related problems and that the effective manager had to be interested in both the personnel and the work. The Hawthorne studies revealed the work organization to be a social system and pointed to the need for consideration of psychological and sociological aspects of organizational behavior. The Hawthorne studies helped light the way for much behavioral research. Since then, the behavioral movement has made great progress. The classical model of the worker has been replaced by a human resources model. In addition, behavioral scientists have entered the field and, by using the scientific method, are helping to unravel many of the mysteries of human behavior at work, such as how to deal with both workaholics and those who subscribe to the leisure ethic. They are also attacking the problems of incorporating women and minorities into the work force and addressing the challenge of international operations. Managers are finding part of the answer in the effective use of motivation. This subject will be the focus of our attention in the next chapter.

KEY TERMS IN THE CHAPTER

human relations	workaholic
scientific management	work ethic
Hawthorne studies	worth ethic
social network	leisure ethic
traditional model	scientific method
human resources model	behavioral scientist
System 1	test group
System 2	control group
System 3	structured interview
System 4	unstructured interview
work	

REVIEW AND STUDY QUESTIONS

1.   What is meant by the term *human relations*? Put it in your own words.

2.   How much did the owner-managers of factories in the latter half of the eighteenth century know about human relations?

3.   Did the scientific managers know anything about human relations? What were their shortcomings in this area?

4.   What were some of the principal findings of the Hawthorne studies? Cite them.

5.   Are happy workers also productive workers? Explain.

6.   How does the traditional model differ from the human resources model? Compare and contrast the two models.

7.   How does a System 1 manager differ from a System 2 manager? How does a System 3 manager differ from a System 4 manager? Which of these systems is most reflective of the human resources philosophy?

8.   In analyzing behavioral problems, practitioners of modern human relations must rely on the scientific method. What is the logic behind this statement?

9.   How do each of the following view work: a workaholic, a work ethic advocate, a worth ethic advocate, a leisure ethic advocate?

10.   In what way are women proving to be a human relations challenge? Minorities? International operations? Explain.

TIME OUT ANSWERS

1.   **False.**   While money is certainly an important motivator, most workers place it in fourth or fifth position. The most commonly cited factors include recognition for a job well done, a chance to succeed, a feeling that the work is important, and an opportunity to contribute to the accomplishment of worthwhile objectives.

2.   **False.**   The work group with high morale will outperform the work group with moderate morale only if the first group's objectives or goals call for higher output than the second group's. If the first group sets low output goals because it is in conflict with the management, the group's output will be low.

3.   **True.**   Workers who do the same job, belong to the same union, or are members of the same unit are more likely to associate with each other than they are to associate with individuals who do none of these things.

4.   **False.** The most efficient workers perform best when placed under moderate stress. Under high stress their output slows because they have to adjust to job-related tension and anxiety.

5.   **True.** Managers tend to use the grapevine far more than workers both in terms of sending and receiving information.

6.   **False.** Top managers tend to be more intelligent than the average of their subordinates. Additionally, while personality is important, it is no substitute for intelligent problem solving and decision making.

7.   **False.** Many managers do not get all of their work done because they fail to establish priorities and do not delegate enough of the minor work to the subordinates.

8.   **False.** While job-related stress does increase as one goes up the hierarchy, it is greatest at the middle to upper-middle ranks. After this it tends to decrease because the executive can delegate many stress-creating tasks to subordinates.

9.   **False.** The major reason is that the organization's machinery is inefficient, the workers are not trained as well as they should be and/or the rewards associated with high output are not sufficiently motivational to encourage personnel to maximize their output.

10.   **True.** Research reveals that eight out of ten managerial communications are downward while only one out of ten involves an upward flow of information.

SCORING:

9–10	Excellent.	Your score is in the top 4 percent of all individuals taking this quiz.
8	Good.	Your score is in the top 26 percent of all individuals taking this quiz.
7	Average.	Your score is just about in the middle. Thirty-seven percent of all individuals taking this quiz received this score.
6 or less	Below average.	Thirty-seven percent of all individuals taking this quiz received this score.

Regardless of your score, you should use this initial quiz only as an indication of the amount of general human relations knowledge you now have. You will be learning a great deal more as you read this book. If your score was lower than you would have liked, do not be discouraged. You will have an opportunity later in the book to take another quiz similar to this one. By then you should be able to improve your score.

CASE: CHARLES'S APPROACH

The Shottlen Company is well known for its door-to-door selling. The company markets a wide variety of home appliances and kitchen-related products using a direct-to-the-customer approach. Prices are slightly higher than those of competitive goods at the supermarket or grocery store, but because of the convenience of at-home buying, customers are willing to pay more for Shottlen products.

Six months ago the firm suffered a severe drop-off in sales that has lasted until the present time. Two factors account for this downturn. First, the three-state region where Shottlen is strongest has been undergoing an economic crunch. Five large manufacturing firms have closed plants in the area, and approximately 6 percent of the total work force in the region has been affected in some way. Second, for the first time in its history, Shottlen finds itself facing strong competition. Two major retail chains in the area have started selling door-to-door.

As sales started dropping off, the company began looking to make operational changes. It finally was agreed that a new sales manager was needed. "We have to be more aggressive if we're going to win this battle," the president told the top management staff. The group concurred, and two months ago Charles Corelli was offered the job of sales manager. Charles has had ten years of sales experience, five of it in door-to-door selling.

After looking over the company and comparing its sales performance to the firm he was leaving, Charles announced that he would join Shottlen on one condition. A new sales bonus plan had to be installed. Salespeople had been receiving 25 percent of whatever they sold, and the average salesperson had been grossing $300 a week. With the downturn in sales, this weekly gross had dropped to $245. Charles's new bonus plan was designed to change this. Everyone who earned 80 percent of their sales quota would continue to receive 25 percent of gross sales. If individuals reached from 81 to 100 percent of quota, however, their take would increase to 35 percent; anything over 100 percent of quota would mean 40 percent of gross sales for the salesperson.

Management did not like the idea initially, but quickly realized that it could be the key to pulling Shottlen out of its sales slump. Charles was given the go-ahead.

Over the last month the firm's sales have increased but the new bonus system does not seem to be accomplishing its objective. A review of the sales commissions shows that everyone is now trying very hard to get into the 81 to 90 percent quota range. This jump from 25 to 35 percent of gross sales is apparently resulting in enough income to make them happy. The best salesperson in the firm recently told Charles, "I'm happy making 35 percent of gross. I don't need to do any better than this." Many of the other salespeople seem to agree.

Nevertheless, in an effort to generate more sales, Charles has been urging everyone to work longer hours. He also took three of the new salespeople under his wing. However, after two weeks all three quit. One of them explained it this way, "Charles will get up at 6 a.m., make his first house call by 8 a.m., and keep going until well after 7 p.m. He's a real workaholic. However, I'm not like that. I want to make a good living but I don't want to kill myself doing it. Charles's idea of the work ethic is a lot different from mine." For his part, Charles has suggested to the president that the lowest 25 percent of the sales force should be fired and replaced by those who have "an appreciation for the American work ethic." The president has said that he will think about his suggestion and get back to him. ∎

QUESTIONS

1.   In your own words, how would you describe Charles's philosophy of work? Is he a workaholic? Explain.

2.   How would you describe the work philosophy of the salespeople? Explain.

3.   Do you agree with Charles's suggestion that the lowest 25 percent of the sales force should be fired? Defend your answer in terms of both work philosophy and human relations.

CASE: A MATTER OF TURNOVER

Milmouth Hospital is a county hospital located in a major southwest city. The hospital offers a large number of services and has a staff of 150 in-house managers, 400 nurses, and 600 support personnel.

Over the last 90 days there has been a dramatic turnover of nurses in both the emergency room and the trauma unit. Because it is so difficult to hire skilled nurses for these areas, the hospital has had to raise salaries by 20 percent in order to retain the current nurses and to attract new ones.

The senior manager of both the emergency room and the trauma unit is Eileen Kostad. Eileen was a head nurse of a large trauma unit in the Washington, D.C. area and came highly recommended for the job. One of her recommendation letters described her as "hard working, intense, and goal-directed." Another called her "dedicated, professional, and highly knowledgeable in her job."

Given the disparity between her strong recommendations and the high turnover of her people, the hospital administrator, George Fallon, decided to discuss the matter with Eileen. He explained his concern over the high employee turnover and then asked Eileen for her explanation of the problem. Here is part of what she said:

The nurses in both emergency and the trauma unit were not doing their jobs properly when I got here. Most of them were not wearing proper dress, they failed to complete all of the necessary daily paperwork, and they often substituted for each other without clearing it with me. They were a care-free, disorganized group that lacked professionalism. I instituted rigorous regulations and straightened out all of this. Those who couldn't shape up have had to ship out.

George was quite surprised by Eileen's remarks. He was unaware that there had been any problems in the emergency and trauma units, and when he mentioned Eileen's comments to one of the in-house physicians, the latter said, "I don't believe it. Why don't you talk to one of the nurses who left and get her input?" George decided that this was good advice and earlier this week he spoke to Samantha Rogers, one of the first nurses to leave the trauma unit. She told George:

Eileen came charging in like a bull in a china shop. She had no prior management experience in running a department. She had been a head nurse for the past 20 years. She knows the technical and work-centered part of the job. However, she doesn't know how to interact with people and get the best out of them. She is rigid, dogmatic, and controlling in her approach. She has no real confidence and trust in her people. The previous manager was much more humanistic and teamwork-oriented. I just couldn't work for Eileen, so I quit. ∎

QUESTIONS

1. Which management system (1, 2, 3, or 4) does Eileen use? Describe the style.

2. Which management system did Eileen's predecessor use? Describe this style.

3. Why is Eileen having trouble? What human relations mistakes is she making? What changes should she make? Explain.

Experiencing Supervisor-Employee Relations

Purpose

- To enrich the student's understanding of the traditional and human resources models.
- To observe supervisor-employee relations using this model for analysis.

Procedure

1.   Two students are chosen to role play the situation described below. One is assigned the traditional management model role (see Table 1.1) and the other the human resources model role.

2.   After the role playing is complete, the class should discuss the following:

     a.   How well did each person represent his or her role?

     b.   Which model provides the "best answer for the situation"?

Situation

You are two store managers of a national retail chain. Your stores sell a wide variety of consumer merchandise including appliances, auto supplies, clothing, electronic goods, garden equipment, household fixtures, and pharmaceuticals. There has been a large amount of tardiness over the past month and this is affecting sales. A regional meeting has been called to discuss the problem. Each of you is to present briefly your approach to handling the situation. The person recommending a traditional approach should speak first and set forth his or her recommendations in 3 to 4 minutes. Then the person recommending a human resources management approach should speak for 3 to 4 minutes. Finally, each should ask the other to elaborate on any points that were unclear. No more than five minutes should be used for this question-and-answer process.

FUNDAMENTALS OF MOTIVATION

GOALS OF THE CHAPTER

One of the most important questions in human relations today is: "How do you get people to do things?" The answer rests in an understanding of what motivation is all about, for it is motivated workers who ultimately get things done, and without such people no organization can hope to be effective.

In this chapter we examine the fundamentals of motivation at work. Our first goal is to look at both how and why people act as they do. We then study the need hierarchy and its relevance to motivation. Finally, we focus attention on expectancy theory and try to answer the question: "What motivates an individual to act in a given way?"

When you have finished reading this chapter, you should be able to:

1. Describe the two sides of motivation: movement and motive.

2. Identify the five basic needs in Maslow's need hierarchy.

3. Describe the two-factor theory of motivation and explain its relevance to the practicing manager.

4. Discuss expectancy theory, noting how both valence and expectancy influence motivational force.

5. Explain the value of money and employee satisfaction in the motivation process.

OPENING CASE

HAPPY WHERE SHE IS

Selling is something that Cecilia Rodriguez always enjoyed; and her sales record shows that she is good at it. Over the last 12 months, Cecilia has been the number one salesperson on three occasions and has finished in the top five every month.

In addition to liking her job, Cecilia works hard. She knows that the average salesperson will make one sale for every five client calls, while an outstanding salesperson will make one sale for every four client calls. Because she is on the road every morning by 7 a.m. and does not stop working until 5 p.m., Cecilia is able to average twelve calls a day. Her average of three sales a day is 50 percent higher than that of the typical salesperson.

Cecilia's company has a "promotion from within" policy. Whenever there is an opening for a sales manager, the job is first offered to a leading salesperson. Last week the company asked Cecilia if she would like to be a sales manager. She turned them down. "Thanks," she said, "but I love to be on the road and to sell. I'd die of boredom in the office. I want to be where the action is, not watching other people carry out the action. Also, the only way I could measure how well I'm doing is through the success of my salespeople. I don't want to depend on other people for my success; I want to win on my own. I know how well I'm doing at the end of each day by just counting my sales. If I'm behind, I work even harder the next day. However, if my salespeople were not doing the job, I'd be frustrated by the situation since I couldn't personally straighten things out."

1.   Is Cecilia a high achiever?

2.   What motivates Cecilia?

3.   What is Cecilia's preference or valence for the office manager's job?

4.   How satisfied is Cecilia with her job?

Write down your answers to these questions and put them aside. We will return to them later. ■

WHAT IS MOTIVATION?

The psychological drive that directs someone toward an objective is **motivation**. The word comes from the Latin word *movere*, "to move." When we see people working very hard we say they are motivated, because we can see they are moving. This is as true for a secretary typing 100 words a minute as it is for an executive slowly reading a complex legal document. Yet motivation involves more than just movement. A student staring at some notes on a piece of paper may be memorizing this information, but we see virtually no movement occurring. Thus, motivation involves both physical *and* mental movement.

In addition, any systematic analysis of motivation must be concerned with both *how* and *why* people act as they do. The former may be easy to pinpoint, but the latter often is not easy to identify. For example, Ralph has been offered time and a half to work on Saturdays and he has agreed to do so. We can, therefore, respond to the question, "How do you get Ralph to work on Saturday?" by answering, "Money." However, we cannot say with certainty why he is willing to work on Saturday. It may be because he wants to buy a boat, go on a vacation, put aside some money for a rainy day, or help pay some hospital bills for an elderly aunt. The "why" is currently unclear, and if we want to know the answer, we must investigate his motives. Motivation, therefore, has two sides: *movement* and *motive*. The former can be seen; the latter can only be inferred. Before reading on, take the accompanying quiz "What Motivates You?" and then read the interpretation of the results at the end of the chapter. This quiz should provide some insights to your own job-related motivation.

■ ■ ■ ■ ■ ■ ■ ■ ■ ■ ■ ■
MOTIVATION HAS TWO SIDES: MOVEMENT AND MOTIVE.

MOTIVES AND MOTIVATION

The "whys" of behavior are the **motives**. Oftentimes they are defined as needs, drives, wants, or impulses within the individual. Regardless of how they are defined, however, motives arouse and maintain activity as well as determine the general direction of an individual's behavior. Many psychologists believe that there are two types of motives: primary and secondary. Primary motives are unlearned. The need for food and shelter are examples. Secondary needs are learned. The need for power, achievement, and affiliation are examples.

In studying how motives prompt people to action, we must first examine two related topics: motive strength and goals. *Motives* are *directed toward goals*. For example, a person who needs money (motive) will opt for overtime (goal). An individual who desires recognition (motive) will strive for promotion to the top ranks of the organization (goal).

■ ■ ■ ■ ■ ■ ■ ■ ■ ■ ■ ■
MOTIVES ARE DIRECTED TOWARD GOALS.

Of course, an individual often has many motives or needs and cannot actively pursue all of them simultaneously. To determine which motives the person will attempt to satisfy through activity, it is necessary to examine *motive strength*. In Figure 2.1 on page 43, a diagram of relative motive strengths, Motive 7 has the greatest strength and will receive the most activity. The individual will work hardest to satisfy this motive. On the other hand, Motive 2 has a very low strength and will be given the lowest priority. Finally, once a motive or need is satisfied, it will no longer

■ ■ ■ ■ ■ ■ ■ ■ ■ ■ ■ ■
MOTIVE STRENGTH DETERMINES BEHAVIOR.

TIME OUT

WHAT MOTIVATES YOU?

There are many things that motivate people. The list below contains 10 work-motivating factors. Read the list carefully and place a 10 next to the factor which has the greatest work-motivating potential for you. Place a 9 next to the second most important work-motivating factor. Continue until you have rank-ordered all ten. If you do not currently work, mentally choose a job for yourself and use it in completing the list.

      7   1. Interesting work
      4   2. Job security
      1   3. Up-to-date equipment
     10   4. A feeling of doing something important
      3   5. Good wages
      9   6. Challenging work
      5   7. Effective supervision by the boss
      6   8. A chance for advancement
      2   9. Pleasant working conditions
      8   10. The opportunity to succeed at what you are doing

The interpretation of your answers can be found in the back of the chapter.

motivate the individual to seek goal-directed behavior. Therefore, after Motive 7 is satisfied, the individual will direct behavior toward activities to help fulfill Motive 3. Once that motive is satisfied, the individual will proceed to seek satisfaction for Motives 5, 4, 8, 6, 1, and finally 2, in that order.

When an individual is given the opportunity to attain a desired goal, the person is positively motivated. He or she will pursue that objective. Sometimes, however, an organization will use negative motivation because an individual has done something wrong, such as commit a major violation of company policy. In this case the person may be turned down for promotion or be suspended from work without pay for a predetermined period of time, such as three weeks. Negative motivation is used to enforce rules and to shape employee behavior.

FIGURE 2.1   **MOTIVES AND MOTIVE STRENGTH**

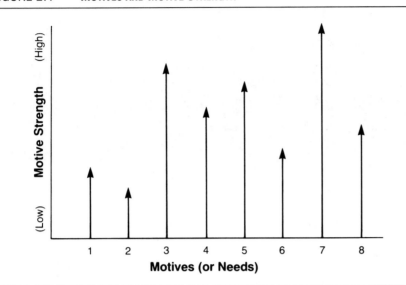

THE NEED HIERARCHY

We have examined motives or needs in very general terms. What kinds of needs do people have that in turn result in goal-directed behavior? Abraham Maslow, the noted psychologist, has set forth five needs that he believes are universal: *physiological, safety, social, esteem,* and *self-actualization* (see Figure 2.2).

PHYSIOLOGICAL NEEDS

The most fundamental of all needs, according to Maslow, are **physiological**. Some common examples are food, clothing, and shelter. A person deprived of everything would want to satisfy these basic needs first. Safety, social, esteem, and self-actualization needs would be, at least for the moment, of secondary importance.

■ ■ ■ ■ ■ ■ ■ ■ ■ ■ ■ ■ ■
PHYSIOLOGICAL NEEDS ARE BASIC REQUIREMENTS SUCH AS FOOD, CLOTHING, AND SHELTER.

In the work place many organizations try to satisfy these needs by providing cafeterias, vending machines, adequate ventilation, lighting, heating, and other physical facilities. In addition, the firms pay the workers a salary with which they can meet these needs by purchasing food and clothing for their families. Although there are many physiological needs, the most basic would get prime attention until satisfied and then would be replaced by other physiological demands with greater need strength.

FIGURE 2.2 **MASLOW'S NEED HIERARCHY WHEN PHYSIOLOGICAL NEEDS ARE DOMINANT**

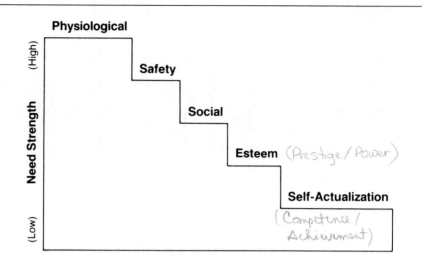

SAFETY NEEDS

■ ■ ■ ■ ■ ■ ■ ■ ■ ■ ■ ■ ■
SAFETY NEEDS PROVIDE FOR
SURVIVAL AND SECURITY.

Once physiological needs are basically satisfied, **safety needs** replace them. These are of two types. First, there is the need for *survival*; this need is so great that many of the laws in our society are designed to protect the life of the individual. Second, there is the need for *security*; this need has both physical and psychological dimensions. On the physical side, businesses often provide safety equipment and safety rules for protecting the worker on the job. They also provide accident, health, and life insurance to help meet safety needs. The psychological aspect of safety is evident in workers' desire for secure jobs in a predictable environment. Individuals who work in government bureaucracies often fall into this category. They want guaranteed employment. Their pay may not be very high, but they are assured of a steady job. Other people find such safety in business bureaucracies where the firm may not pay well, but it just about guarantees continued employment to anyone with minimum performance.

SOCIAL NEEDS

■ ■ ■ ■ ■ ■ ■ ■ ■ ■ ■ ■ ■
SOCIAL NEEDS ARE SATISFIED
THROUGH MEANINGFUL
INTERACTION WITH OTHERS.

When physiological and safety needs are basically satisfied, **social needs** become important motivators. The need involves interaction with others for the purpose of meaningful relationships. On the job, interaction often occurs among people who work near one another and come into frequent daily contact. Over time they build up friendships and look forward to the interaction. In their home lives, people fulfill social needs when they meet their neighbors and socialize with them on a regular basis.

Business firms try to meet this need in their workers by allowing them to interact and talk with each other. On assembly lines, workers know that they can do their routine jobs and interact at the same time. In retail and banking firms, there is an increased opportunity for interaction, since the workers carry out their jobs by socializing to some degree with the customers.

It is important to note that in boring, routine work, social affiliation helps make the job more bearable. When such interaction occurs, morale is higher and productivity tends to remain at least within tolerable ranges. However, when social interaction is denied, workers tend to fight the system by restricting work output or by doing no more than is required by their job descriptions. Allowing the personnel to fulfill social needs on the job often helps prevent these negative behaviors.

These Sun Refining and Marketing Company employees have extended their working relationships to include satisfying their social needs as well.

ESTEEM NEEDS

When social needs are basically satisfied, **esteem needs** come into play. People need to feel important, and self-esteem and self-respect are vital in this process. Esteem is much more *psychological* in nature than the other three needs we have discussed. We can give a person food, clothing, shelter, protection, and social interaction. However, the esteem with which individuals regard themselves is mostly a function of what they allow themselves to believe. For example, a person who is told by his boss that he does an excellent job will only be motivated by this praise if he accepts the laudatory comments. If the individual believes that the manager is only complimenting his work as a matter of course and really does not mean it, the praise has no motivational effect. Research reveals that two motives closely related to esteem are prestige and power.

ESTEEM NEEDS ARE THOSE FOR SELF-IMPORTANCE AND SELF-RESPECT.

PRESTIGE   For many people, **prestige** means "keeping up with the Joneses," or perhaps getting ahead of them. In any event, prestige carries with it respect and status and influences the way people talk and act around the individual. A company president has a lot of prestige and is treated with great respect by organizational members. Out on the golf course, however, the company president may have limited prestige among the players, and the country club's golf pro is given the greatest amount of respect. Thus, one's prestige varies depending on the situation.

PRESTIGE CARRIES WITH IT RESPECT AND STATUS.

POWER   The ability to influence or induce behavior in others is **power**. Power can be of two kinds: position and personal. *Position* power is derived from the individual's position in the company. The president has a

POWER IS THE ABILITY TO INFLUENCE OR INDUCE BEHAVIOR.

great deal more position power than a middle manager in the same organization. *Personal* power derives from an individual's personality and behavior. Anne may have a pleasing personality and an easy-going manner, which results in her being able to cut across departmental lines and get support for her proposals; Andy, however, is considered hard-nosed and bossy and is unable to secure such cooperation. Within bounds, people like power because it provides them with feelings of self-esteem.

SELF-ACTUALIZATION NEEDS

■ ■ ■ ■ ■ ■ ■ ■ ■ ■ ■ ■ ■ ■
SELF-ACTUALIZATION NEEDS ARE
THOSE FOR SATISFYING ONE'S FULL
POTENTIAL.

When all the other needs are basically satisfied, **self-actualization needs** manifest themselves. Because people satisfy this need in so many different ways, behavioral scientists know less about it than the other needs. However, research reveals that there are two motives related to self-actualization, **competence** and **achievement**.

■ ■ ■ ■ ■ ■ ■ ■ ■ ■ ■ ■ ■ ■
COMPETENCE IMPLIES CONTROL
OVER ENVIRONMENTAL FACTORS.

COMPETENCE   Competence is similar to power in that it implies control over environmental factors. At a very early age children begin illustrating their need for competence by touching and handling objects so as to become familiar with them. Later on, they begin trying to take things apart and put them back together again. As a result, children learn tasks at which they are competent.

On the job, the competence motive reveals itself in the form of a desire for job mastery and professional growth. The individual begins matching his or her abilities and skills against the environment in a contest that is challenging but that can be won. Organizations that provide meaningful, challenging work help their people meet this need. In some companies, such as those using assembly lines, such jobs are not in abundance, and the competence motive often goes unsatisfied.

ACHIEVEMENT   Over the last 30 years, a great deal of research has been conducted on people's desire to achieve. One of the leading researchers, David C. McClelland of Harvard University, has been particularly interested in this urge.[1] On the basis of his research, he has set forth the following characteristics of **high achievers**. People who are high

■ ■ ■ ■ ■ ■ ■

[1] See David C. McClelland, J. W. Atkinson, R. A. Clark, and E. L. Lowell, *The Achievement Motive* (New York: Appleton-Century-Crofts, Inc., 1953); David C. McClelland, *The Achieving Society* (Princeton, N.J.: D. Van Nostrand Company, Inc., 1961); and Richard Davidson, "Motivating the Underachiever," *Supervisory Management*, January 1983, pp. 39–41.

achievers: (1) like situations in which they can take personal responsibility for finding solutions to problems; (2) tend to be moderate-risk takers; as opposed to high-risk or low-risk takers; and (3) like concrete feedback on their performance so that they know how well they are doing.

■ ■ ■ ■ ■ ■ ■ ■ ■ ■ ■ ■
CHARACTERISTICS OF HIGH ACHIEVERS.

Although only about 10 to 15 percent of the population in the United States have the desire to achieve, high achievement can be encouraged and developed. McClelland has recommended several methods for individuals who want to become high achievers:

1.   Strive to obtain feedback, so that your successes can be noted and you can make them serve as reinforcement for strengthening your desire to achieve even more.

■ ■ ■ ■ ■ ■ ■ ■ ■ ■ ■ ■
WAYS TO DEVELOP HIGH ACHIEVEMENT.

2.   Pick out people you know who have performed well and use them as models to emulate.

3.   Modify your self-image by imagining yourself as someone who needs to succeed and to be challenged.

4.   Control your daydreaming by thinking and talking to yourself in positive terms.

How can you use these ideas? Human Relations in Action: Increasing Your Achievement Drive offers some specific steps.

On the job, organizations can help create the proper climate for developing high achievement by giving people jobs that provide feedback, increase personal initiative, and allow individuals to take moderate risks. However, while the enterprise can encourage high achievement in its personnel, to a large degree this drive is something that develops in early childhood. Also, high achievers get things done themselves, but they are often ineffective in managing others, so organizations do not want all their employees to possess high achievement drive.

NEED MIX

An important premise of the need hierarchy is that as one need is basically fulfilled, the next most important need becomes dominant and dictates individual behavior. Note that we say "basically fulfilled." This is because most people in our society are *partially satisfied* at each level and *partially unsatisfied*. Greatest satisfaction tends to occur at the physiological level and least satisfaction at the self-actualization level. Maslow put it this way:

IMP

■ ■ ■ ■ ■ ■ ■ ■ ■ ■ ■ ■
PEOPLE ARE PARTIALLY SATISFIED AND PARTIALLY UNSATISFIED AT EACH LEVEL OF THE HIERARCHY.

In actual fact, most members of our society who are normal are partially satisfied in all their basic needs and partially unsatisfied in all their basic needs at the same time. A more realistic description of the hierarchy would be in terms of decreas-

HUMAN RELATIONS IN ACTION

INCREASING YOUR ACHIEVEMENT DRIVE

There are many things you can do to increase your achievement drive. The following are eight of the most helpful.

1. *Put Your Goals in Writing.* This serves two useful purposes. First, it forces you to think through your objectives. Exactly what are you trying to accomplish? Second, it serves as a basis for comparing desired and actual progress.

2. *Make the Goals Challenging Yet Attainable.* If the goals are easy to attain, you really are not achieving much. If the goals are too difficult, you will not be able to reach them. Choose objectives that stretch you, but are within your grasp. In this way, the goals become learning devices that help you grow.

3. *Be Sure That Your Goals Are Compatible.* If your goals are not compatible, you are working at cross purposes with yourself. For example, if one of your objectives is to double your sales this quarter, it is unrealistic to have a second objective of cutting travel and entertainment by 30 percent. If anything, this budget will probably go up because you will have to do more traveling and/or entertaining.

4. *Have Specific Goals.* Where possible, quantify your goals, i.e., reduce production costs by 7 percent; increase sales by 9 percent; increase the number of salespeople by 22. If this is not possible or desirable, write the objective in such a way that progress can be measured.

5. *Establish Timetables.* Tie your goals to a timetable, noting when progress will be achieved. This will help you keep track of how well you are doing. If you start to fall behind, you will be able to identify when and where things are going wrong.

6. *Establish Priorities.* Determine which goals have to be attained first and which can wait. If sales have to be increased as quickly as possible, put this goal high up on your list of things to do. If trips to the field to check on your salespeople can wait until next month, schedule them for next month and get back to work on those things that must be done now.

7. *Review and Revise Your Goals.* Look over your list of goals every 90 days and see how well you are doing. Have any of the goals been attained? If so, remove them from the list. Do any of the current objectives need to be changed? If so, change them. Do any new ones need to be added? Put them on the list. This process keeps your goal-directed behavior properly focused.

8. *Reward Yourself.* Every time you accomplish one of your objectives, reward yourself. When you close that big sale, treat yourself to dinner or buy that suit you have had your eye on. This work/reward approach will encourage you to keep up your efforts. Remember that successful people are good to themselves. If one of your subordinates did something well, you would reward the individual as a way of encouraging a repeat performance. Be no less kind to yourself.

FIGURE 2.3   NEED MIX WHEN PHYSIOLOGICAL AND SAFETY NEEDS HAVE THE HIGHEST STRENGTH

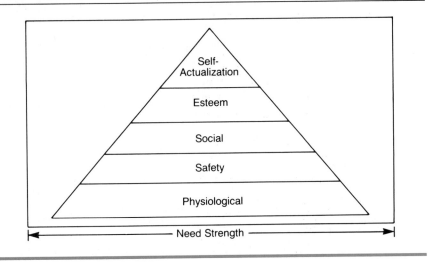

ing percentage of satisfaction as we go up the hierarchy of prepotency. For instance, if I may assign arbitrary figures, . . . it is as if the average citizen is satisfied perhaps 85 per cent in his physiological needs, 70 per cent in his safety needs, 50 per cent in his [social] needs, 40 per cent in his self-esteem needs, and 10 per cent in his self-actualization needs.[2]

As a result, the Maslow need hierarchy cannot be viewed as an all-or-nothing framework. Rather, to understand the fundamentals of human behavior we should regard the hierarchy as useful in predicting behavior on a high or low probability basis. For example, among people who come from abject poverty, the **need mix** pictured in Figure 2.3 is probably highly representative. However, most people in American society are characterized by strong social or affiliation needs, relatively strong esteem and safety needs, and somewhat less important physiological and self-actualization needs; this need mix is illustrated in Figure 2.4. For individuals whose physiological, safety, and social needs are greatly satisfied, esteem and self-actualization are most important. A person born to great wealth would fit into this category. So would a top management executive. The need mix for these people is pictured in Figure 2.5. Of course, these configurations are intended only as examples. Different

. . . .

[2] Abraham H. Maslow, "A Theory of Human Motivation," *Psychological Review*, July 1943, pp. 388–389.

FIGURE 2.4   **NEED MIX WHEN SOCIAL NEEDS HAVE THE HIGHEST STRENGTH**

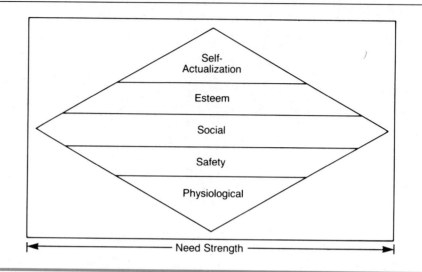

FIGURE 2.5   **NEED MIX WHEN ESTEEM AND SELF-ACTUALIZATION NEEDS HAVE THE HIGHEST STRENGTH**

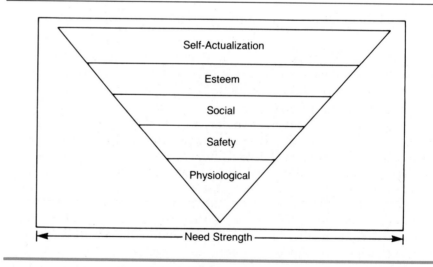

configurations would be appropriate for different people, since in reality the need mix changes from one individual to another.

Maslow's theory is interesting but its practical value is limited. In order to see its application to the motivation of personnel, we must turn to Frederick Herzberg's two-factor theory.

STOP!

Review your answer to the first question and make any changes you would like. Then compare your answer to the one below.

1.   Is Cecilia a high achiever?

She certainly is. Notice how she enjoys taking personal responsibility for finding solutions to problems and likes concrete feedback on her performance so she knows how well she is doing. These are two of the primary characteristics of high achievers. ∎

THE TWO-FACTOR THEORY

The two-factor theory of motivation is a direct result of research conducted by Herzberg and his associates on job satisfaction and productivity among 200 accountants and engineers.[3] Each subject was asked to think of a time when he or she felt especially good about his or her job and a time when he or she felt particularly bad about the job and to describe the conditions that led to these feelings. The researchers found that the employees named different types of conditions for good and bad feelings. This led Herzberg to conclude that motivation consists of two factors: hygiene and motivators (Table 2.1).

HYGIENE FACTORS

The factors associated with negative feelings Herzberg called **hygiene factors**. Illustrations included salary, technical supervision, working conditions, company policies and administration, and interpersonal relations. When the subjects of Herzberg's study were asked what made them feel exceptionally bad about their jobs, typical answers included: "I'm really not satisfied with the salary I'm being paid; it's much too low." "My boss is always too busy to offer me any technical supervision." "The working conditions around here are really poor." All the responses have one thing in common: They relate to the environment in which the work is performed.

·······

[3] Frederick Herzberg, Bernard Mausner, and Barbara Bloch Snyderman, *The Motivation to Work* (New York: John Wiley & Sons, Inc., 1959).

TABLE 2.1   THE TWO-FACTOR THEORY

HYGIENE FACTORS (ENVIRONMENT)	MOTIVATORS (WORK ITSELF)
Salary	Recognition
Technical supervision	Advancement
Working conditions	Possibility of growth
Company policies and administration	Achievement
Interpersonal relations	Work itself

HYGIENE FACTORS ARE ENVIRONMENTALLY RELATED.

Herzberg called these environment-related factors *hygiene* because, like physical hygiene, they prevent deterioration but do not lead to growth. For example, if you brush your teeth (a hygienic step) you can prevent cavities, but your teeth will not become stronger nor will a chipped tooth grow back to its original size. Thus, you have two alternatives: brush your teeth and prevent further damage, or do not brush your teeth and end up losing them. Analogously, Herzberg felt that if you give people hygiene factors you will not give them motivation but you will prevent dissatisfaction.

HYGIENE FACTORS CAUSE DISSATISFACTION BY THEIR ABSENCE.

Using our own percentages as examples, Figure 2.6 provides an illustration of how Herzberg believes hygiene can affect performance. Note that when hygiene factors are satisfied, the workers perform at less than capacity. When these factors are not satisfied, performance drops. Thus, hygiene will not bring about an increase in productivity, but it will prevent a decline.

MOTIVATORS

MOTIVATORS ARE ASSOCIATED WITH POSITIVE FEELINGS.

The factors associated with positive feelings Herzberg called **motivators**. Examples are recognition, advancement, the possibility of growth, achievement, and the work itself. When the subjects were asked what made them feel exceptionally good about their jobs, typical answers included: "My job gives me a feeling of achievement," "I like the recognition I get for doing my job well," "The work is just plain interesting." All these responses have one thing in common: They relate to the work itself. Additionally, they are psychological in nature and relate to upper-level need satisfaction.

MOTIVATORS BRING ABOUT WORKER SATISFACTION.

Herzberg termed these factors motivators because he felt that they caused increases in performance. Using our own percentages as examples, Figure 2.7 provides an illustration of how Herzberg believes

FIGURE 2.6   THE RESULT WHEN HYGIENE FACTORS ARE NOT SATISFIED

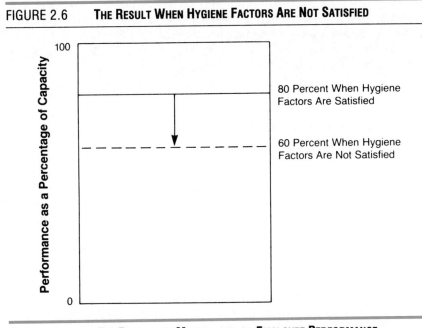

80 Percent When Hygiene
Factors Are Satisfied

60 Percent When Hygiene
Factors Are Not Satisfied

FIGURE 2.7   THE EFFECTS OF MOTIVATORS ON EMPLOYEE PERFORMANCE

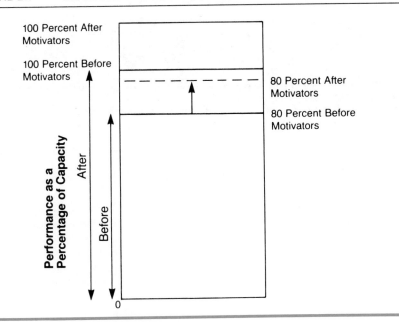

100 Percent After
Motivators

100 Percent Before
Motivators

80 Percent After
Motivators

80 Percent Before
Motivators

motivators can affect performance. Note that the employees represented are performing at 80 percent of capacity. When they are given motivators such as recognition, advancement, and the possibility of growth, their capacity for performance increases to 80 percent of the new amount. In short, as performance potential increases, output goes up.

MOTIVATION-HYGIENE THEORY AND MANAGERS

One of the major reasons that Herzberg's two-factor theory has been so well accepted by managers is that the theory applies Maslow's need concept to the job. For example, Herzberg suggests using hygiene factors to help people attain their lower-level needs. Conversely, he recommends motivators to meet upper-level needs. Figure 2.8 integrates these two concepts. As you can see, Herzberg suggests that physiological, safety, social, and, to some degree, esteem needs can be satisfied with hygiene factors. The remainder of the esteem needs and self-actualization needs can be satisfied with motivators.

A second reason for the popularity of Herzberg's theory is that practicing managers agree with it. In a recent study designed to learn more

FIGURE 2.8   MOTIVATION-HYGIENE AND MASLOW

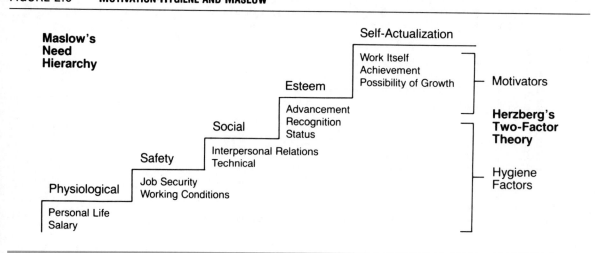

TABLE 2.2   **A COMPARISON OF CAREER MOTIVATIONS FOR FEMALE AND MALE MANAGERS ON A SCALE OF 1 (HIGHEST) TO 8 (LOWEST)**

MOTIVATION	FEMALES	MALES
Sense of achievement	1.68	2.10
Challenge	2.91	2.55
Money	3.45	4.04
Independence	3.48	3.96
Power	5.53	5.71
Security	5.58	5.38
Opportunity to meet interesting people	5.80	5.24
Opportunity to travel	7.00	7.00

Source: Benson Rosen, Mary Ellen Templeton, and Karen Kichine, "The First Few Years on the Job: Women in Management," *Business Horizons*, November–December 1981, p. 27. Copyright 1981 by the Foundation for the School of Business at Indiana University. Reprinted with permission.

about work motivations of men and women, 128 managers were asked to rank eight motives for pursuing a managerial career. The results are reported in Table 2.2. Notice that the top two choices correspond to Herzberg's motivators, illustrating the value of his theory. Also the lists for both groups are quite similar, revealing the application of his theory to managers in general.

MOTIVATION-HYGIENE THEORY IN PERSPECTIVE

Many business people who read about the motivation-hygiene theory are likely to accept it as totally accurate. Certainly, to the extent that it encourages the manager to provide upper-level need satisfaction, the theory is relevant to our study of motivation. However, the theory has several serious shortcomings that merit attention.

First, Herzberg contends that something is *either* a hygiene factor *or* a motivator. The two are independent of each other. Additionally, a lack of hygiene will lead to dissatisfaction, but its presence will not lead to satisfaction. Satisfaction results only from the presence of motivators. We can diagram the relationship as in Figure 2.9. If you give people hygiene factors, you will not motivate them, but you will prevent dissatisfaction. Thus hygiene, according to Herzberg, creates a zero-level of motivation.

Research, however, reveals that some people are indeed motivated by hygiene factors. For example, many individuals say that money is a motivator for them. Some people report that recognition and the chance

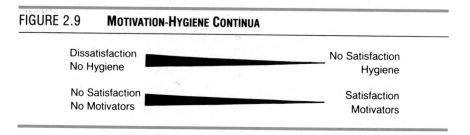

FIGURE 2.9   **MOTIVATION-HYGIENE CONTINUA**

Dissatisfaction   No Satisfaction
No Hygiene   Hygiene

No Satisfaction   Satisfaction
No Motivators   Motivators

■ ■ ■ ■ ■ ■ ■ ■ ■ ■ ■ ■ ■ ■
MOTIVATION-HYGIENE THEORY HAS
SOME SHORTCOMINGS.

for advancement lead to dissatisfaction. For them, these are not motivators. Also, researchers have found that some factors are satisfiers some of the time and dissatisfiers the rest of the time. For example, many people want a chance to achieve, but not every minute of the day. If it is offered too often, they will be unhappy, believing that too much is expected of them. On the basis of findings such as these, Herzberg's critics claim that his initial theory has not been supported well by further investigation.

A second major criticism centers on the way in which the original data were gathered. The researchers asked accountants and engineers what they particularly liked and disliked about their jobs. Critics say that the answers are biased because people tend to give socially acceptable responses when asked such questions. What would you expect people to say that they disliked about their jobs? Stereotyped answers would include salary, supervision, and working conditions. Similarly, people could be expected to say that they liked recognition, advancement, and achievement. A close analysis of these two groups of answers shows that things people dislike about their jobs are related to the work environment, a factor the employee cannot control. The aspects of their jobs that people like are related to their own achievements and accomplishments, and are factors they can control. It is therefore possible that Herzberg's methodology may have encouraged stereotyped answers.

Despite such problems, however, Herzberg's theory sheds some important light on the subject of motivation. In particular, it stresses the importance of helping personnel fulfill *all* their needs, not just basic needs.

■■■■■■■■■■■   ■

STOP!

Review your answer to the second question and make any changes you would like. Then compare your answer to the one below.

2.   What motivates Cecilia?

There are a number of things that motivate Cecilia. These include the work itself, achievement, and recognition. In short, they tend to be more motivators than hygiene factors although money (hygiene) certainly is important because it is a counting device that she uses for feedback on how well she is doing. Notice also, referring to Table 2.2, that the first three items in the table are motivators for her: sense of achievement, challenge, and money. ∎

EXPECTANCY THEORY

While a study of the need hierarchy and blocked need satisfaction is one way of examining motivation, there is now a great deal of interest in **expectancy theory**. Developed by Victor Vroom,[4] and based on earlier work by others, expectancy theory has been expanded and refined by individuals such as Lyman Porter and Edward Lawler.[5] Vroom's motivation formula is a simple, yet powerful one that can be expressed as follows:

■ ■ ■ ■ ■ ■ ■ ■ ■ ■ ■ ■ ■
EXPECTANCY THEORY HOLDS THAT MOTIVATION IS EQUAL TO VALENCE TIMES EXPECTANCY.

$$\text{Motivation} = \text{Valence} \times \text{Expectancy}$$

To understand the theory we must examine the concepts of valence and expectancy.

VALENCE

A person's preference for a particular outcome or objective can be expressed as a **valence**. A valence describes how much someone likes or dislikes something. This preference can range from $+1$ (highest preference) to -1 (lowest preference). For example, Bob wants a promotion to the New York office. On a scale from -1 to $+1$, his valence is $+1$. Suzy, meanwhile, is indifferent to the idea of promotion to the New York office. Her valence is 0. Tom, however, will not take a promotion to the New York office under any conditions. His valence is a -1. Figure 2.10 illustrates the valence range.

■ ■ ■ ■ ■ ■ ■ ■ ■ ■ ■ ■ ■
VALENCE IS A PERSON'S PREFERENCE FOR A PARTICULAR OUTCOME.

Note that expectancy theory forces the manager to answer the question: What motivates the individual? By examining the preference of the workers for various outcomes, ranging from increased salary to a feeling

■ ■ ■ ■ ■ ■ ■

[4] Victor H. Vroom, *Work and Motivation* (New York: John Wiley & Sons, Inc., 1964).

[5] Lyman W. Porter and Edward E. Lawler III, *Managerial Attitudes and Performance* (Homewood, Ill.: Richard D. Irwin, Inc. and Dorsey Press, 1968).

FIGURE 2.10   **RANGE OF AN INDIVIDUAL'S VALENCE**

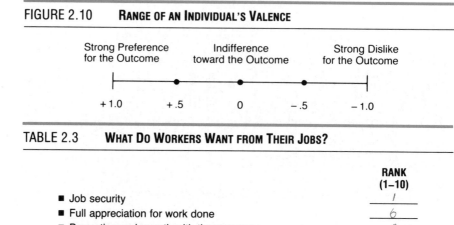

TABLE 2.3   **WHAT DO WORKERS WANT FROM THEIR JOBS?**

	RANK (1–10)
■ Job security	1
■ Full appreciation for work done	6
■ Promotion and growth with the company	2
■ Tactful disciplining	10
■ Good wages	3
■ Feeling in on things	9
■ Interesting work	7
■ Management loyalty to the workers	5
■ Good working conditions	4
■ Sympathetic understanding of personal problems	8

Source: Reported in Paul Hersey and Kenneth H. Blanchard, *Management of Organizational Behavior: Utilizing Human Resources*, 3rd ed. (Englewood Cliffs, N.J.: Prentice-Hall, Inc., 1977), p. 47.

of accomplishment, the manager is in a good position to offer the workers what they want. However, it is important to realize that most managers do *not* know what motivates their workers. Table 2.3 is a list of job qualities for which workers would have varying degrees of preference. This list was given to workers and managers all around the country. The workers were asked to rank the factors from most important to least important. The managers were asked to rank the factors the way they thought the workers would. Before reading further, take time to rank the items on this list by placing a 1 after the item that you think workers said was most important to them, a 2 after the item you think they ranked second, down to a 10 after the item you think the workers ranked last. Then compare your answers to those given at the end of the chapter.

You may find that your list was closer to that of supervisors in industry than to that of the workers themselves. Most students' lists are, because like many managers, they do not know the valences workers actually have for various qualities of the work environment.

EXPECTANCY

The probability that a specific outcome will follow from a specific act is termed **expectancy**. For example, what is the likelihood that Bob will get a promotion to the New York office if he receives the highest efficiency rating in his department? If Bob thinks the chances are very good, he will assign a very high probability such as .99. If Bob believes the likelihood of the promotion is fair (efficiency ratings help, but it really depends most heavily on how well the boss likes you personally), he may assign it a probability of .50. Finally, if Bob believes the high efficiency rating will knock him out of consideration for the New York position (if you are that good they will keep you here rather than let you get away to New York), he will assign it a very low rating, such as .01.

Do not confuse valence and expectancy. Although Bob may have a high valence (+1) for a promotion to New York City, he also may believe that the manager does not like him. So no matter how high his sales, he assigns the probability of his being promoted to New York City (expectancy) as very low, e.g., .10.

■ ■ ■ ■ ■ ■ ■ ■ ■ ■ ■ ■ ■ ■
EXPECTANCY IS THE PERCEIVED PROBABILITY THAT A SPECIFIC OUTCOME WILL FOLLOW A SPECIFIC ACT.

Mary Kay Cosmetics, Inc., employees know that their performance is what counts and that successful sales years will provide them with luxury prizes, such as diamonds, furs, trips, and the pink Cadillacs shown here.

MOTIVATIONAL FORCE

Motivation is a function of both valence and expectancy. One without the other will not produce motivation. This becomes clearer if we apply some illustrations to the expectancy theory formula. Also, let us use the term **motivational force** rather than just motivation, since force or effort is what we are interested in measuring. The formula is:

$$\text{Motivational force} = \text{Valence} \times \text{Expectancy}$$

If either expectancy or valence is 0, the motivational force will be 0. Likewise, if one is high and the other is low, the motivational force will be low.

Let us take an example. The vice-president of sales has just announced that the salesperson with the best sales record for next month will get an all-expenses-paid trip for two to Hawaii at Christmas. The three top salespeople are Charles, Fred, and Maureen. In order to determine each one's motivational force, we have to look at the valence and expectancy each has regarding the free trip.

Charles has a very high valence for this trip (valence = 1.0). He has never been to Hawaii, and he knows his wife would love to go. However, the last time the vice-president made a promise like this he was overridden by the company comptroller, who said the firm could not afford to send two people to Paris for a week. Instead, the winner was given a check for $250. Charles remembers this incident vividly, since he was the winner. As a result, he believes that the possibility of the winner's going to Hawaii is good but not certain (expectancy = .5). We can determine Charles's motivational force as follows:

$$\text{Motivational force} = V(1.0) \times E(.5) = .5$$

Fred would also like to win the free trip to Hawaii. However, as luck would have it, Fred took his wife and family there four months ago for their vacation. Nevertheless, his valence for this trip is still quite high (valence = .7). Furthermore, while he also remembers that the vice-president was prevented from awarding an all-expenses-paid trip last time, Fred believes that this time the contest was probably cleared with the company comptroller and that the winner will indeed travel to Hawaii (expectancy = .9). Fred's motivational force is the following:

$$\text{Motivational force} = V(.7) \times E(.9) = .63$$

Maureen is the only one who is not delighted with the prospect of the trip. Last week she and her fiancé decided that the date for their wedding would be on December 22. They plan to spend the next two weeks honeymooning in Switzerland. The bridegroom's father has a chalet there, right near one of the finest ski resorts in the country. Maureen knows there is simply no way she can take the trip. As a result, she is indifferent about the prize (valence = 0), although she does believe that the winner will be sent to Hawaii (expectancy = 1.0). Her motivational force can be computed this way:

$$\text{Motivational force} = V(0) \times E(1.0) = 0$$

Of the three, Fred is the most motivated toward attaining the highest sales record. A close look at the motivational force computations shows that he had neither the highest valence for the Hawaiian trip (Charles did) nor the highest expectancy (Maureen did). However, the *combination* of the two produced a greater motivational force than that for the others.

EXPECTANCY THEORY IN PERSPECTIVE

It is obvious that no manager is going to spend time trying to determine the motivational force of each worker for each objective. However, expectancy theory is helpful in understanding motivation for many reasons.

First, the expectancy model urges us to look at motivation as a *force* or strength of drive directed toward some objective. As a result, we no longer consider *if* a person is motivated toward doing something, but *how great* the motivation may be. Just about every worker is motivated by money, but some workers are more highly motivated by it than others.

Second, although Maslow's need hierarchy can be applied to everyone in general, it really does not address *individual motivation* and its specific aspects. Expectancy theory does.

Third, the model suggests that people learn what kinds of rewards they like and dislike through *experience*. They also learn to determine the probabilities of their attaining these rewards. Thus, both valence and expectancy are a result of individual experiences, and what highly motivates one person may create no motivational force in another.

Fourth, to a large extent, motivation is determined not only by rewards available but by their degree of *equity* or fairness. If a worker has a higher efficiency rating than anyone else in her department and everyone is given the same raise, she may well stop trying to be so efficient because higher efficiency does not pay off. This issue was indirectly covered in our discussion of valence (the valence for a high efficiency rating declines), but it warrants further discussion here since equity theory is a major topic in modern motivation theory. **Equity theory** holds that workers compare their reward/work ratio to those of others in determining how fairly they are being treated. If Tony and Bill are both receiving the same salary, but Tony feels he works harder than Bill, Tony will also feel he is being treated inequitably. If the organization does not raise his salary above Bill's, Tony is likely to be dissatisfied and may start doing less work or look for a job elsewhere. Remember that this dissatisfaction is a result of perceived inequity. As long as Tony feels there is a lack of equity, the dissatisfaction will remain.

Fifth, if we accept the expectancy model, it follows that to motivate an individual to work we can do only two things. First, we can increase the positive value of outcomes by increasing rewards. Second, we can strengthen the connection between the work and the outcomes. One way of doing this is through effective goal setting. Research shows that clear, specific, attainable goals are more motivational than those which are vague, general, and overly challenging. It also is important to provide people with frequent feedback, so they know how well they are doing and can make any necessary changes.[6]

Sixth, expectancy theory postulates the relationship between a person's valence and expectancy for a particular outcome and his or her satisfaction with this outcome. The relationship can be pictured as in Figure 2.11. Note that goal attainment leads to satisfaction. For example, if Fred wins the trip to Hawaii and is satisfied with the prize, what can we say about Fred's motivation in the future? Certainly it will be high any time the company offers rewards he desires. The same can be said for Tony, if he is given a raise. In short, if people are motivated to attain given objectives and they succeed in their efforts, a "closed loop" is established:

THE EXPECTANCY MODEL IS HELPFUL IN UNDERSTANDING MOTIVATION.

[6]Gary P. Latham and Gary A. Yukl, "A Review of Research on the Application of Goal-Setting in Organizations," *Academy of Management Journal*, December 1975, pp. 824–845; and Edwin A. Locke, Gary P. Latham, and Miriam Erez, "The Determinants of Goal Commitment," *Academy of Management Review*, January 1988, pp. 23–39.

FIGURE 2.11   **A MODEL OF EXPECTANCY THEORY**

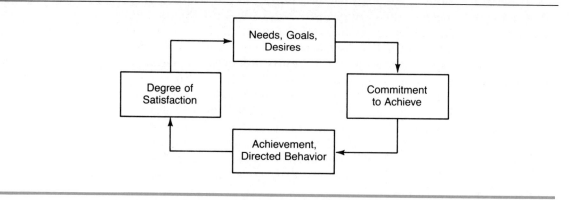

FIGURE 2.12   **NEEDS, GOALS, EXPECTANCY, VALENCE, AND BEHAVIOR: A SYNTHESIS**

They are much more likely to continue to strive for desired objectives. When this process occurs over and over again, we have a highly motivated work force. The process depends, as we noted earlier, on making the desired rewards available to those who attain organizational goals.

Finally, the needs approach to motivation and the expectancy theory of motivation are complementary. Each provides important inputs to the motivation picture. This is seen in Figure 2.12.

STOP!

Review your answer to the third question and make any changes you would like. Then compare your answer to the one below.

3.   What is Cecilia's preference or valence for the office manager's job?

Cecilia's preference or valence of the office manager's job is negative. Using Figure 2.10 as a point of reference, she has a dislike for this job. This means that she would not want the position and would turn it down, if offered. ■

THE PRACTICAL SIDE OF REWARDS

Much of what has been discussed thus far has been theoretical in nature. However, motivation also has a practical side and financial rewards and employee satisfaction play a big role here.[7] There are three reasons for this. First, everyone needs lower-level satisfaction, and money often plays a major role in fulfilling this need. Second, money also can help people attain upper-level need satisfaction. A man who is making 10 percent more than anyone else doing the same job can look himself in the eye and say, "Boy, I must be good. Otherwise, I wouldn't be making so much money." A woman who receives the biggest pay raise in the division can do the same thing. Both are satisfying esteem needs because of money. Third, employee satisfaction is important and rewards, monetary and nonmonetary alike, can influence the extent to which this is present.

FINANCIAL REWARDS

When financial rewards are discussed, most people immediately think of money. The salaries and compensation package paid to top executives (see Table 2.4) is a good example. However, salaries, bonuses, and other similar rewards are usually based heavily on the economic market. Organizations pay what the market demands. If a new secretary can earn $18,000 anywhere in town, the company will generally pay in the range of $18,000. In recent years many firms have supplemented direct pay and bonuses with benefit packages that make the job more enticing. At the lower levels of the hierarchy, typical benefits include paid vacations, medical insurance, life insurance, retirement plans, and prepaid legal plans. The latter (see Table 2.5) provide legal assistance for handling a host of different services, all at a cost of less than $10 per month. At the upper levels of the structure, these benefits often increase in both number and scope and include such perks as a company car, supplemental life insurance, supplemental medical coverage, tax return preparation assistance, club dues and expenses, personal tax and financial planning, and deferred compensation.

Most benefits and perks are nontaxable. This is one of their motivational aspects. Another is that they are of more value to people at the top than those further down the hierarchy. A good example is deferred compensation. When someone is making $250,000 a year, deferring $50,000 will cut current taxes and provide a financial cushion for later years when the individual's earnings may be much lower. Most people making less than $40,000 would not be interested in deferred compensation over

■ ■ ■ ■ ■ ■ ■ ■ ■ ■ ■ ■ ■ ■
PERKS ARE AN IMPORTANT MOTIVATOR.

■ ■ ■ ■ ■ ■ ■

[7] Philip Cochran and Steven L. Wartick, "Golden Parachutes: A Closer Look," *California Management Review*, Summer 1984, pp. 111–125; John Byrne et al., "Who Made the Most and Why?" *Business Week*, May 2, 1988, p. 51.

TABLE 2.4   **SOME OF THE HIGHEST PAID EXECUTIVES**

	COMPANY	TOTAL COMPENSATION*
Jim P. Manzi, Chairman	Lotus	$26,297
Lee A. Iacocca, Chairman	Chrysler	17,896
Paul Fireman, Chairman	Reebok International	15,424
Phillip B. Rooney, President	Waste Management	14,276
Richard M. Furlaud, Chairman	Squibb	13,885
Donald F. Flynn, Senior Vice-President	Waste Management	13,217
John F. Welch Jr., Chairman	General Electric	12,631
Harold A. Poling, Vice-Chairman	Ford Motor	10,555
Jack G. Clarke, Vice-President	Exxon	9,674
Eugene R. White, Vice-Chairman	Amdahl	8,846
J. Richard Munro, Chairman	Time	8,190
August A. Busch III, Chairman	Anheuser-Busch	7,980
Albert Bowers, Chairman	Syntex	7,764
A. William Reynolds, Chairman	GenCorp	7,697
David T. Mitchell, President	Seagate Technologies	7,155

*Thousands of dollars.

Source: *Business Week*, May 2, 1988, p. 51.

TABLE 2.5   **A TYPICAL PREPAID LEGAL PLAN**

BASIC SERVICES

■ Unlimited toll-free telephone calls for advice and consultation with a telephone access law firm.

■ Unlimited letters written on behalf of employees.

■ Unlimited telephone calls by lawyers on behalf of employees.

■ Review of simple documents.

REFERRAL SERVICES

If further service is needed, the employee will receive the name of an attorney (or a list of several attorneys) who practice the legal specialty in which the employee needs assistance. As part of the plan, the attorney (or attorneys) agree(s) to provide services either at reduced hourly fees or at fees that are discounted 10% to 25% from their regular fees.

AVERAGE COSTS

Most plans average $3 to $6 a month. Some may be slightly higher or lower based on group size and type of offer (cafeteria, mandatory benefit, or voluntary payroll deduction).

Source: Reprinted by permission of publisher from Joseph Rader and Ira L. Sharenow, "Picking Prepaid Legal Plans," *Personnel*, October 1986, p. 18. American Management Association, New York. All rights reserved.

and above what they currently are putting into their personal retirement plan. Likewise, tax return preparation can be of great help to a highly paid executive. It has virtually no motivational value for a person making less than $30,000 a year. So basic financial rewards are important motivators.

TAKING THE INDIVIDUAL INTO ACCOUNT   In recent years more and more organizations have begun putting together financial packages that take the needs of each individual employee into account. Quite often these are referred to as flexible benefits.[8] The most common example is *cafeteria incentive plans* in which each person chooses what benefits he or she wants. These plans take a number of different forms. One common arrangement is a series of core benefits such as $10,000 of life insurance, a medical insurance plan, and an annual two-week paid vacation, which are given to everyone. If anyone would like additional coverage, they can purchase it on a payroll deduction basis. A second common arrangement is the offering of a number of different benefit plans, one geared for single people, one for spouses without children, one for people with children, etc. The worker chooses the plan that is of most value. A third arrangement, currently gaining in popularity, gives each employee a certain amount of money that can be used to purchase whatever benefits are desired. Under this arrangement, a young worker with a family can spend the money on medical and term insurance, while an older worker can opt for disability insurance and supplemental retirement benefits.

■ ■ ■ ■ ■ ■ ■ ■ ■ ■ ■ ■
CAFETERIA INCENTIVE PLANS LET PEOPLE CHOOSE THEIR OWN COMBINATION OF BENEFITS.

■ ■ ■ ■ ■ ■ ■ ■ ■ ■ ■ ■
PLANS ARE NOW BECOMING INDIVIDUALIZED.

The same individualized approach is useful for work incentive plans. For example, a retail chain recently offered a three-tiered cafeteria plan to its personnel: one for those with the highest sales, one for those who had better than desired sales, and one for those who attained minimum sales.[9] The benefits are described in Table 2.6. The choice of benefits varied from worker to worker. As seen in Figure 2.13, unmarried employees had preferences that were different from those of married employees. Sex and age also played a role. These results show the importance of tailor-making incentive plans.

EMPLOYEE SATISFACTION

Financial rewards can help increase and maintain satisfaction. So can the environment in which individuals work. Organizations that offer interesting, challenging work and the chance to accomplish meaningful objectives often find that these can compensate for lower salaries or benefit

Zale Corporation understands that its many employees have individual needs. Zale is among the first companies to offer day-care facilities for the children of their employees.

■ ■ ■ ■ ■ ■ ■

[8] Norma A. Fritz, "More Picking and Choosing: Flexible Benefits on the Upswing," *Personnel*, January 1988, p. 7; and Kenneth H. Loeffler, "Flexible Benefits at Ex-Cell-O: A Case Study," *Personnel Journal*, June 1985, pp. 106–112.

[9] Linda Neider, "Cafeteria Incentive Plans: A New Way to Motivate," *Supervisory Management*, February 1983, pp. 31–35.

TABLE 2.6   THREE-TIERED CAFETERIA INCENTIVE PLAN

HIGHEST SALES IN A DEPARTMENT

1. Selection of any merchandise.
2. Dinner for two.
3. Portable TV.
4. $75 gift certificate.

MID-RANGE INCENTIVES

1. Day off with pay.
2. Birthday off with pay.
3. Ten gallons of gas or $15.00 worth of bus tokens.
4. Two sets of movie tickets.
5. Appointment as "Employee of the Day" (get picked up for work, taken out to lunch, and driven home).

MINIMUM-RANGE INCENTIVES

1. Freedom to schedule own average weekly hours (for one week).
2. Coffee breaks free for one week (free coffee or tea).
3. Choice of day off.
4. One-half hour extended dinner/lunch hour (for one day).
5. Assistant manager for a day.

Source: Reprinted with permission of the publisher from "Cafeteria Incentive Plans: A New Way to Motivate," by Linda L. Neider, *Supervisory Management*, February 1983, p. 32. © 1983 AMACOM Periodicals Division, American Management Associations, New York. All rights reserved.

FIGURE 2.13   RANKING OF THE TOP THREE INCENTIVES

| | MARITAL STATUS | | SEX | | AGE | | | |
RANK	SINGLE	MARRIED	MALES	FEMALES	18–21	22–30	31–50	50–UP
1	$75 gift certificate	Day off with pay	Portable TV	Merchandise at cost	Portable TV	Day off with pay	Day off with pay	Schedule own hours
2	Portable TV	Schedule own hours	Dinner for two	Schedule own hours	Day off with pay	Choice of day off	$75 gift certificate	Day off with pay
3	Dinner for two	Choice of day off	10 gallons of gas/bus tokens	$75 gift certificate	Two sets of movie tickets	Dinner for two	Merchandise at cost	"Employee of the day"

Source: Reprinted with permission of the publisher from "Cafeteria Incentive Plans: A New Way to Motivate," by Linda L. Neider, *Supervisory Management*, February 1983, p. 33. © 1983 AMACOM Periodicals Division, American Management Associations, New York. All rights reserved.

packages. This is particularly true in small- and medium-sized firms where the organization would have a difficult time matching the large compensation packages offered by major corporations.

A recent poll by *Inc.* magazine of employees of the 500 fastest growing, small- and mid-sized private companies in America reveals that these employees are very satisfied with their jobs even though they are paid, on average, much less than workers in larger enterprises.[10] This was true for hourly workers who made approximately $8,000 less than their counterparts in large firms as well as managers who earned approximately $39,000 less per year.[11] Specifically, the survey found that 87 percent of the *Inc.* 500 employees were satisfied with their jobs in contrast to 79 percent of the employees of large companies. Similarly, 76 percent of the small- and mid-sized company employees rated their companies favorably compared to 64 percent of the employees in large firms. What accounts for this satisfaction? Some of the primary factors are: (a) challenging, interesting work, (b) a chance to have ideas adopted, (c) a sense of accomplishment, and (d) a feeling of being treated with respect.

Even more interesting was the fact that size had a direct influence on work satisfaction. Employees in smaller companies were more satisfied with their firms than were those in larger enterprises. This pinpoints an important human relations finding: To the extent that an organization can maintain a small company atmosphere, satisfaction will tend to be higher. As the firm gets larger, this close-knit climate often begins to disappear and employee satisfaction declines.[12] The secret of many small firms is their ability to create an environment in which employees are enthusiastic and motivated to do a good job.

STOP!

Review your answer to the fourth question and make any changes you would like. Then compare your answer to the one below.

4.   How satisfied is Cecilia with her job?

Cecilia is very satisfied with her job. The financial rewards are apparently quite satisfactory. (The case indicates that she sells 50 percent more than the average salesperson, so her pay must be quite good.) More importantly, she enjoys the work and is highly satisfied with it. This is particularly evident from the fact that she has turned down the promotion to sales manager. ∎

. . . .

[10] "The Joy of Working," *Inc.*, November 1987, pp. 61–71.

[11] Ibid., p. 62.

[12] Ibid., p. 63.

SUMMARY

In this chapter we examined the fundamentals of motivation. It was noted that motivation has two sides: movement and motive. The former can be seen and the latter can only be inferred. Yet motives are important, for they constitute the "whys" of behavior.

Motives are directed toward goals. The goal that has the highest motive strength is the one the person will attempt to satisfy through goal-directed behavior. Having satisfied that goal, the individual will then go on to the goal with the next highest motive strength.

In examining motives or needs in greater depth, we focused attention on Maslow's need hierarchy. The most fundamental of all needs, according to Maslow, are physiological ones, such as food, clothing, and shelter. When these are basically satisfied, safety needs replace them. Safety needs are of two types: survival and security. Next in the hierarchy are social needs, such as the desire for friendship, affection, and acceptance. The fourth level of the hierarchy contains esteem needs, such as the need to feel important and respected. Research shows that prestige and power are two motives closely related to the esteem need, and to the degree that these motives can be satisfied, the esteem need can be met. At the top of the hierarchy are self-actualization needs. Because people satisfy this need in so many different ways, behavioral scientists know less about it than the other four. However, research does reveal that there are two motives related to self-actualization: competence and achievement. If individuals can satisfy these motives, they can fulfill their drive for self-actualization.

Frederick Herzberg has also found that people desire upper-level need satisfaction. In his famous two-factor theory of motivation, he divided all job factors into two categories: hygiene factors and motivators. Into the former he placed those things that he found do not motivate people but stop them from becoming unmotivated: salary, technical supervision, working conditions, and interpersonal relations. Into the second category he grouped all the factors that motivate people to increase their contribution to the organization: recognition, advancement, the possibility of growth, and achievement. Herzberg contends that hygiene factors do not produce motivation but do prevent dissatisfaction. Conversely, motivators can give satisfaction but never give dissatisfaction. Today the two-factor theory is criticized as incomplete and erroneous. For example, some researchers report that money is a motivator for many people despite Herzberg's claim that it is a hygiene factor. Similarly, some researchers report that workers regard recognition and the chance for advancement as dissatisfiers. At best, then, the two-factor theory is a controversial approach.

The last part of the chapter examined expectancy theory, which holds that motivation can be expressed as the product of valence and expectancy. *Valence* is the measure of a person's preference for a particular outcome. *Expectancy* is the perceived probability that a specific outcome will follow from a specific act. By multiplying the values of valence and expectancy, one can arrive at a motivational force number; the higher the number, the greater the motivation.

Expectancy theory is very helpful in understanding motivation for several reasons. The expectancy model urges us to look at motivation as a force greater in some people than in others. The model suggests that valence and expectancy are a result of individual experiences, and what will highly motivate one person may create no motivational force in another. Expectancy theory makes it possible to study the issue of equity in motivation among specific individuals as opposed to examining general motivation of groups.

Money is a motivator. It helps fulfill both lower- and upper-level needs. Money can take numerous forms including salary and benefits. In recent years organizations have begun adapting financial incentives to individual needs through the use of cafeteria style plans. This allows people to choose those rewards that are best for them. Employee satisfaction is also an important motivator. People will be motivated to the extent that they like the work, feel a sense of accomplishment, have an opportunity to contribute their ideas, and feel they are treated with respect.

KEY TERMS IN THE CHAPTER

motivation	achievement
motive	high achiever
physiological needs	need mix
safety needs	hygiene factors
social needs	motivators
esteem needs	expectancy theory
prestige	valence
power	expectancy
self-actualization needs	motivational force
competence	equity theory

REVIEW AND STUDY QUESTIONS

1. Motives are the "whys" of behavior. What does this statement mean?

2. What are physiological needs? Give some illustrations.

3. How important are safety needs to people just starting their busi-

ness careers? To top executives in large organizations? If your answers differ, what accounts for the difference?

4.   How do people attempt to meet their social needs? Cite some examples.

5.   Research shows that two motives related to esteem are prestige and power. What are these two motives, and how do people try to satisfy them?

6.   One of the ways in which individuals try to satisfy the self-actualization need is through the development of competence. How do they go about doing this?

7.   What are the characteristics of high achievers? How can a high achievement drive be developed?

8.   In Herzberg's terms, what are hygiene factors? Give some illustrations. In Herzberg's terms, what are motivators? Give some illustrations.

9.   According to the two-factor theory, if you give people hygiene factors, you will not motivate them but you will prevent dissatisfaction. Conversely, if you give people motivators, you may get satisfaction but you will never get dissatisfaction. What is meant by these two statements?

10.   The two major terms in expectancy theory are *valence* and *expectancy*. What is meant by each of these terms?

11.   Using the expectancy theory formula, compute the motivational force for Mr. A, whose valence (V) is .8 and expectancy (E) is .7. Compute the motivational force for three other individuals who had the following respective valences and expectancies: Ms. B, $V=.7$, $E=.4$; Mr. C, $V=1$, $E=.5$; Ms. D, $V=.9$, $E=.5$. Which of the four has the greatest motivational force?

12.   Is money a motivator? Explain.

13.   How does a cafeteria incentive plan work? What are its advantages? Describe two of them.

14.   Why are many employees of small- and medium-sized firms more motivated than their counterparts in large firms? Explain.

TIME OUT ANSWERS: INTERPRETATION OF WHAT MOTIVATES YOU

Remember that you gave a 10 to the most important factor and a 1 to the least important factor. So high scores indicate greater motivating potential than low scores. With this in mind, fill in below the number you assigned to each of the 10 factors and then add both columns.

COLUMN A		COLUMN B	
7	1.	4	2.
10	4.	1	3.
9	6.	3	5.
6	8.	5	7.
10	10.	2	9.
42	Total	15	Total

If your total in Column A is higher than that in Column B, you derive more satisfaction from the psychological side of your job than from the physical side. Notice that the five factors in Column A are designed to measure how you feel about the job. These factors are internal motivators. If your score in Column A is over 30, you are highly motivated to succeed and achieve at your current job. Individuals who are most successful in their careers have jobs with higher psychological value than physical value.

If your total in Column B is higher than that in Column A, you derive more satisfaction from the physical side of your job than from the psychological side. Notice that the five factors in Column B all relate to the environment in which you work or the pay you receive for doing this work. These factors are external to you and you have limited control over them. A score of 30 or more indicates that you do not particularly care for the job, but you do like the benefits the company is giving you. Most people who have a higher total in Column B than in Column A rank good wages as one of their top two choices. If you are under 40, it is likely that you will either be promoted to a job with greater psychological value or you will leave the organization. If you are over 40, you may find that your job mobility is reduced, the money is too good to pass up, and you will stay with the organization because of these financial rewards.

CASE: WHY DO PEOPLE WORK?

Harry Barrett, department manager of a well-known retail chain, has been with his store for 23 years, but he has been passed over for promotion and will probably remain a department manager for the rest of his career. This does not greatly concern Harry. He believes that he does the best job he can, and not being promoted is all right with him. Some of Harry's friends, however, feel that Harry killed his chances of moving up by failing to understand human relations. They think Harry does not know how to manage his people very well. One of their complaints is that Harry misunderstands why people work. He believes that salary, working conditions, and security are the three most important objectives. One day Harry remarked that people work only to make a living and then go home to enjoy their lives. The other manager claimed that this simply was not so. "People want more out of a job than just an opportunity to satisfy their physiological and safety needs," he told Harry. "They want to interact with other workers on the job, feel that what they are doing is important, and contribute to the overall good of the organization."

Harry disagreed with this point of view, claiming that his friend had been to too many management courses. "You know, ever since you started working on your master's degree in business, you've come out with some really wild ideas. I'll tell you this: I've been a department manager here for over 10 years and I certainly don't let people socialize on the job. When they are not selling, I want them standing around the counters, alert to the needs of any passing customer. If they get into conversations, they'll lose half their business. And as far as the rest of your ideas about doing important work and contributing to the organization's overall good, that's all philosophical nonsense. People work to make a living and that's all."

Having finished their coffee, the two men stood up to leave. "Harry," said his friend, "you've had the poorest performance record now for almost two years, and evaluations among your personnel reveal that you are considered below average. I've heard some of your workers say that you don't care anything about human relations."

"Oh, I've heard that stuff, too," Harry said. "It's all just sour grapes because I won't buckle under and let them get away with breaking the rules the way some other department managers do."

The two men then returned to their jobs.

QUESTIONS

1.   What types of needs does Harry think people satisfy on the job?

2.   What did the other manager mean when he said that people want more from a job than the opportunity to satisfy their physiological and safety needs?

3.   In what way can Harry's beliefs help account for his department's performance? How could an understanding of Maslow's need hierarchy be of value to Harry? Explain. ■

CASE: WHAT EMPLOYEES WANT

What motivates people? A recent survey attempted to answer the above question by surveying 1,000 industrial sector employees and 100 first-level and second-level supervisors. Each individual was asked to rank ten factors from most important (1) to least important (10). Table 2.7 presents the findings.

TABLE 2.7   WHAT WORKERS WANT, RANKED BY SUBGROUPS

	SUPERVISORS	EMPLOYEES	SEX		AGE				INCOME LEVEL				JOB TYPE				ORGANIZATION LEVEL		
			MEN	WOMEN	UNDER 30	31–40	41–50	OVER 50	UNDER $12,000	$12,001–$18,000	$18,001–$25,000	OVER $25,000	BLUE-COLLAR UNSKILLED	BLUE-COLLAR SKILLED	WHITE-COLLAR UNSKILLED	WHITE-COLLAR SKILLED	LOWER NONSUPERVISORY	MIDDLE NONSUPERVISORY	HIGHER NONSUPERVISORY
Interesting work	5	1	1	2	4	2	3	1	5	2	1	1	2	2	1	2	3	1	1
Full appreciation of work done	8	2	3	1	5	3	2	2	4	3	3	2	1	6	3	1	4	2	2
Feeling of being in on things	10	3	2	3	6	4	1	3	6	1	2	4	5	2	5	4	5	3	3
Job security	2	4	5	4	2	1	4	7	2	4	4	3	4	3	7	5	2	4	6
Good wages	1	5	4	5	1	5	5	8	1	5	6	8	3	4	6	6	1	6	8
Promotion and growth in organization	3	6	6	6	3	6	8	9	3	6	5	7	6	5	4	3	6	5	5
Good working conditions	4	7	7	7	7	7	7	4	8	7	7	6	9	7	2	7	7	7	4
Personal loyalty to employees	7	8	8	8	9	9	6	5	7	8	8	5	8	9	9	8	8	8	7
Tactful discipline	9	9	9	9	8	10	9	10	10	9	9	10	7	10	10	9	9	9	10
Sympathetic help with personal problems	6	10	10	10	10	8	10	6	9	10	10	9	10	8	8	10	10	10	9

Source: Kenneth A. Kovach, "What Motivates Employees? Workers and Supervisors Give Different Answers," *Business Horizons*, September–October 1987, p. 61. Copyright 1978 by the Foundation for the School of Business at Indiana University. Used with permission.

The rankings of the ten factors by both the supervisors and the workers is provided in the first two columns of Table 2.7. The remainder of the table presents information on the workers including sex, age, income level, job type, and organizational level. These data are the first to provide a demographic profile of how different work groups are motivated.[13] They illustrate that many managers have a poor understanding of what really motivates their people. The data also show that motivation can be influenced by a host of factors including age, income level, and organization level.

QUESTIONS

1.   Compare the supervisory responses in Table 2.7 to those provided in Table 2.3. What conclusions can you draw from this comparison?

2.   Which factors (age, income, job type, organization level) have the greatest effect on what workers want from their jobs? Explain.

3.   Which factors have the least effect? Explain. ▪

EXPERIENCING MOTIVATIONAL VARIABLES

PURPOSE

▪   To realize that different people are motivated by different things.
▪   To investigate our own motivational needs.

PROCEDURE

1.   Individually rate the following variables according to how important they are to you at this stage of your life.

2.   As a class or small group, discuss the list of variables according to the Herzberg model. Is each a hygiene or a motivator?

3.   Individually assess your answers. Look at those you ranked one to five. Were they mainly hygiene factors or motivators? How would you interpret these findings?

(Continued)

▪ ▪ ▪ ▪ ▪ ▪ ▪ ▪

[13] Kenneth A. Kovach, "What Motivates Employees? Workers and Supervisors Give Different Answers," *Business Horizons*, September–October 1987, pp. 58–65.

EXPERIENCING MOTIVATIONAL VARIABLES   (Continued)

4.   As a class, discuss the following:

a.   Discuss each of the variables in reference to achievement theory. Which ones are high achievers most likely to pick? How about those with high affiliation needs? High power needs?

b.   Is money a motivator? Do you expect this answer to change as your career develops?

Rank these variables in decreasing order.

_5_ **A.** Good relationship with co-workers
_2_ **B.** Private, nicely furnished office
_3_ **C.** Personal secretary
_10_ **D.** Satisfying work
_9_ **E.** Individual responsibility
_7_ **F.** Creative work
_8_ **G.** Decision-making authority
_1_ **H.** Company car
_6_ **I.** Good rapport with your supervisor
_4_ **J.** Company expense account

■ **ANSWERS TO TABLE 2.3**

	AS RANKED BY	
	WORKERS	SUPERVISORS
Job security	4	2
Full appreciation for work done	1	8
Promotion and growth with the company	7	3
Tactful disciplining	10	7
Good wages	5	1
Feeling in on things	2	10
Interesting work	6	5
Management loyalty to the workers	8	6
Good working conditions	9	4
Sympathetic understanding of personal problems	3	9

PART 2

THE SOCIAL SYSTEM

The overall objective of this part of the book is to study the *social system* of organizations. How and why do people act as they do? In answering this question we must explore three major areas: individual behavior, group behavior, and the informal organization. The individual is the primary unit of behavior in the work place, and studying workers one by one provides a basic understanding of worker behavior. However, it is really not possible to isolate the individual from the group. The individual influences the group and in turn is influenced by it. In short, group behavior is more than the sum of the behaviors of the members. Finally, we need to consider the informal organization. Sometimes people act as formal representatives of the organization, and at other times they resort to informal networks to "get things done." Study of the informal organization provides important insights into the dynamics of behavior in the work place. In this part of the book we examine all three of these areas.

In Chapter 3 we study individual behavior in organizations. We discuss some of the behavioral continua that can be used in describing the individual and then move on to the area of values and perceptions, examining how individual values influence a person's perception. Next we turn to other major components of individual behavior, including attitudes and personality. Finally, we examine some of the ways in which managers can improve their understanding of interpersonal behavior via an understanding of transactional analysis, assertiveness training, and organizational culture.

Chapter 4 is concerned with group behavior. We define the term *group* and then describe the most common types of groups, including functional groups, project groups, and interest-friendship groups. From here we turn to the major characteristics of groups, including roles, norms, status, and cohesiveness. In particular we try to answer the question: "Are highly cohesive groups always high-producing groups?" Then we examine some of the benefits of group decision making vis-à-vis individual decision making, define the *risky-shift phenomenon*, and describe the ways in which this problem can be prevented. The next part of the chapter is concerned with the major factors upon which intergroup performance depends. The last part of the chapter is devoted to an examination of the role, functions, advantages, and disadvantages of committees and how committees can be used effectively in modern organizations. In our analysis of this area, we study some of the ways in which groups try to gain power over other groups and describe some of the strategies that managers can use in resolving intergroup conflict.

In Chapter 5 we examine the informal organization. We start by comparing and contrasting the formal and informal organizations. Then we describe the differences between authority and power and identify which is of greater importance in the informal organization. Next we discuss some of the controls used by members of the informal organization to ensure compliance with group norms. From here our attention is focused on the informal communication network: how it operates, some of the conditions under which people are most likely to be grapevine-active, and some of the primary benefits and disadvantages associated with the informal organization. In the last part of Chapter 5 we discuss some of the ways in which a manager can deal with the informal organization.

When you are finished reading Part 2, you should have a solid understanding of human behavior at work. In particular, you should know a great deal about individual and group behavior in organizations and should be aware of how both individuals and groups use the informal organization to accomplish their objectives.

3
CHAPTER

INDIVIDUAL BEHAVIOR

GOALS OF THE CHAPTER

At the very heart of human relations is the need for an understanding of human behavior. In this chapter we examine this topic. The first goal of this chapter is to review the nature of individual behavior. The second goal is to study some of the major components of individual behavior, including values, perception, attitudes, and personality. The third goal is to examine some of the ways in which managers can improve their understanding of interpersonal behavior.

When you have finished reading this chapter, you should be able to:

1. Identify and describe some of the common values held by all individuals.

2. Describe the term *perception* and explain why it is a determinant of individual behavior.

3. Explain how stereotyping can influence a person's view of another's behavior.

4. Define *attitude* and describe its impact on worker output.

5. Define *personality* and discuss the major forces affecting personality development.

6. Describe how transactional analysis, assertiveness training, and cultural match can help both managers and subordinates improve their understanding of interpersonal behavior.

OPENING CASE

MARK HIS WORDS

"**U**nions may be of value to blue-collar workers, but there is really nothing that they can do for white-collar workers. If they ever get in here, we're in big trouble." This is how Fred Kowalski summed up his feelings, when he learned that a national union was in the process of trying to organize the office personnel. Fred's boss tried to allay his concern, but Fred was adamant. Part of their discussion was as follows:

> Boss: Fred, I think you're overstating things. Sure there's an effort underway to unionize some of our people. However, this has happened before and the union lost. I predict they'll lose again.

> Fred: I don't know. Those guys really worry me. If they get in here, I know that work output is going to go down and costs will rise. Believe me, unions are no good!

> Boss: Well, you obviously have some very strong feelings about this. However, don't you think that if the union does get in that we can all work together as a team?

> Fred: You've got to be kidding. If they get their foot in the door, we're going to be fighting with them from now on. All of those unions are the same. They work to get the best conditions for the workers and then milk the company dry.

> Boss: Obviously, we have a difference of opinion. However, there's one thing about which we are not to have a difference. You are not to say anything to the office workers that can be misinterpreted. Do not attempt to influence the way they vote on this unionization question. Remember that it's against the law to interfere in any way with their right to unionize.

> Fred: Okay, I'll be careful. But I don't like it. Nothing good is going to come from unionization. At the present time all of the office personnel work very hard in supporting the field sales staff. Under unionization we're going to find everyone doing the minimum; initiative will be discouraged; and rules and regulations will dictate work behavior. The team spirit will disappear. Mark my words.

1.   What type of perception problem does Fred have? How does it affect the way he sees this situation?

2.   How can Fred's and his boss's communications be described in transactional analysis terms? What conclusions can be drawn as a result?

3.   What type of organizational culture profile best describes this firm? What profile does Fred believe will describe the firm if the union gains entry? Explain.

Write down your answers to these questions and put them aside. We will return to them later. ∎

THE NATURE OF THE INDIVIDUAL

The individual is a complex being, but this complexity does not stop most people from trying to generalize about human behavior by summing up individuals with a descriptive cliché such as, "People are basically good," or "Everybody has his price; it's just a matter of how much." Some clichés are totally accurate, some partially accurate, and the rest erroneous. In human relations, however, we need to be much more scientific in our analysis of individuals and to realize that people are a *blend of many different types of behavior*. For example, sometimes people are very rational and at other times they are highly emotional; sometimes they are controlled by their environment and at other times they control their environment; sometimes they are interested in economic objectives and at other times they are more concerned with self-actualizing.

■ ■ ■ ■ ■ ■ ■ ■ ■ ■ ■ ■ ■
THERE ARE MANY WAYS OF DESCRIBING PEOPLE.

However, in any examination of individual behavior, we have to look at the *total person*. This requires an examination of the major components of individual behavior. The four major components that merit our attention are: values, perceptions, attitudes, and personality.

VALUES

A **value** is something that has worth or importance to an individual. Values are influenced in many ways. Parents, friends, and teachers all play a role. So do co-workers, business associates, and others with whom one comes in contact. In fact, learning and experience are the two greatest forces in shaping an individual's values.

■ ■ ■ ■ ■ ■ ■ ■ ■ ■ ■ ■ ■
A VALUE IS SOMETHING OF WORTH OR IMPORTANCE TO AN INDIVIDUAL.

One way of examining values is in terms of "terminal" and "instrumental" values. A **terminal value** is expressed in terms of a desired goal or end. An **instrumental value** is the means for achieving the desired goals.[1] Here are some examples:

TERMINAL VALUES (ENDS)	INSTRUMENTAL VALUES (MEANS)
Self-respect	Honesty
A comfortable life	Independence
Family security	Ambition
Wisdom	Courage
A sense of accomplishment	Helpfulness

∎∎∎∎∎∎∎
[1] Milton Rokeach, *The Nature of Human Values* (New York: The Free Press, 1973).

FIGURE 3.1   SPRAUNGER'S VALUE TYPES

THEORETICAL

The overriding interest of the theoretical person is the discovery of *truth*. In pursuing this goal the person often looks for identities and differences, trying to divest himself or herself of judgments regarding the beauty or utility of objects. The chief aim in life of this person is to systematize and order knowledge.

ECONOMIC

The economic person is basically interested in what is *useful*. In addition to self-preservation, the person is concerned with the production of goods and services and the accumulation of wealth. The individual is thoroughly practical and conforms well to the prevailing stereotype of the American business person.

AESTHETIC

The aesthetic person sees highest value in *form* and *harmony*. While not necessarily an artist, the individual's chief interest is in the artistic episodes of life. For example, aesthetic people often like the beautiful insignia of pomp and power but oppose political activity that represses individual thought.

SOCIAL

The highest value for the social person is *love* of people. This individual prizes other people as ends and is as a result kind, sympathetic, and unselfish. The social person regards love itself as the only suitable form of human relationship. This person's interests are very close to those of the religious person.

POLITICAL

The political person is interested primarily in *power*. This individual need not be a politician. Since competition and struggle play a large part in all life, he or she will do well in any career or job in which a high power value is necessary for success, whether this be power over the people (as in the case of a top manager) or the environment (as in the case of an engineer who makes the final decision on how to build something).

RELIGIOUS

The highest value for the religious person is *unity*. This individual seeks to relate himself or herself to the embracing totality of the cosmos. For some there is an attempt to withdraw from active association with the outside world (as in the case of monks in a monastery); for others there is some self-denial and meditation coupled with a life of work among the local people who attend their church or subscribe to the same religious beliefs.

Another way to examine values is in terms of a predetermined list and the preferences people have for these values. Edward Spraunger has identified six values common to everyone: theoretical, economic, aesthetic, social, political, and religious (see Figure 3.1).

Different occupational groups tend to have different value profiles. For example, professors of biology tend to be highest in theoretical interests; business people have very high economic values; artists place great significance on aesthetic values; social workers have high social values; politicians have strong political values; and members of the clergy hold

TABLE 3.1   VALUE PROFILES FOR DIFFERENT GROUPS

SPRAUNGER VALUE	AVERAGE COLLEGE MALE[a]	AVERAGE COLLEGE FEMALE[a]	SUCCESSFUL MALE MANAGER[b]	SUCCESSFUL FEMALE MANAGER[c]
Theoretical	43	36	44	39
Economic	42	37	45	47
Aesthetic	37	44	35	42
Social	37	42	33	31
Political	43	38	44	46
Religious	38	43	39	35

[a] *Study of Values Manual* (Boston: Houghton Mifflin Company, 1970), p. 11.

[b] William D. Guth and Renato Tagiuri, "Personal Values and Corporate Strategy," *Harvard Business Review*, September–October 1965, p. 126.

[c] Richard M. Hodgetts, Mildred G. Pryor, Harry N. Mills, and Karen Brinkman, "A Profile of the Successful Executive," *Academy of Management Proceedings*, August 1978, p. 378.

high religious values. However, to some degree, each of these values is present within and important to each one of us. We must remember that what may be important to the management is *not* necessarily important to the "rank and file." For this reason, values are of major importance in the study of human relations.

STUDY OF VALUES

The most popular test designed to provide information and insight on individual values is the Allport-Vernon-Lindzey *Study of Values*.[2] This test is designed to measure one's preference for each of Spraunger's values. From the responses, a value profile can be constructed for the individual. In fact, the test has been given a sufficient number of times so as to establish value profiles for different groups. Table 3.1 provides such profiles for the average college male, average college female, successful male business manager, and successful female business manager.

Figure 3.2 is a graph of these four profiles. Note that the profile of the successful female manager is similar to that of the successful male manager, and distinctly different from that of the average college female. Apparently, successful managers have the same basic value profiles regardless of their sex.

. . . .

[2] Gordon W. Allport, Philip E. Vernon, and Gardner Lindzey, *Study of Values*. Test Booklet (Boston: Houghton Mifflin Company, 1960).

FIGURE 3.2   VALUE PROFILES

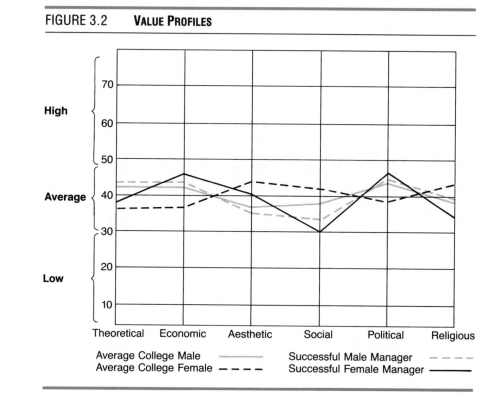

Value tests such as the one described here are useful to an under-standing of human behavior because they identify what is important to an individual. Unless we know what a person holds in high regard, there is little hope that we can motivate or manage the person effectively. The great problem for today's managers, however, is that values appear to be changing. The values of their fathers and grandfathers are different from those of the modern generation. Raised in a period of affluence and reared on television in a high-technology society, young people have different ideas about what is important. When they enter the work force, they bring these new values with them. As a result, modern employees' values are an important focal point of human relations study.

MODERN EMPLOYEE VALUES

Over the last two decades employee values have changed, and they are still in a state of flux. Much of this change has been indirectly explained in Chapter 2, which noted that motivators have greater impact on employee performance than do hygiene factors.

A recent study by *Inc.* magazine found that employee loyalty and overall feelings toward the organization are declining. The survey results showed that large firms, in particular, are not as well rated by their employees as are medium- and small-sized companies. Employees in large firms are more satisfied with their pay and job security and are less likely to leave the organization than are their counterparts in medium- and small-sized firms. On the other hand, personnel in the latter companies report higher degrees of job satisfaction, challenging work, opportunity for advancement, high performance standards, and greater likelihood of getting their ideas adopted.[3]

WORKER LOYALTY IS DECLINING.

— Hygiene Factors

Motivators

A national survey of 7,800 women by *Working Woman* found disturbing results related to employee values. Two-thirds of the women said that men have more opportunities than women. Additionally, while 75 percent of the respondents said they have good salaries and benefits, half of them are thinking of looking for another job.[4]

Black employees also report dissatisfaction. A recent survey by *Black Enterprise* reveals that 60 percent of the respondents feel that they are underpaid, 56 percent say that their career advancement has not been fast enough, and 53 percent say that it would not be possible for them to be promoted into a senior-level management position in their current firm.[5]

What perhaps is most disturbing is that the values of many managers have not changed over the last two decades.[6] This means that there is a "values gap" between the way managers run their organizations and the way lower-level employees want the organizations run. This is likely to create major human relations problems during the 1990s.

PERCEPTION

Perception is a person's view of reality, and it is affected by, among other things, the individual's values. For example, if the person is a member of a union, he or she may discount much of what management says about declining sales, decreased profit margins, and the need for the union and management to work as a team. Most of this talk may be regarded as an attempt by management to exploit the work force for its own gain. Con-

PERCEPTION IS A PERSON'S VIEW OF REALITY.

[3] Curtis Hartman and Steven Pearlstein, "The Joy of Working," *Inc.*, November 1987, pp. 66–67.

[4] Jane Ciabattari, "The Biggest Mistake Top Managers Make," *Working Woman*, October 1986, pp. 54–55.

[5] Richard D. Hylton, "Working in America," *Black Enterprise*, August 1988, p. 66.

[6] James A. Lee, "Changes in Managerial Values, 1965–1986," *Business Horizons*, July–August 1988, pp. 29–37.

versely, many people in management admit that they have a hard time understanding the union's point of view, because they believe that the union is more interested in "ripping off" the company than in working for the overall good of both groups. This is an example of a common situation in which each person agrees with his or her own group's point of view but regards the other group's point of view as incorrect or biased. Human relationists call this *selective perception*. In order to understand why individuals perceive things differently, it is helpful to compare sensory reality and normative reality.

SENSORY REALITY AND NORMATIVE REALITY

■ ■ ■ ■ ■ ■ ■ ■ ■ ■ ■ ■ ■ ■
SENSORY REALITY IS PHYSICAL REALITY.

Physical reality is **sensory reality**. A typewriter, an automobile, and a house are all physical objects that people tend to perceive accurately. However, sometimes physical items present perception problems. Before you read any further, examine the pictures in Figure 3.3 and answer the question accompanying each.

In Figure 3.3A, the two lines are the same length, although most people think that the lower line is longer than the upper one. This perceptual illusion is created by the two diagonal lines at the ends of each line, which make it seem stretched or compressed. In Figure 3.3B, the two lines running across the picture are horizontal, although most people think that the lines bend in at the end. This illusion is a result of the diagonal background lines, which seem to be bowing the center parts of the horizontal lines outward.

■ ■ ■ ■ ■ ■ ■ ■ ■ ■ ■ ■ ■ ■
NORMATIVE REALITY IS INTERPRETIVE REALITY.

In Figure 3.3C we are moving away from sensory reality and toward **normative reality**, which is best defined as interpretive reality. In the first two pictures in Figure 3.3, there was a right answer, whether you saw it there or not. You can verify the answers by simply using a ruler to measure the lines or the distance between them. There is *more* than one right answer in Figure 3.3C, however, and what one person sees, another may not. This is why we call it interpretive reality. Some people see a goblet in this picture; others see the facial profiles of twins, facing each other.

The picture in Figure 3.3D is deliberately ambiguous. Some people see a road, a rock, a tree, and some surrounding terrain. Others see the face of a pirate. Still others see a rabbit. Look at Figure 3.4, in which the clear pictures of the pirate and the rabbit can be seen. Note that the ambiguity is reduced if the artist puts more detail in one part of the picture than in the other.

Figure 3.3E is also a deliberately ambiguous picture. Some people see an old lady; some see a young lady. Figure 3.5 on page 88 is a clear picture of both. Once again, the artist has reduced the ambiguity by putting in the necessary detail.

When we examine individual behavior and the impact of perception on that behavior, it is important to remember that people see what they

FIGURE 3.3   THE PERCEPTUAL PROCESSES

A

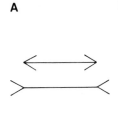

Which of these two
lines is longer?

B

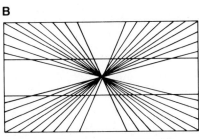

Are the two lines running across this
figure horizontal or not?

C

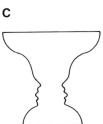
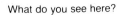

What do you see here?

D

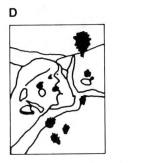

What do you see here?[1]

E

What do you see here?[2]

Sources: 1. From Robert Leeper, "A Study of a Neglected Portion of the Field of Learning—the Development of Sensory Organization," *Pedagogical Seminary and Journal of Genetic Psychology*, March 1935, p. 62.
2. From Edwin G. Boring, "A New Ambiguous Figure," *American Journal of Psychology*, July 1930, p. 444.
3. See also Robert Leeper (No. 1 above). Originally drawn by cartoonist W. E. Hill and published in *Puck*, November 6, 1915.

FIGURE 3.4   THE PIRATE AND THE RABBIT

Pirate

Rabbit

Source: From Robert Leeper, "A Study of a Neglected Portion of the Field of Learning—the Development of Sensory Organization," *Pedagogical Seminary and Journal of Genetic Psychology*, March 1935, p. 62.

FIGURE 3.5   THE OLD WOMAN AND THE YOUNG WOMAN

Old Woman   Young Woman

Source: From Robert Leeper, "A Study of a Neglected Portion of the Field of Learning—the Development of Sensory Organization," *Pedagogical Seminary and Journal of Genetic Psychology*, March 1935, p. 62.

either *want* to see or *are trained* to see. Therefore, in terms of human relations, the manager must try to understand the worker's perception of reality. Personnel willingly accept management's methods only when they perceive those methods to be in their best interests. Otherwise, they will resort to such perceptual pitfalls as selective perception, which we just examined, and stereotyping. For example, Harvey Lester, a new employee, has been having trouble mastering his new job. His boss, Lois, tells him that if he does not improve, she will have to let him go. Feeling that he is on the verge of being fired, Harvey quits. What Lois saw as a mild reprimand designed to improve output is interpreted as a threat resulting in a resignation. Each party interpreted the action differently.

STEREOTYPING

STEREOTYPING IS GENERALIZING A PARTICULAR TRAIT TO ALL MEMBERS OF A GIVEN GROUP.

One of the most common perception problems is that of **stereotyping**, which is generalizing a particular trait or behavior to all members of a given group. The manager who believes that no union can be trusted has a stereotyped view of unions. The worker who believes that management is always out to exploit the personnel also has a stereotyped belief.

Every one of us tries to stereotype people, whether it be in the job environment or in a social setting. We even have standard stereotypes for classes or nationalities. Read the following descriptions and try to identify the nationality described.

- These people are loyal to family ties and always look after their younger brothers and sisters.
- These people believe in fair play, are conservative, and keep a stiff upper lip.

- These people are very scientific, industrious, and hard working.
- These people love caviar, Bolshoi dancing, and music by Tchaikovsky.
- These people love pasta, wine, and, most of all, great opera.

■ ■ ■ ■ ■ ■ ■ ■ ■ ■ ■ ■ ■ ■ ■
SOME TYPICAL STEREOTYPES.

Most people say that the first description is that of the Chinese and the second is that of the English. The remaining three are German, Russian, and Italian. To some degree all these stereotypes are both accurate and inaccurate. For example, in regard to the first description, are not most people loyal to family ties? In regard to the second description, is Britain the *only* country in which fair play is important? And is Germany the *most* scientific and industrious of all nations? Research shows that most people of the world attribute these traits not to the Germans but to the Americans! The last two descriptions are also stereotypes, because they do not describe one group to the exclusion of all others.

Successful businesses do not let stereotyping influence their employment choices. This GM employee is doing what in the past would have been termed "a man's job."

In examining individual behavior, then, it is important to realize that most people employ stereotyping. It is an easy way to generalize about behavior. The effective manager, however, tries to evaluate each person as an individual and to remain aware of his or her own stereotypical beliefs so as to reduce their effect on his or her judgments. For example, what do men have to say about their female counterparts? Successful male managers do not let the old stereotypes influence them. They judge women on the basis of how well the latter do their jobs. In fact, based on survey responses from over 6,500 middle- and upper-level male managers, recent research shows that the higher the educational level of the manager, the more likely it is that he has a high acceptance of women in managerial positions. Additionally, men who work for women generally have a higher acceptance of them as managers than do men who have not had such experience.[7] These findings indicate that stereotypes of women in the work place are beginning to fade. As more and more females enter the ranks of management, negative attitudes and biases against them should continue to lessen.

■

STOP!

Review your answer to the first question and make any changes you would like. Then compare your answer to the one below.

1.   What type of perception problem does Fred have? How does it affect the way he sees this situation?

. . . .

[7] Alma S. Baron and Ken Abrahamsen, "What Men Are Saying About Women in Business," *Business Horizons*, January–February 1982, pp. 10–14.

Fred is guilty of stereotyping. Notice that he classifies all unions into one general category and says that they create low output and high costs and negatively affect teamwork. He does not look at each union on its own merits. Rather, he conveniently generalizes about their collective behavior.

ATTITUDES

■ ■ ■ ■ ■ ■ ■ ■ ■ ■ ■ ■ ■

ATTITUDES ARE A PERSON'S FEELINGS ABOUT OBJECTS, EVENTS, AND PEOPLE.

A person's feelings about objects, activities, events, and other people are termed **attitudes**. These feelings are usually learned over a period of time and are a major factor in determining individual behavior.[8]

COMPONENTS OF ATTITUDES

There are three basic components of attitudes: cognitive, affective, and behavioral. Each plays a major role in attitude formation.

The **cognitive component** is the set of values and beliefs that a person has toward a person, object, or event. For example, a co-worker tells us, "I don't like the boss. He's out to get me." The cognitive component of this attitude is the belief that the boss is unfair or punitive. The cognitive component creates the basis or reason for the negative attitude. If the worker were to change his mind and believe that the boss was fair, the basis for the attitude would change and the worker would now have a positive attitude toward the boss.

■ ■ ■ ■ ■ ■ ■ ■ ■ ■ ■ ■ ■

THE THREE COMPONENTS OF ATTITUDES.

The **affective component** is the emotional feeling that is attached to an attitude. It is the emotion that is felt with regard to a person, object, or event. When we feel happiness or anger or disappointment, this is the affective component. When our favorite baseball team loses an important game and we feel sad, this too is a result of the affective component. The affective component is a result of our feelings toward someone or something. The cognitive component affects the affective component. The person who dislikes the boss may feel happy when he learns that the manager has been transferred to another office.

The **behavioral component** is the tendency to act in a particular way toward a person, object, or event. For example, when the employee learns that the boss is to be transferred, the employee smiles. When your favorite team comes from behind to win a game in the bottom of the ninth, you cheer. If you enjoy your human relations course, you are

■ ■ ■ ■ ■ ■

[8]Elaina Zuker, "Attitudes That Work Against You," *Supervisory Management*, August 1983, pp. 10–16.

FIGURE 3.6   **ATTITUDE QUESTIONNAIRE (PARTIAL FORM)**

Please fill out this questionnaire using the following numbers:
1 = Strongly agree
2 = Moderately agree
3 = Neither agree or disagree
4 = Moderately disagree
5 = Strongly disagree
___ Working conditions here are good.
___ The pay is adequate.
___ The fringe benefit program is better than in most other firms.
___ My boss gives me credit and praise for a job well done.
___ If I have a complaint to make, I feel free to talk to someone up the line.
___ Management encourages suggestions for improvement.
___ I feel I really belong in this organization.
___ The people I work with and I all get along well together.
___ Management is interested in the welfare of the workers.
___ People who get promotions in this firm usually deserve them.
___ My job is very interesting.
___ My boss lives up to his/her promises.
___ I know where I stand with my boss.
___ My job seems to be leading to the kind of future I want.
___ I am proud to work for this organization.

---

likely to show up on time for all classes and participate when asked to do so.

One way to remember the three components of attitude is to think of them in the order that they have been presented. This order moves from the cause of attitudes to the results. The cognitive component is the belief that is the reason for the attitude; the affective component is the emotional feeling that results from this belief; and the behavioral component is the tendency to act in a particular way in response to this feeling.

CAUSE → RESULT

ATTITUDE MEASUREMENT

One way of measuring attitudes is through the use of an **attitude questionnaire**. Figure 3.6 is an example of such an instrument.

Attitude questionnaires are important for several reasons. First, they reflect the attitudes current in the organization. Second, they provide a baseline against which to compare future attitude surveys. (Are attitudes improving or declining?) Third, they serve as a source of information

FIGURE 3.7   ATTITUDES AS AN INTERVENING VARIABLE

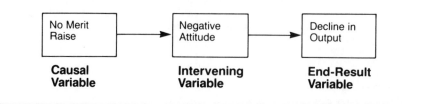

about what areas or issues the organization needs to pay greater attention to and where everything is all right.

In particular, the organization needs to realize that attitudes are an **intervening variable**. They are influenced by causal variables and, in turn, affect end-result variables (see Figure 3.7). In order for an individual's attitude to decline, there must be some cause, such as a change in leadership style, a failure to get a merit raise, or the submission of a poor performance appraisal. This cause brings about a change in the attitude, the intervening variable, which then results in a decline in output, the end-result variable.

Conversely, if attitudes improve because the person is given a merit raise or is told how to obtain a merit raise in the future, his or her output increases. The raise (a causal variable) will improve attitudes (the intervening variable) and result in more output (the end-result variable).

Attitudes are internal. They cannot be seen; they can only be inferred through such end-result variables as output and can be measured by means of attitude surveys. Attention to attitudes, therefore, can be one of the keys to increasing productivity, because how a person feels about the organization will affect his or her output. For example, research shows that those who think positively tend to be more productive than those who do not. Seligman, a university psychologist, has found that individuals with positive attitudes tend to do better jobs than the average worker. Working with the Metropolitan Life Insurance Company, Seligman gave 20-minute written tests to new salespeople in order to determine their attitudes. Within months the new recruits with positive attitudes were dramatically outselling the new recruits who did not have positive attitudes. The company then used the test to screen prospective employees. During the first year of the program, this new hiring practice increased revenues by $10 million. Seligman's research shows the power of positive thinking. Those who felt they would succeed were more successful than those who did not. Their attitudes resulted in a number of important behaviors including: (a) the ability to shrug off bad news; (b) a willingness to take risks; (c) a desire to assume personal con-

■ ■ ■ ■ ■ ■ ■ ■ ■ ■ ■ ■ ■ ■
ATTITUDES ARE AN INTERVENING
VARIABLE.

trol of events rather than just allowing things to happen; and (d) a willingness to set ambitious goals and pursue them.[9]

PERSONALITY

The relatively stable set of characteristics and tendencies that determine similarities and differences between people is termed **personality**. For example, some people are very outgoing while others tend to be introverted. Some are assertive while others are passive. Every individual has a different personality, which we can think of as a composite of all the person's behavioral components as reflected in how he or she acts.

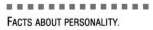

PERSONALITY IS A RELATIVELY STABLE SET OF CHARACTERISTICS.

Sometimes we try to generalize about an individual's overall personality by calling him or her aggressive, hostile, kind, easygoing, or warm. These adjectives are all designed to categorize the person in a word or two; although this may be an incomplete way of describing someone, we all tend to do it. Likewise, most of us look at the way a person walks, talks, and dresses in seeking clues to his or her personality.

Quite obviously, personality consists of *many* factors, making it very difficult to define the term. Psychologists, however, tend to accept certain ideas about personality:

1.   Personality is an organized whole; otherwise the individual would have no meaning.

FACTS ABOUT PERSONALITY.

2.   Personality appears to be organized into patterns. These are to some degree observable and measurable.

3.   Although there is a biological basis to personality, the specific development is a product of social and cultural environments.

4.   Personality has superficial aspects, such as attitudes toward a team leader, and a deeper care, such as sentiments about authority or the Protestant work ethic.

5.   Personality involves both common and unique characteristics. Every person is different from every other person in some respects, while being similar in other respects.

MAJOR FORCES AFFECTING PERSONALITY

What accounts for differences in personality? Four major forces can be cited as directly affecting personality development: heredity, culture, social class, and family relationships (Figure 3.8).

[9]Jill Neimark, "The Power of Positive Thinkers," *Success*, September 1987, pp. 38–41.

FIGURE 3.8   **MAJOR FACTORS INFLUENCING PERSONALITY**

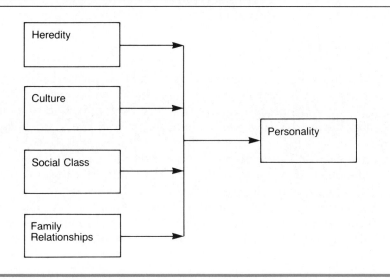

Heredity affects personality because people are born with certain physical characteristics. Intelligence, height, and facial features are all inherited. The person who is highly intelligent may be arrogant toward fellow students; the tall boy may be quiet because he feels awkward; the short boy may compensate for his size by being aggressive in his dealings with others.

Culture is important in that the values and beliefs of the society in which one is raised help determine how a person will act. A society that puts great value on money will be different from one in which leisure is emphasized over work. A society in which education is believed to be important will be substantially different from one in which education is frowned upon.

■ ■ ■ ■ ■ ■ ■ ■ ■ ■ ■ ■
THE FOUR MAJOR FACTORS THAT
AFFECT PERSONALITY.

Social class helps shape personality because an individual's mores are heavily influenced by his or her neighborhood and community life. This social class also affects the individual's self-image, perception of others, and assumptions about authority, work, and money. A manager who wants to understand how people adjust to the demands of organizational life must consider these social class factors.

Family relationships influence personality by rewarding the person for certain behaviors and by not rewarding him or her for others. These actions help shape a pattern of behavior and serve as a basis for interpersonal relations outside the home.

Each of these four factors influences behavior, and the manager has little control over them. This is not to say that the superior cannot direct, channel, or reorient the individual's behavior. This can be done by using the motivational concepts we discussed in Chapter 2. However, unless the manager understands the bases for individual behavior, he or she will have great difficulty managing it.

INTERPERSONAL BEHAVIOR

Values, perceptions, attitudes, and personality are all important components of individual behavior. However, no one lives in a vacuum. People interact with other people. In fact, this is how we develop values, perceptions, attitudes, and, to a large degree, personality. Before finishing our discussion of individual behavior, therefore, we should examine this area of interpersonal behavior. We will do so by first studying the types of interpersonal needs people have and then looking at how the manager can interrelate with the employees on an interpersonal basis.

TRANSACTIONAL ANALYSIS

An interpersonal approach that has gained popularity in recent years is transactional analysis. Although simple to comprehend, this method of analyzing and evaluating interpersonal communications is proving valuable to many organizational managers who want a better understanding of interpersonal behavior.

Transactional analysis (TA) involves the study of social transactions among people. At the heart of TA is a concern for three behavioral patterns known as *ego states*: child, parent, and adult.

TRANSACTIONAL ANALYSIS INVOLVES THE STUDY OF SOCIAL TRANSACTIONS.

CHILD EGO STATE   Each of us has a little child within us. When in the **child ego state** we are likely to sit, stand, walk, think, and feel as we did when we were children. Common facial expressions include pouting, broad grins, twinkling eyes, mischievous winks, and comic distortions. Voice tones are often loud, full of feeling, joyful, whining, or cute. Typical demeanors include playfulness, selfishness, intuitiveness, and creativity. When in the child state, we tend to be spontaneous, open, and happy. An example of a child ego state interaction is:

> Fred: "I wish I could take off work tomorrow and play golf."
> Ernie: "Let's call in sick tomorrow and go over to the country club."

PARENT EGO STATE   Parents serve as models for their children's behavior. When in the **parent ego state** we are likely to think, feel, and act as parents. These behaviors are sometimes supportive and sometimes critical. Common facial expressions include smiling, beaming, and winking or nodding (when being supportive), and body movements such as resting hands on hips, pointing an accusing finger, and pounding the fist (when being critical). Voice tones reflect encouragement, warmth, and friendliness (when being supportive) and are accusing, lecturing, and scolding (when being critical). Typical demeanors include teaching, coaching, and being protective (when being supportive), and being bossy, moralistic, and very proper (when being critical). An example of a supportive parent ego state transaction is:

> Marie: "I told Nancy to go home and I'd cover for her."
> Gladys: "Poor thing; she hasn't felt well for a week."

An example of a critical parent ego state transaction is:

> Frank: "My secretary Nancy went home ill again today; she's so undependable."
> Bob: "What can you expect from women?"

ADULT EGO STATE   The **adult ego state** deals objectively with reality. Problem solving and rational thinking are products of the adult ego state. This state is related not to age but to education and experience. When activated, the adult ego state enables a person to collect and organize information, predict the possible consequences of various actions, and make conscious decisions. By using the adult ego state, a person can help minimize regrettable actions and increase his or her potential for success. Common facial expressions indicate alertness, thoughtful attention, and self assurance. Voice tones are controlled, judicious, and confident. Typical demeanors include listening, attentiveness, and concentration. An example of an adult ego state interaction is:

> David: "What is the annual salary of this job?"
> Patricia: "It starts at $15,000."

TYPES OF TRANSACTIONS

These three ego states serve as a basis for analyzing interpersonal transactions. For our purposes, there are two types that merit consideration: complementary and crossed. A **complementary transaction** is one that progresses along expected lines. A **crossed transaction** is one that does not progress along expected lines. Figures 3.9 through 3.12 illustrate two examples of each type. Note that in the complementary transactions the manager understands human relations and adopts the right ego states. When the subordinate asks an adult question, the boss answers as an adult. When the subordinate adopts the child ego state and talks to the manager as a parent, the boss responds as a parent addressing a child.

If the manager does not choose the right ego state, a crossed transaction can occur, and interpersonal problems are likely. For this reason the manager needs to understand transactional analysis and, where possible, to try to communicate with the personnel on an adult-to-adult

■ ■ ■ ■ ■ ■ ■ ■ ■ ■ ■ ■ ■ ■
COMPLEMENTARY TRANSACTIONS
PROGRESS ALONG EXPECTED LINES.

■ ■ ■ ■ ■ ■ ■ ■ ■ ■ ■ ■ ■ ■
CROSSED TRANSACTIONS DO NOT
PROGRESS ALONG EXPECTED LINES.

FIGURE 3.9 **A COMPLEMENTARY TRANSACTION**

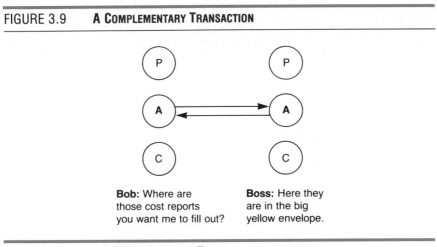

Bob: Where are those cost reports you want me to fill out?

Boss: Here they are in the big yellow envelope.

FIGURE 3.10 **A COMPLEMENTARY TRANSACTION**

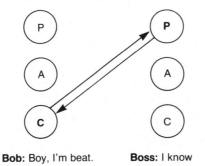

Bob: Boy, I'm beat. Those reports are time consuming.

Boss: I know what you mean. Go home now, you can finish up tomorrow.

FIGURE 3.11 **A CROSSED TRANSACTION**

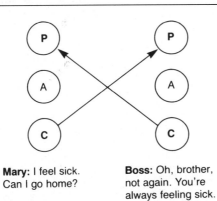

Mary: I feel sick. Can I go home?

Boss: Oh, brother, not again. You're always feeling sick.

FIGURE 3.12   **A Crossed Transaction**

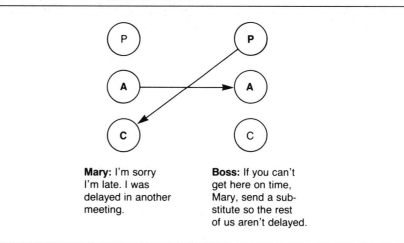

Mary: I'm sorry
I'm late. I was
delayed in another
meeting.

Boss: If you can't
get here on time,
Mary, send a sub-
stitute so the rest
of us aren't delayed.

TA GUIDELINES.

basis. Harris, one of the leading proponents of TA, offers the following guidelines:

1.   Learn to recognize your child, its vulnerabilities, its fears, its principal methods of expressing these feelings.

2.   Learn to recognize your parent, its admonitions, injunctions, fixed positions, and principal ways of expressing these admonitions, injunctions, and positions.

3.   Be sensitive to the child in others, talk to that child, stroke that child, protect that child, and appreciate its need for creative expression. . . .

4.   Count to ten, if necessary, in order to give the adult time to process the data coming into the computer, to sort out parent and child from reality.[10]

STOP!

Review your answer to the second question and make any changes you would like. Then compare your answer to the one below.

2.   How can Fred's and his boss's communications be described in transactional analysis terms? What conclusions can be drawn as a result?

....

[10]Thomas A. Harris, *I'm OK–You're OK: A Practical Guide to Transactional Analysis* (New York: Harper & Row, Publishers, 1966), pp. 95–96.

The communication is a crossed transaction. Notice that Fred's boss continues to communicate on an adult-to-adult basis. His statements are factual and unemotional. Fred, on the other hand, uses a child-to-parent transaction. He is excitable, argumentative, and emotional in his approach. Note that his boss has to warn him about getting carried away and saying anything that could get the company into trouble. There are two conclusions that can be drawn from this transaction. First, the two men are not truly communicating with each other. Second, Fred needs to analyze his attitudes and behavior and begin to communicate on an adult-to-adult basis. ■

ASSERTIVENESS TRAINING

Another way to develop improved interpersonal relations is with **assertiveness training**. The purpose of such training is to teach people appropriate ways of asserting themselves in work and social situations. The goals of the training are threefold:

1. The individual is taught how to determine personal feelings.

2. The person learns how to say what he or she wants.

3. The individual learns how to get what he or she wants.

Assertiveness training can be particularly helpful for those individuals who are bottling up too much inside themselves; they are becoming so uptight that psychologically they are going to explode. Before reading on, test how uptight *you* are in the accompanying Time Out section.

■ ■ ■ ■ ■ ■ ■ ■ ■ ■ ■ ■ ■ ■
THE GOALS OF THE TRAINING ARE THREEFOLD.

PASSIVE, AGGRESSIVE, AND ASSERTIVE BEHAVIOR   The term *assertiveness training* is something of a misnomer since the word *assertive* often conjures up thoughts of pushiness or belligerence. However, this is not what the term means. Actually, in assertiveness training the objective is to teach the individual how to make a clear statement of personal desires without being obnoxious or abusive. This can be made clear with an example. Consider the case of Mary Harrison, who has been asked to meet an incoming job applicant at the airport first thing in the morning, show the individual around the organization, make sure the person gets to all of his scheduled interviews, and see that he gets back to the airport on time for his departure flight. Mary does not want to take on this assignment because she is snowed under with work. There are three types of behavior available to her in responding to the situation: passive, aggressive, and assertive. Here is how each response would be used by Mary.

> Passive: Mary is angry and really wants to tell her boss off. However, she grits her teeth, puts her work aside, and makes plans to get to the airport on time.

TIME OUT

HOW UPTIGHT ARE YOU?

The following descriptive statements are designed to measure how uptight you are. The interpretation of your quiz can be found at the end of the chapter. Circle the appropriate number (1−4) for each of the following statements. Then total your score.

	NONE OR A LITTLE OF THE TIME	SOME OF THE TIME	GOOD PART OF THE TIME	MOST OR ALL OF THE TIME
1. I prefer things to be done my way.	1	2	3	(4) ✓
2. I am critical of people who don't live up to my standards or expectations.	1	2	3 ✓	(4)
3. I stick to my principles, no matter what.	1	2	(3)	4 ✓
4. I am upset by changes in the environment or the behavior of people.	1	(2)	3 ✓	4
5. I am meticulous and fussy about my possessions.	1	2	3	(4) ✓
6. I get upset if I don't finish a task.	1	2 ✓	3	(4)
7. I insist on full value for everything I purchase.	1	2	3	(4) ✓
8. I like everything I do to be perfect.	1	2 ✓	3	(4)
9. I follow an exact routine for everyday tasks.	1	2	(3)	4 ✓
10. I do things precisely to the last detail.	1	2 ✓	(3)	4
11. I get tense when my day's schedule is upset.	1	2	(3)	4 ✓
12. I plan my time so that I won't be late.	1	2 ✓	(3)	4
13. It bothers me when my surroundings are not clean.	1	2	3	(4) ✓
14. I make lists for my activities.	1 ✓	2	(3)	4
15. I think that I worry about minor aches and pains.	(1)	2 ✓	3	4
16. I like to be prepared for any emergency.	1	2 ✓	3	(4)
17. I am strict about fulfilling every one of my obligations.	1	2 ✓	3	(4)
18. I think that I expect worthy moral standards in others.	1	2 ✓	3	(4)
19. I am badly shaken when someone takes advantage of me.	1	2	(3)	4 ✓
20. I get upset when people do not replace things exactly as I left them.	1	2 ✓	(3)	4
21. I keep used or old things because they might still be useful.	1	2 ✓	3	(4)
22. I think that I am sexually inhibited.	(1)	2 ✓	3	4
23. I find myself working rather than relaxing.	1	2	(3) ✓	4
24. I prefer being a private person.	1 ✓	(2)	3	4
25. I like to budget myself carefully and live on a cash basis.	1	2	(3)	4 ✓
Total Score	2	4	30	44 / 80

2   22   9   36 / 69

Source: Reprinted with permission of Barbara M. Weinel, Greenville Technical College, Greenville, South Carolina.

Aggressive: Mary tells her boss, "Hell, I'm not going to do that. I'm up to my nose in work. Get someone else who is not that important. I'm not going to be treated like this, so don't ask me to do it again."

Assertive: Mary says to her boss, "I appreciate your thinking of me, but I'm really snowed under with work. I don't have the time to do this. However, I don't think you'll have any trouble getting someone. There are a number of people in the department who have light work loads this week."

Notice that when using assertive behavior Mary employed an adult-to-adult TA transaction. She stood her ground without being rude or discourteous.

BECOMING MORE ASSERTIVE   How can an individual increase his or her assertiveness? Over the last decade many assertiveness-training programs have been offered by both organizations (for their own personnel) and professional consultants and trainers (for organizational personnel and the general public). While these various workshops employ different techniques for improving individual assertiveness, there are a series of basic steps that every participant should know. Phrased in the form of questions, the list includes the following: *To BE ASSERTIVE :*

1.   Clarify the situation and focus on the issue. What is my goal? What exactly do I want to accomplish?

2.   How will assertive behavior on my part help me accomplish my goal?

3.   What would I usually do to avoid asserting myself in this situation?

4.   Why would I want to give that up and assert myself instead?

5.   What might be stopping me from asserting myself?

    a.   Am I holding on to irrational beliefs? If so, what are they?

    b.   How can I replace these irrational beliefs with rational ones?

    c.   (For women only) Have I, as a woman, been taught to behave in ways that make it difficult for me to act assertively in the present situation? What ways? How can I overcome this?

    d.   What are my rights in this situation? (State them clearly.) Do these rights justify turning my back on my conditioning?

6.   Am I anxious about asserting myself? What techniques can I use to reduce my anxiety?

7.   Have I done my homework? Do I have the information I need to go ahead and act?

8.   Can I do the following:

    a.   Let the other person know I hear and understand him/her?

■ ■ ■ ■ ■ ■ ■ ■ ■ ■ ■ ■ ■

KEY QUESTIONS FOR BECOMING MORE ASSERTIVE.

HUMAN RELATIONS IN ACTION

WHAT YOUR BOSS WANTS YOU TO KNOW

One of the biggest reasons why some people in organizations succeed and others fail is that the former know what their boss wants them to know. Whether it is explicitly spelled out or learned through experience or intuition, successful people know the things the boss is looking for. Eight of the most common include the following:

1.   *Do more than what is expected.* Your boss expects everyone to do his or her job. If you do more, however, you will stand out as a superior performer.

2.   *Forget about making up excuses.* The boss expects you to do things right. When you do not, it may cause problems but it will do you no good to blame someone else. Even if you are right, the boss does not want to hear about it. He or she has more important things to do than trying to assign blame. It is your job to get the work done right the first time. If you did not, work harder to do so the next time.

3.   *Anticipate things going wrong.* If you do, you will seldom be disappointed. However, you will be prepared to deal with them before they become too serious. If part of your job calls for getting information from other people and processing it before passing it on to others, anticipate getting the information late or finding that some of it is erroneous. Allow yourself time to check the data and get it corrected.

4.   *Remember that punctuality and attendance count.* Do not be late for work or meetings. Even if nothing important happens, you are expected to be on time. If you are continually tardy or absent, your boss will see this as an attitude problem, and it will count against you later on.

5.   *Get along with your fellow workers.* Bosses like to think that everyone in their unit is a team player. If there is internal dissension the boss will not want to know who is right or wrong. The boss is not there to referee employee squabbles. Everyone involved will have a black mark against him. Make it a point to stay on good terms with everyone in the unit.

6.   *Be protective of the organization.* Do not say anything that will negatively reflect on the enterprise or anyone who works there. Keep organizational politics and problems within the enterprise and, if you must do anything that reflects on another, go out of your way to minimize its negative effect.

7.   *Learn to read your boss.* Listen closely to what your boss tells you and learn to interpret its meaning. If your boss says, "this really warrants our looking into," it may mean that you should drop everything you are doing and start working on the matter he has been talking about. On the other hand, if he says, "this sounds very interesting," it may mean that the matter is a minor one and should be ignored. Every boss has a specific way of communicating. Figure out what your boss is really talking about.

8.   *Never lie.* The biggest problem with lying is that it calls your integrity into question. What other lies have you told? What exactly are you up to? Your boss may begin feeling that you are not as reliable as he or she thought. When this happens, your credibility comes into question, and your future with the organization may be affected. If you cannot tell the truth, limit what you say so you can stay within this guideline.

    b.   Let the other person know how I feel?

    c.   Tell him/her what I want?[11]

Assertiveness training is an excellent complement to effective behaviors such as those spelled out in Human Relations in Action: What Your Boss Wants You to Know.

ORGANIZATIONAL CULTURE

Individual behavior does not occur in a vacuum. People interact with each other in an organizational setting. Each has needs, desires, and goals he or she would like to attain. Similarly, the organization has objectives that it would like to reach. To the extent that the personnel and the enterprise can work together harmoniously, there will be a cultural match.

CULTURAL MATCH

The similarity of individual and organizational culture is the **cultural match**. It is a reflection of how well the personnel "fit" into the enterprise. **Individual culture** is the norms, attitudes, values, and beliefs that a person brings to the job. These can vary from the type of work philosophy (how hard people should work), to their willingness to take risks (high, moderate, or low), to their desire for power and control (high or low). **Organizational culture** is the environment in which the individual works. Some organizations are very bureaucratic, while others are very participative. Some are highly innovative, while others encourage "doing it by the book." Some are very supportive of their people while others encourage individuality and tolerate limited intragroup conflict.[12]

    Effective organizations look for people who can fit into the culture that will be most effective for the enterprise. Table 3.2 provides an overall description of the four most common cultures. Notice in the table that organizational culture can be described in terms of two characteristics: risk-taking and feedback. In some organizations success depends on the ability to take high risks, while in others success is achieved with low risks. In some successful organizations feedback on results is very fast, while in others it is quite slow.

■ ■ ■ ■ ■ ■ ■ ■ ■ ■ ■ ■ ■
INDIVIDUAL CULTURE IS THE NORMS AND VALUES A PERSON BRINGS TO THE JOB.

■ ■ ■ ■ ■ ■ ■ ■ ■ ■ ■ ■ ■
ORGANIZATIONAL CULTURE IS THE ENVIRONMENT IN WHICH A PERSON WORKS.

■ ■ ■ ■ ■ ■ ■

[11]Lynn Z. Bloom, Karen Coburn, and Joan Pearlman, *The New Assertive Woman* (New York: Dell Publishing, 1976), pp. 175–176.

[12]For more on this see Ellen J. Wallach, "Individuals and Organizations: The Cultural Match," *Training and Development Journal*, February 1983, pp. 29–36.

TABLE 3.2   **ORGANIZATIONAL CULTURE PROFILES**

	TOUGH-GUY MACHO	**WORK HARD/ PLAY HARD**	**BET-YOUR- COMPANY**	**PROCESS**
Risks assumed	High	Low	High	Low
Feedback from decisions	Fast	Fast	Slow	Slow
Organizations that often have this kind of culture	Construction, TV, radio, management consulting	Retail sales, auto distrib- utors, real estate	Capital goods, aerospace, investment banks, military	Banks, insur- ance com- panies, many governmental agencies
How successful people in this culture behave	Have a tough attitude, are individualistic, can live with all-or-nothing decisions	Friendly, super sales types, work well in groups	Can stand long-term ambiguity, are technically competent, check and recheck their decisions	Very cautious, always follow accepted pro- cedures, are good at taking care of details
Strengths of successful people in this culture	Can get a lot done in a short period of time	Are able to quickly produce a great deal of work	Can generate high quality inventions and major scientific breakthroughs	Bring order and system to the work place
Weaknesses of successful people in this culture	Short-run in orientation, ignore the benefits of cooperation	Look for quick- fix solutions, are more inter- ested in action than in problem- solving	Slow in getting things done, cannot adjust well to short- term changes	Initiative is discouraged, there is lots of red tape, the work is often boring
Habits of successful people in this culture	Dress in fashion, live in "in" places, enjoy one-on- one sports like tennis	Avoid extremes in dress, prefer team sports like softball	Dress according to hierarchical rank, enjoy sports like golf where outcome is unclear until the end of the game	Dress according to hierarchical rank, enjoy process sports like swimming and jogging

Source: Terrence E. Deal and Allan A. Kennedy, *Corporate Cultures* © 1988, Addison-Wesley Publishing Co. Inc., Reading, Massachusetts. Adapted from Chapter 6, pages 107–127. Reprinted with permission.

The important thing to remember about cultural match is that the needs of people and organizations must *both* be accommodated. Creative people have to find work in organizations where creativity is encouraged and rewarded. Detail people must seek employment in organizations where concern for precision and detail are given high priority. When an organization is not successful or when its environment changes, a change in culture often is necessary. This calls for a rethinking of one's values and interests, and an assessment of how well they mesh with those the organization is now seeking. In the final analysis, many people are successful because they have figured out how to bring about a cultural match between themselves and their organization.[13]

CULTURE IN ACTION

Successful firms understand their culture and operate within it. In turn, this culture reflects the enterprise's values, beliefs, and philosophy. For example, Hershey Foods, the giant chocolate manufacturer, stresses five important values that reflect its culture: (1) honesty and integrity, (2) people-oriented behavior, (3) quality-consciousness, (4) consumer-consciousness, and (5) results-orientation. In recent years the company has expanded its operation by purchasing the Friendly Restaurant chain, Y&S Candies, the Cory Coffee service, and the San Giorgio-Skinner pasta group. However, Hershey's values and culture have remained the same.[14]

The Wal-Mart Corporation is another good example. The basic beliefs and values of Sam Walton, the founder, continue to guide the giant retailer. When Walton started his retail discount chain in the early 1960s, he stressed three things: (a) customer service, (b) low price, and (c) quality merchandise. In his enterprise there are no "subordinates"; everyone is known as an "associate." This human relations approach has helped create high morale and productivity. By the late 1980s when other giant retailers were limping along with annual sales growth of 3 to 5 percent, Wal-Mart continued to maintain its historic average of 33 percent. Today, with yearly sales in excess of $20 billion, the organization's culture remains the same as it was two decades ago.

However, not all organizations have been able to maintain their cultures. Many have had to adapt to changing conditions. The automakers are a good example. Japanese imports have forced General Motors, Ford, and Chrysler to introduce more assembly line technology and to switch their focus from high production/low cost to high quality/competitive price. In the process, the organizations' cultures have changed and the unions, in particular, have found this threatening. Employee attitudes toward management attempts to streamline operations and increase market competitiveness were negative at first. However, as the Japanese, Germans, Swedes, and now the Yugoslavians and South Koreans, have

Wal-Mart is noted for its corporate culture, which is based on employee participation in decisions. Employees are referred to as "associates" and are made to feel they have an important role to play in ensuring the company's success.

....

[13] See "Changing a Corporate Culture," *Business Week*, May 14, 1984, pp. 130–138; and Jeremy Main, "Waking Up AT&T: There's Life after Culture Shock," *Fortune*, December 24, 1984, pp. 66–74.

[14] Sally J. Blank, "Hershey: A Company Driven by Values," *Personnel*, February 1987, pp. 46–51.

invaded the U.S. auto market, these attitudes have changed. Today the unions and management are working together much more harmoniously. The new culture is one that stresses the management objectives of productivity and quality and the union objectives of profit sharing and job security. The new culture is much more market-responsive and should help the automakers in their fight to maintain and build market share.[15]

Most organizations find that even if they do not have to change their organizational culture, they must often fine tune it. Cliques must be discouraged; proper behaviors must be rewarded; leaders who no longer represent the new culture must be transferred or removed. Some of the steps often followed in this process include: (1) encouraging the use of delegation and participation so as to develop a well-trained, experienced work force; (2) allowing constructive dissent; (3) promoting cooperation, initiative, creativity, and fairness; (4) recruiting and selecting people whose personal values are consistent with those of the organization; (5) using meetings, parties, and dinners to reward good behavior and encourage its continuance; and (6) developing a spirit of teamwork and camaraderie which creates a cohesive, well-motivated work force. Commenting on the importance of corporate culture to the success of the enterprise, Reimann and Wiener point out that:

> A better understanding of their corporate cultures can give top executives some important clues about possible biases that may adversely affect their strategic choices. It can also help managers anticipate or even avoid strategy-implementation problems. Furthermore, the analysis of culture should not be limited to their own corporations or subunits. An appreciation of the dominant culture of a competitor can be extremely useful in anticipating future moves and competitive responses.
>
> . . . The resulting strategic culture tends to support, rather than inhibit, strategic change and adaptation to environmental realities. It will support the implementation of corporate strategies from entering new markets or adapting new technologies to mergers and acquisitions. While a strong strategic corporate culture is no guarantee of success, a keen awareness of the importance and fragility of cultural processes is essential to the long-run strategic management of the corporation.[16]

▪▪▪▪▪▪

[15] For more material on changing organizational culture, see Larry B. Meares, "A Model for Changing Organizational Culture," *Personnel*, July 1986, pp. 38–42; and Robert Desatnick, "Management Climate Surveys: A Way to Uncover an Organization's Culture," *Personnel*, May 1986, pp. 49–54.

[16] Bernard C. Reimann and Yoash Wiener, "Corporate Culture: Avoiding the Elitist Trap," *Business Horizons*, March–April 1988, p. 44.

STOP!

Review your answer to the third question and make any changes you would like. Then compare your answer to the one below.

3.   What type of organizational culture profile best describes this firm? What profile does Fred believe will describe the firm if the union gains entry? Explain.

Based on Fred's description of the current work environment, the firm operates in a work hard/play hard culture. Fred believes that if the union wins the election, the company's culture will eventually change to a process culture. Notice the words he uses to describe how things will be in the future regarding people doing the minimum, initiative being discouraged, and rules and regulations dictating work behavior. ∎

SUMMARY

Individuals are complex beings. Nevertheless, many descriptive clichés have been used in trying to sum them up in a word or two. In human relations, we need to be much more scientific in our analysis of individuals and to realize that people are a blend of many different types of behavior. For example, sometimes they are rational and at other times they are emotional; sometimes they are motivated by economic considerations and at other times they are self-actualizing. In order to more fully understand individual behavior, we examine four of the major components: values, perceptions, attitudes, and personality.

A *value* is something that has worth or importance to an individual. People have, in overall terms, six values: theoretical, economic, aesthetic, social, political, and religious. When examined in a job context, values can be studied in terms of worker satisfaction. The most recent research shows that many employees are dissatisfied with their jobs, feel they do not have equitable promotion opportunities, and are underpaid.

Perception is a person's view of reality. There are two types of perception: *sensory* (physical) and *normative* (interpretive). Normative perception is particularly important in the study of human relations, since people's interpretations of reality will influence their behavior. In particular, it can result in selective perception and stereotyping, perceptual problems that the effective manager tries to avoid.

Attitudes are a person's feelings about objects, activities, events, and other people. Attitudes have three basic components: cognitive, affective, and behavioral. It is common to find organizations using instruments such as questionnaires to measure these feelings in their employees because attitudes are often key variables affecting output.

Personality consists of a relatively stable set of characteristics and tendencies that determine both similarities and differences between one person and another. Some of the major forces affecting personality are heredity, culture, social class, and family relationships.

The manager should also be aware of the available approaches to understanding interpersonal behavior. After all, values, perceptions, attitudes, and, to a large degree, personality are developed through interpersonal relations. Transactional analysis views interpersonal behavior in terms of ego states and kinds of transactions. Assertiveness training teaches people how to determine personal feelings, verbalize them, and get what they want without being abusive or obnoxious. An understanding of corporate cultures helps people understand their own values and those of the organization at large.

Now that we have examined individual behavior, we turn our attention to group behavior, which is the focus of Chapter 4.

KEY TERMS IN THE CHAPTER

value	affective component
terminal value	behavioral component
instrumental value	attitude questionnaire
theoretical value	intervening variable
economic value	personality
aesthetic value	transactional analysis
social value	child ego state
political value	parent ego state
religious value	adult ego state
perception	complementary transaction
sensory reality	crossed transaction
normative reality	assertiveness training
stereotyping	cultural match
attitudes	individual culture
cognitive component	organizational culture

REVIEW AND STUDY QUESTIONS

1.   What is meant by the term *value*? What types of values do people have? Describe some.

2.   Are work values in America changing? Support your answer with examples.

3.   How does sensory reality differ from normative reality?

4.   How can attitude measurement be of value to an organization? Explain.

5.   What is meant by personality? What are some of the ideas that psychologists tend to accept about personality?

6.   What is transactional analysis? What are the three basic ego states in TA?

7.   How does a complementary transaction differ from a crossed transaction?

8.   How can an understanding of TA be of value to the modern manager? Explain.

9.   Of what value is assertiveness training to the modern manager? Would it have any value for subordinates? Explain.

10.   How does a tough-guy macho culture differ from a work hard/ play hard culture? Compare and contrast the two. How does a bet-your-company culture differ from a process culture? Compare and contrast the two.

11.   What do individuals need to understand about cultural match? How can the basic idea be used effectively? Explain.

12.   How can an organization fine tune its culture? What steps would be useful? Explain.

TIME OUT ANSWERS: INTERPRETATION OF HOW UPTIGHT ARE YOU?

SCORING

25–45	Not compulsive or uptight.
46–55	Mildly uptight. Your compulsiveness is working for you, and you are successfully adaptive.
56–70	Moderately uptight. You are adaptive but uptightness has crept into your personality function, and you experience uncomfortable days of high tension.
71–100	Severely uptight. You are adaptive but quite uptight, insecure, and driving hard. You have many days of nervous tension that should be eased off.

The closer you are to the rating of 100, the nearer you come to playing brinksmanship at the ragged edge that borders on exhaustion of your adaptive reserve and a slump into depression. One way of overcoming these problems is by following the suggestions offered in the section of the chapter where assertiveness training was discussed.

CASE: A MATTER OF PERSONALITY

Frank Payne is a store manager for a southwest retail chain. He has been with the organization for five years, and his store's sales have been rated "low average" in comparison with sales of similar stores in locales with the same general population and per capita income. Frank's boss, Eloise Sutter, has been with the organization for 12 years. For five of those years, Eloise was a store manager, during which time her sales were the highest in the region, and she was rated as excellent by her employees.

Eloise believes that one of the most important characteristics of an effective store manager is a good personality. The individual has to like people, to be willing to listen to customer complaints without taking the matter personally, and to express a sincere interest in the well-being of the workers. To Eloise, Frank seems to lack all of these traits. He acts as if he has a chip on his shoulder, and Eloise is afraid that this type of personality is likely to lead to the loss of customer goodwill.

During her recent visit to Frank's store, Eloise watched him talk to a customer who wanted to return some merchandise. The woman insisted that the merchandise was damaged when she opened the package, and she wanted to exchange it for an undamaged item.

Frank refused to accept the return. "We don't sell damaged goods," he told the lady. "It must have been damaged after you took it from the store."

The customer was furious, and in a loud voice she began telling Frank what she thought of the store and its personnel. Many of the other customers in the store at the time heard the ruckus, and Eloise noticed that most of them left without buying anything.

When Frank resumed his discussion with Eloise, he explained that the woman had been wrong in saying that the merchandise was damaged and that the store should not be expected to take the loss. Eloise tried to help Frank see the customer's point of view, but she was unable to do so. She thereupon dropped the subject and turned to other business matters, including the decline in sales.

"Things haven't been going too well since you took over," she told Frank. "What seems to be wrong?"

Frank talked about some of the areas where he felt there were problems that needed to be straightened out. They all related to inventory control and the need for more motivated personnel. At no point during the conversation did Frank indicate that he might be causing any of the problems because of his personality or his leadership style.

Before leaving, Eloise walked around the store and talked to some of the employees. From her brief conversations with them she learned that they did not care much for Frank as a store manager. One of the workers referred to him as "uncaring," while another said he had "the personality of an army drill sergeant." Eloise decided that she would let Frank run the store for another three months but that if sales kept slipping she would have to replace him.

QUESTIONS

1.   What type of personality would you expect to find in a successful store manager?

2.   How might Frank's personality affect the attitudes of the workers? Explain.

3.   Using what you know about transactional analysis, describe how you would advise Frank about being more effective. Do you think you would succeed? Explain. ■

CASE: NOT HER CUP OF TEA

When Maria Delvalle was graduated from nursing school, she had six job offers. Her choice was County Hospital, located near her family's home. It was only a five-minute drive to the hospital and her folks liked the fact that she was working in the local area and staying at home.

During the seven years that Maria was at County, she was a floor nurse and then a supervisor. The latter job required Maria to see that the nurses in her charge filled out all the necessary paperwork and got the doctors to do the same. If there were any problems, Maria would get involved and make a decision regarding what to do. She was also responsible for performance appraisals and salary recommendations. For the most part, however, her job consisted of seeing that the rules were followed and that everything ran according to hospital procedure. As she told one of her new nurses, "If you do things by the book, you'll never go wrong."

One year ago Maria was approached by the director of nursing for a large psychiatric hospital. The hospital was expanding rapidly and wanted to hire nurses with psychiatric and/or managerial nursing experience. Although Maria had never worked with psychiatric patients, the director explained to Maria that her job would be similar to the one she had currently. "We need people with management experience," the director explained. "We are growing rapidly due to the increase in insurance coverage for psychiatric care. At the rate we are going, our hospital is going to double its size within 12 months. That's why we want you to come and work for us." The director offered Maria an increase of 33 percent over her current salary and Maria accepted. Her mother was sorry to see her move away from home, but because the psychiatric facility is more than 40 minutes driving time from home, Maria felt it best to rent an apartment closer to her new job.

Unfortunately, things at the hospital have not worked out very well. One of the major reasons is that Maria's job involves a great deal more than just overseeing nurses. There is an average of two staff meetings a week which, for the most part, consist of discussions on how to hold down costs and generate more revenues. Because the hospital has the highest daily rates of any hospital in the region, the occupancy rate is now declining. Over the past two months, only patients with insurance coverage or wealthy families have been using the facilities. As a result, everyone in management is being urged to become a salesperson and to help build the image of the hospital as the best psychiatric facility in the region. In fulfilling this role, Maria has been asked to be a luncheon speaker at Rotary, Lions, and other organizations on six occasions this year. She has also been asked to talk to the families of patients about the fine facilities and what the hospital can do for their relatives. The objective of meeting with the families is to allay any fears they may have and to reduce the likelihood that they will move their relatives to one of the other psychiatric hospitals in the area.

Maria feels that these types of duties should be handled by other people. "I'm a nurse," she told her mother, "not a public relations or marketing person. I don't feel comfortable selling psychiatric services. I know it has to be done, but that wasn't why they hired me. I'm interested in patient welfare, but my concern is limited to the individual. If they want someone to perform marketing services, they should get a specialist in this area."

Maria has mentioned her concern to some of the other nursing supervisors at the hospital, but none seem to agree with her. They believe that marketing and family relations are part of the job. On the other hand, Maria has also noted that all of her colleagues have had experience in psychiatric nursing.

Earlier this week, Maria had a call from County Hospital. They are looking for a senior-level nursing administrator. Given her experience in the field, they believe Maria would be the best person for the job and they have asked her to apply for the position. Maria has decided to do so. "If I get the job, I'm going to move back home," she told her mother. Her mother did not respond, but Maria could tell by the way she smiled that her mother would like that very much.

QUESTIONS

1.   In what type of organizational culture did Maria work at County Hospital? Describe it using Table 3.2 to help you.

2.   In what type of organizational culture is Maria working at the psychiatric hospital? Describe it using Table 3.2 to help you.

3. Why is Maria interested in returning to County Hospital? Use your answers to the questions above to help explain your reasoning. ■

EXPERIENCING VALUE ORIENTATIONS

PURPOSE

▪ To understand Spraunger's value model explained in the chapter.
▪ To examine value profiles and identify them on the basis of occupation or career.
▪ To demonstrate why people in different occupational groups will have different value profiles.

PROCEDURE

1. Review the Spraunger model and be sure that you understand the basic differences among the six values: economic, theoretical, aesthetic, social, political, and religious.

2. Examine six value profiles and match them with an individual from six occupational groups.

3. Discuss the reasons for the differences in value profiles and how these can affect the way individuals behave.

SITUATION

You have just been given six value profiles. They are the following:

VALUE	A	B	C	D	E	F
Theoretical	62	46	49	26	43	25
Economic	51	66	42	44	55	40
Aesthetic	29	27	64	22	34	23
Social	33	30	24	59	23	50
Political	47	49	41	41	66	41
Religious	18	22	20	48	20	61

These six profiles are from the following individuals:

Clergyman
Industrial engineer
Chief executive officer
Aerospace engineer
Salesperson
Drug counselor

Experiencing Organizational Culture

Purpose

- To identify individual behaviors representative of the four basic organizational cultures.
- To role play work-related situations in each of the four basic organizational cultures.
- To examine problems that result from a lack of cultural match.

Procedure

1. Review Table 3.2 and familiarize yourself with each of the four basic organizational cultures.

2. Your instructor will choose four students and assign each to adopt one of the four basic organizational cultures, without letting the rest of the class know which culture has been assigned to each.

3. Two of the four students will role play the first of the following situations. The remaining two students will then role play the second situation. Each student must act within the characteristics of his or her assigned culture.

4. After role playing each situation, discuss the problem of cultural match and how the organization can resolve any problems. Be as practical and detailed as possible in your answer.

Situation

1. A manager is asking for ideas on how to sell more creatively. The individual believes that new approaches are needed if the firm's market share is to be expanded.

2. A manager wants all weekly cost control reports completed and submitted by 3 p.m. every Friday. In the past these reports have been submitted a week or two late, and this has prevented the firm from taking immediate steps to monitor cost control problems effectively.

4
CHAPTER

Group Behavior

Goals of the Chapter

Individuals may act on their own, but the perceptions, values, and attitudes that cause their behavior are often a result of group interaction. People are influenced by those around them. Therefore, we cannot adequately study human relations without considering group behavior. In this chapter we examine how people act within groups as well as how groups interact with each other.

The first goal of this chapter is to define the term *group* and to examine three of the most common types of groups. Then we answer the question: "Why do people join a group?" The second goal of this chapter is to study the major characteristics of groups, including roles, norms, status, and cohesiveness. The third goal is to look at decision making within groups. The fourth goal is to study intergroup behavior, noting some of the ways a group tries to gain power over other groups and how a manager can resolve intergroup conflict. The final goal is to examine the nature of committees and how these groups can be effectively employed in modern organizations.

When you have finished reading this chapter you should be able to:

1. Describe functional group, project group, and interest-friendship group.

2. Explain the importance of role, norms, and status to group behavior.

3. List some of the benefits of group decision making vis-à-vis individual decision making.

4.   Cite the common symptoms of *group think* and some of the ways it can be prevented.

5.   List some of the ways in which groups try to gain power over other groups.

6.   Relate the four guidelines for making committees more effective.

OPENING CASE

HEALTH CARE SERVICES FOR SALE

Over the last five years hospitals have undergone dramatic changes. In particular, they have found that success no longer depends exclusively on their ability to provide outstanding medical care. They also must be able to market their services effectively because, to most people, one hospital is the same as another. Hospitals have also found that they need to develop one or two major strengths and focus on these in their marketing campaign.

University Hospital, a large metropolitan hospital located in the Midwest, recently formed a special committee to help redefine its marketing strategy. The five-member group, made up of people from a variety of departments around the hospital, decided that the best way to handle the situation would be to list the possible strengths around which it could build a marketing campaign. The group listed seven strengths. Then they began to list the possible marketing themes that could be developed for each of these strengths. "We wanted to identify services for which we were unique or which we could market in an attractive, appealing way," the chairman explained. The process for generating ideas for the marketing themes was quite simple. Someone would call out an idea and everyone else could either piggyback on this idea or call out one of their own. As the group began moving from one theme to the next, the members sometimes backed up and added additional ideas to an earlier theme. When they were finished, each marketing theme had from seven to nineteen ideas associated with it.

The committee then decided which of the themes would be most effective for marketing purposes. "We found that the one with nineteen ideas did not offer any distinctive competencies for the hospital," the chairman explained. "It was a standard health care service. The two we finally ended up with were emergency room care and outpatient services. Our emergency room care is not only the finest in the area, but we guarantee that if you are physically injured you will be provided medical assistance by a doctor or intern within three minutes of the time you come in the door. Our outpatient service is directed toward providing friendly, convenient, and inexpensive health care. We guarantee that our price for this service is the lowest in this geographic region or we will refund you 50 percent of the fee. These two health care services will gain us a distinctive niche in the market."

1.   What type of group is this special committee? Explain.

2.   What type of creative thinking process did the group use in determining the services which the hospital would emphasize in its marketing campaign?

3.   Did the group use right-brain or left-brain thinking in analyzing the alternative strategies? Explain.

4.   Was this an ad hoc group or a standing committee? Explain.

Write down your answers to these questions and put them aside. We will return to them later. ■

DEFINITION OF A GROUP

What is a group? Unfortunately, there is no universally accepted definition of the term. However, there are three characteristics groups seem to have in common.

First, a group is a social unit of two or more members, all of whom engage, at some time or other, in *interaction* with each other. In work groups this interaction often occurs on a face-to-face basis, although some groups are geographically dispersed and interact through letters and telephone conversations.

Second, the members are all *dependent* on one another. In the pursuit of their objectives, each member realizes the need for the others. In a work setting, the individual is aware that the overall job cannot be done without assistance from the other people.

GROUPS HAVE THREE CHARACTERISTICS: INTERACTION, DEPENDENCE, AND SATISFACTION.

Third, the members of the group receive some *satisfaction* from their mutual association. Otherwise they will drop out of the group. In a work setting, for example, they will ask for a transfer to another department or locale or will simply resign.

Now that we have examined the three major characteristics of a group, let us incorporate them into a meaningful definition. A **group** is a social unit consisting of two or more interdependent, interactive individuals who are striving to attain common goals.

A GROUP IS A SOCIAL UNIT OF TWO OR MORE INTERDEPENDENT, INTERACTIVE PEOPLE STRIVING FOR COMMON GOALS.

TYPES OF GROUPS

Many types of groups can be found in organizations (see Figure 4.1). Most of them, however, can be classified as one of the following: functional group, project group, or interest-friendship group.

FIGURE 4.1   DIFFERENT TYPES OF GROUPS

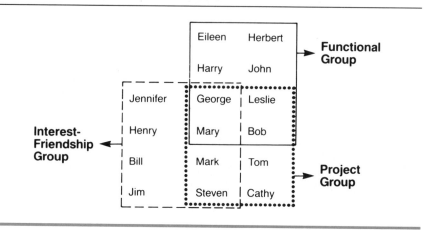

FUNCTIONAL GROUP   A **functional group** is composed of individuals performing the same tasks. In a manufacturing firm, for example, it is common to find major functional groups or departments, such as marketing, production, and finance, and further breakdowns of the personnel within each group. In the marketing department, for example, there is often an advertising group and a personal selling group, and within the latter there are sales forces for product lines or geographic territories. In all these breakdowns, functional groups have been formed by the company for the purpose of promoting internal efficiency.

■ ■ ■ ■ ■ ■ ■ ■ ■ ■ ■ ■ ■ ■
INDIVIDUALS IN FUNCTIONAL GROUPS PERFORM THE SAME TASKS.

PROJECT GROUP   A **project group** consists of individuals from many different areas or backgrounds. The group's purpose is to attain its objective within predetermined time, cost, and quality limits, after which the group is disbanded and everyone goes back to his or her regular department. Project groups are often used in building spacecraft, skyscrapers, bridges, and ships. They have also been employed in designing new products and solving particularly complex problems. Whatever the objective, however, a project group draws personnel from many different areas of expertise and combines their talents in hopes of attaining the project goal.

■ ■ ■ ■ ■ ■ ■ ■ ■ ■ ■ ■ ■ ■
A PROJECT GROUP HAS MEMBERS FROM MANY DIFFERENT BACKGROUNDS.

INTEREST-FRIENDSHIP GROUP   An **interest-friendship group** is formed on the basis of common beliefs, concerns, or activities. On the job, interest-friendship groups are sometimes found within departments, while in other instances they cut across departmental lines. For example, people who have been in an organization for a long time tend to

■ ■ ■ ■ ■ ■ ■ ■ ■ ■ ■ ■ ■ ■
INTEREST-FRIENDSHIP GROUPS ARE FORMED ON THE BASIS OF COMMON BELIEFS, CONCERNS, OR ACTIVITIES.

have many contacts, and they often find it possible to ask friends in other departments to expedite a process or to put a high priority on a particular job.

These types of groups also function away from the job, as in the case of the three members of the accounting department and the three from production who are on the company bowling team. Their primary interest is to win the bowling league title. However, such friendships carry back to the job, and it is not uncommon to find people using their friendships to help attain job-related objectives.

Thus, it should be obvious that people are often members of two or more groups. Figure 4.1, for example, depicts three groups. Half the members of the functional group are members of the project group. Two of them are also members of the interest-friendship group. Such overlapping membership indicates that intragroup and intergroup behavior can be a very complex area, resulting in many kinds of behavioral problems. We examine some of these later in the chapter.

These four Dow Corning employees are building teamwork in the Challenger's Trophy sporting event. Their mutual interest in competitive sports is an extension of their work relationship known as an interest-friendship group.

STOP!

Review your answer to the first question and make any changes you would like. Then compare your answer to the one below.

1.   What type of group is this special committee? Explain.

This group is a project group. It consists of people from a variety of departments around the hospital. This obviously was done so that the group would have members who could provide a wide array of insights regarding the hospital's strengths. ■

CHARACTERISTICS OF GROUPS

All groups have certain characteristics. Some of the most important are roles, norms, status, cohesiveness, and size.

ROLES

A **role** is an expected behavior. In many organizations, job descriptions provide the initial basis for determining one's role. The individual can read this description and obtain a general idea of what he or she is supposed to be doing. Of course, the description does not cover everything, but it will give the person enough general information to begin doing the job.

A ROLE IS AN EXPECTED BEHAVIOR.

■ ■ ■ ■ ■ ■ ■ ■ ■ ■ ■ ■ ■
ROLE AMBIGUITY OCCURS WHEN
THE JOB DESCRIPTION IS VAGUE.

One of the most serious and most common role-related problems occurs when job duties are unclear either because the job description is vague or because no description has ever been written for the work. We call this **role ambiguity**, because what the individual is supposed to do is uncertain or vague. For example, many workers find that when they are promoted to the rank of supervisor, they are told to, "Get out there, manage those people, and get the work done." This statement is too general. They do not understand the specific roles that they are supposed to assume. One of the most effective ways of preventing role ambiguity is to have job descriptions that are clear and which describe in detail the responsibilities and tasks of the position.

■ ■ ■ ■ ■ ■ ■ ■ ■ ■ ■ ■
IN ROLE CONFLICT TWO ROLES ARE
MUTUALLY INCOMPATIBLE.

A second major role-related problem is **role conflict**. This occurs when an individual faces a situation in which he or she must assume *two* roles, and the performance of one *precludes* the performance of the other. For example, a manager is told to do everything she can to build morale in the department. At the same time she is instructed to reprimand anyone who comes late to work. In this case, the manager may face a role conflict problem because she feels she cannot perform both of these tasks. If she is to build morale, she will have to be lenient with those who are tardy while working to change their behavior. If she reprimands anyone, she may feel that this action will affect morale negatively. Clearly, there is a role conflict problem.

NORMS

■ ■ ■ ■ ■ ■ ■ ■ ■ ■ ■ ■
NORMS ARE RULES OF CONDUCT
ADOPTED BY GROUP MEMBERS.

The rules of conduct adopted by group members are termed **norms**. These norms indicate how each group member *ought* to act. Usually norms are few in number and relate only to those areas that have *significance* for the group. For example, a work group will often have norms related to output (how much you ought to do), participation (whether or not you should help out slower workers), and communication with management (what you should and should not say to the boss). It will not have norms related to where you should live, how you ought to raise your children, or what church you should attend.

Additionally, there are *degrees* of conformity. For example, you ought to turn out 480 pieces per day, plus or minus 20. There is thus an *acceptable range*, and those individuals who want to remain in good standing with the group will conform to it.

Overall, there are some conclusions that we can draw about individuals and their conformity to group norms.

1.   Adults tend to be less conforming than children.

2.   Women, because of our cultural values, tend to be more conforming than men.

3.   Highly intelligent people tend to be less conforming than people of low intelligence.

4.   If all other members agree on something, the remaining person is likely to go along with them.

5.   If a person in the group disagrees with the others but receives support from one of them, the person is much less likely to conform. The individual will take heart from the fact that some support has been forthcoming and will often cling tenaciously to his or her original position.

6.   If a person does not understand what is going on, he or she is more likely to follow the direction of a group member who does seem to have a grasp of the situation.

Any individual who does not conform to at least the major norms of the group is denied membership. The person is not permitted to participate in group activities and, in some cases, is ostracized or is subjected to various forms of harassment by the members.

The manager must be aware of group norms because they play a key role in determining what a group will and will not do. If the group's informal work norm, for example, is much lower than the quota set by the company, the group is likely to have low productivity. The manager's awareness of such informal norms, however, can serve as the basis for developing a change strategy, by which the manager can influence the group to increase its informal work norms. (These change strategies are explored further in Chapter 13.)

STATUS

The term that refers to the relative ranking of an individual in an organization or group is **status**. Status can be achieved in a number of ways.

In our society, a Rockefeller has status merely through being *born* into a rich, influential family. On the job, people can achieve status through the *position* they hold. For example, the president of the organization has more status than a vice-president.

STATUS IS THE RELATIVE RANKING OF AN INDIVIDUAL OR GROUP.

Other people achieve such status by the *job* they do. For example, in some firms the advertising manager has greater status than the purchasing manager.

A third way to achieve job status is through *personality*. An individual who gets along with others, is easy to work with, and is always ready to say a kind word is more likely to be given status by the other members of the organization than an individual with whom no one can work because he or she is unpleasant to others.

A fourth work status determinant is *job competence*. The better a person knows his or her job, the more likely it is that the person will be accorded status by members of the peer group. For example, in a group that values high productivity, those individuals who are the highest producers will be afforded the highest status.

Of course, to determine *exactly* how group status will be accorded we have to examine the specific situation. In some groups competence (what

FIGURE 4.2   **CHANGING STATUS**

	ACADEMIA	BANK	BOWLING ALLEY
High Status	Professor of Finance	Bank President	Graduating Senior in Zoology (195 average)
	Assistant Professor of Biology	Professor of Finance	MBA Student (180 average)
	MBA Student	MBA Student	Assistant Professor of Biology (170 average)
	Graduating Senior in Zoology	Assistant Professor of Biology	Bank President (150 average)
Low Status	Bank President	Graduating Senior in Zoology	Professor of Finance (135 average)

the person can do) is very important but in other groups job title (what position the person holds) is of greatest value in obtaining status. Additionally, if we were to move from one organization to another we might well find different status determinants. This would be particularly obvious if we were to put six people—two professors, two bank executives, and two students—into three different group settings. As seen in Figure 4.2, the status of these individuals will vary from one situation to the next. Yet if one were to give them scores, 1 point for first place through 5 points for fifth place, in all three group settings, one would find that the overall score per person is about the same. In short, they all have about the same *average* status across the three groups, but this status varies dramatically within the group. For example, in a university setting, the full professor has the highest status, followed by other faculty, and then students, and finally members of the group whose occupations are not academic. In a bank, the president has the highest status, followed by individuals knowledgeable in finance, students working for degrees in business (MBA), and then members of the group whose occupations do not relate to finance in any way. Finally, in a bowling alley, the status of each is accorded strictly on the basis of bowling skill.

In order to fully understand the importance of status within groups, it is necessary to realize that there can be status problems. The most serious is **status incongruency**, which occurs when there is a discrepancy between a person's supposed status and the way he or she is treated. For example, if all of the senior-level managers except one are given new desks, there is a discrepancy between the way this last person is being treated and the way this person's peers are being treated. Unless there is reason for this discrepancy such as the fact that the manager does not want a new desk and prefers to continue using the old one, the manager's status may be in jeopardy. People will begin to wonder why the manager is not being treated as well as the other senior-level managers. In fact, in some organizations this is the way managers are told that they are "on the way out." They are not given things that are provided to other managers at their organizational level.

A second status-related problem is **status discrepancy**, which occurs when people do things that do not fit with their status in their group. For example, in an organization where there are bitter feelings between management and the union, members of these two groups do not associate with each other. Anyone who is seen being friendly to a member of the other group is considered a traitor and his or her status will decline. Members of the management team who act friendly toward union representatives may soon find such actions negatively affecting promotion potential. Union representatives who are friendly with management personnel may soon be voted out of office. We can sum it up this way: Status is accorded to people for "acting properly," and any time people do things that do not fit into this category, they threaten their own status.

COHESIVENESS

The closeness or interpersonal attractions that exist among group members are referred to as **cohesiveness**. If cohesion is high, members are motivated to remain in the group. If cohesion is low, members often leave the group.

■ ■ ■ ■ ■ ■ ■ ■ ■ ■ ■ ■ ■ ■ ■

COHESIVENESS REFERS TO THE CLOSENESS AMONG GROUP MEMBERS.

However, cohesiveness does *not* guarantee high productivity. The individuals may all like each other very much and may also have an informal norm of low output; they have all agreed to do as little work as possible. Figure 4.3 provides an illustration. Note that Group X has the highest productivity. Everyone in this group is turning out more work than is required by the organization norm. In fact, all the high producers are in this group. Conversely, all the low producers are in Group Z. Their average is far below that of the other two groups. However, cohesiveness is very high. Everyone in the group is conforming to an informal work norm. Note how little each person's productivity deviates from this norm; this is why we can conclude that it is indeed an informal norm. Otherwise, there would be several high and low producers. For example, in Group X there is a greater variation between high and low producers, indicating less acceptance of a group norm. In Group Y the variation is even more significant. We can conclude that Group Z has the greatest cohesion and that Group Y has the least.

Apple Computer Company's engineering team demonstrated that cohesiveness is an important factor in a group project. These team members and their co-workers were involved in the design and development of the Macintosh SE and Macintosh II.

Group cohesiveness presents two major challenges to the manager. First, the manager needs to work closely with low-producing groups to motivate them to increase their productivity norms to the level established by the organization. Many of the ideas presented in Chapter 2 can be used in doing this.

Second, the manager has to protect the cohesiveness of the high-producing groups. Changes in the work or transfer of people into or out of the group can all negatively affect cohesion. One of the most famous

FIGURE 4.3   COHESION AND PRODUCTIVITY

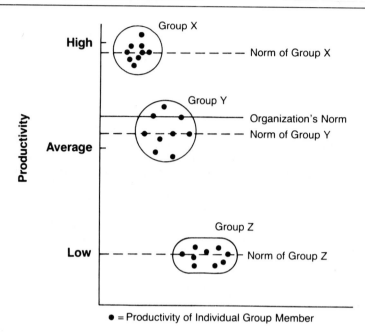

● = Productivity of Individual Group Member

cases of this has been provided by the coal mining industry in Great Britain, which introduced new technology and procedures into the mines after World War II. Before the change, the miners had worked together in teams and there was high cohesion within these groups. However, the new technology disrupted these arrangements. Many of the small cohesive groups were reorganized into larger teams and some of the work previously done by the miners was now done by machine. The restructuring destroyed group cohesiveness, and the coal miners began to slow down their production. It became necessary for the companies to again reorganize some of their operations, this time, however, to better accommodate the miners.

Quite obviously, every organization needs to consider both the technology and the people. If technology is overemphasized, cohesiveness declines and productivity falls. Conversely, if the people are accommodated at the expense of technology, the firm suffers in comparison with other companies that have adopted the latest technological breakthroughs. A balance is needed, as illustrated in Figure 4.4.

GROUP SIZE

Some work groups are quite small (3 or 4 people) while others are very large (20 or more). Research has found that as the size of the group in-

---

FIGURE 4.4   TECHNOLOGY, PEOPLE, AND PRODUCTIVITY

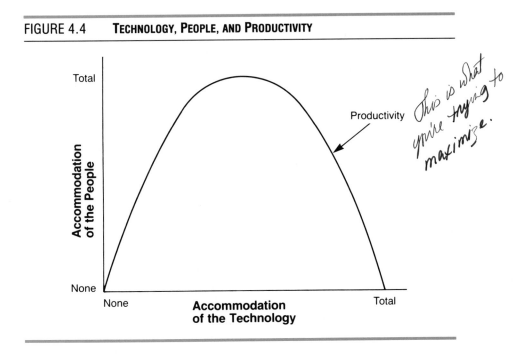

This is what you're trying to maximize.

creases, the way in which members interact with each other undergoes change. As group size goes up, the time and attention given to creating and maintaining group harmony go down. This is in contrast to small groups where members typically exhibit greater agreement on things and seek each other's opinions more frequently. In large groups it is also common to find the need for group approval diminishing; people begin focusing more on getting the job done and less on how their co-workers feel about their actions.

Research also reports that as groups become larger, turnover tends to increase and satisfaction tends to decline. One explanation that has been offered is that in a large group people are less able to fulfill their upper-level needs, and this leads to dissatisfaction. Conversely, in small groups there tends to be greater cohesion, more concern for fellow workers, and greater satisfaction, with the result being lower employee turnover.[1]

• • • • • • •

[1] For more on this topic, see Robert F. Bales and Edgar F. Borgatta, "Size of Group as a Factor in the Interaction Profile," in A. P. Hare, Edgar F. Borgatta, and Robert F. Bales (eds.) *Small Groups* (New York: Knopf, 1955), pp. 396–413; and Lyman W. Porter and Richard M. Steers, "Organizational, Work, and Personal Factors in Employee Turnover and Absenteeism," *Psychological Bulletin*, August 1973, pp. 151–176.

INTRAGROUP BEHAVIOR

Two major activities within groups are of primary interest to those studying human relations: communication and decision making.

COMMUNICATION

The social system of the group helps dictate the way information is communicated. The role that is played by each individual typically is a result of that individual's knowledge and personality and the needs of the group.

INTRAGROUP ROLES   Depending on the size of the group, a varying number of roles may be assumed by the members. In a small group, an individual may assume more than one communication role. In large groups, two or more people may assume the same role, while others have no specific role. Five of the most common roles are the following:

▪   The **opinion leader** is often the informal leader of the group. This person typically receives more communiques than anyone else in the group and is most responsible for determining group goals and actions.

▪   The **gatekeeper** regulates the flow of information to other members of the group. If this individual chooses not to tell something to someone, the latter is deprived of the information because the gatekeeper is the only one in a position to provide this information.

▪   The **liaison** links the group to other groups. He or she is the contact person who communicates with the other groups and gets information from them.

▪   The **isolate** is a person who is generally ignored by the group and receives very little communication. He or she is treated as an outsider, even though the person is a member of the group.

▪   The **follower** goes along with whatever the opinion leader or the group at large wants done. He or she is a loyal group member who can be counted on to "stay in line."

DECISION MAKING

How are decisions made within groups?[2] This is a difficult question to answer because it is multifaceted. However, we know some things about group decision making that are related to risk taking and to creativity.

▪▪▪▪▪▪▪

[2] For more on this, see Jane Whitney Gibson and Richard M. Hodgetts, *Organizational Communication: A Management Perspective* (Orlando, Fla.: Academic Press, 1986), pp. 233–234.

RISK TAKING   A number of important findings have been uncovered about risk taking within groups. First, groups are often *more* effective than individuals in decision making. For example, when faced with the task of evaluating ambiguous situations, groups appear to be superior to individuals. They are also more effective in generating unique ideas or accurately recalling information. However, they are not as effective as individuals in solving problems that require long chains of decisions.[3]

Second, individuals tend to take greater risks when they are in groups than when they are acting alone. This is known as the **risky-shift phenomenon**.[4] Behavioral scientists studying this phenomenon have used measures similar to the questionnaire you will find in the end-of-chapter section Experiencing Risk Taking. The individual is asked questions alone and then is placed in a group, which is asked the same questions. The people in groups tend to be greater risk takers. Why is this so? A list of some of the explanations offered for this phenomenon follows:

■ ■ ■ ■ ■ ■ ■ ■ ■ ■ ■ ■ ■
INDIVIDUALS ARE GREATER RISK TAKERS WHEN ACTING IN A GROUP.

1.   If the decision proves to be wrong, the individual feels less guilt or concern because there were other people involved and responsibility is diffused among everyone.

2.   In group discussions, risky people tend to be more influential than their conservative counterparts. As a result, the viewpoints of the former tend to win out.

3.   Risk is a function of knowledge. The less someone knows about a given area or problem, the greater the risk he or she assumes in trying to remedy the situation. Since group thinking often leads to deeper consideration of, and greater familiarization with, the possible pros and cons of a particular course of action, the risk tends to be reduced. Thus a high risk decision for an individual can be a moderate risk for a group.

■ ■ ■ ■ ■ ■ ■ ■ ■ ■ ■ ■ ■
BEHAVIORAL EXPLANATIONS FOR THE RISKY-SHIFT PHENOMENON.

4.   Risk taking is socially desirable in our culture. As a result, individuals in groups often choose a risk level that is equal to or greater than that risk which is acceptable to the average person.[5]

We should note, however, that groups do *not* always encourage higher risk taking. Sometimes they motivate a manager to be even *more*

■ ■ ■ ■ ■ ■ ■

[3] Bertram Schoner, Gerald L. Rose, and G. C. Hoyt, "Quality of Decisions: Individuals Versus Real and Synthetic Groups," *Journal of Applied Psychology*, August 1974, pp. 424–432.

[4] Dorwin Cartwright, "Risk Taking by Individuals and Groups: An Assessment of Research Employing Choice Dilemmas," *Journal of Personality and Social Psychology*, December 1971, pp. 361–378; Russell D. Clark III, "Group Induced Shift Toward Risk: A Critical Appraisal," *Psychological Bulletin*, October 1971, pp. 251–270; Dean G. Pruitt, "Choice Shifts in Group Discussion: An Introductory Review," *Journal of Personality and Social Psychology*, December 1971, pp. 339–360.

[5] Earl A. Cecil, Larry L. Cummings, and Jerome M. Chertkoff, "Group Composition and Choice Shift: Implications for Administration," *Academy of Management Journal*, September 1973, pp. 413–414.

moderate in setting goals. For example, in many organizations it is common to find the head of the sales department encouraging the managers to strive for 20 percent higher sales. However, sometimes the individual manager's sales force reports that the market is not increasing and that at best a 10 percent rise in sales can be expected; the manager may then be influenced by the sales force to set a more realistic objective for the group. In short, group pressure, toward risky or more moderate goals, influences management behavior.

■ ■ ■ ■ ■ ■ ■ ■ ■ ■ ■ ■ ■ ■
THERE ARE FOUR PHASES TO
CREATIVE THINKING.

CREATIVITY   Sometimes decisions require creative thinking.[6] This process has four phases: preparation, incubation, illumination, and verification. During the *preparation* stage the group members get mentally prepared to make the decision. This phase is characterized by information gathering. During the *incubation* stage the group often will sit back and let the subconscious mind work on the problem. Quite often the result will be a better decision than one that is forced or made in a hurry. On the other hand, if group members are unable to come up with an effective approach after, say, one week, they will go back to the preparation stage and start the process anew by gathering additional data or reviewing what is there. The *illumination* phase is characterized by the group realizing the best decision to make. Sometimes the decision will suddenly hit them; other times it will slowly dawn on them. In any event, they now know what to do. The final stage is *verification*. This is when the group modifies or makes final changes in the solution. Quite often the decision will need some fine tuning because of minor problems. Once this is done, the decision can be implemented.

■ ■ ■ ■ ■ ■ ■ ■ ■ ■ ■ ■ ■ ■
BRAINSTORMING IS A POPULAR
TECHNIQUE.

BRAINSTORMING   It is difficult, if not impossible, for the average group member to be creative on the spur of the moment. However, there are techniques that can help stimulate creative thinking. The most popular is **brainstorming**. A typical brainstorming session begins with the group leader, often the manager, telling the participants the problem under analysis and urging them to be as creative and imaginative as they can. Initial emphasis is placed on generating as many ideas as possible without too much consideration of their realism. As people call out ideas, the others are encouraged to build on them or use them as a basis for developing their own ideas.

Brainstorming is particularly popular when seeking creative solutions to nontechnical problems such as effective advertising campaigns.[7]

■ ■ ■ ■ ■ ■ ■

[6]Ernesto J. Poza, "A Do-It-Yourself Guide to Group Problem Solving," *Personnel*, March–April 1983, pp. 69–77.
[7]See also David A. Pierson, "A Technique for Managing Creative People," *Personnel*, January–February 1983, pp. 12–26.

The technique is also widely used by consumer product firms such as Campbell Soup which is continually developing new foods based on consumer research and creative packaging concepts. Moreover, brainstorming has become so critical in the development of auto products that firms like Nissan actually use examples of brainstorming sessions in their advertisements to help viewers understand how the firm decides the final design and production of its cars.

Aerospace Corporation engineers use brainstorming as a method of discussing and solving highly technical problems in the design of military space equipment for government installations.

SYNECTICS Another creative approach, similar to brainstorming, is **synectics**, which uses analogies to provide mental images to the brain. The approach can be used with groups or by individuals working alone. One of the most common methods in using synectics is to project oneself into the essence of the problem. For example, if a product development engineer is trying to develop a more efficient engine for a vacuum cleaner, the individual might imagine himself or herself as a motor in the cleaning unit. Or the individual might think of a direct analogy such as small engines in other machines that might be modified for use in the vacuum cleaner. Sometimes the individual will use a symbolic analogy such as was done by the synectics group that designed Pringles potato chips. The group wanted to compress potato chips into a small space without squashing them. They eventually found an analogy in leaves which can be compressed and undamaged as long as they are wet at the time of compression. It was decided to make the potato chips by compressing them while still wet, and Pringles became a commercial product. Creativity has become so important to organizations that many of them are beginning to look into left-brain and right-brain thinking.

STOP!

Review your answer to the second question and make any changes you would like. Then compare your answer to the one below.

2.   What type of creative thinking process did the group use in determining the services which the hospital would emphasize in its marketing campaign?

The group used brainstorming. The case explains that an individual would call out ideas associated with one of the major themes and the other members would either piggyback on this theme or call out an answer of their own. They were also free to go back to themes that had been discussed earlier and add ideas to them. This "freewheeling" approach is characteristic of the brainstorming process. ∎

LEFT-BRAIN, RIGHT-BRAIN THINKING In recent years attention has been focused on creativity and brain function. Most people are either left-brain dominant or right-brain dominant. The left brain controls the right side of the body and the right brain controls the left side of the body. This dominance also dictates the way people do things. For example, **left-brain people** tend to be very logical, rational, detailed, active, and objectives-oriented. **Right-brain people** are more spontaneous, emotional, holistic, nonverbal, and visual in their approach to things. Left-brain people have a preference for routine tasks or jobs that require precision, detail, or repetition. Right-brain people like jobs that are nonroutine or call for idea generation.[8] Left-brain people like to solve problems by breaking them into parts and approaching the problems sequentially and logically. Right-brain people like to solve problems by looking at the entire matter and approaching the solution through hunches and insights.

Most people are left-brain dominant. They tend to be less creative and imaginative than right-brain dominant people. In an effort to get individuals to use both sides of the brain, some organizations are now giving their employees "whole brain" training in which the participants learn how to use each side of the brain (see Human Relations in Action: Whole-Brain Thinking). The focus is on making highly rational thinkers more creative and getting highly intuitive types to supplement their approach with greater emphasis on detail, logic, and procedure. The approach is proving to be an excellent supplement to standard creative thinking approaches such as brainstorming.[9] (Before continuing, take the Time Out: What Type of "Thinker" Are You? quiz to find out if you are more right-brain or left-brain dominant.)

A good example is provided in the case of the Hawaii Telephone Company (HTC). Industry deregulation greatly affected this firm by creating both problems and opportunities. In an effort to deal with these, HTC decided to tap the intuitive skills of its personnel.

First HTC administered a diagnostic test to identify left-brain and right-brain managers. Left-brain managers were then introduced to other left-brain managers while right-brain managers were grouped with other right-brain managers. Then the firm set forth its objectives for the future. Some of these objectives were best pursued by right-brain man-

••••••••

[8] Daniel Robey and William Taggart, "Measuring Managers' Minds: The Assessment of Style in Human Information Processing," *Academy of Management Review*, July 1981, pp. 375–383.

[9] For more on this see Tim Smithin, "Maps of the Mind: New Pathways to Decision-Making," *Business Horizons*, December 1980, pp. 24–28; Weston H. Agor, "Brain Skills Development in Management Training," *Training and Development*, pp. 78–83; Patricia Hayes, "Problem Solving Through Visualization," *The Executive Female*, May–June 1984, pp. 29–32; and Dudley Lynch, "Is the Brain Stuff Still the Right (or Left) Stuff," *Training and Development Journal*, February 1986, pp. 23–26.

HUMAN RELATIONS IN ACTION

WHOLE-BRAIN THINKING

Most people are left-brain thinkers. They are analytical, rational, goal-oriented, explicit, and sequential in their approach to decision making. They have been encouraged to think and act this way and in the process have failed to develop right-brain approaches characterized by thinking that is spontaneous, emotional, nonverbal, artistic, and holistic. Today there is a major effort to get people to use *both* sides of their brain, which is called whole-brain thinking. While there are a number of ways of developing this thinking, some are quite simple and can be used on a day-to-day basis. The following examines some of these ways.

RIGHT-BRAIN THINKING	LEFT-BRAIN THINKING
Doodle, draw, or print on a piece of paper.	Outline things, solve math problems, or do a crossword puzzle.
Shift the phone to your left ear, allowing for empathic listening.	Shift the phone to your right ear, allowing for analytic listening.
Carry a clipboard, notes, or other comfortable symbols.	Use a dictating machine, a pointer, or some symbol of authority.
Be aware of the colors, space, and sounds around you.	Estimate the value of your net worth.
Hum, joke, chuckle with others.	Ask questions, make puns.
While sitting at your desk, take a minute to lean back, close your eyes, and daydream.	Go off alone and write a memo related to a major problem you are facing.

These approaches may seem a little silly depending on which list you are using; however, this is because you are more accustomed to doing one set of activities than the other. By switching from left to right or vice versa, you enter a mental world that is somewhat strange to you. Yet that is what whole-brain thinking is all about—getting yourself to use that part of your brain that usually lies dormant.

agers; some were best pursued by left-brain managers; and some were best approached by having right-brain managers provide initial suggestions and then having left-brain managers critique and complement these ideas. This "dual" approach to dealing with uncertainty and competitive problems has proven very effective for HTC.

TIME OUT

WHAT TYPE OF "THINKER" ARE YOU?

Are you a left-brain or a right-brain person? Find out by answering the following questions. An interpretation is provided at the end of the chapter.

1. Do you express yourself well verbally?
   a. _✓_ Yes   b. ____ No

2. Are you a very systematic person?
   a. ____ Yes   b. _✓_ No

3. Do you enjoy moving the furniture in your room and changing things around so that they look different?
   a. _✓_ Yes   b. ____ No

4. When you are learning a new dance, which of the following do you prefer to do?
   a. _✓_ Get the feel of the music and begin to move to the tempo.
   b. ____ Have someone show you the steps and then imitate them.

5. Are you a goal-oriented person?
   a. _✓_ Yes   b. ____ No

6. When you want to remember directions to a location, how do you do it?
   a. _✓_ Visualize the information.
   b. ____ Write down the information.

7. How well do you remember faces?
   a. ____ Not very well   b. _✓_ Very well

8. When you are communicating with someone, do you prefer to be the listener or the speaker?
   a. _✓_ Listener   b. ____ Speaker

9. Without looking at a clock, can you usually tell what time it is?
   a. _✓_ Yes   b. ____ No

10. Do you like to work alone or in groups?
    a. _✓_ Alone   b. ____ In groups

11. Which type of social situation do you prefer?
    a. _✓_ Planned   b. ____ Spontaneous

12. Which of the following subjects did you prefer in school?
    a. ____ Algebra   b. _✓_ Geometry

13. Do you ever print when you are taking notes?
    a. _✓_ Often   b. ____ Never or very seldom

14. Do you like to take risks?
    a. _✓_ Yes   b. ____ No

15. After hearing a song for the first time, which of the following are you able to do best?
    a. _✓_ Hum the music   b. ____ Recall the words

16. Do you have frequent mood changes?
    a. ____ Yes   b. _✓_ No

STOP!

Review your answer to the third question and make any changes you would like. Then compare your answer to the one below.

3.   Did the group use right-brain or left-brain thinking in analyzing the alternative strategies? Explain.

The group used both right-brain and left-brain thinking. Remember that right-brain thinking involves spontaneous, innovative, and imaginative responses. This would be needed in generating the initial ideas regarding how to market each of the hospital's strengths. Left-brain thinking involves logical, rational, and objectives-oriented thinking. This would be needed in examining all of the material and deciding which themes were most useful and could serve as the basis of an effective marketing campaign. ∎

GROUP THINK

START

One final question must be asked about decision making within groups. When are group-generated decisions *not* superior to individual decisions? The answer is: when group think comes into play.

Group think refers to social conformity to group ideas.[10] It requires the individual to stop challenging the thinking of the group and go along with the consensus. Group think occurs when members of a decision-making body decide to avoid being too harsh in their judgments of the group's ideas. They adopt a "soft line" of criticism. Here is a description of some of the thinking that commonly accompanies this phenomenon:

GROUP THINK IS SOCIAL CONFORMITY TO GROUP IDEAS.

1.   The group's ideals are seen as humanitarian and as based on high-minded principles so there need be no concern about unethical behavior.

2.   In order to be a member of the group, one has to avoid criticizing it and to help ensure cohesion by suppressing critical thoughts.

3.   Amiability and esprit de corps among the members are very high, with the result that the members believe that other groups criticizing them are irrational.

The primary symptoms of group think include:

1.   The group has the illusion, whether or not it is ever expressed, of invulnerability. It cannot be wrong.

· · · · · · ·

[10] Much of the material in this section can be found in Irving Janis, "Group Think," *Psychology Today*, November 1971, pp. 43–46, 74–76.

2.   Any warnings that the group's actions may be wrong are ignored or rationalized away.

3.   If any member disagrees, there is pressure put on the person to express such doubts only within the group and to keep disagreement within acceptable bounds.

4.   There is the illusion of unanimity among the members, especially in regard to the major areas of concern.

5.   Individuals who are victims of group think often protect the leader and fellow members from adverse information that might shake the complacency they share.

Group think illustrates the serious consequences of a work team's becoming victim of its own group norms. Fortunately, managers can combat this phenomenon by following a handful of simple rules. First, the manager must encourage the open airing of objections and doubts. Second, one or more outsiders should be invited into the group to challenge the views of the members. Third, one member of the original group should be appointed to function as a lawyer who is challenging the testimony of the other members. Finally, after reaching a preliminary decision, the group should hold a "second chance" meeting at which every member expresses, as vividly as possible, all his or her doubts and the group thinks through the entire issue again before making a final decision.

INTERGROUP BEHAVIOR

Intergroup behavior is interactions between or among *two* or more groups. Sometimes these groups are in the same department; sometimes they are in different departments. In any event, the groups, for some reason, have to coordinate their efforts to attain organizational goals. The purpose of intergroup behavior is to achieve high performance. However, sometimes power struggles develop between the groups, and conflict resolution is required.

ACHIEVING HIGH INTERGROUP PERFORMANCE

High intergroup performance depends on a number of factors.

First, each group has to know what it is supposed to be doing. *Goals* must be clear. If Group A is charged with building Part A, Group B is responsible for constructing Part B, and Group C is supposed to assemble the two parts into a finished product, any delay by the first two groups will slow up Group C. Groups A and B both have to understand how to build the parts and to know how much output is required of them.

Second, there must be *cooperation* among all three groups, since a slow-up or bottleneck in *any* of them will result in a drop in production. Each group is a vital link in the production process.

Third, there must be *careful planning* of all interfaces between them, so that if one of the groups falls behind, the manager knows about it and can start correcting the problem before the situation gets out of control. One way this can be done is through daily monitoring of output. If production in any group falls off, the supervisor or department head is aware of it within 24 hours. Another way is to designate a liaison or coordinating manager, who works out any bottlenecks. For example, if Group A is falling behind because it has run out of raw materials, the coordinating manager checks with the purchasing department to see that the materials are rushed to the group. If some members of Group B stay home sick with the flu, the coordinating manager arranges for temporary replacements from other departments.

■ ■ ■ ■ ■ ■ ■ ■ ■ ■ ■ ■ ■
CLEAR GOALS, COOPERATION, AND CAREFUL PLANNING ARE NEEDED.

Such planning and liaison work can do much to ensure high intergroup performance. However, this is not always enough. Sometimes the problem is that groups are squabbling with each other, a common occurrence when power struggles develop.

POWER STRUGGLES

Power is influence over others; and although struggles for power can be detrimental to organizational efficiency, they are an inevitable part of intergroup behavior. Sooner or later one group will try to gain power over others by means of several behaviors.

PROVIDING SERVICES   One of the most common ways to gain power over other groups is to provide services for them that they either cannot or will not provide for themselves.

■ ■ ■ ■ ■ ■ ■ ■ ■ ■ ■ ■ ■
PROVIDE IMPORTANT SERVICES.

For example, many large- and medium-sized businesses in industrial states are unionized. In order to deal with the union members, each company usually has an industrial relations department, which negotiates a contract with the union and works out the finer points of management-union prerogatives. What type of seniority system will there be to protect the rights of union members who have worked for the company for a long time? If some union people are laid off, in what order must they be rehired? What right of appeal does a member have if he or she is threatened with demotion or dismissal? Most departments look to the industrial relations department for help in resolving any problem related to

FIGURE 4.5   **INTEGRATIVE IMPORTANCE OF GROUPS**

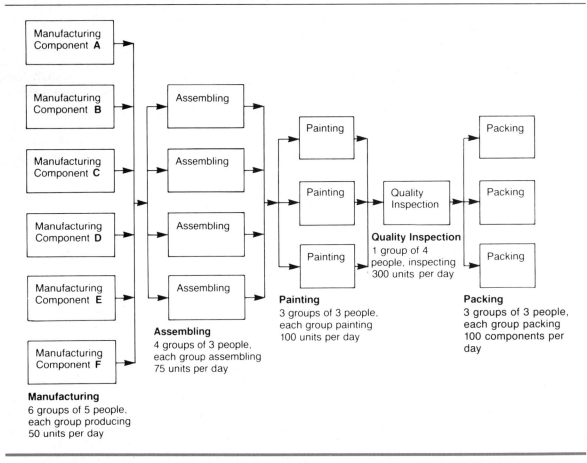

these issues. As a result, in the area of labor-management issues, the industrial relations department holds power over the others.

■ ■ ■ ■ ■ ■ ■ ■ ■ ■ ■ ■ **INTEGRATIVE IMPORTANCE**   A second power struggle is directly re-
PLAY AN IMPORTANT INTEGRATIVE   lated to the degree of integrative importance. If a group has an im-
ROLE.   portant integrative role in a process involving many groups, the other
groups depend on it.

Consider the case of the manufacturing firm that produces a specialized power tool for industrial use. Figure 4.5 is a representation of the production process. There are five steps: manufacturing, assembly, painting, quality inspection, and packing. There are six major components to be manufactured. These are then sent to one of four assembly groups, each of which assembles an identical product. From here the products are forwarded to the painting groups, each of which is charged with painting 100 units a day. The products are then sent to the quality inspection group, which has a special machine that checks each for paint quality and determines that it works properly. If there is some failure in the product, the inspector identifies the problem, writes a ticket on it, and, depending on what is wrong, sends it back to the assembly or painting group. If the product passes inspection, it is sent to the packing group, where it is carefully boxed and made ready for shipment. A close study of Figure 4.5 reveals that, of all the groups, quality inspection has the greatest integrative importance. There is only one such group and it performs a very important role. The group can either accept or reject the work of the other groups. Additionally, the other groups are larger in number or perform identical tasks. If one of these groups, such as assembly, is short of manpower because of illness, the other assembling groups can take up the slack. However, if the quality inspection people slow down, there is no one else to help them catch up, and the whole organization can be adversely affected. Therefore, because of its integrative importance, the quality inspection group has a degree of power over the others.

BUDGET ALLOCATION   A third common power struggle between groups is related to budget allocation. Most organizational groups, especially at the departmental level, would like to increase their budgets. Under favorable economic conditions, when the average annual increase is 10 percent, they will fight for a 15 to 20 percent increase. If sales or revenues have not been good and budgets are being reduced by 10 percent, departmental groups will strive to maintain their original allocation.

One of the most effective ways of succeeding in budget battles is to show top management that the department is doing a better job than most of the other departments. For example, the manufacturing group argues that its production costs have dropped and it is turning out more goods than ever before; if the group is given an increase in budget, more machines can be purchased and efficiency can be further improved. The marketing department produces statistics showing that sales per dollar of advertising are way up so its budget should be increased. Meanwhile the finance department opposes the manufacturing and marketing groups, arguing that the company is spending too much too fast and that it would be wiser to pay off some of the long-term debt, maintain a more liquid financial position, and add more finance personnel for control and evaluation purposes.

■ ■ ■ ■ ■ ■ ■ ■ ■ ■ ■ ■ ■
GET A BIGGER BUDGET ALLOCATION.

Quite obviously, each group has its own ax to grind, and a big increase in one group's budget can come only at the expense of the others. If the manufacturing group is given a 20 percent increase, the marketing and finance groups will feel slighted. If the large increase is given to marketing, the production and finance departments will be unhappy. If the finance department's argument convinces the top management to withhold increases, the other groups will be angry.

This group power struggle arises because of **goal conflict**. Each group must learn that its goal may not benefit other groups and that decisions must sometimes be made that appear to be detrimental to that group's welfare.

CONFLICT RESOLUTION

The astute manager is aware of these intergroup power struggles but also realizes that there are ways of eliminating or diminishing their negative effects. The individual works to accomplish this through what is called conflict resolution. There are a number of ways to resolve intergroup conflict. Four of the most common are: confrontation, collaboration, compromise, and altering the organizational structure.[11]

■ ■ ■ ■ ■ ■ ■ ■ ■ ■ ■ ■ ■
CONFRONTATION INVOLVES FACE-
TO-FACE PROBLEM SOLVING.

CONFRONTATION   Problem solving on a face-to-face basis is termed **confrontation**. If the manager finds that several groups in the department are unable to get along and decides to use confrontation, the groups or their leaders are asked to meet to discuss their differences. Sometimes they are able to express their dissatisfaction with one another quickly and easily; sometimes it is a long process. In any event, there are some common complaints: "Those guys don't want to work with us. They're always doing something to slow up the flow of operations." "Whenever we're slow with our end of the work, those guys gripe, but if they're slow, they get angry if we say anything." "We don't know what the problem is with that group, but we just don't feel we can trust them, so we don't like working with them."

These standard responses are often the result of misunderstanding among the groups. By encouraging each group to express its objections, the manager can usually cultivate a feeling of harmony among them. Each group begins to see how the other groups view it and obtains better understanding of its own behavior. Then the groups are asked how they are going to increase their interaction with one another and what steps should be taken to insure that they do not slip back into their old habits.

This confrontation method is one of the most successful approaches to conflict resolution because it concentrates on solving the problem directly rather than trying to bypass it or to smooth over the issues.

■ ■ ■ ■ ■ ■ ■
[11] For others see George H. Labowitz, "Managing Conflict," *Business Horizons*, June 1980, pp. 30–37.

COLLABORATION　　　Sometimes goals desired by two or more parties cannot be reached without the cooperation of those involved; this is when collaboration can be effective. **Collaboration** calls for all parties to work out their differences and to realize that without full cooperation all of them will fail. A common illustration is the case of the powerful union that wants a lucrative contract from a company on the verge of bankruptcy. It is obvious that if the union insists on its demands, the firm will go out of business. The only way to resolve the situation is for the union to take less money and to cooperate with the company in working to attain a more profitable position. When the company is stable, the union can resubmit its demands for a lucrative contract.

■ ■ ■ ■ ■ ■ ■ ■ ■ ■ ■ ■ ■ ■
COLLABORATION REQUIRES FULL COOPERATION OF EVERYONE.

COMPROMISE　　　When each party gives up something and no one group is the clear "winner" **compromise** occurs. Consider the case of the foreman who fires a worker for being late four days in a row. During the ensuing labor-management meeting required by the contract, the union argues that the offense has not justified such a harsh penalty. Both sides, the company and the union, then compromise on the situation: they agree that laying the worker off for five days (without pay) is sufficient punishment. Thus the worker has not been fired, but he has not escaped punishment for blatant infringement of the rules.

■ ■ ■ ■ ■ ■ ■ ■ ■ ■ ■ ■ ■ ■
IN COMPROMISE EACH PARTY GIVES UP SOMETHING.

ALTERING THE ORGANIZATIONAL STRUCTURE　　　If the manager finds that a particular group cannot get along with some of the other groups, he or she may decide to resolve the conflict by reorganizing the department structure. For example, using Figure 4.5 again, the manager finds that some of the members of the quality control group cannot get along with members of the other groups. He or she may simply remove the people by transferring them to other departments or work assignments and replacing them with more congenial workers. Or, if the manager finds that the assembling and painting departments resent the fact that their work can be sent back to them by quality control people, a supervisor may be appointed to make the final decision regarding what is to be returned as unacceptable. In this way the manager interposes someone between the antagonist (quality control) and the antagonized (assembly and painting groups). This type of organizational rearrangement has been found to be very effective in cases in which workers object to "taking orders" from other workers.

■ ■ ■ ■ ■ ■ ■ ■ ■ ■ ■ ■ ■ ■
REORGANIZATION CAN SOMETIMES HELP.

COMMITTEES

An important type of group, commonly found in modern organizations, is the committee. There are two basic kinds of committees: ad hoc and standing. An **ad hoc committee** is formed for a particular reason, and

■ ■ ■ ■ ■ ■ ■ ■ ■ ■ ■ ■ ■ ■
AN AD HOC COMMITTEE IS FORMED FOR A SPECIFIC PURPOSE.

■ ■ ■ ■ ■ ■ ■ ■ ■ ■ ■ ■ ■ ■
A STANDING COMMITTEE EXISTS
INDEFINITELY.

when this objective has been accomplished, the group is disbanded. An example is a committee to review a new product offering before putting it on the market. A **standing committee** exists indefinitely. The most common example is the board of directors of a corporation.

■ ■ ■ ■ ■ ■ ■ ■ ■ ■ ■ ■ ■ ■
THERE ARE ADVANTAGES.

There are a number of advantages to committees. Three of the most commonly cited include: (1) the opportunity for collective judgment, often producing a better decision than one person working alone, (2) the benefit it can provide in coordinating plans and transmitting information throughout the organization, and (3) the motivational value it creates among the members who often derive both enthusiasm and support for their decisions.

■ ■ ■ ■ ■ ■ ■ ■ ■ ■ ■ ■ ■ ■
AND THERE ARE DISADVANTAGES
AS WELL.

On the other hand, there are disadvantages to committees. Three of the most commonly cited include: (1) they can be a big waste of time and money, (2) they are sometimes used for making decisions that can be best handled by an individual manager, and (3) when a deadlock is reached, the decision of the committee is sometimes a compromise that produces a truly inferior result.

Overall, however, the use of committees in modern organizations is growing. If they are employed properly, they can be very effective.

USING COMMITTEES EFFECTIVELY

There are four basic guidelines that should be employed in using committees effectively. If these guidelines are followed, the committee can well be worth its cost in time and money.

■ ■ ■ ■ ■ ■ ■ ■ ■ ■ ■ ■ ■ ■
GUIDELINES FOR EFFECTIVENESS.

1.   Choose well-qualified individuals to serve on the committee. This choice must be directly tied to the objectives of the group. If the goal is to review production schedules, members should have a working knowledge of what these schedules are and how they are currently employed. If the goal is to formulate a more effective pay package, the members must know something about wage and salary administration.

2.   Have a specific agenda drawn up and delivered to each of the members prior to the meeting. This allows everyone to come prepared to discuss the issues, and, if any reading or preparatory work must be done, there is ample time to do it.

3.   Have enough members to get the job done but not so many that they are continually getting in each other's way. The effective chairperson should encourage each individual to contribute ideas and opinions; however, if the committee is too large, this process will literally take up most of the time set aside for the meeting.

4.   Have the chairperson keep the meeting heading toward its stated objective. From time to time the discussion will get off the main point. The chairperson must steer the group back on track.

These four guidelines cannot guarantee committee success. However, they have been found to improve committee performance markedly because they are designed to overcome specific common pitfalls.[12]

STOP!

Review your answer to the fourth question and make any changes you would like. Then compare your answer to the one below.

4.   Was this an ad hoc group or a standing committee? Explain.

This was an ad hoc group. It was created for the purpose of developing an advertising campaign. The group members will now disband. Standing committees remain in existence for an indefinite time period. ■

SUMMARY

A group is a social unit consisting of two or more interdependent, interactive individuals who are striving to attain common goals. There are three types of groups: functional groups, project groups, and interest-friendship groups. Functional groups are composed of individuals performing the same tasks. Project groups consist of individuals from many different areas or backgrounds who are gathered together to carry out some task; when its task is completed the group is disbanded and its members return to their original departments. Interest-friendship groups are formed on the basis of common beliefs, concerns, or activities.

All groups have certain characteristics. These include roles, norms, status, and cohesiveness. A role is an expected behavior; it indicates what a person is supposed to do. Some of the most serious role-related problems include role ambiguity and role conflict. A norm is a behavioral rule of conduct that is adopted by group members. Norms dictate how each group member ought to act. The manager needs to be aware of group norms because they play a key role in determining what a group will and

- - - - - - -

[12] For more on this topic see H. Kent Baker, "How to Make Meetings More Meaningful," *Management Review*, August 1978, pp. 45–47; "The Art of Running a Meeting," *Working Woman*, July 1984, p. 54; Ellen Goldman, "A New Approach to Managing Meeting Discussions," *Supervisory Management*, March 1984, pp. 32–37; William Leebov, "Problems, Plans, and Sharing: A Format for Productive Meetings," *Supervisory Management*, June 1984, pp. 35–37; Christopher P. Andersen, "Running Your Own Meetings," *Working Woman*, April 1986, p. 125; and Julie Bailey, "The Fine Art of Leading a Meeting," *Working Woman*, April 1987, pp. 68–71.

will not do. Status is the relative ranking of an individual in an organization or group. There are many ways of achieving job status, including position, the nature of the job, personality, and job competence. Two of the greatest job status-related problems with which the manager must be familiar are status incongruency and status discrepancy. Cohesiveness is the closeness of interpersonal attractions among group members. However, cohesiveness does not guarantee high productivity; a group can have high cohesion and low output. This situation occurs when the group members have all agreed to do as little work as possible. Group size influences member interaction and satisfaction. Small groups tend to be more satisfied than large groups.

The manager must also understand intragroup and intergroup behavior. Intragroup behavior consists of behavioral interactions within the group. Of primary interest in this chapter were communication and decision making among the group members. A number of communication roles are played by group members. Five of the most common are: opinion leader, gatekeeper, liaison, isolate, and follower. All group members play at least one of these roles, and some may play more than one. Groups are often more effective than individuals in decision making, particularly when faced with estimating or evaluating ambiguous situations, generating unique ideas, or accurately recalling information. Creative thinking techniques such as brainstorming can also help. Additionally, when making decisions in a group, individuals tend to be greater risk takers, a phenomenon known as the risky-shift. Furthermore, if groups are not careful they may become victims of group think, or social conformity to group ideas.

Intergroup behavior consists of behavioral interactions between or among groups. High intergroup performance can be achieved by making group goals clear, obtaining cooperation, and carefully planning all interfaces between the various groups. When such performance drops off, it is often a result of power struggles in which one group achieves or strives for some influence over the others. Some of the most common ways of gaining power are: providing services for other groups that they either cannot or will not provide for themselves; playing an important integrative role among the other groups; and defeating other groups in budgetary allocation battles. Some of the ways for resolving such conflicts include confrontation, collaboration, compromise, and altering the organizational structure.

The committee is an important type of group found in modern organizations. There are a number of advantages and disadvantages associated with the use of the committee. In order to obtain the greatest effectiveness from the committee, four guidelines are important: well-qualified members, a specific agenda, a manageable group size, and a continual focus on the purpose of the meeting. If the group follows these guidelines, committee performance can be markedly improved.

KEY TERMS IN THE CHAPTER

group
functional group
project group
interest-friendship group
role
role ambiguity
role conflict
norms
status
status incongruency
status discrepancy
cohesiveness
opinion leader
gatekeeper
liaison

isolate
follower
risky-shift phenomenon
brainstorming
synectics
left-brain people
right-brain people
group think
goal conflict
confrontation
collaboration
compromise
ad hoc committee
standing committee

REVIEW AND STUDY QUESTIONS

1. What are the three characteristics that all groups have in common? Identify them and give your definition of the term *group*.

2. Why do people join groups? Cite at least three reasons.

3. On the basis of the information provided in this chapter, what conclusions can be drawn about individuals and their conformity to group norms? Cite at least four.

4. What is meant by the term *cohesiveness*? Are all high-producing groups highly cohesive? Do all low-producing groups have low cohesiveness?

5. What role is played by each of these group members: opinion leader, gatekeeper, liaison, isolate, follower.

6. What impact does group size have on member satisfaction and employee turnover? Explain.

7. How does the risky-shift phenomenon help explain some of the decision making that goes on in groups?

8. What are the four phases of creative thinking? Describe them.

9. Why would an organization be interested in knowing which of its managers are right-brain dominant and which are left-brain? Explain.

10. What are some of the common symptoms that accompany group think? How can group think be prevented?

11. What are some of the ways groups try to gain power over other groups? Cite and explain at least two.

12. How can a manager go about resolving intergroup conflict? Give some examples.

13.   Of what value are committees? What are four guidelines chair-people should follow in effectively managing committees?

TIME OUT ANSWERS: WHAT TYPE OF "THINKER" ARE YOU?

Take your answers and circle them on the answer sheet below. For example, if your first answer was an "a" and your second was a "b," put a circle in Column I for answer 1 and in Column II for answer 2. Continue this for all 16 answers and then total the number of circles you have in each column.

ANSWER	COLUMN I	COLUMN II
1.	(a)	b
2	a	(b)
3.	(b)	a
4.	b	(a)
5.	(a)	b
6.	b	(a)
7.	a	(b)
8.	b	(a)
9.	b	(a)
10.	(a)	b
11.	(a)	b
12.	a	(b)
13.	b	(a)
14.	(a)	b
15.	b	(a)
16.	(b)	a
Total	7	9
	Left	Right

INTERPRETATION   Your answers in Column I indicate your preference for left-brain thinking. Your answers in Column II indicate your preference for right-brain thinking. Highly analytical people have higher scores in Column I; highly creative people have higher scores in Column II. Of course, these sixteen questions are not enough to adequately determine if you are left-brain or right-brain dominant. However, they should provide you insights regarding your preference. Most people have scores that indicate they are more left-brain than right-brain dominant.

CASE: THE NEW SUPERVISOR

When Gary Paterson was put in charge of the small-products assembly department, output was at an all-time low. Bob Willard, the retiring supervisor, had been in charge of the department for the last 10 years, during which time the output had slowly declined. When Bob had first taken over the department, the average worker was assembling 200 units a day but the company norm was 225. During his decade as supervisor, the firm introduced some technological advances, and the norm was raised to 250 units per day. However, the average output declined to 193.

The management's time-and-motion studies showed that the figure of 250 units was well within the ability of the average worker, and the manual dexterity tests given to members of the department revealed that each was physically capable of attaining this objective. Bob, however, explained the situation in terms of changing values. "People are different today," he said. "They no longer want to work hard. They've lost the old work ethic, especially our young people, and that's who works in the assembly department. Why, the average age there has declined from 29 to 23 in the last 8 years. I don't know. I guess lower output is just something we're going to have to learn to live with."

These remarks had Gary very worried. He wondered how he might keep the output from declining even more. After serious thought, he decided to call the department together and talk to everyone as soon as he took over. During this talk he emphasized three points to the assembled workers. First, he told them that he wanted them to continue working in their present groups. Since the members of all eight groups knew one another very well, he said, there was no sense breaking up satisfied work teams. However, if someone did want to change to another work group, he promised to help him or her do so, although it would require a mutual exchange of personnel with the other group. Second, he urged them all to come talk with him if they had any problems. Third, he asked their assistance in boosting output to 225 units per person per day.

During the next three months, Gary was asked to make a few changes in group composition. He also resolved several job-related technical problems. Overall, however, he found the groups to be congenial and fun to supervise. In addition, output began to move up slowly. At the end of 90 days, the average daily output was 219 units.

One of the women in the department, when asked why production was up, said, "We like this new supervisor. He's a good guy. He talks to us, helps us solve problems, and doesn't keep emphasizing output. He lets us work at our own pace. It's such a change from when Bob Willard was here."

QUESTIONS

1.   Is group cohesion in the small-products assembly department high or low? Has cohesion changed since Gary took over?

2.   Have group production norms changed since Gary took over? Explain your answer.

3.   What role do the workers want the supervisor to assume? How did Bob err in this regard? What is Gary doing right?■

CASE: A FUND-RAISING APPROACH

Every year Private University has a fund-raising drive. Last year the university raised $11 million. The year before it raised $7 million. This year's goal is $20 million.

Because the campaign goal is so high, the president of the university has created a special committee consisting of 25 business and civic leaders. Most are alumni but some have been chosen for their organizational and fund-raising skills. Approximately half were members of last year's fund-raising committee including the chairman, Morris Rosenberg, who was assistant chairman last year.

At their first meeting the chairman suggested that the committee follow the same strategy as last year. The country will be divided into eight geographic regions and each region will have its own fund-raising group. The group will be responsible for meeting a specific target from $1 million (for the far western region where there are few alumni) to $7 million (for the state where Private University is located and two of the adjoining states).

During this organizational meeting, a number of the members suggested different or supplemental approaches for fund raising. One of these suggestions was set forth by Joan Transam, president of a small management-consulting group. She suggested that the group begin its activity by giving all of the members a psychological test to measure whether they are left-brain or right-brain oriented. "Then we take those who are right-brain thinkers and have them formulate creative ideas for raising money," she continued. "The left-brain people would then review and critique the suggestions of the first. In this way, we would get each person on the committee to contribute his or her mental talents. There are many creative strategies that the right-brain people could think up that would get us publicity and would encourage contributions from alumni and business."

A number of the committee members like Joan's ideas, although they are unsure of how difficult it will be to implement them. They are particularly concerned that a great deal of time will be spent analyzing their thinking processes, and this will be time taken away from the campaign. Others think that Joan's idea is an excellent one and will result in a far more successful campaign than any previous one. Still others, including the chairman, believe that it would be best simply to stick with last year's strategy because it has been proven effective.

Despite their reservations, however, all of the members have agreed to complete a brain-skills management test and participate in either formulating or critiquing creative approaches to raising money. In particular, Joan wants to have the committee sponsor an auction that would sell university memorabilia and other items contributed by donors. "We should be able to raise at least $500,000 from this activity," she told the chairperson. Another member of the committee has suggested that the university hold a large campaign-kickoff dinner with tickets selling for $1,000 each. Other members have suggested an attention-getting brochure that would announce the campaign and solicit a donation by mail. This would be combined with a follow-up telephone campaign that would reach every member of the alumni organization.

"It appears that we have plenty of ideas for this campaign," Morris noted. "However, I think we have to be careful not to drift too far afield in our creative efforts. Fund-raising campaigns are serious business. I suggest we start by completing the brain-skills management test, divide into the two groups to formulate and critique the campaign, and then implement our ideas. We have 90 days to get the campaign under way, so let's not waste any time." Everyone agreed.

QUESTIONS

1.   What will be the function of those members of the committee who are found to be right-brain dominant? Left-brain dominant? Explain.

2.   How will the creative thinking process be of value to the committee? How does this process work? What can the committee expect from these efforts?

3.   How willing is Morris to accept risks and develop a creative, imaginative fund-raising strategy? Has the committee had any impact on his thinking? Will they have any impact in the future? Why or why not? ∎

EXPERIENCING RISK TAKING

PURPOSE

■   To determine your personal willingness to take risks.

■   To evaluate your score and those of other students.

■   To examine how your willingness to take risks changes when you are in a group.

(Continued)

EXPERIENCING RISK TAKING (Continued)

PROCEDURE

1. Complete the risk-taking questionnaire provided below. When you are finished, enter your scores on the answer sheet that is provided and then total them.

2. Work with a group of 2 to 4 students and collectively complete the same questionnaire. For each statement, there must be agreement among the group members on which alternative to choose. When you are finished, total the scores for the group.

3. Compare your individual scores to the group scores and explain the reason for the differences.

SITUATIONS

There are 10 situations presented below. In each case read the situation and then choose the lowest probability or odds that you would accept.

1. You have just learned that you have a serious heart ailment. If you choose not to have an operation, you can live another 10 years only. If you choose to have the operation, there is a chance that you will not survive the operation. Should you survive, however, you will have a normal life expectancy. Check the lowest probability of survival that you would consider acceptable:
   _____1 out of 10 _____3 out of 10 _____5 out of 10
   _____7 out of 10 _____9 out of 10 _____You would not take the chance

2. You are playing chess against a much better player. Early in the game you notice that you have a chance for a quick win, providing your opponent does not see through your strategy. If he does, you are finished. Check the lowest probability you would consider acceptable for the risky play:
   _____1 out of 10 _____3 out of 10 _____5 out of 10
   _____7 out of 10 _____9 out of 10 _____You would not take the chance

3. You have $5,000 in conservative stock holdings returning you 9 percent a year. You have learned from your cousin that she is in the process of selling stock in her new firm. If her company survives the next five years, your stock will quadruple in value. Check the lowest probability of survival that you would consider acceptable for investing the $5,000 in her company.
   _____1 out of 10 _____3 out of 10 _____5 out of 10
   _____7 out of 10 _____9 out of 10 _____You would not take the chance

4. There are two colleges to which you are thinking about applying for admission. College A has a national reputation but also flunks out over 50 percent of all those admitted. College B has only a local reputation but the flunk-out rate is less than 2 percent. Check the lowest survival probability that you would accept in opting for College A.

(Continued)

EXPERIENCING RISK TAKING   (Continued)

_____1 out of 10 _____3 out of 10 _____5 out of 10
_____7 out of 10 _____9 out of 10 _____ You would not take the chance

5. You have a good steady job at a moderate rate of pay. Your best friend has offered you a job in his firm at a much higher rate of pay. However, his company is small and may not survive the next two years. Check the lowest probability of survival you would look for in this new firm.

_____1 out of 10 _____3 out of 10 _____5 out of 10
_____7 out of 10 _____9 out of 10 _____ You would not take the chance

6. You are thinking about getting married. Your intended is a wonderful person but is also emotional and sometimes very hard to get along with. On the other hand this individual makes you happier than anyone you have ever met. Check the lowest probability of your marriage surviving which you would accept before going ahead with the wedding.

_____1 out of 10 _____3 out of 10 _____5 out of 10
_____7 out of 10 _____9 out of 10 _____ You would not take the chance

7. You are the coach of a football team. You are going for the state title and are one point behind, having scored a touchdown just as the final gun went off. If you kick the extra point, you will have a tie. If you try a trick play, you can go for two points. What is the lowest probability of success with the trick play that you would accept?

_____1 out of 10 _____3 out of 10 _____5 out of 10
_____7 out of 10 _____9 out of 10 _____ You would not take the chance

8. You have saved $3,500 over the last two years and are considering buying a bond paying 13.5 percent annually. Your brother, an oil wildcatter, wants you to invest the money with him. If he is successful, you will double your money in one year. If he is not, you will lose it all. What is the lowest probability of success you would accept for investing with your brother?

_____1 out of 10 _____3 out of 10 _____5 out of 10
_____7 out of 10 _____9 out of 10 _____ You would not take the chance

9. You have the option of taking a steady job in the personnel department where your future with the firm is just about guaranteed. Or you can go with the advertising department. It will take five years of hard work before you know whether you will succeed in this department, but if you do your salary will be almost double that in the personnel department. If you fail, you will have to find another job elsewhere. What is the lowest probability of success in the advertising department that you would be willing to accept?

_____1 out of 10 _____3 out of 10 _____5 out of 10
_____7 out of 10 _____9 out of 10 _____ You would not take the chance

10. You can keep your current stateside job or take one in the Far East. If you stay here, you will receive moderate increases and promotions for the indefinite future. If you opt for the overseas assignment and do well, you will be a vice-president within five years and will be one of the highest paid people in the firm. If you do not do well, you will be fired. What is the lowest probability of success in the overseas assignment that you would be willing to accept?

_____1 out of 10 _____3 out of 10 _____5 out of 10
_____7 out of 10 _____9 out of 10 _____ You would not take the chance

(Continued)

EXPERIENCING RISK TAKING   (Continued)

Scoring Instructions   Fill in your answers below by transferring the numbers you chose in each case. For example, if you chose "1 out of 10," put in a 1. If you chose "5 out of 10," put in a 5. If you opted not to take the chance, put in an answer of 10. Then total your scores for both the individual and group assignments.

ANSWER SHEET

SITUATION	INDIVIDUAL SCORE	GROUP SCORE
1.	___	___
2.	___	___
3.	___	___
4.	___	___
5.	___	___
6.	___	___
7.	___	___
8.	___	___
9.	___	___
10.	___	___
Total	___	___

THE INFORMAL ORGANIZATION

GOALS OF THE CHAPTER

In Chapters 3 and 4 we examined individual behavior and group behavior. To complete our discussion of the social system, we now study the informal organization, which engages in both individual and group behavior.

The first goal of this chapter is to examine the nature of the informal organization. How does it differ from the formal organization? The second goal is to study the communication patterns that exist within informal organizations, with particular emphasis on grapevines and grapevine activity. The third goal is to examine the benefits associated with the informal organization. The fourth goal is to review some of the drawbacks of the informal organization. The fifth goal is to look at some of the ways the manager can deal with the informal organization.

When you have finished reading this chapter you should be able to:

1. Compare and contrast the formal and informal organizations.

2. Discuss some of the behavioral controls used by members of the informal organization to ensure compliance with its norms.

3. Explain how the informal communication network functions.

4. Identify the primary benefits and disadvantages associated with the informal organization.

5. Cite some of the ways in which a manager can deal with the informal organization.

OPENING CASE:

INSIDE INFORMATION

The Coughlin Corporation is a major conglomerate in the manufacturing, smelting, and mining industries. The president, George Bakker, typically works sixteen hours a day, six days a week. The demands of the operation are so great that his work day is often put together weeks in advance by his assistant, Gladys Adler.

Gladys has been with the company for thirty-five years and has been Mr. Bakker's personal assistant for five years. He relies heavily on Gladys to ensure that his time is spent profitably. This means, among other things, that only those who have important business requiring his direct attention are given appointments. Since Gladys keeps Mr. Bakker's day book, it is impossible to see him without first going through her.

After Mr. Bakker, the three senior-level managers in the company are the vice-presidents of marketing, manufacturing, and finance respectively. Gladys likes the vice-president of marketing because the man is always cheerful and goes out of his way to praise Mr. Bakker and offer him encouragement. Gladys feels that the vice-president of manufacturing is a sourpuss who often asks for a much larger budget than is justified. The vice-president of finance, in Gladys's opinion, is a constant worrier. This woman is always painting the bleakest possible economic future for the firm. On a number of occasions, Gladys has noted that the woman's pessimism has upset Mr. Bakker.

Gladys goes out of her way to ensure that the vice-president of marketing can see the president whenever he wants. However, she often turns the other two vice-presidents away by telling them, "He can't see you today. You'll have to check with me tomorrow, and I'll see if I can get his calendar clear in the late afternoon." These two managers are convinced that Gladys is deliberately refusing them entry to the president, but they would not dare raise this issue with Mr. Bakker because they know that he is very supportive of Gladys.

Last week Gladys learned from Mr. Bakker that he was thinking of buying a large manufacturing operation in the Southwest. This firm would provide the company with entry to the electronics business. Gladys passed on this information to the vice-president of marketing, and the latter had his people investigate the marketing implications of the possible acquisition.

At a special management meeting yesterday, Mr. Bakker asked his three vice-presidents what they would think about the company acquiring a large manufacturing operation in the electronics industry. The manufacturing and finance vice-presidents said it would be a poor idea. The marketing vice-president said he thought it was an excellent idea and cited statistics related to the potential growth of this industry during the 1990s. The president was elated with these latter remarks, and then announced his plan to go ahead with the acquisition.

The vice-president of finance was convinced that Gladys had leaked the information to the marketing people. However, she was unable to get anyone, including a middle-level marketing manager who is a friend of hers, to confirm her suspicion. Nevertheless, she visited Gladys earlier today and directly accused her of leaking the information. Gladys was incensed and said she intended to report the incident to Mr. Bakker. She then called the vice-president of marketing and asked him to drop by. When he did, Gladys told him about the incident. He had never seen Gladys so angry. When she was finished talking, he calmly discussed the situation with her, helped her realize that no one was going to find out what had happened, and after assuring himself that she had gotten over her anger, went back to his office.

1.   Does Gladys have a great deal of authority? Power?

2.   Which informal network best describes the situation in this case?

3.   What are two benefits of the grapevine that were illustrated in this case?

4.   Which of the three vice-presidents is likely to be the most effective over the next couple of years? Why?

Write down your answers to these questions and put them aside. We will return to them later. ∎

NATURE OF THE INFORMAL ORGANIZATION

The informal organization plays a significant role in the dynamics of human behavior at work. As a result, no discussion of human relations would be complete without consideration of this area. In this part of the chapter, we examine the nature of the informal organization by pointing out how it differs from the formal organization. In particular we direct our attention to four major areas: (1) interpersonal relations, (2) informal leadership, (3) behavioral control, and (4) dependency. Before reading on, however, take the informal organization quiz in the Time Out section and obtain a preliminary evaluation of both your use and understanding of this organization.

INTERPERSONAL RELATIONS

In the formal organization, relationships between people are clearly defined. For example, all the members of an assembly group are charged with assembling 30 units an hour and placing the completed items on a

TIME OUT

THE INFORMAL ORGANIZATION: AN INITIAL APPRAISAL

The following 15 statements are designed to measure your understanding and use of the informal organization. Assume you are a manager and answer each statement from that viewpoint. An interpretation of your answers is provided at the end of the chapter.

	TRUE	FALSE
1. I always work through formal channels.	_____	_____
2. I don't care how my people get things done as long as they get them done.	_____	_____
3. Everyone should have a job description and stick to it exclusively.	_____	_____
4. If I can get things done faster, I cut across formal channels and use whatever means necessary.	_____	_____
5. All rules and procedures are made to be obeyed.	_____	_____
6. I use the informal organization to both give and get information.	_____	_____
7. I discourage grapevine activity.	_____	_____
8. Almost all of the grapevine communications are inaccurate.	_____	_____
9. The grapevine can be influenced by management.	_____	_____
10. The grapevine is inevitable.	_____	_____
11. Workers will form into informal groups regardless of what the organization does.	_____	_____
12. The grapevine's basic objective is to undermine management's efforts.	_____	_____
13. Most informal communiqués are passed to others on a purely random basis.	_____	_____
14. The goals of the informal organization are almost always in conflict with those of the formal organization.	_____	_____
15. Just about all grapevine messages are started by individuals with an ax to grind.	_____	_____

large table. Everyone is supposed to be doing the same job and turning out an identical number of items. Most organizations, however, do not work this way.

Over time, workers begin to form friendships with one another. This in turn results in their going beyond their job descriptions and carrying out activities that are more to their liking. Consider the case of the assembly group we mentioned previously. Although each person is supposed to be working independently of the others, we know that in every group there are slow workers and fast workers. Additionally, some

FIGURE 5.1   **Who Helps Whom?**

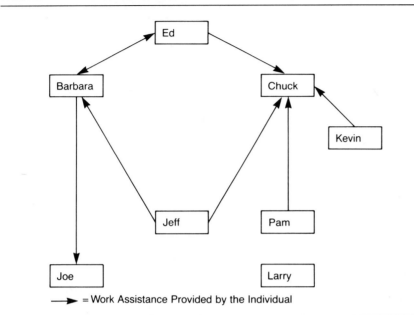

of these workers are so well liked that their peers help them with their work. Conversely, some will be disliked and will be ignored by their fellow workers.

   Figure 5.1 is an illustration of the degree of assistance that some members of a work group give to others. Note that Jeff is helping two of his co-workers but is not receiving any help in return. This indicates that Jeff is probably a very fast worker. Chuck receives assistance from four of his fellow workers, so Chuck is not a fast worker. However, the other members of the group like him and are therefore willing to assist him in assembling the units. Barbara and Ed help each other. Joe receives help from Barbara but does not reciprocate. Finally, Larry neither receives help from anyone nor does he give any.

   Figure 5.1 is an illustration of a **sociogram**, a schematic drawing that shows the social relationships that exist between members of a group. In this case the relationship is being measured in terms of who helps whom. Sociograms provide interesting insights to informal group behavior because they help pinpoint those members who are most popular, those who do all the work, those who get help from others, and those with whom no one interacts.

A SOCIOGRAM SHOWS INTRAGROUP SOCIAL RELATIONSHIPS.

INFORMAL LEADERSHIP

In a formal organization the leader is designated by the management, while in an informal organization the leader is chosen by the members of the group. If the formal leader does a good job, he or she is often promoted away from the department. If the informal leader does a good job, he or she maintains that position, but if he or she does a poor job, someone else will be chosen who can help the group meet its objectives.

When we compare formal and informal leaders, therefore, we can see that the formal leader has authority and the informal leader has power. **Authority** is the right to command, and it is given by the superior to the subordinate. **Power** is the ability to influence, persuade, or move another person to one's own point of view. The informal leader uses his or her power in two ways: (1) to achieve informal group objectives, such as persuading the foreman that since the workers are doing the best they can there is no need to crack down any harder, and (2) to maintain his or her position of leadership in the group.

■ ■ ■ ■ ■ ■ ■ ■ ■ ■ ■ ■ ■ ■

AUTHORITY IS THE RIGHT TO COMMAND.

■ ■ ■ ■ ■ ■ ■ ■ ■ ■ ■ ■ ■ ■

POWER IS THE ABILITY TO INFLUENCE.

AUTHORITY AND POWER   What makes these concepts of authority and power in the formal and informal organizations so interesting is that the person who has the authority may *not* always have the power.[1] We can illustrate this with Figures 5.2 and 5.3, which represent the organization of a fictional department. In both illustrations, the closer a name is to the top of the figure, the more power the individual has in the department. Figure 5.2 shows the formal organization chart. Note that Harry is in charge of five subordinates, and each of them has three subordinates. Figure 5.3 shows the informal organization. Here we see quite a difference. For example, although Harry is the designated leader, Andy is the person with the real power. For some reason, Harry listens to Andy and goes along with whatever he says. One common explanation for such an arrangement is that Harry is new on the job, and Andy has been around for a long time and is the informal group leader. Realizing that he must rely heavily on Andy's help, Harry defers to him on most matters.

There are other interesting facts revealed by the informal organization chart. For example, Andy's three subordinates have more power than the other 12 subordinates. (Look how high up in the informal power structure they are located.) Also, although Mary and Bob are equal in authority (see Figure 5.2), Bob has more power than Mary. Moreover, Charles is supposed to be in charge of Bill, Mark, and Tony, but a close look at Figure 5.3 shows that Bill is giving the orders in the group and Charles has the *least* amount of power. Finally, although all

■ ■ ■ ■ ■ ■ ■

[1] A. J. Patellis, "Your Power to Produce Results," *Supervisory Management*, January 1985, pp. 2–6.

FIGURE 5.2   **FORMAL AUTHORITY**

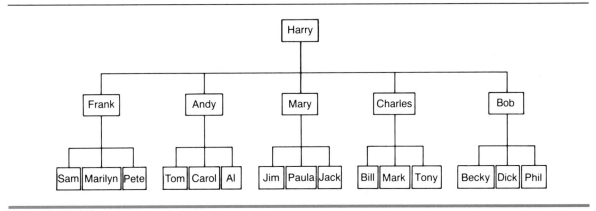

FIGURE 5.3   **INFORMAL POWER**

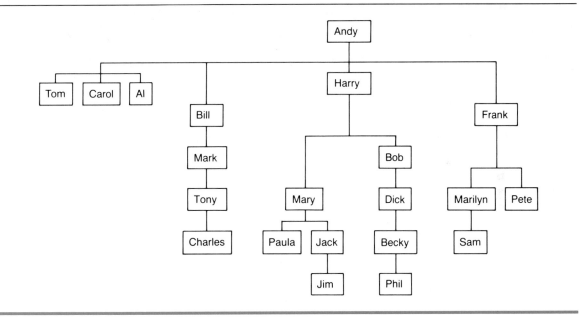

the subordinates are supposed to be equal, some are more equal than others. A look at Bob's subordinates, Becky, Dick, and Phil, shows that Dick has the greatest power and Phil has the least.

Some people like to define the formal organization as the one the company creates and the informal organization as the one the people

---

FIGURE 5.4   **ORGANIZATIONAL GOALS AND INDIVIDUAL-GROUP GOALS**

THE ORGANIZATION GOALS

- Good profit
- High return on investment
- Adequate worker efficiency
- High quality goods and services
- Strong competitive posture
- Low tardiness and absenteeism
- Low turnover

THE INDIVIDUAL-GROUP GOALS

- Good pay
- Job security
- Adequate fringe benefits
- Challenging work
- A chance to achieve
- Work satisfaction

---

themselves re-create. Certainly there is a give-and-take between the needs of the organization and those of its personnel. A commercial firm, for example, is most interested in attaining economic goals such as profit and return on investment. The people in the organization are most concerned with getting good pay, adequate fringe benefits, and satisfying work. The company needs to make the workers see its point of view, and they must persuade the top management to understand theirs (Figure 5.4).

Who usually wins this conflict between organizational goals and individual-group goals? Usually, neither side emerges totally victorious. Each side takes less than it deems ideal, but neither accepts anything less than it regards as minimal. In human relations terms, we say that each side engages in **satisficing behavior** by agreeing to accept adequate or satisfactory payoffs from the other. Let us take an illustration. The company announces that beginning Monday all workers must clock in. The news is not well received by the informal organization, which decides to work around the rule if possible. One way of doing so is to have the group member who arrives first clock everyone else in and to rotate the assignment at the end of the day by having everyone take turns clocking out all the group members. In this manner, the company's rules are obeyed, and the group finds a way to live with them.

Another illustration of satisficing behavior occurs in the case of the company that offers its people a 3 percent increase in salary and a 3 percent increase in fringe benefits. This offer is ideal for management, because if the union accepts it, the company will be able to surpass its goals of a 15 percent return on investment. The union, meanwhile, counters with a demand of 9 percent for both salary and benefits. The two then compromise on 5 percent. Each side gets less than it wanted originally, but both can live with the contract because it provides them with satisfactory output or results that are "good enough."

■ ■ ■ ■ ■ ■ ■ ■ ■ ■ ■ ■
SATISFICING BEHAVIOR LEADS TO
SATISFACTORY PAYOFFS.

TABLE 5.1   TACTICS USED IN ORGANIZATIONAL POLITICS (*n* = 87)

TACTIC	CHIEF EXECUTIVE OFFICERS (%)	STAFF MANAGERS (%)	SUPERVISORS (%)
Attacking or blaming others	60.0	50.0	51.7
Use of information	56.7	57.1	48.3
Image building/impression management	46.7	39.3	24.1
Support building for ideas	43.3	46.4	69.0
Praising others, ingratiation	46.7	39.3	24.1
Power coalitions, strong alliances	26.7	17.9	31.0
Associating with the influential	16.7	35.7	20.7
Creating obligations/reciprocity	3.3	14.3	30.7

Source: Robert W. Allen, Dan L. Madison, Lyman W. Porter, Patricia A. Renwick, and Bronston T. Mayes, "Organizational Politics: Tactics and Characteristics of Its Actors," © 1979 by the Regents of the University of California. Reprinted from *California Management Review*, Volume XXIII, No. 1, p. 79.

STOP!

Review your answer to the first question and make any changes you would like. Then compare your answer to the one below.

1.   Does Gladys have a great deal of authority? Power?

Gladys has a great deal of authority because she is the personal assistant of the conglomerate's president. However, her real impact is a result of her power. She can deny people access to the president. Additionally, she is privy to information that she can share with others if she wants. This means that she is able to greatly influence what happens (or does not happen) in the company. ∎

POLITICS AT WORK   The use of power typically requires political behavior. Rather than run roughshod over someone, the effective manager often uses a well thought-out political approach. In this way, the individual gets what he wants done while causing the fewest number of hard feelings or problems.[2] Table 5.1 shows some of the most commonly used

. . . .

[2] Victor Murray and Jeffrey Gandz, "Games Executives Play: Politics At Work," *Business Horizons*, December 1980, pp. 11–23.

approaches. Notice that while some of these tactics are obvious (attacking or blaming others), most are subtle (image building, praising others, creating obligations). Additionally, the type of tactics used tends to vary by hierarchical level. Chief executive officers tend to attack or blame others; staff managers try to associate with influential people; supervisors try to form power coalitions and create obligations among others.

BEHAVIORAL CONTROL

When people in the formal organization do something right, they are given rewards; when they do something wrong, they are punished. If Barry reduces overhead in his department by 5 percent, he may be placed on a list of "up-and-coming" young executives. On the other hand, if departmental overhead increases dramatically and he is unable to control it, he may be labeled as incompetent and may lose the chance of ever being promoted.

In the informal organization, also, rewards and punishments are dispensed to the members. These, however, usually take the form of giving or denying need fulfillment. If Paula conforms to group norms, she is included in group activities and provided with social interaction. If she violates group norms or refuses to act "properly," she is ostracized and may even be subjected to pressure and ridicule and made to look foolish in the eyes of the other members. In Figure 5.1, a sociogram illustrated who in a department was helping whom; Larry neither helped anyone else nor was helped by them. From this we can conclude that he is not a member of the informal group, since one of the most common informal norms is that of assisting one's peers.

DEPENDENCY

Despite the strength of the informal group leader, the formal leader has a greater capacity for rewarding and punishing the personnel. The formal leader can give both physical and psychological rewards to those who obey organizational directives and do things well. Because the informal leader can give only psychological rewards, not everyone conforms to informal group norms. Some people resist because they believe there is more to be gained by *not* joining the informal group, and not even the most extreme form of ostracism budges them. This was clearly seen a number of years ago in the case of the West Point cadet who was accused of cheating, judged guilty by his peer review board (made up of other cadets), and told to resign his commission. However, the man was not found guilty by those in authority and was allowed to stay at the academy. Because he refused to abide by the decision of his peers, none of them talked to him or interacted with him for the remainder of his stay at West Point. Despite such pressures, the cadet remained at the academy and graduated with his class.

Those individuals who agree with the informal group's norms, however, strive for membership and depend on the group for social interaction and support. As a result, we have three subgroups in an informal organization structure. First is the **nucleus group**, which consists of full-fledged members of the informal organization who interact with each other. Second is the **fringe group**, consisting of those seeking admission to the informal organization. These people are often new members of the work force who are being screened for membership by the nucleus group. Finally, there is the **outer group**, consisting of individuals who have been rejected for membership. These people have failed to measure up to the requirements set for admission to the group. Numerous reasons can be cited for this failure: doing too much work, doing too little work, having an unpleasant personality, and "squealing" to a supervisor about a member of the nucleus group.

THE NUCLEUS GROUP CONTAINS FULL-FLEDGED MEMBERS OF THE INFORMAL ORGANIZATION.

THE FRINGE GROUP MEMBERS ARE SEEKING ADMISSION.

THE OUTER GROUP MEMBERS HAVE BEEN REJECTED.

INFORMAL COMMUNICATION

One of the most interesting behavioral aspects of the informal organization is its communication pattern. Commonly referred to as the **grapevine**, this communication network is used to carry information between members of the informal organization. In this section, we examine the pattern of grapevine communication and four of the most likely causes of this activity.

THE GRAPEVINE IS THE INFORMAL COMMUNICATION NETWORK.

HOW THE GRAPEVINE WORKS

The grapevine arises from social interaction and tends to be an oral, as opposed to written, form of communication. Bud in engineering can send a message through the interdepartmental mail asking Doris in accounting if she is going to the party on Friday. However, it is more likely that Bud will either call and ask Doris or wait until they meet later in the day.

Much of the information carried by the grapevine deals with matters that are of current interest to the personnel. The introduction of new work procedures in the metals department, the details of an accident in Plant 2, and the installation of a new computerized accounting system in the comptroller's offices are the kinds of topics commonly discussed via the grapevine. As you can see, these topics are sometimes of interest to people in many departments, so the number of individuals on a grapevine can be extremely large. This is particularly true when the message is viewed with concern or fear. For example, when the personnel throughout the firm learn about the introduction of new work procedures in the metals department, they may see this as the beginning of an efficiency move by management. If this does prove to be the case, the various departments have been forewarned and each will have already taken action to ensure that its own efficiency is already as high as can be expected. Meanwhile, if the message proves to be total fabrication and no new work procedures have been introduced, grapevine activity related to this topic will cease. Since grapevine members begin checking on the truth of a rumor almost immediately, one of these two actions will be initiated very shortly.

GRAPEVINE NETWORKS   Many people believe that the grapevine consists of a long chain of people with each individual passing the message to the next person in the chain. The type of communication network, known as the **single strand**, is illustrated in Figure 5.5; it is the least frequently used.

Another way in which informal messages can be communicated is by one person telling all the others. This is called the **gossip chain** (Figure 5.5). While more commonly used than the single strand, the gossip chain is also one of the less frequently used grapevine networks.

A third way in which information is passed through the grapevine is on a random basis. One person arbitrarily tells another, who goes on and tells one or two others (Figure 5.5). This is known as the **probability chain**, and of the three we have discussed, it is the most widely used.

■ ■ ■ ■ ■ ■ ■ ■ ■ ■ ■ ■ ■ ■

THE MOST COMMON GRAPEVINE
NETWORK IS THE CLUSTER CHAIN.

However, the most common grapevine network of all is known as the **cluster chain**. It works this way: one person tells two or three people who in turn either keep the information to themselves or pass it on to two or three other people. As a result, we have one individual passing the message to a cluster of people, and those who pass it on also tell it to another cluster. In Figure 5.5, for example, Al tells the message to Wayne and Nancy. Wayne keeps it to himself, while Nancy passes it on to Don, Lois, and Ken. Al and Nancy are the links with their respective clusters.

Carrying this idea a step further, we can conclude that if 100 people learn of a particular happening, such as the firing of a top manager, it is very likely that the word was spread by only 15 or 20 people. These individuals are known as *liaison* people, because they serve as the links between those who have the information and those who do not. Commenting on the predominance of the cluster chain, Davis has reported that in one company he investigated, a quality control problem had occurred and 68 percent of the executives knew about it. However, only 20 percent of them had spread the information. In another firm he studied, 81

FIGURE 5.5   **INFORMAL COMMUNICATION NETWORKS**

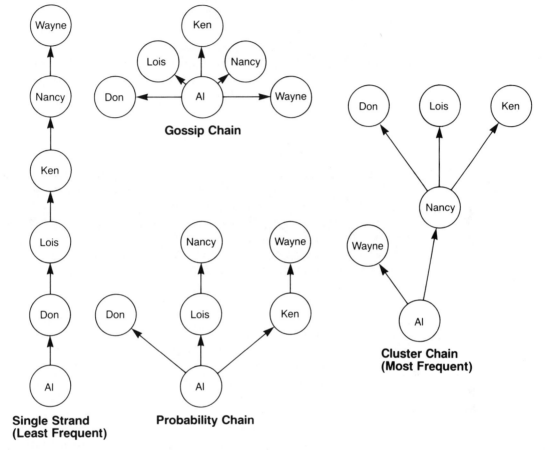

percent of the executives knew that a top manager planned to resign, but only 11 percent had passed the news to the others.[3]

Liaison people are very *selective* in the way they communicate. There are some people to whom they pass information and others whom they bypass. For example, Ed Anderson has just learned that he is to be promoted to vice-president of international operations. However, the formal announcement will not be made for 10 days. Ed is very anxious to tell

▪▪▪▪▪▪▪

[3] Keith Davis, *Human Behavior at Work: Organizational Behavior*, 6th ed. (New York: McGraw-Hill Book Company, 1981), p. 339.

someone but he has to be selective in leaking the news, for he does not want to tell anyone who will circulate the story back to top management for fear they might reverse the promotion decision. Ed chooses his best friend, Bob James, to tell about the impending promotion. Bob is delighted and, realizing the confidential nature of the communiqué, passes the information to other people who he knows will treat the matter confidentially. Ten days later the formal announcement is made, and to most people in the organization, it comes as a surprise. Furthermore, even those who knew of the promotion through the grapevine are careful not to let on. If any one of them does indicate prior knowledge, he or she will be bypassed by future grapevine messages.

Bypassing people, however, is *not* always a sign of distrust or unreliability. The grapevine bypasses those who are not supposed to get a particular message. For example, in one company the president planned a party for 25 top executives. The grapevine learned about the party but did not know for sure which executives were on the list. As a result, only those they thought would be invited were told about the party by informal communicators. As it turned out, 23 executives learned of the upcoming announcement, and of these 22 were *actually* on the list. The cluster chain is indeed a selective communication network.

GRAPEVINE ACTIVITY   Some people tend to be very active on the grapevine and others are fairly inactive. However, given the proper situation and motivation, just about anyone will be "grapevine-active." In fact, research reveals that there is little difference between the activities of men and of women on the grapevine. If people feel they have cause to be grapevine-active, they will be. Let us discuss four of the most likely causes of grapevine activity.

■ ■ ■ ■ ■ ■ ■ ■ ■ ■ ■ ■ ■ ■
WHEN PEOPLE LACK INFORMATION THEY TEND TO BE GRAPEVINE-ACTIVE.

First, if people lack information about a situation, they try to fill in these gaps via informal channels. Sometimes these efforts lead to distortion of facts or fabrication of rumors. For example, not long ago a senior executive was informed by the company president that his office was to be refurbished. He was to be given a new desk, bookcases, furniture, and a very expensive rug. This was a reward for the successful advertising program he had developed for one of the firm's new product lines. As soon as the man's office was torn up, the grapevine began to hum. Before the afternoon was over, rumor had it that the executive had been fired and that his office was being made ready for a new advertising manager. Also, the personnel associated with the manufacture and sale of the new product line all became very concerned, fearing that the next step would be a reduction in their own work force.

■ ■ ■ ■ ■ ■ ■ ■ ■ ■ ■ ■ ■ ■
THE SAME IS TRUE WHEN THERE IS INSECURITY IN A SITUATION.

Second, people are active on the grapevine when there is insecurity in a situation. Continuing our illustration above, the first thing that people associated with the new product did was contact the sales manager to ask if there were any truth to the rumor. The manager informed them that sales for the product were running 37 percent ahead of projections. After putting these facts together with those about the work being done in the senior executive's office, the workers realized that he was being rewarded for the product's success. They then passed this information back through the grapevine, and informal communications related to this development ceased. There was nothing more to talk about.

Third, there is grapevine activity whenever people have a personal interest in a situation. For example, if Mary and her boss get into an argument over the monthly cost control report, Mary's friends will tend to be grapevine-active. Likewise, if the management decides to lay off 15 salespeople, the rest of the sales force will be interested in the situation because they have a stake in what is going on. People want to share among themselves any information about what is happening in the part of the world that is important to them.

■ ■ ■ ■ ■ ■ ■ ■ ■ ■ ■ ■ ■ ■
OR WHEN PEOPLE HAVE A PERSONAL INTEREST IN THE SITUATION.

Fourth, people are most active on the grapevine when they have information that is recent rather than stale. Research shows that the greatest spread of information occurs immediately after it is known. When most people learn the news, grapevine activity slows down.[4]

■ ■ ■ ■ ■ ■ ■ ■ ■ ■ ■ ■ ■ ■
OR WHEN THEY HAVE NEW INFORMATION.

STOP!

Review your answer to the second question and make any changes you would like. Then compare your answer to the one below.

2.   Which informal network best describes the situation in this case?

The cluster chain best describes the informal network used in this case. Notice that the information was passed on selectively. Only the people in marketing knew about the impending acquisition. Notice also that while the vice-president of finance has a friend in the marketing department, the friendship did not help her learn anything because this individual did not know the information was leaked. Undoubtedly, the people in marketing who received the news knew that this individual is a friend of the finance vice-president and deliberately kept the information away from this person. This is another example of the selectivity of the cluster chain. ■

- - - - - - -

[4] For more on grapevine activity see Roy Rowan, "Where Did that Rumor Come From?" *Fortune*, August 13, 1979, pp. 130–137; and William A. Delaney, "The Secretarial Grapevine," *Supervisory Management*, March 1983, pp. 31–34.

BENEFITS OF THE INFORMAL ORGANIZATION

Every organization has an informal structure. By definition, then, there must be some very important benefits to be derived from its existence; otherwise it would cease to function. One of the most obvious reasons for an informal organization is that most of the personnel, both workers and managers, like it, want it, use it, and benefit from it! In this section we examine five major benefits to be derived from the informal organization: (1) getting things done, (2) lightening managerial work loads, (3) providing job satisfaction, (4) serving as a safety valve for employees' emotions, and (5) providing feedback to the manager.[5]

GETTING THINGS DONE

■ ■ ■ ■ ■ ■ ■ ■ ■ ■ ■ ■ ■ ■
THE INFORMAL ORGANIZATION CAN HELP GET THINGS DONE.

One of the primary benefits of the informal organization is that it supplements the formal organization in getting things done. Howard, a supervisor in the components assembly department, needs some help in securing parts from an outside supplier. The company's purchasing department is dragging its feet on the matter. Howard's friend Claire is the comptroller's secretary and a cousin of Greg, who is in charge of purchasing. Howard calls Claire and tells her his problem. Claire contacts Greg, who calls in Eddie, one of his assistants. Their discussion might go something like this:

"How come Howard down in the manufacturing section is having trouble getting parts from outside suppliers?"

"Is he calling to complain again?"

"No, I got the message from someone else in the firm. Apparently this order is jeopardizing the production schedule. What is its current status?"

"Well, it's sitting on my desk, but I wanted to get some of my other paperwork cleared up before sending the order to the supplier."

"Forget about sending it. Call it in this afternoon and tell them we need those parts by tomorrow."

"Okay, I'll get on it right now."

Later in the afternoon, Howard gets a call from Eddie telling him that the parts are on the way, and they arrive the next morning.

We can diagram this flow of communication in Figure 5.6. Note that Howard used the authority of the purchasing manager to help him get the needed parts. However, he worked through the informal organiza-

■ ■ ■ ■ ■ ■

[5] For still other benefits see Pyung E. Han, "The Informal Organization: You've Got to Live with It," *Supervisory Management*, October 1983, pp. 25–28.

FIGURE 5.6   **THE INFORMAL ORGANIZATION IN ACTION**

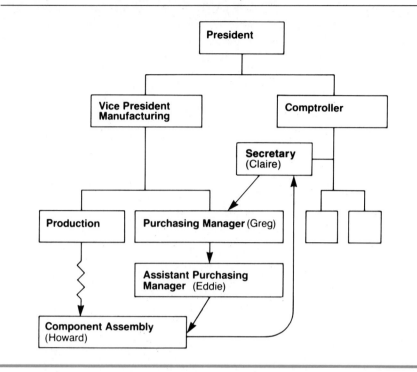

tion in contacting Claire, and she used the network in reaching Greg. Without the informal organization everyone would go "through channels" and it would take a lot longer to accomplish anything. Many of the organization's best workers would leave, and those who remained would simply stop putting out extra effort. After all, who wants to spend all his or her time fighting organization red tape?

LIGHTENING MANAGERIAL WORKLOADS

Another benefit of the informal organization is to lighten managerial work loads. When managers realize that the informal organization is on their side, they are more likely to delegate authority and to rely on their subordinates to get things done. This results in looser, more generalized control and often creates a feeling of trust among the workers, who respond by showing the manager that they are indeed reliable. The outcome is higher productivity.

■ ■ ■ ■ ■ ■ ■ ■ ■ ■ ■ ■ ■ ■
IT CAN LIGHTEN THE MANAGER'S WORKLOAD.

PROVIDING JOB SATISFACTION

An accompanying benefit is job satisfaction, a term that relates to the favorableness or unfavorableness with which the personnel view their work. This topic is discussed in greater depth later, but let us briefly examine a few of its aspects here. Satisfaction is a relative matter in that whether people are satisfied or dissatisfied is determined by how well their expectations fit with what they are given. If Tony has been led to believe that the company stresses imagination and creativity and finds himself instead saddled with rules and procedures, he will be dissatisfied. Conversely, if Dick expects his new job to pay well but to be boring, and to his surprise finds the work both interesting and challenging, he will be very satisfied.

Ford Motor Company Parts and Service Division head Joe Kordick meets informally on a regular basis to get input from employees.

Job satisfaction is also related to absenteeism, turnover, and productivity. The higher the satisfaction, the lower the likelihood of both absenteeism and turnover and the higher the likelihood of productivity.[6] When personnel find the work satisfying, they derive a sense of meaningfulness and tend to remain on the job. Much of this satisfaction is related to the social environment in which the work is done. Thus the informal organization helps create a climate conducive to high productivity.

SERVING AS A SAFETY VALVE

The grapevine also functions as a safety valve for employees' emotions. It lets the workers blow off steam and release some of their job pressures. When a person is angry over something, he or she needs some release for the frustration and resentment. This is where the informal organization plays a role. For example, if Don and his boss were to have an argument and he were to tell the boss where to get off, he could be fired. Instead, Don complains to his fellow workers. By sharing his problem with other employees, Don is able to release much of his pent-up anger in a way that does *not* threaten his job. Also, after he talks about the issue for a while, it is likely to appear minor and he can turn his attention back to doing his job.

PROVIDING FEEDBACK

Perhaps the greatest overall benefit of the informal organization is that of providing the manager with feedback. The grapevine, in particular, reflects how the workers feel about the company, the managers, and the

■ ■ ■ ■ ■ ■ ■

[6]For more information about this issue see Benjamin Schneider and Robert A. Snyder, "Some Relationships between Job Satisfaction and Organizational Climate," *Journal of Applied Psychology*, June 1975, pp. 318–328; Ray Wild, "Job Needs, Job Satisfaction, and Job Behavior of Women Manual Workers," *Journal of Applied Psychology*, April 1970, pp. 152–162.

work. By tapping the communication flow, the manager can learn what is going on. If a manager makes a bad decision or does not know how to supervise the subordinates properly, this information will eventually be carried back to the boss. What better way to protect one's job than by learning of problems through the grapevine and working to correct them before the boss asks, "What's this I hear about you having trouble with . . . ?"

STOP!

Review your answer to the third question and make any changes you would like. Then compare your answer to the one below.

3.   What are two benefits of the grapevine that were illustrated in this case?

One of the benefits of the grapevine is that it helps get things done. Notice that Gladys wanted someone to support the president's acquisition decision, so she leaked the information to the person who was best equipped to do this. Second, when Gladys wanted to let off steam she talked to the marketing executive because she knew she could be forthright with him and not be concerned about any negative repercussions. ∎

DRAWBACKS OF THE INFORMAL ORGANIZATION

Despite its potential benefits, the informal organization has drawbacks. The most common include: (1) resistance to change, (2) goal conflict, (3) conformity problems, and (4) rumor.

RESISTANCE TO CHANGE

One of the greatest drawbacks of the informal organization is its resistance to change. Quite often the organization systematically ignores or only partially carries out directives related to such changes as new work procedures or rules. The overriding philosophy of many informal organizations is "Live and let live." They do not want the status quo changed. This behavior is often referred to as *homeostasis*, which is the tendency of a group to maintain things as they are.

Of course, change is inevitable. Technological innovations, plant redesign, and competitive developments in the external environment all require the organization to adapt operations to meet these conditions. If

THE INFORMAL ORGANIZATION SOMETIMES FIGHTS CHANGE.

an innovative press is developed that will reduce current printing costs by 33 percent, a printing company has to buy it. However, part of this cost savings may be a result of manpower reduction. This is why the informal organization will fight the change. It does not want any of its members to be fired. Nor, as noted about group cohesion in Chapter 4, does the informal organization approve of any people being reassigned. If the company breaks up a cohesive group, productivity may drop off (see Figure 4.3).

Another reason the informal organization resists change is that work standards or quotas are often increased. In many cases, change generates new job demands; in *all* cases, it brings about higher efficiency (or at least attempts to achieve efficiency). For example, if a company establishes new work procedures, it is usually because a faster way of doing the job has been discovered. If work assignments are changed, it is because the firm has found a way to get more output with the same number of people. The informal organization resists such efficiency moves for three reasons. First, as mentioned, the people like the status quo and believe that any change will disrupt their pleasant work environment. Second, if they conform and do more work, the management may believe that it can introduce change any time it wants, and it may begin regarding the people as mere factors of production who need not be consulted in advance about changes. By resisting, the informal organization insures that management keeps the human element in mind when introducing change. Third, many members of the informal organization believe that it is unfair of management to introduce efficiency measures and keep all the profit for the company. If the people are going to do more work, they should be paid more money. Keep in mind, however, that this is not always a fair argument. If the firm buys a new machine for $500,000, the cost savings may allow it to pay for the machine and keep costs at a competitive level but may not increase profit. Of course, not being privy to such financial data, the informal organization may simply assume that changes in the work environment always increase profit.

GOAL CONFLICT

■ ■ ■ ■ ■ ■ ■ ■ ■ ■ ■ ■ ■
IT CAN LEAD TO GOAL CONFLICT.

Whenever someone is asked to pursue two objectives that work against each other, **goal conflict** occurs. For example, Joe wants to be a member of the informal organization but also wants to meet the work quota assigned by management. The informal organization quota is only 80 percent of the company quota. Clearly, Joe cannot be totally loyal to both.

As we discover later in this chapter, management must carefully cultivate mutual interests with informal groups so as to integrate the goals of both. This is not an area where the firm will ever achieve perfect harmony, since there will always be some differences between the formal and informal organizations, but management must strive to reduce the differences to an "acceptable" level.

CONFORMITY

Closely related to goal conflict is the problem of **conformity**. Group norms and sanctions are used in persuading members to accept informal goals. Sometimes these norms and sanctions are so strong that individuals feel compelled to go along with the group in spite of their own inclinations. More likely, however, the informal organization becomes so much a part of the employees' work lives that they are unaware of its presence. As a result, they conform without consciously weighing the pros and cons of such action; even if their conformity were pointed out to them, they would be unwilling to deviate from these informal norms.

■ ■ ■ ■ ■ ■ ■ ■ ■ ■ ■ ■ ■ ■
IT CAN RESULT IN CONFORMITY.

RUMOR

The most undesirable feature of the informal organization is **rumor**. Many people believe that the word is synonymous with the total product of the grapevine, but this is not so. Rumor is the unverified or untrue part of grapevine information. Communication theorists often define rumor as a product of interest and ambiguity.[7]

■ ■ ■ ■ ■ ■ ■ ■ ■ ■ ■ ■ ■ ■
IT CAN CAUSE RUMORS.

$$Rumor = Interest \times Ambiguity$$

The logic behind this equation is quite simple. First, there can be no rumor unless the issue is of interest to someone. You undoubtedly have never heard a rumor about the impact of the ice age on the existence of the penguin. However, you may have passed on a rumor about the type of examination given by a math professor in whose class you were currently registered. Second, if all the facts about a situation are known, there is no cause for rumor. If the professor told you that the final exam would come from the last 10 chapters of the book, ambiguity would be much less than if the questions were to be drawn from all 20 chapters and all class discussion. Ambiguity would be further reduced if the professor gave out a list of 50 equations from which the 25 exam problems would be drawn exclusively. Ambiguity could never be totally eliminated (which 25 equations?), but it would be reduced.

To avoid grapevine rumors when the company was introducing its new personnel benefits plan, Ed France, Senior Vice President of Fischer & Porter Company, explained the new plan to all Department Managers.

Rumor is both maintained and magnified through the use of selective filtering and elaboration. **Selective filtering** involves the screening of rumor so that part of the story is maintained and the rest is discarded.

■ ■ ■ ■ ■ ■ ■

[7]See, for example, Gordon W. Allport and Leo Postman, *The Psychology of Rumor* (New York: Holt, Rinehart and Winston, Inc., 1974), p. 33.

Usually, the part that is kept is the part that is of greatest interest to the person repeating the rumor. This is then elaborated upon: details are added and are rearranged to fit the individual's point of view. **Elaboration** thus contributes to the further modification of a rumor.

DEALING WITH THE INFORMAL ORGANIZATION

In dealing with the informal organization, the manager must undertake two major tasks: (1) recognize the inevitability of the informal network, and (2) attempt to influence its direction so that the goals of both the formal and informal organizations are in harmony. The manager must also stay abreast of changes within the informal organization.

RECOGNIZE ITS INEVITABILITY

Some managers believe that the disadvantages of the informal organization more than outweigh the benefits. As a result, they try to develop means of "stamping it out." However, this approach is never really successful. Using the grapevine as a representative segment of the informal organization, Davis has offered the following explanation of its inevitability:

THE GRAPEVINE CANNOT BE ELIMINATED.

> ... In a sense, the grapevine is a human birthright, because whenever people congregate into groups, the grapevine is sure to develop. It may use smoke signals, jungle tom-toms, taps on the prison wall, ordinary conversation, or some other method, but it will always be there. Organizations cannot "fire" the grapevine because they did not hire it. It is simply there.[8]

Because the informal organization is inevitable, the manager must develop methods for influencing it.

INFLUENCE ITS DIRECTION

One of the most direct ways for a manager to influence the informal organization is by tapping its grapevine, learning what is being communicated, and countering any negative rumors by getting the organization's message into the channel. This can be done by learning who the liaison people in the informal network are and using them as a point of entry.

Of course, if the manager begins feeding rumors or half-truths back

------

[8]Davis, *Human Behavior at Work*, pp. 337–338.

into the grapevine, the liaison people will either modify the message or simply refuse to carry another organization message. The manager cannot fight rumor with rumor. He or she must determine whether the information in the grapevine is accurate or not, and when it is inaccurate, must substitute correct information.

Do managers really use the grapevine to influence the informal organization? Research shows that they do. Knippen studied the grapevine in a large grocery store and found that although employees knew only 42 percent of the grapevine information, managers knew about 70 percent. Furthermore, while the managers accounted for only a small percentage of the 170 employees, they initiated almost 50 percent of the grapevine information. On the average, each manager told eight other people, while the typical employee told four. The managers were not waiting to see what information the employees were passing through the grapevine. Rather, they were using this informal channel to get their own messages across.[9]

■ ■ ■ ■ ■ ■ ■ ■ ■ ■ ■ ■ ■ ■ ■
THE MANAGER SHOULD SEEK TO INFLUENCE IT.

The purpose of these management-initiated messages should be to smooth the way for more cooperation between the formal and informal organizations. The manager's objective should be to create conditions that help align the goals of both groups (see Human Relations in Action: Influencing the Informal Organization). When this is accomplished, the manager will find that resistance to change is minimized, rumors are reduced, and overall organizational cooperation is achieved.

STAY ABREAST OF CHANGES

The informal organization is continually undergoing change. Some people are dropping out of its ranks, others are becoming members. Sometimes this is a result of the membership itself which accepts and rejects members and thus keeps membership in a state of flux. Many times it is a result of people leaving the company or being transferred to other units or departments. Since the latter are no longer in the nearby vicinity, they will drop out of the local informal organization and, in all likelihood, be replaced by others. Managers who want to deal effectively with the informal organization have to keep abreast of the changing membership.

Managers also have to remember that different problems will bring different informal leaders to the fore. If a university is having a problem with its part-time employees and they are unionized, the shop steward or union spokesperson will probably be the informal leader. This individual is chosen because he or she is perceived as someone who can help the

------

[9] Jay Knippen, "Grapevine Communication: Management Employees," *Journal of Business Research*, January 1974, pp. 47–58.

HUMAN RELATIONS IN ACTION

INFLUENCING THE INFORMAL ORGANIZATION

There are a number of ways of influencing the informal organization. Most of them relate to how you interact with members of this group. In particular, there are four things you have to keep in mind.

First, when you communicate with the informal organization, always convey the fact that the message you are providing has importance. Do not wait too long or your listener will begin to mentally wander off and you will have trouble getting him back. For example, if you want to tell Jack something of importance, say it right up front. "Jack, this is something that you'll be interested in. It directly relates to the type of problem you've been investigating in the shipping department." Notice how quickly you have zeroed in on your main point.

Second, speak authoritatively and with conviction. Do not end your sentences with a question. Phrase them so that they are factual and accurately represent your point of view. If you can make them sound like the other party should also accept them as such, so much the better. Also remember to maintain eye contact as you talk.

Third, do not give the other person much chance to disagree or attempt to prove that you are wrong. This undermines your efforts. For example, if you need to have something done, do not say, "Tim, I think this is a good time for you to handle that cost control report." This sounds too wishy-washy and Tim may say, "No, I don't think it is." Now you are going to be in an argument regarding whether or not the time is right. A better way to handle the situation is to say, "Tim, now is the time for you to handle that cost control report." He may still disagree, but you have reduced the chances of this happening. Remember that if you nar-

group achieve its goals. This person is seen as able to wield power. If a hospital is having a salary dispute with its nursing staff, the nurse who informally represents the group may be chosen because of her job experience and tenure. She is chosen on the basis of work-related expertise. If a work team on a loading dock sets a goal of loading 10 percent more trucks than any other team, the individual who is the fastest worker may be chosen as the informal leader. This person's informal authority is based on his or her job expertise.

Since informal organizational membership is continually in a state of flux, the manager must continually ask the question: Who is in charge of the informal group and why? The answer will help the manager decide how to influence or deal with the informal group most effectively.

row the options, you improve your chances of dealing effectively with the informal organization. For example, instead of asking someone when she would like her vacation, figure out what weeks are available and offer them only, "Mary, would you like your vacation during the first two weeks of August or the first two weeks of September?" This approach saves you time because it eliminates all the other weeks of the year, which have already been taken by people in the unit who have more seniority.

Know when to listen. Sometimes you can influence the informal organization by listening to others. For example, if you are interested in finding out why so many people throughout the organization are coming late to work, you might ask, "Frank, why is everyone showing up late all the time?" Frank may know the answer, and this information will be useful to you. One company vice-president recently found out the reason that so many people were leaving work early. It was he, himself. Every day the senior vice-president would leave at 4:30 p.m. and the rest of the personnel would begin leaving within five minutes. They reasoned that if the senior vice-president did not think it was important to stay until 5 p.m., why should they? During one of his informal chats with some of the personnel, the vice-president indirectly learned of the effect that his behavior was having. From that day on, he made it a point to stay until 5 p.m. or later. He listened and learned.

In dealing with the informal organization, it is important to know when to take the initiative and when to hold back and listen. Both can be important strategies in influencing people.

STOP!

Review your answer to the fourth question and make any changes you would like. Then compare your answer to the one below.

4.   Which of the three vice-presidents is likely to be the most effective over the next couple of years? Why?

Obviously the marketing vice-president is likely to be the most effective. He gets along better with Mr. Bakker than do the other two vice-presidents, and he is privy to information that is likely to improve his standing in the future. ■

SUMMARY

The informal organization plays a significant role in the dynamics of behavior at work. Comparison with the formal organization shows that the two organizations differ in terms of interpersonal relations, leadership, behavioral control, and dependency. One of the informal organization's most interesting behavioral aspects, however, is its communication network. Commonly referred to as the *grapevine*, this communication network is used to carry information between members of the informal organization. Four common types of grapevine network are the single strand, gossip chain, probability chain, and cluster chain. The cluster chain, which involves the selective transmission of messages, is the most common.

Some people tend to be very active on the grapevine, but others are fairly inactive. However, given the proper situation and motivation, just about everyone will be grapevine-active. Research reveals that some of the most likely causes for such activity are lack of knowledge about a situation, insecurity, personal interest in a situation, and the possession of recent information.

Some of the commonly cited benefits of the informal organization are: getting things done, lightening managerial workloads, providing job satisfaction, serving as a safety valve for employee emotions, and providing feedback to the manager. Despite such benefits, however, there are some major disadvantages to the informal organization: resistance to change, goal conflict, conformity, and rumor.

In any event, the informal organization is inevitable. It cannot be stamped out, so the manager will do well to understand its presence and, if possible, to influence its direction so that the goals of both the formal and informal organizations are brought into harmony. Some of the most effective ways of doing this include tapping the grapevine to learn what is going on, countering rumor with fact, and creating conditions that help align the goals of both groups. If this can be accomplished, the manager will find that resistance to change is minimized, rumors are reduced, and overall organizational cooperation is achieved.

KEY TERMS IN THE CHAPTER

sociogram	gossip chain
authority	probability chain
power	cluster chain
satisficing behavior	goal conflict
nucleus group	conformity
fringe group	rumor
outer group	selective filtering
grapevine	elaboration
single strand	

REVIEW AND STUDY QUESTIONS

1.   One of the ways in which the informal organization differs from the formal organization is that of interpersonal relations. What is meant by this statement?

2.   How does the formal leader differ from the informal leader?

3.   In what way is authority different from power? Which is of greater importance in the informal organization?

4.   What kinds of power tactics do managers use? Explain.

5.   What are some of the behavioral controls used by members of the informal organization to ensure compliance with its norms?

6.   How does each of the following grapevine networks function: single strand, gossip chain, probability chain, cluster chain? Explain.

7.   In your own words, when are people most likely to be grapevine-active? Give at least three illustrations.

8.   In what way does the informal organization help in getting things done?

9.   One of the biggest complaints about the informal organization is that it tends to resist change. Is this true? Defend your answer.

10.   How should the manager deal with the informal organization? Make your answer complete.

TIME OUT ANSWERS: INTERPRETATION OF THE INFORMAL ORGANIZATION INITIAL APPRAISAL

This quiz consists of two parts. Questions 1–7 measure your use of the informal organization. Questions 8–15 measure how much you really know about the informal organization.

Do you use the informal organization? The following key is for scoring your answers to Questions 1–7. For each answer you have that agrees with this key, give yourself a point.

1. False   5. False
2. True   6. True
3. False   7. False
4. True

The higher your score, the greater the likelihood that you use the informal organization. However, if you have a score of 6 or 7, you have to be careful that you are not simply ignoring the formal structure. A high score can indicate total disregard for organizational policies and procedures, but only you can determine this. Most effective managers have a score of at least 5 on this part of the quiz.

What do you know about the grapevine? Questions 8–15 are designed to measure your knowledge of the informal organization. For each answer you have that agrees with this key, give yourself a point.

8. False	12. False
9. True	13. False
10. True	14. False
11. True	15. False

If you currently know a great deal about the informal organization, your score here will be in the 6–8 range. In any event, as you read the material in this chapter, you will learn the logic behind each of the above answers.

CASE: A CASE OF LAYOFFS

The rumor mill in Betty Harrigan's department has been in full operation this week. It seems that everyone's mind is on the new equipment that is being installed. The machinery was approved by a management committee more than six months ago and is the result of company efforts to modernize the facilities. The machines are state-of-the-art but, despite their sophistication, still require just as many people to run them as did the old machines. Nevertheless, this has not stopped the rumors about impending layoffs.

In an effort to deal with the situation, Betty called a meeting of her staff and explained to them that three months before she became department manager, a committee had approved the purchase of this new machinery. She was unable to explain why no one in the unit knew about the impending purchase, but she assured everyone that there would be no layoffs or cutbacks in the number of hours worked. "These machines are going to help us increase the quality of work but they will not increase the quantity. We are going to need everyone in the department and will probably have to hire two more people." The group listened quietly as Betty spoke. When she was finished she asked if there were any questions. One of the young men in the back said, "Are we the only department getting new equipment?" Betty explained there were two other units that also were having new machinery installed. She then hastened to add, "And like us, neither of them is going to have any layoffs either." With this the meeting broke up.

As soon as she returned to her office, Betty had a call from her boss. "Look, I don't want to panic you," he said, "but I've just had a call from the vice-president of administration. The other departments that got new equipment are going to have some layoffs because they were overstaffed to begin with. However, you will not have any. You are understaffed and, as we agreed, you will be getting two new people within the month. Unfortunately, none of the people being laid off has the qualifications you need, or we would simply transfer them to your department. The reason I wanted to call was to let you know that you have nothing to worry about." Betty thanked him and hung up. Just then there was a knock at her door. The young man from the meeting came in and said, "I just heard that people in those other two departments are to be laid off. I was wondering what effect this would have on the new hires in our department. If I'm going to get laid off, I'd like to start looking for a new job as soon as possible." Betty asked the man to sit down.

QUESTIONS

1.   How did the young man find out about the layoffs in the other departments? Explain.

2.   Will Betty's comment about no layoffs in her department now be regarded with skepticism? Why? What did Betty do that might make people doubt her?

3.   What would you advise Betty to say to the young man? Explain. ∎

CASE: *FOREWARNED IS FOREARMED*

Tim Shaugnessy is a department manager in a large governmental agency. Tim likes to get to work early so he can spend 15 or 20 minutes having coffee with the employees. During this time, Tim finds he can pick up a lot of information about what is going on around the agency, both in his department and in others.

Last week, when Tim entered the large agency dining area, he found a group of employees discussing upcoming work changes. One of them seemed quite upset over the amount of work that would be generated as a result of these changes. "You know," she said, "no matter what happens around here, the word-processing people always end up having to shoulder more of the burden. In fact, I know that a number of word-processing people are trying to transfer to other agencies."

Tim has three word-processing people in his department. Most of the other departments have more because they are larger. The woman's remarks intrigued Tim. He wondered if the woman was just talking out loud or had made her comments based on sound information. "Do you think all of the word-processing people are going to be trying to transfer?" he asked. The woman did not know who Tim was, but assumed he was one of the office personnel. She turned to him and said, "I know at least six people who are thinking about transferring." She then proceeded to identify them. Two of them work for Tim, but he did not tell her this. He simply listened and nodded his head. "If you have any word-processing work you need handled, I'd suggest you get it in early," she cautioned. Tim smiled and thanked her.

Back in his department, Tim decided to take immediate action. He called in the three word processors and began to review the impact that the new departmental guidelines would have on their work load. Tim went out of his way to downplay the need for them to work overtime or harder than they are currently working. "We're going to maintain the same pace as before," he told them. "Let the other departments work their people to the bone. I'm submitting a request for two more word-processing people, and am going to personally sift through all of the work that you are going to have to be doing. Some of this stuff has got to be unimportant and can be ignored or delayed for a while. We can't have you being overworked just because the agency decides to change regulations." At no time during this talk did Tim let on that he knew about the transfer plans of the two word processors. However, he could tell that they were pleased with his decision and when they left his office, he could see the three of them huddled in quiet conversation at a desk at the far end of the room.

Earlier today Tim's boss called an immediate meeting. He had just learned that four of the word-processing operators had applied for transfers to other departments. "This is going to leave some of your departments very short of help. Tim, you're the only one who is not going to be directly affected. Can you help out by loaning one or two of your people to the other departments?" Tim carefully explained that his people would be even further swamped with work if he did this. "I've already put in a request for two more people. I can't spare anyone." The boss then looked at the other departmental managers and said, "Well, for the time being at least, you guys are going to have to get by with your current work staff. I'll get you some help just as soon as I can."

QUESTIONS

1.   What does this case relate about the selectivity of the grapevine process? Explain.

2.   Why did the other managers not know that the word-processing people felt overworked and were trying to transfer?

3.   Why did Tim not tell the other departmental managers when he learned the news? What does your answer relate about the role of power in informal group operations? Explain. ■

EXPERIENCING GRAPEVINE COMMUNICATIONS

PURPOSE

- To understand how the grapevine works.
- To use each of the four basic grapevine networks to convey information.
- To evaluate the grapevine networks in terms of speed and accuracy.

PROCEDURE

1. Teams of six people are formed. The instructor will give each team a set of four messages. These messages are labeled 1, 2, 3, and 4 respectively.

2. Each team will form a single strand informal communication network and pass message number one from one team member to the next. The last person to receive the message will write it down.

3. Each team will then form a gossip chain. The individual in the center will convey message number two to everyone in the group. Everyone will then write down their interpretation of the message.

4. Each team will then form a probability chain to pass message number three and then form a cluster chain to pass message number four. In each case, the last persons to receive the message will write it down.

5. Review each of the four informal networks. Which was easiest to use? Which resulted in the fastest conveying of information? Which was slowest? Which was most accurate? Which was least? Finally, when choosing an informal network, when would each of the four be the first choice? When would each be the last choice?

PART 3

THE TECHNICAL SYSTEM

The overall objective of this part of the book is to study the technical system of organizations. In Part 3 we examine individual behavior and group behavior that occur within a prescribed organizational framework or structure commonly referred to as the *technical system*. The primary focus of attention in the technical system is the organization structure. However, modern human relationists are interested in more than just the structure itself. They also want to know the particular factors of organization design, including technology, and the ways in which jobs can be redesigned to be more rewarding for the personnel and more efficient for the organization. Thus, the technical system has three major components: (1) the impact of technology on people at work, (2) a focus on productivity and quality improvement, and (3) job redesign and job enrichment.

In Chapter 6, we examine technology and its impact on people at work. This relationship, often referred to as the *sociotechnical system*, is important for modern human relations because it forces the manager to pay increased attention to the technical-human interface in modern organizations, an interface that is of major importance because of the great acceleration in the evolution of technology in the last 50 years. In the first part of Chapter 6, we trace the evolution of technology from the handicraft era to the era of cybernated technology and note the impact of knowledge on technological growth. Then we identify and describe the four major characteristics of a post-industrial society, discuss the effect of technology on work values, and describe how technology can lead to alienation. Finally, we explain how technological advances can engender fear of replacement by machine and outline some of the ways in which effective planning can result in an integration of technology and the organizational personnel. At this point we discuss industrial democracy and participative management.

In Chapter 7, we study productivity and quality improvement, two major challenges facing modern organizations. The current status and future direction of management efforts to improve productivity and quality are reviewed. Then attention is focused on techniques and methods that are being used in meeting these two challenges. Included in this group are quality circles, no-smoking regulations, alternative work arrangements, effective organization designs, and intrapreneurship. The end of the chapter examines Japanese management techniques and their value in improving productivity and quality improvement.

In Chapter 8, we study how modern organizations deal with the challenge of technology and its dysfunctional effects. One of the ways of doing so is to redesign jobs and enrich them with psychological motivators, and the overall goal of the chapter is to study how this can be done. We explain what job design is and explore some of the ways in which jobs can be redesigned, including job rotation, job enlargement, and job enrichment. Then we describe core job dimensions and illustrate how selected enrichment principles can be used to fulfill these dimensions. The end of the chapter illustrates job enrichment and describes some of the current challenges in job design.

When you have finished reading this part of the book you should have a solid understanding of the technical system. In particular, you should: be aware of the impact of technology on the organizational personnel and the ways in which such technology can lead to alienation, be able to explain how technology can bring about fear of job replacement, and be capable of outlining some of the ways in which effective planning can bring about the needed integration of technology and organizational personnel. Additionally, you should know what is meant by job redesign, how organizations redesign jobs, and what the important job core dimensions and job enrichment principles are that play such a key role in job redesign. Most importantly, you will be aware of the all-important personnel–organizational structure interface and how modern human relations managers try to integrate the needs of both groups in attaining overall efficiency.

TECHNOLOGY AND PEOPLE AT WORK

GOALS OF THE CHAPTER

There are many factors to which the organization must respond. One of the most important is that of technology, for as technology increases the organization finds itself bombarded with change. The relationship of technology to people at work is known as **sociotechnical systems**, and modern managers are finding that they must give increased attention to this technical-human interface. In particular, today's workers report that they are dissatisfied with formal organization designs that fail to take into account their personal needs. In many cases, the result is alienation, as reflected in feelings such as powerlessness, isolation, and self-estrangement.

The goal of this chapter is to examine technology and its effect on the organizational personnel. First, we trace the evolution of technology from the handicraft era to the cybernated technology stage. Then we examine the impact of knowledge on technology and review some of the reasons why the modern technological engine is moving at an ever faster clip. Next we look at the post-industrial society and identify the four major characteristics that differentiate it from earlier societies. Then we study technology and its effect on people at work, with primary attention to work values, alienation, and the replacement of personnel by technology. The last part of the chapter is devoted to identifying some of the ways in which the technical-human interface can be resolved.

When you have finished reading this chapter you should be able to:

1.   Trace the evolution of technology from the handicraft era to the cybernated technology stage.

2.   Identify and describe the four major characteristics of a post-industrial society.

3.   Discuss the effect of technology on work values.

4.   Explain how technology can bring about fear of replacement by machine.

5.   Discuss how industrial democracy and participative management can bring about an integration of technology and the organizational personnel.

OPENING CASE

USING RESOURCES EFFECTIVELY

"**P**roductivity. That's the name of the game. If you can't produce things cheaper and with better quality than the competition, you're history. We intend to make the competition in this industry a part of history." With these words, the president of Grindling Inc. cut the ribbon that stretched across the front gate of the company's new plant, and the assembled managers, workers, newspeople, and guests all walked into the new plant. After a brief tour of the facilities, lunch was served in the cafeteria. As the president left the plant, he turned to Pablo Gutierrez and said, "Pablo, this is your plant. Run it effectively and you'll be a senior-level manager within five years. No one in the industry can touch us in terms of automation. This is a state-of-the-art plant. We're capable of producing the finest electronic equipment in the industry. You've got 200 workers running a facility that three years ago would have required 1,400 people. Treat them well and get the most out of them, and we'll all prosper." With these words, the president got into his limousine and headed for the airport.

During the eleven months the plant has been open, Pablo has found himself facing a wide variety of challenges. In particular, the workers quickly became upset with the high automation. "We're just a bunch of small cogs in a big machine," one of them complained. "We don't count for much around here." Another said, "We're at the mercy of these computerized monsters. I want a job where I personally can get involved." Pablo has been trying to deal with this problem by creating worker committees that are charged with deciding how to change things to accommodate the personnel. Although the plant is highly automated, there are things that can be done by the workers. In particular, quality control can be improved by more careful inspection of the finished products. There are also some automated operations that are not working out as intended. It appears that the machines are not as efficient as people. "I want to more fully integrate the personnel into the work place," Pablo told the president recently. "This may require some reorganization of the operations." The president told Pablo to make whatever changes he thought were in the best interests of the company. "If you can do a better job by shutting down some of the automated line and having the work done by the people, do so. Get the best blend of worker and machine that you can. This is the only way that we can ensure that human resources are being most effectively used." Pablo told the president that he would keep him informed regarding any changes that were made.

1.   What type of technology does this firm use?

2.   Is the company more interested in profit maximizing or quality of work life?

3.   In what way is technology causing alienation?

4.   Is Pablo's use of committees an example of industrial democracy or participative management? Explain.

Write down your answers to these questions and put them aside. We will return to them later. ∎

THE EVOLUTION OF TECHNOLOGY

One of the most dramatic events of the twentieth century has been the dynamic development of technology. Today people are traveling faster than ever before, residing in houses made of material that was unavailable 25 years ago, using home appliances and tools that make their lives more enjoyable, and, thanks to medical technology, living longer than ever. However, technology has had its price. Many people are now living at a very fast rate, being subjected to what Alvin Toffler has called **future shock**—the effect of enduring too much change in too short a time.[1] How has our society arrived at this advanced state of technology? We attempt to answer this question by examining the eras of technological development through which mankind in general and the United States in particular have progressed.

FUTURE SHOCK IS THE EFFECT OF ENDURING TOO MUCH CHANGE IN TOO SHORT A PERIOD OF TIME.

[1] Alvin Toffler, *Future Shock* (New York: Bantam Books, 1971).

HANDICRAFT ERA

The first phase of technological development was the **handicraft era**. During this period people made things by hand. They built their own houses, made their own clothes, and developed their own medicines and herbs to combat illness. In short, they were self-sufficient. The only specialists during this era were carpenters, cobblers, and tailors, who provided the local population with their services and in turn received goods or money with which to buy food, clothing, and shelter. However, these craftsmen were to be found only in larger towns where their services were required. In outlying areas such as farm communities, for example, there was little need for a tailor or a cobbler, although a blacksmith might be able to eke out a living. In any event, there was a minimum of specialization. Almost everyone was a jack-of-all-trades.

If mankind was to progress, however, it was necessary for people to specialize, for with specialization come increases in productivity and output. Many individuals welcomed such advances because they saw the chance to obtain cheaper and more abundant goods and services.

■ ■ ■ ■ ■ ■ ■ ■ ■ ■ ■ ■ ■ ■
THE HANDICRAFT ERA WAS CHARACTERIZED BY SELF-SUFFICIENCY.

MECHANIZATION ERA

In the **mechanization era**, machine labor replaced human labor.[2] One of the most significant developments of this era was job specialization, by which workers were assigned a limited number of tasks that were to be repeated over and over again. One of the earliest examples was reported by Adam Smith in his famous book, *The Wealth of Nations* (1776). Commenting on job specialization, or *division of labor* as it is often called, as it was applied to the manufacture of pins, he wrote:

■ ■ ■ ■ ■ ■ ■ ■ ■ ■ ■ ■ ■ ■
THE MECHANIZATION ERA SAW THE USE OF MACHINE LABOR.

> A workman not educated to this business . . . nor acquainted with the use of machinery employed in it . . . could scarcely, perhaps, with his utmost industry, make one pin in a day, and certainly could not make twenty. But, in the way in which this business is now carried on not only the whole work is a peculiar trade, but it is divided into a number of branches, of which the greater part are likewise peculiar trades. One man draws out the wire, another straightens it, a third cuts it, a fourth points it, a fifth grinds it at the top for receiving the head; to make the head requires two or three distinct operations; to put it on, is a peculiar business, to whiten the pins is another; it is even a trade by itself to put them into the paper, and the important business of making a pin is, in this manner, divided into about eighteen

■ ■ ■ ■ ■ ■ ■

[2]Daniel A. Wren, *The Evolution of Management Thought*, 2nd ed. (New York: The Ronald Press, 1979), pp. 44–46.

distinct operations, which, in some manufactories, are all performed by distinct hands.[3]

With this method of job specialization, Smith found, a group of workers could make about 12 pounds of pins in a day. This tremendous increase in output could be traced directly to (1) the increase in dexterity of each worker, (2) saving time that was formerly lost as the worker switched from one job (drawing the wire) to another (straightening it), and (3) the invention of new machines that enabled one employee to do the work of many.

During this period mankind began to harness energy and use it to drive machinery; the spinning jenny and the power loom are illustrations. There was thus an increase of mechanization on two fronts: the workers and the machines. Each was seen as a complement to the other, and between them productivity increased dramatically. The age of mechanization was upon us.

MECHANISTIC TECHNOLOGY

A further increase in the use of machines and job simplification was represented by **mechanistic technology**. Eli Whitney, best known for his invention of the cotton gin, introduced standardized interchangeable parts in his production plant and was soon turning out muskets and clocks in greater quantities and at lower cost than ever before. A century later this basic idea was further extended through the development of the modern assembly line, such as that used by Henry Ford in building his Model T. Now the pace of technology was increasing and the role of the worker was diminishing. The number of tasks the person had to perform was decreasing and the amount of skill required was also declining. The employer no longer hired John Jones because of his experience and skill; he simply hired a person who could perform certain simple functions on a product coming down the assembly line. If the individual did the job poorly, could not keep up with the pace of the line, or simply did not like the work and decided to quit, a replacement could be easily obtained.

■ ■ ■ ■ ■ ■ ■ ■ ■ ■ ■ ■ ■
MECHANISTIC TECHNOLOGY BROUGHT THE ASSEMBLY LINE.

AUTOMATED TECHNOLOGY

In many organizations, *automated technology* has replaced mechanistic technology. Automated technology involves the linking together and integrating of assembly-line machines in such a fashion that many functions are performed automatically without human involvement. Some people have contended that this development represents the beginning

■ ■ ■ ■ ■ ■ ■ ■ ■ ■ ■ ■ ■
AUTOMATED TECHNOLOGY MODERNIZED THE ASSEMBLY LINE.

■ ■ ■ ■ ■ ■ ■

[3] Adam Smith, *The Wealth of Nations* (New York: The Modern Library, 1937), pp. 4–5.

of a second industrial revolution. Modern auto assembly lines are an excellent illustration. So are office computer systems that are linked one to the other, allowing managers using a microcomputer to interface with a giant mainframe. No wonder recent research shows that even small businesses are now computerizing operations.[4]

CYBERNATED TECHNOLOGY

■ ■ ■ ■ ■ ■ ■ ■ ■ ■ ■ ■ ■ ■

WITH CYBERNATED TECHNOLOGY MACHINES RUN OTHER MACHINES.

At present, a fifth stage, **cybernated technology**, is emerging. The term *cybernetics* refers to automatic control; today, by means of cybernated technology, machines are running and controlling other machines. A classic example is provided by modern computers which can monitor the temperature throughout a plant or building and order the heating and air conditioning units to turn off or on as needed. This form of environmental control is helping to reduce costs throughout industry. Computers are also being programmed to operate machines and to handle jobs automatically that once had to be performed by humans. As a result, robotics are gaining a foothold in many enterprises.[5]

STOP!

Review your answer to the first question and make any changes you would like. Then compare your answer to the one below.

1.   What type of technology does this firm use?

The firm uses automated technology. A close look at the various forms of technology described in this chapter indicates that this new plant goes beyond mechanistic technology through its use of modern equipment and state-of-the-art machines. ■

R&D, KNOWLEDGE, AND TECHNOLOGY

How has mankind been able to accomplish such tremendous breakthroughs in technology? One way is through the billions of dollars annually invested in research and development (R&D). At the present time

■ ■ ■ ■ ■ ■ ■

[4] Roxanne Farmanfarmaian, "Does Computerizing Really Pay Off?" *Working Woman*, March 1988, pp. 42–46.

[5] Roger H. Mitchell and Victor A. Mabert, "Robotics for Small Manufacturers: Myths and Realities," *Business Horizons*, July–August 1986, pp. 9–16.

the United States spends more than $125 billion annually on R&D. This sum is greater than that of England, France, West Germany, and Japan combined, and helps explain why the United States is the world's leading producer of basic research. Commenting on America's R&D prowess, *Fortune* recently noted that:

- Americans write 35 percent of all scientific and technical articles published.
- U.S. researchers get more patents than the rest of the world combined.
- Since World War II, 127 American scientists have won the Nobel Prize, compared with 98 Europeans and 5 Japanese.
- Federal research facilities, such as the National Institute of Health and the Department of Energy labs at Los Alamos, New Mexico, and Livermore, California, are doing pioneering research in theoretical physics, molecular biology, and computer science.
- Independent research institutes, such as Rockefeller University in New York and Woods Hole Oceanographic Institution in Massachusetts are leaders in their specialties.
- The 100 or so U.S. research universities that perform more than 60 percent of the nation's basic research are unequaled. Says Erich Bloch, director of the National Science Foundation: "It's no surprise that our universities draw students from all over the world and attract investment from foreign companies. In the competitive educational market, they deliver the best product."[6]

Technology such as robotics is important to General Motors. Executives at GM believe that the ultimate success of technology depends on the effective integration of people into all phases of the technological process.

These R&D expenditures are bringing about the development of all sorts of new products. The results can be seen in any large retail store—more goods than ever before. And it does not stop here. Thanks to research breakthroughs, we have supersonic transport, telecommunication satellites, and computers for medical research. In short, at work or at home, the employee is surrounded by technological innovation. Furthermore, there is no going back. Technology is speeding up, and the modern organization is being forced to accommodate many breakthroughs. What is the basic cause of this accelerative technological thrust? The answer is found in *knowledge*, technology's fuel.

■ ■ ■ ■ ■ ■ ■ ■ ■ ■ ■ ■ ■ ■
THERE HAVE BEEN TREMENDOUS ADVANCES IN SCIENCE.

Every year more and more people receive college degrees. The number of highly educated people in the population is increasing. Many of these graduates have studied physical sciences, and organizations employ them to discover new ideas that can be marketed to the general public.

On the basis of our discussion so far in this chapter, we can draw three conclusions:

■ ■ ■ ■ ■ ■ ■

[6] Stuart Gannes, "The Good News about U.S. R&D," *Fortune*, February 1, 1988, p. 49.

1.   There have been some tremendous technological breakthroughs over the past century.

2.   More money is being spent on R&D every year.

3.   A well-educated, highly intelligent segment of our society is seeking still further technological advances. Relying upon just this information we could postulate that such advances will be coming faster and faster; research shows that this is indeed what has been happening over the past century.

KNOWLEDGE IS TECHNOLOGICAL FUEL

Operating as an independent division, the New Business Development Group of Alberto Culver contributes to corporate growth by researching and developing internally generated new product concepts, seeking out and evaluating ideas submitted through other sources, and identifying promising product acquisitions.

The rate at which information has been gathered has been spiraling upward for 10,000 years. The first great breakthrough occurred with the invention of writing. The next great leap forward did not occur until the invention of movable type by Gutenberg in the fifteenth century. Prior to this period, Europe was producing about 1,000 book titles per year, and it was taking about 100 years to turn out a library of 100,000 titles. In the 550 years since Gutenberg's accomplishment, a tremendous acceleration occurred; by 1950 Europe was producing 120,000 titles per year. What had once taken a century now required only 10 months. Today the world's output of books is more than 2,500 titles per day.

Naturally, every book will not lead to a technological breakthrough, but the accelerative curve in book publication crudely parallels the rate at which mankind discovers new knowledge. Advances in science support this statement. For example, before the movable type press, only 11 chemical elements were known and it had been 200 years since the last one, arsenic, had been discovered. The twelfth element was discovered while Gutenberg was working on his invention. Over the next 550 years, more than 70 additional elements were discovered, and since 1900 scientists have been isolating new elements at the rate of 1 every 3 years.

Much of this advance must be attributed to the fact that 90 percent of all the scientists who ever lived are now alive and new discoveries are being made every day. This is evident from a reading of local newspapers and magazines. For example, some of the latest technological developments and research breakthroughs include the following:

▪   Computer researchers at Sandia National Laboratories in Albuquerque have developed a formula that allows computers to tackle massive problems by dividing up the work to be done and then having the various calculations performed simultaneously.

▪   Scientists at Epoulon Inc. in Boston are developing a substance that will rebuild bone tissue and teeth lost to periodontal disease.

▪   Startup Micro Dry Inc. of Tulsa has designed a microwave clothes-drying machine that dries clothes from the inside out, working on the same basic principles as the microwave oven.

■   Interpro Inc. of Haverhill, Massachusetts, has invented a lotion that protects hands from harsh solvents and alkaline lubricants and can be used by factory workers to prevent scratches, abrasions, and general abuse suffered on a typical day at the plant.[7]

Scientific discoveries are being brought to fruition at a faster rate. For example, in 1836 a machine was invented that mowed, threshed, tied straw into sheaves, and poured grain into sacks. The machine was based on technology that even then was 20 years old, but it was not until 1930 that such a combine was actually marketed. The first English patent for a typewriter was issued in 1714, but it took 150 years for typewriters to be commercially available. Today such delays between idea and application are almost unthinkable. It is not that we are more eager or less lazy than our ancestors, but we have, with the passage of time, invented all sorts of social devices to hasten the process. Thus, we find that the time between the first and second stages of the innovative cycle—between idea and application—has been cut radically. Frank Lynn, for example, in studying 20 major innovations including frozen foods, antibiotics, integrated circuits, and synthetic leather, found that since the beginning of this century more than 60 percent has been slashed from the average time needed for a major scientific discovery to be translated into a useful technological form. Today a vast and growing research and development industry is consciously working to reduce the lag still more.[8]

In addition, the number of consumer goods is increasing so rapidly that the time between introduction and decline is getting smaller. Cheaper, better-quality, or more useful goods are being produced. To a large degree, technology is creating a disposable product society. In the process, the United States has found itself entering a post-industrial society, in which changes in the external environment are bringing about a whole different set of internal values. Technology is changing America in general and employees in particular.

POST-INDUSTRIAL SOCIETY

In the past 30 years the United States has progressed from an industrial society to a **post-industrial society**. This transition has involved four major changes: (1) a service-oriented work force, (2) a dynamic increase in the number of professional and technical workers, (3) an increase in the importance of theoretical knowledge, and (4) the planning and controlling of technological growth.

■■■■■■■

[7] These examples can be found in *Business Week* March 23, 1988, p. 75; *Business Week*, May 23, 1988, p. 109; and *Business Week*, May 30, 1988, p. 101.

[8] Toffler, *Future Shock*, pp. 27–28.

SERVICE-ORIENTED WORK FORCE

■ ■ ■ ■ ■ ■ ■ ■ ■ ■ ■ ■ ■ ■
OVER HALF OF ALL U.S. WORKERS
ARE IN SERVICE JOBS.

Unlike the work force in other countries, the majority of the U.S. work force is no longer engaged in manufacturing or agriculture; it is engaged in services. Workers in transportation, utilities, trade, finance, insurance, real estate, services, and government now constitute approximately two-thirds of the total work force. The remaining one-third are in agriculture, forestry, fisheries, mining, construction, and manufacturing. In order to release such a large number of people from manufacturing and maintain our production output, we had to have made great technological advances. The result, quite obviously, has been a dramatic change in the work environment.[9]

DYNAMIC INCREASE IN NUMBER OF PROFESSIONAL AND TECHNOLOGICAL WORKERS

■ ■ ■ ■ ■ ■ ■ ■ ■ ■ ■ ■ ■ ■
THERE HAS BEEN A TREMENDOUS
GROWTH IN PROFESSIONAL AND
TECHNICAL JOBS.

Another characteristic of post-industrialism is the dynamic growth in numbers of workers in professional and technical occupations. In particular, the number of white-collar and service workers is increasing while that of blue-collar and farm workers is declining. At the present time white-collar workers constitute approximately 70 percent of the labor force; blue-collar workers are about 30 percent.

INCREASE IN THE IMPORTANCE OF THEORETICAL KNOWLEDGE

■ ■ ■ ■ ■ ■ ■ ■ ■ ■ ■ ■ ■ ■
THEORETICAL KNOWLEDGE IS VERY
IMPORTANT.

A third characteristic of a post-industrial society is an increase in the importance of theoretical knowledge. Industrial societies are interested in the practical side of things. They concentrate on what works and ignore the rest. A post-industrial society, however, is concerned with more than just this short-run, heavily pragmatic view. For example, in hospitals today a great deal of research is being done. Medical institutions are collecting all sorts of data on their patients: From what ailment is the person suffering? How old is the patient? What is the patient's height, weight, age, sex, and religion? Is there any variable to which the problem can be traced, and if so, can we make any generalization about how people with this ailment might be cured? In many cases the data are analyzed, but no answer is found. Nevertheless, medical personnel keep this information stored in a computer. They do not need to find any short-run value for it. Perhaps in a few years they will have enough data from which to postulate a theory regarding the causes and cures for the ailment. The same is

■ ■ ■ ■ ■ ■ ■

[9]Marvin S. Katzman, "When Robots Dominate the U.S. Workplace," *Supervisory Management*, June 1983, pp. 37–43; and Terry Feulner and Brian H. Kleiner, "When Robots Are the Answer," *Personnel Journal*, February 1986, pp. 45–47.

TABLE 6.1   HUMAN, SOCIAL, AND ORGANIZATIONAL EVOLUTION

ERA OR SOCIETY	PREVAILING ETHIC	PROCESS OR MECHANISM	HUMAN NEEDS	PREDOMINANT GOALS
Handicraft era	Individualism Craftsmanship	Family Guilds Entrepreneurism	Physiological Safety/Security Belonging Esteem	Human survival Personal identity Independence
Mechanization and assembly-line eras	Individualism Competition Mass production Supremacy of the organization	Job simplification Scientific management Bureaucracy	Physiological Safety/Security Belonging	Human survival Organizational efficiency Profit
Post-industrial society	Collaboration Industrial democracy Individual-organizational congruency	Automation Job enrichment Adhocracy Human resources management	Physiological Safety/Security Belonging Esteem Self-actualization	Adaptability Optimization of human and organizational objectives Institutional interdependency

true in many other areas, from physics and chemistry to psychology and sociology. The purpose of this theoretical knowledge is to serve as a base for projecting and planning for the future. A post-industrial society is more future-oriented than its predecessors. (See Table 6.1 for a more detailed comparison of these societies or eras.)

PLANNING AND CONTROLLING TECHNOLOGICAL GROWTH

The fourth and final characteristic of post-industrial society is an attempt to plan and control technological growth. When we examine the first three characteristics of a post-industrial society, we realize that it is an environment totally different from anything we have yet seen. It is a society in which highly educated people work in "think jobs" and in which a tremendous amount of money is spent each year on research and development, with much of the new knowledge being stored for future use. What will the year 2000 look like? The prospect scares many people and helps account for the fact that planning and control have now become important considerations. Without giving attention to monitoring our technological environment and deciding how we want it to grow, mankind faces a truly uncertain future. Toffler recognizes the challenge.

■ ■ ■ ■ ■ ■ ■ ■ ■ ■ ■ ■ ■ ■
THERE ARE ATTEMPTS TO PLAN AND CONTROL TECHNOLOGICAL GROWTH.

> Our first and most pressing need, therefore, before we can begin to gently guide our evolutionary destiny, before we can build a humane future, is to halt the runaway acceleration that

is subjecting multitudes to the threat of future shock while, at the very same moment, intensifying all the problems they must deal with—war, ecological incursions, racism, the obscene contrast between rich and poor, the revolt of the young, and the rise of a potentially deadly mass of irrationalism.[10]

As the external environment changes, the environment within organizations alters as well. Technology permeates the organization's boundaries, affecting not only the structure but the personnel as well.

TECHNOLOGY AND PEOPLE AT WORK

Technology has an effect on people at work for two reasons. First, technology is causing a change in people's values, which they bring to the work place with them. Second, technology is leading to changes in the work environment, from the machines people use in creating output and making decisions[11] to the way in which their offices and work stations are designed.[12] In analyzing this people–work environment–technology interface, we should consider five areas: (1) technology and work values, (2) alienation in the work place, (3) the fear of replacement by machine, (4) how workers feel about their jobs, and (5) the quality of work life issue. Before doing so, however, take the Time Out quiz on your job and you.

TECHNOLOGY AND WORK VALUES

Technology carries the connotation of efficiency. For example, new machines are brought into the work place because they can do the job faster than either the workers or the old machines. This emphasis on efficiency may have been one of the central themes of industrialism, but as we noted in our discussion of post-industrial societies, efficiency no longer occupies a central position.

The result is a discerning employee who believes that many of the organization's rules are outmoded and that its philosophy needs to be completely revised. One writer described typical young employees this way:

They tend to see themselves as basically rejecting the Calvinist Work Ethic, as being more honest, more open to new ideas and

・・・・・・・

[10] Toffler, *Future Shock*, p. 486.

[11] Eliezer Giesler, "Artificial Management and the Artificial Manager," *Business Horizons*, July–August 1986, pp. 17–21.

[12] "Ergonomics," *Personnel Journal*, June 1986, pp. 95–102.

TIME OUT

YOUR JOB AND YOU

This quiz is designed to examine the relationship you have with your job. How comfortable do you feel doing your work? What role is played by technology? After you read each statement, try to be as candid as possible in your answer. Interpretations are provided at the end of the chapter.

	HIGHLY DISAGREE	DISAGREE	INDIFFERENT	AGREE	HIGHLY AGREE
1. While you have certain things you have to do every work day or work week, you set the pace at which you work; management simply judges you on whether or not you have reached your overall objectives.	___	___	___	___	___
2. Basically, you do the same thing day after day, and the work is downright dull.	___	___	___	___	___
3. Your job is mentally challenging; it requires rigorous thought.	___	___	___	___	___
4. Your job is meaningless; anyone could do it and, to be quite frank, you are embarrassed when someone asks you what you do for a living.	___	___	___	___	___
5. On your job, you feel extremely tense and anxious, even though you may not know why.	___	___	___	___	___
6. There is virtually no chance for you to socialize on your job.	___	___	___	___	___
7. No matter how fast you work, there is always more to do; you can never get finished.	___	___	___	___	___
8. Your work environment is a very comfortable, enjoyable place; it is relaxing and encourages high productivity.	___	___	___	___	___
9. Your job requires a variety of skills, and people in the organization admit that it takes real talent to do what you do.	___	___	___	___	___
10. Face it, on your job you are a small cog in a big machine; if you cannot master the latest technology, the organization will find someone who can.	___	___	___	___	___

experimentation, more concerned with beauty, more interested in world events, more self-centered, more optimistic about the future, and less impressed with formal authority.

TECHNOLOGY CAN AFFECT VALUES.

The other kinds of changes they would like to see in society are: more participation in decisions that affect them, less emphasis on material things, more acceptance of other people's peculiarities, more emphasis on work being meaningful in its own right, and more freedom to do their own thing providing it doesn't hurt anybody.[13]

Most organizations would disagree with these ideas, believing that they would be detrimental to the enterprise at large.

FIRST CAME THE PROFIT-MAXIMIZING ERA.

Without addressing this thesis directly, let us note that management in the United States has witnessed three managerial phases. First, there was the era of **profit maximizing**, in which all decisions were directed toward making the greatest amount of money possible. Self-interest and the free market system were used in determining the most efficient allocation of resources. Underlying these basic values was a philosophy of hard work, competition, and the belief that the workers were merely factors of production. Some organizations today, especially small business firms, seem still to adhere to this model.

FOLLOWED BY TRUSTEESHIP MANAGEMENT.

During the Depression and the post-World War II period, many organizations made a transition to **trusteeship management**. In many cases, the owners were no longer the managers, and the organization became much more interested in its interface with society at large. Some of the values of trusteeship management are: consideration of employee needs for security, belonging, and recognition (the middle portions of Maslow's need hierarchy); a belief that the employee has rights to be respected; recognition of the importance of trading off profit for social good; and a decline in the support of the maxim of survival of the fittest. Most organizations still operate within the confines of this management philosophy.

AND QUALITY-OF-LIFE MANAGEMENT.

The most recent system to emerge is known as **quality-of-life management**. Continuing the trend established by the trusteeship management era, organizations operating with this philosophy believe that people must be managed more humanistically than ever before; profit is to be considered more as a means to an end than as an end itself; and there must be a trade-off between profit and responsibility to society and the workers. The values adhered to by these organizations include emphasis on cooperation between management and personnel, and redesign of work life so that it meets some of the demands the workers bring to the work place (job redesign is examined in greater depth in

·······

[13] Eugene Koprowski, "The Generation Gap, From Both Sides Now," *Management of Personnel Quarterly*, Winter 1969, p. 4.

TABLE 6.2	SOME UNDERLYING REASONS FOR VALUE CHANGES AMONG YOUNG PEOPLE	
THEY WERE:	**SO THEY:**
Raised in affluence	Take technological conveniences for granted
Physically more mature	Resent being treated as children
Raised on TV	Expect immediate action
	Have been exposed to masses of information
	Are aware of incongruities in society
	Respond to action rather than words
	Have been exposed to violence
Raised on protest	Are aware of injustice, poverty, and discrimination
	Have no live heroes

Chapter 8). While there is an emerging interest in this philosophy of work, quality-of-life management has not yet been widely accepted by American managers. We should note, however, that while most managers are operating in the trusteeship management stage, most of the incoming young workers are demanding a philosophy much closer to that of quality-of-life management. (See Table 6.2.) In short, the values of the organization and the personnel are growing farther and farther apart. The impact of technology in people's daily lives is encouraging them to seek a higher quality of life, but the impact of technology within the organization is being used to promote the trusteeship management philosophy. There appears to be a clash between the effects of technology on the personnel and on the organization!

STOP!

Review your answer to the second question and make any changes you would like. Then compare your answer to the one below.

2.   Is the company more interested in profit maximizing or quality of work life?

There are two answers to this question. It appears that the president is interested in profit maximizing although his comments could also be interpreted to mean that he is equally interested in the quality of work life. Pablo seems very interested in the personnel's quality of work life, although his directives from the boss indicate that profit maximizing must also remain a major concern. ∎

TECHNOLOGY AND ALIENATION

Of all the behavioral implications of technology, the most important seems to be that of alienation. This concept incorporates (1) powerlessness, (2) meaninglessness, (3) isolation, and (4) self-estrangement.

POWERLESSNESS   Many workers feel they are at the mercy of technology. Their sense of **powerlessness** can lead to alienation. Workers on the assembly line, for example, remain at their stations and the work comes to them. If the line is moving very fast, they have to work faster to accommodate it. Sometimes the speed of the line is so rapid that no one can keep up. In order to avoid getting in trouble, many workers come in early and begin building a backlog of stock for when they get behind. One management researcher worked on an assembly line for four months to study the quality of work life there. His first job consisted of installing stabilizer bars, which give the car stability in cornering. Try as he might, he was unable to install the bar in the allotted 75–80 seconds. Yet this was the time established for the job by engineering. Feeling powerless in his efforts to keep up, he complained to the foreman.

> After I had complained to the foreman about the difficulty of the job, and after other workers had also complained to both the foreman and the union committeeman, the company clocked the job. When the time study was completed, the company seemed surprised to discover what we had known all along— that the job required 150% of the time the engineers had allotted to it. No wonder I was always behind! The company then removed some of the tasks from the job, which made it slightly easier. The job was still difficult, however, and required building stock ahead of time each day.[14]

MEANINGLESSNESS   Many employees are unable to determine what they are doing or why they are doing it. Individuals who put a bolt on a widget, assemble two minor parts of a major system, or test a component that will be placed in a giant machine feel no relationship with the finished product. Technology helps create this **meaninglessness** through its emphasis on job specialization, as in assembly-line work.

How do workers adapt to these conditions? Some simply fail to show up for work. It is not uncommon to find assembly plants with manpower shortages when the hunting season opens. Those who do show up for

■ ■ ■ ■ ■ ■ ■ ■ ■ ■ ■ ■ ■ ■
TECHNOLOGY MAKES WORKERS FEEL AT THE MERCY OF TECHNOLOGY.

■ ■ ■ ■ ■ ■ ■ ■ ■ ■ ■ ■ ■ ■
IT CAN LEAD TO MEANINGLESS JOBS.

■ ■ ■ ■ ■ ■ ■

[14]John F. Runcie, "By Day I Make the Cars," *Harvard Business Review*, May–June 1980, pp. 107–108.

work often spend a large percentage of their workday playing mental games (doing multiplication tables in their mind) or daydreaming.

> Counting cars was one conscious method I used to pass the time; other methods came unconsciously. One time I realized I was doing my job to the rhythm of an aria from an opera I had heard the last weekend. Another time I found myself a thousand miles away, driving an imaginary automobile down a highway I had not been on in years. How many chassis went by during my mental lapses—and whether I even did my job—I don't know and never found out.[15]

ISOLATION   The individual becomes detached from society. People who find the clamor and pace of big-city life to be too much are now leaving with their families to seek isolation in the countryside. A few are going beyond and, far from civilization, setting up communes that offer their members a chance for a relaxed, slower-paced way of life. On the job people cannot run away from technology. If only to keep up with the competition, it is a part of their work life. Here, then, the individual is locked in, forced to cope with technology. However, there is still **isolation** in many cases, for the person is often confined to one locale, as in the case of a worker on an auto assembly line who must remain at a particular place on the line for the entire work day; a computer operator who has to stay near the machine, checking on jobs being run, and remaining alert for any machine malfunctions; or a press operator who is confined to the general area of the printing press, constantly observing the speed and feed of the paper, prepared to adjust or stop the machine should something go awry. All these people are isolated within a given area and, depending on the specific situation, isolated from other workers. At best, the technology allows them to interact only with those in their immediate vicinity; at worst, the demands of the job sometimes stop them from associating with anyone for extended periods of the work day.

■ ■ ■ ■ ■ ■ ■ ■ ■ ■ ■ ■ ■
IT CAN LEAD TO LONELINESS ON THE JOB.

SELF-ESTRANGEMENT   The worker can no longer find intrinsic satisfaction in what he or she is doing. The work becomes merely a means to earn a living. There is no fun or challenge associated with it. If another job offered more money, he or she would quit. Technology creates **self-estrangement** by reducing the scope and importance of the work itself. As we saw in Chapter 2 when we discussed Herzberg's two-factor theory, the things people liked best about their jobs were related to the work itself: they were intrinsic motivators, such as achievement, responsibility, and the possibility of growth. Technology eliminates many of these.

■ ■ ■ ■ ■ ■ ■ ■ ■ ■ ■ ■ ■
IT CAN RESULT IN THE ELIMINATION OF INTRINSIC MOTIVATION.

■ ■ ■ ■ ■ ■
[15] Ibid., p. 109.

Faunce has summed up much of what we have said about technology and alienation: [16]

> The most persistent indictment of industrial society is that it has resulted in the alienation of industrial man. Loneliness in the midst of urban agglomeration; loss of social anchorage in mass society; the absence of a predictable life trajectory in an era of unprecedented social change; and the powerlessness of man within the complex social, economic, and political systems he has created are common themes in the social criticism of the industrial way of life. [16]

Of course, not all workers suffer the negative effects of technology. Research reveals that some employees seem to experience little alienation. This is particularly true among workers in small-batch technology firms where small numbers of products are produced and in process-production companies such as oil refineries. Those in mass-production industries, however, do suffer alienation. After conducting a review of the literature in this area, Luthans has reported:

> Blauner studied four diverse technological situations—a print shop, a textile mill, an automobile assembly line and a highly automated chemical plant. He found that alienation was a direct function of the type of technology in operation. For example, in the automobile assembly line, alienation of the workers was widespread. On the other hand, in the chemical plant, which operated on a continuous-process form of technology, alienation was noticeably absent. The reasons given were that on the assembly line the workers were powerless and suffered from self-estrangement, whereas in the chemical plant the workers had meaningful jobs in which they had a great deal of responsibility and control. Thus, there is little doubt that technology has an effect on the alienation of workers, but it appears to be highly selective in nature. [17]

FEAR OF REPLACEMENT BY MACHINE

■ ■ ■ ■ ■ ■ ■ ■ ■ ■ ■ ■ ■ ■ ■

TECHNOLOGY CAN CAUSE FEAR OF JOB LOSS.

Another problem created by technology is the workers' fear that they will be replaced by machines. [18] This fear is typical among people who are not highly skilled or who are performing paperwork functions, such as checking forms, filling out structured reports, or entering data in accounting

■ ■ ■ ■ ■ ■ ■

[16] William A. Faunce, *Problems of an Industrial Society* (New York: McGraw-Hill Book Company, 1968), p. 84.

[17] Fred Luthans, *Organizational Behavior*, 2nd ed. (New York: McGraw-Hill Book Company, 1977), pp. 91–92.

[18] "Replaced by a Computer: An Interview with Nils Nilsson," *Whole Earth Software Review*, Spring 1984, pp. 116–121.

ledgers. All of them could possibly be replaced by a computer—and sometimes they are. Consider, for example, the insurance company that computerized most of its routine paper-processing tasks. Realizing that their jobs could be threatened by such a move, the workers sought to delay implementation of the machine while seeking transfers to other departments. The management assured the workers that all efforts would be made to find work in other units for any displaced persons, and within the first month of the machine's installation, 30 percent of the personnel were transferred to other units. However, this merely served to increase the anxiety among those remaining, who believed that there were fewer jobs available in the company for them.

> As one of them said, "You mark my words. There just aren't enough jobs in the company to absorb everyone. So it's just a matter of time before the company announces that it will be laying off some of us." The statement seemed to reflect the sentiments of the other members because at about this time the management noticed a decline in cooperation from these people. Both the managers and the systems engineers who were revising the work schedules found many of the workers unwilling to answer questions about their work assignments or providing only minimal information. In fact, one manager described the workers as "downright hostile." Another said, "They think they're going to be fired, so they're doing everything they can to screw us up."
>
> As a result it took three weeks longer than anticipated to get everything straightened out and transferred to the computer. Meanwhile, what about the personnel? Well, true to their fears, 20 per cent of the original department was laid off.[19]

Situations like this are typical in many organizations in which machines can be used in place of workers. The United States Post Office is another illustration. Years ago, a mail clerk stood before a bank of labeled pigeonholes called cells and quickly sorted the envelopes according to neighborhood, post-office branch, and even carrier route. At top speed, most could sort around 30 letters a minute or 1,800 an hour. If they were talking to one another, the rate would be slightly lower. Today much of this has changed. In many post offices around the country, the clerks no longer talk to one another, nor do they have control over the pace of their work. Now they sit with earphones clamped over their heads listening to prescribed radio programs, many of which play rock music that shuts out the noise around them and builds a psychological tempo that encourages them to sort the mail faster. In addition, there is a

· · · · · · ·

[19] Richard M. Hodgetts, *Management: Theory, Process and Practice* (Philadelphia: W. B. Saunders Co., 1975), pp. 417–418.

letter sorting machine that puts envelopes before them at the rate of 60 per minute or 3,600 an hour. In the second that the envelope is before the mail sorter, he or she taps a key, which assigns the envelope to one of the cubbyholes along a conveyor belt. In the old days, a good worker could sort mail into 77 different cells. The machine is not only twice as fast but more accurate as well.

While technology is inevitable, there are ways of dealing with it from a human relations standpoint. Human Relations in Action: Dealing with Technology describes some of them.

HOW WORKERS FEEL ABOUT THEIR JOBS

Despite the feelings of alienation which many workers find in their jobs, the effect of technology can be lived with. In fact, most workers report that there are many things they like about their jobs.

■ ■ ■ ■ ■ ■ ■ ■ ■ ■ ■ ■ ■ ■
THEY LIKE THE PAY AND BENEFITS.

One of the primary advantages is pay and benefits. A typical response to the question "How long do you intend to work for this company?" is "Until I retire." Many workers believe that given their education and training they could not do as well in another organization.

A second advantage is, despite their feelings of alienation, that the organization is a good place to work. For example, Runcie surveyed over 200 assembly-line workers and found that many of them had enough seniority to transfer to easier jobs in the plant. However, they did not want to do so. They liked their current jobs regardless of the problems that went along with them.

■ ■ ■ ■ ■ ■ ■ ■ ■ ■ ■ ■ ■ ■
BUT NOT SUPERVISORY
FAVORITISM.

On the other hand there are problems. As seen in Table 6.3, workers in one plant had some particular gripes including the need to take a day off, feelings that the supervisor did not treat everyone fairly, and the belief that who you knew was more important than how much you knew.

These findings are not surprising; nor are they limited to production plants. A survey among 400 research and development (R&D) managers found that over 60 percent wanted, among other things: (1) more time for innovative, substantive projects rather than routine R&D work; (2) more and better communication with their superiors about the objectives of R&D; and (3) more encouragement to develop new ideas into commercial realities.[20] The quality of work life in a high-tech environment is often less than ideal. This finding has been further reinforced by a recent survey which examined work satisfaction among a variety of different groups. The results, reported in Table 6.4, show that work satisfaction tends to be lowest among those who work in the most heavily technical areas and highest among those who work in highly nontechnical areas.

■ ■ ■ ■ ■ ■ ■

[20] Renato Tagiuri, "Work Changes Desired by R&D Managers," *Research Management*, September–October 1985, p. 24.

HUMAN RELATIONS IN ACTION

DEALING WITH TECHNOLOGY

Technology is making many jobs easier. At the same time it can cause concern among personnel who are convinced that computers, robots, or some other form of advanced technology will replace them. There is nothing that can be done to prevent the advance of technology. However, there are human relations steps that can be followed to help with the personnel challenge. Five of the most useful are these:

1. *Become familiar with the jobs that your people are doing.* This has two benefits. First, if new technology is to be introduced into the work, you will have a pretty good idea of what it can do. Second, most workers object to any changes that are likely to lead to their being displaced. If you understand how their jobs work, you are in a better position to help them confront this problem.

2. *Be aware of the negative impact technology can have.* When people become adjuncts of the machines they operate, their self-esteem and job satisfaction often drop. You cannot help your people deal with this problem until you realize that it is a common response to technology. It does no good to tell a person that his job is interesting if he does not see it that way. Try to empathize with those who are most affected by the impact of technology. Then you will be better able to help them adjust.

3. *Get worker input regarding how to use technology.* This is one of the most effective ways of introducing work changes. The personnel often have good ideas for using new machinery and equipment; after all, they are the ones who do the job. If there are any shortcuts that can be worked out, or problems in making the machine do what it is supposed to, they will find them. There is no better source for evaluating job technology than the workers themselves.

4. *Keep your people apprised of what is going on.* If you and your boss have been talking about putting in new automated machinery, tell this to the workers as soon as the decision is made. If you wait until the machines are delivered, the impact of the change will cause panic. You need to introduce change slowly. Sure, some of the workers may accuse you of trying to undermine their jobs and threaten to quit. However, most of the workers know that as manager it is your job to maintain high productivity, and if new machines are needed, they will have to be purchased.

5. *Be honest with your people.* Some workers will be displaced by new technology. This is particularly true of those doing simple jobs or unable to learn new work procedures. In many cases these people will be able to obtain work elsewhere in the organization. If this is not possible, be open with them and tell them that they are going to be laid off. No one likes to give people this kind of news but it is better to be honest with them so they can make plans than to keep them in the dark until the last minute. The way you treat workers who are being let go will influence the morale and trust of those who remain in the department. Honesty is always the best policy.

TABLE 6.3   HOW WORKERS FEEL ABOUT LIFE IN THE PLANT*

	YES	NO	UNCERTAIN
Do you have to take a day off every once in a while?	54.3%	43.3%	2.4%
Is absenteeism a big problem in the plant?	86.1	9.1	4.8
Do you ever drink at lunchtime?	40.4	59.6	—
Have you ever gotten high while working on the line?	32.7	66.3	—
Have you seen others in the plant get high while working on the line?	50.9	49.1	—
Do you think it's not important how much you know but who you know that counts?	78.4	12.0	9.6
Does your supervisor treat everyone fairly?	43.8	48.1	8.2
Would the company be better off without a union?	2.9	88.0	9.1

---

*These are only some of the attitudinal questions used in the larger research project. In the questionnaire, attitudes were measured on a five-point scale rather than on the three-point scale shown here, and the percentages represent only those workers who actually answered each question.

Note: Several of the statements presented to the workers have been edited into question form for this article, but the substance remains the same.

Source: Reprinted by permission of the *Harvard Business Review*. An exhibit from "By Day I Make the Cars" by John F. Runcie (May–June 1980). Copyright © 1980 by the President and Fellows of Harvard College; all rights reserved.

TABLE 6.4   OVERALL WORK SATISFACTION

OCCUPATIONAL GROUP	NUMBER OF RESPONDENTS	AVERAGE SCORE*
Factory worker	249	2.57
Police officer	440	2.81
Factory foreman	68	2.85
Registered nurse	342	2.81
Administrative personnel	167	3.10
University faculty	169	3.17
Elementary school teachers	108	3.18

---

*Rankings were on a scale of 1 (lowest) to 5 (highest)

Source: Clifford J. Mottaz, "Work Satisfaction among Hospital Nurses," *Hospital & Health Services Administration*, Spring 1988, p. 61.

THE QUALITY OF WORK LIFE ISSUE

A major sociotechnical issue is the quality of work life (QWL). QWL is concerned with the overall work climate, with specific attention on: (1) the effect of work on both people and organizational effectiveness and (2) worker satisfaction in organizational problem solving and decision making.[21] For example, employees who work in large batch or mass production technology have the highest reported levels of alienation. However, these workers also seem to be at a loss in determining what can be done. Runcie reports that, "Workers see only a few places where changes . . . would be effective."[22] Examples include better manufactured parts that meet all design specifications and more objective (no favoritism) supervision.

Additionally, when management and workers have formed QWL committees, there has not been very active support from the employees. Many workers distrust these types of joint committees, believing that, in the long run, the only change will be to speed up the assembly line. A number of managers also feel that these committees are of no real value. The result is a stereotyped view of the workers.

THEY DISTRUST QWL COMMITTEES.

> The technology of the assembly line fosters the idea that the people should be like the products rolling off the line. All the workers should think the same, act the same, do the same things. When a person comes along who does not play by the rules and wants simply to be seen as an individual, the members of the system react to bring the person back to the norm. But no one person totally fits the mold. Everyone is different and people can only adapt so far. Maybe how they are treated has to change. Some supervisors, union officials, and workers realize this— but sadly, not enough do.[23]

What then is the answer in dealing with sociotechnical problems? One part of the solution is the use of job enrichment and other redesign techniques discussed in the next chapter. Another part of the answer must be found in the industrial environment itself. In many European countries industrial democracy is used. In the United States participative management is more prevalent. Both offer possibilities for meeting the sociotechnical challenge.

STOP!

Review your answer to the third question and make any changes you would like. Then compare your answer to the one below.

3.   In what way is technology causing alienation?

·······

[21] Fred Luthans, *Organizational Behavior*, 5th edition (New York: McGraw-Hill Book Company, 1989), p. 273.

[22] Runcie, "By Day I Make the Cars," p. 111.

[23] Ibid., p. 115.

The technology is resulting in powerlessness. Notice that the personnel feel that they are just small cogs in a big machine and that they do not count. They want to get more actively involved in the production of the product. ■

MEETING THE SOCIOTECHNICAL CHALLENGE

The dysfunctional effects of technology can be traced, in large part, to the fears it creates among the personnel. Human relations management requires that the employees' interests be both considered and protected by management. The workers need to feel confident that in the long run they will gain from technology. In other words, there must be a supportive climate between the personnel and the management. If this climate can be created, the workers will be more receptive to the changes being thrust upon them by technology. Two alternatives to attaining this objective are industrial democracy and participative management.

INDUSTRIAL DEMOCRACY AND PARTICIPATIVE MANAGEMENT

The two major trends in management-worker relations over the last 25 years are those of industrial democracy and participative management. Both involve shared decision making between the workers and management. However, despite their similarity of intent, there are fundamental differences in their methods. **Industrial democracy** is a formal, and usually legally sanctioned, arrangement of worker representation in the form of committees, councils, and boards at various levels of decision making. **Participative management**, on the other hand, is an informal style of face-to-face leadership in which management and workers share decision making in the work place. It is sometimes called *shop-floor democracy*. Some countries of the world make more use of one than the other.

■ ■ ■ ■ ■ ■ ■ ■ ■ ■ ■ ■ ■
INDUSTRIAL DEMOCRACY IS
LEGALLY SANCTIONED.

■ ■ ■ ■ ■ ■ ■ ■ ■ ■ ■ ■
PARTICIPATIVE MANAGEMENT IS
INFORMAL IN NATURE.

GERMANY   In Germany, for example, companies with more than 500 workers have supervisory boards that set company policy. These boards are two-thirds shareholder representatives and one-third worker representatives. Firms with more than 2,000 employees have 50 percent worker representation on these boards. By law, industrial democracy is a way of life in Germany. German workers also have much more operating authority than do American workers. For example, the workers are allowed to rotate jobs to prevent the work from becoming boring. Some firms even allow their workers to vary the number of hours they work throughout the year. They can work less during some months as long as they work more during other months. One individual, explaining how the concept was used in an insurance company, noted:

. . . management worked with the staff to develop a monthly accounting system by which an employee did not have to work a fixed number of hours per month. . . . management came to an agreement with employees whereby daily and weekly hours could be chosen rather freely, although employees were warned not to ignore the necessities of their particular jobs. The result was that employees worked less when there was less work to be done or when they wanted time off, and worked more when the work had to be done.[24]

One of the primary reasons for the high degree of participative management in Germany is that the unions and management have a much more cooperative relationship than in the United States. The two sides try to work out their differences in a way that is beneficial to both.

SCANDINAVIA   In the Scandinavian countries—Norway, Sweden, and Denmark—there are also statutory requirements regarding worker representation on governing boards. For example, for almost 40 years Sweden has required that companies with more than 50 employees have work councils with representatives from management and labor which meet regularly to solve problems and exchange information.

> INDUSTRIAL DEMOCRACY IS PREVALENT.

However, Scandinavians also lead the way in terms of shop-floor democracy. In some of their factories autonomous work groups have been introduced. These groups have decision-making discretion that allows them to determine for themselves how to do their jobs. Their range of authority often extends from the receipt of orders to final inspection. These groups consist of councils and committees that have been formed to encourage employee involvement in identifying and implementing changes that will improve work place ambience and help sustain high morale and positive employee attitudes.[25]

> AS IS PARTICIPATIVE MANAGEMENT.

BRITAIN   The United Kingdom and Ireland are the only countries in the European community that do not have statutory requirements for information dissemination, consultation, or worker representation on boards. However, this appears to be changing. Current legislative efforts are likely to require that firms with more than 500 people discuss all major proposals affecting the workers with their trade union representatives. The government also believes that employees should have a right of representation on the boards of their companies. Some organizations

> INDUSTRIAL DEMOCRACY IS INCREASING.

[24] Bernhard Terlet, "Flexiyear Schedules in Germany," *Personnel Journal*, June 1982, p. 428.
[25] For more on this see Richard M. Hodgetts and Galen Kroeck, *Personnel/Human Resource Management* (Chicago: SRA, 1990), Chapter 21; and Ron Zemke, "Scandinavian Management—A Look at Our Future?" *Management Review*, July 1988, pp. 44–47.

are already moving to meet these recommendations. For example, the post office has expanded its board of directors from 7 to 19. Seven of the representatives are from management, seven are from trade union members, two are independents chosen from a list submitted by the government minister responsible for the post office, two are members who represent the consumers' interests, and the last is a chief executive from the management side.

THE UNITED STATES   In the United States participative management and industrial democracy have both developed. The former, if only because of the American traditions of individualism and democracy, always has been very popular. However, industrial democracy is also gaining in importance.

▪▪▪▪▪▪▪▪▪▪▪▪▪
PARTICIPATIVE MANAGEMENT IS POPULAR.

In the early 1970s General Foods opened a pet-food plant in Topeka, Kansas, and designed the facilities so that things could be run with a minimum of supervision. The workers took over many of the traditional management tasks including interviewing job applicants, assigning jobs, and deciding pay raises. The result was that commitment and satisfaction among the workers dramatically increased.

Yet, industrial democracy is also quite present in the United States. By the early 1920s paternalistic firms had elected bodies of worker representatives who had some input regarding management decisions. More recently companies like the Eaton Corporation have begun employing the concept. Overall, however, industrial democracy has not made the inroads in the United States that it has in Europe. Yet the concept has important value in helping management meet the sociotechnical challenge.

Increased employee involvement in decisions that directly affect their jobs is an important objective at General Motors. This participative management approach is expected to bring higher levels of quality and operational effectiveness.

MATCHING THE APPROACH AND THE SITUATION

Should organizations use greater participative management, more industrial democracy, or a combination of the two? The answer will depend on both the country and the specific situation. For example, research reveals that Americans tend to like a participative approach much more than do other cultures. Table 6.5 shows that over 50 percent of the American subordinates in a major research study reported satisfaction in decision-making situations with a participative supervisor. Additionally, this research study reported that Americans, more than any other group, felt they profited from self-planning.

Several reasons can be offered for this. Sense of accomplishment may be greater when executing one's own plan rather than the assigned plan. There may be more commitment to see the validity of a plan by executing it successfully and more confidence that it can be done. Understanding of the plan is likely

TABLE 6.5	**REPORTED SATISFACTION OF SUBORDINATES FOLLOWING DECISION MAKING WITH PARTICIPATIVE SUPERIORS**

NUMBER	CULTURE	PERCENT OF SUBORDINATES MOST SATISFIED IN DECISION-MAKING MEETINGS WITH PARTICIPATIVE SUPERVISOR
65	Dutch-Flemish	64.7
50	Nordic: Danish, Norwegian, Swedish, Austrian, West German, German-Swiss	56.4
202	Anglo-Americans: British-Northern Irish, American, Australian	53.1
179	Latin: Brazilian, Colombian, French, Italian, Spanish, French-Swiss, Walloon	52.6
28	Japanese	50.0
37	Indian	29.4

Source: Adapted from Wayne F. Cascio, "Functional Specialization, Culture, and Preference for Participative Management," *Personnel Psychology*, Winter 1974, p. 599.

Reprinted with permission.

to be greater. Human resources may be better utilized. There may be a perception of more flexibility and more room for modification and initiative to make improvements in an assigned plan. There are likely to be fewer communication problems and consequent errors and distortions in pursuing instructions. Finally, competitive feelings aroused between planners and those who must execute the plans are avoided because planners and doers are the same persons.[26]

American firms doing business in the states are likely to find a participative management approach of great value in meeting the sociotechnical challenge. In overseas countries, industrial democracy must be heavily relied upon. However, this is not an either-or situation. America has exported participative management to the world and is now beginning to import some of the industrial democracy practices from abroad. The result is an emerging mutual support between participative management and industrial democracy. The eventual key to whether this support will continue rests in the degree to which participative management brings about self-planning in the organization. As Bass and Shackleton have noted, "Self-planning is the key to the complementarity of participative management and industrial democracy."[27] As technology

·······

[26] Bernard M. Bass and V. J. Shackleton, "Industrial Democracy and Participative Management: A Case for Synthesis," *Academy of Management Review*, October 1979, p. 395.

[27] Ibid., p. 400.

TABLE 6.6   ISSUES THAT CAN BE DEALT WITH BEST BY INDUSTRIAL DEMOCRACY, PARTICIPATIVE MANAGEMENT, OR BOTH

ISSUES	INDUSTRIAL DEMOCRACY	PARTICIPATIVE MANAGEMENT	REASON
Pay benefits	Yes	No	Principles of equity, company finances, need to avoid maximizing self-interest.
Job satisfaction	No	Yes	Participative management will directly improve.
Career development	Yes	Yes	Broad policies need to be set at higher levels, but career planning is best as self-planning.
Working conditions: sociotechnical issues	Yes	Yes	Plant-wide problems and community affairs are best dealt with by council and staff. On the other hand, changes may be instituted and implemented best through participation in the decision process at the local level.
Job security	Yes	Yes	Market conditions and finance of the firm as a whole require organization-wide attention. Yet some commitment to strategies, such as sharing reductions in hours, can be best accomplished at local levels via participative endeavor.

Source: Bernard M. Bass and V. J. Shackleton. "Industrial Democracy and Participative Management: A Case for Synthesis," *Academy of Management Review*, October 1979, p. 401. Reprinted with permission.

■ ■ ■ ■ ■ ■ ■ ■ ■ ■ ■ ■ ■ ■
THE TWO APPROACHES CAN HELP
MEET THE SOCIOTECHNICAL
CHALLENGE.

advances the worker will have to take over more and more of the industrial process.

Can industrial democracy and participative management help organizations deal with sociotechnical issues? Researchers, in particular, argue that it can do this and more. As seen in Table 6.6, the development of both areas can be helpful in dealing with a large range of modern industrial problems from sociotechnical issues to pay and benefits, job satisfaction, career development, and/or job security.

The primary way in which the sociotechnical challenge is being met currently is through the use of job enrichment and job design. These topics are the focus of our attention in the next chapter.

STOP!

Review your answer to the fourth question and make any changes you would like. Then compare your answer to the one below.

4.   Is Pablo's use of committees an example of industrial democracy or participative management? Explain.

Pablo's use of committees is an example of participative management. Industrial democracy calls for a sharing of formal power between management and the workers. Quite often it results in the personnel having seats on the board of directors. In this case the workers are being given a greater role to play in producing the products. They are being allowed to participate more actively. ■

SUMMARY

Technology has gone through five stages. The first was the handicraft era, in which people made things by hand. Next came the mechanization era, characterized by machine labor replacing human labor. This was followed by the mechanistic technology stage, as seen in the case of the early auto assembly lines. Next came automated technology, in which assembly-line machines were linked together in such a way that many functions were performed automatically. At present a fifth stage, cybernated technology, is emerging, in which machines are running and controlling other machines.

These technological breakthroughs have been possible because large amounts of money are being spent annually on R&D and because more and more members of our society are attaining higher levels of education. When these R&D funds and highly educated people are brought together, the result is an accelerative thrust from which more and more goods and services can be produced at an ever-increasing rate. At the same time, the United States has entered the stage of post-industrialism, which is characterized by: (1) a service-oriented work force, (2) a dynamic increase in the number of professional and technical workers, (3) an increase in the importance of theoretical knowledge, and (4) the planning and controlling of technological growth.

In the work place, technology has some specific effects on the personnel. First, the values they bring to the work place are changing, because technology is affecting their daily lives. People now reject the work ethic, are less impressed with formal authority, and demand more participation in decisions that affect them. Within the organization, technology is leading to a more structured environment that rejects these basic values. This results in a clash between the types of values promoted by technology in the external environment and those developed by it in the internal (work) environment.

Technology is causing alienation in the work place. This alienation is taking a number of different forms, including powerlessness, meaninglessness, isolation, and self-estrangement.

Additionally, technology is causing some workers to fear they will be replaced by machines. This is particularly true among those who are not highly skilled or who are performing paperwork functions that can be handled by computers.

Despite these feelings, many workers find life in a modern factory quite livable. In particular, they like the pay and benefits and, to a large extent, seem unclear as to how the quality of work life could be improved.

One way in which the sociotechnical problem is being addressed is through participative management practices. A second way, which seems to be gaining in favor, is the use of industrial democracy.

KEY TERMS IN THE CHAPTER

sociotechnical systems	trusteeship management
future shock	quality-of-life management
handicraft era	powerlessness
mechanization era	meaninglessness
mechanistic technology	isolation
automated technology	self-estrangement
cybernated technology	industrial democracy
post-industrial society	participative management
profit-maximizing management	

REVIEW AND STUDY QUESTIONS

1.   What was the basic characteristic of the handicraft era? What was the basic characteristic of the mechanization era? How does mechanistic technology differ from automated technology? How does automated technology differ from cybernated technology? Explain.

2.   Alvin Toffler has said, "If technology is to be regarded as a great engine, a mighty accelerator, then knowledge must be regarded as its fuel. And thus we come to the crux of the accelerative process in society, for the engine is being fed a richer and richer fuel every day." What is meant by this statement?

3.   What are the four characteristics of a post-industrial society? Describe each.

4.   How did the prevailing ethic change as mankind progressed from the handicraft era, to the mechanization and assembly-line eras, to the post-industrial era? Explain.

5.   Which needs, in Maslow's need hierarchy, are considered to be most important in the handicraft era? The mechanization and assembly-line eras? The post-industrial era?

6.   The impact of technology on people's daily lives is encouraging them to seek a higher quality of life, but the impact of technology within the organization is being used to promote the trusteeship management philosophy. What is meant by this statement?

7.   How can technology cause powerlessness, meaninglessness, isolation, and self-estrangement? Discuss each condition separately.

8.   How does technology lead personnel to fear replacement by machines? Explain.

9.   The major step the modern organization must take in integrating technology and people is to determine the effect that technology is likely to have and to develop a plan for reducing its dysfunctional effects. What is meant by this statement?

10.   What role can be played by industrial democracy and participative management? Explain.

TIME OUT ANSWERS: INTERPRETATION OF YOUR JOB AND YOU

This quiz is designed to measure the effect that the technological surroundings of your job have on you. Keeping in mind that there are five possible responses to each statement, here is the way to score each:

	HIGHLY DISAGREE	DISAGREE	INDIFFERENT	AGREE	HIGHLY AGREE
1.	−2	−1	0	1	2
2.	2	1	0	−1	−2
3.	−2	−1	0	1	2
4.	2	1	0	−1	−2
5.	2	1	0	−1	−2
6.	2	1	0	−1	−2
7.	2	1	0	−1	−2
8.	−2	−1	0	1	2
9.	−2	−1	0	1	2
10.	2	1	0	−1	−2

If you have a positive score, the impact of technology and stress on your job is not at all negative. In fact, you are doing quite well in beating the dysfunctional effects of technology and stress. A score of 4 or better is a very good sign. Conversely, a score of −4 or less indicates that technology and job-created stress is getting to you. A score of −7 or less is a sign that you should consider switching jobs.

CASE: THE OLD VERSUS THE NEW

Sue Ryan was a secretary at Wilshire Community College for three years. During this time she received three salary raises and was now at the top of her salary range.

Sue enjoyed working at Wilshire because the work was not extremely demanding, and she liked the interaction with both the faculty and her fellow workers. However, one day she realized that if she remained at the college she would never increase her salary more than five to seven percent a year. This dismayed Sue, because she had just bought a new car and had been hoping to vacation in Europe with some school friends next year. With her current salary, she could afford the car but not the trip.

Then she learned that a new factory had opened in town. The plant was owned and managed by a national corporation, which had decided to assemble some of its consumer products in the area. According to a newspaper ad she read, the starting salary for assemblers was 25 percent higher than her current salary, and there was a guaranteed cost-of-living raise.

Sue decided to find out more about the job. She went to the company's personnel office, talked to someone about the job qualifications, and learned that in addition to what she knew already, there was also a very good medical and pension plan—far better than what was in effect at the community college. After giving the matter serious thought, Sue decided to quit her secretary's job and go to work for the assembly plant.

For the first four weeks things went quite well. Sue was so busy trying to master her job and keep up with the speed of the line that she had little time to think about anything else. At night she was so tired that she went right home and fell into bed. However, as she began to gain control of the job and to learn some of the shortcuts, Sue realized that her job was quite different from the one she had at the college. For one thing, there was no one working very close to her. The nearest person was 35 feet away, and because of the machine noise, Sue had to almost shout if she wanted to talk to the woman. In addition, the line was moving so fast that Sue really did not have time for any extended talking. It was all she could do to keep up.

As the next few months passed Sue began to reevaluate her decision. She realized that while the assembly line job certainly paid well, it was not very enjoyable work. In fact, she disliked it. As a result, at the end of the fourth month, she called her former boss at Wilshire and asked if she could return to the community college. He told her she could, and two weeks later Sue resigned her job at the assembly plant. As she went into the personnel department to pick up her paycheck and sign some termination papers, she noticed that she was not alone. Seven other women were also terminating their employment that day. On the way out she heard one of the personnel people saying into the phone, "I don't know what the problem is over here, but we've got a turnover rate of almost 40 percent and we haven't been operating six months yet."

QUESTIONS

1.   What did Sue dislike about her assembly line job? Incorporate into your answer a discussion of alienation.

2.   What particular features of her old job do you think enticed Sue to return to the community college?

3.   How can the assembly plant deal with the problem of high turnover? Explain. ■

CASE: THE SILENCE WAS DEAFENING

The county manager's office used to be a hub of noisy activity. One reason was because a secretarial pool of five typists used to be located in an area to the right of the manager's desk. Anyone entering the large office would be greeted with the clacking of typewriters and the typically loud conversations going on among the group members. Quite often the typists knew the person who had entered the office, and there would be a friendly exchange of greetings. The pool of typists was generally regarded as below average in performance, but an extremely friendly, highly cohesive group.

Six months ago the county manager resigned. The new manager, Jose Gonzalez, was hired from outside. Jose had been an assistant city manager in a large metropolitan area. He had five years experience in this position and was, in the view of the county commissioners who hired him, just the individual to whip the county into sound financial shape. Jose's expertise is in the finance area, and he quickly set about axing what he felt were costly and inefficient programs. The county zoo's budget was cut by 15 percent, the bus system's budget was reduced by 12.5 percent, and an all-county hiring freeze was enacted. These efficiency measures even extended into the county manager's office.

Under a new organizational arrangement, Jose had all of the typists placed in a separate room away from the main office. The typists were then given word-processing training and their work assignments were changed. Instead of just typing material associated with the county manager's office, they were assigned work from many different departments. "With their new word-processing skills," Jose explained, "they'll be able to do a lot more work than before and now that they are out of the limelight of the central office, they will have fewer distractions."

Since these changes went into effect, there has been a dramatic turnover in the typing pool. Two of the typists have quit, and one of the others has transferred to another department. The office manager, Sara

Fonetella, was asked by Jose to find out what the problem is in keeping word-processing people. Sara decided that the easiest way to handle this assignment, and not get personally involved in the conflict, would be to interview the current word-processing personnel. She did and then wrote a two-page memo to Jose. Here is what part of the memo said:

> The word-processing people do not like the new office arrangement. They are located in a very small room that they find to be confining. The work is boring and their opportunities to talk to each other are limited because there is a never-ending flow of work. The word-processing individuals who have been here the longest feel that it was unfair to move the typing pool from the outer office without consulting with them and giving them some voice in the decision. They also feel that the only reason the typists were trained in word processing was to increase their work output. No consideration was given to how these changes would affect them psychologically.
>
> My overall impression of the word-processing group is that the turnover will continue to be high. The work is boring, the personnel have no personal power over their jobs, and most of them feel isolated and alone. When they were in the outer office, there was a feeling of togetherness; this no longer exists. If we do not reorganize the work, this situation is going to continue.

QUESTIONS

1.   What are some of the problems that the workers are encountering as a result of the new technology and work arrangement? Identify and discuss three of them.

2.   Could a participative management approach have helped prevent these problems? Explain.

3.   What would you recommend doing to help correct the problem? What human relations steps would you suggest? Explain. ■

EXPERIENCING TECHNOLOGY EVOLUTION

PURPOSE

- To understand the evolution of technology from the handicraft era to the cybernated technology stage.
- To examine the work ethic underlying each stage of technology.

PROCEDURE

1.   The class is divided into five groups, each representing one of the eras of technology: handicraft, mechanization, mechanistic, automated, or cybernated. Discuss the nature of work in your era. Describe the work ethic of the times. What values would be most appropriate for the era? What type of employee would you want to hire?

2.   In turn, each group, starting with the handicraft era and proceeding onward, describes its findings.

3.   As a class, discuss the current "work ethic." What are its characteristics? What problems can we foresee as we enter the cybernated technology era?

7
CHAPTER

PRODUCTIVITY AND QUALITY IMPROVEMENT

GOALS OF THE CHAPTER

Two of the major objectives of modern organizations are to increase productivity and to improve quality. At first blush these may appear to be goals that can be achieved with improved technology. However, this is only one side of the coin. The other side is the people who must use this new technology. Without their support and assistance, the organization will not achieve these two goals.

The first goal of this chapter is to examine the nature of the productivity and quality challenges facing America. The second goal is to examine some of the methods being used to attack the problem directly. The third goal is to study some of the participative management approaches that are useful in improving productivity and quality. The fourth goal is to review two of the new philosophical approaches that are being considered in management's overall effort to achieve productivity and quality improvement.

When you have finished reading all of the material in this chapter, you will be able to:

1. Describe the current status and future directions of management efforts to improve productivity and quality.

2. Discuss how a quality circle works and its value in increasing both productivity and quality.

3. Explain why no-smoking regulations are important to improved productivity.

4. Relate the value of alternative work arrangements and effective organization design to increased productivity and quality.

5. Define the term *intrapreneurship* and relate its value to improved organizational productivity and quality.

6. Compare and contrast the American and Japanese approaches to management and explain the benefits of adopting some of the Japanese practices.

OPENING CASE

GO FOR IT

Johnson's, a large retail chain in the Northeast, has been growing at an annual rate of 22.4 percent. The chain has been particularly effective because of its locations and competitive prices. Johnson's has 25-year leases in a large number of shopping malls that are located in rapidly growing rural areas. Recent research by the marketing department reveals that the company is doing a very good job of attracting new customers, but is having some trouble keeping old customers. Ten percent of those who shop at Johnson's report that they are displeased with the service and, if there is a nearby store with competitive prices, they will shop there rather than come back to Johnson's.

The senior management staff at Johnson's has decided to take steps to correct this problem. In particular, they believe that store managers should begin putting together quality circles and and using these to identify and address problem areas. "If we intend to give better customer service, we have to start with the people who are directly providing this service," the president of the firm contends. Top management would like to take a series of additional steps to improve overall efficiency. One step is to eliminate smoking at both the stores and the central management offices. Management believes this will increase work productivity and reduce operating expenses. Management also would like to see the stores experiment with flexible work schedules such as changing the workweek from five 8-hour days to four 10-hour days. "I think this could increase morale and boost our bottom-line performance," notes the vice-president of operations. Top management also would like to see an increase in the average span of control at the store level. They believe this will increase the average worker's responsibility and motivation. Finally, management would like to see the training department offer a course in intrapreneurship. "If we can get everyone to act like an in-house entrepreneur," notes the president, "we'll have the best work force in the industry. Morale will soar, customer service will increase, and our profitability will be the envy of Wall Street. Of course, these changes are going to take a lot of effort, but I think they're well worth the time and effort they will require. It's an investment that is well justified. I say, go for it!"

1.   How does a quality circle work? Could it be used to improve customer relations?

2.   Will the elimination of smoking increase productivity?

3.   What are three factors that should be considered in deciding whether or not to expand the average span of control?

4.   How can intrapreneurship be promoted? Offer three recommendations.

Write down your answers to these questions and put them aside. We will return to them later. ■

THE PRODUCTIVITY AND QUALITY CHALLENGES

Productivity is typically measured by the equation: output/input. Beginning in the mid-1970s the United States began to feel the effects of growing productivity from foreign competition. The Japanese and Germans, in particular, began making more effective use of their labor and other resources and thus producing output at a lower cost per unit than many American firms. Japanese manufacturing companies, for example, were able to produce autos at $2,000–3,000 per car below the cost per car of their American competitors. In the international services arena, increased productivity was evident in the form of lower prices and better service in the airline, hotel, and restaurant industries, to name but three. Quite obviously the United States was falling behind in terms of productivity growth. America needed to focus more attention on increasing output (goods and services) and/or lowering input (salaries, wages, benefits, materials, machinery, and equipment).

PRODUCTIVITY IS EQUAL TO OUTPUT/INPUT.

At the same time, quality became a major issue. Auto firms found that quality was more important than price in consumer purchase decisions. Airlines started discovering that equipment safety and on-time arrivals, two major quality issues, were becoming two of the most critical factors for customers deciding which airline to fly. Hospitals found that high quality service was becoming critical in meeting patient expectations and competitive pressures from other health care outlets. Similarly, restaurants were discovering that service was often more important than price. During this same time period, one major research study found that, "Businesses that improved quality increased their market share five or six times faster than those whose products declined in quality, and three times faster than those whose relative quality was similar to their competitors."[1] Obviously, something had to be done.

QUALITY IS A MAJOR ISSUE.

[1]Y. K. Shetty, "Product Quality and Competitive Strategy," *Business Horizons*, May–June 1987, p. 50.

American Airlines has established a Quality Assurance Department to stimulate excellence in every aspect of the airline's operation. To help avoid frustrating delays or flight cancellations due to equipment problems, American's mechanics strive to keep their aircraft in perfect working order.

CURRENT STATUS, FUTURE DIRECTIONS

At the present time, the United States is working hard to increase both productivity growth and quality. Figure 7.1 shows that many American companies are raising their hourly output. However, since the competition is doing the same, this means that the United States will have to continue its efforts. In particular, as seen in Figure 7.2, the service industry is falling far behind manufacturing in terms of productivity.

How can American firms meet this challenge? To a large extent that answer is found in the use of effective human relations practices. These practices can take a variety of forms, but they have one thing in common: They help the organization increase its output and/or lower its input. One of the most obvious steps is that of reducing the number of organizational personnel. If an organization can trim its work force by 10 percent while maintaining current output, the enterprise will increase productivity. Unfortunately, this strategy can have negative effects. A reduction in the work force will often result in a decline in worker morale followed by a drop in output. So the strategy can backfire.

A second common strategy is to introduce new machinery and equipment and thus help people work more efficiently. However, this strategy also has its down side in terms of human relations. Quite often the personnel will believe that the new capital equipment will be used to replace

---

FIGURE 7.1   HOW COMPETITIVE IS AMERICAN BUSINESS?

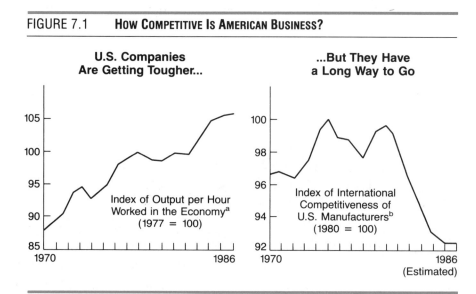

[a] Data: Data Resources Inc.

[b] Based on worldwide market share. Data: Paul R. Krugman.

Source: Reprinted from October 5, 1987, issue of *Business Week* by special permission, copyright © 1987 by McGraw-Hill, Inc.

FIGURE 7.2   SERVICES FALL FAR BEHIND MANUFACTURING IN PRODUCTIVITY

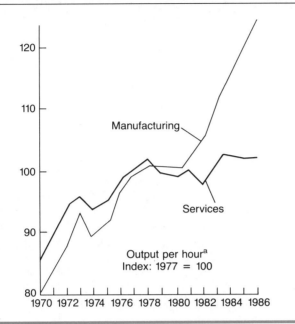

^aData: American Productivity Center, BW.

Source: *Business Week*, April 5, 1987, p. 55. Reprinted with permission of Roger J. Gorman.

them, so they fight implementation. Or they believe that the machinery will require them to do more work than before. In either event, there is resistance from the personnel.

There are a number of ways in which organizations deal with the human relations challenges accompanying productivity and quality efforts. These typically coordinate a concern for both people and work.[2] Mischkind, for example, has suggested seven steps in creating systematic productivity improvement. (See Figure 7.3.)

■ ■ ■ ■ ■ ■ ■ ■ ■ ■ ■ ■ ■
STEPS FOR CREATING SYSTEMATIC
PRODUCTIVITY IMPROVEMENT.

1.   Develop an effective communication system that involves communication between all levels of the hierarchy.

2.   Set goals that are clear, challenging, and inspirational.

3.   Have the necessary infrastructure of people, technology, and finance needed to achieve the predetermined goals.

4.   Create a desire within the personnel to pursue the goals.

■ ■ ■ ■ ■ ■ ■

[2]Roland A. Dumas, Nancy Cushing, and Carol Laughlin, "Making Quality Circle Theories Workable," *Training and Development Journal*, February 1987, pp. 30–33.

FIGURE 7.3   **Systematic Productivity Improvement**

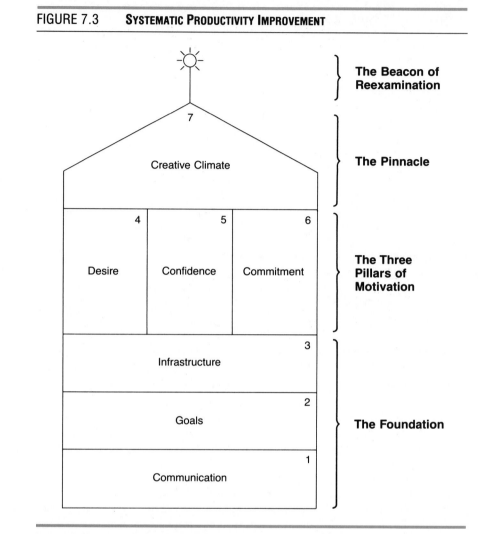

5.   Give people caring and coaching and thus build their self-confidence.

6.   Create commitment by helping the personnel deal with any problems that arise.

7.   Maintain a creative climate within which the people function.[3]

· · · · · · ·

[3]Louis Mischkind, "Seven Steps to Productivity Improvement," *Personnel*, July 1987, pp. 22–30.

The remainder of this chapter examines some of the major human relations approaches that are proving to be effective in handling the productivity/quality challenge.

ATTACKING THE PROBLEM DIRECTLY

There are some steps that can be taken to attack the problem directly. Two of the most common are the use of quality control circles and the elimination of smoking on the job.

QUALITY CIRCLES

A **quality circle** is a group of five to ten well-trained employees and a team leader that study job-related problems and make recommendations for improvements. Over the last 10 years, individuals and organizations interested in improving productivity and quality have turned to the use of these circles. Some of the best-known organizations using them include General Electric, Honeywell, Lockheed, and the federal government.

■ ■ ■ ■ ■ ■ ■ ■ ■ ■ ■ ■ ■
A QUALITY CIRCLE FOCUSES ON MAKING RECOMMENDATIONS FOR IMPROVEMENT.

GETTING THEM STARTED   The objective of a quality circle is to improve productivity, increase quality, and/or raise morale—all at a relatively low cost.[4] While some circles have slightly different approaches, most work the same way. The circle will focus on production or service problems that fall within its scope of work. In most cases the circle will undertake a project that can be handled within a three- to six-month time frame. During this time, the group will meet for an hour or two each week to study a problem that the members have identified. Typical examples include production bottlenecks, quality control problems, improperly designed parts, and inadequate service procedures. Circle members will then suggest steps that should be undertaken to correct the problems. If these steps can be taken by the members of the circle, they implement their own suggestions. If the problem is more comprehensive in nature, the members often confine themselves to recommendations. In any event, a solution is eventually identified and implemented. Commenting on their use in Japan, Ouchi, who has gained an international reputation for his study of Japanese management, has noted that:

■ ■ ■ ■ ■ ■ ■ ■ ■ ■ ■ ■ ■
CIRCLES MEET WEEKLY TO STUDY PROBLEM AREAS.

> The underlying messages are many. . . . Perhaps the first message . . . is that a firm can realize the full potential of its employees only if it both invests in their training and then shares with them the power to influence decisions. Without training,

■ ■ ■ ■ ■ ■ ■

[4]James F. Harmon, "The Supervisor and Quality Circles: Study a Problem Area," *Supervisory Management*, March 1984, pp. 38–43.

Campbell Soup Company has established almost 500 quality-control circles worldwide. Both production and office employees participate in discussing ways to improve quality and increase productivity.

the invitation to participate in decision making will lead only to frustration and conflict. Without a sharing of decision-making power, an investment in training will be both frustrating and wasteful. That . . . firm that hopes to learn from the Japanese example need only do that which the Japanese have done. Just as they have studied the United States industrial system and have blended together the best aspects of both, so we must do the same.[5]

A number of American firms are heeding Ouchi's advice. For example, Honeywell, the giant electronics and computer firm, currently has 150 quality circles throughout its North American operations. In most cases, the circles are made up of a half-dozen assembly workers and a team leader who meet every two weeks to examine productivity problems. In the process, the members find that the increase in autonomy is beneficial to the quality of work life, and that tardiness and average absenteeism go down while efficiency rises.[6]

Lockheed, another high-technology firm, has also had positive results with quality circles. In the first two years, with only 15 circles in operation, the firm reported saving over $2.8 million. In one operation alone, the company reduced rejects from 25 to 30 per 1,000 hours to fewer than 6 per 1,000 hours. Furthermore, of those employees who participated in the study, 97 percent indicated a strong preference to continue with the program.[7]

The White Sands Missile Range in southeastern New Mexico recently set up four circles. During the first year of operation, $33,000 was saved. The concept is now being expanded to other areas of the organization.[8]

KEEPING THEM GOING   The quality circle concept is not a panacea for organizations facing productivity and quality problems. However, if used properly, it can be extremely useful in meeting these challenges. Some of the most important human relations ideas which must be kept in mind include the following:

1.   Quality control circles are a method of employee development as well as a means for improving organizational output and efficiency. If the development side is ignored, the efficiency side will suffer.

▪▪▪▪▪▪

[5] William G. Ouchi, *Theory Z: How American Business Can Meet the Japanese Challenge* (Reading, Mass.: Addison-Wesley Publishing Company, 1981), p. 268.

[6] Mike Michaelson, "The Decline of American Productivity," *Success Unlimited*, October 1980, p. 28.

[7] Ed Yager, "Examining the Quality Control Circle," *Personnel Journal*, October 1979, p. 684.

[8] Arthur A. Whatley and William Hoffman, "Quality Circles Earn Union Respect," *Personnel Journal*, December 1987, pp. 89–93.

2.   Membership in a quality circle should be voluntary. No one ought to be forced to join a quality circle; this can negatively affect the person's contribution to the group.

3.   Participants should all be fully trained. This training should not only be technical but also provide the individuals with insights regarding conference techniques and/or group dynamics so they will know how to work more effectively in groups.

4.   Quality circles are group efforts, not individual efforts. Showing off and competition must be minimized and cooperation and interdependent behavior must be encouraged.

5.   The quality circle's project should be related to the members' actual job responsibilities. In this way the members are working to improve the quality of their own jobs, something in which they ought to have a high interest.

■ ■ ■ ■ ■ ■ ■ ■ ■ ■ ■ ■ ■ ■
QUALITY CIRCLE GUIDELINES.

6.   The quality circle program should help employees see the relationship between their work and the quality of the goods or services being generated by their efforts. This quality and improvement awareness development should be used to further commit the members to quality.

7.   If there is a quality control department in the organization, the relationship between the department and the quality control circle should be clarified before the circle begins its job. This will prevent intergroup fights and squabbling. The best way usually is for the circle to complement the quality control department.

8.   If the organization is just starting the quality control concept, a pilot study is in order. Then, if the circle produces results and wins acceptance of the managers and employees alike, use can be expanded.

9.   Management should use the suggestions set forth by the quality control circle. If none of the recommendations are adopted, the circle will lose effectiveness, and both membership and morale in the circle will drop off.

10.   Management must be willing to grant recognition for all ideas that are set forth by the circle. If this is not done, the program is likely to backfire.[9]

■ ■ ■ ■ ■ ■ ■
[9]The ideas in this section can be found in: Robert J. DuBrin, *Contemporary Applied Management* (Plano, Texas: BPI, 1982), pp. 120–122); Gerald D. Klein, "Implementing Quality Circles: A Hard Look at Some of the Realities," *Personnel*, September–October 1981, pp. 11–20; James F. Leonard, "Can Your Organization Support Quality Circles? A Practical Model," *Training and Development Journal*, September 1983, pp. 66–72; Larry R. Smeltzer and Ben L. Kedia, "Training Needs of Quality Circles," *Personnel*, August 1987, pp. 51–55; Gopal C. Pati, Robert Salitore, and Sandra Brady, "What Went Wrong with Quality Circles," *Personnel Journal*, December 1987, pp. 83–87.

In recent years, many firms have found that their quality circles are not as effective as they were previously. The circles seem to be running out of ideas.[10] Critics are beginning to refer to them as nothing more than fads. Yet this need not be the case. Guidelines such as those presented in Human Relations in Action: Keeping the Circle Alive can help prevent the problem.

STOP!

Review your answer to the first question and make any changes you would like. Then compare your answer to the one below.

1.   How does a quality circle work? Could it be used to improve customer relations?

A quality circle is a small group of well-trained employees who study job-related problems and make recommendations for action. It certainly could be used to improve customer relations because the employees are knowledgeable about how to deal with customers and they should be able to pinpoint problems and identify ways of correcting the situation. ∎

ELIMINATION OF SMOKING

Although seldom equated with productivity, smoking is a major cause of absenteeism and lost output. For this reason, many organizations are now beginning to adopt no-smoking policies or are limiting smoking to restricted areas of their facilities. Although this action can create human relations problems, the gains to be achieved often justify the expenses.

SMOKING DIRECTLY AFFECTS PRODUCTIVITY.

EFFECTS ON PRODUCTIVITY   Smoking in the work place can have significant effects on the cost of operations. The Congressional Office of Technology Assessment estimates that each smoker costs his or her employer between $2,000–5,000 annually.[11] Weis, after making a detailed

----

[10] Sud Ingle, "How to Avoid Quality Circle Failure in Your Company, *Training and Development Journal*, June 1982, pp. 54–59; and Edward E. Lawler III and Susan A. Mohrman, "Quality Circles after the Fad," *Harvard Business Review*, January–February 1983, pp. 65–71.

[11] Jim Collison, "Workplace Smoking Policies: 16 Questions and Answers," *Personnel Journal*, April 1988, p. 72.

HUMAN RELATIONS IN ACTION

KEEPING THE CIRCLE ALIVE

Although quality circles are very popular today, some firms are finding their circles being phased out. The group seems to outlive its usefulness. Yet this is not an inevitable development. There are ways of keeping quality circles alive. The following are six of the most important steps in doing so.

1.   *Train personnel in problem analysis and problem solving.* Quality circle members cannot do a good job if they do not know how to examine their work and identify techniques for solving job-related problems. This requires more than just job experience. Formal training is required.

2.   *Do not expect too much immediately.* Quality circles take time to pay off. The members have to learn how to identify and resolve problems, and then they have to implement these ideas. It sometimes takes up to a year before bottom-line performance begins to show up.

3.   *Weekly meetings should be held and the findings should be reported.* This has a number of benefits. First, it ensures that the group will meet regularly. Second, by publicizing the results, members get recognition for their contributions. Third, when other groups learn about what this group is doing, it gives them ideas for problem identification and resolution of their own.

4.   *Management must be involved.* Quality circles cannot survive without middle and top management support. One way of winning their support is by getting them involved in the effort. If they attend weekly meetings, listen to the progress of the groups, and ask questions of their own, their support is likely to increase. Another way is to have all dollar savings verified by the accounting department. This shows management that predicted cost savings are not just off-the-cuff estimates but factual statements regarding the bottom-line efficiency of the quality circle.

5.   *Committee membership should be rotated.* It is not uncommon to find quality circle members simply running out of ideas regarding new problems to study. Some of them will feel that the circle has gone as far as it can. This usually is not true, although the individual member may have gone as far as he or she can go. In order to prevent this burnout from affecting the rest of the group, it is helpful to rotate membership and put fresh life on the committee. The average committee member often needs to be replaced after the second or third year, but then can be rotated back onto the committee after a 6–12 month period.

6.   *Morale should be kept high.* By focusing on how well the group is doing and how much money has been saved over the last 12 months, it is possible to maintain high morale. Continued psychological support and understanding of participants' efforts also is crucial to maintaining high morale. While many circles have failed or simply been phased out, those which have managed to keep morale high have remained in operation.

TABLE 7.1   THE ORGANIZATIONAL COST OF SMOKING

EFFECT OF SMOKING	COST TO THE ORGANIZATION (IN 1986 DOLLARS)
Absenteeism (50% greater for smokers than nonsmokers)	$ 250
Medical care (50% higher for smokers)	288
Lost earnings to employer due to absenteeism, sickness, or early death of smoker	956
Insurance costs (other than health) due to smokers	113
Lost productivity caused by smoking breaks and smoking rituals	2,275
Damage to employer property from burns, extra cleaning, and maintenance from smoking pollution	1,250
Health impact on nonsmokers in the nearby area	608
Total	$5,740

Source: Mario Colosi, "Do Employees Have the Right to Smoke?" *Personnel Journal*, April 1988, p. 80.

analysis of smoking-employee costs has estimated the expense, in 1986 dollars, at $5,740.[12] His breakdown is shown in Table 7.1.

This is a very large sum of money. When coupled with the fact that approximately one-third of all adult Americans smoke, the organizational cost becomes clearer. In an effort to deal with the problem, many organizations are developing no-smoking policies.

NO-SMOKING REGULATIONS   Smoking is an issue that concerns not just organizations but society at large. Figure 7.4 shows that in recent years there has been a dramatic trend toward restricting smoking in public areas. The same trend is evident in both private businesses and public organizations.

Smoking policies have taken various forms. A recent survey of International Personnel Management Association and National Public Employee Labor Relations Association members found that 38 percent of the polled public agencies (cities, counties, school districts, state agencies, federal agencies) had smoking policies. In some cases a no-smoking pledge was a hiring requirement.

HUMAN RELATIONS CHALLENGES

From a human relations standpoint, there are two important questions that organizations must answer. First, does the enterprise have a right to

▪▪▪▪▪▪▪

[12] Mario Colosi, "Do Employees Have the Right to Smoke?" *Personnel Journal*, April 1988, p. 80.

FIGURE 7.4   A GUIDE TO LIGHTING UP[a]

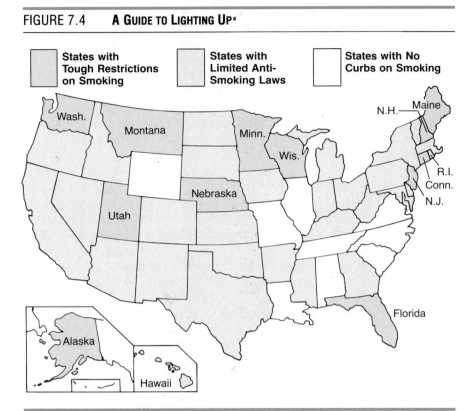

| States with Tough Restrictions on Smoking | States with Limited Anti-Smoking Laws | States with No Curbs on Smoking |

[a]Source: Action on Smoking and Health. IB Ohlsson-Newsweek.

Source: *Newsweek*, April 18, 1988, p. 25. All rights reserved. Reprinted by permission.

deny smoking privileges to its people? Second, and related, is this policy legal? The answers are intertwined; a response to one typically addresses the other.

The legal issues have been tested in the courts. The answer is that firms do have a right to limit or ban smoking on the job, and nonsmoking employees can bring legal action to protect this right. In 1982 the Missouri Court of Appeals ruled that an employee was entitled to a reasonably safe work place and ordered Western Electric to take the necessary steps. In that same year a U.S. district court in Seattle ruled that the Veterans Administration was within its authority when it separated smoker desks from nonsmoker desks and installed air purifying equipment in order to accommodate employee sensitivity to tobacco smoke. A similar finding was provided by the Ninth Circuit Court of Appeals. More recently the Supreme Court in New Jersey upheld the right of New Jersey Bell Telephone to ban smoking on the job.

The major human relations challenge is that of implementing smoking policies so that they are acceptable to the personnel and thus result in

■ ■ ■ ■ ■ ■ ■ ■ ■ ■ ■ ■ ■
SMOKING BANS OR LIMITS ARE LEGAL.

productivity increases. A number of strategies have been used effectively. One, employed by Blue Cross and Blue Shield of Maryland, used a three-step program. During Phase I, smoking was banned in all meetings, conferences, and training sessions. Smoking breaks, however, were allowed in meetings lasting more than one hour. In Phase II, introduced nine months later, all work areas were made smoke-free, but certain areas were designated for smoking. Phase III, which went into effect three months later, prohibited smoking on all company premises.[13] At the present time 20 percent of all employees still smoke, but they must do so in designated outdoor areas.

Many organizations offer assistance to their employees in breaking the habit. This often begins immediately after the new policy is announced and is designed to help people cope with the upcoming challenge.[14] Organizations typically pay part of the fee for outside sponsored "stop smoking" courses or provide them in-house for free. In some cases, incentives are offered. One company gives employees $3 a week as a bonus for every week that they do not smoke. If they start, they are honor-bound to tell the firm and give up the bonus. Another company allows its people to bet between $1–100, with a double or nothing return, on 12 months of abstinence from smoking. A third uses a lottery system. Each individual who does not smoke gets a lottery ticket for each week of abstinence. Weekly and monthly drawings are held and prizes are awarded. A fourth organization holds award ceremonies to recognize former smokers and give them certificates suitable for framing.[15]

Yet, regardless of what human relations strategies they use for implementation purposes, organizations are on their way to smokeless environments. The ultimate result will be safer and more productive work places.

■■■■■■■■■■■■■■■
SOME FIRMS OFFER INCENTIVES TO NONSMOKERS.

STOP!

Review your answer to the second question and make any changes you would like. Then compare your answer to the one below.

2.   Will the elimination of smoking increase productivity?

It should. After all, when people are smoking they are not devoting their full energies to their jobs. Additionally, if smoking is reduced, it should

■■■■■■■

[13] Sherry C. Hammond, David A. De Cenzo, and Mollie H. Bowers, "How One Company Went Smokeless," *Harvard Business Review*, November–December 1987, pp. 44–45.

[14] Howard Potter, "Clearing the Air about No-Smoking Policies," *Management Solutions*, August 1987, p. 39.

[15] Collison, "Workplace Smoking Policies," p. 83.

be possible for the company to cut expenses associated with such things as maintenance and insurance. It should also be possible to reduce tardiness and absenteeism, thereby further increasing productivity. ■

PARTICIPATIVE MANAGEMENT APPROACHES

Some approaches to improving productivity and quality are based on getting the employees more involved in the effort by giving them greater authority in the work place. Two of the most popular are alternative work schedules and effective organization design.

ALTERNATIVE WORK SCHEDULES

An *alternative work schedule* is a variation in the times at which employees begin and end work each day. There are a number of ways that this can be done. The three most common are the compressed workweek, flextime, and shift work.

COMPRESSED WORKWEEK   The **compressed workweek** allows an individual to work a shorter workweek than the typical five-day week. The arrangement might involve four 10-hour days or three 12-hour days. When work is compressed into four days, it is typical to find the personnel working Monday through Thursday or Tuesday through Friday. Firemen have long used this arrangement. So have some manufacturing firms which have found that a four-day workweek reduces cleanup and start-up time and cuts back on three to five paid holidays a year. In industries such as petroleum and chemicals, many personnel work a three-day, 36-hour schedule.

■ ■ ■ ■ ■ ■ ■ ■ ■ ■ ■ ■

A COMPRESSED WORKWEEK HAS LONGER WORK DAYS.

    Some of the major reasons cited for adopting a compressed workweek include: an increase in employee leisure time; an increase in work quality, production, and employee satisfaction; a decrease in employee tardiness, turnover, and accidents; and lower setup and cleanup costs.

    Is the compressed workweek a good idea? Research reveals that most employees favor it and that it takes only about a month to adjust to the fatigue factor. However, the arrangement does not work well where the personnel are carrying out heavy physical or taxing mental work.[16] In these cases, many employees have opted for flextime.

FLEXTIME   There are a number of different versions of **flextime**, but all require that the personnel be on hand during certain times, which are

■ ■ ■ ■ ■ ■ ■

[16]Randall B. Dunham, Jon L. Pierce, and Maria B. Casteneda, "Alternative Work Schedules: Two Field Quasi-Experiments," *Personnel Psychology*, Summer 1987, pp. 215–242.

■ ■ ■ ■ ■ ■ ■ ■ ■ ■ ■ ■ ■ ■ ■ ■ known as *core hours*.[17] One of the most common arrangements calls for
EVERYONE HAS TO BE ON HAND FOR everyone to be at work by 10 a.m. and not to leave before 3 p.m.: 10–3
CORE HOURS. are the core hours. Those who choose to come in later in the morning
can arrive at 10 a.m. and go home at 6 p.m. Those who prefer to arrive at
7 a.m. can leave at 3 p.m. Under another common arrangement the personnel can take their lunch period any time during the core hours. A
third arrangement is to allow the personnel to work as many hours in a
day as they like just as long as they are present for all core hours and
work their total number of weekly hours. A fourth arrangement is to use
the same approach as the third one except that each employee's hours
are checked for completeness on a monthly instead of weekly basis.
When there are a large number of employees, work scheduling often is
handled with a computerized system. This system matches employee
work preferences with the demand for workers so that the necessary
number of employees are on hand at all times.[18]

Many enterprises have had success with flextime. In one recent
study of 900 firms, 300 each in the banking, insurance, and utilities industries, researchers focused on the benefits of flextime among clerical
workers. They found that some of the major advantages included: increased worker satisfaction, higher work quality, greater efficiency, reduced tardiness, lower absenteeism, and less overtime.[19] On an overall
basis, the researchers reported that 83 percent of the utilities, 85 percent
of the banks, and 97 percent of the insurance firms believed that flextime, in comparison with fixed hours, increased effectiveness.

Is flextime a good idea? Most researchers have found that it is. In
addition to the above stated advantages, other benefits include: reduced
employee commuting time, less stress to get to work on time, lower absenteeism, and more job freedom.[20]

Many organizations have found that in deciding whether or not to
implement a flextime approach, it is advisable to begin by putting a small
number of personnel on flextime, work out any problems with the program, and then extend it to include more people. The approach often
used in doing this is the following:

1.   Get top management's support.

2.   Solicit involvement from employees at all levels.

3.   Appoint someone, who will have the respect of both management
and workers, to oversee the entire program.

■ ■ ■ ■ ■ ■ ■

[17] Barney Olmsted, "(Flex)Time is Money," *Management Review*, November 1987, pp. 47–52.

[18] James E. Bailey, "Personnel Scheduling with Flexshift: A Win/Win Scenario," *Personnel*,
September 1986, pp. 62–67.

[19] J. Carroll Swart, "Clerical Workers on Flextime: A Survey of Three Industries," *Personnel*,
April 1985, p. 44.

[20] Jean B. McGuire and Joseph R. Liro, "Absenteeism and Flexible Work Schedules," *Public
Personnel Management*, Spring 1987, pp. 47–59.

4.   Set up a committee or task force to coordinate work assignments, hold meetings to explain the procedures necessary to implement the program, and keep two-way communication channels open.

5.   Train the management staff by acquainting them with how flextime works, its advantages and drawbacks, and what they need to know about managing their people under this work arrangement.

6.   Conduct a pilot test of the program to help pinpoint any problems that will have to be overcome before the arrangement is carried to the organization at large.

7.   Formulate guidelines for handling problems that may arise.

8.   Set up procedures for monitoring work schedules.

9.   Evaluate the results.

■ ■ ■ ■ ■ ■ ■ ■ ■ ■ ■ ■ ■ ■
GUIDELINES FOR IMPLEMENTING FLEXTIME.

SHIFT WORK   Most enterprises use **shift work** with 8 to 5 or 9 to 5 being the most common shifts. Some industries have round-the-clock shifts because of the demand for their output. Manufacturing firms with a large backlog of orders are likely to go to a second, and perhaps a third, shift until the backlog is eliminated. Police and fire departments and hospitals have round-the-clock shifts every day of the year. Hood and Milazzo report that in 46 percent of all dual-worker couples, one or both spouses begin work after noon. This means that in many families where both the husband and wife work, shift work influences their lives.[21]

There are a number of advantages to shift work. One is that the pay usually is better for those on the second and third shift. Another is that there usually is less commuting time for people on these shifts. A third is that these shifts are often less hectic and allow the worker more job autonomy.

Is shift work a good idea? Many organizations feel it is. In some cases, no alternative exists. Police and fire departments, for example, have no other way of providing 24-hour protection. In other enterprises, management has found that people soon adjust to their new work shifts and, as their seniority increases, they are able to switch to other shifts that better meet their social and personal preferences. For these reasons, shift work will continue to be an imporant alternative work schedule.

EFFECTIVE ORGANIZATION DESIGN

In improving productivity and quality, organizations have also begun examining general organization design. Is one type of structure more conducive to high productivity or increased quality? Research shows that

■ ■ ■ ■ ■ ■ ■

[21] Jane C. Hood and Nancy Milazzo, "Shift Work, Stress, and Well-Being," *Personnel Administrator*, December 1984, p. 95.

benefits can be derived from various types of structures. In particular, more and more firms are trying to create small work groups within large departments, and thus capture some of the morale and esprit de corps common to small enterprises. To do this, organizations are turning their attention to two areas: (1) span of control and (2) decentralization and delegation of authority.

■ ■ ■ ■ ■ ■ ■ ■ ■ ■ ■ ■ ■ ■
SPAN OF CONTROL IS THE NUMBER OF SUBORDINATES REPORTING TO A SUPERIOR.

SPAN OF CONTROL   The number of subordinates who report to a specific superior is the **span of control**. Early organization theorists believed that narrow spans (3 to 6 subordinates) were superior to wide ones (7 to 10 or more). By definition, this line of thinking encourages **tall structures**, as in Figure 7.5, as opposed to **flat structures**, as in Figure 7.6. Note that with a span of control of 2 it takes 6 hierarchical levels to organize 63 people (Figure 7.5), whereas a span of 8 needs 3 levels to organize 73 people (Figure 7.6).

For years, organizational theorists have argued the relative merits of tall and flat structures. So far, no research has shown conclusively that one is always superior to the other; however, there are times when one offers better results than the other. For example, Porter and Lawler have reported that in companies with fewer than 5,000 employees, the flat structure tends to provide greater job satisfaction but in larger companies, the tall structure brings about higher job satisfaction.[22] It also appears that upper-level managers experience greater satisfaction in tall structures and lower-level managers are more satisfied in flat structures.[23]

THE HUMAN RELATIONS ELEMENT   Table 7.2 presents some of the major factors that influence spans of control on a more *individualized* or human relations basis. Work experience, job difficulty, and managerial style are all important determinants of span of control. However, this list is not all-inclusive; there are far too many factors for us to consider here. For example, technology seems to have an impact on span of control. Firms in industries with a high level or a low level of technology usually have narrow spans of control, whereas firms in industries with a middle level of technology tend to have wide spans of control. If all the subordinates work in one location, the most effective span of control tends to be wider than if they are divided among three or four locations. Drawing

■ ■ ■ ■ ■ ■ ■

[22] Lyman W. Porter and Edward E. Lawler III, "The Effect of 'Tall' Versus 'Flat' Organization Structure on Managerial Job Satisfaction," *Personnel Psychology*, Summer 1964, pp. 135–148.
[23] Chris J. Berger and L. L. Cummings, "Organization Structure, Attitudes and Behavior: Where Are We Now?" *Academy of Management Proceedings*, 1975, pp. 176–178.

FIGURE 7.5   **TALL ORGANIZATION STRUCTURE (SPAN OF 2)**

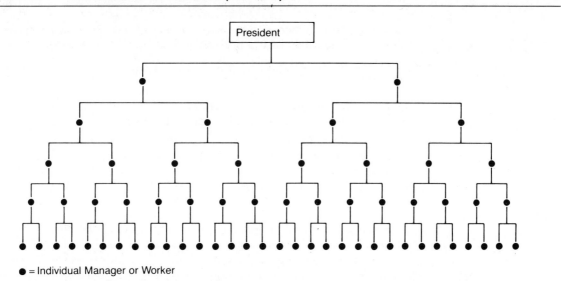

● = Individual Manager or Worker

FIGURE 7.6   **FLAT ORGANIZATION STRUCTURE (SPAN OF 8)**

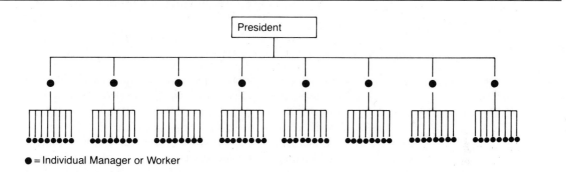

● = Individual Manager or Worker

TABLE 7.2   **SOME MAJOR FACTORS DETERMINING SPAN OF CONTROL**

NARROW SPAN	WIDE SPAN
Subordinates have fewer than 5 years of job experience.	Subordinates have 10 or more years of job experience.
Subordinates have no assistants.	Subordinates have assistants of their own.
Subordinates are supervised exclusively by the superior.	Subordinates are supervised in part by others.
Subordinates all carry out different functions.	Subordinates all carry out similar functions.
Organization is large.	Organization is small.
Work is nonroutine.	Work is routine.
Worker error will prove to be a costly mistake.	Worker error will not prove very costly.
Coordination among the subordinates is of major importance.	Coordination among the subordinates is not of major importance.
Manager wants close control of subordinates.	Manager prefers loose control of subordinates.
Manager is located high up the organization.	Manager is located in the middle to lower levels of the hierarchy.

together all the evidence currently available, however, we can make the following generalizations:

1.   The optimal span of control in most situations is in the range of 5 to 10.

2.   In determining the ideal span, consideration of the costs associated with both wide and narrow spans must be studied.

3.   In establishing a span for a specific situation, factors such as the desirability of group solidarity, the need for job satisfaction, the amount of control required, the nature of the work, the stability of the environment, and the extent of assistance to the manager have to be taken into consideration.[24]

By adhering to such guidelines, the organization addresses the issue of optimum spans and attempts to find the right span for each manager and situation.[25] In so doing, the enterprise also addresses the human relations side of span of control: how one balances organizational efficiency (lowest possible costs, greatest possible productivity and profit) with personnel needs and desires (autonomy, decision-making authority, and a chance to be creative).

DECENTRALIZATION AND DELEGATION OF AUTHORITY

■ ■ ■ ■ ■ ■ ■ ■ ■ ■ ■ ■ ■ ■

CRITERIA FOR MEASURING DECENTRALIZATION.

In recent years more and more firms have begun decentralizing decision making, pushing responsibility for decisions further down the line toward the operating level. How does one know if an organization is basically centralized or decentralized? This question can be answered by looking at such criteria as: (1) whether a large or small number of decisions are made lower down the management hierarchy, (2) whether these decisions are important ones or just minor issues, and (3) how much checking is being made on the decisions by higher management. If a large number of decisions are being made, many of them are important, and there is a minimum of checking, the organization is **decentralized**. If the reverse is true, the organization is centralized.

■ ■ ■ ■ ■ ■ ■ ■ ■ ■ ■ ■ ■

DELEGATION INVOLVES DISTRIBUTION OF WORK TO SUBORDINATES.

Delegation, meanwhile, involves the distribution of work to subordinates. If the manager gets the people actively involved in carrying out departmental assignments, there will be a great deal of delegation. We know, however, that many managers tend to delegate only minor matters and to keep most of the work for themselves. In so doing they fail to develop the real potential of their subordinates and may overwork themselves in the process.

■ ■ ■ ■ ■ ■ ■

[24] John B. Miner, *The Management Process: Theory, Research, and Practice*, 2nd ed. (New York: MacMillan Publishing Company, 1978), p. 291.

[25] See also Joseph F. Michlitsch and Debra L. Gipson, "Managing the Span of Control," *Supervisory Management*, June 1984, pp. 13–18.

DECENTRALIZATION CONSIDERATIONS   Should every organization decentralize to as great a degree as possible? The answer is no. In past years firms like DuPont, General Motors, Standard Oil of New Jersey, and Sears, Roebuck and Company have decentralized. Some students of management have been quick to cite them, claiming that if the big successful organizations are decentralizing, every other company should also. However, decentralization is not an overwhelming trend. Many firms in industries such as copper, nickel, aluminum, and steel have tended to remain basically centralized (International Nickel, Alcoa, and Bethlehem Steel). The decision to decentralize depends on size and environmental changes. Firms that are in highly competitive environments or have been diversifying are much more likely to decentralize than those that are in stable environments and are not increasing their operations through merger or acquisition. Table 7.3 compares some of the benefits and drawbacks associated with centralization and decentralization. Some contingency questions, however, must be asked before a decision about decentralization is made. They include:

TABLE 7.3   CENTRALIZATION OR DECENTRALIZATION?

	CENTRALIZATION	DECENTRALIZATION
BENEFITS	Assures uniformity of standards and policies among the organization units. Permits the use of outstanding talent in managers by the whole organization rather than a single unit. Ensures uniform decisions. Helps eliminate duplication of effort and activity.	Reduces the total responsibility to more manageable units. Encourages more involvement of the personnel in the decision-making process. Shortens lines of communication. Brings decision making closer to those affected by the decision. Disperses power and authority among many people.
DRAWBACKS	Makes great demands on a few managers instead of spreading responsibility. Forces top managers to possess a broad view, which may be beyond their ability. Gives vast amounts of authority and power to a few people. Reduces a sense of participation for all but a few.	Allows a lack of uniformity of standards and policies among organizational units. Necessitates making of decisions without capable managers, who may be unavailable or unwilling to participate. Can create coordination problems among the various organizational units. Can lead to interunit rivalry, which can interfere with the organization's overall effectiveness. Requires training programs, which can be time consuming and costly.

1. *How much coordination will be needed between units or individuals?* The more coordination required the greater the need for centralization. If only limited coordination is needed, decentralization is possible.

2. *Where can planning be accomplished best?* If planning must be performed by individuals possessing a broad overview of the entire organization, centralization will be needed. If, however, planning can be oriented to local, more specialized functions and duties, decentralization will be best.

3. *Are rigid controls necessary?* If strict performance standards are essential, centralization will be preferable; if not, decentralization is more likely to be possible.

4. *Are the individuals who will be a part of the decentralized unit capable of self-direction, self-motivation, and self-control?* The more capable subordinates are of handling authority, the more authority they can be given.

5. *Are the individuals who will be part of the decentralized unit willing to assume the self-generating responsibilities of decentralization?* The attitude of the affected individuals must be favorable toward receiving more authority if the change is to be successful.

6. *Will initiative and morale be significantly improved by decentralization?* Decentralization typically improves the initiative and morale of the affected (decentralized) unit, but what will be the effect on other levels? Ideally, the response to decentralization will be favorable from all quarters; however, this is not always the case.

DELEGATION CONSIDERATIONS   Some managers are reluctant to delegate authority, and some subordinates are afraid to accept it.[26] Table 7.4 provides some reasons for both of these occurrences. Research reveals that regardless of job descriptions or company directives, subordinates who want to exercise authority will either encourage their boss to delegate it to them or will simply take it upon themselves to do the tasks.[27] Similarly, subordinates who do not want authority to be delegated to them will simply refuse to accept it. In the final analysis, however, the problem rests with the manager.[28]

■ ■ ■ ■ ■ ■ ■

[26] A. T. Hollingsworth and Abdul Rahman A. Al-Jafary, "Why Supervisors Don't Delegate and Employees Won't Accept Responsibility," *Supervisory Management*, April 1983, pp. 12–17.

[27] Patrick J. Montana and Deborah F. Nash, "Delegation: The Art of Managing," *Personnel Journal*, October 1981, pp. 784–787.

[28] For still other ideas see Don Caruth and Bill Middlebrook, "How to Delegate Successfully," *Supervisory Management*, February 1983, pp. 36–42; and Burt K. Scanlan and Roger M. Atherton, Jr., "Participation and the Effective Use of Authority," *Personnel Journal*, September 1981, pp. 697–703.

TABLE 7.4   **WHY DELEGATION DOES NOT TAKE PLACE**

THE BOSS IS RELUCTANT BECAUSE HE OR SHE:	**THE SUBORDINATE IS RELUCTANT BECAUSE HE OR SHE:**
Feels he or she can do better personally.	Would rather ask the boss than do it personally.
Is unable to instruct the subordinates.	Is afraid of harsh criticism.
Lacks confidence in the subordinates.	Lacks self-confidence.
Has inadequate systems for catching errors in time.	Does not have the necessary resources.
Dislikes taking a chance.	Has inadequate positive incentives for accepting the work.

Adapted from William H. Newman, E. Kirby Warren, and Jerome Schnee, *The Process of Management*, 5th ed. (Englewood Cliffs, N.J.: Prentice-Hall, 1982), p. 227.

Formal delegation may be less important to the final outcome than the individual tendencies of managers to make their own decisions or defer to superiors. Clearly many managers are unwilling to take the risk of making decisions and being held accountable. They claim that their freedom of action is restricted, when in fact they merely do not want to accept responsibility for their own decisions. It seems apparent from . . . research that if delegation is to prove effective, managers must be found or developed who can accept delegation and make decisions in accordance with the requirements of this . . . role.[29]

How well do you personally do as a delegator? In answering this question, take the accompanying Time Out quiz to see how effective you are as a delegator.

STOP!

Review your answer to the third question and make any changes you would like. Then compare your answer to the one below.

3.   What are three factors that should be considered in deciding whether or not to expand the average span of control?

Three factors that should be considered are subordinate experience, the similarity of functions, and the degree to which the work is routine. Others include: work errors should not be costly, there should be little need for coordination, and management must be willing to operate under conditions of loose control. ■

▪▪▪▪▪▪▪
[29]John B. Miner, *The Management Process: Theory, Research, and Practice*, pp. 278–279.

TIME OUT

HOW EFFECTIVE ARE YOU AS A DELEGATOR?

The following questions are designed to measure how well you delegate. If you are a manager, answer the questions from that point of view. If you are not a manager, use your personal insights to help identify how you would respond to each if you were put in a managerial position. An interpretation of your answers is provided at the end of the chapter.

	YES	NO
1. Do you make sure your people get all of the information they need to carry out delegated assignments?	___	___
2. Do you ensure that your people are trained to handle tasks before you delegate the work to them?	___	___
3. If your people make decisions that you think you can handle better, do you overrule them?	___	___
4. Do you use subordinate mistakes to weed out incompetents and serve as a lesson to others to shape up or ship out?	___	___
5. If a subordinate makes a decision and it proves to be wrong, do you assume a portion of the responsibility yourself because final accountability rests with you (as opposed to letting this person take the entire blame)?	___	___
6. When someone comes to you asking for help with a decision, do you make the decision rather than spend time helping them work it out?	___	___
7. Do you define the limits of delegated authority so your people know the authority they have and do not have?	___	___
8. Do you trust your people enough to let them handle any situations on their own?	___	___
9. If your people do make mistakes, do you use them to find out what went wrong and how they can be prevented in the future (as opposed to punishing your people for the error)?	___	___
10. Have you a follow-up system for evaluating how well things are going without having to continuously look over your subordinates' shoulders?	___	___

ADOPTING NEW PHILOSOPHICAL APPROACHES

Increased productivity and quality are also a result of new philosophical approaches to the management of people at work. One example is the creation of an environment where entrepreneurial spirit is nurtured and developed. A second is the adoption of Japanese management techniques which place a strong focus on concern for humanistic principles.

DEVELOPING INTRAPRENEURSHIP

An **intrapreneur** is an entrepreneur who works within the confines of an enterprise. Sometimes the individual is referred to as an in-house entrepreneur. In any event, many organizations are beginning to realize that intrapreneurs are critical in their efforts to increase productivity and quality. Brandt has put it this way.

█ █ █ █ █ █ █ █ █ █ █ █ █
INTRAPRENEURS ARE IN-HOUSE ENTREPRENEURS.

> The challenge is relatively straightforward. The United States must upgrade its innovative prowess. To do so, U.S. companies must tap into the creative power of their members. Ideas come from people. Innovation is a capability of the many. That capability is utilized when people give commitment to the mission and life of the enterprise and have the power to do something with their capabilities. Noncommitment is the price of obsolete managing practices, not the lack of talent or desire.

> Commitment is most freely given when the members of an enterprise play a part in defining the purposes and plans of the entity. Commitment carries with it a de facto approval of and support for the management. Managing by consent is a useful managing philosophy if more entrepreneurial behavior is desired.[30]

CREATING THE RIGHT CLIMATE   There are many approaches that can be used in creating and nurturing an intrapreneurial climate. Four of the steps that many enterprises have taken include: (1) setting explicit, mutually agreed upon goals so that employees know what is expected of them; (2) providing feedback and positive reinforcement so that people know how well they are doing and are encouraged to continue their efforts; (3) placing emphasis on individual responsibility that builds confidence, trust, and accountability; and (4) giving results-based rewards that encourage risk-taking and high achievement.

Other steps are designed to create an innovative environment. Some of the most useful are:

1. Encourage action.
2. Use informal meetings whenever possible.
3. Tolerate failure and use it as a learning experience.
4. Be persistent in getting an idea to market.
5. Reward innovation for innovation's sake.

The intrapreneurial spirit is strong at AT&T. Product developer Jim McLaughlin designed a new circuit board for the 75XE digital PBX, a new product in the area of information movement and management.

██████

[30] Steven C. Brandt, *Entrepreneuring in Established Companies* (Homewood, Ill.: Dow Jones–Irwin, 1986), p. 54.

6.   Plan the physical layout of the enterprise to encourage informal communication.

7.   Expect clever adaptations of other employees' ideas.

8.   Put people on small teams for future-oriented projects.

9.   Encourage personnel to circumvent rigid procedures and bureaucratic red tape.

10.   Reward and/or promote innovative personnel.[31]

DEVELOPING INTRAPRENEURING STRATEGIES   Intrapreneuring strategies are designed to create an environment in which creative, innovative employees flourish. In this environment, the manager often assumes a number of roles including those of coach, teacher, and mentor. The employees, meanwhile, are encouraged to develop ideas that will result in higher productivity and quality, without concern about making mistakes and losing their jobs. Intrapreneurial organizations often supplement their strategies with rewards that encourage both effort and commitment. Examples include bonus plans, stock incentive plans, stock option plans, and profit sharing.

Intrapreneurial strategies often have two phases. The first phase creates the necessary environment; the second gains participant support. During the first phase, top management will determine the types of entrepreneurial ideas it is interested in and the rules that will be used in managing intrapreneurs. Management will also use this time to identify potential intrapreneurs and target them for attention. The second phase is dedicated to convincing these personnel to formulate and implement intrapreneurial projects and helping them to do so. General Electric is a good example.

■ ■ ■ ■ ■ ■ ■ ■ ■ ■ ■ ■ ■ ■
INTRAPRENEURIAL STRATEGIES
TYPICALLY HAVE TWO PHASES.

The company carefully selects young, high-technology people with only a few years' work experience, and often no formal management education, and literally sets them up in businesses. Basically, General Electric gives these new entrepreneurs a product line and a time period, and then asks them to make the company grow. They must compete against each other for allocation of funds and resources, and they must learn to assess markets and prioritize and deploy resources. This process is enhanced through the active support of the supervisors who regularly meet with their intrapreneurs. Finally, at the end of the time period, these venture managers are assessed by how well

■ ■ ■ ■ ■ ■ ■

[31] Donald F. Kuratko and Richard M. Hodgetts, *Entrepreneurship* (Hinsdale, Ill.: The Dryden Press, 1989), p. 549.

TABLE 7.5   OBJECTIVES AND PROGRAMS DESIGNED FOR INTRAPRENEURIAL STRATEGIES

OBJECTIVE	SPECIAL PROGRAMS
1. Make sure that the current systems, structures, and practices do not present insurmountable roadblocks to the flexibility and fast action needed for innovation.	Reduce unnecessary bureaucracy. Reduce segmentation and encourage communication across departments and functions. Change internal budgeting and accounting procedures.
2. Provide the incentives and tools for entrepreneurial projects.	Use internal "venture capital" and special project budgets. (This has been termed *intracapital* to signify a special fund for intrapreneurial projects.) Set aside discretionary funds to allow for expansion of projects. Allow discretionary time for projects (sometimes referred to as "bootlegging" time). Establish performance review and compensation procedures for intrapreneuring. This means newer forms of rewards and bonuses must be set up to encourage and support intrapreneurial activity.
3. Seek synergies across business areas so that new opportunities are discovered in new combinations while at the same time business units retain operating autonomy.	Encourage joint projects and ventures among divisions, departments, and companies. Use conferences and exchange ideas to foster the communication and information flow across company boundaries. Allow and encourage employees to discuss and brainstorm new ideas.

Source: Adapted by permission of the publisher from Rosabeth Moss Kanter, "Supporting Innovation and Venture Development in Established Companies," *Journal of Business Venturing*, Winter 1985, p. 57. Copyright 1985 by Elsevier Science Publishing Co., Inc.

they have attained their objectives and how much money they have made. Compensation is related to this contribution.[32]

However, regardless of the specific steps taken by an organization, all have similar patterns. They seek a proactive change in the status quo and a new, flexible approach to the management of operations. In doing so, organizations pursue three common objectives as set forth in Table 7.5. They also tend to undertake the following steps:

1.   Encourage individuals to be willing to assume the challenges of intrapreneurship.

▪▪▪▪▪▪▪

[32] *Ibid,* p. 553.

2.   Give intrapreneurs the authority and freedom to do the job their own way.

3.   Let the individuals see their ideas through to completion.

4.   Fund intrapreneurial efforts.

5.   Have many intrapreneurial projects going on at the same time.

6.   Encourage risk taking and tolerate mistakes.

7.   Stick with entrepreneurial ideas long enough to see if they will work.

8.   Encourage people from different departments and areas of interest to pool their interdisciplinary skills.

9.   Allow the formation of autonomous teams that have full responsibility for developing their ideas.

10.   Let intrapreneurial teams have authority to use the resources of other divisions and outside vendors if they choose.[33]

THEORY Z THINKING

No discussion of productivity and quality improvement would be complete without consideration of Japanese management practices. Today it seems that many American firms are looking at the way the Japanese manage and are asking the question: What can we learn from them? One of the most detailed responses to this question has been provided by Ouchi in his best-selling book, *Theory Z: How American Business Can Meet the Japanese Challenge.* Ouchi presents and describes the seven dimensions that characterize Japanese management. These dimensions have helped Japanese firms become more competitive in the world market and, in many instances, successfully compete against American companies. Before examining these dimensions, it should be noted that while they have helped Japanese companies deal with challenges confronting them, there is no proof that these same approaches would work in America. On the other hand, Japanese management experts like Ouchi believe that a *modified* Japanese approach can work well in the United States.[34]

LIFETIME EMPLOYMENT   In large Japanese firms individuals are virtually guaranteed a lifetime of employment. This policy relieves managers of the pressure to obtain an immediate return from the individual and permits long-term training and development programs. The employees

• • • • • • •

[33] Gifford Pinchot, "Innovation through Intrapreneuring," *Research Management*, March–April 1987, pp. 14–19.

[34] Ouchi, *Theory Z: How American Business Can Meet the Japanese Challenge* (Reading, Mass.: Addison-Wesley Publishing Company, 1981).

also adopt a long-term view of career development and are more willing to operate within the bounds of organizational norms.

CONSENSUAL DECISION MAKING   Unlike in the United States, in Japan a decision is not implemented until all affected parties have considered the problem, offered their views, and indicated their support for the final decision. This process is slow in producing a decision, but implementation is rapid and effective because of the prior agreement of those involved.

COLLECTIVE RESPONSIBILITY   Since responsibility for the success or failure of a project is borne collectively by all who are involved, the process eliminates the ability to judge performance and confer awards on the basis of individual contribution. It also leads to performance through peer pressure and creates a high degree of cohesiveness within the group.

SLOW EVALUATION AND PROMOTION   Japanese firms follow a practice of slow evaluation and promotion. The evaluation frequently involves a number of supervisors who are familiar with all aspects of the individual's performance. This process prevents a rapid rise to the top by the bright young star, but it also reduces errors in selecting those who enter the ranks of top management.

■ ■ ■ ■ ■ ■ ■ ■ ■ ■ ■ ■ ■ ■ ■
THE JAPANESE MODEL HAS SEVEN MAJOR DIMENSIONS.

INFORMAL CONTROL   Control of activities within Japanese firms is very informal and unstructured. The basic assumption in the firm is that when an individual fully understands the philosophy of the organization, he or she will make the appropriate decision without the need for formal guidelines and controls. While this approach is not set down in writing, the theory is communicated through a common culture shared by key managers and, to some extent, all other employees.

NONSPECIALIZED CAREER PATHS   The Japanese train their employees in all aspects of the business. This policy improves communication between departments, leads to loyalty to the company rather than the profession, and decreases the likelihood that someone will quit and move to another firm. Since the person is trained for one company specifically, much of the individual's knowledge is of limited value to anyone else.

WHOLISTIC CONCERN   Japanese organizations pay close attention to their people, both off and on the job. This approach is cultural to Japan.

Many years ago when industrialization began to flourish, parents were reluctant to allow their children to come to the large cities to work in factories and industrial establishments unless they could be sure that the children would be taken care of. As a result, the owners built dormitories, provided healthful food, and ensured that the children would receive the moral, intellectual, physical, and domestic training that would prepare them for life. Today Japanese firms use this wholistic concern to create a work environment that nurtures high morale and team spirit among employees.

■ ■ ■ ■ ■ ■ ■ ■ ■ ■ ■ ■ ■

THEORY Z IS A MODIFIED
APPROACH FOR AMERICAN FIRMS.

THE AMERICAN MODEL   Can American firms follow the Japanese example in meeting sociotechnical challenges? Ouchi believes it is possible by means of a modified American approach, which he calls **Theory Z**, that combines some features of Japanese firms with some from American firms. In particular he recommends consideration of lifetime employment, consensual decision making, slower evaluation and promotion, informal control, a moderately specialized career path, and wholistic concern. This modified approach incorporates five of the features of Japanese management along with one half-way step (career paths). Can it be done? Can American businesses emulate the Japanese model and be successful? Some firms are looking into the value of using Theory Z including General Motors, Ford, Chrysler, Hewlett-Packard, General Electric, Westinghouse, IBM, Texas Instruments, Honeywell, Lockheed, Fairchild Camera and Instrument, and Brunswick, to name a dozen. The great challenge will be getting people to go along with the changes, especially since these ideas are so closely tied to Japanese cultural values.[35] On the positive side, however, if it will take a change toward Theory Z management to survive, organizations are likely to make the transition. Experts like Gmelch and Miskin have suggested that American firms use techniques such as quality circles, but not fall into the trap of outrightly mimicking Japanese management methods.[36] Cosier and Dalton agree with this flexible approach, noting that truly excellent firms are adaptable and have been willing to change their products, markets, technology, and management in response to changing conditions.[37] In any event, American business in the 1990s can certainly profit from studying Japanese management practices, if not outrightly adopting them.

■ ■ ■ ■ ■ ■ ■

[35] Linda S. Dillon, "Adopting Japanese Management: Some Cultural Stumbling Blocks," *Personnel*, July–August 1983, pp. 73–77.

[36] Walter H. Gmelch and Val D. Miskin, "The Art of High Productivity," *Personnel*, April 1986, pp. 34–38.

[37] Richard A. Cosier and Dan R. Dalton, "Search for Excellence, Learn from Japan—Are These Panaceas or Problems," *Business Horizons*, November–December 1986, p. 68.

STOP!

Review your answer to the fourth question and make any changes you would like. Then compare your answer to the one below.

4.   How can intrapreneurship be promoted? Offer three recommendations.

Three recommendations are: (1) encourage individuals to assume challenges; (2) reward them for their performance; and (3) tolerate mistakes. Others include: (1) encourage risk taking; (2) stay with entrepreneurial ideas long enough to see if they will work; and (3) form pools of people with interdisciplinary skills. ∎

SUMMARY

Two of the major challenges facing organizations today are those of increasing productivity and improving the quality of goods and services. Productivity is measured by the equation: output/input. Over the last decade American productivity has been declining vis-à-vis foreign competitors such as the Japanese and Germans. The same is true for quality. This chapter examines some of the major human relations-oriented approaches that are being used to turn things around.

Two of the steps that are being taken to attack the problems directly are the introduction of quality circles and the elimination of smoking on the job. A quality circle is a group of five to ten well-trained employees and a team leader that study job-related problems and make recommendations for improvement. These circles typically focus on a problem or project that can be handled within 3–6 months. During this time the members meet for an hour or two each week to study the problem and formulate solutions. The group then implements the solutions or makes recommendations for action.

Smoking is a major issue because of its impact on the overall productivity of the enterprise. In 1986 dollars, the average cost per smoking employee was over $5,700. As a result, many organizations are establishing no-smoking or restricted smoking policies and are developing plans including incentive schemes to encourage their people to give up the habit.

Other approaches encourage participative management. Alternative work arrangements allow people some control in determining when they will come to work and when they will go home. These include such work schedules as the compressed workweek, flextime, and shift work. Effective organization design efforts focus on flattening the structure, decentralizing, and delegating more authority to the personnel.

A third major approach in improving productivity and work quality is the introduction of new philosophical approaches. One is the development of intrapreneurship by encouraging entrepreneurial activity within the enterprise. This usually takes two steps. First, the right climate is created. Second, employees are designated as having intrapreneurial potential, are encouraged to engage in entrepreneurial activity, and are rewarded for their efforts. Another philosophical approach is the adoption of Theory Z concepts. The essence of this approach is to determine those Japanese management concepts that are of most value to the firm and then modify or directly incorporate them into everyday practices.

KEY TERMS IN THE CHAPTER

productivity	tall structure
quality circle	flat structure
compressed workweek	decentralization of authority
flextime	delegation of authority
shift work	intrapreneur
span of control	Theory Z

REVIEW AND STUDY QUESTIONS

1.   What is meant by the term *productivity*? Of what importance is productivity to American enterprise?

2.   Are American productivity and quality improving or declining? Defend your answer.

3.   How does a quality circle work? Of what value would a circle be in improving productivity and quality? Give an example.

4.   Why are many organizations introducing either no-smoking or restricted smoking policies? What relationship does your answer have to efforts to increase productivity?

5.   How are enterprises using human relations techniques in their efforts to eliminate or restrict smoking on the job? Cite and explain at least two examples.

6.   How do the following work: compressed workweek, flextime, shift work. Give an example of each.

7.   In what way do alternative work schedules help increase work productivity and quality? Defend your answer.

8.   In what way would a flat structure be of value to an organization that is seeking to increase productivity or improve quality? Be complete in your answer.

9.   What considerations do managers have to keep in mind when they delegate authority? Identify and discuss three of them.

10.   What is an intrapreneur? How can organizations encourage intrapreneurship? Cite five examples.

11.   Why would organizations seeking to increase their productivity and work quality be interested in encouraging intrapreneurship?

12.   What is meant by the term Theory Z? Would these ideas be of any practical value to organizations seeking to improve their productivity or work quality? Defend your answer.

TIME OUT ANSWERS: INTERPRETATION OF HOW EFFECTIVE ARE YOU AS A DELEGATOR?

Give yourself one point for each of the following answers.

1. Yes	6. No
2. Yes	7. Yes
3. No	8. Yes
4. No	9. Yes
5. Yes	10. Yes

A good score is eight or above; an excellent score is nine or above. If you failed to get the right answer for any of the questions, go back and read the questions again. By examining the logic and reasoning behind the statement, you can develop the most effective philosophy for delegating authority.

CASE: A CHECK-IN AND CHECKOUT PROBLEM

Pellier Hotel is very popular with both businesspeople and visitors to the city. This can be seen from the long lines in the lobby. Beginning around 7 a.m. every day there is always a waiting line to check out. Just prior to 1 p.m., final checkout time, the line sometimes extends the length of the lobby. Then around 2 p.m. the check-in line begins to grow. On a typical afternoon, there will be at least 20 check-ins in line at any given time.

One of the major reasons for these lines is that the Pellier's front desk area is not large enough to accommodate the growing number of customers. The hotel was expanded by 350 rooms last year, but no one realized the problem this would create for those at the front desk.

The manager of the hotel, Celeste Renford, has had numerous suggestions regarding how to streamline the check-in and checkout process. Some of these are already in practice. For example, everyone receives a copy of their bill the night before checking out. There is no need for them to wait in line unless they have had additional charges such as breakfast. In this case, they can pay for breakfast at the restaurant and proceed on their way. Unfortunately, some of them do not know this, so they wait in line to pay the bill at the front desk. Others want to question some of the items on the bill, so they too line up. As a result, despite the hotel's efforts, the checkout lines remain long. Checking in is even more time consuming. The front desk can handle no more than three people at a time and each check-in usually takes around five minutes. It has been suggested to Celeste that a small table be put in the corner of the lobby to add another check-in line. However, since the person managing this desk would not have a computer hookup to the main desk, the process would still be very time consuming.

In an effort to deal with the problem, Celeste plans to form a group of six to eight people to investigate the problem and decide what to do. She believes that people from reservations, the front desk, and the lobby area should be part of the team because they are directly affected by the problem and are more apt to know what types of solutions are likely to work. Celeste intends to convene the committee tomorrow, ask them to present their recommendations to her within three weeks, and then, if all goes well, allow them to implement their solutions.

QUESTIONS

1.   What do you think of Celeste's idea of forming a committee to work on the problem? Give your evaluation.

2.   Are there any characteristics of Japanese management techniques that will be used by the committee Celeste is forming? Identify and describe three of them.

3.   Should Celeste delegate the authority to the committee to implement their recommended solutions, or should she reserve the right to review them first? Why? Explain. ■

CASE: A PRODUCTIVE APPROACH

Karl Landis recently bought a collection agency. The agency handles bills that are turned over to it by organizations that believe these debts are uncollectible. Karl's firm receives 40 percent of all monies collected. The agency also does bill collecting for the county. A large number of parking tickets go unpaid each year, even though residents are denied renewal of their licenses if they have any outstanding violations. Many of these people will not pay until they are forced to do so. However, the county does not want to wait for its money, so it has agreed to give Karl's agency 40 percent of all fines that are collected.

Collection work can be very time consuming and costly. For this reason, Karl's firm relies exclusively on telephone collection. This method is fairly effective given the fact that most people would like to pay their bills but are financially strapped. What Karl finds is that most people will pay their overdue bills if they are put on a time payment plan. They just need someone to coax them into agreeing to it and then follow up to ensure that they are sticking to their agreement. In the case of overdue parking tickets, most people are surprised to get a call at home and often pay the bill within 10 days. The secret of success in the business is to find the person's telephone number and get through to that person. Sometimes the person has no phone; other times it is unlisted; still other times the person answering the phone will say that the person is not at home. In the collection business, experienced bill collectors are vital to success.

To maximize his agency's income, Karl has taken five steps. First, he has purchased a computer software program that keeps track of the names, addresses, and phone numbers of every person from whom his agency is trying to collect. This program is also used to keep track of those who have agreed to pay their bills and how much they have paid. The system provides the collection personnel with accurate information when they call back to follow up on slow-paying customers. Second, after a one-week training program in which personnel are taught how to collect, Karl turns them loose on their own. He gives each of them full authority to handle the collection process. He does not interfere with his people. Third, he allows his people to set their own hours collectively. In the group of 15 full-time people who work for him, there are some who prefer to begin work early in the morning while there are others who prefer to come in around 1–2 p.m. Karl does not care when his personnel come and go just as long as among them they get the work done. Fourth, Karl requires that each person be on the phone talking to a customer or placing a call at least 50 minutes out of every hour. Research shows that there should be one successful collection every 50 minutes, so Karl knows that each person should get collections from eight people per day. Fifth, anyone who is responsible for collecting more than $1,000 in any day is given a 5 percent bonus for all sums in excess of this amount.

Since he introduced these five steps, Karl's collections have increased by 55 percent a week. Additionally, he has not lost one employee although the turnover is extremely high at most collection agencies. In fact, there is a waiting line of job applicants.

QUESTIONS

1.   What type of an alternative work arrangement is Karl using? Explain.

2.   In what way is Karl encouraging productivity among his people? Give an example.

3.   Does Karl use any Japanese management approaches? Explain. ∎

EXPERIENCING QUALITY CIRCLES AT WORK

PURPOSE

- To better understand how a quality circle works.
- To provide individuals an opportunity to study and improve a situation which directly affects them.

PROCEDURE

1.   In groups of five to eight, students should choose an activity at their college or university that directly affects them. It may be the long lines at the cafeteria or the bursar's office. It may be the service at the library.

2.   Divide the activity among the members with each person studying one phase and looking for ways to shorten the process or improve the delivery of the service. Interview personnel who are directly involved.

3.   Meet and review your findings with an eye toward what can realistically be done about the situation. Be as practical as possible, keeping in mind the need to improve quality and reduce costs.

4.   Write up your recommendations for action and submit them to the appropriate university or college official.

JOB REDESIGN AND JOB ENRICHMENT

GOALS OF THE CHAPTER

How can modern organizations deal with the challenge of technology and the dysfunctional effects it creates? One of the primary ways is to redesign jobs and enrich them with psychological motivators, such as increased autonomy, feedback, and task variety. In this chapter we study how this can be done.

The first goal of this chapter is to examine the current status of work in America and the need for an improved quality of work life (QWL). The second goal is to examine the nature of job redesign and some of the most commonly used job redesign techniques. The third goal is to study core job dimensions and job enrichment principles employed in redesign programs. The fourth goal is to look at some successful job enrichment programs. The fifth goal is to examine some of the current challenges in job redesign.

When you have finished reading this chapter you should be able to:

1. Explain what job design is all about.

2. Tell how job rotation, job enlargement, and job enrichment work.

3. Describe the five core job dimensions and illustrate selected enrichment principles that help create these dimensions.

4. Cite some illustrations of job enrichment in action.

OPENING CASE

A VERY REWARDING JOB

When his company decided to build the most automated assembly plant in the industry, Chris Robinson was not surprised. He knew that the firm was determined to increase its market share and one way of doing this was to improve product quality and reduce cost per unit. What did surprise Chris was the announcement that he would be the new plant manager.

The personnel in this new plant were all transferred from a nearby facility. They are familiar with assembly line work, although the new layout is different. In the old plant, each individual would assemble one part of the product and then pass it on to the next person. In the new plant, each person builds a product from start to finish. One of these products, a lightweight, state-of-the-art videocassette recorder is a good example of how the new production system works. The assembler is required to put together 60 recorders a day. Some people prefer to work faster in the morning and then slow up in the afternoon. Others do their best work in the afternoon. Management does not care how fast they work each hour just as long as they meet their daily quotas.

Each person works at a separate table, with the parts to be assembled located around the table. There is a machine for testing the product and ensuring that it works properly. If it does not, the individual must disassemble it, find the problem, and then reassemble it. If the product does pass inspection, it is placed on a special cart and is taken directly to the shipping dock.

Management has conducted a series of interviews with the workers over the last month regarding how well they like the new arrangement. The personnel are quire pleased with their conditions. One worker told management, "I feel like I really make a contribution, and I can see a finished product. I'm not just producing a small part of a large product. I'm doing the whole thing." Another said, "This job gives me a chance to use technical skills and personal judgment. It's just great." A third remarked, "I like the opportunity to set my own pace. I'm basically an afternoon person and at the old assembly plant, they were always on my back first thing in the morning because I wasn't working fast enough. None of that occurs in this plant."

1.   Compare the way the work used to be done in the old plant with the way it is done now. Is this a case of job enlargement or job enrichment? Explain.

2.   Which of the five core job dimensions are present in the work? Explain.

3.   What are some of the job enrichment principles the company used in designing the work for this new factory?

4.   Could job redesign be used with nonproduction jobs in this company? Explain.

Write down your answers to these questions and put them aside. We will return to them later. ∎

WORK IN AMERICA

Many workers today admit that they are bored with their jobs. They feel no challenge or desire to do a particularly good job. There is no excitement in their work lives.

What can management do about this? There are four alternatives available:

1.   The organization can do nothing.

2.   The management can offer the workers more money for accepting these dull, repetitive, uninteresting jobs.

3.   The organization can try to replace the workers with machines by automating many of the jobs.

4.   The company can redesign the work so that it has meaning for the employees.

THERE ARE NUMEROUS WAYS TO DEAL WITH BORING JOBS.

The most important of these alternatives in the study of human relations is the last.

There is a need to give workers more of a challenge, more of a whole task, more opportunity to use advanced skills, more opportunity for growth, and more chance to contribute their ideas. The classical design of jobs was to construct them according to the technological imperative, that is, to design them according to the needs of technology and give little attention to other criteria. The new approach is to provide a careful balance of the human imperative and the technical imperative. *Jobs are required to fit people as well as technology*. This is a new set of values and a new way of thinking that focuses on QWL.[1]

Much of what we discuss in this chapter relates to lower-level jobs. The reason is quite simple—most of the dull, repetitive jobs are located at the bottom of the hierarchy. Of course, middle-level and top-level managers also quit their jobs because they can find no meaning in them. However, their number is quite small in contrast to that of their counter-

[1] Keith Davis, *Human Behavior at Work: Organizational Behavior*, 6th ed. (New York: McGraw-Hill Book Company, 1981), p. 287.

Before computer technology was introduced at American Family Insurance Company, employees handled claims in an assembly-line fashion. Jobs were often boring and offered little opportunity for advancement.

The introduction of computers led to a job-redesign experiment where 12-member teams processed claims from start to finish, resulting in a wider range of tasks.

parts farther down in the organization. The major focus of QWL efforts is at the lowest levels where productivity gains through more meaningful jobs can be achieved by work life improvements. How can this be done?[2] One of the primary ways is to redesign the work itself.

THE NATURE OF JOB REDESIGN

JOB REDESIGN REFERS TO ANY WORK CHANGES THAT INCREASE WORK QUALITY OR PRODUCTIVITY.

Any activities involving work changes with the purpose of increasing the quality of the worker's job experience or improving the worker's productivity are referred to as **job redesign**.[3] Under this term can be included such commonly used job redesign techniques as job rotation, job enlargement, and job enrichment.

Job redesign is a unique way of improving organizational efficiency. This is true for four reasons.

First, job redesign alters the basic relationship between the worker and the job, which has long been a human relations problem.[4] The scientific managers tried to deal with the problem by blending the physical requirements of the work with the physical characteristics of the workers, and screening out those who did not measure up. When behavioral scientists entered industry, they attempted to refine this process by improv-

[2] Edward M. Glaser, "Productivity Gains through Worklife Improvement," *Personnel*, January–February 1980, pp. 71–77; and Jim M. Grath, "Let's Get a Handle on QWL," *Supervisory Management*, June 1983, pp. 26–34.

[3] J. Richard Hackman and J. Lloyd Suttle, eds., *Improving Life at Work* (Santa Monica, Calif.: Goodyear Publishing Company, 1977), p. 98.

[4] John C. Crystal and Richard S. Deems, "Redesigning Jobs," *Training and Development Journal*, February 1983, pp. 44–46.

ing the selection and training of the workers. As with the scientific managers, however, the concentration of effort was still on the people doing the job. The work was treated as a fixed commodity that could not be altered. Job redesign breaks with this tradition and is based on the assumption that the work itself can be a powerful influence on employee motivation, satisfaction, and productivity.

Moreover, after jobs are changed, it usually is difficult for workers to slip back into old ways. The old ways simply are inappropriate for the new tasks, and the structure of those tasks reinforces the changes that have taken place. Thus, one need not worry much about the kind of backsliding that occurs so often after training or attitude modification activities, especially those that occur off-site. The task-based stimuli that influence the worker's behavior are very much on-site, every hour of every day. And once those stimuli are changed, behavior is likely to stay changed—at least until the job is again redesigned.[5]

Second, job redesign does not attempt to change attitudes first (such as inducing workers to care about work results in a zero-defects program that is designed to reduce, and then to eliminate, all product errors) but assumes that positive attitudes will follow if the job is redesigned properly. Initial attention is given to determining how the job ought to be done. Once this is worked out, the individual doing the work will be forced to change his or her old behavior and hopefully will like the new arrangement so much that attitude toward the job will then be positive.

■ ■ ■ ■ ■ ■ ■ ■ ■ ■ ■ ■ ■
JOB REDESIGN IS A UNIQUE WAY OF IMPROVING ORGANIZATIONAL EFFICIENCY.

Third, job redesign helps individuals regain the opportunity to experience the kick that comes from doing a job well. There is more here than just satisfaction; there is a sense of competence and self-worth in which people feel themselves stretching and growing as human beings.

Fourth, sometimes when an organization redesigns jobs and solves people-work problems, other opportunities for initiating organizational change are presented. For example, technical problems are likely to develop when jobs are changed, offering management the opportunity to smooth and refine the entire work system. Interpersonal issues are also likely to arise, often between supervisors and subordinates, providing the organization a chance to do developmental work aimed at improving the social and supervisory aspects of the work system.

In any event, job redesign is a very important tool, for it provides a basis for developing and utilizing the organization's resources. Some experts like to say that it is a way for the enterprise to work "smarter" rather than "harder."[6] In the next section we examine three job redesign techniques commonly used in this process.

■ ■ ■ ■ ■ ■ ■

[5] Hackman and Suttle, *Improving Life at Work*, p. 102.

[6] Bernard J. Reilly and Joseph A. DiAngelo, Jr., "A Look at Job Redesign," *Personnel*, February 1988, pp. 61–65.

Job Redesign Techniques

Job redesign techniques are methods used to change work procedures and, depending on the situation, increase or decrease work demands. These techniques are very useful in helping deal with morale problems caused by boring or meaningless work. When employees do not feel challenged by their jobs or believe that their work is of little importance, morale tends to decline. Conversely, if these individuals feel challenged by the work and are convinced that their jobs are important, morale tends to rise and remain high. Job redesign techniques are often, although not always, used to improve morale. There are three popular job redesign techniques: (1) job rotation, (2) job enlargement, and (3) job enrichment.

Job Rotation

■ ■ ■ ■ ■ ■ ■ ■ ■ ■ ■ ■ ■ ■
IN JOB ROTATION THE WORKER
MOVES FROM ONE JOB TO
ANOTHER.

Moving a worker from one job to another for the purpose of reducing boredom is termed **job rotation**. For example, six workers are charged with assembling, soldering, testing, painting, and packaging a piece of sophisticated machinery. As seen in Figure 8.1, the first person assembles Components A, B, and C; the second assembles D, E, and F; and each of the other workers performs a specific function on the unit. The arrows in the figure illustrate how job rotation works. Each person moves to the task immediately following the one he or she has been doing. The person assembling Components A, B, and C now assembles Components D, E, and F; the worker soldering the unit and putting it into a casing now tests the unit to be sure it works; the individual packaging the unit now moves to assembling Components A, B, and C. Continually moving all the workers in this manner can often keep them more interested in their work than if they each did the same thing day after day. Another benefit of job rotation is the perspective it provides the individual as to how his or her activity fits into the overall work flow. A third benefit is that the individual's identification with the final output increases. A fourth benefit is that job rotation turns workers from narrow specialists who can do but one task into broad generalists who can do many.[7] All these benefits can help increase work motivation.

Job Enlargement

■ ■ ■ ■ ■ ■ ■ ■ ■ ■ ■ ■ ■ ■
JOB ENLARGEMENT GIVES THE
WORKER MORE TO DO.

Giving the worker more to do is **job enlargement**. Usually this new work is similar to what the person has done before. For example, if Joe is wiring, Ralph is soldering, and Mary is testing the product, the three of them may have their jobs enlarged by allowing each to perform all three

■ ■ ■ ■ ■ ■ ■

[7]Steve Lohr, "How Job Rotation Works for Japanese," *New York Times*, July 12, 1982, pp. 19, 22.

FIGURE 8.1   **Job Rotation**

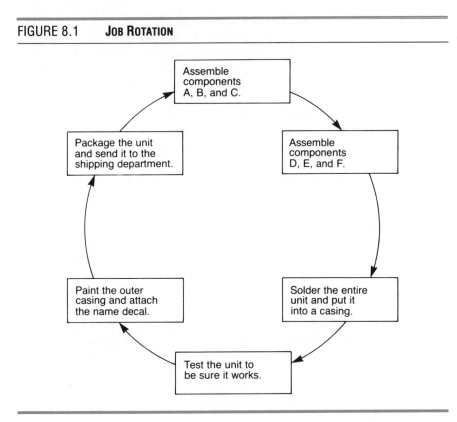

functions. One of the ways in which this job redesign can result in efficiency is through the time saved by not having to pass the product from one person to the next. Additionally, there is the psychological reward associated with completing a unit as opposed to performing just one small task on a large product. Some researchers have reported that the main advantages of job enlargement appear to be increased job satisfaction and improved quality of work.[8]

Job Enrichment

A technique that is more behaviorally sophisticated than job enlargement is **job enrichment**, which attempts to build psychological motivators, as described by Herzberg's two-factor theory, into the job. In particular, job enrichment programs attempt to give the worker more authority in planning the work and controlling the pace and procedures used in doing the job.

JOB ENRICHMENT GIVES THE WORKER MORE AUTHORITY IN PLANNING AND CONTROLLING THE WORK.

••••••

[8] Alan C. Filley, Robert J. House, and Steven Kerr, *Managerial Process and Organizational Behavior*, 2nd ed. (Glenview, Ill.: Scott, Foresman and Company, 1976), p. 345.

Industrial research reveals that a number of firms have had success with job enrichment, including American Telephone and Telegraph (AT&T), General Foods, and Travelers Insurance. At AT&T, for example, employees who were handling insurance correspondence with stockholders were chosen for a job enrichment program. Using a test group and a control group, the researchers enriched the jobs of the test group by permitting them to sign their own names to the letters they prepared, encouraging them to become experts in the kinds of problems that appealed to them, holding them accountable for the quality of their work, and providing them with expert assistance in carrying out these duties. After six months, the group's quality, attitudes, and productivity had increased, and their tardiness, absenteeism, and work costs had declined. The control group's performance on these factors, meanwhile, had remained the same.[9] However, job enrichment is not without costs and those who do not approach it with enough determination to do it right often will fail.[10] This is especially true if they fail to consider core job dimensions.

STOP!

Review your answer to the first question and make any changes you would like. Then compare your answer to the one below.

1.   Compare the way the work used to be done in the old plant with the way it is done now. Is this a case of job enlargement or job enrichment? Explain.

This is a case of job enrichment. Notice from the comments of the workers that they like the new arrangement a lot more than the old one. It is psychologically satisfying. This is not simply a situation of the workers being given more work because it will save time and allow the company to produce more units at a lower price. The personnel really like what they are doing. They can control the pace of their work and are responsible for the quality of the total final product so the job is intrinsically motivational. ∎

∎∎∎∎∎∎

[9] Robert N. Ford, *Motivation through the Work Itself* (New York: American Management Association, 1969), pp. 20–44.

[10] Howard R. Smith, "The Uphill Struggle for Job Enrichment," *California Management Review*, Summer 1981, pp. 33–38.

CORE JOB DIMENSIONS

Why do redesign techniques such as the three discussed in the previous section often lead to increases in productivity and higher satisfaction among the personnel? The answer rests not only in the physical changes that take place in the work environment, but also in the psychological changes that take place within the employees. In particular, it has been found that certain dimensions can be built into the work that will bring about higher output, lower absenteeism, higher quality, and greater internal work motivation. Research reveals that there are five **core job dimensions** that are extremely useful in enriching jobs: (1) skill variety, (2) task identity, (3) task significance, (4) autonomy, and (5) feedback.[11] These core dimensions are typically a result of redesigning jobs so that they are more psychologically rewarding and result in higher morale and job satisfaction. Research shows that when these core job dimensions are present, morale and job satisfaction tend to increase and when they are not present, morale and job satisfaction will often decrease.[12]

Using a "craft station" concept, Buick now assembles some of its automobiles by team operations. At each station, a small team performs its functions. The team must be satisfied with the job before the car is moved to the next station.

SKILL VARIETY

The degree to which a job requires the completion of different activities, all of which involve varying talents and capabilities, is the **skill variety**. The two most common types of skills are motor skills and intellectual skills. Motor skills help one with "doing" tasks, and intellectual skills are used with "thinking" tasks. If a job can draw on both, it will provide greater variety than if only one of them is needed.

■ ■ ■ ■ ■ ■ ■ ■ ■ ■ ■ ■ ■
SKILL VARIETY IS THE DEGREE TO WHICH JOBS REQUIRE A COMPLETION OF DIFFERENT ACTIVITIES.

> Bob Williams is a salesman for a large machine manufacturer. The machine he sells is very complex and requires a technical sales pitch. Advertising is also very important in gaining customer attention and arousing initial interest. The typical sales strategy is to mail an advertising brochure to potential customers and then follow up by sending in a salesperson to those who express interest.
>
> Bob had been the company's number one salesman for three years and had been thinking about quitting because the challenge of selling was losing its excitement. He started to feel that the requisite technical sales presentation did not allow him to exercise his creativity. He decided to stay on, however, after

■ ■ ■ ■ ■ ■ ■

[11] J. Richard Hackman and Greg R. Oldham, "Development of the Job Diagnostic Survey," *Journal of Applied Psychology*, April 1975, pp. 159–170.
[12] Lisa A. Mainiero and Robert L. DeMichiell, "Minimizing Employee Resistance to Technological Change," *Personnel*, July 1986, pp. 32–37.

the vice-president of sales asked him to help write the advertising brochure.

"We need some input from you regarding how to make the initial pitch to the customer," the vice-president told him. "You know how these people think; we'd like to put your ideas into the brochure." Delighted with the chance to do some "think" work, Bob dropped his plans to leave the company.

TASK IDENTITY

■ ■ ■ ■ ■ ■ ■ ■ ■ ■ ■ ■ ■

TASK IDENTITY INVOLVES THE DEGREE TO WHICH A JOB REQUIRES COMPLETION OF AN IDENTIFIABLE PIECE OF WORK.

The degree to which the job requires completion of a whole or identifiable piece of work is termed **task identity**. The more an individual does on the job, the more likely he or she will identify with the task. Assembly-line employees who put a bolt on a car or weld part of the structure have little task identity. Those who complete a major part of the car (working as a member of a group) have much greater task identity.

Jane Copeland is an assembler-packer for a consumer goods manufacturer. A year ago Jane used to assemble two parts of a seven-part consumer product. Then, thanks to a job redesign program, she was given all seven parts to assemble as well as the responsibility of packaging the product. The result—in Jane's group there was a 90 percent decline in absenteeism and turnover and a seven percent increase in output.

TASK SIGNIFICANCE

■ ■ ■ ■ ■ ■ ■ ■ ■ ■ ■ ■ ■

TASK SIGNIFICANCE IS THE DEGREE TO WHICH A JOB HAS A SUBSTANTIAL IMPACT ON OTHERS.

The degree to which a job has a substantial impact on the lives or work of other people is its **task significance**. When employees are able to see how the work they do influences others, they tend to be more motivated to do a good job.

Alice Bodelyn is a manuscript editor for a college textbook publishing firm. Generally, Alice is assigned two manuscripts at the same time and for the next two to three months she reads the material, edits it for grammar, makes style and substance recommendations, and then sends it back to the respective author in batches of three to four chapters for the author's comments. As the edited manuscript reaches completion, Alice discusses the content of the book with a member of the design department, who will work up a cover for the text. Finally, the author visits the publishing house, meets Alice and the cover designer, and spends a few days with them and the marketing people who are putting together the advertising campaign.

Alice has been a manuscript editor for four years and she has received a personally autographed copy of each book from its author. When asked what she likes best about her work, she says, "I feel an integral part of an important team. When I look at the finished book I see part of myself in it."

AUTONOMY

The degree to which the job provides the worker freedom, independence, and discretion in scheduling the work and determining how to carry it out is **autonomy**. As people begin to plan and execute their assignments without having to rely on others for direction and instructions, they develop feelings of strong personal responsibilities for job success and job failure and are motivated to do the best possible job.

■ ■ ■ ■ ■ ■ ■ ■ ■ ■ ■ ■
AUTONOMY IS THE DEGREE TO WHICH A JOB PROVIDES THE WORKER WITH FREEDOM IN CARRYING IT OUT.

> Dick Jackson is a life insurance agent for a large company based in New York. Dick usually begins his workday at 10 a.m., calling on one or two prospective customers and taking a third to lunch. Then he returns to the office to answer correspondence and prepare material for people he will be meeting later in the day. From 4 p.m. to 6 p.m., Dick talks to customers in the office, and three days a week he works evenings. Last year Dick was again a member of the million dollar club, having sold $1.92 million of life insurance.
>
> This past week the district manager asked Dick if he would like to leave his current job and become an office manager. "What for?" asked Dick. "I've got freedom in my current job. Who wants to be tied down to a nine-to-five office schedule?"

FEEDBACK

The degree to which the work required by the job results in the individual's receiving direct, clear information about the effectiveness of his or her performance is termed **feedback**. Feedback allows people to monitor their own work rather than depend on someone else to do it for them.

■ ■ ■ ■ ■ ■ ■ ■ ■ ■ ■ ■
FEEDBACK IS THE DEGREE TO WHICH THE WORK PROVIDES THE WORKER WITH PERFORMANCE INFORMATION.

> Group A is charged with wiring the panels for a complex telecommunications satellite. If the wiring of these panels is done incorrectly, it could result in a malfunction of the entire system during or after launching into earth orbit. To prevent such an occurrence, there are a few simple tests that can be conducted on the panels. Owing to the complexity of the wiring, however, it is not uncommon for each panel to have three or four incorrectly placed wires. When this occurs, errors are caught by the test group and are noted on an error chart. The panel is then returned to Group A for partial rewiring.
>
> Group A has recently protested this procedure, claiming that it is virtually impossible to wire a panel correctly on the first

try. There are bound to be a few errors, and the group is embarrassed when a panel is sent back by the test group. The members of Group A have asked management to redesign their work and incorporate testing as one of their functions while, of course, maintaining a small test group to make a final check of the panel. The company agreed, and over the last four weeks none of the 40 panels sent to the test group has been returned. "Once we know there's an error," said a member of Group A, "we can correct it before sending it on. This type of feedback, from our own group, reduces tension and helps us to do a better job."

MOTIVATING POTENTIAL SCORE

Researchers have used the five core job dimensions described in this section to develop a **motivating potential score** formula:

$$\text{Motivation potential score (MPS)} = \left[\frac{\text{Skill variety} + \text{Task identity} + \text{Task significance}}{3} \right] \times \text{Autonomy} \times \text{Feedback}$$

Although we do not need to get into the mathematics of the formula, one overriding conclusion can be drawn from it. If the organization wants to redesign jobs so that the employees are motivated, it must build in autonomy, feedback, and at least one of the three remaining dimensions. This last statement becomes clear when we see that if there is no autonomy or no feedback, the MPS will be zero, since these two dimensions are multiplicative. Likewise, if all the three other dimensions are zero, the MPS will be zero.

Testing of these job core characteristics has provided some breakthroughs in job design. In particular, researchers have found that if these dimensions are present, individuals with high growth needs will be more motivated, productive, and satisfied than if they work on tasks without these dimensions.

JOB PROFILE CHARTS

In addition, it is possible to construct **job profile charts** so that enrichment programs can more effectively be designed. For example, in Figure 8.2, Job 1 is low on skill variety, task identity, and task significance. Job 2 is low on task significance, autonomy, and feedback. Job 3 is low on skill variety, task significance, and feedback. The first question the organiza-

FIGURE 8.2   **PROFILE CHART OF CORE JOB DIMENSIONS FOR THREE JOBS**

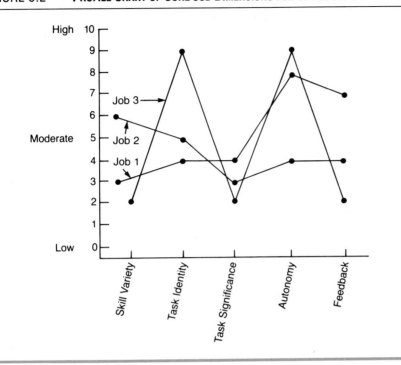

tion must answer is: can the particular job be enriched; i.e., can Job 1 be redesigned so that it has greater skill variety, task identity, and task significance? If the answer is yes, then the people charged with the redesign program know where to begin. If the answer is no, the employees must be made to realize that there is nothing that can be done to restructure the job.

A JOB PROFILE CHART HELPS IDENTIFY CORE JOB DIMENSIONS.

Before our discussion of this point closes, one thing should be made very clear: some jobs cannot be enriched. There may be no way of increasing the task significance of a dishwasher's job. Nor can American auto-assembly lines, under present conditions, provide a person with skill variety. In some cases the individual must conform to the work pattern because the work pattern cannot be altered.

How much of these core dimensions can you find in your own job? One way of answering this question is to analyze your work views systematically with the help of the short Time Out quiz on how you view your work.

TIME OUT

HOW YOU VIEW YOUR WORK

The quiz is designed to provide insights into how you view your work. If you do not currently work full time, refer to your last full-time job in answering the questions. If you have not had a full-time job, think of one you would like to have (be reasonable in your choice), and use it throughout the quiz. Interpretations are provided at the end of the chapter.

I. Read the following job-related questions very carefully and decide how accurate each is in describing your job. Then answer each using the following scale:

1. None
2. Very little
3. A little
4. A moderate amount
5. Some
6. Quite a bit
7. A lot

1. To what degree does your job allow you to do a whole series of different things, employing a variety of skills and talents in the process? _____
2. To what degree does your job allow you to complete a whole piece of work in contrast to just a small part of an overall piece of work? _____
3. How much significance or importance does your job have? _____
4. How much freedom do you have to do your job your own way? _____
5. To what degree does the job itself provide feedback on how well you are doing? _____
6. To what degree do your boss or fellow workers let you know how well you are doing? _____

II. Determine how accurate each of the following statements is in describing your job. Use the following scale to record your answer:

1. Highly inaccurate
2. Mostly inaccurate
3. Slightly inaccurate
4. Uncertain
5. Slightly accurate
6. Mostly accurate
7. Highly accurate

1. Your job is simple and repetitive. _____
2. Your boss and co-workers never give you feedback on your work progress. _____
3. Your job provides you no chance to use personal initiative or judgment in carrying out tasks. _____
4. Your job is not really very significant or important. _____
5. Your job provides independence and freedom in doing the work your way. _____
6. Your job provides the chance to completely finish pieces of work that you begin. _____
7. How well you do your work really affects a lot of other people. _____
8. Just by the way the work is designed, you have many opportunities to evaluate how well you are doing. _____
9. Your job calls for you to use a lot of complex and/or high-level skills. _____
10. Superiors often let you know how well you are doing your job. _____
11. Your work is set up in such a way that you do not have the chance to do an entire piece of work from beginning to end. _____
12. Your job provides few clues regarding how well you are performing your tasks. _____

STOP!

Review your answer to the second question and make any changes you would like. Then compare your answer to the one below.

2.   Which of the five core job dimensions are present in the work? Explain.

All five of the core job dimensions are present. The personnel have a greater opportunity to use their skills. They are able to identify with the task and feel that it is significant. They also like the autonomy and, thanks to the testing equipment, they get immediate feedback on how well they are doing and what changes, if any, are required. ■

JOB ENRICHMENT PRINCIPLES

There are many ways of enriching jobs so as to provide more meaningful work. In this section, we examine five job enrichment principles: (1) formation of natural work units, (2) establishment of worker-client relationships, (3) combining of tasks, (4) vertical loading, and (5) opening of feedback channels. We study how each principle can be used in redesigning work. Figure 8.3 illustrates how each principle is tied to one or more of the core job dimensions.

FORMATION OF NATURAL WORK UNITS

In many organizations, the workers all contribute to providing a product or service but do not have any basis for identifying with the work. A secretary in the typing pool types all the correspondence and reports as-

NATURAL WORK UNITS GIVE A WORKER SOME JOB OWNERSHIP.

FIGURE 8.3   EXAMPLE OF THE RELATIONSHIP BETWEEN SELECTED JOB ENRICHMENT PRINCIPLES AND CORE JOB DIMENSIONS

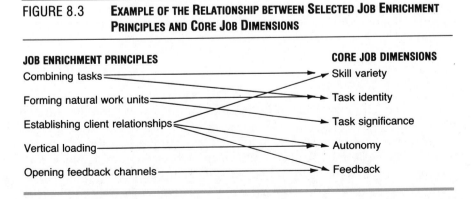

JOB ENRICHMENT PRINCIPLES — CORE JOB DIMENSIONS

Combining tasks — Skill variety
Forming natural work units — Task identity
Establishing client relationships — Task significance
Vertical loading — Autonomy
Opening feedback channels — Feedback

signed by the supervisor of the pool. On a given day there may be letters from five or six departmental managers as well as part of a speech for the vice-president of personnel. After a while, all the work blurs together and the secretary identifies with none of it. He or she is simply a producer of typed material. This analogy holds for a person on an auto-assembly line who is installing upholstery. One car looks like another. The job has no real meaning.

One way of enriching jobs such as these is through the formation of natural work units, in which the employee obtains some ownership of the work. For example, responsibility for all the work requested by a single department or person could be assigned to one typist. Instead of typing one part of a large report, the typist now types it all. Over time, the person begins to identify with the task and to see how the material is of value to those who receive the finished product. The formation of natural work units contributes to two core job dimensions: task identity and task significance (see Figure 8.3).

ESTABLISHMENT OF WORKER-CLIENT RELATIONSHIPS

■ ■ ■ ■ ■ ■ ■ ■ ■ ■ ■ ■ ■ ■
WORKER-CLIENT RELATIONSHIPS
CONTRIBUTE TO SKILL VARIETY,
AUTONOMY, AND FEEDBACK.

Workers seldom come in contact with the ultimate user of their product or service. If such a relationship can be established, however, job commitment and motivation will usually be enhanced. There are three steps in the establishment of worker-client relationships: (1) identify the client, (2) determine the most direct contact possible between the worker and the client, and (3) set up a system by which the client can evaluate the quality of the product or service and convey the judgments directly to the worker.

Establishing worker-client relationships can contribute to three core job dimensions: skill variety, autonomy, and feedback. Skill variety increases because the worker has the chance to exercise interpersonal skills in both managing and maintaining the client relationship. Autonomy increases because the person is given responsibility for deciding how to manage the client relationship. Feedback increases because the worker has the opportunity to receive both praise and criticism for his or her output.

COMBINING OF TASKS

■ ■ ■ ■ ■ ■ ■ ■ ■ ■ ■ ■ ■ ■
COMBINING OF TASKS CAN
INCREASE MOTIVATION.

The principle of combining tasks is based on the assumption that higher work motivation can result when a series of simple tasks is combined to form a new and larger work module. For example, a few years ago a Corning Glass Works plant redesigned the job of assembling laboratory hot plates by combining a number of tasks that had been separate. The redesigned job called for each operator to assemble an entire hot plate.

Costs declined and motivation increased as a result of the redesign effort. The combining of tasks contributes to two core job dimensions: skill variety and task identity. The enlarged job requires a greater variety of skill, and as the individual begins turning out finished products, task identity increases. The assembler can see the unit taking shape as the various pieces are affixed and soldered.

VERTICAL LOADING

When the gap between the "doing" and "controlling" aspects of the job is reduced **vertical loading** occurs. In particular, responsibilities that formerly were reserved for management are now delegated to the employee as part of the job. Some ways of vertically loading a job include the following:

VERTICAL LOADING CLOSES THE GAP BETWEEN THE DOING AND CONTROLLING ASPECTS OF THE JOB.

- Give the worker the responsibility for deciding work methods and for advising or helping to train less experienced workers.
- Provide increased freedom to the worker including decisions about when to start and stop work, when to take breaks, and how to assign work priorities.
- Encourage the workers to do their own troubleshooting and manage work crises rather than immediately calling for a supervisor.
- Provide workers with increased knowledge of the financial aspects of the job and the organization, and increased control over budgetary matters that affect their work.[13]

When a job is vertically loaded, autonomy increases and workers begin feeling personal responsibility and accountability for the outcome of their efforts.

OPENING OF FEEDBACK CHANNELS

In most jobs there are ways of opening feedback channels so each worker can monitor his or her own performance. One way, discussed already, is to establish direct worker-client relationships by which the individual can learn what the client likes and dislikes about the product or service being provided. Another is to place as much control as possible in the hands of the worker. For example, rather than having quality checks performed by people in the quality assurance department, let the worker do the checking. Such a move ensures immediate feedback and allows the individual to exercise self-control. Placing quality-control functions in the hands of workers can result in higher quantity and quality of out-

FEEDBACK CHANNELS ALLOW FOR SELF-CONTROL.

[13] Hackman and Suttle, *Improving Life at Work*, pp. 138–139.

put. This principle helps overcome one of the main human relations problems—failure to tell people how well they are doing.

Tradition and established procedure in many organizations dictate that records about performance be kept by a supervisor and transmitted up (not down) the organizational hierarchy. Sometimes supervisors even check the work and correct any errors themselves. The worker who made the error never knows it occurred and is therefore denied the very information that could enhance both internal work motivation and the technical adequacy of his performance. In many cases, it is possible to provide standard summaries of performance records directly to the workers. This would give the employees personally and regularly the data they need to improve their effectiveness.[14]

STOP!

Review your answer to the third question and make any changes you would like. Then compare your answer to the one below.

3. What are some of the job enrichment principles the company used in designing the work for this new factory?

One of the job enrichment principles the company used in designing the work for this new factory was that of combining tasks. Now the workers carry out a series of tasks, not just one or two. The company also used vertical loading. The personnel now have autonomy to work at their own pace. The firm also opened feedback channels by giving the workers testing equipment so they could check assembled units to make sure that the units were properly put together. ■

JOB ENRICHMENT IN ACTION

There have been a number of successful applications of the job enrichment concepts we discuss in this chapter. Perhaps the best known is that by Volvo, the Swedish car manufacturer. Job enrichment has also been effective in many other organizations, ranging from manufacturing firms to insurance companies.[15] Let us examine some cases of job enrichment in action.

∎∎∎∎∎∎

[14] *Ibid.*, pp. 139–140.

[15] David A. Whitsett and Lyle Yorks, "Looking Back at Topeka: General Foods and the Quality-of-Work-Life Experiment," *California Management Review*, Summer 1983, pp. 93–109.

VOLVO

In the early 1970s, Volvo built a new auto assembly plant in Kalmar, Sweden. Instead of having the work come to the people, however, the management decided to construct an assembly line in which the people went to the work. The company felt that people would do a better job if it was the product that stood while the personnel did the moving. Additionally, the management believed that people want to have social contact on the job, and on the typical assembly line this is not possible because the employees are physically isolated from one another. If the work were patterned according to the people, the Volvo management believed, the employees could act in cooperation, have more time to discuss work-related problems, and decide among themselves how best to organize their jobs. This new approach was to be based on stimulation rather than restriction.

> The design for Kalmar incorporated pleasant, quiet surroundings, arranged for group working, with each group having its own individual rest and meeting areas. The work itself is organized so that each group is responsible for a particular, identifiable portion of the car—electrical systems, interiors, doors, and so on. Individual cars are built up on self-propelling "carriers" that run around the factory following a movable conductive tape on the floor. Computers normally direct the carriers, but manual controls can override the taped route. If someone notices a scratch in the paint on a car, he or she can immediately turn the carrier back to the painting station. Under computer control again, the car will return later to the production process wherever it left off.
>
> Each work group has its own buffer areas for incoming and outgoing carriers so it can pace itself as it wishes and organize the work inside its own area so its members work individually or in subgroups to suit themselves. Most of the employees have chosen to learn more than one small job; the individual increase in skills also gives the team itself added flexibility.[16]

In addition, each team does its own inspection. After a car passes three work group stations, it goes through a special inspection station where people with special training test it. If there are any persistent or recurring problems, a computer-based system flashes the results to the proper group station, informing them of the particular problem and reviewing how they solved it the last time.

    This design employs many of the ideas we discussed in this chapter, including the five core job dimensions, and Volvo has reported success with its approach. In fact, since the success with the Kalmar plant, the

■ ■ ■ ■ ■ ■ ■ ■ ■ ■ ■ ■ ■ ■ ■

VOLVO HAS HAD GOOD SUCCESS WITH JOB ENRICHMENT.

- - - - - - -

[16] Pehr G. Gyllenhammer, "How Volvo Adapts Work to People," *Harvard Business Review*, July–August 1977, p. 107.

FIGURE 8.4   JOB DESIGN GUIDELINES FROM VOLVO

---

1. Each unit should be free to develop individually without interference or detailed control from headquarters.
2. A positive management attitude toward change is a prerequisite for positive results.
3. Positive achievements seem related to the extent that managers understand that the change process will, sooner or later, affect several organizational levels.
4. Problems can be encountered if change is formalized and targets, minutes, and figures are requested too early.
5. Progress seems to be fastest when a factory or company starts by forming a joint management and union steering committee to look at its own problems.
6. The fastest way to get ideas flowing is to set up discussion groups of less than 25 people in each working area.
7. A new plant, product, or machine provides an opportunity to think about new working patterns.
8. An investment in one new facility or work group area often results in spontaneous changes in related facilities or groups.
9. Most factories have a number of tasks that need not be done on assembly lines. Once a few have been found, others will reveal themselves.
10. So that change suggestions will emerge from inside, changes of work organization must be integrated with a structure of employee consultation.

Source: Reprinted by permission of the *Harvard Business Review*. An exhibit from "How Volvo Adapts Work to People" by Pehr G. Gyllenhammer (July/August 1977). Copyright © 1977 by the President and Fellows of Harvard College; all rights reserved.

company has introduced this job design program in four other plants. In addition, a recent survey among the unionized employees at Kalmar reports that almost all of them are in favor of the new working patterns. Figure 8.4 lists findings and suggestions that resulted from the Volvo program.

FEDERAL BUREAU OF INVESTIGATION

The Federal Bureau of Investigation (FBI) is another example of an organization that has successfully used job enrichment. While the bureau has approximately 9,000 special agents in the field, most of its employees work in various support capacities. FBI headquarters recently undertook an effort to improve productivity of its support help. The focus of attention was a 60-person unit responsible for generating criminal arrest and suspect records and entering the data into a mainframe computer.[17] These individuals worked in a highly structured environment and their

· · · · · · ·

[17] Donald C. Witham and John D. Glover, "Recapturing Commitment," *Training and Development Journal*, April 1987, pp. 42–45.

morale was very low. Additionally, because the work load was so great, nearly 10 percent of the unit's records were outdated and unusable. Moreoever, some of the records that were processed were done inaccurately. The bureau decided to reorganize the unit, raise the morale, reduce the work backlog, and increase the group's accuracy.

A review of the worker's personnel records revealed that many of them were in their twenties and that this was their first job. Productivity among the group members varied widely, as did their error rates. Most of them saw little relationship between their performance and the FBI's effectiveness.

In turning the unit around, the bureau began by first setting achievable goals for the employees. Group members and the management jointly participated in this process. The organization then introduced a job enrichment program. Instead of having some of the workers enter record data into the computer and others check the accuracy of the work, the latter jobs were eliminated. Now all employees were given autonomy and control over their own work in terms of both entering information and checking it for accuracy. The management also relaxed the rules regarding conversation among employees and eliminated requirements for simultaneous scheduling of lunch and breaks.

ACHIEVABLE GOALS WERE SET.

> In addition the unit formed a problem-solving team comprising people elected by their peers. This invaluable group identified and suggested ways of overcoming obstacles to higher performance. The team initiated a number of changes in the work area, making it more informal and private. Team members work hand in hand with supervisors to correct problems. Several workers stated that they had regained their initial enthusiasm about working for the FBI and that they finally felt like valued members of the agency.[18]

As a result of the job enrichment program, the unit's productivity soared by more than 60 percent while error rates plummeted. At the same time, absenteeism fell by 20 percent, turnover dropped by more than 50 percent, the backlog of records dropped by almost half, and employee satisfaction went up. Informal discussions with the unit workers revealed substantially improved morale and attitudes. As a result of these efforts, the FBI is now expanding its job enrichment program to include other units.

PRODUCTIVITY ROSE DRAMATICALLY.

ROHM & HAAS BAYPORT, INC.

In the mid-1980s Rohm & Haas Bayport introduced job redesign and job enrichment into the operation of its LaPorte, Texas chemical plant

[18] *Ibid.*, p. 45.

■ ■ ■ ■ ■ ■ ■ ■ ■ ■ ■ ■ ■ ■
A FLAT STRUCTURE WAS USED.

through the use of a flat organization structure.[19] Although there are 67 people in the facility, there are only three levels in the hierarchy. At the top is the plant manager; below this person are two manufacturing managers who head up the operating units; below these people are the process technicians and technical people (engineers and chemists) who run the operation. Unlike plants that operate under traditional rules, there are no shift supervisors at Bayport.

Half the technicians work in the operating unit that produces a herbicide used on soybeans; the other half manufacture a chemical used in making auto paint and film for photographic plates. Neither of the two manufacturing managers gives much direction to the personnel. The employees are expected to make operating decisions by themselves. Working in teams of four to seven people, they decide how to staff the facilities 24 hours a day, 7 days a week. The technicians are cross-trained so that everyone can do all of the jobs in the group, and they rotate jobs with other team members every four to twelve weeks. This practice keeps motivation high and boredom low.

Any major problems are handled by a task force consisting of process technicians, technical people, and management. In this way, there is input from all levels of the hierarchy.

Even the performance evaluation system has been changed to increase its usefulness and to make it less threatening to the personnel. In the past, for example, the technicians would complete written evaluations on each other every six months and submit these to the manufacturing manager. The latter would then individually discuss the evaluations with each technician. Under the newly designed arrangement, each person evaluates only the individuals in his or her own work group. People like this arrangement better and admit that no one knows their work as well as other members of their own group.

■ ■ ■ ■ ■ ■ ■ ■ ■ ■ ■ ■ ■ ■
PARTICIPATIVE MANAGEMENT HAS
PROVEN SUCCESSFUL.

The results from redesigning jobs and introducing participative management have been startling. Before the redesign, the plant had a turnover rate of almost 50 percent. Today the rate is less than 10 percent. Additionally, volume shipped has gone up and the quality rating of the plant by outside contractors is one of the highest in the industry. One reason for the success of the plant is that the employees like the new arrangement much better than the old one. One individual put it this way:

> For me, if I never get a promotion until the day I retire, it's still worth it to work in this environment. I can live without ever being a foreman because people listen to a lot of the things I have to say. That makes me feel good about myself . . . At most places, people don't care what you think. That's the way you

■ ■ ■ ■ ■ ■ ■

[19] Don Nichols, "Taking Participative Management to the Limit," *Management Review*, August 1987, pp. 28–32.

need to do it, and that's all you need to know. You want to work a little harder here, I think.[20]

The Bayport plant is so well thought of by the company, that other plants around the country are beginning to study its methods. As the plant manager put it, "The idea of team participation and team management is diffusing into the company. But we're still way out ahead of the others. I like to think that we've created a good system of working that benefits both our people and Rohm & Haas."[21]

OTHER EXAMPLES

There are many other cases of organizations using job redesign and job enrichment. These include both white-collar and blue-collar operations.

PAUL REVERE COMPANIES   At Paul Revere Companies, the giant insurance firm, the organization decided to identify those factors that helped increase productivity and to build a program around them. They found that from 70 to 90 percent of productive potential was a result of: (1) self-esteem, (2) responsibility, (3) co-worker relationships within work groups, (4) employee capability, and (5) the availability of resources.[22] The firm then set about creating an environment that would tap this potential. They began emphasizing personal responsibility for quality and recognizing achievement. A reward system was developed that featured everything from lapel pins and bracelet charms to catered work-team lunches; articles and pictures in the company newspaper; gift certificates; and personal congratulations from senior-level managers. The company also began creating a formal communication system that would tell people how well they were doing in their job. At the same time the firm started to increase the amount of training it was giving to its people. The primary focus was put on skill improvement programs that would help people do a better job. As a result of these redesign and job enrichment efforts, the company has produced more than $10 million in direct and indirect savings over the last two years.

■ ■ ■ ■ ■ ■ ■ ■ ■ ■ ■ ■

JOB REDESIGN AND JOB ENRICHMENT PAID OFF.

MAJOR WEST COAST BANK   A major west coast bank has used a joint work-team approach to create order out of chaos. As the bank began expanding rapidly, many middle managers and loan officers were hired to

■ ■ ■ ■ ■ ■

[20] *Ibid.*, p. 32.

[21] *Ibid.*

[22] Jac Fitz-Enz, "White-Collar Effectiveness, Part 1: The Employees' Side," *Management Review*, May 1986, p. 52.

HUMAN RELATIONS IN ACTION

IMPLEMENTING JOB ENRICHMENT

Many firms have successfully implemented job enrichment programs, but some company efforts have failed. The reasons some programs have been unsuccessful can often be linked directly to one of the five critical steps in implementing a job enrichment program. The five critical steps follow:

1.   *Be willing to make changes in jobs.* The first step in any job enrichment program is the willingness to change work procedures or job requirements in an effort to increase the motivational potential of the tasks. Unless an organization is willing to make such changes, there is no chance for a job enrichment program to succeed.

2.   *Get the workers involved.* No one knows more about a job than those who are doing it. If the work is boring, excessively demanding, or poorly organized, the workers are aware of this. By getting them involved in redesigning the job, an organization increases the chances that the new work will be more motivational and/or result in increased productivity.

3.   *Stay the course.* Will a newly designed job result in increased output or improved service? It may, but the results often take time; the company has to be willing to wait and see how things turn out. If a job is totally reorganized, for example, the workers may like the new arrangement but need a couple of months to master the new procedures and techniques. Only then can management draw valid conclusions regarding the overall effect of the program.

4.   *Be prepared for more changes.* Sometimes changes in one job result in the need for changes in other jobs. For example, if assembly-line workers are given greater authority over their tasks, supervisors' jobs may become less challenging and need to be redesigned as well. This ripple effect may be felt throughout the entire department or plant and result in the need for job redesign in many areas.

5.   *Know how to measure the results.* The organization should know how it will measure the results of any redesign effort. Typical examples include productivity, service, and personnel-related results such as absenteeism, tardiness, and turnover. Is efficiency increasing? This is commonly measured by comparing the amount of output with the cost of producing the goods. Is service improving? This is usually measured in terms of customer feedback. Are absenteeism, tardiness, and turnover going down? These are typically measured through time cards, supervisory feedback, and personnel records.

staff new branches. These people had varied backgrounds and beliefs about how branch banks should be run. As a result, there was internal conflict regarding work responsibilities, and a lack of clear-cut business objectives. Analysis showed that differences of opinion about lending and operations within the branches were blocking progress. The bank then brought together the branch officers to examine the problems.

Each person was asked to review independently a list of branch office tasks and mark those for which they had either primary or back-up responsibility. Comparisons of the lists revealed many duplications and gaps. Through intragroup discussion and additional training, these discrepancies were clarified. As a result, clear-cut objectives were set, and the branches began running smoothly. Within six months, most of the units were exceeding their earnings targets.[23]

■ ■ ■ ■ ■ ■ ■ ■ ■ ■ ■ ■ ■ ■
CLEAR-CUT OBJECTIVES RESULTED IN IMPROVED EARNINGS.

AT&T SHREVEPORT   AT&T's Shreveport works plant decided to make itself competitive on a world scale by reducing the offshore flow of residential telephone production, retooling its factory, and focusing on increased output quality. It began by grouping together workers who shared chores that were interrelated. In this way, high group cohesion and interdependency were developed. At the same time, the company gave the personnel the authority to stop the line whenever errors occurred and to seek out the reasons for problems on the line. Additionally, quality task groups were created and given authority to deal with these problems.

■ ■ ■ ■ ■ ■ ■ ■ ■ ■ ■ ■ ■ ■
HIGH GROUP COHESION WAS DEVELOPED.

> According to Walters [the AT&T manager who coordinated the program], quality is an ongoing commitment that's "spreading beyond classical production operations to every area of the factory." For instance, administrative process improvement teams are looking at paperwork, streamlining flows, eliminating redundancy and "basically challenging" all the steps in the process.
> Throughout, Walters says, Shreveport "is stressing individual responsibility and authority in simplifying jobs and improving techniques." He sees the rewards of that approach going way beyond statistically better products. "We think that attention to the process and individual responsibility will take care of the basic quality question. But we'll get an even bigger enhancement to total quality by building a working environment that seeks perfection and involves everyone in the quest."
> The work force appears to agree. "People on the line are wildly enthusiastic," Walters says. "When we decided to give individual operators the responsibility and authority to stop production, it was a breakthrough. Suddenly, they were full partners in the manufacturing process. They responded by solving problems—or demanding help to solve them—rather than working around the problems. It's exciting."[24]

■ ■ ■ ■ ■ ■ ■

[23] *Ibid.*, pp. 53–54.

[24] Hank Johansson and Dan McArthur, "Rediscovering the Fundamentals of Quality," *Management Review*, January 1988, p. 37.

CURRENT CHALLENGES IN JOB DESIGN

Job design is a very important issue in human relations. After all, designing work so that the employees achieve a sense of task identity and task significance and are provided with skill variety, autonomy, and feedback stimulates motivation. Much of what we have discussed in this chapter has been directed toward this end. However, there are some current job design challenges of which the modern manager should be aware.

First, we need to learn more about the theory and practice of job design. It is not a preassembled innovation that can simply be plugged into an organization and forgotten. Considerable skill and sophistication are needed to design, install, and maintain such programs successfully.

Second, better ways have to be found to diffuse job redesign throughout the organization. For example, Walton studied eight organizations in which successful job design projects had been conducted.[25] In only one of them did he find that significant diffusion took place. Quite obviously, strategies for facilitating job design innovations throughout the organization must be devised.

■ ■ ■ ■ ■ ■ ■ ■ ■ ■ ■ ■ ■ ■

HOWEVER, THERE ARE STILL JOB ENRICHMENT PROBLEMS TO BE SOLVED.

Third, more attention has to be given to improving the jobs of lower-level managers. These jobs are often poorly designed with limited autonomy and feedback. Additionally, lower-level managers tend to be caught in the middle. They are too high in the hierarchy to associate with the rank and file and too far down to be accepted by the other managers. They also have problems when their subordinates' jobs are redesigned and theirs are not. More decision making and special tasks traditionally reserved for management are given to the workers, and the job of the manager becomes less meaningful. If work redesign is to be diffused throughout the organization, the jobs of those lower-level managers must be improved.

Fourth, the role of labor unions in initiating and executing job redesign programs has to be expanded and elaborated.[26] The position of many organized labor representatives is one of suspicion. They do not understand the value of job redesign and are concerned that management will use it to increase work output or exploit the employees in some other way. In Europe, union-management cooperation is common; in fact, unions often take the initiative in suggesting work redesign. At present in this country, little is known regarding how best to achieve union participation in such activities. Clearly, research in this area is needed.

In sum, the challenge facing unions, management and behavioral scientists in articulating and elaborating the role of unions

■ ■ ■ ■ ■ ■ ■

[25] R. E. Walton, "The Diffusion of New Work Structures: Explaining Why Success Didn't Take," *Organizational Dynamics*, Winter 1975, pp. 3–22.

[26] James W. Thacker and Mitchell W. Fields, "Union Involvement in Quality-of-Worklife Efforts: A Longitudinal Investigation," *Personnel Psychology*, Spring 1987, pp. 97–111.

in work redesign activities is a substantial one. But it is also a challenge that is worthy of considerable effort on the part of those who care about improving the quality of life in organizations. For without the active involvement of organized labor, it is doubtful that work redesign can ever evolve into a strategy for change that actively *develops*—not just utilizes—human resources in organizations.[27]

STOP!

Review your answer to the fourth question and make any changes you would like. Then compare your answer to the one below.

4.   Could job redesign be used with nonproduction jobs in this company? Explain.

It certainly could. The firm could use the basic ideas presented in this chapter including the core job dimensions and the job redesign principles to help it identify how work could be redesigned. However, the firm would also have to be aware of the fact that there are potential pitfalls in the process and make every effort to avoid these problems. ∎

SUMMARY

Many workers are bored with their work, feeling no challenge or desire to do a particularly good job. What can management do about this? There are various alternatives available, but the most practical is that of redesigning the work so that it has meaning for the employees. There are a number of ways of doing so: job rotation, job enlargement, and job enrichment. The last is the most commonly employed approach.

How does one go about enriching jobs? Some of the latest research reveals that five core job dimensions are extremely useful in this process: skill variety, task identity, task significance, autonomy, and feedback. Researchers have used these five core job dimensions to develop a motivating potential score with which to evaluate a job. The formula shows that in order to redesign jobs so that the employees are motivated, the work must have autonomy, feedback, and at least one of the other three core job dimensions. The common job enrichment principles that can be used in obtaining these dimensions include formation of natural work units,

- - - - - - - -
[27] Hackman and Suttle, *Improving Life at Work*, p. 162.

establishment of worker-client relationships, combining of tasks, vertical loading, and opening of feedback channels.

A number of successful applications of job enrichment are discussed in this chapter, including those at Volvo, the FBI, Rohm & Haas Bayport, Paul Revere Companies, a major west coast bank, and AT&T Shreveport. In the last part of the chapter, current challenges in job design were examined. Two of the most important include improving the jobs of lower-level managers and stimulating labor unions to initiate and support redesign programs.

KEY TERMS IN THE CHAPTER

job redesign	**task significance**
job rotation	**autonomy**
job enlargement	**feedback**
job enrichment	**motivating potential score**
core job dimensions	**job profile chart**
skill variety	**vertical loading**
task identity	

REVIEW AND STUDY QUESTIONS

1.   Explain how each of the following job redesign techniques works: job rotation, job enlargement, and job enrichment.

2.   In your own words, what is meant by each of the following core job dimensions: skill variety, task identity, task significance, autonomy, and feedback?

3.   How have researchers used the five core job dimensions described in this chapter to develop a motivating potential score formula? Be sure to incorporate a discussion of the formula in your answer.

4.   Define each of the following job enrichment principles: formation of natural work units, establishment of worker-client relationships, combining of tasks, vertical loading, opening of feedback channels. How does each work?

5.   Which of the core job dimensions does each of the job enrichment principles (discussed in the answer to the preceding question) help fulfill? Explain, using a figure or drawing to relate each principle to its respective core job dimension(s).

6.   What are the six commonly accepted guidelines for job redesign programs? Explain each.

7.   How has Volvo used job enrichment to redesign its assembly line at Kalmar, Sweden?

8.   How has the FBI used job enrichment to increase work productivity? Explain.

9.   How have organizations used autonomous work teams to improve work productivity and quality? Use Rohm and Haas Bayport, a major west coast bank, and AT&T Shreveport as examples.

10.   What are the current challenges in job redesign? Describe them.

TIME OUT ANSWERS: INTERPRETATION OF HOW YOU VIEW YOUR WORK

This quiz is designed to measure the five dimensions discussed in the chapter. (Feedback has more questions associated with it because information on feedback from both the job itself and the personnel in the organization were obtained.) Here is how to get your score for each dimension: (1) take all six of your answers to Part I and enter them in the appropriate place on the answer sheet; (2) take your answers in Part II for each of the numbers 1, 2, 3, 4, 11, and 12, and subtract each one from 8 before entering the result in the appropriate place below; and (3) take your answers in Part II for numbers 5, 6, 7, 8, 9, and 10, and enter them in the appropriate place. As you can see, the answers from Part II that have an asterisk were handled with reverse scoring; a low answer received a high score and vice versa.

SKILL VARIETY
I.   1. _____
II. 1.* _____
     9. _____

TASK IDENTITY
I.   2. _____
II. 6. _____
     11.* _____

TASK SIGNIFICANCE
I.   3. _____
II. 4.* _____
     7. _____

AUTONOMY
I.   4. _____
II. 3.* _____
     5. _____

FEEDBACK (FROM THE JOB)
I.   5. _____
II. 8. _____
     12.* _____

FEEDBACK (FROM OTHERS)
I.   6. _____
II. 2.* _____
     10. _____

The largest total you can have for any of the above job dimensions is 21 and the smallest is 3. Divide all of your answers by 3 to determine your average score per job dimension. Average scores tend to be in the range of 4.5–6.0. If you score lower than 4.5, your job is low on this particular job dimension; if you score higher than 6, your job is high on this particular job dimension. If you do not like your current job, you can probably determine why if you examine work from the standpoint of these job dimensions. The reverse is also true; if you like your current job, you should be able to determine why from your totals.

CASE: The Best Job He Ever Had

When Emile Veras was in college, he worked part-time for a small accounting firm. His duties were highly routine. Emile would clock in at 4 p.m. and clock out at 8 p.m. every weekday. During these four hours he was responsible for addressing and mailing all packages and letters left in the "to be mailed" box. He was also responsible for taking phone messages and filing reports, letters, memos, and tax returns.

Emile found the work to be boring, but at $7.25 an hour he knew that it would be impossible to find a higher paying job that required so little mental effort. Additionally, he knew that once he was graduated he would find a job that would be more psychologically rewarding that would start him on a meaningful career.

Eight months ago Emile finished his undergraduate degree in English and landed a job as a copy editor at a publishing house. The publisher specializes in trade books. Emile's job is to read and copyedit books for the business market. Typical titles include *30 Steps to More Effective Negotiating*, *Building Confidence in 5 Minutes a Day*, and *Creating Excellence in Your Own Company*. These titles appeal to those interested in "how-to-do-it" books. They are very popular with businesspeople, especially young managers and entrepreneurs. Sometimes the books are chosen by business book clubs as the monthly selection. In any event, it is common to find the author being interviewed on radio talk shows and television programs, while the publisher works hard to support the sales effort through newspaper advertising and mail brochures.

While most authors believe that their book can stand on its own merits, Emile's company understands the importance of everyone on the sales team knowing the message the author is trying to convey. For this reason, the publisher will invite the author to its headquarters to meet those who will be working on the project from the copy editor and the designer to the chief of advertising and the head of the sales force. These individuals will listen to the author explain what he or she is trying to convey in the book, and then they will have the opportunity to ask questions. Once everyone understands the basic message of the book, it is much easier to produce and market it. Advertising has a firmer idea of the book's unique features; the sales people know the right "hooks" that they can point to in reinforcing why a bookstore should carry the title. Even Emile has found that by listening and talking to an author, he can gain valuable insights for copyediting purposes. "Anyone can copyedit a book," he told his mother. "But to copyedit it with a slant toward the author's message, that is the difference between an average book and a best seller."

In addition to meeting the author, Emile is assigned to a work team that consists of all in-house personnel who will be responsible for turning out the book. This group is responsible for making all of the decisions associated with its publication. Typically Emile is asked to copyedit a book within 20 working days. The rest of his time on the project is spent discussing the cover with the design artist and the promotion program with the advertising people. When recently asked what he likes about his job, Emile said, "This work really gives me an opportunity to be creative and show what I can do. I love helping turn out a completed project and then watching its release and sale to the public. I feel like I'm helping create something rather than just reworking words on a page. This is the best job I've ever had."

QUESTIONS

1.   Which of the core job dimensions are present in Emile's current job? Identify and briefly describe each.

2.   How does his current job differ from his previous job? Be complete in your answer.

3.   Using Figure 8.2 as your point of reference, how do you think Emile would describe his current job? What conclusions can you draw as a result of this profile? ∎

CASE: VISITING THE CLIENT

Clara Wilson owns her own computer software company. The firm specializes in writing programs for clients. Most of Clara's business results from a firm calling her up and telling her the type of program it wants. Clara, along with a couple of members of her staff, then visits the client and makes notes regarding the company's needs. Back at the office she and her people compare notes and discuss the type of software that would be appropriate. They then write the program and deliver it to the client. This is the basic approach that Clara has used since she started her business five years ago.

Unfortunately, there are two major problems with this approach. First, the company is always waiting for clients to contact it. Second, the work is boring and it is difficult to keep programmers.

In an effort to deal with these problems, Clara recently hit on a new approach. The school system, she learned, currently spends over $5 million for computer equipment and programs. Most of these programs, however, are provided by the manufacturers of the hardware. The faculty and students are dissatisfied with these "canned" software programs, because they need programs that are written specifically for the courses they are involved in. With this in mind, Clara decided to take a team of her people to talk with some of the teachers at one of the major high schools in town. After sitting in on some of the math and science classes, she had a joint meeting with teachers and students. "What types of computer programs would you like?" she asked. Both the faculty and the students offered similar suggestions.

Clara and her team took these ideas back to the office and began working on them. Within a month they had developed special software packages for basic algebra, geometry, physics, and biology. They then took these programs to the school board and showed the members what they had done. "These programs are a result of meetings that we conducted with students and faculty in the school system. They are designed to provide higher quality education than the packaged programs provided by the computer manufacturers." The school board listened quietly and then voted that the superintendent of schools be directed to review these programs and, if they met with his approval, purchase them for all high schools in the system.

Last month Clara received word that her programs had been purchased by the school system. They wanted 500 copies of each program and also wanted to know if she could develop additional ones for the other math and science courses in the curriculum. Clara was delighted with the request but felt that she might have problems writing these programs if she could not keep her programmers. She decided that before doing anything, she should have a meeting with them. During the meeting, she learned three things: (1) all of the programmers are quite happy with their work, which is a major change from what she was hearing three months ago; (2) the group particularly likes going out to the schools, talking to the students and faculty, and learning the types of programs these people would like; and (3) they hope that when they are done with the math and science programs that they can move to still other subject areas.

Clara was delighted with the results of the meeting. "I thought my idea of going into the schools would generate more sales for us," she told her assistant. "I had no idea it also would be a job enrichment technique."

QUESTIONS

1.   Have the programmers' jobs been enlarged or enriched? Defend your answer.

2.   What core job dimensions are now present in the programmers' jobs that were not there before? Explain.

3.   What job enrichment principles did Clara use in motivating the programmers? Explain. ■

*EXPERIENCING JOB ENRICHMENT**

PURPOSE

- To understand the concepts of job enrichment and job enlargement.
- To apply these concepts to redesigning specific jobs.

PROCEDURE

1.   In small groups, students should choose one specific job to study. It may be the actual job of a group member or of someone who one of the group members knows well. It should also be a job that the group feels would be well served by job redesign. The person whose job or whose friend's job is being analyzed should brief the group on the job, giving them as much detail as possible.

2.   The group should develop a job redesign program for the job that would be motivational to the employee yet realistic within the organizational context. Remember job enlargement means adding other duties at a similar level of responsibility whereas job enrichment means adding other duties at increased levels of responsibility.

3.   Each group in turn should describe its chosen job and the recommended redesign of that job to the rest of the class.

4.   Discuss the following: Is job redesign as easy as you originally thought it would be? Why or why not?

■ ■ ■ ■ ■ ■ ■

*Adapted from: "Redesigning Jobs" in Jane W. Gibson and Richard M. Hodgetts, *Readings and Exercises in Organization Behavior* (Orlando: Academic Press, 1985, p. 184).

PART 4

THE ADMINISTRATIVE SYSTEM

The overall objective of Part 4 is to study the *administrative* system of organizations. In Parts 2 and 3 we examined the social and technical systems of organizations, noting the role of both individuals and structure in the work place. The interaction of people and structure can have dysfunctional results, unless there is an effective administrative system to handle the situation. This system can be defined in one word—leadership. In this part of the book we study leadership: what it is, how it works, and the importance of systematically appraising and rewarding job performance.

In Chapter 9 we start by studying the fundamentals of leadership. We define the term *leadership*, present some of the leadership characteristics found in effective managers, and describe some of the personal qualities that appear to be related to managerial effectiveness, including superior intelligence, emotional maturity, motivation drive, problem-solving skills, managerial skills, and leadership skills. Then we introduce and explain what is meant by Theory X and Theory Y and discuss the importance of the immaturity–maturity theory to the study of leadership. Next, we examine the two major dimensions of leadership, concern for people and concern for work, and explain one of the most popular contingency models of leadership, giving primary emphasis to the type of leader who is most effective in each situation. Finally, we consider the value of the managerial grid and path-goal theory in the study of human relations.

Having examined the fundamentals of leadership, we then turn to the leader's role in the organization. What do effective leaders do? In Chapter 10 we discuss the leader's "linking pin" function, explain what is meant by the term *teamwork*, and identify the three key factors necessary to develop teamwork. Then we turn our attention to the leader's role as a counselor and review the kinds of counseling often given by managers. Next we define the term *power*, explain the various types of leader power, and note which are used most widely by effective managers and which are not. In the final part of the chapter we explain the importance of time management to the effective leader and identify important steps for managing time well. Finally, we discuss how the manager should deal with stress.

Then, in Chapter 11, we study how a leader appraises and rewards performance. We begin by discussing the performance appraisal cycle and explaining some of the currently popular evaluation methods, including graphic rating scales, the paired comparison method, assessment centers, behaviorally anchored rating scales, and management by objectives. Then we describe the major problems associated with performance appraisal. Next we outline the most common intrinsic and extrinsic rewards, discuss the role of equity in performance appraisal, and examine the link between performance and rewards. Finally, we identify the discipline used when performance is inadequate and explain how the "red-hot stove rule" can be used in effectively employing discipline.

When you have finished reading this part of the book you should have a solid understanding of the administrative system in modern organizations. In particular, you should know the definition of leadership, the role the leader must attempt to play in the organization, and the various ways in which performance can be measured, rewards can be given, and discipline can be carried out.

FUNDAMENTALS OF LEADERSHIP

GOALS OF THE CHAPTER

The goals of this chapter are to examine the nature of leadership, to study leadership behavior, and to investigate two of the most famous contingency leadership models. In the first part of the chapter we review some of the leadership and personal characteristics effective leaders often possess and examine the assumptions that many leaders hold regarding the nature of organizational personnel. Then we look at various styles of leadership: authoritarian, paternalistic, participative, and laissez-faire. Finally, we examine contingency leadership with particular attention to Fiedler's contingency model and the path-goal theory of leadership.

When you have finished reading this chapter you should be able to:

1.   List leadership characteristics found in effective managers.

2.   Describe some personal characteristics that appear to be related to managerial effectiveness, including superior intelligence, emotional maturity, motivation drive, problem-solving skills, managerial skills, and leadership skills.

3.   Compare and contrast Theory X and Theory Y.

4.   Compare and contrast the four styles of leadership.

5.   Describe the two major dimensions of leadership, concern for people and concern for work.

6.   Explain Fiedler's contingency model, giving primary emphasis to the type of leader most effective in each situation, and discuss the value of the managerial grid and the path-goal theory of leadership to the study of human relations.

OPENING CASE

LOOKING FOR SOMEONE TO GET TOUGH

For the last three years the Josephson Insurance brokerage has lost money. There are a number of reasons for this development. One is that the current president did not stay in control of operations. Agency representatives in other states were allowed to carry on business with little direction from the home office. In three cases, agents failed to turn in premiums that they received. When claims on these policies came due, the central office refused to pay. It argued that the policies had not been properly issued. However, the state court ruled that the firm had to pay these claims because the brokers were agents of the insurance company. These court rulings resulted in the company losing over $22 million last year.

The board of directors has decided that it is time to replace the president with someone who can keep things under control. "We need a chief executive officer who'll crack down and make sure that we don't have the types of losses we had last year. This is a very cost-control business," remarked the chairman of the board. "If we have a loss on an account, we have to pay perhaps 50 times the premium. This means that we have to write a lot of policies in order to ensure a small amount of profit. And if we have a large number of claims, we are sure to lose a great deal of money. We can prevent this from occurring by hiring top managers who will keep close control of things."

There are two people whom the company has been considering for the chief executive job. Both are very experienced in the field and have been in charge of small, highly profitable insurance firms. One was trained primarily in sales before going into administration. The other is quantitatively oriented with a strong background in accounting, statistics, and actuarial science. The company hopes to choose a new operating officer by the end of next week.

1.   What personal characteristics should an effective leader possess?

2.   Is the current president a Theory X or Theory Y manager? Explain.

3.   How would you describe the leadership behavior of the current president?

4.   In terms of the managerial grid, what type of leader is the current president? How will the new leader be different? Explain.

Write down your answers to these questions and put them aside. We will return to them later. ∎

THE NATURE OF LEADERSHIP

Leadership is the process of influencing people to direct their efforts toward the achievement of some particular goal(s). Good leaders have visions of where they want the organization to go, and they have the ability to create enthusiasm among their followers to pursue their goals. Some managers are highly effective leaders, but most are, at best, only moderately successful.[1] What accounts for this difference? Some people believe the answer rests in **leadership characteristics**, such as drive, originality, and tolerance of stress, which, they say, are universal among successful leaders. If you have these qualities, you will do well in leading others; if you lack them, you will be ineffective in the leadership role.

> LEADERSHIP IS THE PROCESS OF INFLUENCING PEOPLE TO DIRECT THEIR EFFORTS TOWARD PARTICULAR GOALS.

Others argue in favor of **personal characteristics**, such as superior mental ability, emotional maturity, and problem-solving skills. They claim there is no universal list of leadership characteristics, so we must turn to personal characteristics that interact with one another to produce the desired outcomes. Only through an awareness of how these characteristics influence managerial effectiveness can we truly understand the nature of leadership. To begin our study of this subject, we examine both approaches, leadership characteristics and personal characteristics, and then address the importance of managerial assumptions regarding the nature of organizational personnel.

LEADERSHIP CHARACTERISTICS

Recent leadership studies have pointed out the importance of environmental influences on leadership effectiveness. However, published research indicates that, regardless of the situation, certain characteristics favor success in the leadership role.

From 1920 to 1950 the study of leadership characteristics, known as trait theory, sought to isolate those factors that contribute to leader effectiveness. This approach assumed that attributes such as initiative, social dominance, and persistence were the primary factors in leadership success and failure. Unfortunately, the research studies conducted during this period failed to produce a universal list of traits. Additionally, in most cases, no consideration was given to the possibility that different situations might require different characteristics, or that a specific situation might demand so little of the leader or might be so unfavorable that leadership characteristics would be of little, if any, value. Despite the arguments for situational leadership, however, Ralph Stogdill, one of the leading authorities in the field, concluded that a selected group of char-

> TRAIT THEORY IS AN ATTEMPT TO ISOLATE THOSE FACTORS THAT CONTRIBUTE TO LEADER EFFECTIVENESS.

[1] John Lawrie, "What is Effective Leadership?" *Management Solutions*, May 1987, pp. 25–30.

acteristics do, in fact, differentiate leaders from followers, effective from ineffective leaders, and high-echelon from low-echelon leaders.

The leader is characterized by a strong drive for responsibility and task completion, vigor and persistence in pursuit of goals, venturesomeness and originality in problem solving, drive to exercise initiative in social situations, self-confidence and a sense of personal identity, willingness to accept consequences of decision and action, readiness to absorb interpersonal stress, willingness to tolerate frustration and delay, ability to influence other persons' behavior, and capacity to structure social interaction systems to the purpose at hand.[2]

■ ■ ■ ■ ■ ■ ■ ■ ■ ■ ■ ■ ■ ■

WITH TRAIT THEORY, NO COMMON LIST OF LEADERSHIP CHARACTERISTICS HAS BEEN DISCOVERED.

The greatest problem with trait theory, however, is that no common list has been forthcoming. Some traits appear important, but their value is situationally determined. A leader with a capacity to structure social interaction systems may do well when directing subordinates with a high need for social interaction but poorly if the subordinates or the situation does not allow for such interaction. For example, assembly-line work is not designed for manager-subordinate interaction, so the ability to initiate or structure such relationships is of little value to the foreman. As a result, leadership effectiveness appears to be situational in nature. This finding has led many researchers to turn their attention to personal characteristics of effective leaders.

PERSONAL CHARACTERISTICS

Many personal characteristics, including intelligence, emotional maturity, motivation, problem-solving skills, managerial skills, and leadership skills, contribute to managerial effectiveness.

Many personal characteristics appear to be related to managerial effectiveness, but an exhaustive list is beyond our current needs. We will, however, examine some major personal characteristics that significantly contribute to leadership effectiveness. They are: superior intelligence, emotional maturity, motivation drive, problem-solving skills, managerial skills, leadership skills, and a desire to lead.

SUPERIOR INTELLIGENCE   Research reveals that effective managers tend to have superior intelligence.[3] By this we mean that there is a minimum level of mental ability below which we are unlikely to find successful leaders. Conversely, there may well be a ceiling above which we are again unlikely to find effective leaders. Williams, for example, reports

■ ■ ■ ■ ■ ■ ■

[2] Ralph Stogdill, *Handbook of Leadership* (New York: The Free Press, 1974), p. 81.

[3] Glen Grimsley and Hilton Jarrett, "The Relation of Managerial Achievement to Test Measures Obtained in the Employment Situation: Methodology and Results," *Personnel Psychology*, Spring 1973, pp. 31–48.

that psychological assessments he conducted over a 15-year period suggest that:

> IQs from about 120 to 135 are the ideal range for managerial success. This ranges from the 91st to the 99th centiles of the general population on the best adult intelligence test. . . . Individuals with IQs from 115–119 are acceptable in some managerial positions but seldom in top companies with strong competition for promotion. Managers with IQs below 115 are at a distinct disadvantage when competing with other managers, except at the first-line supervisory level. Those with unusually high IQs (say, over 135) sometimes become undesirably theoretical and/or become bored with the routine that exists in many line positions.[4]

THERE SEEMS TO BE AN IDEAL IQ RANGE.

Keep in mind, however, that intelligence is a relative matter. Some geniuses are excellent leaders, while some people with IQs (intelligence quotients) in the 120–135 range lack the personality to manage effectively. Additionally, one can have a superior intellect and be in the wrong job. For example, a person with high verbal skills and abstract reasoning ability and low quantitative ability might do poorly in an accounting firm or a bank, and an individual with low verbal skills and high quantitative abilities might be a total failure as a personnel manager. Yet both have high IQs and their mental abilities are comparable.

EMOTIONAL MATURITY   Successful leaders are emotionally mature. They are self-confident and capable of directing their subordinates in a calm, conscientious manner. If a subordinate makes a mistake, the effective leader tries to use the experience as an opportunity to teach and counsel the person so as to prevent recurrence of the problem. The leader realizes that little is to be gained from bawling out the subordinate (except maybe to embarrass the latter in front of his or her peers), especially if the person really wanted to do the job right.

LEADERS ARE SELF-CONFIDENT AND CALM.

Effective leaders also have a sense of purpose and meaning in life. They know who they are, where they are going, and how they are going to get there. They are practical and decisive and have confidence in their own abilities. Additionally, the goals they set for themselves are often challenging as well as realistic.

Finally, because they are emotionally mature, successful leaders are neither ulcer-prone nor workaholics. They know how to deal with stress, to delegate work that is either minor in importance or is best handled by someone more technically skilled, and to handle the challenges of the job

[4]J. Clifton Williams, *Human Behavior in Organizations*, 2nd ed. (Cincinnati: South-Western Publishing Co., 1982), pp. 413–414.

FIGURE 9.1   **LEADERSHIP SUCCESS AND NEED DRIVE**

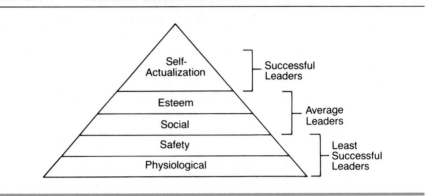

without resorting to alcohol or drugs. Because they know and understand themselves, they are able to cope with the demands of both their business and personal lives. For example, the divorce rate among successful leaders is no greater than that in the general population.

THEY HAVE HIGH DRIVE.

MOTIVATION DRIVE   Effective leaders have high motivation drive. In particular, they seem most motivated by the opportunity to achieve the chance for power or control over a situation and by the need to self-actualize.[5] Additionally, as we noted in our discussion of money in Chapter 2, they are motivated by increased personal income, because it is a sign of how well they are doing. Effective leaders often measure their progress in quantitative terms: how much money they are making, how many promotions they have had, how many subordinates they control. If we were to compare highly successful, moderately successful, and unsuccessful leaders in terms of need motivation we could assign each to specific levels of Maslow's need hierarchy, as in Figure 9.1.

Additionally, we know from research that successful leaders tend to have subordinates who are also interested in fulfillment of self-actualization and esteem needs. Average leaders have followers who are most concerned with esteem and social needs. The least successful leaders have subordinates who are most interested in safety and physiological needs. In short, successful leaders tend to attract a particular type of subordinate, as do the average and least successful leaders, and these subordinates have need drives similar to those of their superiors.[6] In large

■■■■■■■

[5] See, for example, David C. McClelland and David H. Burnham, "Power is the Great Motivator," *Harvard Business Review*, March–April 1976, pp. 100–110.

[6] Jay Hall, "To Achieve or Not: The Manager's Choice," *California Management Review*, Summer 1976, pp. 5–18.

measure, highly motivated leaders attract or develop highly motivated subordinates.

PROBLEM-SOLVING SKILLS   Effective leaders also possess problem-solving skills. They see a problem as both a challenge and an opportunity to prove their managerial abilities. As such, these skills are closely related to high motivation drives, for without such motivation leaders might be unwilling to assume the risk that comes with problem-solving. These individuals also have a great deal of self-confidence. Conversely, average leaders and, especially, ineffective leaders tend to shun problem-solving because they either are unprepared to deal with the issues or have learned through experience that they are not up to the task.

■ ■ ■ ■ ■ ■ ■ ■ ■ ■ ■ ■ ■
THEY ARE PROBLEM-SOLVERS.

MANAGERIAL SKILLS   Effective leaders, especially at the upper levels of the hierarchy, have managerial skills. These skills are of three types, technical, human, and administrative.

Technical skills: The knowledge of how things work. This is very important for lower-level managers such as foremen.

Human skills: The knowledge of how to deal with people. This is very important for middle-level managers who must lead other managers. Without a solid understanding of such behavioral areas as interpersonal communication, motivation, counseling, and directing, middle-level managers would be ineffective in leading their subordinates.

Administrative skills: The knowledge of how all parts of the organization or department fit together. This skill covers many activities, from formulating organizational objectives, policies, and procedures, to developing techniques for handling office work flow, to coordinating a host of seemingly unrelated functions that enable the enterprise to operate as an integrated unit.[7]

■ ■ ■ ■ ■ ■ ■ ■ ■ ■ ■ ■ ■
THEY POSSESS ADMINISTRATIVE
SKILLS.

As shown in Figure 9.2, the leader's place in the hierarchy determines the degree of managerial skill he or she must have. As managers prove their effectiveness and begin moving up the ranks, they need to learn more about human and, in particular, administrative skills. Some will develop great administrative proficiency and continue their upward climb; others will find they are unable to develop the requisite degree of administrative skill and will remain where they are. In the final analysis, administrative skill makes the difference between leaders who will head the organization and leaders who must be content to manage at the intermediate and lower levels.

■ ■ ■ ■ ■ ■ ■

[7] William D. Litzinger and Thomas E. Schaefer, "Something More—The Nature of Transcendent Management," *Business Horizons*, March–April 1986, pp. 68–72.

FIGURE 9.2   **SKILLS NEEDED AT DIFFERENT HIERARCHICAL LEVELS**

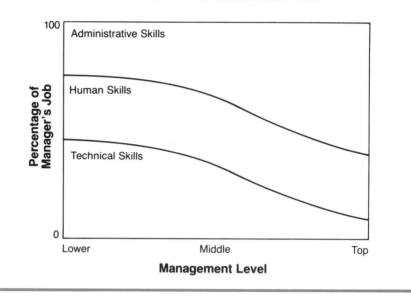

LEADERSHIP SKILLS   Although what leadership style is effective depends on the situation, some personal characteristics seem to contribute to the leadership skills of managers. Some are task-related, while others are more social in nature. The task-related characteristics of effective leaders, as isolated by Stogdill, include initiative, need to excel or achieve, task orientation, drive for responsibility, and responsibility in pursuit of objectives. Some of the social characteristics of effective leaders are administrative ability, interpersonal skills, tact and diplomacy, ability to enlist cooperation, popularity, social participation, cooperativeness, and attractiveness.[8]

■ ■ ■ ■ ■ ■ ■ ■ ■ ■ ■ ■ ■ ■
THEY TEND TO HAVE CERTAIN
LEADERSHIP SKILLS.

DESIRE TO LEAD   In order to be effective as a leader, individuals must want to lead and they must be willing to assume the responsibilities associated with the position. Recent research reveals that many young college graduates do not have the same desire to lead as did their counterparts of twenty years ago. The American Telephone and Telegraph Company (AT&T) did a study in which the values and motivational profiles of young managers were compared with those of the late 1950s.[9] The two

■ ■ ■ ■ ■ ■ ■

[8] Stogdill, *Handbook of Leadership*, pp. 80–81.

[9] Ann Howard and James A. Wilson, "Leadership in a Declining Work Ethic," *California Management Review*, Summer 1982, pp. 33–46.

groups proved to be quite different. Today's young workers have less of a desire for upward mobility, are not as willing to exercise leadership, and are more pessimistic about the future of their careers with a firm than were managers of the late 1950s. These young people also have a greater desire to be liked by their fellow workers and their subordinates. Such findings indicate that many young people entering the ranks of management do not want to lead, which bodes poorly for their future in the organization. On the positive side, however, nonleaders who desire to influence managers or other subordinates can exercise leadership. The necessary leadership and personal characteristics are possessed by many individuals. The most important of these include: above average intelligence, clear-cut goals, a desire to succeed, the ability to solve problems, effective human skills, high motivation, and emotional maturity. In fact, to the extent that leaders can nurture such behaviors among their personnel, the efficiency and effectiveness of their work groups will increase. In a manner of speaking, this approach encourages every employee to be a leader and, in the process, makes the formal leader's job an easier one.

STOP!

Review your answer to the first question and make any changes you would like. Then compare your answer to the one below.

1.   What personal characteristics should an effective leader possess?

The case does not spell out these characteristics, but it is evident that the company wants someone who can exercise closer control than the previous president. So some of these characteristics will undoubtedly include superior intelligence, motivation drive, problem-solving skills, managerial skills, leadership skills, and perhaps most important of all, a desire to lead. ■

THE NATURE OF ORGANIZATIONAL PERSONNEL

Leadership characteristics and personal characteristics provide insights regarding who leaders are. However, it is also important to understand why leaders act as they do. Part of this explanation can be found in the opinions leaders have about their people. Are the subordinates content with satisfying lower-level needs or do they strive also for esteem and self-actualization fulfillment? How important is money to them? As managers begin to answer these questions, they express their assumptions about the nature of the organization's personnel. One of the finest summaries of such managerial assumptions has been provided by Douglas McGregor. He called these assumptions Theory X and Theory Y.[10]

THEORY X

Theory X assumptions hold that people are basically lazy and that in order to get them to work, it is often necessary to use coercion and threats of punishment. McGregor summarized the assumptions this way:

1.   People, by their very nature, dislike work and will avoid it when possible.

2.   They have little ambition, tend to shun responsibility, and like to be directed.

3.   Above all else, they want security.

4.   In order to get them to attain organizational objectives, it is necessary to use coercion, control, and threats of punishment.[11]

From this summary of their attitudes, we can arrive at two conclusions regarding Theory X managers. First, they like to control their subordinates because they feel such control is in the best interests of both the organization and its personnel. Second, they believe that people work to satisfy their lower-level needs (security above all else) and that upper-level need satisfaction is not very important. Additionally, since lower-level needs are satisfied with physical rewards, such as money, job security, and good working conditions, Theory X managers will withhold these rewards if the workers do not comply with organizational directives.

Quite obviously this management thinking does not provide for those workers who dislike close control or who desire satisfaction of upper-level needs. All management can offer the workers is more physiological and safety rewards. If the workers balk at this, management will resort to punishment, a reaction that accords with the fourth Theory X tenet listed above.

The use of punishment seems to be a logical method of solving the issue; either the workers do the job or management will get tough. However, the problem rests on the fact that management mistakes causes for effects, the result being a self-fulfilling prophecy. Believing punishment is a necessary tool for effective management, the company introduces it the minute the workers start offering resistance, with mental notes, "See, it's like we said. You have to get tough with these people if you want any

■ ■ ■ ■ ■ ■ ■ ■ ■ ■ ■ ■ ■ ■ ■
THEORY X HOLDS THAT PEOPLE ARE BASICALLY LAZY.

■ ■ ■ ■ ■ ■ ■

[10] Douglas McGregor, *The Human Side of Enterprise* (New York: McGraw-Hill Book Company, 1960).

[11] *Ibid.*, pp. 33–34.

performance." Yet it is management's fault that the workers are discontent in the first place.[12]

Why, then, do many managers have trouble motivating their subordinates? The answer rests in the erroneous assumptions they have about the nature of the organizational personnel. Believing that they need to treat their people like children, providing low-level need satisfaction rewards if the work is done well, and withholding these benefits if the work is done poorly, the managers use a "carrot-and-stick" theory of motivation. This approach may be useful in getting a donkey to pull a cart, but it is seldom effective in motivating people. A more realistic set of assumptions are those described in Theory Y.

THEORY Y

Modern behavioral research has provided the basis for formulating assumptions for a new theory of management, which McGregor called **Theory Y**. Its assumptions are:

1.   The expenditure of physical and mental effort in work is as natural to people as is resting or playing.

2.   External control and the threats of punishment are not the only ways of getting people to work toward organizational objectives. If people are committed to objectives, they will exercise self-direction and self-control.

3.   Commitment to objectives is determined by the rewards associated with their achievement.

4.   Under proper conditions, the average human being learns not only to accept but to seek responsibility.

5.   The capacity to exercise a relatively high degree of imagination, ingenuity, and creativity in the solution of organizational problems is widely distributed throughout the population.

6.   Under conditions of modern industrial life, the intellectual potentialities of the average human being are only partially utilized.[13]

> THEORY Y HOLDS THAT UNDER THE RIGHT CONDITIONS PEOPLE WILL WORK.

As you can see, Theory Y presents a much more dynamic view of the organizational personnel. They are now seen as interested in both lower-level and upper-level need satisfaction and as having untapped potential. This theory urges management to reevaluate its thinking and to begin focusing attention on ways of enabling the personnel to attain their

[12] Richard M. Hodgetts, *Management: Theory, Process, and Practice*, 4th ed. (Orlando: Academic Press, 1986), p. 480.

[13] McGregor, *The Human Side of Enterprise*, pp. 47–48.

upper-level needs. Motivation is viewed as a problem that must be solved by management. No longer can the leader hide behind Theory X assumptions, claiming that workers are by nature lazy and unmotivated.

Before continuing, however, we should answer one very important question: is a Theory Y manager always superior to a Theory X manager? Although we have presented Theory Y as a modern, superior view of the workers, it is not without its critics. Some of them point out that Theory Y can be dangerous in that it allows too much freedom to the workers, many of whom not only need but want close direction and control. Additionally, Theory Y assumes that people want to satisfy their needs while on the job. However, many satisfy their needs off the job, as in the case of workers who want a shorter work week so they will have more leisure time.

Therefore, to put these two theories in perspective, we must acknowledge that some people respond better to Theory X management than to Theory Y management. However, many managers tend to underrate the workers, subscribing much more heavily to Theory X than to Theory Y. Chris Argyris has made this very clear with his immaturity–maturity theory.

IMMATURITY–MATURITY THEORY

While at Yale University, Argyris made an examination of industrial organizations for the purpose of determining the effect that management practices had on individual behavior. According to his **immaturity–maturity theory**, seven changes take place in an individual's personality as he or she matures. First, the individual moves from a passive state as an infant to an active state as an adult. Second, as an infant, the individual depends heavily on others for assistance, but as he or she matures there is an increasing degree of independence. Third, an infant is capable of behaving in only a few ways, but with maturity this capability increases dramatically. Fourth, an infant has casual, shallow interests, but as the individual grows older, he or she becomes capable of developing deeper, stronger interests. Fifth, an infant's time perspective is very short and encompasses only the present; as the child matures, however, this perspective increases to include both the past and the future. Sixth, an infant is subordinate to everyone, but with maturity the individual achieves an equal or superior position. Seventh, a child lacks an awareness of "self," but the mature individual is aware of and is able to control the "self" (Table 9.1).

Argyris contends that the healthy personality is one that develops along the continuum from immaturity to maturity. However, many organizations are not geared for mature people. Organizational rules, policies, and procedures are all designed to keep the personnel passive,

■ ■ ■ ■ ■ ■ ■ ■ ■ ■ ■ ■ ■ ■
THE INDIVIDUAL'S PERSONALITY CHANGES AS HE OR SHE MATURES.

TABLE 9.1   IMMATURITY–MATURITY DEVELOPMENT

IMMATURITY		MATURITY
Passivity	→	Activity
Dependence	→	Independence
Capable of behaving in a few ways	→	Capable of behaving in many ways
Casual, shallow interests	→	Deep, strong interests
Current time perspective	→	Past, present, and future time perspective
Subordinate position	→	Equal or superior position
Lack of awareness of "self"	→	Awareness and control of "self"

dependent, and subordinate. They are supposed to respond to management's needs, follow orders, and accomplish organizational objectives. In so doing, they become an extension of the organization's physical assets and are often treated more like things of production than like people. This has led Argyris to report:

> An analysis of the basic properties of relatively mature human beings and formal organization leads to the conclusion that there is an inherent incongruency between the self-actualization of the two. This basic incongruency creates a situation of conflict, frustration, and failure for the participants.[14]

The state that Argyris is referring to as *immature* is the same state that is promoted and nurtured by Theory X management, yet this style of management does not have to be tolerated. Organizations can encourage mature behavior from their people. Argyris, himself, has reported a case in which the president of a company asked him how to motivate the company workers more effectively. The two men visited a company production plant where 12 women were assembling a product similar to a radio. The group also had a foreman, an inspector, and a packer.

Professor Argyris suggested a one-year experiment in which each of the women would assemble the total product herself. The president agreed, and over the ensuing months, production under the new method was closely monitored. During the first month, production dropped 70 percent. The next three weeks saw a continual down slide as workers' morale declined. However, by the eighth week production began to rise. By the end of the fifteenth week output was at an all-time high, error and waste costs had decreased 94 percent, and complaints had dropped 96 percent. By employing a Theory Y-oriented leadership style, the man-

········

[14] Chris Argyris, *Personality and Organization: The Conflict between the System and the Individual* (New York: Harper & Row Publishers, Inc., 1957), p. 175.

agement was able to improve overall performance. How, exactly, does one employ Theory X or Theory Y on the job? This question can be answered best with an examination of leadership behavior. Before doing so, however, examine your own basic beliefs about people by answering the accompanying Time Out quiz on your assumptions about people.

STOP!

Review your answer to the second question and make any changes you would like. Then compare your answer to the one below.

2.   Is the current president a Theory X or Theory Y manager? Explain.

The current president is a Theory Y manager. Notice that he did not exercise close control over the agents who failed to turn in the premiums to the company. He trusted the field people to do their job honestly and correctly. These are all characteristics of a Theory Y manager. ∎

LEADERSHIP BEHAVIOR

Leadership behavior is the way leaders actually carry out their jobs. There are four styles of leadership behavior: authoritarian, paternalistic, participative, and laissez-faire. On a continuum, they range from high concern for work and people to general lack of concern for the work and the personnel. Depending on the situation, any one of these styles can be ideal.

AUTHORITARIAN LEADERSHIP

Leaders who engage in **authoritarian leadership** tend to be heavily work-centered, with much emphasis given to task accomplishment and little to the human element. Such leaders fit the classical model of management in which the workers are viewed as factors of production.

These individuals can be very useful in certain situations. For example, when a crisis occurs and the organization needs a "get-tough" leader, the authoritarian manager is often ideal. Attention should be focused on objectives, efficiency, profit, and other task-related activities, and this is just to the manager's liking.

Unfortunately, there are not that many instances where an authoritarian manager is superior to all others, although there are a fairly large number of such managers in industry today. These people have authoritarian personalities, often developed because their parents were also au-

AUTHORITARIAN LEADERS ARE WORK-CENTERED.

TIME OUT

YOUR ASSUMPTIONS ABOUT PEOPLE

Read the following 10 pairs of statements. In each case, show the relative strength of your beliefs by assigning a weight from 0 to 10 to each statement. The points assigned to each pair *must* total ten points. If you totally agree with one statement and totally disagree with the other, give the first one a 10 and the second a zero. If you like both statements equally, give each 5 points. The interpretation of your answers is provided at the end of the chapter.

1. Most employees are fairly creative but often times do not have the chance to employ this ingenuity on the job. _____ (a)

   Most workers are not creative at all, but then again the job does not lend itself to creativity so nothing is lost. _____ (b)

2. If you give people enough money, this will greatly offset their desire for interesting, challenging, and/or meaningful work. _____ (c)

   If you give people interesting, challenging, and/or meaningful work, they are less likely to complain about money and fringe benefits. _____ (d)

3. Workers who are allowed to set their own goals and standards of performance tend to set them higher than management would. _____ (e)

   Workers who are allowed to set their own goals and standards of performance tend to set them lower than management would. _____ (f)

4. People want freedom to do work the way they believe is right. _____ (g)

   People want to be told what to do; freedom actually makes them nervous. _____ (h)

5. The better an individual knows his or her job, the more likely it is that the person will work only hard enough to produce the minimum amount acceptable to management. _____ (i)

   The better an individual knows his or her job, the more likely it is that the person will find satisfaction in the work and try to produce at least as much as the average worker in the organization. _____ (j)

6. Most workers in a modern organization are not up to the intellectual challenge presented by their jobs. _____ (k)

   Most workers in a modern organization have more than sufficient intellectual potential to do their jobs. _____ (l)

7. Most people dislike work, and if given the chance, they will goof off. _____ (m)

   Most people like work, especially if it is interesting and challenging. _____ (n)

8. Most employees work best under loose control. _____ (o)

   Most employees work best under close control. _____ (p)

9. Above all else, workers want job security. _____ (q)

   While workers want job security, it is only one of many things they want, and it does not rank first on all lists. _____ (r)

10. It increases a supervisor's prestige when he or she admits that a subordinate was right and he or she was wrong. _____ (s)

    A manager is entitled to more respect than a subordinate, and it weakens the former's prestige to admit that a subordinate was right and he or she was wrong. _____ (t)

thoritarian. They were taught early in life to be submissive toward superior authority and, in turn, have used this parental model to dominate those who hold positions subordinate to theirs. As a result they tend to be "yes men" when talking to their bosses and to demand the same type of behavior from their own personnel.

PATERNALISTIC LEADERSHIP

■ ■ ■ ■ ■ ■ ■ ■ ■ ■ ■ ■ ■ ■
PATERNALISTIC LEADERS TEND TO
BE PROTECTIVE.

Leaders who practice **paternalistic leadership** are heavily work-centered but, unlike authoritarian leaders, have some consideration for the personnel. They tend to look after their people the way a father does his family. Their basic philosophy, far out of step with the needs of most employees, is "work hard and I'll take care of you." This style of management was prevalent in the late nineteenth century, when some businesses went so far as to provide the workers with lodging, medical services, a company store, and even churches for religious worship. The Pullman Corporation, famous for the Pullman railroad sleeping car, was such a company, and like other firms that built company towns, it eventually found the workers fighting its paternalism. We know from human relations studies that people do not want to be treated like children or to feel they are owned by the company.

■ ■ ■ ■ ■ ■ ■ ■ ■ ■ ■ ■ ■ ■
THEY ARE SOFT THEORY X TYPES.

Many managers in this country are paternalistic leaders; they believe their subordinates want someone to look after them and provide job security, cost-of-living raises, insurance programs, retirement plans, and other extrinsic rewards. Actually, these leaders are confusing management with manipulation. In terms of Theory X and Y, they are soft Theory X managers. They do not believe people are totally lazy or security-oriented, but they do feel workers have a tendency toward acting this way. By playing the role of the parent, these leaders believe they can get the most productivity out of their people. Unfortunately for them, most workers resent this type of leadership, although there are some who like it. Employees who have been smothered with affection and security by their parents often welcome a boss who acts the same way. They now have a surrogate parent who takes care of them when they are on the job. However, these people are exceptions to the rule; most workers dislike paternalism.

PARTICIPATIVE LEADERSHIP

■ ■ ■ ■ ■ ■ ■ ■ ■ ■ ■ ■ ■ ■
PARTICIPATIVE LEADERS HAVE HIGH
CONCERNS FOR PEOPLE AND WORK.

Leaders who have a high concern for both people and work are engaged in **participative leadership**. They encourage their subordinates to play an active role in operating the enterprise, but they reserve the right to make the final decision on important matters. In short, they delegate authority but do not abdicate in favor of subordinate rule. Some manage-

James L. Ketelsen, Chairman and CEO of Tenneco, shown here at the company's annual all-employee meeting, believes that feedback from employees is essential to effective management.

ment experts have contended that no manager can perform effectively over an extended period of time without some degree of employee participation. This is certainly true of U.S. managers, for it is an accepted norm in this country that workers have a voice in what goes on.

One way in which this is commonly done is through delegating authority to the lowest possible organizational level. A second way is through encouraging feedback from the subordinates. While an authoritarian manager is busy telling the personnel what to do, the participative leader is getting information on what is going well and what is going poorly. From this feedback, the manager is able to decide what should be done next. No leader can be truly effective without the support of the subordinates, and feedback is a key indication of such support. Finally, participative leaders discuss objectives with their people and then give them the opportunity to attain these objectives. This is in contrast to authoritarian leaders who keep objectives to themselves, distrust their subordinates, delegate very little, and try to do too many things themselves. The participative manager builds esprit de corps by sharing objectives and providing the chance for subordinates to fulfill their esteem and self-actualization needs. The personnel, in turn, like this approach and work harder for the leader.

FIGURE 9.3   **LEADER-SUBORDINATE INTERACTIONS**

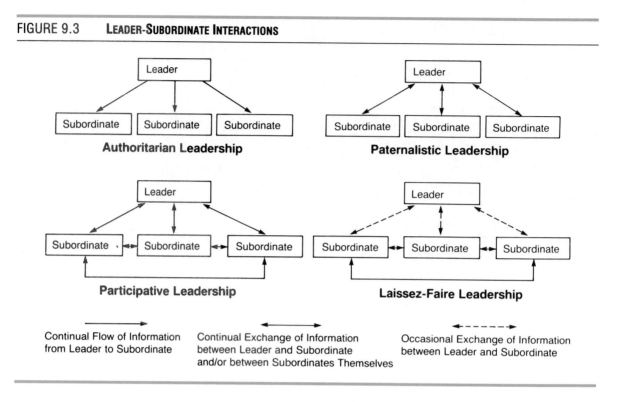

LAISSEZ-FAIRE LEADERSHIP

■ ■ ■ ■ ■ ■ ■ ■ ■ ■ ■ ■ ■

LAISSEZ-FAIRE MEANS
NONINTERFERENCE.

Laissez-faire is a French term meaning noninterference. As we move across the continuum from authoritarian to participative leadership, the subordinates begin playing an increasingly larger role. If a leader continues this transition, however, he or she will come very close to abdicating the leadership position. We can diagram the comparisons between leadership behaviors we have discussed, as in Figure 9.3. Note that the subordinates in the **laissez-faire leadership** diagram are interacting with one another to get the work done. The leader is only checking in on occasion to see how things are going.

Are there some subordinates for whom this style is effective? Yes, although they are not very common. University professors are an example. Very seldom does the department chairperson check up on the professor to see if the individual is having any problems, meeting classes on time, or conducting appropriate research activities. The chairperson usually meets with the professor prior to the beginning of the academic year to discuss objectives and assignments and relies on him or her to fulfill these obligations by the end of the school year. This approach works for highly skilled professionals in any area. The office manager of a research and development laboratory leaves the scientists alone to get their work done. Only occasionally does the manager check in to see that everything is running smoothly. In a business setting, some managers employ a laissez-faire style with their outstanding copywriters and design people, and a board of directors uses it with a president who has led the company into a new period of prosperity. In each case, the subordinates play a tremendous role in running the show. Keep in mind, however, that although this style can work effectively with some people, it does not work well with most. On average, the participative style tends to be most effective.

ON AVERAGE, PARTICIPATIVE LEADERSHIP IS MOST EFFECTIVE.

COMMON LEADERSHIP BEHAVIORS

In understanding effective leadership, it is also important to realize that there are a number of things that effective leaders try to do in influencing and directing their people. One is that they strive to get their subordinates to become "self leaders" and to learn to motivate and direct themselves. This reduces the amount of time the leader must spend on direct supervision.[15]

Leaders also support their personnel and provide them with assistance and guidance as needed. In this way there is a mutual exchange between the two that is rewarding to both parties.[16]

Leaders also tend to follow basic rules that have proven effective in the past. Examples include: (1) be decisive; (2) do not promise what you cannot deliver; (3) praise people in front of others for a job well done and reprimand them in private when they have made a mistake; and (4) when possible, promote from within.[17]

STOP!

Review your answer to the third question and make any changes you would like. Then compare your answer to the one below.

3. How would you describe the leadership behavior of the current president?

[15] Charles C. Manz, "Self-Leadership: Toward an Expanded Theory of Self-Influence Process in Organizations," *Academy of Management Review*, July 1986, pp. 585–600.

[16] Richard M. Dienesch and Robert C. Liden, "Leader-Member Exchange Model of Leadership: A Critique and Further Development," *Academy of Management Review*, July 1986, pp. 618–634.

[17] "Rules to Lead By," *Nation's Business*, August 1988, p. 26.

The president appears to believe in letting people do their jobs and not checking up on them too closely. This helps explain the problem with the field agents. He also tends to run a looser ship than the chairman of the board is seeking. In terms of Figure 9.3, the president is a combination of a participative and a laissez-faire leader. He certainly is not an authoritarian or paternalistic leader. ▪

LEADERSHIP DIMENSIONS

Each of the four leadership styles we have just examined contains some degrees of concern for work and for people. These two **leadership dimensions**—concern for work and concern for people—have been found to be *independent* dimensions. This means, for example, that someone can be high in one of the dimensions without having to be low in the other. As a result, there are four basic leadership behaviors:

FOUR INDEPENDENT DIMENSIONS.

- High concern for work, high concern for people.
- High concern for work, low concern for people.
- Low concern for work, high concern for people.
- Low concern for work, low concern for people.

Figure 9.4 is a leadership grid incorporating these behaviors. While effective leaders have a preferred style of leadership, there are times when each of these four basic styles will be used. For example, the high

FIGURE 9.4   **A LEADERSHIP GRID**

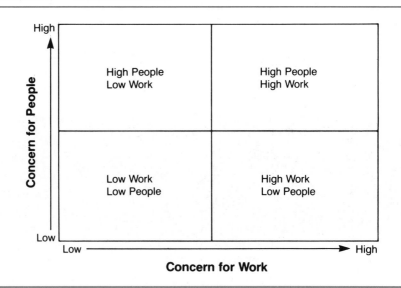

concern for work and people typically is employed when the leader
wants to develop high teamwork, wants to set challenging goals, or must
act decisively. A high concern for work and low concern for people often
is used when the leader strongly needs to control the personnel, must
have strict compliance, or is faced with an emergency that must be quickly
resolved. A low concern for work and high concern for people is often
used when the leader is eager to help, is sympathetic because of a personal problem facing a worker, or wants to praise someone for doing a
good job. A low concern for work and people is often used when the
leader feels that a situation will work itself out without any personal
intervention. An example is when a new worker has been told how to do
a job and must now be left alone to accomplish the task. Although the
leader may want to help, he or she may feel that the best approach is to
allow the new worker to carry out the task without any interference or
assistance. Later the leader and the worker can evaluate the situation and
decide what needs to be done. For the moment, however, a low concern
for the work and the people is the preferred leadership style.

Keeping in mind that any one of these can be an effective leadership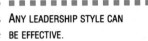
style, depending on the situation, let us examine some specific examples   ANY LEADERSHIP STYLE CAN
of each style and place them in the grid in Figure 9.5. First, let us take the   BE EFFECTIVE.
foreman on an assembly line. The foreman is charged with seeing that
the workers keep up with the line. The most effective style for such
a person is usually one that stresses high concern for work (for this is

FIGURE 9.5   **CONTINGENCY LEADERSHIP STYLES APPLIED TO A LEADERSHIP GRID**

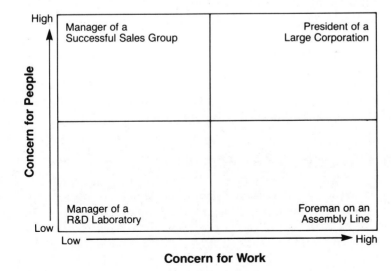

where the emphasis is needed) but low concern for people. (After all, what can a foreman do for them since the whole operation is automated?)

Conversely, the manager of a successful sales group has little need to be concerned with a work emphasis. The people are doing the job; sales are very high. The leader can therefore concentrate attention on praising the salespeople and encouraging them to keep up the good work. The individual needs a style with high concern for people and low concern for work.

The president of a large corporation, meanwhile, has to have high concerns for work and for people. This individual must be concerned with long-range planning, budgets, and programs and must be friendly, approachable, and willing to look out for the personal welfare of all the employees.

Finally, in the lower left corner of Figure 9.5 is the manager of a research and development lab. This individual has highly competent personnel, so there is no need to be concerned with production. These workers are self-motivated. Likewise, there is no need for the manager to praise them for a job well done, because they are skilled scientists who receive intrinsic satisfaction when they are praised by their peers. Such praise from their boss, however, means very little to them, since the manager of such a laboratory is usually not a scientist and so would be less able to value their work. As a result, the most effective style for the leader is low concerns for both people and work. The manager should be prepared to help them if called upon, but for the most part he or she should stay out of the way.

We should keep one thing in mind about this discussion. The examples we have used in Figure 9.5 are all presented to conform to one of the four leadership dimension combinations. However, we are not saying that every foreman on an assembly line should have high concern for work and low concern for people or that every president of a large company ought to have high concerns for both work and people. It all depends on the situation. In an effort to more fully understand leadership, many researchers have turned to an investigation of contingency leadership models. This represents the latest development of leadership theory, and every student of human relations should be familiar with it.

CONTINGENCY LEADERSHIP MODELS

Today we are in a *contingency* phase of leadership study. The human relations manager must adapt his or her style to meet the situation. Drawing upon our discussion of leadership and personal characteristics, we now address the question, "What specific style of leadership is best in which type of situation?" To answer this question, we need to match the styles with the environmental demands. In this section, we examine three contingency approaches: (1) Fiedler's contingency model, (2) the managerial grid, and (3) the path-goal theory of leadership.

FIEDLER'S CONTINGENCY MODEL

The best-known contingency model of leadership effectiveness was developed by Fred Fiedler and his associates.[18] **Fiedler's contingency model** represents a significant departure from earlier trait and behavioral leadership models because he contends that group performance is contingent on both the motivational system of the leader and the degree to which the leader can control and influence the situation. In order to classify leadership styles, Fiedler and his colleagues developed the least-preferred co-worker scale.

■ ■ ■ ■ ■ ■ ■ ■ ■ ■ ■ ■ ■
IT IS THE BEST-KNOWN CONTINGENCY MODEL.

The **least-preferred co-worker scale** (LPC) uses a questionnaire that asks the leader to describe the person with whom he or she can work least well. From the responses, an LPC score is obtained by adding the item scores. This score reveals the individual's emotional reaction to people with whom he or she cannot work well.

■ ■ ■ ■ ■ ■ ■ ■ ■ ■ ■ ■ ■
THE LPC ASKS, "WITH WHOM CAN YOU WORK LEAST WELL?"

Fiedler found that the leader with the high LPC score describes a least-preferred co-worker in favorable terms. The individual tends to be relationship-oriented and obtains great satisfaction from establishing close personal relations with the group members.

Conversely, the leader with a low LPC score describes his or her least preferred co-worker in unfavorable terms. The individual tends to be task-oriented and obtains much satisfaction from the successful completion of tasks, even if it comes at the risk of poor interpersonal relations with the workers.

SITUATIONAL VARIABLES   In addition to administering the LPC test to each individual, Fiedler sought to determine the major situational variables that could be used to classify group situations. He discovered three:

Leader-member relations are very important. The leader who is trusted by the subordinates can often influence group performance regardless of his or her position power. Conversely, the leader who is distrusted by the members must often rely solely on position power to get things done.

■ ■ ■ ■ ■ ■ ■ ■ ■ ■ ■ ■ ■
LEADER-MEMBER RELATIONS ARE IMPORTANT.

Task structure is the degree to which the leader's job is programmed or specified in step-by-step fashion. If the job is highly structured, the leader knows exactly what is to be done, and if there are any problems,

■ ■ ■ ■ ■ ■ ■ ■ ■ ■ ■ ■ ■
SO IS THE DEGREE OF TASK STRUCTURE.

■ ■ ■ ■ ■ ■ ■

[18] Fred E. Fiedler, *A Theory of Leadership Effectiveness* (New York: McGraw-Hill Book Company, 1967).

the organization can back the leader up. If the job is highly unstructured, there is no one right solution to the problem, and the leader will have to rely on personal relationships in getting the group to do things his or her way.

■ ■ ■ ■ ■ ■ ■ ■ ■ ■ ■ ■ ■ ■
AND THE LEADER'S POSITION
POWER.

Leader position power is the authority vested in the leader's position. For example, the president has more power than the vice-president, and the division head has more power than the unit manager.[19]

FIEDLER'S FINDINGS   Fiedler then brought together the LPC scores (which identified leadership style) with the situational variables to find what leadership style works best in each situation.

Figure 9.6 illustrates all the variables in the model. At the bottom of the graph are the eight possible combinations of situational variables (leader-member relations, task structure, and leader position power). Note that in Situation 1, on the left, things are very favorable for the leader; leader-member relations are good, the task is highly structured, and leader position power is strong. Meanwhile in Situation 8, on the right, things are very unfavorable for the leader. Leader-member relations are poor, the task is unstructured, and the leader's position power is weak. As we move across the continuum from the first to the eighth situation, things get progressively worse for the leader.

■ ■ ■ ■ ■ ■ ■ ■ ■ ■ ■ ■ ■ ■
THE TASK-CENTERED LEADER
IS BEST IN VERY FAVORABLE OR
UNFAVORABLE SITUATIONS.

What type of individual does best in each of these eight situations? As can be seen from the model, a task-oriented leader does best in very favorable situations (1, 2, and 3) or very unfavorable situations (7 and 8), and the relationship-oriented leader does best in the moderately favorable and moderately unfavorable situations (4, 5, and 6). Fiedler explained it this way:

■ ■ ■ ■ ■ ■ ■ ■ ■ ■ ■ ■ ■ ■
THE RELATIONSHIP-CENTERED
LEADER IS BEST IN MODERATELY
FAVORABLE OR UNFAVORABLE
SITUATIONS.

The results show that a task-oriented leader performs best in situations at both extremes—those in which he has a great deal of influence and power, and also in situations where he has no influence and power over the group members.

Relationship-oriented leaders tend to perform best in mixed situations where they have only moderate influence over the group. A number of subsequent studies by us and others have confirmed these findings.

The results show that we cannot talk about simply good leaders or poor leaders. A leader who is effective in one situation may or may not be effective in another. Therefore, we must specify the situations in which a leader performs well or badly.[20]

■ ■ ■ ■ ■ ■ ■

[19] For more on this see Rosabeth Moss Kanter, "Power Failure in Management Circuits," *Harvard Business Review*, July–August 1979, pp. 65–75.

[20] Fred Fiedler, "Style or Circumstance: The Leadership Enigma," *Psychology Today*, March 1969, p. 42.

FIGURE 9.6   IDENTIFYING THE EFFECTIVE LEADER

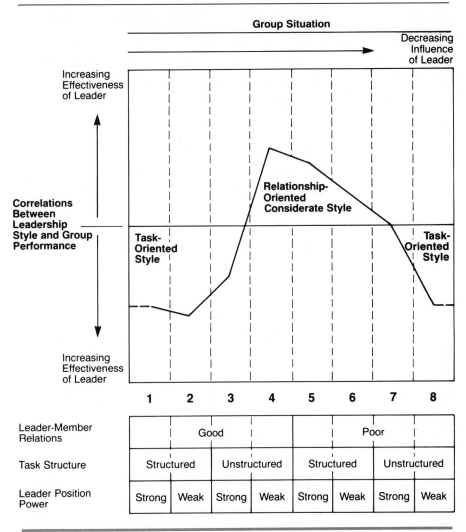

Source: Fred Fiedler, "Style or Circumstance: The Leadership Enigma," *Psychology Today*, March 1969, p. 42. Reprinted with permission from *Psychology Today* Magazine, © 1969 (PT Partners, L.P.).

FIEDLER'S THEORY AND HUMAN RELATIONS   Fiedler's theory offers several important alternatives for improving human relations. First, the organization as well as the leader is responsible for the latter's success, since a leader can be effective or ineffective depending on the situation. Many personnel psychologists and managers tend to view the executive's position as fixed and to turn their attention to changing the person's basic leadership style. However, this is the wrong approach. In order to change a leader's style one has to alter his or her personality. This can take from one to several years; a few lectures or some brief but intensive training will not do it.

What then should be done? The answer is: develop training programs that provide a leader with the opportunity to learn in which situations he or she can perform well and in which failure is likely.

Second, engineer the job to fit the leader. This recommendation is based on the fact that it is a lot easier to change the leader's work environment than his or her personality. Any one of the three situational variables can be altered. For example, the leader's position power could be improved by giving him or her a higher rank, or it can be reduced by forcing the leader to consult with the subordinates rather than make unilateral decisions. Similarly, the leader's task can be made more explicit or can be changed to be more vague. Finally, leader-member relations can be altered. The group can be made more homogeneous or more interdisciplinary, or the leader can be reassigned to a group that gets along well or one that is continually engaged in squabbling.

Applying these recommendations to Figure 9.6, we can move the leader back and forth on the grid depending on our objectives. For example, a task-centered manager operating in Situation 5 will not be very effective. A relationship-centered leader would do better. However, if we can do something to change leader-member relations from poor to good, we will have moved the leader to Situation 1. (You can verify this by comparing the three major variables for Situations 1 and 5 and noting what happens when the leader-member relations are changed.) Likewise, a relationship-oriented manager operating under the conditions in Situation 8 will be ineffective. However, the person would do quite well in Situation 4. This can be arranged simply by working to improve the leader-member relations from poor to good. (Again, you can prove this by comparing the three major variables for Situations 8 and 4 and noting what happens when the leader-member relations are changed.) If the leader were aware of his or her strengths and weaknesses, the individual could try to change the group situation to match his or her leadership style.

■ ■ ■ ■ ■ ■ ■ ■ ■ ■ ■ ■ ■ ■ ■ ■
DEVELOP TRAINING PROGRAMS
FOR LEADERS.

■ ■ ■ ■ ■ ■ ■ ■ ■ ■ ■ ■ ■ ■ ■ ■ ■
ENGINEER THE JOB TO FIT
THE LEADER.

THE MANAGERIAL GRID

The grid approach is most closely associated with Robert Blake and Jane Mouton.[21] The **managerial grid** consists of two dimensions: concern for production and concern for people. As can be seen in Figure 9.7, there

■ ■ ■ ■ ■ ■ ■

[21] R. R. Blake and J. S. Mouton, *The Managerial Grid* (Houston, Texas: Gulf Publishing Company, 1964).

FIGURE 9.7   **The Managerial Grid**

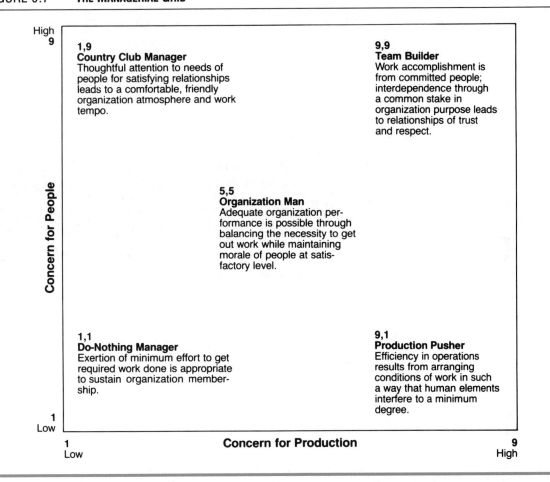

are 9 gradients or degrees associated with each dimension, so there are 81 possible combinations of concern for production and concern for people. A 1 represents low concern for the dimension and a 9 represents high concern.

Rather than trying to direct attention to all 81 combinations, grid development practitioners tend to focus on 5 critical combinations. The combinations are usually referred to by number, and when people become familiar with the grid they know what the numbers mean. Although they are briefly described in Figure 9.7, let us examine each combination in more detail.

The **1,1 managerial style** is used to describe the *do-nothing manager*. This individual tends to put people in jobs and then leave them alone. He or she does not check up on their work (concern for production) or try to interact with them by offering praise and encouraging them to keep up the good work (concern for people).

The **9,1 managerial style** describes the *production pusher*. This manager has a high concern for production and a low concern for people. He or she plans the work and pushes to get it out. Little interest is shown in the workers; if they cannot keep up, they are replaced by others who can.

The **1,9 managerial style** has been called *country club management* because of high emphasis given to concern for people's feelings, comfort, and needs. The manager is interested in obtaining loyalty from the subordinates and tries to motivate them to do their work without putting pressure on them.

The **5,5 managerial style** typifies the *organization manager*. This person assumes that there is an inherent conflict between the concerns for production and people. Therefore, he or she tries to compromise and balance the two dimensions.

The **9,9 managerial style** is used by the *team builder*. It is regarded by many as the ideal style, as the one that both managers in particular and the organization in general should employ. This style focuses on people's higher-level needs, involves subordinates in decision making, and assumes that the goals of the people and the goals of the organization are in harmony. As a result, the 9,9 manager believes that maximum concern for both dimensions will result in the greatest overall efficiency.

Which of these basic styles is best? The answer will depend on the needs of the subordinates, the manager, and the organization. *There is no such thing as one ideal style for all situations.* This can be made clear by giving you the opportunity to choose a leadership style on your own.

IDENTIFYING YOUR STYLE   A modern manager must perform many functions. Four of the most important are planning, decision making, leading, and controlling. In carrying out these functions, various degrees of concern for both people and work can be employed. In Figure 9.8, we have listed for each of these functions five leadership behaviors that can be used to implement them. Read the five behavior descriptions that accompany each function and place a 1 next to the behavior that you feel is *most* descriptive of you. Put a 2 next to the second most descriptive behavior, and so on, to a 5 for the *least* descriptive. If you are not currently a manager, imagine that you are in a managerial position while you take the test.

When you have finished assigning numbers to all of the behaviors, write your answers in the columns of the table below Figure 9.8. Be sure to enter the numbers properly. If you assigned a 3 to alternative b in the

■ ■ ■ ■ ■ ■ ■ ■ ■ ■ ■ ■ ■
THERE ARE FIVE BASIC STYLES.

FIGURE 9.8   MANAGEMENT STYLE IDENTIFICATION TEST

PLANNING

a _____ I sit down with my people, review the whole picture, and get reactions, ideas, and commitments from them. Schedules, goals, responsibilities, and control points are developed during this interaction period.

b _____ I plan the work for each of my people after discussing such things as targets and schedules with the person involved. I then make individual assignments but also ensure that each person knows to check back with me whenever further assistance is needed.

c _____ I suggest steps and offer assistance to my people in arranging their activities.

d _____ I let my people have planning responsibilities for their own parts of the job.

e _____ I plan for my people, set quotas where they are needed, and assign steps to be followed. I also establish check points that can be used for measuring performance.

DECISION MAKING

a _____ I make decisions, and after they are made, I stick with them.

b _____ My decisions follow the thinking of my boss; I think as he (or she) does.

c _____ I discuss decisions with those who will be affected by them, give them the facts from my point of view, and, in turn, get facts from them. After evaluation of alternatives, decisions are reached based on mutual understanding.

d _____ I sit down with each person who is affected by the decision and listen to the person's point of view. Then I make the decision and communicate it to those who will be affected, along with my reasons for making that particular decision.

e _____ I try to get a picture of what the subordinates want and use it as a basis for my decisions.

LEADING

a _____ Once assignments and plans have been clearly explained, I keep up with each person's performance and review their progress with them. If someone is having difficulty getting the job done, I lend assistance.

b _____ After assignments have been given to the people, I prefer to take little on-the-spot action. I think it is best for people to solve their own problems.

c _____ Once upcoming assignments are discussed, I keep in touch with my people in order to show that I am interested in how each is getting along.

d _____ Once plans have been determined, I keep up with the progress of the subordinates. I contribute time and effort as required by defining problems and removing roadblocks.

e _____ After I have set out plans and instructions, I keep a close eye on the subordinates' work performance and make changes as necessity dictates.

CONTROLLING

a _____ As work progresses, if any problems or changes need to be made, I make them on the spot. When the job is completed, I evaluate everyone's performance, correct those who have done a poor job, and give recognition to those who have performed well.

b _____ I sit down with my subordinates and review progress in detail, and when the job is totally finished I study how the entire operation was handled. Correct decisions, good work, errors, and misjudgments are all noted and examined

(Continued)

FIGURE 9.8 (*Continued*)

	in detail so that the former can be reinforced and the latter can be prevented in the future. When deserved, recognition for contribution is given on both a joint and an individual basis.
c _____	When I receive a reaction to their work, whether it is praise or a complaint, I pass this information on to the respective subordinates.
d _____	I compliment my subordinates when they do a good job and invite their suggestions for improvements. I believe that criticism tends to arouse tension and make people defensive.
e _____	I point out weaknesses as well as strengths to each subordinate. Each person then gets a chance to introduce his or her own suggestions for improvements.

	I	II	III	IV	V
Planning	b _____	d _____	e _____	a _____	c _____
Decision Making	d _____	b _____	a _____	c _____	e _____
Leading	a _____	b _____	e _____	d _____	c _____
Controlling	e _____	c _____	a _____	b _____	d _____
TOTAL	_____	_____	_____	_____	_____

Planning part, put a 3 in Column I in the table. If you gave a 5 to alternative d in the Planning part, put a 5 in Column II. Then add each column and put the total on the bottom line of each.

The short survey quiz is designed to determine the type of leadership style you use in carrying out each of the four functions we discussed. Which overall leadership style is your favorite? That will depend on the total scores of the columns. Remember, the *lower* the total the *higher* your support for that leadership style. (You gave a 1 to your favorite choice and a 5 to the least preferred.)

Column I reveals your preference for the 5,5 style. Column II measures your preference for the 1,1 style. Columns III, IV, and V measure preference for the 9,1 style, the 9,9 style, and the 1,9 style, respectively. Which is your most preferred style? Your least preferred style? Could you have predicted this, or are the findings a surprise to you?

The grid is important in the study of human relations because it offers the opportunity to close the gap between one's current and ideal leadership styles. The current style is the one identified in the management style test. The ideal style is the one that would be best in managing subordinates. The gap is the difference between the current and ideal styles. For example, if a person feels that the 9,9 leadership style would be most effective but currently is relying most heavily on the 5,5, that person must become more people- and work-oriented. On the other hand, if the person's current style is 1,9, he or she must become more work-oriented.

STOP!

Review your answer to the fourth question and make any changes you would like. Then compare your answer to the one below.

4.   In terms of the managerial grid, what type of leader is the current president? How will the new leader be different? Explain.

While it is difficult to fully describe the current president in terms of the grid, it is obvious from the description in the case that the individual is a behaviorally oriented leader. He is a combination of 9,9; 5,5; and 1,9. The leader whom the board is seeking is going to be a 9,9; 5,5; and 9,1 person. The company will see the top manager move from being heavily people-oriented to being more work-oriented. ■

PATH-GOAL THEORY OF LEADERSHIP

Path-goal leadership theory draws heavily on expectancy motivation theory and high concerns for both people and work. The theory has been proposed by Robert House and has been expanded and refined by him and others over the last decade.[22] The **path-goal theory of leadership** can be summarized as follows:

1.   The leader can improve subordinate motivation by making the rewards for performance more attractive. By giving the people raises, promotions, and recognition, the leader can increase the subordinates' valence (preference) for goal achievement.

2.   If the workers' assignments are poorly defined, the leader can increase motivation by providing structure in the form of helpful supervision, subordinate training, and goal clarification. Reducing the ambiguity of the job makes it easier for the subordinates to pursue the goals. Expectancy (the likelihood of attaining this first-level outcome) should increase.

TENETS OF PATH-GOAL THEORY.

If we take these two steps together, we can see that in the first, valence is increased, and in the second expectancy is increased. Recall the expectancy theory: Motivational force = Valence × Expectancy. It is obvious that path-goal theory is designed to increase worker motivation.

3.   If the work of the subordinates is already greatly structured, as in the case of assembly-line workers or machinists, the leader should refrain

----

[22] Robert J. House, "A Path-Goal Theory of Leader Effectiveness," *Administrative Science Quarterly*, September 1971, pp. 321–338; and Robert J. House and Terence R. Mitchell, "Path-Goal Theory of Leadership," *Journal of Contemporary Business*, Autumn 1974, pp. 81–97.

from introducing any more structure. Such actions will be viewed as unnecessary and overly directive. Instead of worrying about the work, the leader should now spend more time being concerned with the personal needs of the people by giving them attention, praise, and support.

At present there is some research support for the path-goal approach to leadership,[23] although it does appear that more work needs to be done in both expanding and refining the original theory.[24] One reason is that in some unstructured situations subordinates react negatively to attempts by the leader to clarify goals and reduce ambiguity. The employees would rather handle the situation themselves. On the other hand, there is fairly strong evidence to support the path-goal theory proposition that increasing consideration for subordinates whose work is already highly structured will increase their job satisfaction.

For human relations study, path-goal theory provides three important benefits. First, it helps integrate expectancy theory and contingency leadership. Second, it reemphasizes the importance of high leader concerns for both the work and the people. Third, it encourages the leader to analyze the situation in determining the right degree of each—concern for structure and concern for people—that will be required. Drawing together the ideas in this chapter, Human Relations in Action provides some of the most important steps for managers to follow.

SUMMARY

Leadership is the process of influencing people to direct their efforts toward the achievement of particular goal(s). What makes a leader effective? Some people believe the answer rests in leadership characteristics such as drive, originality, and the tolerance of stress. The greatest problem with this trait theory approach, however, is that it does not take the

■■■■■■■

[23] Robert J. House and G. Dessler, "The Path-Goal Theory of Leadership: Some Post Hoc and A Priori Tests," in J. G. Hunt and L. L. Larson, eds., *Contingency Approaches to Leadership* (Carbondale, Ill.: Southern Illinois University Press, 1974), pp. 29–55; and H. P. Sims, Jr. and A. D. Szilagyi, "Leader Structure and Subordinate Satisfaction for Two Hospital Administrative Levels: A Path Analysis Approach," *Journal of Applied Psychology*, April 1975, pp. 194–197.

[24] John E. Stinson and Thomas W. Johnson, "The Path-Goal Theory of Leadership: A Partial Test and Suggested Refinement," *Academy of Management Journal*, June 1975, pp. 242–252; Andrew D. Szilagyi and Henry P. Sims, Jr., "An Exploration of the Path-Goal Theory of Leadership in a Health Care Environment," *Academy of Management Journal*, December 1974, pp. 622–634; H. Kirk Downey, John E. Sheridan, and John W. Slocum, Jr., "Analysis of Relationships among Leader Behavior, Subordinate Job Performance and Satisfaction: A Path-Goal Approach," *Academy of Management Journal*, June 1975, pp. 253–262; and Charles Greene, "Questions of Causation in the Path-Goal Theory of Leadership," *Academy of Management Journal*, March 1979, pp. 22–41.

HUMAN RELATIONS IN ACTION

LEADING EFFECTIVELY

A great deal of research has been conducted on leadership. Drawing together much of this information from a human relations standpoint, we find there are four things managers should know in their quest to lead effectively.

1.   *Know your biases.* Are you a Theory X person? A Theory Y person? A combination of the two? If the latter, do you lean more to the X side or the Y side? If you can answer these questions accurately, you know something about your leadership biases. This is important because, like it or not, you eventually resort to that leadership style with which you feel most comfortable.

2.   *Know the situations in which you function best.* Do you do well when there is a crisis? Are you good at handling situations that are out of control? Or are you best when things are on an even keel? In answering these questions, think of a time when you have done extremely well as a leader. Then think of a situation when you performed poorly. What was the difference in the two situations? Your answer helps you understand your "best" environments.

3.   *Understand the leadership preferences of your people.* What leadership style do your subordinates like best? Your answer will undoubtedly include a range of behaviors but group them all under one of the four basic styles: authoritarian, paternalistic, participative, and laissez-faire.

4.   *Match your style with the situation and the people.* Pull everything together: your style, the demands of the situation, and the needs of the subordinates. Do the best you can to lead from your strengths by employing that style with which you have had the most success. You may have to alter this style a bit, but stay within the leadership parameters you know best. Use Fiedler's ideas to change the environment to suit your style rather than vice versa. Also remember that in the short run you may have to use a style which you do not prefer. Be flexible and adapt to this brief inconvenience, while working to get things back to where you can employ your most effective style.

situation into account. A leadership style that is effective in one situation may not be effective in another.

In an effort to address the situational nature of leadership, many people have turned to personal characteristics. Some of the most commonly cited personal characteristics of leaders include superior intelligence, emotional maturity, motivation drive, problem-solving skills, managerial skills, and leadership skills. The degree and importance of each is situationally determined. For example, some situations require the leader to rely heavily on human skills, but others demand administrative skills.

In order to lead personnel effectively, it is also necessary to form some opinions about them. Some managers are adherents of the Theory X philosophy, which holds that people are basically lazy and that in order to get them to work, it is often necessary to use coercion and threats of punishment. Other managers support Theory Y, which holds that people are interested in both lower-level and upper-level need satisfaction, have untapped potential, and, if given the right rewards, exercise self-direction and self-control in attaining organizational objectives.

Many organizations keep the people in a state of immaturity. This has led Argyris to conclude that there is a basic incongruence between the needs of the healthy personality and the demands of the average organization. Yet this does not have to be the case. Experiments in job design, for example, have illustrated that people who are given increased responsibility and the chance for upper-level needs satisfaction often produce far more than they have in the past.

Leadership styles also vary. Some situations require authoritarian leadership behavior, but others call for a paternalistic leader; some are best handled with a participative leadership style, and others require a laissez-faire manager. Each of the four styles can be described in terms of two dimensions: concern for work and concern for people. Every leader exercises some degree of each, and since they are independent dimensions, the individual can be high in one without having to be low in the other. The person can be high in both or, for that matter, low in both.

Today, we are in a contingency phase of leadership study. The best-known contingency model is that of Fred Fiedler, who has found that task-centered leaders do best in very favorable or very unfavorable situations and relationship-oriented leaders are most effective in situations that are moderately favorable or moderately unfavorable. He recommends matching the leader to the situation rather than trying to change the individual's personality to fit the job.

The managerial grid approach is well-liked by practicing managers. It is useful in helping participants to understand the five basic styles of leadership and to close the gap between current and desired leadership styles.

The path-goal theory of leadership draws heavily on expectancy motivation theory and leader concern for both people and work. In essence the theory holds that (1) the leader can improve subordinate motivation by making the rewards for performance more attractive, (2) if work assignments are poorly defined, the leader can increase motivation by providing structure in the form of helpful supervision, subordinate training, and goal clarification, and (3) if the work is already greatly structured, the leader should concentrate on the personal needs of the individuals by giving them attention, praise, and support. At present, some research supports the path-goal approach to leadership, but more work needs to be done to expand and refine the theory.

KEY TERMS IN THE CHAPTER

leadership	leadership dimensions
leadership characteristics	Fiedler's contingency model
personal characteristics	least-preferred co-worker scale
technical skills	leader-member relations
human skills	task structure
administrative skills	leader position power
Theory X	managerial grid
Theory Y	1,1 managerial style
immaturity–maturity theory	9,1 managerial style
authoritarian leadership	1,9 managerial style
paternalistic leadership	5,5 managerial style
participative leadership	9,9 managerial style
laissez-faire leadership	path-goal theory of leadership

REVIEW AND STUDY QUESTIONS

1. How do leadership characteristics differ from personal characteristics? Explain.

2. Are there any leadership characteristics that appear to account for success in the leadership role? What are they?

3. In terms of need drive, how do successful leaders differ from average leaders? From least successful leaders?

4. What are the three types of managerial skills every leader must have? Explain.

5. What are the basic assumptions of Theory X? How accurate are they? What are the basic assumptions of Theory Y? How accurate are they?

6. Is a Theory Y manager always superior to a Theory X manager? Explain.

7. According to Argyris, what are the seven states through which an individual progresses as he or she matures?

8. The two leadership dimensions—concern for work and concern for people—have been found to be independent dimensions. What does this statement mean?

9. What type of leader would do best in a situation requiring high concern for work, low concern for people? High concern for both? Low concern for both? Explain your answers.

10. According to Fiedler, what type of leader is most effective in which kind of situation? Be complete in your answer.

11. In what way is Fiedler's theory useful in the study of human relations?

12.   What is meant by each of the following: 1,1 management, 9,1 management, 1,9 management, 5,5 management, 9,9 management?

13.   Of what value is the managerial grid in the study of human relations? Explain.

14.   In your own words, what is the path-goal theory of leadership all about? How can an understanding of this theory contribute to one's knowledge of human relations? Explain.

TIME OUT ANSWERS: INTERPRETATION OF YOUR ASSUMPTIONS ABOUT PEOPLE

This test measures your tendency to support Theory X and Theory Y beliefs. In getting your scores for each, fill in the answer sheet below and then plot a graph by placing a dot at the point where your Theory X and Theory Y scores intersect.

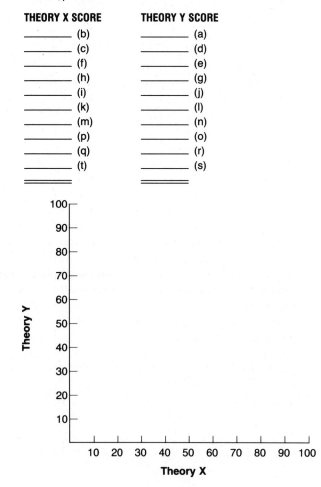

THEORY X SCORE

_____ (b)
_____ (c)
_____ (f)
_____ (h)
_____ (i)
_____ (k)
_____ (m)
_____ (p)
_____ (q)
_____ (t)
══════════

THEORY Y SCORE

_____ (a)
_____ (d)
_____ (e)
_____ (g)
_____ (j)
_____ (l)
_____ (n)
_____ (o)
_____ (r)
_____ (s)
══════════

Look at the dot you have placed on the graph. Now draw a line from the origin through the dot and on outward to the end of the graph. At the end of this line place an arrowhead. This line points the direction in which your beliefs about people move. Based on the direction of the arrow, you can tell if you are basically a Theory X person, a Theory Y person, or a strong blend of the two.

CASE: BACK TO SQUARE ONE

Ted Abbott was brought into Kendrick Works to straighten things out. Ted had worked for one of Kendrick's competitors for eight years and had earned an enviable reputation during this time. Starting out at the foreman level, Ted worked his way up to senior vice-president. Along the way, he streamlined the company's operations, brought in new machinery and equipment that increased productivity, cut waste and inefficiency, and reduced the overall payroll from 55 percent of total expenses to under 42 percent. Ted was in line for promotion to president when Kendrick contacted him and asked if he would consider taking over their reins. Since it would be at least five years before his firm's president stepped down, Ted accepted Kendrick's offer.

For more than three years Kendrick had been losing money. Top management hoped that under Ted's direction all of this could be changed. Over the next two years, they were not disappointed with their decision. Ted started cutting waste and inefficiency and getting the firm on a more competitive basis. Within six months, the company started to show a profit. A year later the board announced that it was paying back its outstanding long-term debt and was issuing a special dividend on all stock. The firm was making more money than it ever had before.

Then things started to turn around. Costs began to rise and employee turnover increased. At the lower and middle ranks of management, more and more people began leaving. The union entered into prolonged negotiations with management, arguing that with the increase in profit the firm should raise wages by 10 percent more than was standard in the industry. When Ted held the line, there was a 45-day strike, which worsened the company's position. Kendrick soon found itself heading back into the red.

Over the past 18 months Kendrick has continued losing money, and at a faster rate than when Ted took over. Some members of the board of directors have suggested that they get rid of Ted and bring in someone else. One of them put it this way, "What good is Ted to us? Thanks to him we're back to square one." On the other hand, Ted has a strong following on the board and they are unwilling to let him go. As one of them argued, "Look, the guy turned things around before. We all know that.

Well, here's a chance for him to work his magic again. I don't know anyone else who can straighten out a mess better than he can, and a mess is certainly what we have. I recommend that we keep Ted on and see what we can do to help him turn things around again." The majority of the board agreed.

QUESTIONS

1.   What type of a leader is Ted? Refer to Figure 9.6 in your answer.

2.   Why was Ted effective in turning the company around? Why is he having trouble now? Explain.

3.   If you were on the board, would you vote to replace Ted? Why or why not? Defend your answer. ■

CASE: MAKING SOME NECESSARY CHANGES

Helen Knighter and Sam Schwede are assistant store managers for a large retail chain located throughout the midwestern and southern parts of the country. Helen began her career with the firm three years ago. The company was hiring people for its personnel department, and Helen's degree in psychology helped land her the job. Although most of the new people who were hired were put into training and development, Helen was assigned to counseling. In this job she talked to store people who were having a variety of personal problems from drinking to failure to interact effectively with customers. Helen's job was to provide them assistance and guidance in straightening out their lives. After a six-week training program, she was assigned a number of cases and performed very well. Her performance ratings were always in the top 10 percent of the department.

Although Helen liked her job, she realized that there was a limited career track for people in counseling. If she wanted to succeed with the firm, she needed to get a job in one of the firm's retail stores. At the end of her second year, she applied for a position as assistant store manager and was assigned to a unit four months ago. Since then Helen has worked very hard to learn her job. Last week she attended a managerial training program. During one of the sessions, the participants measured their leadership style. Before interpreting this style, the trainer asked each of the participants to identify the style that they thought would be most effective for them in getting their jobs done. Helen chose the 9,9 style. When her test results were interpreted, however, it turned out that Helen was using a 1,9 style.

Sam Schwede was sitting next to her during the training program. Sam has been with the company for only four months. He was hired directly out of college where he majored in management and minored in marketing. Sam has had little experience in retail management. This is why his store manager sent him to the training program. Like Helen, Sam identified the 9,9 style as the one that would be ideal for him in managing the store personnel. However, his leadership style test indicated that he was using a 5,5 style.

When the trainer discussed the results of the test with both Helen and Sam, he pointed out that both will have to make changes in order to bring their current styles more into line with their desired style. "This won't be as hard as it seems," he told them, "but it will take some work on your part."

QUESTIONS

1.   In your own words, describe the five basic styles on the managerial grid.

2.   What changes will Helen have to make? Be complete in your answer.

3.   What changes will Sam have to make? Explain. ∎

EXPERIENCING FOUR SYSTEMS OF LEADERSHIP

PURPOSE

- To better understand leader-subordinate interactions under authoritarian, paternalistic, participative, and laissez-faire leadership.
- To analyze leadership behavior under these four systems.

PROCEDURE

1.   The class is divided into four groups and each group organizes itself around one of the four systems as assigned by the teacher. A leader is identified in each group. A non-participating observer is also assigned and, before continuing, each group should discuss how leaders and members behave under the assigned system. For example, those in the paternalistic group need to consider how the leader will behave with respect to his or her employees. How do members typically respond?

(Continued)

EXPERIENCING FOUR SYSTEMS OF LEADERSHIP   (Continued)

2.   After ten minutes of such discussion, the group solves the following problem, keeping strictly in the assigned character. Each group has ten minutes to come to a decision.

3.   Each group relates to the class its decision, how it was reached, and how they as individuals are satisfied. Each observer comments on how the group acted. Did they stay in character?

4.   Discuss the following:
  a.   Which group came to the fastest decision? Why?
  b.   Which group was most committed to the decision reached? Why?

SITUATION

The group consists of plant manager and first line supervisors. Budgetary problems require that they lay off two production employees immediately. Chances are they will not be rehired. Who is laid off?

1.   Robert Sanderson, age 25, good producer, 6 months with the company, unmarried, attending night school for a bachelor's degree in business administration.

2.   Mark Riley, age 32, average producer, B.S. degree, 7 years with the company, married with 2 kids, one on the way.

3.   Marilyn Smith, age 30, excellent producer, 5 years with the company, no degrees, married and pregnant.

4.   Cheryl Whitman, age 50, average producer, technical school graduate, 15 years with the company, married with 3 grown kids.

5.   Mary Sampson, age 25, average producer, 4 years with the company, enrolled in high school equivalency program, unmarried.

6.   Raul Sanchez, age 21, excellent producer, 1 year with the company, high school dropout, no family in the United States.

10
CHAPTER

THE ROLE OF THE LEADER

GOALS OF THE CHAPTER

In Chapter 9 we examined the fundamentals of leadership; in particular, we studied the nature of leadership, leadership behavior, and contingency leadership styles. Now we want to turn to the role of the leader by answering the question, "What do effective leaders do on a day-to-day basis?" Although there are many tasks the leader must perform, six are of primary importance: representing and supporting the subordinates, developing teamwork, counseling wisely, using power properly, managing time well, and managing stress well. The goal of this chapter is to examine these tasks, beginning with leader-member related activities and then moving to tasks that tend to be performed by the leader alone.

When you have finished reading this chapter you should understand the role of the leader and should be able to:

1. Explain what is meant by *teamwork* and describe the three key factors necessary to the development of teamwork.

2. Tell why employees need counseling and cite the kinds of counseling often given by managers.

3. Define *power* and explain the various types.

4. Explain the three ways of managing time and tell how effective leaders manage their time well.

5. Discuss how the manager should deal with stress.

OPENING CASE

THE BUSY MANAGER

Greg Ransforth is regarded as one of the best managers in his company. Greg interacts well with both his own personnel and with upper-level management. Two months ago management decided to implement a new monthly cost control report. Greg gathered the necessary information regarding how the report was to be filled out and filed and why this new report was important. He then convinced his people of the need to complete and submit the report by the first of every month. Greg can also be relied upon to support his personnel. Two weeks ago one of his people needed to take three personal days. The company seldom allows more than two personal days at a time. However, Greg was able to convince his boss that this was a special situation, and the woman was granted the three days.

While Greg likes to help his people, he tries to stay out of their business. If someone has a personal problem, Greg does not ask questions. He offers advice only if he is asked. However, a few weeks ago something happened that has made Greg wonder whether he should get more actively involved in his employees' personal problems. Howard Taylor, a new employee, was taking a report out of his desk to hand to Greg. As he removed it from the lower drawer, Greg could see that there was a small bottle of liquor there. The bottle was half empty. Greg did not say anything because he had never seen Howard drinking on the job. Greg thought that Howard might have accidentally brought the bottle into the building in his attache case and was going to take it out that evening.

A few days later the janitor reported to Greg that someone had deposited an empty liquor bottle in the trash can in the men's rest room. Yesterday the janitor reported another such incident. Has Howard been drinking on the job? Greg is not sure, but if Howard has been doing so, Greg intends to take action. Greg hopes that this is not the case because he already has his hands full with all of the other things he is trying to do. As he noted to his wife recently, "I can't get all of my work done anymore. There's just too much. I need to start working smarter, not harder."

1.   What is the linking pin function and what relevance does it have to this case?

2.   Aside from directly asking him, what can Greg do to determine if Howard has been drinking? What symptoms might he look for?

3.   If Howard has been drinking on the job, what types of power can Greg use in resolving this problem? Cite and describe two.

4.   What could Greg do to work smarter, not harder? Offer him three recommendations for action.

Write down your answers to these questions and put them aside. We will return to them later. ∎

REPRESENT AND SUPPORT THE SUBORDINATES

One of the primary roles of the leader is to represent the subordinates to his or her boss. The leader must be the interface between the work group and higher management. At the same time, he or she must be personally supportive of the group members.

LINKING PIN FUNCTION

One way of looking at leaders is as **linking pins** that represent or connect their group to the one directly above it in the hierarchy. Made famous by Rensis Likert, the idea is depicted in Figure 10.1.[1] The lowest-level managers, the supervisors, are links between each of their three subordinates (below) and their own group managers (above). In turn, the group manager represents the three supervisors to the department manager. This idea, if continued up the line, results in an integrated organization. If the linking pin connection is weak, however, effectiveness will suffer.

LEADERS ARE LIKE LINKING PINS.

SUPPORTIVE BEHAVIOR

In addition to representing members of the group to the upper management, the effective leader must strive to remove roadblocks, define tasks, and motivate the subordinates toward goal attainment. This may require further training of the workers, purchase of new equipment, or more efficient scheduling of material delivery.

THE LEADER MUST BE SUPPORTIVE

In any event, the foundation of supportive behavior is trying to understand employee needs. What kinds of support are required for the workers to do a better job? Often the answer is found in **social exchange theory**. If the leader wants something from the subordinates, he or she must be willing to give something in turn. This quid pro quo serves to help overcome apathy and reduce turnover and absenteeism. The effective leader knows the value of supportive role behavior.[2]

∎∎∎∎∎∎∎

[1] Rensis Likert, *New Patterns of Management* (New York: McGraw-Hill Book Company, 1961), pp. 113–115.

[2] Richard M. Dienesch and Robert C. Liden, "Leader-Member Exchange Model of Leadership: A Critique and Further Development," *Academy of Management Review*, July 1986, pp. 618–634.

FIGURE 10.1   **THE LINKING PIN FUNCTION**

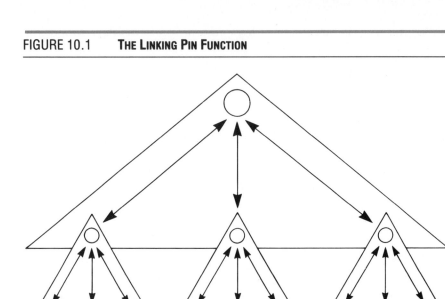

DEVELOP TEAMWORK

A second important role of the leader is to develop *teamwork*. Whenever a leader is placed in charge of an operating team for which each person in the group must contribute some effort toward goal attainment, teamwork is necessary.

KEY FACTORS IN DEVELOPING TEAMWORK

There are three key factors in the development of teamwork: the leader, the subordinates, and the environment (Figure 10.2). They are interdependent. For example, if the leader cannot get along with the subordinates, the group members do not like the leader, or the environment is not conducive to effective teamwork, overall group efficiency suffers.[3]

·······

[3] For more on this topic see Mary Walsh Mossop, "Total Teamwork: How to Be a Leader, How to Be a Member," *Management Solutions*, August 1988, pp. 3–9; and Marc Bassin, "Teamwork at General Foods: New & Improved," *Personnel Journal*, May 1988, pp. 62–70.

FIGURE 10.2   **TEAMWORK DETERMINANTS**

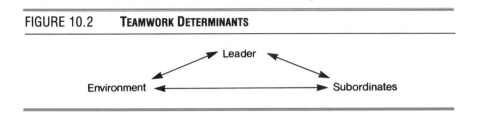

THE LEADER   The leader must build an environment in which team-work can happen. Research shows that between the leader and the sub-ordinates there must be trust, cooperation, and compatibility. Some lead-ers have the training, experience, and personality that allow them to build teamwork among their people almost immediately. Others require more time because the subordinates are reluctant to trust them, the work environment is not conducive to teamwork, or they lack the personal characteristics needed to create the right environment.[4] Once the proper environment is created, the leader must maintain the situation and en-sure that the subordinates do not lose interest.

■ ■ ■ ■ ■ ■ ■ ■ ■ ■ ■ ■ ■
THE LEADER MUST BUILD THE
ENVIRONMENT FOR TEAMWORK.

THE SUBORDINATES   No matter how hard the leader tries to develop teamwork, the subordinates have a key role to play in this effort. If the norms of the group restrict output, the leader is starting out in a weak position. If there has been bitter union-management conflict over a re-cently negotiated contract, the leader may find no basis for developing effective teamwork. If the leader is paternalistic but the subordinates want a participative leader, there will be teamwork problems. Finally, if some of the group members do not get along with one another, there will be minimum cooperation among them. This will reduce group teamwork.

■ ■ ■ ■ ■ ■ ■ ■ ■ ■ ■ ■
SUBORDINATES MUST HELP IN THIS
PROCESS.

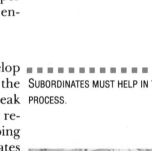

THE ENVIRONMENT   Most teamwork problems are a result of several interacting influences that cannot be attributed solely to the leader or the subordinates. Rather, they arise from the way the work is organized and the operations are carried out. Two questions will always reveal them. What tasks are the individuals in the group doing? Is there a basis for teamwork, or are the people being rewarded for competing with one another?

In some organizations, for example, the marketing department is rewarded for selling, the production department for manufacturing, and

At Citgo Petroleum Corpora-tion, a new safety awareness program was begun recently. It stresses teamwork and in-dividual responsibility for safety and rewards outstand-ing performers.

■ ■ ■ ■ ■ ■ ■
[4]Dale E. Zand, "Trust and Managerial Problem Solving," *Administrative Science Quarterly*, June 1972, pp. 229–239; and W. Brendan Reddy and Anne Byrnes, "Effects of Inter-personal Group Composition on the Problem-Solving Behavior of Middle Managers," *Journal of Applied Psychology*, December 1972, pp. 516–517.

the finance department for carefully monitoring and controlling overall budgets and capital expenditures. What the top manager fails to realize, however, is that all three cannot succeed. One or two win at the expense of the third. In particular, if finance holds down expenditures, marketing may be unable to initiate its advertising program, sales will not be greater, and production may be unable to buy new machines so the cost per unit will be higher. Finally, with a smaller marketing effort and a higher product cost, the net profit will be below the forecast. The top manager must strive to develop teamwork among his or her key people by reducing this built-in goal conflict as much as possible.

AND THE ENVIRONMENT MUST BE RIGHT.

A similar situation is that of salespeople who are selling the same product line in different geographic locales. In contrast to the previous illustration in which intergroup cooperation is needed to accomplish overall goals, however, this is a classic case of "Every man for himself." Each salesperson is given a quota and urged to meet it. There is no reward for cooperation or teamwork. Danny may know of a potential customer in Sue's territory, but he neglects to convey this information to her because he may endanger his chances of being the company's top salesperson this year. In order to overcome this problem, the leader must revise the sales incentive plan so that people are rewarded for teamwork. If the current sales environment does nothing to encourage team players, it must be changed.

STOP!

Review your answer to the first question and make any changes you would like. Then compare your answer to the one below.

1.   What is the linking pin function and what relevance does it have to this case?

The linking pin function is the process of representing one's group to the one directly above it in the organizational hierarchy. Greg does this by supporting his people with upper-level management and trying to get them the necessary support and assistance. ■

COUNSEL WISELY

COUNSELING INVOLVES THE DISCUSSION OF AN EMOTIONAL PROBLEM.

A third important role of the leader is to counsel wisely. **Counseling** is the discussion of an emotional problem with an employee with the purpose of eliminating or reducing it. Many people in the work place need counseling because the demands of their jobs create emotional disequilibrium.

Why Employees Need Counseling

Many factors can cause an employee to need counseling. Three of the most important are frustration, conflict, and stress.

FRUSTRATION   A result of a blocked need drive is **frustration**. We can represent it as in Figure 10.3. A person who sees his or her efforts blocked often becomes uneasy, anxious, or nervous. A worker may be unable to accomplish a task because of interference by other employees or failure of equipment.

> ■ ■ ■ ■ ■ ■ ■ ■ ■ ■ ■ ■ ■
> FRUSTRATION RESULTS FROM A
> BLOCKED NEED DRIVE.

What the manager needs to realize is that the higher the worker's motivation to reach a desired goal, the higher the person's frustration over failure; and conversely, the lower the person's motivation, the lower the frustration over failure. Since the manager wants to encourage high motivation, it is imperative that some form of counseling be given to employees who are encountering frustration reactions. Additionally, where possible the manager should use his or her power to directly reduce the barriers by, for example, personally investigating why certain raw materials have not arrived and expediting their delivery.

Another common cause of frustration is unfair or discriminatory treatment in the work place. In some organizations, minorities are not accorded the same treatment as larger groups. Research shows that blacks and women, on average, have lower salaries than do their white male counterparts. Here, again, counseling can be useful in helping these people formulate career strategies that will overcome these problems.

CONFLICT   When individuals or groups in the organization clash over some issue that, at least to them, is important, **conflict** occurs. Sometimes this occurs on an interpersonal basis, and at other times it takes place be-

> ■ ■ ■ ■ ■ ■ ■ ■ ■ ■ ■ ■ ■
> CONFLICT OCCURS WHEN PEOPLE
> DISAGREE ABOUT AN ISSUE.

FIGURE 10.3   **BLOCKED NEED DRIVE AND FRUSTRATION**

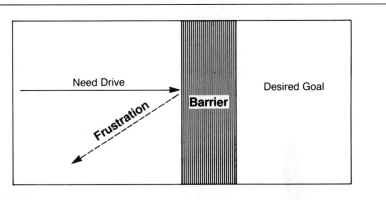

tween groups. One person may defeat another for a promotion; one group may have new machinery installed in its department before the other gets new machines. One division may be given 15 percent more merit money than another.

Conflict is not always bad, but when it leads to a deterioration of co-operation, trust, and loyalty among the personnel, counseling is in order. This is particularly true when parties to the conflict engage in win-lose situations, in which one party's gain is the other's loss. By counseling those involved, the manager can often reduce conflicts and redirect the efforts of the personnel toward more meaningful objectives.

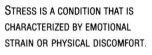

STRESS IS A CONDITION THAT IS CHARACTERIZED BY EMOTIONAL STRAIN OR PHYSICAL DISCOMFORT.

SmithKline Beckman managers relieve some of their work-related stress by exercising regularly.

STRESS   The condition that is characterized by emotional strain or physical discomfort and that, unrelieved, can impair one's ability to cope with the environment is termed **stress**. A small amount of stress can be good. In many people it stimulates performance. If stress is increased or is maintained for an extended period, however, it can be dangerous. In the short run it can lead to a headache or upset stomach; in the long run it can result in ulcers, a heart condition, or nervous disorders.

Research shows that workers and managers report about the same degree of job stress. If one assumes that managerial jobs are more stressful, these findings indicate that the management selection process in many organizations apparently weeds out those least likely to withstand the pressure.[5] However, this does not negate the need for counseling. Workers must still withstand the stress associated with job insecurity, role ambiguity, role conflict, and job overload. Additionally, many employees suffer stress in their home lives and bring these pressures with them to the job. Counseling can help alleviate much of this problem.

COUNSELING FUNCTIONS

The overall purpose of counseling is to provide support to the employees in dealing with their emotional problems. The manager's objective should be that of increasing the employee's understanding, self-confidence, and ability to work effectively as a member of the team. Here are some of the most commonly accepted counseling functions.

THE MANAGER MUST ADVISE THE SUBORDINATE.

ADVICE   When the manager advises the subordinate, he or she lays out a course of action to be followed. The manager takes the lead, the subordinate follows. Some professional counselors have pointed out the

■■■■■■■

[5] Vernon E. Buck, "Working under Pressure," *Management and Organization Studies* (Seattle, Washington: University of Seattle), Autumn 1974, pp. 1–3.

dangers in trying to understand another person's complicated emotions and to recommend a path of action. In spite of the possible dangers, however, this approach to counseling is widely used, because managers believe they should do it and workers expect it to be done. Many employees admit that they would rather have the manager suggest a course of action (even if it might be wrong) than to plan one themselves.

REASSURANCE   Closely related to advice is reassurance. Some people, for example, encounter stress because they are unsure of how well they are doing their jobs. The manager may tell a subordinate that he or she is doing fine and may encourage him or her to keep it up. To a worker who is experiencing job stress the manager may point out, "This is all temporary. Our busy season ends next week and everything will go back to normal." Sometimes reassurance is just what the person needs to reduce frustration or stress.

     In other cases the individual needs to be assured that organizational rules and regulations will be enforced. A good example is sexual harassment on the job. Managers not only need to be aware of this form of behavior, but must be prepared to take action as soon as they learn about it. (See Human Relations in Action: Dealing with Sexual Harassment.)

> GIVE THE PERSON REASSURANCE.

RELEASE OF EMOTIONAL TENSION   Many times all the worker needs is a sympathetic ear. Once he or she pours out what has been bottled up inside, the tension declines. Of course, this may not solve the problem, but it often removes mental blocks and permits the worker to face the problem squarely. Few people can resolve their problems when seething with anger and tension. This counseling function can help alleviate such emotions.

> PROVIDE A SYMPATHETIC EAR.

REORIENTATION   Sometimes employees need to be reoriented. They require additional training for a new job, a revision of their aspirations so that they are more in line with their abilities, or a rethinking of their current goals and values vis-à-vis those of the organization. These problems can sometimes be handled by the manager, but if they are severe, it is necessary to call on professional help. If, for example, an executive becomes an alcoholic, helping him or her become reoriented can be beyond the ability of the average manager.[6] When one's subordinate has this problem, it is best to let more professional help take over.

> GIVE NECESSARY REORIENTATION.

▪▪▪▪▪▪▪

[6]"Business Dries Up Its Alcoholics," *Business Week*, November 11, 1972, pp. 168–169, 173; and "More Firms, Unions Establish Programs to Fight Alcoholism," *Wall Street Journal*, October 18, 1978, p. 19.

HUMAN RELATIONS IN ACTION

DEALING WITH SEXUAL HARASSMENT

Many women in the work place feel that they are sexually harassed. In the past, this problem was confined to the woman and the person who was doing the harassing. This no longer is true. Many organizations have formal policies that specifically forbid sexual harassment. Additionally, the latest court cases now make the employer responsible if such harassment was known, or should have been known, and the situation was not corrected. In dealing with sexual harassment, there are five things managers should do.

1.   *Know the organization's policy on sexual harassment.* If you do not have a copy of the rules, get one and read it. If there is no written policy, assume that any complaint by a female worker that she is being "bothered" by a male employee will be construed by the courts to be sexual harassment.

2.   *If there is a formal policy, make sure that everyone in your work unit knows about it and understands it.* If there is no formal policy, tell your people that sexual harassment will not be tolerated and urge those who feel they have been victims to report the matter to you.

3.   *Take all complaints seriously.* Do not assume that someone has hidden motives and is trying to get another worker in trouble. Meet with the complaining employee, taking notes and asking any questions that will help you get a better understanding of what has happened. Also make it clear that the organization does not tolerate sexual harassment in any form and you will not allow it in your work unit. It is important to convey the seriousness with which you approach this matter. If it ever gets into court, one of the first things the prosecution will attempt to prove is that you knew of the situation and treated it lightly.

4.   *Act immediately.* Call in whoever has been named in the sexual harassment charge and talk to the person. Try to resolve the situation at this point. Perhaps this person regards the entire matter as nothing more than a joke. Make it clear to the person that these matters are not funny. Perhaps the individual says that the woman misunderstood some innocent remark. Make it clear that any remarks that can be misconstrued as sexual harassment can get an individual into serious trouble. If the matter is serious enough, in your view, have the woman present and make it clear to both of them that you expect no further problems along this line. It may be embarrassing to the woman to be present at the meeting, but if it will help you convey the seriousness of the matter to the male employee, you should have her there.

5.   *Follow up your actions.* After a week has gone by, check with the woman to be sure that she is not being subjected to further harassment. Let her know that you have not forgotten the matter and if it arises again, you want to know about it at once. It is unlikely that you can stamp out sexual harassment in the work place. However, you can reduce its occurrence and its negative impact by following the above five steps.

COUNSELING AND THE MODERN EMPLOYEE

In most cases the leader's counseling role will be one of providing general guidance and advice.[7] Sometimes, however, the leader will be dealing with a troubled employee who may be having problems with self-confidence, be suffering from depression, or be facing increased family pressures. Or the problem may go deeper and be the result of alcohol or drug abuse. The following examines how these problems should be addressed.

TROUBLED EMPLOYEES   Sometimes employees will be troubled over job-related or home-related problems. If the manager feels the problem is best handled by letting it go, of course, no action is required. However, if the manager believes some action is needed, three courses are available: (1) tell the employee to shape up or ship out, (2) discipline the person, or (3) discuss the problem with the employee in an effort to work out a solution. This last approach requires effective counseling or coaching by the leader. Some of the most useful guidelines that can be employed include the following:

1.   Talk to the employee early in the work week rather than just before the weekend. In this way you can follow up the next day if additional coaching or counseling is needed.

2.   Talk to the employee early in the day rather than just before quitting time. This will allow you ample time to at least cover your main points and give the worker a chance to respond.

3.   Talk to the individual privately, away from other workers and managers. Let the person know there are just two of you involved—at least at this stage.

4.   Get to the point immediately. Describe the problem situation or behaviors you have been noticing and present them from *your* point of view rather than someone else's. For example:

Do say:
I am becoming concerned about the number of accidents you are having.

As opposed to:
You are so nervous that you are having too many accidents.

Do say:
I am upset over your failure to follow my instructions.

As opposed to:
You make me mad by failing to follow my instructions.

■ ■ ■ ■ ■ ■ ■ ■ ■ ■ ■ ■ ■ ■
GUIDELINES FOR COACHING TROUBLED EMPLOYEES.

■■■■■■■
[7] Donald J. Reed, "One Approach to Employee Assistance," *Personnel Journal*, August 1983, pp. 648–657.

Do say:

I have some concerns about your work.

As opposed to:

Some concerns have been voiced about your work.

5. If the worker finds it difficult to talk, provide reassurances and let the individual proceed at his or her own pace. Acknowledge what the person says without passing judgment or giving advice.

6. When the employee is done talking, discuss how he or she can improve work performance. Let the person know you are available if assistance is needed.

7. If the individual's problem requires professional counseling, do not offer it yourself. The problem is beyond your training. Help identify the problem and then have the organization's counseling service handle the matter. If no such service is available, prepare a list of community referral services to which the worker can turn. Typical examples of problems for which referrals should be made include:

recurring bouts of anger, sadness, or fear

feelings of loneliness, isolation, moodiness, or depression

suicidal thoughts

inability to concentrate or sleep

lack of self-confidence

family problems

high stress levels

constant anxiety[8]

8. Respect the employee's confidentiality. Do not discuss his or her situation with co-workers or others who have no need to know about the matter.

ALCOHOLISM Frustration and stress are very common in modern organizations. In dealing with these problems, some people turn to alcohol because they believe it helps them unwind. The unfortunate fact is that alcoholism in industry has now become a major problem resulting in accidents, absenteeism, wasted time, ruined materials, and premature job termination. The annual cost to American industry is now in the neighborhood of $100 billion. Some of the specific statistics that help explain this enormous loss include: (1) each alcoholic worker costs a business over $2,500 in unnecessary expenses; (2) these employees are 2½ times more likely to be absent than their co-workers; and (3) alcoholic em-

·······

[8]Terry L. Smith, "Coaching the Troubled Employee," *Supervisory Management*, December 1981, p. 35.

FIGURE 10.4   OBSERVABLE BEHAVIOR PATTERNS

STAGE	ABSENTEEISM	GENERAL BEHAVIOR	JOB PERFORMANCE
I Early	Tardiness Quits early Absence from work situations ("I drink to relieve tension")	Complaints from fellow employees for not doing his or her share Over-reaction Complaints of not "feeling well" Makes untrue statements	Misses deadlines Commits errors (frequently) Lower job efficiency Criticism from the boss
II Middle	Frequent days off for vague or implausible reasons ("I feel guilty about sneaking drinks"; "I have tremors")	Marked changes Undependable statements Avoids fellow employees Borrows money from fellow employees Exaggerates work accomplishments Frequent hospitalization Minor injuries on the job (repeatedly)	General deterioration Cannot concentrate Occasional lapse of memory Warning from boss
III Late Middle	Frequent days off; several days at a time Does not return from lunch ("I don't feel like eating"; "I don't want to talk about it"; "I like to drink alone")	Aggressive and belligerent behavior Domestic problems interfere with work Financial difficulties (garnishments, etc.) More frequent hospitalization Resignation; does not want to discuss problems Problems with the laws in the community	Far below expectation Punitive disciplinary action
IV Approaching Terminal Stage	Prolonged unpredictable absences ("My job interferes with my drinking")	Drinking on the job (probably) Completely undependable Repeated hospitalization Serious financial problems Serious family problems; divorce	Uneven Generally incompetent Faces termination or hospitalization

(Left vertical label: ALCOHOL ADDICTION TIME)

---

ployees collect over three times the amount of sick-leave payments than other employees.[9]

How does a manager know when one of the workers is drinking too much? This is a difficult question to answer, but there are some signs for which the individual can remain alert (see Figure 10.4). Among white-

• • • • • • •

[9] Gene Milbourne, Jr., "Alcohol and Drugs: Poor Remedies for Stress," *Supervisory Management*, March 1981, p. 40.

■ ■ ■ ■ ■ ■ ■ ■ ■ ■ ■ ■ ■ ■

WHITE-COLLAR SYMPTOMS.

■ ■ ■ ■ ■ ■ ■ ■ ■ ■ ■ ■ ■ ■

BLUE-COLLAR SYMPTOMS.

collar workers these include such things as elaborate (and often bizarre) excuses for work deficiencies, pronounced and frequent swings in work pace, avoidance of the boss and associates, and increased nervousness. Among blue-collar workers, the clues include a sloppy personal appearance, signs of a hangover, frequent lapses of efficiency leading to occasional damage to equipment or material, increased nervousness, and increased off-the-job accidents.[10] Perhaps the biggest problem managers face in dealing with alcoholics is that they are very skillful in denying the problem, especially when confronted by the boss.

> Alcoholic employees have an uncanny knack for manipulating the feelings of supervisors. In many cases they sense the onset of angry outbursts and know how to play for the counter-feelings that will block supervisory urges to act decisively. A favorite ploy is the "whipped child" syndrome characterized by the hang-dog look and the "I can't do anything right" verbalizations. Almost invariably these behaviors tug at parental heart-strings, and suddenly a supervisor finds himself or herself comforting and supporting the alcoholic employee rather than confronting the individual. At other times outbursts of righteous indignation by an employee will frighten the supervisor and cause him or her to back off.
>
> Alcoholics have a great deal of experience at playing these games. Unless they know what is going on, supervisors do not have a chance.[11]

Regardless of how effective they are in initially hiding their problem, however, it eventually becomes obvious to the boss. This is particularly true if the organization has trained its managers in how to identify the excessive drinker. At this point the problem worker should be sent either to the firm's medical department or personnel department for counseling or further referral. Since the manager is not likely to be an expert on alcohol rehabilitation, the individual must be careful about what he or she says. For example, it is a mistake for the manager to moralize to the employee about the dangers of drinking or try to diagnose why the person has become a problem drinker. Instead, the manager should stress that the problem will be handled confidentially and alcoholism can be successfully treated. From here it is a matter of providing assistance to the person in getting the necessary treatment. Many organizations have their own program designed to deal with alcoholism; this is the ideal situation.[12]

■ ■ ■ ■ ■ ■ ■

[10] *Ibid.*

[11] Donald A. Phillips and Harry J. Older, "Alcoholic Employees Beget Troubled Supervisors," *Supervisory Management*, September 1981, p. 5.

[12] "The Sobering of America: A Push to Put Drinking in Its Place," *Business Week*, February 25, 1985, pp. 112–113.

According to William Dunkin, assistant director of labor management services at the National Council on Alcoholism, employee programs are the best way to treat alcoholism because of the employee's desire to keep his or her job. The costs of such programs are minimal compared to the cost of alcoholism. One small company estimated that its 102 problem drinkers cost the firm $100,650 annually, but a successful program to treat these workers cost only $11,400 a year. One consultant estimates that an effective program costs a company only 35 to 50 cents per month per employee.[13]

Some firms have found that managers do not like to be the ones to confront a subordinate about a drinking problem. The confrontation can be awkward and the manager is often defensive about having to take the action. As a result, some firms are now using a team approach in which a subordinate's associates and peers are involved in the evaluation process. As Edwards and Sproull have noted, "An alcoholic may be able to hide behaviors from a boss, but it is unlikely that . . . associates will be fooled."[14]

STOP!

Review your answer to the second question and make any changes you would like. Then compare your answer to the one below.

2.   Aside from directly asking him, what can Greg do to determine if Howard has been drinking? What symptoms might he look for?

The easiest way to do this is to watch Howard's job performance. Notice from Figure 10.4 that there are symptoms that often occur in the early, middle, late middle, and terminal stages of alcoholism. Since Howard is new on the job, there is no prior performance record with which to compare current performance. However, if Howard begins giving any sign of the types of job performance problems presented in Figure 10.4, Greg could immediately seek advice regarding how to proceed from here. Of course, Greg's suspicions may be entirely unfounded, but it is better to be safe than sorry. ∎

· · · · · · ·

[13] Milbourne, "Alcohol and Drugs: Poor Remedies for Stress," *Supervisory Management*, p. 41.

[14] Mark R. Edwards and J. Ruth Sproull, "Confronting Alcoholism through Team Evaluation," *Business Horizons*, May–June 1986, p. 82.

DRUG ABUSE   Employee drug abuse is also on the rise. In one recent study over 87 percent of the surveyed organizations reported that they had to deal with drug problems.[15] There are various reasons for this rise in drug use. Generally people take drugs at work to reduce the boredom, tension, or anxiety that accompanies the work. The symptoms of drug abuse are similar to those of alcoholism: slurred speech, dilated eyes, unsteady walk, lack of dexterity, and uncontrollable laughter or crying. Also like alcoholism, programs have been developed for dealing with drug abusers. A typical program, in a large organization, will be designed and implemented in four stages:

1.   A committee is formed. If there is a union, it will be adequately represented. If there is a medical department, there will be one representative in the group.

■ ■ ■ ■ ■ ■ ■ ■ ■ ■ ■ ■ ■ ■

TYPICAL DRUG ABUSE PROGRAM DESIGN AND IMPLEMENTATION.

2.   A policy statement expressing the philosophy of the organization toward the effect of drug abuse on job performance will be developed.

3.   If there is a union, a joint labor/management policy statement recognizing the effect of drug abuse on health and behavior will be developed.

4.   Supervisors and management personnel will be trained in identifying drug-related problems and the proper ways to deal with them most effectively, including monitoring rehabilitation progress as measured by job performance.[16]

Those found to be using drugs are removed from the work place and often provided with assistance. If they accept this help and overcome their drug dependency, no disciplinary action is taken. Otherwise, they are dismissed.[17]

One of the major drug-related issues currently facing many organizations is whether or not to conduct random drug testing. A recent survey of Fortune 100 industrial firms found that 50 percent of the companies test all job applicants.[18] However, most do not test all employees. There are various reasons for this. One is concern over the accuracy of the tests.[19] A second is the disagreement regarding how much of a drug a worker has to ingest before work performance suffers. As Rosen notes,

■ ■ ■ ■ ■ ■ ■

[15] James W. Schreier, "A Survey of Drug Abuse in Organizations," *Personnel Journal*, June 1983, pp. 478–484.

[16] Milbourne, "Alcohol and Drugs: Poor Remedies for Stress," *Supervisory Management*, p. 42.

[17] R. Wayne Mondy, Shane R. Premeaux, and Larry Worley, "People Problems: Substance Use and Abuse," *Management Solutions*, February 1987, pp. 22–24.

[18] Dale Masi, "Company Responses to Drug Abuse from AMA's Nationwide Survey," *Personnel*, March 1987, p. 44.

[19] James T. Wrich, "Beyond Testing: Coping with Drugs at Work," *Harvard Business Review*, January–February 1988, p. 126.

"It should be pointed out that we now have legal definitions for alcohol intoxication based on blood levels. However, there are no such definitions for intoxication due to other drugs. In the work place, supervisors must determine problem behaviors or unsatisfactory work performance strictly by observation."[20] A third is that the precise legal status of drug and alcohol testing remains undefined and may result in problems for the firm.[21] A fourth is that random drug testing can be costly and have a negative effect on employee morale; the workers may view the tests as attempts by management to invade their privacy and gather evidence that will lead to their dismissal.[22] A fifth is that many tests have proven inconsistent.[23] A sixth is that some personnel such as professional athletes have contracts that prohibit mandatory testing even of a random nature,[24] although these barriers are beginning to be negotiated away. A seventh is that many personnel oppose the practice because it is not preceded with probable cause.[25]

How then should drug testing be handled? Many experts recommend that an employee assistance program (EAP) be created which offers confidential and professional help to those employees who are drug abusers.[26] Many firms have an alcohol-related EAP, so it is merely a matter of expanding the program's focus. Rather than putting the emphasis on catching drug users and firing them, however, attention is devoted to prevention and rehabilitation. During the 1990s this is going to be the front-line defense for many organizations in their fight to deal with drug abusers in the work place.[27]

■■■■■■■

[20] Theodore H. Rosen, "Identification of Substance Abusers in the Workplace," *Public Personnel Management*, Fall 1987, p. 203.

[21] Rusch O. Dees, "Testing for Drugs and Alcohol: Proceed with Caution," *Personnel*, September 1986, pp. 53–55; Robert J. Aalberts, "Business and the Law," *Business*, January–March 1988, pp. 52–56; Jan P. Muczyk and Brian P. Heshizer, "Mandatory Drug Testing: Managing the Latest Pandora's Box," *Business Horizons*, March–April 1988, pp. 14–22; and Elizabeth Grillo Olson, "The Workplace is High on the High Court's Docket," *Business Week*, October 10, 1988, pp. 88, 92.

[22] Miriam Rothman, "Random Drug Testing in the Workplace: Implications for Human Resource Management," *Business Horizons*, March–April 1988, p. 24.

[23] Anne Marie O'Keefe, "The Case against Drug Testing," *Psychology Today*, June 1987, pp. 34–38.

[24] Joan W. Hoffman and Ken Jennings, "Will Drug Testing in Sports Play for Industry?" *Personnel Journal*, May 1987, pp. 52–59.

[25] Cecilia Preble, "Air Traffic Controllers Sue to Block FAA Drug Testing," *Aviation Week & Space Technology*, March 2, 1987, pp. 32–33.

[26] William A. Balzer and Kenneth I. Pargament, "The Key to Designing a Successful Employee Assistance Program," *Personnel*, July 1987, pp. 48–54.

[27] For more on this see Wrich, "Beyond Testing: Coping with Drugs at Work," pp. 120–130; and James W. Schreier, "Combatting Drugs at Work," *Training and Development Journal*, October 1988, pp. 56–60.

USE POWER PROPERLY

A fourth important leadership role is that of using one's power properly.[28] Teamwork and effective counseling both require the leader to act as a motivator without throwing his or her weight around. One of the best ways to understand how to use power properly is to begin by analyzing the various types of power the leader can hold.

TYPES OF POWER

There are many types of power.[29] Five of the most commonly cited are: reward power, coercive power, legitimate power, referent power, and expert power.[30]

■ ■ ■ ■ ■ ■ ■ ■ ■ ■ ■ ■ ■ ■ ■
REWARD POWER INVOLVES THE
USE OF EXTRINSIC SATISFIERS.

REWARD POWER   Power that is held by leaders who can give extrinsic satisfiers to subordinates who do their jobs well is known as **reward power**. Some of the most common forms of extrinsic reward are increases in pay, bonuses, and promotions. In human relations terms, the leader has power over the subordinates because he or she can give or withhold these rewards, depending upon subordinate performance. Sometimes this performance is measured in terms of physical output (Did Steve do all that was expected?), and at other times it is measured in less quantitative terms (Is Doris a team player or does she do whatever she wants?). Leaders who use reward power are, in their own way, employing some of the ideas we encountered in our discussion of behavior modification. By giving positive reinforcement to those who do things the way the leader wants them done and failing to reward those who do otherwise, the leader attempts to keep everyone in line. On the positive side, if the leader's reward philosophy is regarded as fair by the workers and results in attainment of organizational objectives, it may be unnecessary to challenge its use.

■ ■ ■ ■ ■ ■ ■ ■ ■ ■ ■ ■ ■ ■ ■
COERCIVE POWER INVOLVES THE
USE OF FIRING OR DEMOTIONS.

COERCIVE POWER   Power that is held by those who can fire, demote, or dock subordinates who do not comply with their directives is termed **coercive power**. They can also threaten to use these negative reinforcers

■ ■ ■ ■ ■ ■ ■

[28] Janet Hagberg, "The Good, the Bad and the Ugly: Understanding Power Styles," *Working Woman*, December 1984, pp. 124–125, 176, 178, 180–181; and Gary Yukl and Tom Taber, "The Effective Use of Managerial Power," *Personnel*, March–April 1983, pp. 37–44.

[29] Hugh R. Taylor, "Power at Work," *Personnel Journal*, April 1986, pp. 42–49.

[30] John R. P. French, Jr., and Bertram Raven, "The Bases of Social Power," in *Studies in Social Power*, ed. D. Cartwright (Ann Arbor, Mich.: Institute for Social Research, 1959), pp. 150–167.

(although they may not carry through on the threat). These leaders derive their power from the workers' expectation that they will be punished if they do not conform.

LEGITIMATE POWER   The form of power that is vested in the manager's position in the organizational hierarchy is **legitimate power**. For example, a vice-president has greater legitimate power than a foreman, and a district manager has greater legitimate power than a unit manager. Legitimate power is often referred to as "delegated authority."

LEGITIMATE POWER IS VESTED IN THE MANAGER'S POSITION.

REFERENT POWER   Power that is based on the followers' identification with the leader is **referent power**. If the followers like the leader, the leader's power is greater than if they are indifferent about the leader. Leaders with charisma, reputation for fairness, or "winning" personalities commonly hold referent power.

REFERENT POWER IS BASED ON THE FOLLOWERS' IDENTIFICATION WITH THE LEADER.

EXPERT POWER   Leaders have **expert power** when their employees attribute knowledge and expertise to them. They are regarded as knowing what they are doing. Leaders who have demonstrated competence to implement, analyze, evaluate, and control group tasks are often seen as knowledgeable in their jobs, and they acquire expert power.

EXPERT POWER IS BASED ON KNOWLEDGE AND COMPETENCE.

POWER AND THE LEADER

Depending on the individual and the situation, a leader can possess varying amounts of all the sources of power we just discussed.[31]

However, are there any types of power that the effective leader can rely on consistently? Are there any types that a leader should avoid using?[32] Although any answer must be tempered by the specifics of the situation, research shows that coercive power brings great resistance from the subordinates but that they will comply if this power is very strong. People tend to like legitimate power better than coercive power. Additionally, they like expert power, and the leader who proves to be an expert on one task is likely to find an increase in his or her ability to exert influence on a subsequent task.[33]

· · · · · · ·

[31] David Calabria, "CEOs and Paradox of Power," *Business Horizons*, January–February 1982, pp. 29–31.

[32] Robert C. Benfari, Harry E. Wilkinson, and Charles D. Orth, "The Effective Use of Power," *Business Horizons*, May–June 1986, pp. 12–16.

[33] John Scholler, "Social Power," in *Advances in Experimental Social Psychology*, ed. Leonard Berkowitz (New York: Academic Press, 1965), pp. 177–218.

More directly related to our study of human relations, however, is the relationship between a manager's power and the resulting satisfaction and performance of the subordinates. On the basis of studies of five organizations, including a branch office, a college, an insurance company, a utility company, and some production work units, one group of researchers was able to make the following conclusions: [34]

SOME CONCLUSIONS ABOUT POWER.

1.   Expert power is most strongly and consistently related to satisfaction and performance.

2.   Legitimate power, along with expert power, was rated as the most important basis of complying with a leader's wishes, but was an inconsistent factor in determining organizational effectiveness.

3.   Referent power was of intermediate importance as a cause for complying with leader directives, while at the same time was positively correlated with organizational effectiveness.

4.   Reward power was also of intermediate importance for complying with leader directives, but had an inconsistent correlation with performance.

5.   Coercive power was by far the least valuable in bringing about compliance to leader directives, and it was negatively related to organizational effectiveness.

These findings indicate that informal bases of power can have a more favorable impact on organizational effectiveness than formal bases. This means that the effective leader must be greatly concerned with persuading the subordinates to follow orders and setting a good example through demonstration of expertise and should not rely exclusively on position power. People obey orders only when they feel it is in their best interests to do so. Quite obviously, we could argue that a person who is told to "obey or else" may well choose to follow the leader's command. However, sometimes people accept the punishment rather than comply. Given this fact, it should be apparent that the effective leader tempers his or her orders with a concern for the needs of both the people and the organization. No leader is effective unless the subordinates obey. Thus we can think of power as a two-way street: the leader has power and the subordinates have the right to either comply or refuse to do so. The effective leader learns how to use negotiation in dealing with subordinates. [35]

■■■■■■■

[34] Jerald G. Bachman, David G. Bowers, and Philip M. Marcus, "Bases of Supervisory Power: A Comparative Study in Five Organizational Settings," in *Control in Organizations*, ed. Arnold S. Tannenbaum (New York: McGraw-Hill Book Company, 1968), p. 236.

[35] Joseph F. Byrnes, "Ten Guidelines for Effective Negotiating," *Business Horizons*, May–June 1987, pp. 7–12.

STOP!

Review your answer to the third question and make any changes you would like. Then compare your answer to the one below.

3.   If Howard has been drinking on the job, what types of power can Greg use in resolving this problem? Cite and describe two.

There are a number of types of power that Greg can employ. One is coercive power. Howard can be formally reprimanded, given days off without pay, or be fired. Greg could rely on his legitimate power in enforcing these sanctions. However, it is important to remember that whatever type of power is used, this should be done only after Greg has been advised regarding how to proceed. Remember that Greg is not a counselor with psychological training. If Howard does have a problem and agrees to do something about it, Greg could then rely on reward power to reinforce these desired behaviors. ∎

MANAGE TIME WELL

A fifth important leadership role, which is often overlooked, is that of managing time well.[36] No leader can afford to be so bogged down in work that he or she lacks the time to carry out managerial tasks such as planning, decision making, organizing, communicating, counseling, and developing teamwork. On the other hand, the leader must set priorities and realize that every matter cannot be given primary attention.[37] This is easily seen by the data in Table 10.1 which shows the price of executive time. In large part, effective leaders get things done because they know how to budget their time to address major issues and to delegate minor ones. In doing so, they have learned how to deal with each of the three kinds of management time.

KINDS OF MANAGEMENT TIME

There are three different kinds of management time: boss-imposed, system-imposed, and self-imposed.

■ ■ ■ ■ ■ ■ ■

[36] Dennis E. Miller, "Time: A Manager's Most Important Asset," *Supervisory Management*, May 1983, pp. 16–19.

[37] Warren Keith Schilit, "A Manager's Guide to Efficient Time Management," *Personnel Journal*, September 1983, pp. 736–742.

TABLE 10.1   THE VALUE OF AN EXECUTIVE'S TIME

ANNUAL SALARY	WEEKLY SALARY*	BENEFITS (40% OF WEEKLY SALARY)	SALARY PER WEEK	COST PER HOUR	COST PER MINUTE
$ 50,000	$ 961.54	$ 384.62	$1,346.16	$ 33.65	$0.56
60,000	1,153.85	461.54	1,615.39	40.38	0.67
75,000	1,442.31	576.93	2,019.24	50.48	0.84
100,000	1,923.08	769.23	2,692.31	67.31	1.12
250,000	4,807.70	1,923.08	6,730.78	168.27	2.80

*Assuming a 40-hour week

BOSS-IMPOSED TIME IS USED FOR DOING WHAT THE BOSS WANTS DONE.

Boss-imposed time is used to accomplish those activities that one's superior wants done. Responding to a boss's command to complete and submit a monthly cost control report by the end of the week is an example. The manager cannot disregard these activities, so the time needed to carry them out must be allocated.

SYSTEM-IMPOSED TIME IS USED TO HANDLE REQUESTS FROM OTHER MANAGERS.

System-imposed time is used to handle requests from other managers. Sometimes they need assistance or support in coordinating activities or planning operations. These time demands are often not as important as those imposed by the boss, but the manager must try to respond to them.

SELF-IMPOSED TIME IS USED BY THE MANAGER FOR HANDLING OTHER RESPONSIBILITIES.

Self-imposed time is used for doing the tasks the manager originates or agrees to do personally. Much of this is often referred to as *subordinate-imposed time* and will be spent answering questions and providing assistance to group members. The remaining portion is *discretionary time*, which the manager can use in any way he or she desires.[38]

The effective leader realizes that boss-imposed and system-imposed time demands cannot be ignored. This leaves only self-imposed time from which to take the hours necessary to carry out all remaining tasks. To use this remaining time well, the leader needs to be aware of several vital principles of time management.

HANDLING THE MONKEY

One of the primary ways a manager finds self-imposed time being used up is by subordinates who continue to drop by the manager's office and talk him or her into doing their work. Often, the approach is very subtle and the manager is unaware of what has happened until the subordinate

[38] For more see William Oncken, Jr., "The Manager's Time Machine," *Success*, October 1987, p. 14.

has left. Other subordinates do not wait to get into the office; they waylay the manager in the hallway.

> Let us imagine that a manager is walking down the hall and he notices one of his subordinates, Mr. A, coming up the hallway. When they are abreast of one another, Mr. A greets the manager with, "Good morning. By the way, we've got a problem. You see. . . ." As Mr. A continues, the manager recognizes in this problem the same two characteristics common to all problems his subordinates gratuitously bring to his attention. Namely, the manager knows (a) enough to get involved, but (b) not enough to make the on-the-spot decision expected of him. Eventually, the manager says, "So glad you brought this up. I'm in a rush right now. Meanwhile, let me think about it and I'll let you know." Then he and Mr. A part company.
>
> Let us analyze what has just happened. Before the two of them met, on whose back was the "monkey"? The subordinate's. After they parted, on whose back was it? The manager's. Subordinate-imposed time begins the moment a monkey successfully executes a leap from the back of a subordinate to the back of his superior and does not end until the monkey is returned to its proper owner for care and feeding.[39]

By accepting the monkey, the manager has taken a subordinate position. It is now up to the manager to make the next move. As a result, his or her self-imposed time is being reduced.[40]

How can the manager prevent this problem in the future? Several ground rules should be followed:

1.   The manager should offer assistance but should never agree to handle the problem.

2.   The manager must tell the subordinate that assistance is given only to someone who needs it—in other words, to the person who has the monkey. If the subordinate wants the manager to *take* the monkey, there is no basis for assistance.

3.   When the conversation is over, the monkey should be where it was initially—on the subordinate's back.

4.   In those rare instances in which the manager must temporarily accept the monkey, the next move must be worked out by both manager and subordinate together.

■ ■ ■ ■ ■ ■ ■ ■ ■ ■ ■ ■ ■ ■ ■
SOME TIME MANAGEMENT GROUND RULES.

■ ■ ■ ■ ■ ■ ■

[39] William Oncken, Jr., and Donald L. Wass, "Management Time: Who's Got the Monkey?" *Harvard Business Review*, November–December 1974, p. 76.

[40] William Oncken, Jr., "Get Those Monkeys Off Your Back," *Working Woman*, April 1985, pp. 116–119.

FIGURE 10.5   **TIME MANAGEMENT CHART**

WHAT MUST BE DONE TODAY	TIME FOR EACH ACTIVITY	A MUST PERSONALLY BE DONE	B COULD BE DELEGATED	C SHOULD BE DELEGATED
1. 2. 3. 4. 5.				
Total Time ____	= ____	+ ____	+ ____	

By following these guidelines, the manager can reduce the amount of self-imposed time that is taken up by others.[41]

TIME PRIORITIES AND WORK DELEGATION

Even if the manager can eliminate the attempts of subordinates to pass the buck upward (or the monkey over), he or she must still be concerned with the remaining duties. As we noted in the previous chapter, many subordinates want participative leadership, and most managers find their people willing to help out, especially if they have created good rapport with the group. What can be delegated and what should be handled personally?

■ ■ ■ ■ ■ ■ ■ ■ ■ ■ ■ ■ ■ ■ ■
DEVELOP A TIME MANAGEMENT CHART.

One way of deciding this question is to develop a time management chart for either the day or the week, on which the manager can assign priorities, determine what must personally be done, and decide what can and should be delegated. Figure 10.5 is an example of such a chart. Notice that at the bottom of the chart the initial total time for all the manager's daily activities is equal to the sum of Columns A, B, and C, but that the actual total time is equal to the sum of Column A and whatever in Column B the manager is willing to do.

In trying to use time effectively, most managers make three critical mistakes. First, they fail to delegate, believing that good managers assume responsibilities rather than pass them on. What they do not realize is that an effective manager is not a workaholic; he or she does not have to be doing something every minute of the day. The best managers as-

■ ■ ■ ■ ■ ■ ■

[41] See also William Oncken, Jr., "Keeping the Monkeys Off Your Back," *Success,* December 1987, p. 18.

sign the work that can be handled by the subordinates and keep only what is left. They know the importance of pacing themselves and never getting caught in these all-too-common time traps.

Second, managers fail to schedule their work time. Some of the most commonly employed techniques for scheduling include:

1.   Using a calendar as a major scheduling document.

2.   Scheduling on a short-interval basis—day-to-day or week-to-week.

3.   Not letting the activities of other departmental personnel interfere with their planned activities.

■ ■ ■ ■ ■ ■ ■ ■ ■ ■ ■ ■ ■
SOME SCHEDULING TECHNIQUES.

4.   Not letting the schedule get filled with routine tasks when their energy could be better utilized.

5.   Reviewing objectives and priorities before making the schedule final.

Third, and last, many managers do not believe that they can manage their time well. Effective managers, however, are certain that with careful planning they can accomplish their assigned goals within the allotted time. They try to devote their energies to working smarter, not harder.[42] Table 10.2 provides some of the rules they follow in doing so.

STOP!

Review your answer to the fourth question and make any changes you would like. Then compare your answer to the one below.

4.   What could Greg do to work smarter not harder? Offer him three recommendations for action.

There are a number of things that Greg can do. One is to prioritize his time. A second is to delegate work to others. A third is to make up a list of "things to do" and use this list to guide his daily work activities. Others include: (1) read standing up; (2) concentrate effort on one thing at a time; and (3) when a particularly difficult or important task is completed, take some time off as a reward. ■

■ ■ ■ ■ ■ ■ ■

[42] For additional guides to managing time see Larry D. Alexander, "Effective Time Management Techniques," *Personnel Journal*, August 1981, pp. 637–640; Cynthia Katz, "Use the Phone Instead," *Working Woman*, December 1984, pp. 63–68; Everett T. Suters, "Overdoing It," *Inc.*, November 1988, pp. 115–116; Charles R. Hobbs, "Thirteen Ways to Procrastinate Efficiently and Gain Control of Your Time," *Working Woman*, October 1987, pp. 96–97; and Jimmy Calano and Jeff Salzman, "How to Get More Done in a Day," *Working Woman*, April 1988, pp. 99–101.

TABLE 10.2   TEN RULES OF TIME MANAGEMENT FOR EFFECTIVE LEADERS

---

1. Carry a "to do" list with you; jot down notes on those things you have to do and cross out those that you have finished.
2. When reading memos, mail, or short reports, do so standing up. You read faster in this position.
3. As you read memos and letters that call for a reply, answer each as you go along. Otherwise you will have to read each again later when you get around to formulating a response.
4. Concentrate your efforts on one thing at a time.
5. Give your primary attention to those tasks which are most important and work at delegating minor jobs to your subordinates.
6. If you have an appointment to visit someone, bring work with you so that if you are forced to wait you can put the time to good use.
7. When you finish a particularly important or difficult task, give yourself time off as a special reward.
8. Try not to work on weekends.
9. Examine your work habits for ways of streamlining your current procedures and saving time.
10. If you do not get all you wanted accomplished in a given day, tell yourself you will get to it the next day. Do not feel guilty over any failure to meet your daily work plan. As long as you are doing your best, tell yourself that this is good enough.

MANAGE STRESS WELL

Effective leaders also learn how to manage stress well: both their own and that of their subordinates.[43] What the leader needs to remember is that most people are unable to function well on the job unless they have some stimulus to get them going. However, if this stress is allowed to continue for a long period of time, it can be dangerous to their health. This danger is most prevalent among individuals who are known as Type A people.

TYPE A PEOPLE

■ ■ ■ ■ ■ ■ ■ ■ ■ ■ ■ ■ ■ ■ ■
TYPE A PEOPLE TRY TO GET MORE
AND MORE DONE IN LESS AND LESS
TIME.

In 1974 two California cardiologists proposed a nickname for achievement-oriented, competitive behavior patterns found in hard-driving individuals who strove to get more and more accomplished in less and less time. They called these people **Type A persons** and pointed out that the behaviors that characterized these people could bring about heart attacks.[44] Yet it was very difficult for these high achievers to break their old

■ ■ ■ ■ ■ ■ ■

[43] Jane Ciabattari, "The Kind of Stress Managers Know Best," *Working Woman*, September 1987, pp. 125–130.

[44] Meyer Freedman and Ray H. Rosenman, *Type A Behavior and Your Heart* (New York: Fawcett Crest Books, 1974).

TIME OUT

ARE YOU A TYPE A OR TYPE B PERSON?

Below are ten combinations of statements related to your work and personal habits. In each case read the A and B statements and decide which is most descriptive of you. If A is totally descriptive of you and B is not at all descriptive, give 10 points to A and none to B. If both statements are descriptive of you, divide the 10 points between A and B based on their degree of descriptive accuracy. If B is totally descriptive of you and A is not at all descriptive, give 10 points to B and none to A. An interpretation is provided at the end of the chapter.

POINTS

1. A — Even when it is not necessary I find myself rushing to get things done.
   B — I seldom rush to get things done, even if I am running late.

2. A — I often get upset or angry with people even if I do not show it.
   B — I seldom get angry with people if there is no real reason for it.

3. A — When I play a game or compete in an event, winning is my primary objective.
   B — When I play a game or compete in an event, my greatest enjoyment comes from the social interaction with others.

4. A — I am a tense, anxious person, but I try to cover this up by smiling a lot and trying to be social.
   B — I am basically a relaxed, easy-going individual; I seldom get tense or uptight.

5. A — Even when I am sitting down watching TV I am usually moving about, checking my nails, tapping my foot or carrying out some similar physical activity.
   B — When I sit down to watch TV, I get totally involved in the program and seldom move about or change position.

6. A — I set high goals for myself and become angry if I fail to attain them.
   B — I set reasonable goals for myself and if I fail I try not to let this get me down.

7. A — I write down how I intend to spend my day and I rigidly stick to this schedule.
   B — I note objectives that I want to attain during the day but try to remain flexible; if something is not finished today, I will get to it tomorrow morning.

8. A — I hate to wait for people; it makes me edgy and nervous.
   B — If I have to wait for others, I try to spend the time doing something relaxing like reading, talking to others, or quietly walking around.

9. A — Meals interrupt my schedule, and I often find myself doing work at the same time I am eating.
   B — I enjoy meals and eat them slowly and in a relaxed fashion; if there is any work to do, it can wait until I am finished eating.

10. A — At the end of the day, I often find myself extremely tired and run down.
    B — I like to get things done but not at the cost of physical exhaustion.

habits because for years they had trained themselves to work at a feverish pace. Type B people can also be achievement-oriented, but they take things at a slower pace. Are you a Type A or Type B person? Before continuing, take the accompanying Time Out quiz to find out which type you are.

If you have examined your results to this quiz, you have a fairly good idea of what a Type A and Type B person is like. More specifically, you can understand why Type A people are often described this way:

1.   thinking or doing two or more things at the same time

2.   scheduling more and more activities into less and less time

3.   hurrying the speech of others

4.   believing that if you want something done well, you have to do it yourself

■ ■ ■ ■ ■ ■ ■ ■ ■ ■ ■ ■ ■ ■
SOME OF THE CHARACTERISTICS OF
TYPE A PEOPLE.

5.   gesticulating when you talk

6.   making a fetish of always being on time

7.   using explosive speech patterns or obscenities

8.   playing nearly every game to win, even when playing against children

9.   measuring your own and others' success in terms of numbers (number of articles written, patients seen, sales made, etc.)

10.   becoming impatient when watching others do things you think you can do better or faster.[45]

STRESS AND PRODUCTIVITY

As noted earlier, everyone needs some stress to get them going.[46] However, few people work well under high stress; this is especially true if the stress continues for an extended period of time. Figure 10.6 illustrates this idea. For the average person a moderate amount of stress will bring about high performance. However, under high stress the individual begins to falter and fail. He or she is unable to cope with the extreme anxiety, tension, and nervousness that result.

Individuals facing this type of situation are often caught in what is called the *fight-versus-flight dilemma*. On one hand, they want to stay and fight the stress; on the other hand, they want to run away from it. In many instances, especially among up-and-coming managers, the decision is made to stay and fight. These people learn to live with the pressures

■ ■ ■ ■ ■ ■ ■

[45] For more on this, see Jane E. Brody, "Study Suggests Changing Behavior May Prevent Heart Attack," *New York Times*, September 16, 1980, pp. C1, C3.

[46] Sandra L. Huber, "Managing Stress for Increased Productivity," *Supervisory Management*, December 1981, pp. 2–12.

FIGURE 10.6   STRESS AND JOB PERFORMANCE: THE RELATIONSHIP FOR MOST PEOPLE

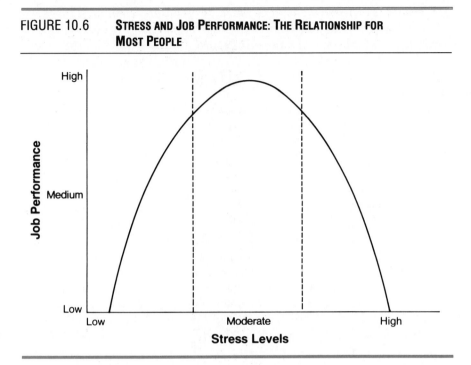

and hope that their health will not fail as a result. Nor is it necessary to confine our attention exclusively to high-achieving managers to find individuals suffering the negative effects of stress. Personal life events can bring the same results to the average worker. Some of the most common include: the death of a spouse, a divorce, a jail term, marital separation, the assumption of a mortgage on a first house, and a change in eating habits. Some of the most serious business-related events that cause stress include: being fired, retiring from work, changing to a different line of work, trouble with the boss, and being moved to a new city by the company. All of these are called *life stressors*; they cause tension and anxiety.

■ ■ ■ ■ ■ ■ ■ ■ ■ ■ ■ ■ ■ ■
PERSONAL AND JOB-RELATED EVENTS CAN CAUSE STRESS.

TROUBLED EMPLOYEES, TROUBLED MANAGERS

Stress is faced by both employees and managers, so the leader has two primary challenges. The first is to identify and help employees deal with their own stress-related problems. The second is to identify and deal with stress from a personal standpoint.[47]

■ ■ ■ ■ ■ ■

[47] Herbert Benson and Robert Allen, "How Much Stress is Too Much?" *Harvard Business Review*, September–October 1980, pp. 86–92.

The first of these challenges was addressed, in large part, when we discussed how to deal with troubled employees. When workers are under stress, they exhibit many of the symptoms of Type A people; they seem to be in a nervous hurry or they withdraw into themselves because the stress is too much for them to handle. Equally as important, they appear to have a cynical attitude toward life and this compounds the problem.[48]

Managerial stress is an even greater problem because although many managers have learned to identify stress in others, they have not learned how to identify it in themselves. The result is that they push themselves too long and too hard. The eventual outcome is called **burnout**, a condition in which the manager is both mentally and physically exhausted.[49] Levinson has provided an excellent example of managerial burnout.

■ ■ ■ ■ ■ ■ ■ ■ ■ ■ ■ ■ ■ ■
BURNOUT IS A CONDITION OF
PHYSICAL AND MENTAL
EXHAUSTION.

> A vice-president of a large corporation did not receive an expected promotion so he left that company to become the CEO of a smaller, family-owned business, which was floundering and needed his skills. Although he had jumped at the opportunity to rescue the small company, once there he discovered an unimaginable morass of difficulties, including continuous conflicts among the family owners. He felt he could not leave, but neither could he succeed. Trapped in a kind of psychological quicksand, he worked nights, days, and weekends for months trying to pull himself free. His wife protested to no avail. Finally, he was hospitalized for exhaustion.[50]

LEARNING TO COPE

How can leaders help their people cope with the negative aspects of stress? How can they, themselves, deal with these same problems? The first way is by learning to recognize its symptoms. This can be done by asking and answering stress- and burnout-related questions such as those posed in the short Time Out quiz on stress, burnout, and you.

Second, leaders must be willing to take these symptoms seriously. When someone begins to manifest signs of burnout, or they, themselves, feel they are working too hard and too fast, action must be taken that will slow the person down. Many times leaders let these symptoms go unaddressed, believing that they are only temporary. The result is burnout.

Third, those suffering from excessive stress must learn to realign their goals. They are trying to do too much too fast. They have to reduce their objectives to a more realistic and attainable level. Here is where the

■ ■ ■ ■ ■ ■ ■

[48] Joshua Fischman, "Type A on Trial," *Psychology Today*, February 1987, pp. 42–50.

[49] John Grossman, "Burnout," *Inc.*, September 1987, pp. 89–96.

[50] Harry Levinson, "When Executives Burn Out," *Harvard Business Review*, May–June 1981, p. 74.

TIME OUT

STRESS, BURNOUT, AND YOU

Read and answer each of the following as accurately as you can. An interpretation is provided at the end of the chapter.

	BASICALLY YES	BASICALLY NO
1. Do you feel you are working harder but accomplishing less?	_____	_____
2. Have you lost your vim and vigor lately?	_____	_____
3. Is your job beginning to get you down?	_____	_____
4. Are you snapping at people a lot more lately?	_____	_____
5. Do you feel your job is taking you on a road to nowhere?	_____	_____
6. Is your temper getting shorter?	_____	_____
7. Do you have a lot of aches and pains, even though you have not been ill lately?	_____	_____
8. Is your job enthusiasm beginning to go downhill?	_____	_____
9. Do you find it is hard to laugh at a joke about yourself?	_____	_____
10. Are you more tired lately than you used to be?	_____	_____

leader must offer counseling to others and also be prepared personally to accept and follow such advice.

Fourth, if possible, the individual under stress should restructure his or her job so that some of the work which causes this stress is shifted to others or totally eliminated. The leader can be extremely important here in helping ensure that the employee's job is changed and made less stressful.

Fifth, those suffering from overwork should strive to keep themselves in a positive mental state. One of the most effective ways of doing so is by pampering oneself with small rewards, praising oneself for doing a good job, and telling oneself that it is all right to slow down and do less work.

Sixth, relaxation techniques should be considered. Many individuals find that by forcing themselves to take 15 minutes in the morning and again in the afternoon to do nothing but sit quietly in a chair with their eyes closed and their minds working to force their bodies to totally relax, they are able to overcome many job-created tensions. Others report that by getting involved in an active sport such as tennis, racquetball, or jogging, they are able to work out some of the stress that comes from the job.

Seventh, and finally, individuals suffering from stress and burnout need to view the fight against stress and burnout as a lifelong battle. It

■ ■ ■ ■ ■ ■ ■ ■ ■ ■ ■ ■ ■
THERE ARE WAYS OF EFFECTIVELY DEALING WITH STRESS.

can never be totally won. The person must continually work to maintain a positive attitude toward self-development and self-improvement. In this way the individual not only develops antistress, antiburnout techniques but continues to use them every day.[51]

Eighth, managers need to realize that their own leadership styles can be the cause of stress and to work to correct these behaviors. For example, some researchers have found that putting people into task forces can reduce their stress. The groups reinforce and support the morale of the personnel and help the individual members cope with job stress.[52] Managers also need to understand what causes stress for their people and to work to provide them with assignments that are within each worker's ability to cope.[53] Chusmir and Duran have noted that for a variety of reasons women often have greater stress on the job than men. Managers can help reduce this stress by taking steps such as: (1) encouraging workers to include women in all informal groups; (2) learning to accept and encourage women in equal roles; (3) finding male mentors for women with advancement potential; and (4) encouraging other female employees to help newcomers.[54]

SUMMARY

The leader has a number of important roles to play. One of these is to represent and support the subordinates. In a manner of speaking, the individual must be a linking pin with the manager directly above. In this way the leader represents the people to his or her boss. The leader's job also is to provide supportive assistance to the subordinates.

A second important role of the leader is to develop teamwork. The three key factors in this process are the leader, the subordinates, and the environment. Each plays an important part, but of the three, the environment is often the most crucial.

■■■■■■■

[51] For more on this topic see Harriet B. Braiker, "A New Way to Manage Stress that Really Works for Women," *Working Woman*, August 1984, pp. 80–87; James C. Quick, "Thinking Styles and Job Stress," *Personnel*, May 1986, pp. 44–48; Robert W. Eckles, "Stress—Making Friends with the Enemy," *Business Horizons*, March–April 1987, pp. 74–78; Jane Ciabattari, "Managing Your Way Out of Office Stress," *Working Woman*, May 1987, pp. 110–111; Steven Lurie, "A Dozen Ways to Control Stress," *National Business Employment Weekly*, November 22, 1987, pp. 9–10; Annetta Miller *et al.*, "Stress on the Job," *Newsweek*, April 25, 1988, pp. 40–45; Janette Scandura, "Mastering the Art of Mellow: A High Achiever's Guide to Stress," *Working Woman*, April 1988, p. 121; Gordon Bakoulis, "11 Common Stress Symptoms and How to Outsmart Them," *Working Woman*, April 1988, pp. 123–124.

[52] M. Michael Markowich, "Using Task Forces to Increase Efficiency and Reduce Stress," *Personnel*, August 1987, pp. 34–38.

[53] David Hingsburger, "Learning How to Face That Stressful Situation," *Management Solutions*, February 1988, pp. 41–45.

[54] Leonard H. Chusmir and Douglas E. Durand, "Stress and the Working Woman," *Personnel*, May 1987, p. 43.

A third important role of the leader is to counsel wisely. Counseling is discussing an emotional problem with an employee with the purpose of eliminating or reducing it. Some of the major factors that cause an employee to need counseling are frustration, conflict, and stress. Counseling functions that the manager can use to help employees deal with their emotional problems include advice, reassurance, release of emotional tension, and reorientation.

A fourth important leadership role is that of using one's power properly. The most commonly cited kinds of power are reward, coercive, legitimate, referent, and expert. Use of each kind has benefits and drawbacks.

A fifth leadership role is the management of time. Since boss-imposed and system-imposed time demands usually cannot be reduced, it is up to the leader to manage self-imposed time demands well. Some of the ways of doing this are not letting the subordinate put the monkey on one's back, setting time priorities and delegating minor tasks, and developing a schedule for one's daily work time.

A sixth leadership role is that of managing stress. Many managers are Type A individuals characterized by a chronic, incessant struggle to achieve more and more in less and less time. Yet some stress is necessary if work is to be accomplished. The leader's primary concern should be that of identifying and dealing with the negative aspects of stress, from both a personal and employee standpoint, so that burnout does not result.

Having now discussed the fundamentals of leadership and the role of the leader, we turn to a final area of consideration—how the leader goes about evaluating and rewarding performance. This is the focus in Chapter 11.

KEY TERMS IN THE CHAPTER

linking pin function	legitimate power
social exchange theory	referent power
counseling	expert power
frustration	boss-imposed time
conflict	system-imposed time
stress	self-imposed time
reward power	Type A person
coercive power	burnout

REVIEW AND STUDY QUESTIONS

1.   One way of looking at a leader is as a linking pin. What is meant by this statement?

2.   What is meant by *teamwork*? Put it in your own words.

3.   There are three key factors in the development of teamwork: the leader, the subordinates, and the environment. What is meant by this statement?

4.   How should a manager counsel a troubled employee? Describe at least five useful guidelines.

5.   What do managers need to know about alcohol and drug-related employee problems? How should the individual go about dealing with these problems?

6.   In your own words, define each of the following types of power: *reward*, *coercive*, *legitimate*, *referent*, and *expert*.

7.   How can leaders manage their time well? Cite some principles of time management in your answer.

8.   What is the relationship between stress and productivity?

9.   How can a manager identify Type A people or those suffering burnout symptoms? Be complete in your answer.

10.   How can leaders help their people cope with stress? How can they, themselves, learn to cope with it? Offer at least five practical steps.

TIME OUT ANSWERS: INTERPRETATION OF ARE YOU A TYPE A OR TYPE B PERSON?

Add up your total points for the A statements and the B statements.

If your total for A is:
80–100   You exhibit strong Type A behavior.
60–79   You exhibit moderate Type A behavior.

If your total for B is:
80–100   You exhibit strong Type B behavior.
60–79   You exhibit moderate Type B behavior.

Any other combination is a mixture of Type A and B behavior which does not exhibit a clear pattern.

TIME OUT ANSWERS: INTERPRETATION OF STRESS, BURNOUT, AND YOU

If you answered basically yes to 8 or more of the questions, you may well be suffering from too much stress and be on the road to burnout. Should this be the case, think seriously about discussing the situation with your boss or changing to another line of work.

CASE: SHE'S NOW NUMBER ONE

Christine Mankowitz has been in charge of Work Group 4 for six months. In the beginning it was difficult. Christine is the first female manager her company has ever had at the work group level. There was a lot of pressure on her to succeed, and she has. The monthly productivity data came out yesterday and for the second month in a row, Christine's work group was at the top of the list.

One of the people who works on the company's in-house newspaper came by to talk to Christine and write a story about her. "People throughout the organization like to read success stories," she told Christine, "and you certainly are one. How did you do it? How have you managed to take a work group that six months ago had the lowest productivity in the area and get it up to number one?" Christine thought for a moment and then said, "It hasn't been easy. In the beginning the teamwork was very poor. Everyone was out for himself. I had to work on getting my group to trust me and understand that I could do more for them if they pitched in and helped me out. Perhaps the best early example was the new lockers on the west side of the work area. For three years management had promised an improvement in working conditions including new work lockers, but nothing had been done. I took this as a priority item and went to my boss. When he approved the expenditure, I took this back to my people and said, 'See, I can get things done for you. Now let's talk about how together we can get things done in the work group.' This was the beginning of our teamwork efforts and it has lasted to the present day. So when you say I have been a success story, you really are talking about the people in my work group as well."

The reporter was impressed by Christine's story. "Can you cite me another example of something you did to help build teamwork in your unit?" Again Christine thought for a minute before responding. "Last week we received the vacation schedule. It calls for most of my people to take vacations during June and July. This is the way it's been for the last five years. However, most of the people in my department have children who are now in high school and college and they would like to get part of their vacation during August when their children are out of school, as opposed to June when most of them are still in class. I asked my boss if we could put this on the agenda for the next meeting of the work group managers and he agreed. During the meeting, I asked if any of the groups that had August vacation times would be willing to switch with me and some were. We worked out a new vacation schedule among all of us and everyone is happier as a result."

After completing her interview with Christine, the reporter visited people in her work group to find out what makes her such an effective manager. The comments she heard most often were, "She goes to bat for us. She is reliable. She gets things done. She is true to her word. She cares about what happens to us."

QUESTIONS

1.   Based on the information in the case, in what way is Christine a linking pin? Cite an example.

2.   Using Figure 10.2 as your reference, how does Christine go about creating teamwork in the unit? Explain.

3.   What type of power does Christine use? Explain. ■

CASE: IF YOU WANT IT DONE RIGHT

Henry Albertini was a star salesperson for 20 years. Two years ago, in an effort to support its expanding sales program, the president of his company asked Henry to come in off the road and assume the job of sales manager for the eastern region. Reluctantly, Henry agreed.

There are 12 states in Henry's region with the territory divided up among 19 salespeople. Henry's job is to coordinate their activities, ensure that they have the support help they need, and spend an average of one day a week in the field providing direct assistance. At least, this is the way the job was explained to him. However, Henry found it impossible to go into the field just one day a week. "Half of our people in the field don't know what they're doing," he explained to his secretary. "They are inexperienced and unable to effectively close sales. Our quota for this year is never going to be met if we rely on their efforts. I have to get out there and help out."

This is exactly what Henry did. During the first 18 months as sales manager, he was in the field an average of 2½ days a week. Over the last six months this has increased to 3 days a week, and it appears that Henry's efforts have been fruitful. Over the past 24 months sales in the eastern region have been 22 percent over quota, and for the second straight year, Henry has been named sales manager of the year.

Early yesterday Henry's secretary entered his office and found him lying on the floor. She immediately called 911 and an emergency unit was on the scene within eight minutes. Henry has been diagnosed as having suffered a mild heart attack. He can be back at work within four weeks. However, the doctor had a long talk with Henry's boss. Here is part of what he said:

Henry is being overworked. This heart attack is the first major sign that he has to change his lifestyle. He needs to slow down and let others help him get the work done. From what I can glean from talking to his wife, he has been on the road more days than he's been in the office. This has to stop or he's going to suffer another heart attack, and that one may be fatal. You are going to have to figure out the type of support help Henry needs and get it for him. At the same time, you are going to have to help him readjust his work life. When he comes back, it can't be "business as usual."

Henry's boss has promised to help. However, he is somewhat puzzled regarding what he can do to help Henry. "It seems to be," the boss told the president, "that Henry brought this problem on himself. He is a Type A person who believes that if you want something done right, you have to do it yourself. How can I get him to break this habit? Sometimes I think people are born a given way and there is no way to change their behavior." Nevertheless, Henry's boss intends to talk to Henry and see if there are some changes that can be made that will prevent a recurrence of yesterday's unfortunate event.

QUESTIONS

1. Is Henry a Type A person? Explain.

2. What things might the boss do to help Henry prevent a second heart attack? Offer at least three recommendations.

3. What things will Henry have to do in order to minimize the chances of a second heart attack? Offer at least three recommendations. ■

EXPERIENCING POWER

PURPOSE

- To identify the five types of power.
- To understand how to use each type of power.
- To examine the benefits and drawbacks of each type of power.

PROCEDURE

1.   Groups of six students each are formed.

2.   Five of the students in the group each draw two cards from a prepared stock and use the designated type of authority on the card as a guide in attempting to convince an employee to accept a transfer to a branch office. The sixth group member plays the role of the subordinate who is being transferred.

3.   In round-robin fashion, each student reads one of their cards and using the assigned type of power tries to convince the subordinate to accept the transfer.

4.   The student playing the subordinate writes down the type of power that is being employed by each of the other members of the group.

5.   After everyone has finished their two "power" presentations, the sixth student attempts to identify the type of power used in each situation.

6.   Participants then discuss which type of power was most successful in influencing the subordinate and which was least successful. What conclusions can be drawn as a result of these findings?

DEVELOPING, APPRAISING, AND REWARDING PERSONNEL

GOALS OF THE CHAPTER

An effective leader has productive subordinates. Three functions of the leader which we have not yet discussed are developing subordinates, appraising their performance, and rewarding those who merit it. Successful personnel development means that subordinates learn the most productive ways of doing their jobs. Valid performance appraisal means that the leader is able to identify those who do the best job. A well-designed reward system ensures that those who do their jobs properly are equitably rewarded. In carrying out these three tasks, the leader first needs to choose the most effective means of developing the personnel. This is then followed by an appraisal of their performance and a reinforcement of their efforts through the allocation of proper rewards.

The first goal of this chapter is to study what personnel development is all about. The second goal is to examine the performance appraisal cycle. The third is to review five appraisal tools commonly used in employee evaluations. The fourth is to study some of the problems often associated with performance appraisal. The fifth is to look at some of the extrinsic and intrinsic rewards used in rewarding performance and to review the link between performance and rewards. The final goal is to examine discipline and methods of employing it.

When you have finished reading this chapter, you should be able to:

1.   Describe how an effective orientation program works.

2.   Identify and discuss the four common approaches to personnel training.

3.   Discuss the performance appraisal cycle.

4.   Explain how graphic rating scales, paired comparison, assessment centers, and behaviorally anchored rating scales can be used in appraising performance.

5.   Explain how management by objectives can be used in performance appraisal and why this approach is so popular today.

6.   Describe four of the major problems associated with performance appraisal.

7.   Examine the link between performance and rewards.

8.   List the types of discipline used when performance is inadequate.

Opening Case

The Consultants' Report

Things in Racquel Bamforth's department are not going well. There has been a 35 percent annual turnover rate for the last 20 months and this is not improving. The same is true for most of the other major departments in the organization.

A consulting team was brought in last month to find out what could be done to improve the situation. The group's report was submitted to the board of directors last week, and Racquel received a copy of the report earlier today. Here are some of the major recommendations it contained:

1.   The orientation program is extremely poor. It should be expanded from one-half day to five days and cover a wide variety of topics such as an introduction of the firm's overall purpose and mission; a presentation of the company's major product lines including what the future is likely to hold in the way of new products; and a series of brief motivational seminars to help create a high esprit de corps.

2.   The current graphic rating scale approach to performance evaluation should be dropped and a management by objectives approach should be instituted.

3.   A concerted effort should be made to stop giving all employees an "average" performance rating and start giving them "excellent," "good," "fair," and "poor" as merited.

4.   There should be closer linking of rewards and job performance.

5.   There should be implementation of a more effective discipline program. At the present time many of the employees report that: (a) they have been disciplined for doing things they did not know were infractions

of the rules and (b) some people are not disciplined even though the supervisor knows they broke the rules.

Racquel agrees with these findings and feels that the consultants have done a good job of analyzing current problems. However, she is not sure that their recommendations will be accepted by top management. "We've been doing things the wrong way for a long time," she explained to a friend, "and I'm not sure that we will be able to change." Nevertheless, if management decides to implement these recommendations, Racquel intends to give the changes her full support.

1.   Can orientation really help a company reduce its turnover rate?

2.   What is a graphic rating scale? What is MBO all about? Is MBO a better choice for performance appraisal? Explain.

3.   What performance evaluation rating error is made when a manager always gives people an "average" rating and nothing higher or lower?

4.   Would a linking of productivity and rewards really pay off? Explain.

5.   What type of discipline approach would solve the problem described in this case?

Write down your answers to these questions and put them aside. We will return to them later. ∎

DEVELOPING PERSONNEL

The development of personnel begins when individuals enter the organization and does not end until they leave. From a human relations standpoint, this subject is important because every person in an organization will be affected by the ways the enterprise develops its people. This process typically involves orientation, training, appraising, and rewarding. Students of human relations should be familiar with the way in which these processes are carried out. This is particularly true for the last two, appraising and rewarding performance, to which the greatest amount of attention will be devoted. We begin our study of the area by examining the orientation process, which is the initial way in which organizations start to develop their personnel.

ORIENTATION

Orientation is the process of introducing new employees to their work group, their superior, and their tasks. Some of the most common items on an orientation agenda include: a brief discussion of the company's history and general policies, a description of its services and products, an

ORIENTATION IS THE PROCESS OF INTRODUCING NEW EMPLOYEES TO THEIR JOBS.

explanation of the organizational structure, a rundown of personnel policies, an explanation of general rules and regulations, and a formal introduction to the group in which the individual will be working. In small organizations, much of this is handled orally; in large organizations, new employees typically are given booklets or brochures that explain and elaborate on the verbal presentation.

■ ■ ■ ■ ■ ■ ■ ■ ■ ■ ■ ■ ■ ■
ORIENTATION CAN PAY OFF.

Many important advantages are associated with an effective orientation. Among them are (1) a reduction in the costs of instruction, (2) a lessening of anxiety regarding job failure, (3) a reduction in employee turnover, (4) a saving in time spent on assistance, and (5) an increase in the employee's job satisfaction.

A number of studies have been conducted on the benefits of orientation programs. Texas Instruments, for example, gave one group of new employees its standard orientation and another group a more detailed, comprehensive orientation. The firm found that the latter group had 50 percent less tardiness and absenteeism, required 50 percent less training time, and had 80 percent less waste.[1] Well-designed orientation programs do indeed pay off.

TRAINING

Commercial Credit Company recently opened four regional training centers. These centers provide individualized training for branch personnel in systems, procedures, selling, and customer service.

There are a number of types of training that can be given to the personnel. The first step, however, is to identify the objectives of the training.[2] What does the individual need to know?[3] The answer to this question will determine the appropriate training method. The four principal types of employee training are apprentice, vestibule, on-the-job, and off-the-job.

Apprentice training is given to people who are new to a job. The training is designed to teach them the rules for getting the work done and to provide an opportunity for applying these procedures. Apprentice training is done both on and off the job.

Vestibule training takes place in an environment that simulates the actual work place. For example, a trainee who is being taught to run a lathe will be sent to a special area of the plant where a trainer will provide close supervision. Once the trainee learns the job, he or she will then be sent to the shop floor and assigned to a lathe.

■ ■ ■ ■ ■ ■ ■

[1] For more on this see Daniel N. Kanouse and Philomena I. Warihay, "A New Look At Employee Orientation," *Training and Development Journal*, July 1980, pp. 34–36, 38; and Edmund J. McGarrell, Jr., "An Orientation System that Builds Productivity," *Personnel*, November–December 1983, pp. 32–41.

[2] Theodore E. Zorn, Jr., "A More Systematic Approach to Employee Development," *Supervisory Management*, June 1983, pp. 10–12; and Jack J. Phillips, "Training Programs: A Results-Oriented Model for Managing the Development of Human Resources," *Personnel*, May–June 1983, pp. 11–18.

[3] Francis X. Mahoney, "Targets, Time, and Transfer: Keys to Management Training Impact," *Personnel*, November–December 1980, pp. 23–34.

On-the-job training is provided by the immediate superior and by fellow workers. It can be formal or informal in nature and usually consists of coaching the individual in the most effective ways of getting the job done.[4] The major benefit of on-the-job training is that it teaches the individual the right way to do the job, bypassing the inefficiencies of trial-and-error.

THERE ARE FOUR PRINCIPAL TYPES OF TRAINING.

Off-the-job training is done away from the work place. Quite often it is used when people need to be trained in activities or ideas that are nontechnical in nature. Examples include training in effective communication, motivation, and leadership. These areas are often best handled by trainers who teach both theory and practice.

These training methods help the individual learn the job quickly and correctly. In a way, they help match the individual to the job[5] and improve the person's chance of getting a good performance appraisal.

STOP!

Review your answer to the first question and make any changes you would like. Then compare your answer to the one below.

1. Can orientation really help a company reduce its turnover rate?

It certainly can. In fact research shows that effective orientation programs can reduce turnover, anxiety regarding job failure, and the costs of instruction, while increasing employee job satisfaction. ■

APPRAISING SUBORDINATES

Every effective organization wants to reward its best performers and ensure that they remain with the enterprise. How does one separate the best from the average or poor performers? The answer is through a well-designed performance appraisal process.[6] If this process is carried out properly, and the employees realize that management intends to be equitable in its reward system, personnel morale will be high and teamwork can be both developed and nurtured by the enterprise.[7]

---

[4] Ellen J. Wallach, "Performance Coaching: Hitting the Bull's Eye," *Supervisory Management*, November 1983, pp. 19–22.

[5] Ann Coil, "Job Matching Brings Out the Best in Employees," *Personnel Journal*, January 1984, pp. 54–60.

[6] Virginia Bianco, "In Praise of Performance," *Personnel Journal*, June 1984, pp. 40–50.

[7] J. Peter Graves, "Let's Put Appraisal Back in Performance Appraisal: Part I," *Personnel Journal*, November 1982, pp. 844–849; and J. Peter Graves, "Let's Put Appraisal Back in Performance Appraisal: Part II," *Personnel Journal*, December 1983, pp. 918–923.

So in essence, performance appraisal is more than a control process; it is a human relations tool which provides a basis for ensuring that everyone is treated fairly. Without such a process, it is quite difficult to reward performance on anything but a random basis. After all, how does management really know who deserves the most if it has no basis for evaluating contribution to organizational effort? Everything begins with the performance appraisal process.

In order to fully understand the performance appraisal process, we must: (1) examine the performance appraisal cycle, which describes how the entire evaluation process should be conducted, (2) examine the appraisal tools that can be used in carrying out the evaluation, (3) compare the attributes of appraisal techniques, and (4) learn to recognize the problems that can accompany a performance appraisal and the ways to reduce or avoid them.

PERFORMANCE APPRAISAL CYCLE

PERFORMANCE STANDARDS MUST BE ESTABLISHED.

Performance appraisal is a four-step process referred to as the **performance appraisal cycle**. First, there must be some *established performance standards* that specify what the worker is supposed to be doing. These standards are often quantified, i.e., the machinist is supposed to process 25 pieces an hour or the typist is expected to type an average of 60 words a minute. Such performance standards establish a basis against which to evaluate the individual.

INDIVIDUAL PERFORMANCE MUST BE MEASURED.

Second, there has to be a *method of determining individual performance*. To say "Barry does a good job" or "Kathleen is an asset to the department" is not a sufficient measure of individual results. The organization needs appraisal instruments that measure desired performance. In the case of the machinist, we would want to consult daily output records to see if his or her average is 25 pieces an hour; in the case of the typist we would want to check the number of pages of material turned out in a typical day. Of course, appraisals will not be conducted on a daily basis, but if proper evaluation instruments are designed, output can be recorded periodically and can be evaluated later.

COMPARISON OF PERFORMANCE AND STANDARDS MUST BE MADE.

Third, there must be some *comparison of performance against standards*. At some point, usually once a year, the individual's work record should be compared with the standards set for the job.

EVALUATION OF PERFORMANCE MUST BE MADE.

Fourth, an *evaluation of performance* should be made on the basis of the comparison. This process can take numerous forms. Sometimes the boss meets with the subordinate, reviews progress in general terms, and then announces the basic direction for the upcoming year. At other times, the manager has a detailed work report on the subordinate and is able to pinpoint strengths and weaknesses in great detail. In either case, this step is not finished before the manager has told the subordinate how well he or she is doing. The more definitive the manager is, the more

---

FIGURE 11.1   **PERFORMANCE APPRAISAL IN ACTION**

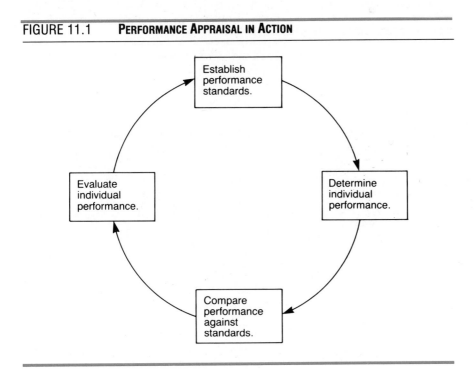

useful the feedback will be in directing and motivating the subordinate. Once this fourth step is completed, the manager and the subordinate are ready to establish performance standards for the next evaluation period. Building on current successes (and sidestepping failures), the two can determine the department's needs and the subordinate's abilities and then work to mesh them. This overall performance appraisal cycle, presented in Figure 11.1, provides the primary basis for any evaluation program.[8]

PERFORMANCE APPRAISAL TOOLS

Many kinds of appraisal tools can be used to evaluate employee performance.[9] Five of the most common are graphic rating scales, the paired comparison method, assessment centers, behaviorally anchored rating scales, and management by objectives.

▪▪▪▪▪▪▪

[8] For more on appraisals see Martin G. Friedman, "10 Steps to Objective Appraisals," *Personnel Journal*, June 1986, pp. 66–71.

[9] John D. McMillan and Hoyt W. Doyel, "Performance Appraisal: Match the Tool and the Task," *Personnel*, July–August 1980, pp. 12–20.

FIGURE 11.2   ILLUSTRATION OF A GRAPHIC RATING SCALE (PARTIAL FORM)

Employee _____   Date _____

Department _____   Rater _____

RATING / FACTOR	1 Unsatisfactory Totally Inadequate	2 Fair Meets Minimal Requirements	3 Good Exceeds Minimal Requirements	4 Superior Always Does Above the Basic Job Requirements	5 Exceptional Is Consistently Outstanding
Quantity The Volume of Output Produced					
Quality The Accuracy and Thorough- ness of the Output					
Supervision The Need for Direction, Correction, and/or Advice					
Attendance Dependability, Regularity, and Promptness					

THE GRAPHIC RATING SCALE IS THE MOST WIDELY USED PERFORMANCE APPRAISAL TOOL.

GRAPHIC RATING SCALES   The most widely used of all performance appraisal tools are **graphic rating scales**. One of the major reasons is undoubtedly the ease with which they can be developed and used. Figure 11.2 illustrates such a scale. In the chart the factors on which the employee is to be evaluated are identified and the degrees of evaluation are spelled out. The rater, usually the subordinate's boss, merely has to read each of the factors and then check the appropriate box. By totaling the value associated with every factor degree (i.e., from 1 for unsatisfactory up to 5 for exceptional), the rater can obtain a total score for the subordinate.

THE PAIRED COMPARISON METHOD IS MORE DISCRIMINATING IN ITS APPROACH.

PAIRED COMPARISON METHOD   The **paired comparison method** is regarded by many managers as superior to the graphic rating scale because it is more discriminating in its approach. Rather than just giving a person an overall evaluation, in which each might end up receiving an excep-

FIGURE 11.3   THE PAIRED COMPARISON METHOD FOR RATING EMPLOYEES ON WORK QUANTITY AND QUALITY

ON THE BASIS OF WORK QUANTITY

As Compared to:	PERSONNEL BEING RATED				
	Anderson	Brown	Carpenter	Davis	Evans
Anderson		−	+	−	+
Brown	+		+	+	+
Carpenter	−	−		−	+
Davis	+	−	+		+
Evans	−	−	−	−	

↑
Evans has the highest ranking for work quantity.

ON THE BASIS OF WORK QUALITY

As Compared to:	PERSONNEL BEING RATED				
	Anderson	Brown	Carpenter	Davis	Evans
Anderson		−	+	+	+
Brown	+		+	+	+
Carpenter	−	−		+	+
Davis	−	−	−		−
Evans	−	−	+	+	

↑
Davis has the highest ranking for work quality.

Note: A plus (+) indicates higher than and a minus (−) indicates lower than. The individual with the greatest number of pluses is the one with the highest ranking.

tional score, this method compares each employee to every other one in the group with respect to a number of factors (see Figure 11.3). In this way, while everyone may be doing good work, it is still possible to determine who is best and who is poorest. It is no longer simply a matter of how well a person is performing the job, but how the individual compares with all the other workers. In Figure 11.3 work quality and quantity are measured. A rater may end up with five to ten paired comparison forms before compiling the scores and getting an overall evaluation for each employee. Regardless of the number of factors rated, however, only one person ranks at the top of the list when all the ratings are completed.

ASSESSMENT CENTERS   During the last 10 years, the assessment center has become a popular form of performance appraisal. Unlike most other appraisal techniques, the **assessment center** focuses on evaluating the long-range potential of an employee. For this reason, it is a very useful tool for identifying managers with potential for assuming higher-level positions.

Assessment centers are currently used by many well-known organizations including IBM, GE, Merrill Lynch, J.C. Penney, and the FBI. The approach is basically the same regardless of the enterprise. It consists of six fundamental steps:

1.   A series of assessment techniques are used. At least one of these must be a simulation or exercise in which the applicants are required to use behaviors related to dimensions of performance on the job. This simulation may be a group exercise, fact-finding exercise, interview simulation, etc.

2.   A number of assessors must be used. These people must have had thorough training so they know exactly what to look for in the applicants.

3.   The final decision regarding what to do (hire, promote, etc.) must be a result of a group decision by the assessors.

4.   The simulation exercises that are used must have been developed to tap a variety of predetermined behaviors, and have been pretested prior to use to ensure that they provide reliable, objective, and relevant behavioral information.

5.   The techniques used in the assessment center must be designed to provide information that can be used in evaluating the dimensions, attributes, or qualities previously determined.

6.   The assessment by the evaluators must be made after the exercises are completed, not during the exercises.[10]

On the positive side, a number of organizations have reported great success from their assessment centers. At IBM, for example, 1,086 non-management employees were classified as either having or not having the potential for successful assignment beyond the first management level. Of those assessed as having such potential, 20 percent achieved second-level positions. Conversely, only 10 percent of those rated first-level were promoted beyond this level. Additionally, 20 percent of those

·······
[10]"When Is an Assessment Center Really an Assessment Center?" *Training/HRD*, March 1980, p. 24.

promoted against the prediction were eventually demoted in contrast to only 9 percent of those who were promoted in accordance with the prediction.[11]

On the other hand, there is some concern about the fact that most of the validation studies to date have been restricted to large business organizations. A second concern is that unless the organization knows how to carry out an assessment center, the evaluators may not really know what they are doing or why they are doing it. A third area of concern is whether these assessment centers can be defended in a court of law. In one recent case, an assessment center was used to select the deputy police chief of a large Midwestern city. While the judge upheld the validity of the process, he questioned some of the methods used.

What does the future hold for assessment centers? Because they are so well thought of, they will continue to gain in popularity during the 1990s. At the same time, there will be a continuation of the current trend toward improving the various techniques that are used and in the process, reducing the cost. Some of the developments that we are likely to see include: (1) the use of video technology to present scenarios on videotapes (in some cases interactive videos); (2) mini-simulations in the form of role plays that will be conducted by individuals who will also help assess the job applicant; and (3) panel interviews that will be used to investigate the applicant's skills in various areas.[12]

BEHAVIORALLY ANCHORED RATING SCALES   In recent years a new appraisal method, known as **behaviorally anchored rating scales (BARS)**, has been developed.[13] Advocates of this appraisal method claim that it provides more detailed and equitable evaluations than anything else available in the field.[14] As we have just seen, the graphic rating scale requires the organization to develop a series of factors and ratings for each, and the paired comparison requires the identification of factors and the comparison of each person in the group against every other on the basis of these factors. BARS uses a different approach, usually consisting of five steps: [15]

▪▪▪▪▪▪▪

[11] Ron Zemke, "Using Assessment Centers to Measure Management Potential," *Training/HRD*, March 1980, p. 30.

[12] Frederic D. Frank, David W. Bracken, and Michael R. Struth, "Beyond Assessment Centers," *Training and Development Journal*, March 1988, pp. 65–67.

[13] Louis Oliva, "Using Assessment Centers for Individual and Organizational Development," *Personnel*, May–June 1980, pp. 63–67.

[14] Cheedle W. Millard, Fred Luthans, and Robert L. Otteman, "A New Breakthrough for Performance Appraisal," *Business Horizons*, August 1976, pp. 66–73.

[15] Donald P. Schwab, Herbert G. Heneman III, and Thomas A. DeCotiis, "Behaviorally Anchored Rating Scales: A Review of the Literature," *Personnel Psychology*, Winter 1975, pp. 549–562.

1.   People who have knowledge of the job(s) to be appraised are asked to develop specific illustrations of effective and ineffective behavior. These critical incidents serve as a foundation for the rest of the development of the appraisal form.

2.   The people are then asked to cluster these incidents into smaller sets, usually five to ten, of performance dimensions. Each of these clusters or dimensions is then defined. Illustrations of common clusters include: knowledge and judgment, operating skill, and conscientiousness.

3.   Another group of people who are familiar with these jobs is then given the cluster definitions and critical incidents, and asked to review and, where necessary, reassign each incident to the proper cluster, i.e., critical incidents associated with knowledge and judgment are put in one group, while critical incidents associated with operating skill are placed in another.

4.   Then the second group is asked to rank the critical incident behaviors on a one-to-nine point scale, with the value of one or two given to ineffective behavior up to seven or nine for highly effective behavior. At this point only those critical incidents which best describe effective and ineffective behavior are used.

5.   The overall instrument is then constructed and used to evaluate the personnel.

Figure 11.4 is an example of a behaviorally anchored rating scale for an employment interview. Note that the performance criterion in this case is knowledge and judgment. This, of course, is only one of many that would be developed for the interviewer's job. Others would generally include job involvement, interpersonal relationships, and adaptability. As also can be seen in Figure 11.4, there is a scale for rating performance from 1 to 9. The scale is "behaviorally anchored" in that the critical incidents specify what is meant by effective and ineffective behavior.

Critics of the BARS approach point to some obvious shortcomings. The process can be very time consuming and expensive. Many things have to be done. A rating scale for quite a few performance criteria, such as knowledge and judgment, job involvement, interpersonal relationships, and adaptability, must be constructed. Then the rater has to evaluate each individual on each of these scales. Finally, an overall evaluation must be determined. The process may take as much as 30 to 60 minutes per employee, compared with 5 to 10 minutes for the graphic rating scale.

However, the BARS approach has a number of advantages. First, the standards of measurement are clear. The rater should have no trouble distinguishing between poor, average, good, and outstanding performance. Second, the instrument is put together by individuals who know the job

BARS CONSISTS OF FIVE STEPS.

DISADVANTAGES OF BARS.

ADVANTAGES OF BARS.

FIGURE 11.4   BEHAVIORALLY ANCHORED RATING SCALE (PARTIAL FORM)

Knowledge and Judgment = familiarity, understanding, and application of information needed to meet employment needs of applicant and/or employers.

Employment interviewers and claims deputies must possess and apply job knowledge in order to perform their jobs. Some understand thoroughly the many policies and procedures, application files, and labor market information. Others do not seem to understand and to apply even what should be common knowledge about their jobs and why certain things are done.

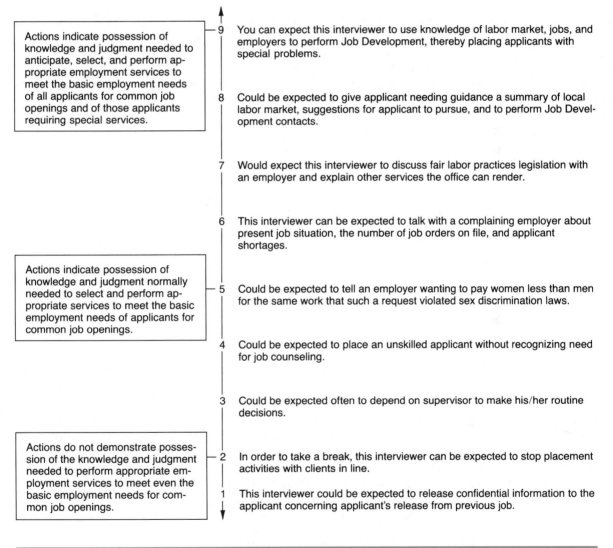

Actions indicate possession of knowledge and judgment needed to anticipate, select, and perform appropriate employment services to meet the basic employment needs of all applicants for common job openings and of those applicants requiring special services.

9 — You can expect this interviewer to use knowledge of labor market, jobs, and employers to perform Job Development, thereby placing applicants with special problems.

8 — Could be expected to give applicant needing guidance a summary of local labor market, suggestions for applicant to pursue, and to perform Job Development contacts.

7 — Would expect this interviewer to discuss fair labor practices legislation with an employer and explain other services the office can render.

6 — This interviewer can be expected to talk with a complaining employer about present job situation, the number of job orders on file, and applicant shortages.

Actions indicate possession of knowledge and judgment normally needed to select and perform appropriate services to meet the basic employment needs of applicants for common job openings.

5 — Could be expected to tell an employer wanting to pay women less than men for the same work that such a request violated sex discrimination laws.

4 — Could be expected to place an unskilled applicant without recognizing need for job counseling.

3 — Could be expected often to depend on supervisor to make his/her routine decisions.

Actions do not demonstrate possession of the knowledge and judgment needed to perform appropriate employment services to meet even the basic employment needs for common job openings.

2 — In order to take a break, this interviewer can be expected to stop placement activities with clients in line.

1 — This interviewer could be expected to release confidential information to the applicant concerning applicant's release from previous job.

Source: From Cheedle W. Millard, *The Development and Evaluation of Behavioral Criteria for Measuring the Performance of Non-Operational Employees*, Ph.D. Dissertation, University of Nebraska, 1974, p. 185.

and the requirements, so the evaluation form tends to be highly valid and reliable. Third, by putting together a series of five or six performance dimensions (knowledge and judgment, job involvement, and so on), the rater has a much better idea of what is being rated. This is superior to a scale on which he or she is working with just one or two factors (such as concern for work and ability to work well with fellow employees) that are so encompassing that it may be impossible to appraise the employee objectively. Finally, having five to six performance dimensions makes it much easier to point out to people where they have not performed well and how they can improve in the future.

■ ■ ■ ■ ■ ■ ■ ■ ■ ■ ■ ■ ■ ■ ■
MBO IS AN OVERALL APPRAISAL SYSTEM.

MANAGEMENT BY OBJECTIVES   Management by objectives (MBO) is an overall appraisal system used at all levels of the employment hierarchy.[16] Many organizations prefer MBO because it is systematic, all-encompassing, and easy to understand. Because of its great popularity, we shall study it in much greater depth than the other appraisal tools. Before doing so, however, let us define the term. **Management by objectives** is a process in which the superior and the subordinate jointly identify common goals, define the subordinate's major areas of responsibility in terms of expected results, and use these measures as guides for operating the unit and assessing the contribution of each member.

HOW MBO WORKS   There are six basic steps in the MBO process. Figure 11.5 illustrates the typical cycle employed in implementing it.

First, the manager identifies the goals that his or her unit should pursue over the next evaluation period. These goals can often be expressed in terms of profit, revenues, margins, competitive position, or employee relations.

Second, the organization must be clearly described. Who is in the department? What does each person do? Having answered these questions, the manager then reviews each individual's past work, noting what can be expected of that person.

■ ■ ■ ■ ■ ■ ■ ■ ■ ■ ■ ■ ■
THERE ARE SIX STEPS IN MBO.

Third, the manager sets objectives for the next evaluation period for the workers individually. This is done by (1) asking each subordinate to list those objectives he or she has in mind for the next year and setting a date for discussing them, (2) making a personal list of objectives one would like to see the subordinate attain, (3) reviewing both lists and then jointly agreeing on a final set of objectives for the subordinate, (4) having two copies of the final draft of objectives typed, one for the superior and

------

[16] George S. Odiorne, *Management by Objectives* (New York: Pitman Publishing Corporation, 1965).

FIGURE 11.5   **THE BASIC MBO CYCLE**

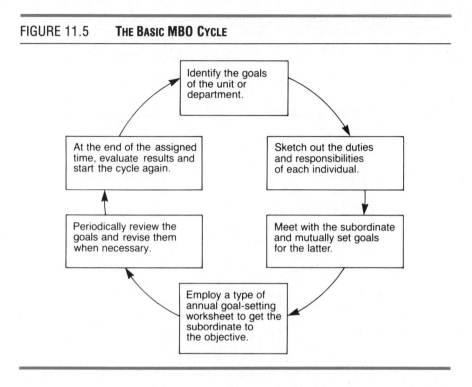

one for the subordinate, and (5) making oneself available to help the subordinate accomplish the assigned goals.

Fourth, an annual goal-setting worksheet is designed to help the subordinate reach these objectives. Figure 11.6 is an example. As can be seen in the figure, the worksheet is divided into three parts: (1) objectives, (2) major steps planned for achieving the objectives, and (3) the way in which progress is to be evaluated; in short, what is to be done, how it will be accomplished, and what way(s) will be used to show how well it is being accomplished.

Fifth, during the year each subordinate's goals are checked to see if the objectives are being reached. In particular, the manager needs to know how close the person is coming to attaining these targets, whether any of the goals need to be amended, and what kinds of assistance the person requires to reach the goals.

Sixth, results are measured against goals. Near the end of the MBO cycle, which commonly coincides with the budget year, the superior asks each subordinate to prepare a brief statement of performance. Then the two meet to review how well the subordinate has done and to establish objectives for the next budget year.

FIGURE 11.6   AN ANNUAL GOAL-SETTING WORKSHEET (PARTIAL FORM)

NAME Hal Lymer	DATE January 2, 1990
POSITION Superintendent of Engine Manufacturing	SUPERVISOR Les Rodgers

OBJECTIVES	MAJOR STEPS FOR ACHIEVING PLANNED OBJECTIVES	THE WAY IN WHICH PROGRESS WILL BE EVALUATED
Increase the number of production hours in the engine departments from 30,000 to 40,000.	Conduct methods study of the bottleneck operations in engine assembly and make necessary changes. Reduce machining time on the planer type mill by employing an assistant operator during peak periods. Add 3 floating foremen to give round-the-clock supervision to the bottleneck operations.	Progress will be measured in terms of shipments reported on the monthly cost control report.
Reduce supervisory overtime by cross-training foremen.	Cross-train foremen in the large machine, small machine, and engine assembly departments. Determine how general foremen can be used as substitutes for foremen and assistant foremen. Use these general foremen on at least 4 Sundays per calendar quarter.	In the first 6 months of last year foremen and assistant foremen in engine manufacturing worked an average of 20 of 26 Sundays. The target for the first 6 months of this year is to reduce this to no more than 15 of 26 Sundays.
Reduce scrap cost from 4 percent to 3 percent of production.	In conjunction with quality assurance have manager conduct a study to identify the specific causes of scrap losses. Determine ways to measure scrap and rework costs by shift. Put together a task force for determining alternative ways to reduce this scrap. Develop an incentive plan for rewarding the shift with the best scrap record. Determine the feasibility of disciplining employees who cause major scrap losses.	Measure progress in terms of scrap and rework costs reported on the monthly cost control report.

■ ■ ■ ■ ■ ■ ■ ■ ■ ■ ■ ■ ■
THE SUBORDINATE PARTICIPATES.

WHY MBO IS SO POPULAR   MBO has proved to be a very popular approach because it is both comprehensive and easy to understand. One of its primary advantages is the attention given to the subordinate in the goal-setting process. Rather than telling the individual what goals he or she should pursue, there is now a give-and-take process in which the subordinate has the opportunity to participate.

■ ■ ■ ■ ■ ■ ■ ■ ■ ■ ■ ■ ■
OBJECTIVES ARE QUANTIFIABLE
AND TIED TO A TIME DIMENSION.

Another advantage of this approach is that MBO places a strong emphasis on quantifiable objectives that are tied to a time dimension. For example, performance standards are stated in specific, measurable terms such as percentages, dollars, ratios, costs, and quality. If a manager is going to reduce tardiness, this goal will be stated in a percentage: "We will cut tardiness by 18 percent." In addition, a period will be set for the attainment of the objective. Expanding the above statement, then, we can bring together the quantifiable goal and the time dimension in this way: "We will cut tardiness by 18 percent within the first 6 months of the upcoming fiscal year." Objectives for other major areas of organizational performance might be:

- Raise return on investment to 15 percent within the next four operating quarters.
- Complete the management control reporting system for all operating decisions by December 31.
- Install the new computerized information system by April 30.

Note that each objective is written in such a way that what is to be attained (the goal) and when it is to be attained (the time dimension) are clearly stated.

A third advantage of MBO is that there is a concentration on the organization's key objectives. Each manager ties his or her unit's objectives to those of the organization at large. As a result, all units are working in the same direction.

THERE IS CONCENTRATION ON KEY OBJECTIVES.

In the MBO approach, emphasis is given to working with a small, manageable number of objectives. Goals assigned to each person are usually limited to five or six. These are the key goals that must be accomplished if the manager is to be effective. Condensing all the individual's targets into a handful of goals makes it easier for the person to channel his or her energies toward goal accomplishment and for the superior to monitor progress and to review performance.

CONSIDERATION IS LIMITED TO 5 OR 6 GOALS.

MBO helps coordinate the activities of the units by linking each with those above, below, and on the same level. For example, Mary is in charge of Department B. When she meets with her boss, Ted, who is in charge of a group of departments, to determine objectives for her, Ted integrates her objectives with his own. He will do the same for the other departments, A and C, which report to him, as will Mary with the subordinates in her department who report to her.

MBO HELPS LINK THE ORGANIZATION TOGETHER.

Another advantage of MBO is that it encourages the manager to delegate time-consuming activities and to devote his or her energies to overall planning and control. With MBO the manager knows what everyone is supposed to be doing. The initial delegation of authority is very systematic. Additionally, MBO helps the manager to evaluate the subordinates and to learn in the process what each can do well and what each does poorly. With this information, the manager can then determine what work to delegate to each subordinate in the future. Who does Job A well? Who is best assigned to Job B? Who is the best performer on Job C? In delegating these tasks, the manager is able to pass off much of the busy-work he or she has performed in the past because now the man-

IT ENCOURAGES THE MANAGER TO DELEGATE TIME-CONSUMING ACTIVITIES.

TABLE 11.1   ADVANTAGES AND DISADVANTAGES OF SELECTED PERFORMANCE APPRAISAL TECHNIQUES

DIMENSION	GRAPHIC RATING SCALE	PAIRED COMPARISON	BARS	ASSESSMENT CENTER	MBO
Amount of time required to develop the appraisal tool	Low	Low	High	High	High
Cost of developing the appraisal tool	Low	Low	High	High	Medium
Acceptability of the technique to superiors	Low	Low	High	High	High
Acceptability of the technique to subordinates	Low	Low	High	High	High
Potential for rating errors	High	High	Low	Low	Low
Usefulness for counseling employees	Poor	Poor	Good	Good	Good
Value for allocating rewards	Poor	Poor	Good	Fair	Good
Value for identifying those who are most promotable	Poor	Poor	Fair	Good	Fair

ager knows the strength of the subordinates better. Additionally, the manager's boss will encourage such delegation. One of the primary benefits of MBO is its philosophy of delegating busy-work and concentrating one's time on "think-work." An effective top manager will not let the subordinate manager delegate work that should be handled personally while hanging on to time-consuming activities.

Overall, MBO has been well accepted in many modern organizations. In particular managers like its systematic approach and the emphasis it gives to the key managerial functions of planning, organizing, and controlling. In both public and private sectors, it holds a great deal of promise for the future.[17]

COMPARISON OF APPRAISAL TECHNIQUES

Which of these five appraisal techniques is the best one to use? The answer depends on what the organization is looking for. Examples include a low-cost appraisal instrument, one that is easy to use, one that is of value in allocating rewards, one of use in identifying potentially promotable managers, and so on. Table 11.1 provides such a comparison.

A close look at the table shows that management usually gets what it pays for. The easier it is to develop the appraisal technique and the lower

• • • • • • •

[17] Jack N. Kondrasuk, "Studies in MBO Effectiveness," *Academy of Management Review*, July 1981, pp. 419–430.

the costs involved, the higher the potential for rating errors. If management wants to increase the overall effectiveness of its evaluation process, it must be prepared to invest the time and money needed to develop a valid and reliable instrument. If it does not, several types of problems can result.

STOP!

Review your answer to the second question and make any changes you would like. Then compare your answer to the one below.

2.   What is a graphic rating scale? What is MBO all about? Is MBO a better choice for performance appraisal? Explain.

A graphic rating scale is a performance evaluation that uses a combination of evaluation factors and degrees of each factor in arriving at an overall evaluation of each person. MBO is an evaluation that involves mutual goal setting on the part of superiors and subordinates in determining those goals that will be pursued by the latter and how and when evaluations will occur. In the case presented here, MBO certainly does seem like a better choice for performance appraisal. It has the advantage of being highly acceptable to both superiors and subordinates. ∎

PERFORMANCE APPRAISAL PROBLEMS

Performance appraisal helps the manager identify those who should be rewarded for adequate or superior performance and those who should not. However, such an approach can yield erroneous results if the appraisal form is improperly designed or the rater is biased.[18]

CLARITY OF THE APPRAISAL FORM   One of the most common appraisal problems relates to clarity of the form. If every appraiser does not have an identical interpretation of what the factors and their ratings mean, uniformity is impossible. In Figure 11.2, for example, quantity, quality, supervision, and attendance are briefly defined. So, too, are the ratings for each. But how does the appraiser determine when a person should get a rating of fair and when he or she should be rated good?

RATERS MUST FULLY UNDERSTAND ALL THE FACTORS.

[18] Ann M. Morrison and Mary Ellen Kranz, "The Shape of Performance Appraisal in the Coming Decade," *Personnel*, July–August 1981, pp. 12–22.

Unless the factors are precisely defined and this information is made available to the evaluator, an employee might be rated fair by one manager and good by another. The situation is even worse if the factors or their ratings are not described at all. If each manager is using only his or her own judgment, performance evaluations will not be uniform throughout the organization.

To overcome this problem it is necessary to describe on the evaluation form the factors and degrees on which the employee will be evaluated and to ensure that the appraisers have a uniform interpretation. When is an individual's performance to be considered good? When is it to be rated superior? Many organizations find it very helpful to have all the people who are rating one group of employees, such as salespeople, meet, discuss the evaluation form, and determine the ground rules for the appraisal. In this way, all employees doing similar work can be rated in uniform terms.

THE HALO EFFECT   A **halo effect** occurs when the appraiser gives a worker the same rating on all factors, regardless of actual performance. For example, the manager has noticed that Paul is occasionally late for work. The manager believes that Paul does not care much for his job, and this impression carries over to the manager's rating of Paul. Regardless of how much work Paul does or how high the quality of the work output is, he continually receives a fair rating. Conversely, Mandy is always on time for work and has a very pleasant personality. This biases the manager's rating of her, and she is always rated excellent in all categories. Many firms find that a training program can alleviate this problem by helping the manager identify these built-in biases and work to correct them.

CENTRAL TENDENCY   A second common rater-generated problem is that of **central tendency**, in which everyone receives an average rating, regardless of how effective he or she has been. For example, Andy is one of the department's poorest workers and Karl is one of the best. However, their performance ratings are always identical. The manager continually rates both as good. Such an approach helps Andy, who should be given a rating of fair, but it punishes Karl, who should be given a rating of superior.

One of the greatest problems faced by managers who rate their people this way is that the best workers begin looking for new jobs. After all, their chances for increased salary or promotion are being severely limited. Another problem is that the evaluations are now useless. The organization cannot rely on them to identify those who should be advanced and those who should be terminated. One way of overcoming this prob-

A HALO EFFECT OCCURS WHEN THE APPRAISER GIVES A WORKER THE SAME RATING ON ALL FACTORS, REGARDLESS OF ACTUAL PERFORMANCE.

THE HALO EFFECT CAN BIAS THE RATING.

WITH CENTRAL TENDENCY, EVERYONE RECEIVES AN AVERAGE RATING.

lem is to use a paired comparison evaluation or an MBO approach in which results are quantified or described in such terms that the manager is required to give the person a more precise rating.

LENIENCY   A third common rater-generated problem is that of **leniency**, where managers give all their people the highest possible rating. Here again, failure to distinguish between those doing an outstanding job and those doing a poor one results in inaccurate ratings. Many organizations in recent years have worked around this problem through use of a paired comparison evaluation.

■ ■ ■ ■ ■ ■ ■ ■ ■ ■ ■ ■ ■
WITH LENIENCY, THE HIGHEST POSSIBLE RATINGS ARE GIVEN OUT.

DEALING WITH APPRAISAL PROBLEMS   The problems we have identified in this section are caused by either the rating form or the rater. By investigating the various advantages and disadvantages of each rating approach, an organization can determine which one best meets its needs. Additionally, training the raters in how to use the form can eliminate many bias problems.[19]

Remember, two major issues must be dealt with in performance appraisal: validity and reliability. By **validity** we mean that the instrument measures what we want it to measure. If work quantity is important, then this factor should be on the rating form. If cooperation with others is of no value because the individual works alone, it should not appear on the form. By **reliability** we mean that the instrument measures the same factor over and over. If we are interested in work quality but not work quantity, we want to be sure that the raters understand this. Otherwise, the way a person is rated by two managers might differ.

■ ■ ■ ■ ■ ■ ■ ■ ■ ■ ■ ■ ■
VALIDITY MEANS THE INSTRUMENT MEASURES WHAT IT IS DESIGNED TO MEASURE.

■ ■ ■ ■ ■ ■ ■ ■ ■ ■ ■ ■ ■
RELIABILITY MEANS THAT THE INSTRUMENT MEASURES THE SAME FACTOR OVER AND OVER.

A good example of validity and reliability problems is provided by the typical true or false or multiple-choice test given in college. Since all the students are taking the same test, there is reliability. The instrument is continually measuring the students' knowledge of certain material. However, if the test has not been designed properly, a large number of questions may not really measure a student's command of the subject. Some questions may be trivial, some may be ambiguous, and some may be based on information not contained in the text. There is no validity. Some behavioral scientists have pointed out that it is much easier to obtain reliability in testing than to obtain validity. In the future, people constructing tests for the purpose of measuring knowledge will have to address the issue of validity. Some of the ways of avoiding these pitfalls are presented in Human Relations In Action: Conducting an Effective Performance Appraisal.

■ ■ ■ ■ ■ ■ ■

[19] Mark R. Edwards, Michael Wolfe, and J. Ruth Sproull, "Improving Comparability in Performance Appraisal," *Business Horizons*, September–October 1983, pp. 75–82.

HUMAN RELATIONS IN ACTION

CONDUCTING AN EFFECTIVE PERFORMANCE APPRAISAL

There are many things that managers need to know about carrying out an effective performance appraisal. The following five guidelines present much of this in capsulized form.

1.   *Be familiar with the jobs being evaluated.* The best way of making an effective appraisal is to know what the person has been doing. Some people can look productive while performing simple or meaningless tasks. They could be overrated. Conversely, an effective worker might be underrated by someone unfamiliar with the job. There is no substitute for work familiarity.

2.   *Know the factors to be evaluated.* The following criteria can be used in deciding how well the individual is performing the job: work quantity, work quality, speed, accuracy, ability to get along with others, and communication effectiveness. These factors should be job related so that individuals who do well on the job also receive high ratings.

3.   *Let personnel know the factors that are being evaluated.* This has a number of advantages. One is that the workers are aware of what they need to do to get a good evaluation. A second is that the amount of tension and anxiety often associated with being evaluated tends to decline. A third is that it lets the workers know that the evaluation is job related and not tied to personal factors such as an ability to get along with the boss.

4.   *Measure the evaluation criteria appropriately.* Some jobs can be measured on a daily or weekly basis. For example, secretaries or office workers often handle short-term assignments. Progress can be evaluated from week to week. On the other hand, salespeople often have certain seasons of the year that are better than others and you cannot evaluate their overall performance until you see how well they have done during the best sales months.

5.   *Use the evaluation to help people do better.* Evaluations should not be punitive instruments. Using them to show people where they have made mistakes creates anger and resentment. Instead, evaluations should be used as learning tools for showing people where their performance needs to be improved. An effective evaluation can serve as a basis for personnel training and development.

STOP!

Review your answer to the third question and make any changes you would like. Then compare your answer to the one below.

3.   What performance evaluation rating error is made when a manager always gives people an "average" rating and nothing higher or lower?

The manager is guilty of central tendency. This error occurs when a rater gives personnel average performance evaluations when, in fact, there are some who deserve much better and some who deserve much less. ■

REWARDING PERFORMANCE

The manager is in a position to reward (or not reward) a subordinate on the basis of the performance appraisal. In determining the type and degree of reward to give, it is necessary to examine three important areas: (1) extrinsic and intrinsic rewards, (2) performance and rewards, and (3) discipline. The first two areas are discussed in Chapter 2, but here we want to apply them directly to performance rewards. Discipline is important because sometimes the manager has to give out negative rewards.

EXTRINSIC AND INTRINSIC REWARDS

Extrinsic rewards are external and physical, taking such forms as money, increased fringe benefits, and use of a company car. **Intrinsic rewards** are internal and psychological, taking such forms as a feeling of accomplishment, increased responsibility, and the opportunity to achieve.

■ ■ ■ ■ ■ ■ ■ ■ ■ ■ ■ ■
EXTRINSIC REWARDS ARE EXTERNAL AND PHYSICAL.

Money is both an extrinsic and an intrinsic reward. In and of itself, money is extrinsic, but with it often come psychological rewards, such as esteem ("I'm important; look how much the organization is paying me"), a feeling of accomplishment ("Well, I did it: I finally made $75,000 in one year"), and a sense of achievement ("I'm good at what I do, a real achiever; that's why I'm being paid so much").

■ ■ ■ ■ ■ ■ ■ ■ ■ ■ ■ ■
INTRINSIC REWARDS ARE INTERNAL AND PSYCHOLOGICAL.

The effective leader realizes that a mixture of extrinsic and intrinsic rewards is needed. What mix will be best? This depends on the subordinate, and to be more definitive in our answer, we must apply expectancy theory to the specific situation.

■ ■ ■ ■ ■ ■ ■ ■ ■ ■ ■ ■
THE RIGHT MIX OF EXTRINSIC AND INTRINSIC MOTIVATORS MUST BE USED.

Remember that expectancy theory is: Motivational force = Valence × Expectancy. Valence is the individual's preference for an outcome; for example, John may prefer a $100-a-week raise to a company car. Expectancy is the perceived probability that a particular act will be followed by a particular outcome; if John has the highest sales in the region he will be given a one-week, all-expenses paid trip to San Francisco. Knowing a person's valence and expectancy is no easy task. However, effective leaders understand their people and soon learn to know what rewards will motivate them.

Maureen Wilson is the head of advertising for a large cosmetics firm. Maureen is making more than $100,000 a year in salary and 50 percent more in bonuses tied directly to sales. The more effective the advertising program, the more likely that sales, and her bonus, will rise.

Realizing that money will not motivate Maureen very much, her boss has scheduled her to go to sales meetings in London, Paris, and Rome during the next month. The boss knows that Maureen likes to travel and that her husband, who owns a successful retail store, can get away any time he wants. The two of them can spend three weeks in Europe and the cosmetics firm will pay most of their expenses. Next year Maureen will be going to the Far East.

It is obvious that Maureen's boss knows how to motivate her. The reward schedule is designed to meet Maureen's specific needs. The boss gave her a combination of extrinsic and intrinsic rewards. The free travel saved her the cost of going to Europe on her own (her income tax bracket is very high, so if the cost of her trip were $8,000, she would have to make around $12,000 to have this amount after taxes) and also shows her how much the firm appreciates her talents.

On the other hand, some people want extrinsic rewards and are little influenced by psychological payoffs. This is especially true for people just starting their careers and raising a family at the same time.

Tony Farino is a middle manager in a manufacturing plant. He is married and has three children. He bought a house for $90,000, and his car is two years old. Tony's salary is $27,500, but with overtime, including Saturday and occasionally Sunday work, he can gross $35,000. Last month there was an opening for a manager in the purchasing department. This department has had more than its share of problems. The company's sales are growing so quickly that the department is in a constant state of turmoil trying to check on orders, verify deliveries, and see that suppliers are paid promptly.

When the department manager resigned, Tony was offered the job. The salary was $35,000 with the opportunity of making another 25 percent through overtime. Tony accepted and so far has been very happy. Although he is working harder than ever before, he feels that the higher pay more than compensates. Also, with the increased salary, he and his wife are planning to take the family on a week's vacation, something that would have been impossible with his former salary. Tony realizes that he is working long hours and not seeing very much of his family, but he feels that within 12 to 18 months, things will turn around. The car will be paid for, and the cost-of-living increase that management gives the employees will raise his salary enough to ease the burden of the house payments. Then he will be able to relax and spend more time with the children. For the time being, however, he is willing to sacrifice his leisure time for increased extrinsic rewards.

In both our illustrations, the manager knows how to motivate the subordinate, offering each what he or she wants. Involved in the two cases was the issue of equity, something that merits closer attention than we have yet given to it.

LINKING PERFORMANCE AND REWARDS

One of the most important questions in modern compensation theory is: How closely should performance and rewards be linked? From a human relations standpoint, this question relates less to the specific types of rewards that can be given than it does to the reward system itself. The system can offer three types of rewards: wages, incentive programs, and benefit programs.

WAGES, INCENTIVE PROGRAMS, AND BENEFIT PROGRAMS   Wages are agreed upon or fixed rates of pay. For an hourly employee making $6 an hour, we need merely multiply the number of hours worked by $6 to determine the person's pay for the time period under consideration. Most people, however, do not work for an hourly wage; they are salaried. Managerial personnel, in particular, are paid an annual amount, such as $26,000 a year. This salary is then broken down by pay period, i.e., $500 a week before taxes and other deductions.

Some organizations also have **incentive payment plans**. When offered on an individual basis, they typically take the form of production or sales incentive plans. In a production incentive plan, a worker is paid a higher rate for producing output over and above an established level. For example, a firm might pay $1 per manufactured piece per week up to 200 and $1.25 for any output in excess of 200. In a sales incentive plan, the salesperson's pay is tied to sales dollars generated. Quite often the individual receives a guaranteed draw, such as $50 a week, and a percentage of sales, such as 5 percent of all receipts generated.

THERE ARE INDIVIDUAL INCENTIVE PLANS.

Group incentive programs can also be found in some organizations. In these cases the program is similar to the individual incentive plan. For example, the production output of the group, or the sales of the unit, are combined in determining how much of an incentive has been earned by these employees.

GROUP INCENTIVE PLANS.

Some organizations have found they can save money by instituting an organization-wide incentive program. In this case, everyone in the enterprise participates. The logic is simple. Management believes that with a joint worker-management effort increased efficiency and cost savings can be effected. Table 11.2 provides a comparison of these three different types of incentive plans.

AND ORGANIZATION-WIDE INCENTIVE PLANS.

TABLE 11.2   A COMPARISON OF INDIVIDUAL AND GROUP AND
               ORGANIZATION-WIDE INCENTIVES

INDIVIDUAL INCENTIVE PLANS	GROUP AND ORGANIZATION-WIDE INCENTIVES
TYPICAL CHARACTERISTICS OF THE PLAN	
Rewards are based directly on what the individual produces.	Rewards are based on group performance.
Performance is determined by the individual worker.	A committee typically determines performance standards.
Rewards are provided every payday.	Performance is only indirectly controlled by employees.
Individuality and competitive spirit are encouraged.	Rewards are paid on a monthly, quarterly, semiannual, or annual basis.
The incentive relies heavily on monetary rewards.	Teamwork and unity are encouraged.
COMMONLY CITED ADVANTAGES	
There is a strong sense of individualism.	The incentive motivates a large number of employees.
Rewards are in direct proportion to output.	The approach can be used for a wide variety of tasks.
	All employees in the organization can be included.
	Group cooperation is encouraged.
COMMONLY CITED DISADVANTAGES	
Seldom are all of the employees included in the plan.	Employees are not all rewarded according to their own productivity.
This incentive tends to be restricted to mass-produced and relatively simple operations.	Individual initiative and effort are often discouraged.
The incentive cannot be easily adapted to high-quality jobs.	
Employee grievances are a continual headache.	

■ ■ ■ ■ ■ ■ ■ ■ ■ ■ ■ ■ ■ ■ ■

AS WELL AS BENEFIT PROGRAMS.

Benefit programs also come in many different versions. Some of the most common include life, health, and accident insurance, sick leave, workers' compensation, pension plans, and unemployment insurance. An increasing number of organizations are also making use of "cafeteria benefits" in which each worker can pick and choose the benefits he or she wants within a dollar limit established by the firm. This allows people to tailor the benefit package to meet their own particular needs. For example, during the 1990s one of the fastest growing benefits will be child care assistance.[20]

■ ■ ■ ■ ■ ■ ■

[20] Toni A. Campbell, "71% of Employers Say They Could Be Part of the Child Care Solution," *Personnel Journal*, April 1988, pp. 84, 86.

TABLE 11.3   USE OF NONTRADITIONAL REWARD SYSTEMS

NONTRADITIONAL REWARDS	NUMBER OF FIRMS (n = 1,598)	PERCENT OF TOTAL SAMPLE[a]
Profit sharing	507	32%
Lump-sum bonus	484	30
Individual incentives	440	28
Gainsharing	211	13
Small group incentives	223	14
All-salaried	174	11
Two-tier systems	171	11
Earned time off	101	6
Total number using more than one nontraditional reward	1,190	75

[a]Sums adding up to more than 100% are due to multiple responses.

Source: Reprinted by permission of publisher from Carla O'Dell and Jerry McAdams, "The Revolution in Employee Rewards," *Management Review*, March 1987, p. 32. American Management Association, New York. All rights reserved.

CAUSAL LINK?   Is there a link between people's performance and their rewards? Experts like Peters, of *In Search of Excellence* fame, contend that the problem in most organizations is that few enterprises offer incentives to their people to do a better job.[21] So the first step is to institute the proper rewards system. In recent years many companies have shown a willingness to set up a compensation plan that does promote this linkage, and the latest research reveals that more and more firms are doing so. In fact, there currently is a revolution taking place in employee rewards in the form of pay-for-performance plans. Workers like them, and organizations are finding that they are effective in promoting productivity and quality improvement.

Child-care assistance will be one of the fastest-growing benefits in the 1990s. Procter & Gamble provided the start-up funding for a child development center where their employees can obtain quality day care during working hours.

Many of these pay-for-performance plans make use of what are called nontraditional rewards. Table 11.3 provides the findings from a survey by the American Productivity Center and the American Compensation Association. These rewards are tied to productivity and output and include such compensation forms as profit sharing; bonuses; individual incentives; gainsharing programs that divide cost reductions among all members of the organization; small group incentives; payment for knowledge; and the granting of earned time off in lieu of a monetary reward. (See Table 11.3.)

An organization can link rewards and performance only when four conditions are present:

----

[21] Tom Peters, "Letter to the Editor," *Inc.*, April 1988, pp. 80–82.

■ ■ ■ ■ ■ ■ ■ ■ ■ ■ ■ ■
CONDITIONS FOR DIRECTLY LINKING
REWARDS AND PERFORMANCE.

1.   Individual performance can be measured objectively.

2.   There is a low degree of interdependence among the individuals in the system.

3.   It is possible to develop measures for all the important aspects of the jobs.

4.   Effort and performance are closely related over a relatively short time span.[22]

In establishing this linkage, many managers find it helpful to focus on actions that reward people for work well done. Some of the specific steps that are followed in this process include:

1.   Reward solid solutions instead of quick fixes. This is done by specifically identifying what people are to do and then evaluating their performance over the long-term rather than every 3–6 months.

2.   Reward risk taking. This is done by encouraging people to take well thought-out calculated risks and being willing to encourage those who fail as well as those who succeed.

3.   Reward applied creativity. This is done by giving people bonuses and other forms of monetary payment when their creative ideas result in profits for the organization.

4.   Reward decisive action. This is done by encouraging people to set deadlines and make decisions within this time period rather than continually procrastinating and doing more thinking and research, thus falling victim to "paralysis by analysis."

5.   Reward people for working smarter rather than just harder. This is done by giving people the information and tools they need to get the job done right, correcting poor work habits, and letting them go home when they have attained their goals rather than making them sit around and wait until closing time.

6.   Reward simplification. This is done by encouraging people to use direct communications such as calling on the phone rather than writing a memo, to avoid creating bureaucratic red tape and to simplify procedures.

7.   Reward quietly effective people. This is done by not letting the squeaky wheel get all of the attention and rewards, but rather seeking out and rewarding the quiet heroes who are responsible for getting things done.

8.   Reward quality. This is done by seeing that people are well trained, encouraging them to improve their techniques and methods, and giving

■ ■ ■ ■ ■ ■ ■

[22] Wayne F. Cascio and Elias M. Awad, *Human Resources Management: An Information Systems Approach* (Reston, Va.: Reston Publishing Company, Inc., 1981), p. 392.

recognition and monetary rewards to those who produce the highest quality output.

9.   Reward loyalty. This is done by providing job security, promoting from within, keeping communication lines open, offering fair pay and benefits, and providing people continuous education, training, and development.[23]

STOP!

Review your answer to the fourth question and make any changes you would like. Then compare your answer to the one below.

4.   Would a linking of productivity and rewards really pay off? Explain.

It should. Research shows that when individuals are rewarded for their productivity efforts, they tend to repeat these efforts. Conversely, when rewards are not provided, people tend to be less productive. ∎

DISCIPLINE

Sometimes, instead of giving rewards to employees, the leader must discipline some of them. Often this is referred to as a *negative reward*. The use of this approach will depend on the employee and the situation. For example, as seen in Table 11.4, problem employees can be divided into four categories. In dealing with each category, the manager must consider the primary and secondary goals to pursue. (Again, see Table 11.4.) For purposes of human relations, the manager must integrate this information with an understanding of (1) the types of discipline and (2) the way in which discipline should be administered.

TYPES OF DISCIPLINE   Most formal disciplinary processes employ what is called *progressive discipline*, beginning with an oral warning and, if things do not straighten out, terminating with firing.[24]

If a.1 employee breaks a rule, especially a minor one, the first step is usually a clear **oral warning**, pointing out that repetition of the act will result in discipline. At this point the manager hopes that the worker will refrain from breaking the rule in the future.

FIRST, USUALLY, COMES AN ORAL WARNING.

[23] Michael LeBoeuf, "The Greatest Management Principle in the World," *Working Woman*, January 1988, pp. 70–72, 100–101.

[24] Roger B. Madsen and Barbara Knudson-Fields, "Productive Progressive Discipline Procedures," *Management Solutions*, May 1987, pp. 17–24.

TABLE 11.4   **TYPES OF PROBLEM EMPLOYEES**

TYPE	PRIMARY GOAL	SECONDARY GOAL
Type I does not intentionally violate the rules, does so unintentionally and infrequently.	To correct the behavior, to inform and train.	To maintain the individual's motivation.
Type II will violate the rules when he or she considers some treatment unfair; will occasionally violate the rules.	To correct the behavior *and* to avoid discipline problems with others.	To identify and deal with why the person feels treated unfairly. Otherwise, future problems will occur.
Type III will violate the rules whenever he or she can get away with it, generally creates problems, and is often disciplined.	To avoid discipline problems with others.	To document the use of discipline (toward eventual termination).
Type IV is not so much a problem employee as an employee with a problem.	To get help for the individual and to provide a reason to use that help.	To document if the individual is unwilling to seek help or the problem recurs.

Source: Reprinted by permission of publisher from John Seltzer, "Discipline with a Clear Sense of Purpose," *Management Solutions*, February 1987, p. 34. American Management Association. All rights reserved.

THEN A WRITTEN WARNING.

If the employee breaks the rule again or if the first offense was a major one, some firms require **written warnings**. These become part of the employee's records and can be cited as evidence if it is decided to terminate the individual in the future.

THEN A DISCIPLINARY LAYOFF.

A **disciplinary layoff** is the next most severe form of discipline. In this case the person is required to not come to work for a specified period and forfeit the pay for that period. A layoff varies in length from one day to two weeks. Some organizations, however, do not believe in disciplinary layoffs, because they are unable to find a replacement for a few days or weeks. Instead, they simply fire the employee.

THEN DISCHARGE.

Discharge is the ultimate penalty. In recent years this approach has been used less and less, principally because the penalty is often regarded as too harsh. The effective leader strives to avoid this situation by preventing rule violations. When they do occur, the individual is consistent and impersonal in employing discipline.[25] In discharging someone, Suters recommends the following six guidelines:

1.   Be firm and unemotional and present the decision as irrevocable.

2.   Give straight, honest reasons for the dismissal.

3.   Do not be drawn into an argument or counterproductive discussion over the reasons for the termination.

[25] Other approaches to discipline are offered by Brian Heshizer, "An MBO Approach to Discipline," *Supervisory Management*, March 1984, pp. 2–7; and Donald F. Barkman, "Team Discipline," *Personnel Journal*, March 1987, pp. 58–63.

4.   Ease the blow by pointing out that the action is a mutual disap-pointment.

5.   Do not terminate anyone when you are upset.

6.   Do not blame the decision on anyone else.[26]

THE "RED-HOT STOVE RULE"   One of the most effective methods of employing discipline is the **red-hot stove rule**. This rule draws an anal-ogy between touching a red-hot stove and receiving discipline. When someone touches a red-hot stove the burn is *immediate*. There was *ad-vance warning* in the form of heat emanating from the stove, which should have alerted the person to the danger. Anyone who touches the stove is burned, and this *consistency* holds for everyone else who touches it. The burn is *impersonal* in that everyone touching the stove is burned regardless of who they are. These four characteristics are applied to discipline.

DISCIPLINE SHOULD BE IMMEDIATE   As soon as the manager knows that a worker has broken a rule, discipline should follow. If the manager waits, there is the likelihood that the worker will not associate the disci-plinary action with the violation of the rule. When this happens, bitter feelings are likely to result.

By immediate discipline we do not mean hurried action. The facts of the case should be clear, and only if there is an obvious infraction of the rules should discipline be given. In many organizations a worker is sus-pended until the investigation is complete. If the worker is found in-nocent, he or she is reinstated and given back pay for the suspension period. Conversely, if the worker is found guilty of the offense, the pre-scribed discipline is carried out.

DO NOT WAIT; DISCIPLINE IMMEDIATELY.

THERE SHOULD BE ADVANCE WARNING   The organization should make its rules clear and the employees should know what the penalties are for breaking them. One of the most common ways of doing this is to famil-iarize workers with the rules during the induction period. Any future rule changes should then be communicated by the immediate superior or, if workers are unionized, should be included in the union contract.

Two important guidelines must be followed by management in giv-ing advance warning. *Never have too many rules.* If people are given 5 rules to follow, they will generally adhere to them. However, if they are asked to abide by 105 rules they will generally ignore them. The degree of im-

MAKE SURE EVERYONE KNOWS THE RULES.

[26]Everett T. Suters, "The Toughest Job Around," *Inc.*, November 1986, pp. 138, 140.

portance tends to decline as the number of rules increases. *Clearly state and uniformly apply the penalties for infractions.* If management does otherwise, the workers will protest disciplinary procedures. For example, if Paul, a new worker, sees people walking around the construction site without hard hats, he will feel discriminated against if the foreman disciplines him for not wearing his hat. In addition, when such cases go to arbitration, it is likely that the company will lose because disciplinary action has not been taken for previous offenses. "Why," the arbitrator will reason, "should the firm suddenly decide to start enforcing the rule now?"

■ ■ ■ ■ ■ ■ ■ ■ ■ ■ ■ ■ ■ ■

MATCH THE DISCIPLINE TO
THE OFFENSE.

DISCIPLINE SHOULD BE CONSISTENT   If two people commit the same offense, each should be given the same discipline. The biggest problem for the manager is that of identifying everyone who breaks the rules. If the manager can catch only 20 percent of the workers who violate a particular rule, those who are caught are often angry, because discipline seems to be more a matter of chance than anything else.

■ ■ ■ ■ ■ ■ ■ ■ ■ ■ ■ ■ ■ ■

TREAT EVERYONE THE SAME.

DISCIPLINE SHOULD BE IMPERSONAL   The manager should make it clear to the workers that they are all on the same team but that this does not mean the workers can violate the rules with impunity. Some workers are more productive than others. Some are informal group leaders and others are followers. The manager would, quite obviously, want to cultivate the friendship of the more productive or leading workers. However, this cannot be done at the expense of either the other workers or the organization.

On the other hand, the manager should not be excessively harsh when disciplining a worker. After ensuring that the worker has indeed broken the rule, the effective manager tries to learn why and then to work with the individual to prevent another violation.

If the manager handles the situation properly, it is often possible to prevent feelings from being hurt. To a large degree, the manager's success in handling this matter will be determined by his or her negotiating ability.[27] In fact, appraising, rewarding, and disciplining employees requires effective skills. Before proceeding, take the accompanying Time Out quiz to rate your effectiveness in reward-discipline situations as measured by your negotiating ability.

■ ■ ■ ■ ■ ■ ■

[27] For more on this topic see Don Caruth, Bill Middlebrook, and Trezzle A. Pressley, "This Matter of Discipline," *Supervisory Management*, April 1983, pp. 24–31; and Ronald J. Bula, "Absenteeism Control," *Personnel Journal*, June 1984, pp. 56–60.

HOW GREAT IS YOUR NEGOTIATING ABILITY?

Performance appraisal, the allocation of rewards, and the effective use of discipline require a manager to be, among other things, a skilled negotiator. The individual must be able to evaluate performance diplomatically and effectively and withstand the pressures that come about when subordinates complain that they are being treated unfairly. How great is your negotiating ability? In each of the following 20 statements decide whether the statement is basically true or basically false in describing you.

	BASICALLY TRUE	BASICALLY FALSE
1. When I need to get someone or some group to do something, I can do so.		
2. I really like to be liked.		
3. I get a real kick out of going out to shop where prices are fixed and managing to get a discount on what I buy.		
4. I am not a very good listener, but I am an excellent talker.		
5. I try not to do formal preparation for any negotiation because it detracts from my spontaneity and creativity; I prefer to play things by ear.		
6. I am not really much of a compromiser; I know what I want and I fight to get it all.		
7. Under pressure, I can really handle myself well.		
8. People who know me well find me to be both tactful and diplomatic.		
9. I do not like taking short-range losses even at the prospect of long-range gains.		
10. I find that most things in life are negotiable.		
11. No matter what salary increase is offered to me, I try to get more.		
12. I take what people say at face value.		
13. Whenever possible, I try to avoid conflict and confrontation.		
14. I do not care how the other side feels about the results of my negotiation efforts; that is their problem not mine.		
15. I am willing to work long and hard to gain a small advantage.		
16. I do not like to haggle with people over prices; I pay what is asked or walk away from the deal.		
17. A person's facial expressions often tell me more about what is being said than do the words.		
18. I am not particularly adept at expressing my point of view.		
19. In most cases I am not willing to compromise on issues.		
20. I find it easy to smile even when engaged in a serious discussion.		

The interpretation of your self-assessment can be found at the end of the chapter.

DISMISSAL AND THE LAW

Over the last few years a new dismissal-related problem has arisen. Employees who have been discharged by their firms are now suing their companies and many have been winning large settlements.[28] At the heart of the matter are the issues of "employment at will," which means that the organization has a right to dismiss an employee at any time regardless of cause, and the right of employees to expect fair and equitable treatment from the employer. Sometimes these two issues are in conflict. A good example is when a loyal longtime employee is fired for a minor rule infraction or summarily dismissed even though he or she has been receiving very good performance evaluations. Do employees have the right to continued employment or is this provided at the discretion of the employer?

■ ■ ■ ■ ■ ■ ■ ■ ■ ■ ■ ■ ■

EMPLOYEES CAN SUE FOR WRONGFUL DISCHARGE.

Forty-six states currently give employees the right to sue for "wrongful discharge." This means that if an employee feels that he or she has been fired without just cause, he or she can bring a lawsuit. At the present time there are 25,000 pending wrongful discharge lawsuits compared with only 200 ten years ago. In an effort to deal with this emerging social phenomenon, Montana has passed a law that requires employers to submit these cases to arbitration and limits to four years' back wages the damages that can be awarded. The law also prohibits firing anyone who has completed a probationary period unless there is just cause for such action.[29]

Many firms are now developing procedures for handling these situations. The most popular is an arbitration procedure that relies upon neutral outside arbitrators to listen to the facts and then make a ruling. The Northrop Corporation has used this procedure for decades. BankAmerica, NBC, Aetna Life Insurance, and most recently, Chrysler Corporation have followed suit.[30]

During the 1990s we are likely to see a continuation of this trend. Some employers are beginning to fight back by having their employees sign statements which indicate that they can be dismissed at the discretion of the company. However, except in the case of new employees who sign these forms at the beginning of their employment, the courts are setting them aside and allowing wrongful-discharge suits which, in many cases, are proving to be quite costly to employers. As a result, there is going to be a continued trend toward impartial arbitration in handling these matters.

■ ■ ■ ■ ■ ■ ■

[28] Aaron Bernstein, "More Dismissed Workers Are Telling It to the Judge," *Business Week*, October 17, 1988, pp. 68–69.

[29] John Hoerr, "It's Getting Harder to Pass Out Pink Slips," *Business Week*, March 28, 1988, p. 68.

[30] Bernstein, "More Dismissed Workers Are Telling It to the Judge," p. 69.

STOP!

Review your answer to the fifth question and make any changes you would like. Then compare your answer to the one below.

5.   What type of discipline approach would solve the problem described in this case?

The company needs to use a discipline approach in which everyone knows the rules, infractions are disciplined immediately, and the discipline is consistent and impersonal in nature. ■

SUMMARY

In this chapter we deal with the issues of personnel development, appraisal of performance, and rewarding of performance. Personnel development should begin with an effective orientation program. Research shows that well-designed and well-implemented orientation programs can cut tardiness and absenteeism and increase productivity. Another important phase of personnel development is training. There are four basic types of training: apprentice, vestibule, on-the-job, and off-the-job. Each is discussed in the chapter.

We next consider the four-step process of performance appraisal: (1) performance standards are established, (2) individual performance is determined, (3) a comparison of individual performance and performance standards is made, and (4) overall performance is evaluated. When this fourth step is completed, the cycle starts again.

Many kinds of appraisal tools can be used to evaluate employee performance. The simplest is the graphic rating scale in which all the factors (and degrees of each factor) on which the employee is to be evaluated are listed. The manager's job is then to check the appropriate degree of every factor and total the value associated with each to arrive at an overall score for the individual.

The paired comparison method of evaluation requires the manager to compare each employee in the group with every other. Often there are five to ten factors on which all are compared. On the basis of the comparisons on all factors, the manager is able to rank the workers from the best to the poorest.

Assessment centers are used for evaluating employee long-range potential as well as short-range performance. Employing a series of assessment techniques as well as a number of assessors, this method requires the employee to use behaviors related to dimensions of actual performance on the job. The final decision regarding what to do (hire, promote, etc.) is the result of a group decision by the assessors.

Behaviorally anchored rating scales (BARS) rely heavily on an identification of critical incidents that represent effective and ineffective behaviors. After these behaviors are put in clusters, they are used to develop a rating scale for a particular cluster or dimension. The rating usually extends from 1 (ineffective behavior) up to 7 or 9 (effective behavior).

Management by objectives (MBO) can be used at all levels of the employment hierarchy. The MBO process consists of six steps: (1) identifying the goals of the unit or department, (2) describing the duties and responsibilities of the personnel, (3) meeting with the subordinate and mutually setting goals for the latter, (4) employing a goal-setting worksheet to help the subordinate work toward the objective, (5) periodically reviewing the goals and revising them where necessary, and (6) evaluating the results and starting the cycle again.

In every performance appraisal, the manager must be aware of problems. The most common problems are attributable to: (1) lack of clarity of the form itself, (2) the halo effect, (3) central tendency, and (4) leniency. While noting ways in which these problems can be overcome, we stress the need for validity and reliability in performance appraisal instruments.

The last part of the chapter is devoted to the subject of performance rewards. After reviewing common types of extrinsic and intrinsic rewards, we discuss the link the organization establishes between performance and rewards. Some organizations attempt to do this through the use of incentive payment plans; others make strong use of performance appraisal. In most cases, the reward-performance linkage is not very great, and the manager must rely most heavily on providing an environment in which workers can attain psychological rewards.

The manager must also be able to exercise discipline, sometimes referred to as a negative reward. Most formal disciplinary processes employ progressive discipline, beginning with an oral warning and moving to a written warning, a disciplinary layoff, and, ultimately, discharge. In carrying out discipline many managers use the red-hot stove rule. Effective discipline has four characteristics: (1) it should be immediate, (2) there should be advance warning of discipline penalties, and if the individual still violates the rule, the discipline should be (3) consistent and (4) impersonal. If dismissal is required, just cause should be provable.

KEY TERMS IN THE CHAPTER

performance appraisal cycle	validity
graphic rating scales	reliability
paired comparison method	extrinsic rewards
assessment center	intrinsic rewards

behaviorally anchored rating
   scales (BARS)
management by objectives (MBO)
halo effect
central tendency
leniency

incentive payment plans
oral warning
written warning
disciplinary layoff
discharge
red-hot stove rule

REVIEW AND STUDY QUESTIONS

1.   Of what value is an orientation program? What are some of the benefits it offers?

2.   There are four basic types of training. What are these types? Identify and describe each.

3.   How does the performance appraisal cycle work? Be sure to discuss all four steps.

4.   How does the graphic rating scale help the manager appraise subordinates?

5.   How do assessment centers work? Explain.

6.   What are some of the major advantages of a BARS appraisal method? List three.

7.   Why is MBO so popular? Explain.

8.   What are some of the major performance appraisal problems? Cite three.

9.   What is meant by *validity*? *Reliability*? Which is more difficult to attain? Explain your answer.

10.   When it comes to rewarding performance, which is more important, extrinsic rewards or intrinsic rewards? Explain.

11.   How can performance and rewards be linked? Offer five human relations steps.

12.   According to the red-hot stove rule of discipline, what are the four characteristics of appropriate discipline? Explain each.

13.   If an individual must be fired, what guidelines should the manager follow? Discuss four.

14.   Can an employer dismiss an employee regardless of cause? Explain.

TIME OUT ANSWERS: INTERPRETATION OF HOW GREAT IS YOUR NEGOTIATING ABILITY

Take your answers to the self-assessment quiz and compare them to those below. For each one you have that is identical to the scoring key presented here, give yourself one point.

1.	Basically true	11.	Basically true
2.	Basically false	12.	Basically false
3.	Basically true	13.	Basically false
4.	Basically false	14.	Basically false
5.	Basically false	15.	Basically true
6.	Basically false	16.	Basically false
7.	Basically true	17.	Basically true
8.	Basically true	18.	Basically false
9.	Basically false	19.	Basically false
10.	Basically true	20.	Basically true

Your score, assuming your self-evaluation is correct, provides some insights regarding your ability to negotiate well. The following is a general breakdown regarding how effective you are:

17–20	Excellent.	You are a true negotiator.
14–16	Good.	You have real negotiating potential.
11–13	Average.	You do not see yourself as much of a negotiator.
0–11	Below average.	You do not see yourself as a negotiator.

How can you improve your negotiating ability? The best way is by examining your incorrect responses and trying to change your behavior appropriately.

CASE: PROFESSIONAL EVALUATION

A large urban university in the Midwest offers three classes of business law at 7:30 a.m. on Mondays, Wednesdays, and Fridays. All three are taught by practicing attorneys who meet the class and then go downtown to their law offices. The three lawyers all teach the same basic class, but they have totally different grading policies. One of them is a very difficult grader. Most of his students receive C's. Over the last four semesters, the breakdown of his grades has been: A's, 10 percent; B's, 15 percent; C's, 50 percent; D's, 15 percent; and F's, 10 percent. Regardless of how well the students perform in this class, the professor grades them on a bell-shaped curve. The highest 10 percent of the class will receive an A; the lowest 10 percent will get an F. Of course, the top 10 percent seldom have a 90 average, and the lowest 10 percent always have an average well below 50. So all the professor does is decide how much of a curve to put on the grades in fitting them into his predetermined bell-shaped grading format.

The second lawyer is the most lenient of the three. Most of the students in her class receive either A's or B's. The breakdown on grades over the last four semesters in this class has been: A's, 33 percent; B's, 50 percent; and C's, 17 percent. The student body is well aware of this professor's grading practices, and her classes are always filled to capacity during the first day of registration. This woman always divides her final grades into three groups. Those in the top third are given A's regardless of their final score. The lowest one-sixth all get C's, and everyone else is given a B.

The third lawyer has grading policies similar to the first. Over the last four semesters, his grade breakdown has been: A's, 10 percent; B's, 20 percent; C's, 50 percent; D's, 15 percent; and F's, 5 percent. However, he has a soft spot for people who are working their way through college. The students are aware of this and, as a result, many of them show up in work clothes so the professor will realize that they hold jobs in the city. Some of them make it a point to walk out to the parking lot with the professor, while discussing their jobs with him. Realizing that some of them will attempt to pull the wool over his eyes, the professor always asks the dean's office to give him a list of those students who are working full-time (this information must be turned into the dean's office) and thus sidesteps such maneuvers.

Some students objected to the grading policies of the first and third professors (none had anything but praise for the second one), and asked the dean to insist that the professors change their rigid approach to performance evaluation. However, the dean declined to get involved and suggested that the matter be turned over to a university committee. After visiting with the committee and learning that they feel that any attempt to interfere with the professors would be viewed as an infringement of academic freedom, the students decided to drop their action and learn to live with the situation.

QUESTIONS

1.   In terms of performance appraisal errors, what error(s) is (are) the first lawyer making? What about the second lawyer? The third lawyer? Explain.

2.   Is the grade evaluation of each lawyer valid? Is it reliable? Support your reasoning.

3.   Are the lawyers properly rewarding the students for their performance? What suggestions would you make to each? Explain. ∎

CASE: CLOCK-IN TIME

Fred Winslow is a shop steward in a New York City manufacturing firm. He is well liked by the management and the workers. The management feels that Fred is particularly helpful in working out union-management grievances before they reach arbitration. Several times, Fred has served as an intermediary and has always been able to establish harmony between the disagreeing factions.

Last month, for example, one of the unionized employees was charged with stealing some supplies. The supervisor laid the man off immediately and recommended that he be fired. Fred, as the shop steward, came to the man's defense and said that the punishment was too great for "accidentally" walking off the job with $10 worth of supplies. After talking to the man and getting his side of the story, Fred approached the supervisor and suggested a compromise. The worker would admit that he accidentally took some supplies from the premises and would submit to punishment of five days off without pay. The supervisor agreed that the compromise was fair, and everyone was pleased.

In the last two weeks, however, the supervisor, who also happens to be Fred's boss, has encountered a problem. There is a company rule that says anyone who comes in late must be docked an hour's pay for any tardiness less than 60 minutes, two hours' pay if the lateness extends into the second hour, and so on. In addition, a worker who is late twice in one week is laid off for one week. If a worker is late three times in a four-week period, the penalty is a layoff of two weeks. Finally, if the worker is late four times in any four-week period, he is dismissed.

Two weeks ago, Fred was late 30 minutes one day and was docked an hour's pay. He said that the train had been delayed. Earlier this week Fred was again late by 30 minutes and was docked an hour's pay. The supervisor is worried, however, because Fred was late again today. He came in at 8:15 a.m. and immediately went to his work station. The supervisor noticed this, because he had been waiting since 7:30 to talk to Fred. At 7:55, when he had gone to check for Fred's time card, it had not yet been punched.

When the supervisor finally saw Fred enter the work area, he immediately went over to talk to him. The supervisor said nothing about Fred's tardiness, although Fred said that he was sorry he was late getting to his work station but that he had been talking to one of the men in another part of the plant about a union matter.

What has the supervisor concerned is this: Fred has to clock in by 8:00 a.m. regardless of union activities, although he is allowed to go then to other parts of the plant on union business. If he is late, the supervisor feels, Fred should be penalized regardless of his position in the union and his value to management in helping solve union-company problems. The actual proof, of course, is the time card, which should have Fred's actual arrival time on it. The supervisor went over to get the card after talking to Fred. It showed a clock-in time of 7:58 a.m. Now the supervisor is unsure of what to do, for he is certain that Fred was not in the building before 8:15.

QUESTIONS

1.   If you were the supervisor, what would you do first?

2.   If you found Fred to be guilty of tardiness, what would you do?

3.   If you were the supervisor's boss and he came and told you that he had proof that Fred was late but wanted your advice before doing anything, what would you recommend? Explain. ▪

EXPERIENCING MANAGEMENT BY OBJECTIVES

PURPOSE

- To understand how the MBO process works.
- To construct an annual goal-setting MBO worksheet.

PROCEDURE

1.   In groups of three to five students, consider the course you currently are taking. Identify the goals that you should be pursuing. List three or four goals, identifying them as quantitatively as possible. Relate what you specifically want to accomplish. Your particular goals may be somewhat different from those of others on the team, but the desired end results should be similar.

2.   Write down your goals on a goal-setting worksheet similar to the one provided in Figure 11.6.

3.   Write down the major steps that should be taken in pursuing each of the goals you have identified above.

4.   Write down the way in which you will evaluate progress toward each goal.

5.   Discuss your individual worksheet with the other members of the team and, where you see the need for change or improvement, make it. Discuss the value of a goal-setting worksheet in preparing course assignments and studying for exams.

PART 5

BEHAVIORAL EFFECTIVENESS

Parts 2 through 4 examined the social system, the technical system, and the administrative system. However, we have not yet attempted to address the question, "What does the organization do to prevent problems from occurring, and what does it do if it is unsuccessful in this attempt?" In Part 5, we answer this question by examining the two most important areas for ensuring behavioral effectiveness: (1) communication and (2) the management of change.

In Chapter 12 we study how modern organizations go about communicating for effectiveness. We define *communication*, describe the communication process, discuss major communication flows, and examine some of the common barriers to effective communication, including perception, inference, language, and status. Then we study how organizations try to overcome or prevent such problems through understanding the four steps in the communication process, and employing simple and repetitive language, using empathy, learning how to understand body language and to receive and give feedback, developing effective listening habits, and improving speaking and writing skills.

In Chapter 13 the subject of attention is the management of change. In addition to defining *change* and discussing how the change process works, we attempt to answer the question, "Is resistance to change bad?" Then we describe some of the important factors that influence an individual's evaluation of a proposed change, explain the four most common responses to change, cite some of the common reasons for resisting change, describe the three dimensions of change, list the five basic steps in the change process, and explain why time is an important factor in implementing change. Finally we discuss the role of participation and communication in the change process, describe how balance theory can help the manager in introducing and implementing change, and examine the ways in which organizational developmental interventions can be of practical value in the management of change.

When you have finished reading this part of the book, you should have a solid understanding of the communication process and of how modern organizations attempt to manage change. You should also understand the importance of behavioral effectiveness and know how communication and the management of change help to ensure this result.

COMMUNICATING FOR EFFECTIVENESS

GOALS OF THE CHAPTER

One of the most common causes of organizational inefficiency is poor communication. In this chapter we study ways in which managers can communicate effectively. The first goal of this chapter is to study the communication process. In particular we are interested in how messages are put together, transmitted, and interpreted. The second goal is to study downward, upward, lateral, and diagonal communication flows. The third goal is to examine some of the common barriers to communication, including perception, inference, language, and status. The final goal of the chapter is to study ways of achieving effective communication: knowing the steps in the communication process, using simple and repetitive language, using empathy, understanding body language, learning how to get and give feedback, and developing effective listening habits.

When you are finished reading this chapter, you should be able to:

1.   Describe the communication process.

2.   Discuss major communication flows (downward, upward, lateral, and diagonal).

3.   Explain how perception, inference, language, and status can also lead to communication breakdown.

4.   Outline the four steps in the communication process and describe how an understanding of them can help a manager improve his or her communication skills.

5.   Describe the importance of using simple, repetitive language and using empathy in achieving effective communication.

6.   List some of the listening habits and writing and speaking guidelines valuable to effective communication.

OPENING CASE

IS ANYONE PAYING ATTENTION?

When Mary McClintok completed her bachelor's degree in business administration, she looked forward to being transferred to the field. Mary had been working part-time on her degree and it had taken her eight long years. During most of this time she had worked in the shipping department. Now, she was convinced, her career with the firm would take off.

In Mary's company everyone who has made it into the ranks of top management has spent at least a few years in the field. Some individuals choose to forego this experience and stay in the home office. None of these individuals has ever been promoted into the top management ranks, and all of them admit that they made a poor career choice.

When Mary's boss gave no sign that he was going to have her name placed on the list of personnel to be transferred to the field, Mary decided to take action of her own. She wrote a formal memo to her boss and specifically asked to be transferred. When she saw him the next day, he told her, "I received your memo and passed it on to my boss. You should be hearing something in the near future." That was six weeks ago.

Since this time Mary has heard nothing from her boss. However, she did notice that a large number of new graduates were hired and that most of these were immediately assigned to the field. A friend of hers asked, "When are you going to be sent out? If they don't send you soon, there won't be any positions left out there. Those new college kids are filling up most of the current openings."

After four more weeks, Mary began to talk to some of her friends at other companies. One of them told her, "Come on over during your lunch hour and interview with us. I'll bet you get a job immediately. You not only have an undergraduate degree but you've got eight years of practical experience as well." Mary decided to take her friend up on the offer. She interviewed during the lunch hour and at 2 p.m. that day she received a call offering her a job effective in two weeks.

Mary submitted her resignation yesterday. Her boss was surprised and said he was sure she was on the list to be transferred to the field. However, no one seems to know what has happened to Mary's request.

When she called the personnel department to tell them that she would be coming by next week to sign the necessary termination papers, she asked if her name had been put on the latest list of those going to the field. It had not. This led Mary to conclude that leaving the firm is undoubtedly a very wise decision.

1.   What medium did Mary use in communicating her message? What medium might have been more effective?

2.   What communication mistake did the boss make in handling Mary's request? Explain.

3.   How did perception affect Mary's decision?

4.   How could this problem have been avoided?

Write down your answers to these questions and put them aside. We will return to them later. ■

THE COMMUNICATION PROCESS

Communication is the process of transmitting meanings from sender to receiver. These meanings are conveyed through a medium such as a telephone call, a memorandum, or a conversation. In this **communication process** there are five essential elements: (1) the sender, (2) the message being transmitted, (3) the medium used to carry the message, (4) the receiver of the message, and (5) the interpretation given to the message. In conveying meanings from sender to receiver, three functions must be performed. First, the message has to be encoded, or put into a form that will be understood by the receiver. Second, it has to be conveyed through the proper medium or channel. Third, it must be decoded, or interpreted properly by the person to whom it was directed. These functions are described in Figure 12.1.

COMMUNICATION IS THE PROCESS OF TRANSMITTING MEANINGS FROM SENDER TO RECEIVER.

ENCODING

Before a message can be sent from one person to another it has to be **encoded**, or expressed in a code (words, facial expressions, gestures) that is intelligible to the receiver. For example, if a top executive is flying from New York to London to attend a corporate meeting with his counterpart in the United Kingdom, he might call the British executive and say, "I'm arriving on Wednesday at 7 a.m. on Pan Am Flight 201. My secretary tried to get an earlier flight but everything here is booked up because of the heavy tourist travel to your country. Would you be kind enough to have someone meet me at the airport so I won't be late for our meeting at 9:30?" However, if the executive is unable to reach his counterpart by phone, he might send a telegram. In this case the message will be encoded differently. Telegrams are much briefer and leave out a lot

FIRST, THE MESSAGE MUST BE ENCODED.

FIGURE 12.1   THE COMMUNICATION PROCESS IN ACTION

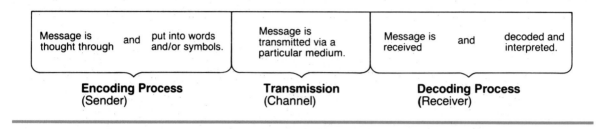

of the window dressing. The executive's telegram might read "ARRIV-ING EARLIEST POSSIBLE FLIGHT WED PANAM 201 STOP WILL REQUIRE TRANSPORTATION STOP." It is up to the British manager to work out the details such as arrival time and transportation.

Note that in the encoding process there are two important steps. First, the sender thinks through the ideas to be communicated. Second, the sender translates these ideas into some code or symbol, which in this case was words.

MEDIUM

■ ■ ■ ■ ■ ■ ■ ■ ■ ■ ■ ■ ■ ■
THEN A COMMUNICATION MEDIUM
MUST BE CHOSEN.

In describing the encoding process, we have already noted two of the most common forms of communication media: the telephone and the telegram. Other forms include conversation, pictures, diagrams, fig-ures, and charts. For example, when one is advertising a product, one frequently uses pictures to convey the idea, as in newspaper ads and billboards. Diagrams, figures, and charts are often used when manag-ers communicate with each other. Much business data is conveyed in these forms.

In addition, we need to consider nonverbal forms of communica-tion. For example, there is body language.[1] People transmit meanings by their facial expressions, eye movements, and how close (or far away) they sit or stand in relation to other people. Even the way they walk tells us something about them.

The physical environment in which people live has an influence on their communication. Dentists' offices have comfortable chairs and pleas-ant decor in the waiting rooms so that patients will be less nervous. Res-taurants have dim lighting and soft music, which encourage people

■ ■ ■ ■ ■ ■ ■

[1] Julius Fast, *Body Language* (New York: Pocket Books, 1971); and Michael B. McCaskey, "The Hidden Messages Managers Send," *Harvard Business Review*, November–December 1979, pp. 135–148.

TABLE 12.1   THE ASSOCIATION OF MOODS WITH COLORS

MOOD	COLOR
Exciting, stimulating	Red
Secure, comfortable	Blue
Distressed, disturbed, upset	Orange
Tender, soothing	Blue
Protective, defending	Red
Despondent, dejected, unhappy, melancholy	Black
Calm, peaceful, serene	Blue
Dignified, stately	Purple
Cheerful, jovial, joyful	Yellow
Defiant, contrary, hostile	Red
Powerful, strong, masterful	Black

Source: From Lois B. Wexner, "The Degree to Which Colors (Hues) Are Associated with Mood-Tones," *Journal of Applied Psychology*, December 1954, pp. 433–434.

to talk softly and stay longer. Even the colors of the room can have an effect on people's mood, resulting in a particular communication pattern. Table 12.1 lists the moods commonly associated with certain colors. If the boss is going to communicate important news to a subordinate and has him or her wait in the orange room, the subordinate may feel the news is bad (orange tends to create a distressed, disturbed mood), but if the subordinate is waiting in a yellow room, he or she might begin to expect good news (yellow tends to create a cheerful, jovial mood).

Finally, we have to consider that the medium is also used in directing the message toward certain people and away from others. This selective process is examined in Chapter 5 in the discussion of informal communication networks and the high degree of selectivity that exists among organizational personnel. Some people are passed information and others are deliberately bypassed.

DECODING

The last phase of the communication process involves a **decoding** or interpreting of the message by the receiver. In understanding how this decoding process works, we must consider three areas: the sender's meaning, the receiver's interpretation, and the degree of overlap between them. Let us consider an exaggerated example of very little overlap.

FINALLY, THE MESSAGE MUST BE DECODED.

> Eddie Jones spent two weeks in South America consulting for the local branch office. The branch manager assigned him a secretary and an office. A few days before his assignment was over,

Enhancing communication skills is just one objective of Comerica's frequent training meetings. The company's public contact staff members must properly decode messages about new products and services.

Eddie told the branch manager that he wanted to show his gratitude to the secretary for a job well done. He planned on getting her a small present on his last day there. The branch manager told Eddie that the secretary would appreciate such a gesture. Following up on his promise, Eddie brought the secretary a dozen roses.

Imagine his surprise when the office manager came by to tease him later. "When you said you were going to get her a gift I thought you were going to buy her something for her home. I should have asked you beforehand what you wanted to get. You see, giving flowers in this country is a sign of *romantic* interest!"

We can diagram the decoding of the message between Eddie (the sender) and the branch manager (the receiver) as in Figure 12.2. Let us take another example.

The hospital administrator told Roy Jones, his associate administrator, that the board of directors would be visiting the hospital the next day and would be looking at the new wing that had just been built. The wing had seven stories and the top five stories contained patients' rooms. "The beds and other furniture arrived yesterday and we should get them put into the rooms as soon as possible," the administrator told Roy, "so the board members can see what the rooms look like when they're furnished." Roy rounded up all the help he could get on short notice and began moving the furniture and arranging the rooms. It took until 1:00 a.m. just to get all the furniture up in the rooms, but by the time the board members arrived at 9:00 a.m., everything was ready. The members examined the first two floors of the building, took the elevator to the third floor to look at some of the patients' rooms, and then returned to the main part of the hospital for lunch.

Later, the hospital administrator said to Roy, "I didn't realize that you were going to furnish all the rooms. I should have

---

FIGURE 12.2   **A MAJOR DECODING PROBLEM**

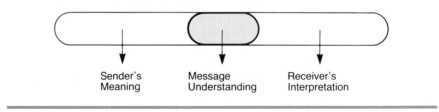

Sender's   Message   Receiver's
Meaning   Understanding   Interpretation

FIGURE 12.3   **A MINOR DECODING PROBLEM**

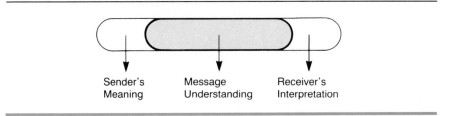

Sender's Meaning   Message Understanding   Receiver's Interpretation

told you that they would only be looking at one of the patients' floors! All of them are the same, so there was really no need for them to go on up any farther. Nevertheless, it's better to have done too much work than too little. We would have had to put all the furniture in those rooms later in the month anyway."

In this case, we can see that there was more than adequate information conveyed. We can diagram the decoding process as in Figure 12.3.

STOP!

Review your answer to the first question and make any changes you would like. Then compare your answer to the one below.

1.   What medium did Mary use in communicating her message? What medium might have been more effective?

Mary used a written memo to send her message. A verbal message might have been more effective, if only as a complement to her written message, because it would have allowed her to follow through more quickly to find out the status of her request rather than sitting back and waiting for a written response. ■

COMMUNICATION FLOWS

The communication process carries messages in four basic directions: downward, upward, lateral, and diagonal. Figure 12.4 illustrates each direction of flow.

FIGURE 12.4   **COMMUNICATION FLOWS**

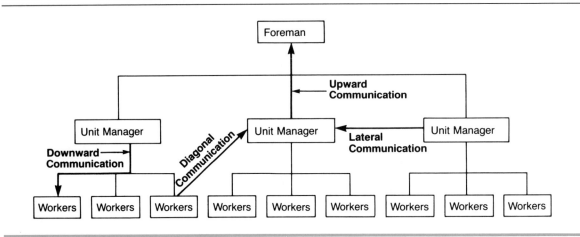

DOWNWARD COMMUNICATION

Downward communication travels from the superior to the subordinate. The most common purposes of this communication flow are to transmit information and instruct employees in the performance of their jobs. Some of the most typical downward communication channels include written directives, face-to-face conversations, use of public address systems, bulletin boards, and company newspapers.

For human relations study, downward communication is important because it provides direction and control for the employees. Remember from the discussion of informal organizations that if there is a lack of information it will be filled by rumor, gossip, or other grapevine activity. Effective downward communication can prevent confusion and distortion.

Additionally, it is important to note that orders coming down the line tend to be expanded in terms of interpretation and impact. A top manager tells a subordinate, "Find out how many people we have working in our San Francisco branch. I know the president is going to ask for this information during our meeting Friday, and I want to be prepared." The subordinate passes the message to a secretary, who calls the San Francisco branch and tells the secretary there, "The president has asked for a complete list of everyone who works in your branch. We need it all within two days." The branch secretary then expands the message by telling the branch manager that the president wants personnel records of all the branch employees sent as soon as possible. Within two hours, five people are assigned to the task. The data arrives at the main office early the next morning in four large boxes shipped air freight.

FIGURE 12.5   OPERATION HALLEY'S COMET

A COLONEL ISSUED THE FOLLOWING DIRECTIVE TO HIS EXECUTIVE OFFICER:

"Tomorrow evening at approximately 2000 hours Halley's Comet will be visible in this area, an event which occurs only once every 75 years. Have the men fall out in the battalion area in fatigues, and I will explain this rare phenomenon to them. In case of rain, we will not be able to see anything, so assemble the men in the theater and I will show them films of it."

EXECUTIVE OFFICER TO COMPANY COMMANDER:

"By order of the Colonel, tomorrow at 2000 hours, Halley's Comet will appear above the battalion area. If it rains, fall the men out in fatigues, then march to the theater where this rare phenomenon will take place; something which occurs only once every 75 years."

COMPANY COMMANDER TO LIEUTENANT:

"By order of the Colonel be in fatigues at 2000 hours tomorrow evening, the phenomenal Halley's Comet will appear in the theater. In case of rain, in the battalion area, the Colonel will give another order, something which occurs once every 75 years."

LIEUTENANT TO SERGEANT:

"Tomorrow at 2000 hours the Colonel will appear in the theater with Halley's Comet, something which happens every 75 years. If it rains, the Colonel will order the comet into the battalion area."

SERGEANT TO SQUAD:

"When it rains tomorrow at 2000 hours the phenomenal 75-year-old General Halley, accompanied by the Colonel, will drive his comet through the battalion area theater in fatigues."

Source: From a speech by Dan Bellus of the Santa Monica firm of Dan Bellus and Associates. Reprinted in the DS LETTER, Vol. 1, No. 3 (1971). Published by Didactic Systems, Inc., Box 457, Cranford, N.J. Reprinted with permission.

This is message expansion. A simple order is distorted as it comes down the line. The top executive merely wanted the subordinate to come up with the number of employees, i.e., 137 people. Instead, the order is turned into a major project involving 10 people. In downward verbal communication, we find that the number of links often determines the extent of message distortion. The more people (links) there are in the chain, the greater the likelihood of communication expansion and distortion (Figure 12.5). To overcome this problem, managers must strive to forge the shortest link between themselves and the person who will carry out the order.

UPWARD COMMUNICATION

Upward communication travels from subordinate to superior. The most common purpose of this information flow is to provide feedback on how well things are going. It also provides the subordinates' superior with the opportunity to represent the subordinates to his or her own boss.

■ ■ ■ ■ ■ ■ ■ ■ ■ ■ ■ ■ ■
UPWARD COMMUNICATION PROVIDES FEEDBACK.

FIGURE 12.6   **UPWARD COMMUNICATION IN ACTION**

MANAGER	MESSAGE BEING RECEIVED
President	The management and the salary structure are outstanding. Fringes and working conditions are good and should get better.
Vice-President	We really like the salary structure and hope that with the new contract fringes and working conditions will improve. We really like the management.
General Manager	Salaries are good; fringes and working conditions are O.K. They should improve over the next year.
Supervisor	Salaries are good; fringe benefits and working conditions are minimally acceptable. We think things will get better.
Foreman / **Workers**	We feel working conditions are poor; work assignments are unclear and the insurance program is lousy. However, we do like the competitive salary and feel the company has the potential to straighten out its problems.

Whereas downward communication tends to be expanded, upward communication tends to be contracted. As information flows up the line it is compiled, examined, reduced, and passed on. Figure 12.6 illustrates this contraction. Note that good news tends to rise, but bad news is filtered out. This is particularly true when managers do not like to hear bad news from their subordinates. Realizing this, the subordinates simply screen out or reduce the amount of bad news they pass on. This often leads to insulation of the top manager, who may make erroneous decisions as a result. The only way to overcome this problem is to make it clear that *all* information, good and bad, is to be conveyed upward. Additionally, top managers must refrain from being critical of subordinates who give them this feedback, for once it becomes obvious that a manager dislikes bad news, selective filtering will occur.

LATERAL AND DIAGONAL COMMUNICATION

■ ■ ■ ■ ■ ■ ■ ■ ■ ■ ■ ■ ■ ■
LATERAL COMMUNICATION
PROVIDES TEAMWORK.

Lateral communication takes place between people on the same level of the hierarchy. The most common reason for this communication flow is to promote coordination and teamwork. For example, the manager in Department A needs to know when the materials from Department B

FIGURE 12.7   **FAYOL'S GANGPLANK THEORY**

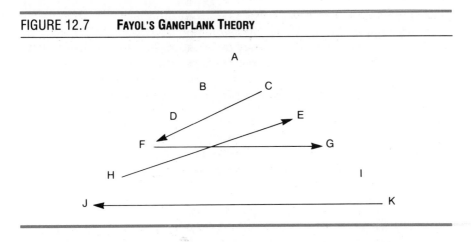

---

will arrive so that none of the members of Department A will be sitting around doing nothing. In communicating with the B manager, the A manager uses lateral communication.

Diagonal communication occurs between people who are *neither* in the same department *nor* on the same level of the hierarchy. For example, an advisor to the president calls the head of Department A to ask when the prototypes of the new consumer appliance product will be ready for inspection, or the head of Department B calls the vice-president of personnel to complain about errors in the computation of some employees' paychecks. In each case, someone communicates either downward or upward with someone in another functional area.

There are a number of potential problems with diagonal and lateral communication. One is that they involve communications outside one's department or unit and can cause interorganizational friction or mis-understanding. A second is that these communications may undermine the authority of one's own boss by making promises or commitments that involve the department or unit. In the same way, they can undermine the authority of a manager in the other unit.

Additionally, some students of human relations believe that it is wrong for managers to use either lateral or diagonal communication be-cause it violates the chain of command. While this is true, this form of cross-communication is widely used in organizations today because it fa-cilitates efficiency. Introduced in 1916 by Henri Fayol, this justification is often referred to as **Fayol's bridge or gangplank theory.**[2] In Figure 12.7, diagonal communication is being used by Manager C to talk to Manager

DIAGONAL COMMUNICATION FACILITATES EFFICIENCY.

---

[2] Henri Fayol, *Industrial and General Administration*, translation by J. A. Coubrough (Geneva: International Management Institute, 1929), p. 28.

F, by Manager F to talk to Manager G, by Manager H to talk to Manager E, and by Manager K to talk to Manager J.

Obviously, both lateral and diagonal communication can be dangerous because they cross the organizational structure and sidestep the long, formal line of command. However, this form of communication should be promoted as long as anyone initiating the communication follows two simple rules:

1.   Obtain permission from one's direct supervisor before undertaking the communication.

2.   Inform the direct supervisor of any significant results of the cross-communication.

STOP!

Review your answer to the second question and make any changes you would like. Then compare your answer to the one below.

2.   What communication mistake did the boss make in handling Mary's request? Explain.

The boss simply passed the message on to his boss. He used an upward communication channel to get rid of the message. As far as he is concerned, it is now out of his hands. If he were effective, he would have ensured that there was also a downward communication link between his boss and himself so that he could have kept abreast of the status of the request. ∎

BARRIERS TO COMMUNICATION

All communication flows are subject to barriers that prevent the receiver from getting the sender's meaning. Some of the most common barriers are: (1) perception, (2) inference, (3) language, and (4) status.

PERCEPTION

PERCEPTION IS A PERSON'S VIEW OF REALITY.

As noted in Chapter 3, **perception** is a person's view of reality. Since no two people have the same experiences and training, no two people see things exactly the same way. However, for effective communication, it is not necessary for them to have the same perception. One person needs to transmit sufficient information for the other person to take appropriate action. The major question for the manager is, "What constitutes

FIGURE 12.8   A COMMUNICATION CONTINUUM

Clear
Communications

Vague
Communications

'sufficient' information?" Some messages may be well thought out and still may be misunderstood by the receiver. Other messages may be vague but the receiver may have no trouble understanding them.

These two ideas—clear and vague—can be placed on a communication continuum as in Figure 12.8. The messages on the left deal with ideas that are easily understood and do not involve matters of opinion or issues that are open to interpretation.

"George, beginning tomorrow you are to occupy Ralph's office. He is being transferred to the Denver office, and you are next in line in seniority so the office is yours." This is a clear message. We can expect George to clean out his desk and move the contents into Ralph's office tomorrow. We would be surprised if we found that George moved into his boss's office, because that would indicate quite a deviation from the originally transmitted message.

"George, if you do well in your current position, you can expect a promotion to the Denver office as well." This message is much more vague than the previous one. Note that the sender of the message does not make clear what is meant by "if you do well." It is implied that George knows, but does he?

DEGREES OF PERCEPTUAL DIFFICULTY   As one moves across the communication continuum in Figure 12.8, there is some point after which the messages become extremely difficult to comprehend. However, it is erroneous to believe that all clear communiqués are error-free. Often people see and hear what they want or expect to see and hear. When this happens, communication breakdown can occur. Let us take an example. After this paragraph there is a sentence containing all capital letters. Read the sentence slowly and carefully so that you understand its entire meaning. When you are finished, go on to the paragraph that follows.

FINISHED FILES ARE THE RESULT OF YEARS OF SCIENTIFIC STUDY COUPLED WITH THE EXPERIENCE OF MANY YEARS.

Before reading further, you may read the above sentence one more time. When you have finished, and *only* when you have finished, continue reading down this page.

The capitalized sentence that you have read consists of seventeen words. It is a somewhat long although not particularly difficult sentence containing a handful of ideas. Within this sentence there are a number of different letters: fourteen E's, four A's, and so on. Count the number of times another letter appears in the above sentence, with the following ground rules. First, you may not use your finger, pen, or pencil in re-reading the capitalized sentence; you may use only your eyes. Second, you are to read the sentence as quickly as possible, taking no more than 10 seconds to do so. (If possible, time yourself.) When you have finished reading the sentence, you may continue to the next paragraph. Ready? Okay. Begin reading the capitalized sentence and count the number of times the letter F appears. Go!

How many times did you find the letter F in the sentence? The most common answers are two, three, four, five, six, and seven. Was your answer one of these? The right answer is included in this list. Regardless of the number you arrived at the first time, go back to the sentence and read it *slowly* and *deliberately*, counting the number of F's very carefully.

If you have counted three—no more, no less—you are typical of most people. Actually, there are six F's in the sentence, in *finished*, *files*, *scientific*, and the three *of*'s. Most people miss these last three because they are accustomed to reading past short words, skimming over them too quickly to notice the spelling. This exercise demonstrates that even when it comes to "clear" messages people make errors because they do not perceive what actually is there.

Let us take another illustration, this time using a vague message. Following this paragraph are nine dots. After studying them for a minute, connect all nine dots with four straight lines. Here are the rules:

1.   You may not take your pen or pencil off the paper.

2.   If you retrace a line by, for example, going from left to right and then back again to the point of departure, you have used two lines.

3.   The lines must indeed be straight; do not curve them in any way.

After you have finished this exercise (take no more than five minutes with it), you can check your answer with the solution given at the end of the chapter. As you will see, the puzzle can be solved *only* by going outside the perimeter formed by the nine dots. If you try to stay within this square area, you cannot solve the problem without using at least five straight lines.

When managers communicate, they often believe that their messages are clear. Often, however, they are vague, and the receiver ends up asking, "What did the boss mean by that?"

INFERENCE

Another common communication problem, closely associated with perception, is inference. An **inference** is an assumption made by the receiver of a message. Inferences are most often present in messages that are very long or that involve a large number of facts. In interpreting their meaning, the receiver is often forced to make assumptions, since the facts are not all clearly transmitted. The Time Out quiz is an illustration.

AN INFERENCE IS AN ASSUMPTION MADE BY THE RECEIVER OF A MESSAGE.

How well did you do? Check your answers with those at the end of the chapter. Most people get no more than eight right.

Inference occurs whenever the sender of the message fails to communicate clearly and completely. In face-to-face communication many of these problems can be overcome, since the listener can quickly stop the conversation and ask a question. However, with written messages this is more difficult, because the receiver is forced to use his or her own best judgment in deciding what the message really means.

LANGUAGE

Language is used to convey meanings in the communication process. This is as true in written as in spoken communication. However, sometimes language proves to be a communication barrier. One of the most common reasons is that people have different meanings for the same words. For example, in engineering firms the word *burn* often means to photocopy. Imagine the surprise of a manager in such a company when he or she tells a new secretary to burn a copy of the original blueprints and then finds that they have to be redrawn!

Communicating in the international area presents special language problems. The use of a translator can help alleviate these problems. Nynex Chairman D. C. Staley speaks to Xiao Guang Fong, a Chinese official, and translator Diana Fu in Beijing, China.

Every profession has its own meanings for words. In the medical profession *OD* stands for overdose, an excessive amount of a drug. However, in the field of management, *OD* signifies organizational development, a strategy used to introduce planned change. Or consider *OB*, which in the medical profession stands for obstetrics but in the management profession signifies organizational behavior, an academic discipline taught in accredited schools of business. Communications theorists like to point out that meanings are not in words but in the people who use them. When we employ language for communication purposes, we sometimes do not have the same meaning for a word that the receiver does, and communication breakdown is all but inevitable.

MEANINGS ARE IN PEOPLE, NOT IN WORDS.

TIME OUT

A MATTER OF INFERENCE

Instructions: Read the following story very carefully. You may assume that everything it says is true, but be aware that parts of the story are deliberately vague. You can read the story twice if you desire, but *once you start reading the statements that follow, do not go back to either the story itself or any previous statements*. Simply read each statement and decide if it is true (the story said so), false (the story said just the opposite), or inferential (you cannot say whether it is true or false; you need more facts). Write your answer (T for true, F for false, I for inferential) on the line after the statement. When you are finished, check your results with the answers given at the end of the chapter.

The story: Bart Falding is head of the research and development department of a large plastics firm located in New England. Bart has ordered a crash R&D program in hopes of developing a new process that will revolutionize plastics manufacturing. He has given five of his top R&D people authority to spend up to $250,000 each without consulting him or the R&D committee.

He has sent one of his best people, Mary Lou Rasso, to a major midwestern university to talk to a Nobel Prize winner there who has just applied for and received a patent that Bart believes may provide the basis for a breakthrough in the plastics field. Three days after Mary Lou left for the university, Bart received a call from her. Mary Lou was very excited and said she and the scientist were flying in to see Bart the next day, although she declined to discuss the matter over the phone.

Bart believes that he will have very good news for the company president when they meet for their biweekly lunch early next week.

Another common language-related problem is that of reading. Many schools no longer teach students to read and write properly. Grammar, sentence construction, and reading skills all go unstressed. Students now enter the work force unprepared to communicate effectively.

STATUS

■ ■ ■ ■ ■ ■ ■ ■ ■ ■ ■ ■ ■ ■
STATUS IS A PERSON'S RELATIVE
RANK.

Status, as defined in Chapter 4, refers to the relative ranking of an individual in a group. In the formal organization, those at the top tend to have much higher status than those at the bottom. When people commu-

THE STATEMENTS

1. Bart is head of the research and development department of a large plastics firm. _____

2. The company is located in Los Angeles, California. _____
3. Bart received orders from the president to engage in a crash R&D program. _____
4. Bart's R&D budget is in excess of $1 million. _____
5. Bart assigned five of his best people to work on developing a new process for revolutionizing plastics manufacturing. _____
6. Mary Lou was sent to talk to a Nobel Prize–winning professor. _____
7. Mary Lou works for the plastics manufacturing department. _____
8. Mary Lou was authorized to spend up to $250,000 without approval from the R&D committee. _____
9. Bart's company wants to buy the patent from the university professor. _____
10. Bart believes that Mary Lou has already offered the professor a deal and the latter is prepared to accept it, but first wants to discuss the matter with top management. _____

11. Mary Lou has agreed to pick up all the scientist's expenses if the latter will consent to come and talk to Bart in person. _____
12. The scientist must be interested in some type of financial or business arrangement with Bart's firm, or the scientist would not have agreed to fly in and meet with Bart. _____

13. The scientist received the Nobel Prize for work he did in the area of plastic processes. _____

14. Bart and the company president have lunch on a biweekly basis. _____
15. Bart believes that he will have good news for the president for he is sure that the scientist will agree to sell the patent to the company if the firm makes a sufficiently high offer. _____

nicate, status affects the process, because they often monitor what they say or write on the basis of who is going to receive the message, and they distort what they hear by judging its accuracy according to who said it.

Management may regard a complaint it receives from the union as nothing more than union rhetoric. However, if a member of management tells the president that the complaint is accurate, the union's message takes on a higher degree of credibility. Conversely, if a union employee is late for work and is laid off for three days, the shop steward may fight to have the punishment reduced. However, if people in the employee's area tell the steward that the employee is always late for work, falls down in assignments, and altogether is more of a hindrance than a help, the shop steward may not argue the employee's case very hard. The steward has been given two messages by the other unionized employees: the worker got what he deserved, and we're happy to see him laid off for a few days, if only to keep him out of our hair.

One of the ways to motivate people is to give them status symbols. The personnel may want equality, but most people want just a little bit more for themselves than the average person is getting. In short, status is important. We all want to feel that we are special. As a result, the organization cannot remove status symbols, so it must learn to adjust to the problems that accompany them, including communication breakdown.

STOP!

Review your answer to the third question and make any changes you would like. Then compare your answer to the one below.

3.   How did perception affect Mary's decision?

Perception affected Mary's decision because she felt that the firm was not going to do anything about her request. As a result, she took action of her own. Her view of reality was that the company either did not care that she had finished her college degree or did not intend to send her to the field. ∎

ACHIEVING EFFECTIVE COMMUNICATION

The barriers we have just examined can prevent the sender from conveying his or her meaning to the receiver, but this need not happen. There are ways to overcome the barriers and achieve effective communication. Some of the most useful are (1) knowing the steps in the communication process, (2) using simple, repetitive language, (3) using empathy, (4) understanding body language, (5) learning how to get and give feedback, (6) developing effective listening habits, and (7) improving writing and speaking skills.[3]

----

[3] In addition to the material in this section, other useful suggestions can be found in Russell W. Driver, "Opening the Channels of Upward Communication," *Supervisory Management*, March 1980, pp. 24–29; Paul Hersey and Joseph W. Ralty, "One-On-One OD Communications Skills," *Training and Development Journal*, April 1980, pp. 56–60; Edward L. Levine, "Let's Talk: Tools for Spotting and Correcting Communication Problems," *Supervisory Management*, July 1980, pp. 25–37; George Miller, "Management Guidelines: Being a Good Communicator," *Supervisory Management*, April 1981, pp. 20–26; and N. Patricia Freston and Judy E. Lease, "Communication Skills Training for Selected Supervisors," *Training and Development Journal*, July 1987, pp. 67–70.

KNOWING THE STEPS IN THE COMMUNICATION PROCESS

If a manager knows the steps in the communication process, many of the breakdowns we have just discussed can be avoided. There are four steps in communication: (1) attention, (2) understanding, (3) acceptance, and (4) action.

ATTENTION   Only when the listener has screened out all the disturbances or other distractions that can interrupt his or her concentration is **attention** possible. The sender can help in this process by remembering that many listeners are confronted with message competition. There are other things on their minds—telephone calls that must be returned, memos and reports that need to be read, people who have asked them for assistance and are awaiting replies. If the sender does not keep the message interesting and informative, there is a good chance that the receiver will begin to daydream or ponder some of the other messages competing for his attention.

■ ■ ■ ■ ■ ■ ■ ■ ■ ■ ■ ■ ■ ■
MESSAGE COMPETITION MUST BE OVERCOME.

UNDERSTANDING   Comprehension of the message results in **understanding**. The receiver must get the meaning. In trying to accomplish this step, many managers ask their people, "Do you understand what I'm saying?" However, this is the wrong approach. One should never ask people *if* they understand, because all the pressure is on them to answer, "Yes." Rather, the manager should ask them *what* they understand. In this way, the listener is forced to restate the message in his or her own words, and the manager can judge the accuracy of understanding. Following is an illustration.

■ ■ ■ ■ ■ ■ ■ ■ ■ ■ ■ ■ ■ ■
ALWAYS ASK *WHAT*, NOT *IF*.

- Manager: Doris, we need this report typed up and sent to the division manager. I want you to get to it as soon as possible.
- Doris: Uh, okay. I'll get to it as soon as possible.
- Manager: Are you sure you understand?
- Doris: Sure.
- Manager: What are you going to do?
- Doris: Well, I'm going to drop that rush job I'm working on and get going on this report for the division manager.
- Manager: No, Doris, that's not what I meant to say. I want you to finish that rush job and *then* do the report for the division manager.
- Doris: Oh, okay. I misunderstood. I'm sorry.
- Manager: That's all right, Doris. The important thing is that we now understand each other. In the future if you have any questions about what I mean, don't hesitate to ask.

Note that the manager initially asked *if* the subordinate understood, but avoided a problem by then asking Doris *what* she understood. The manager also encouraged her to ask questions in the future to ensure continued understanding.

■ ■ ■ ■ ■ ■ ■ ■ ■ ■ ■ ■ ■ ■
ACCEPTANCE REQUIRES
COMPLIANCE.

ACCEPTANCE   When the receiver is willing to go along with the message, **acceptance** occurs. Only in rare cases do subordinates refuse to comply with directives from the boss. They usually obey without giving the matter much thought. However, people balk if they think the order is detrimental to their best interests.

▪   Manager: Jack, I've just gotten a phone call from Morris, and they're shipping over the supplies we ordered last week. They'll be here in about 40 minutes. I'd like you to wait, sign for the supplies, and put them in the storeroom.

▪   Jack: Sir, I've got a night class at the university that starts at 6 p.m. If I don't leave right now, I'll miss it.

Obviously, the manager can try to force Jack to stay. However, if the boss reads the feedback signs, he should be able to see that Jack's acceptance will at best be slow in coming. The manager must be aware of these negative vibrations and either press for acceptance or ask someone else to wait for the supplies. In this case, asking someone else appears preferable. Use of transactional analysis (Chapter 3) can be very helpful in attaining communication acceptance.

■ ■ ■ ■ ■ ■ ■ ■ ■ ■ ■ ■ ■ ■
ACTION REQUIRES THE RECEIVER
TO DO WHAT WAS EXPECTED.

ACTION   The final step in the communication process, **action**, requires the receiver to follow up and do what was requested. A purchase order may have to be placed, a report filed, or a meeting held. It would appear that, if the sender gets to this action stage, the communication process will attain completion with no further problems. However, this is not always so. Sometimes the receiver will encounter unforeseen difficulties. The purchase order may not be filled because the supplier is temporarily out of raw materials; an executive secretary may be on vacation so a particular report may have to wait to be filed until she returns; a vice-president may be on an extended business trip so a meeting may have to be delayed until he or she returns. In all these cases, the message will not get through the action stage.

Another cause for inaction can be found in the receiver, who may be incapable of carrying out the order. For example, if Mary tells Bob to fill out Report A and send it to the comptroller, but Bob has never been told how to do it, the report may be done wrong or not at all. The message may not reach the stage of completed action. Or, if Bob asks Mary for help and she is too busy to see him, he will fill it out as best he can, with the same result.

If the action stage is to be completed, the sender must be available to answer questions and provide assistance to the receiver. If a problem develops, the receiver then has someone to turn to. The action stage ensures that there is feedback in case of trouble. Remember, the sender's communication responsibility does not end until the desired action is completed.

USING SIMPLE, REPETITIVE LANGUAGE

The simpler a message, the more likely it will be understood and acted on properly. Consider the advertisements you see in the daily newspaper. Research shows that the shorter the ad, the higher the reader rate, and the greater the likelihood that the material will be remembered.

Unfortunately, many managers do not carry this simple rule to the work place with them. They tend to communicate long messages in hurried-up fashion. The receivers are unable to follow everything said, but because the sender is in such a rush they are afraid to interrupt either to ask questions or get the sender to repeat the more difficult portions of the message. If the message is in writing, the sender tends to use vague terms and incorporate too many ideas into one sentence. When the receiver has read the memo, only part of the message has been properly decoded.

SIMPLE MESSAGES OFTEN GET THE BEST RESULTS.

Effective managers know that every message should be understandable. If the subject matter is complex, the communication should be done in "small bites," giving the listener the opportunity to ask questions or seek clarification. In addition, the sender should, from time to time, recap part of the message so that the listener finds it easier to follow the flow of information. We illustrate how this can be done further on in the chapter.

USING EMPATHY

Putting oneself, figuratively, in another person's place is termed **empathy**. In so doing one begins to see things as the other person does. Barker has put it this way:

EMPATHY MEANS PUTTING ONESELF IN ANOTHER PERSON'S PLACE.

> Empathy means deep understanding of other people, identifying with their thoughts, feeling their pain, sharing their joy. Such empathy is typical of strong, healthy relationships. Indeed, empathetic communicators know each other so well that they can predict the responses to their messages. For example, Mario says to himself, "I know if I tell May that I'm not crazy about her new dress, she'll be hurt. So instead I'll say, 'May, that dress looks great on you, but I think the green one is even more becoming.'"[4]

[4]Larry L. Barker, *Communication* (Englewood Cliffs, N.J.: Prentice-Hall, Inc., 1978), p. 151.

■ ■ ■ ■ ■ ■ ■ ■ ■ ■ ■ ■ ■
SUCCESSFUL MANAGERS ARE
EMPATHETIC.

We know that successful managers empathize with their subordinates. They know when to be task-oriented and when to be people-oriented, because they are capable of putting themselves in a subordinate's place and answering the question, "What kind of direction does this person need?"

Empathy is particularly important at two stages of the communication process: acceptance and action. When the manager gives an order that the subordinate is reluctant to accept, the manager should be tuned in to pick up the hesitancy. Apparently the subordinate does not understand how important the matter is and how significant his or her role will be. The manager needs to further clarify the situation and explain why the subordinate is being asked to handle the task. If a manager lacks empathy, it is likely that he or she will ignore the hesitancy. The astute manager knows that the problem or issue should be dealt with immediately and laid to rest.

Empathy also helps in the action stage. When the subordinate has trouble carrying out a directive, the empathetic manager is quick to give assistance. He or she realizes immediately that help is needed and does not let the subordinate down. Conversely, the manager who lacks empathy does not check on worker progress and, when he learns that the subordinate is having trouble, lets the subordinate work it out alone. Research shows that empathetic managers are more effective than managers who lack empathy.

UNDERSTANDING BODY LANGUAGE

Body language is one of the most important forms of nonverbal communication. People use this communication form to pass messages to each other, although in many cases they are unaware they are doing so.[5] Common examples of body language include the way a person moves his eyes, where an individual stands in a room in relation to others, the way a person shakes hands or touches another on the shoulder, and the way people dress.

■ ■ ■ ■ ■ ■ ■ ■ ■ ■ ■ ■ ■ ■
EYE MOVEMENT IS IMPORTANT.

In regard to eye movement, many managers believe that if people are lying, they will not look the listener in the eye. This is untrue. Effective liars often do look their listeners right in the eye; they know such eye contact increases their credibility. However, there are things managers can learn by looking at the other person's eye movements. In particular, it is possible to tell when the other party is under stress or emotion. For example, right-handed people tend to look to the left when they are trying to deal with an issue on an emotional level, and they tend to look to

■ ■ ■ ■ ■ ■ ■

[5] Lynn Renee Cohen, "Nonverbal (Mis) Communication Between Managerial Men and Women," *Business Horizons*, January–February 1983, pp. 13–17.

the right when they are unemotional or rational. The reverse is true for left-handed people.

Posture is a second important body language sign. Slouching, look- ■ ■ ■ ■ ■ ■ ■ ■ ■ ■ ■ ■
ing down, or hanging back in the crowd are typical examples of individu- So IS POSTURE.
als who are unsure of themselves. Mehrabian, a communications expert, has found that there is a relationship between how near a person stands to another and how relaxed the individual is. Some of these findings include:

1.   A high degree of relaxation generally indicates a lack of respect or a dislike of the other person while a lesser degree of relaxation indicates a liking for the other person.

2.   An absence of relaxation indicates that the person feels threatened or is being threatening to someone else.

3.   Relaxation is related to status with higher-status people being generally more relaxed than their lower-status counterparts.

4.   Women consistently demonstrate greater immediacy and consequently deliver more positive feelings.[6]

Touch is another important body language sign. When people shake ■ ■ ■ ■ ■ ■ ■ ■ ■ ■ ■ ■
hands, a vigorous handshake (by a man) or a firm one (by a woman) is AND TOUCH.
often regarded as a sign of self-assurance. Touching is used to define power relationships. A manager who wants to emphasize an order will grasp the employee's arm while issuing the order. If the manager wants to congratulate the employee, he or she will pat the person on the back.

Physical location is a fourth important form of body language. This subject is known as **proxemics** and deals with the way people use physical space to communicate. The quiz on physical location and body lan- ■ ■ ■ ■ ■ ■ ■ ■ ■ ■ ■ ■
guage (see quiz on page 438) illustrates this idea. Where people sit or AND PHYSICAL LOCATION.
stand in relation to each other also communicates a message. For example, when communicating personal information, individuals often stand within two feet of each other. When conveying general or social information, the parties generally stand two to six feet apart. The less personal the message, the greater the distance between the people. Of course, these cultural guidelines only hold in the United States and other western countries. When dealing with Arabs or other people from the Middle East, for example, it is customary to conduct general business discussions within a few feet of each other. This "nearness" often makes Americans feel uncomfortable, but if they back away and try to establish a greater distance, they will usually find their Arab counterparts coming closer. The use of proxemics is culturally determined.

·······
[6] Albert Mehrabian, *Nonverbal Communication* (Chicago: Aldine/Atherton, 1972), pp. 25–30.

PHYSICAL LOCATION AND BODY LANGUAGE: A QUIZ

Assume that you are Person A. You would like very much to be cooperative and open to Person F. Are you seated in a correct chair or should you switch chairs with someone else? Think about this for a minute and then compare your answer to that at the end of the chapter.

Clothing also conveys messages. Here are some general guidelines that have been found effective in the choice of executive clothing:

1.   Pinstripe suits for men and women convey power.

2.   Dark suits are a good choice.

3.   Brown suits are better choices for women than for men.

4.   Black is a good color for men because it conveys power, but it is important to use a shirt and tie that complement the suit and keep the wearer from seeming threatening.

5.   Women should avoid wearing orange or yellow suits, although these colors can be used selectively for blouses and dresses.

6.   Purple, mauve, and green are usually poor choices for business suits.

7.   A white suit can be worn during the summer as long as it does not make the wearer look too pale.

8.   Pastel shades convey a less serious image and should be avoided.

■ ■ ■ ■ ■ ■ ■ ■ ■ ■ ■ ■ ■ ■

GUIDELINES FOR CHOOSING
CLOTHING.

LEARNING TO RECEIVE AND GIVE FEEDBACK

The primary way for any manager to improve in communication ability is by learning when his or her messages are being transmitted poorly and working to overcome the breakdown. One way to do so is to solicit feedback.[7] There are a number of effective openers. For example:

> "Could you give some more information about . . . ?"
> "You've given me some things to think over. I'd welcome any other ideas you might have about. . . ."
> "I think the proposed reorganization plan is a good one. What do you think?"

Notice that in each of these opening remarks, the sender is encouraging the receiver to give feedback. The channel is being opened.

In discouraging feedback, the sender closes the channel by either threatening or belittling the receiver. In those cases the receiver is likely to say nothing. The following are illustrations:

> "Let me say straight off that there is no way that I'll go along with any recommendation other than the one that J. R. proposed yesterday."
> "While you may not be aware of all the constraints I'm working under . . . ."
> "Of course, that may be the way you see it, but let's look at the facts."

In each of these statements the sender is closing down the feedback channel. In the first example, the sender is apparently backing up a top manager and daring the receiver to argue the point. In the second, the sender seems to be saying that he or she is overworked and does not want any disagreement or argument from the receiver. In the last example, the sender appears to be labeling the receiver as stupid. Unless the receiver is looking for an argument with the manager, there is little chance that he or she will say anything in response.

Once the manager starts getting feedback, it is important to sustain the flow of information. Numerous stock phrases or statements can be used for this. Here are some of the most effective:

> "Could you tell me more about . . . ?"
> "I see."
> "Right, right. Go on."
> "I appreciate your saying that."
> "Am I going into sufficient detail?"
> "What else?"

Finally, we need to consider the subject of giving feedback. Sometimes the subordinate will not ask questions about matters that merit further discussion or explanation. At these times the effective manager needs to know how to introduce feedback into the process. Some of the best opening lines are:

■ ■ ■ ■ ■ ■ ■ ■ ■ ■ ■ ■ ■

SOLICIT COMMUNICATION
FEEDBACK.

■ ■ ■ ■ ■ ■ ■ ■ ■ ■ ■ ■ ■

SUSTAIN THE FLOW OF
INFORMATION.

■ ■ ■ ■ ■ ■ ■

[7] Nelson W. Aldrich, Jr., "Lines of Communication," *Inc.*, June 1986, pp. 140–144.

"Would you be interested in my reactions to . . . ?"

"You may be at a good point right now for me to give you some feedback on . . . ."

"I like what you did. What sets it apart is . . . ."

In each of these instances the sender (manager) has approached the feedback issue from the standpoint of the receiver (subordinate). Each comment conveys something of help or value to the receiver. For example, in the first opening, the manager is going to give reactions to some matter that apparently involved the subordinate. Note, however, that the manager did not attempt to give these reactions unsolicited. The manager asked if the subordinate would be interested in them. If the subordinate feels feedback will be of little value, he or she can say so, but the opportunity for feedback is there if the subordinate wants it. In the second and third openings, it is obvious that the subordinate is going to be given feedback that is important and, in the last case, laudatory.

These effective openers contrast significantly with ineffective openers that commonly lead the subordinate to tune out the message. Some common examples are:

"You really ought to know better than to . . . ."

"How many times do I have to tell you not to . . . ?"

"Now, Bob, you're just too critical of . . . ."

In each case the listener is not really being given feedback as much as being criticized for particular behavior. The most common response is to ignore it.

How does a manager overcome these common pitfalls and learn how to both receive and give feedback? The answer rests in analyzing one's messages and putting oneself in the receiver's shoes (empathizing).

DEVELOPING EFFECTIVE LISTENING HABITS

Listening is difficult business. Research reveals that most people speak approximately 125 words a minute but are capable of listening to over 600 words a minute. This leaves the brain a great deal of slack, which can be used for such things as daydreaming or thinking up responses to issues that the speaker raises. Instead of really listening to what the person is saying, the listener is trying to formulate a response.[8]

This is unfortunate since effective human relations is based heavily on good listening skills. For example, individuals who are poor listeners are typically also poor negotiators. As a result, they are unable to learn what the other party wants or is willing to settle for, and so they end up with a less-than-ideal settlement. Poor listeners are also ineffective in crisis situations. During this period these individuals need to gather as

----

[8]Ralph G. Nichols, "Listening, What Price Inefficiency?" *Office Executive*, April 1959, pp. 15–22.

much information as possible in determining how to handle the situation. However, they often shut out incoming signals and make decisions that are based on incomplete information.[9]

Fortunately, there are a number of things that can be done to improve one's listening skills. One is to ask questions that will help provide feedback and increase understanding. Another is to remain objective and not get upset by what the other person is saying.[10] A third is to empathize and put yourself in the other person's shoes and try to see things from that individual's point of view.[11] These suggestions are designed to encourage the listener to hear what the other person has to say and to put the information into proper perspective before saying anything. Other useful guidelines include the following:

Effective listening is an important part of effective communication. Honeywell-Bull managers have successfully introduced multi-media presentations which help improve listening skills.

1.   Do not label the speaker as either boring or uninteresting merely because you dislike his or her delivery. Listen to *what* is being said rather than *how* it is being said.

2.   Tell yourself that the speaker has something to say that will be of value or benefit to you. Give him or her a chance to communicate.

3.   If the speaker starts talking about something you find boring, ask a pertinent question to influence him toward more interesting subject matter.

4.   If the presentation becomes too technical or difficult to understand, fight the tendency to tune out the speaker by increasing your determination to listen, to learn, and to remember.

5.   Note the techniques used by the speaker to determine if you should adopt any of them yourself. Did he or she use a lot of facts? Was an emotional appeal ever employed? When? Were either of these approaches effective in presenting the message? Could you use these techniques yourself to improve your own communication skills?

■ ■ ■ ■ ■ ■ ■ ■ ■ ■ ■ ■ ■ ■
TEN WAYS TO DEVELOP EFFECTIVE COMMUNICATION.

6.   Evaluate the relevance of what is being said. Are any new or useful data being communicated that can be of value to you?

7.   Listen for intended meanings as well as for expressed ideas. Are there any hidden messages that the speaker is trying to convey?

8.   Integrate in your mind what the speaker is saying so that it all fits into a logical composite. If any information does not fit into this overall scheme, place it on the sidelines but seek to integrate it later.

9.   Be a responsive listener by maintaining eye contact with the speaker and giving him positive feedback, such as nods and facial expressions.

■ ■ ■ ■ ■ ■ ■

[9] Walter Kiechel III, "Learn How to Listen," *Fortune*, August 17, 1987, pp. 107–108.

[10] Oliver L. Niehouse, "Listening: The Other Half of Effective Communications," *Management Solutions*, August 1986, pp. 26–29.

[11] "Your Attention, Please," *Changing Times*, October 1986, pp. 127–129.

10.   Be willing to accept the challenge of effective listening by telling yourself that it is something you need to develop.[12]

Another way to improve one's listening skills is to become an active listener (see Human Relations in Action: How to Become a More Active Listener). How do you rate in terms of being a good listener? One way of finding out is by taking the accompanying Time Out quiz.

It is not always easy to follow these ten guidelines. In fact, many effective managers report that when they first decided to become better listeners they had to force themselves to follow these guidelines. Effective listening is not simply "doing what comes naturally"; for, as Preston has noted, "everyone has learned to talk, but no one has learned to listen."[13] Listening is a developed skill. This is why, in many organizations today, managers are being given effective listening courses in which they are taught how to become active listeners. In large degree, listening is starting to be regarded as partly a science (rather than totally an art) which can be improved by training and practice.

STOP!

Review your answer to the fourth question and make any changes you would like. Then compare your answer to the one below.

4.   How could this problem have been avoided?

There are a number of things that could have been done to prevent this problem. One is that Mary's boss should have followed up and ensured that some action resulted from the memo. Second, and complementary, feedback channels should have been opened up. Third, the boss should have learned more from Mary regarding her career objectives and used this to help her get her request. ■

IMPROVING YOUR WRITING SKILLS

Whenever communication is discussed, talk usually centers on reading, speaking, and listening; writing typically is given a low priority. Why is this so? Perhaps the main reason is that most managers do not write well and they hate to be reminded of it. Yet written communication is an im-

·······

[12] For more on this topic see "Listening Is a 10-Part Skill," *Nation's Business*, September 1987, p. 40.

[13] Paul Preston, *Communication for Managers* (Englewood Cliffs, N.J.: Prentice-Hall, Inc., 1979), p. 52.

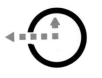

TIME OUT

ARE YOU A GOOD LISTENER?

Read the 14 statements below and rate yourself on each by using the following scale:

A = Always
B = Almost always
C = Usually
D = Sometimes
E = Rarely
F = Almost never
G = Never

1. Do you let the speaker completely express his or her ideas without interruption by you? _____

2. Do you become upset or excited when the speaker's views differ from your own? _____

3. Are you able to prevent distractions from disrupting your ability to listen? _____

4. Do you make continuous notes on everything the other person says? _____

5. Are you able to read between the lines and hear what a person is saying even when there are hidden messages being conveyed? _____

6. When you feel that the speaker or topic is boring, do you find yourself tuning out and daydreaming about other matters? _____

7. Are you able to tolerate silence by sitting quietly and allowing the speaker time to gather his or her thoughts and go on with the message? _____

8. As you listen, do you find yourself trying to pull together what the speaker is saying by thinking of what has been said and what seems to be coming? _____

9. As you listen to the speaker, do you note that person's body language and try to incorporate this into your interpretation of the message? _____

10. If you disagree with what the speaker is saying, do you provide immediate feedback by shaking your head no? _____

11. Do you move around a great deal when listening, changing your posture, crossing and recrossing your arms and/or legs, and sliding back and forth in your chair? _____

12. When you listen, do you stare intensely into the speaker's eyes and try to maintain this direct contact throughout the time the person is speaking? _____

13. When the other party is finished speaking, do you ask pointed and direct questions designed to clarify and amplify what was said? _____

14. If the speaker has been critical of you, do you try to put down that person before addressing the substantive part of the message? _____

The interpretation of your answers is at the end of the chapter.

HUMAN RELATIONS IN ACTION

HOW TO BECOME A MORE ACTIVE LISTENER

Effective listening involves more than just paying attention. It includes active, empathetic, and supportive behaviors which tell the speaker, "I understand. Please go on." This is the way an active listener behaves. However, there are four other types of listener to watch out for: directing, judgmental, probing, and smoothing. Here is a brief description of each.

The directing listener leads the speaker by guiding the limits and direction of the conversation. This individual likes to use phrases such as, "If I were you I'd . . ." and "Don't worry about it, everybody agrees that . . . ." The directing listener really does not listen; he or she takes control of the situation.

The judgmental listener introduces personal value judgments into the conversation. This individual offers advice or makes statements regarding right or wrong conduct. Some of the most common statements he might use include, "Well, you're just going to have to understand that . . ." or "You're right to say that Bill is tough to get along with because . . . ." Rather than hearing the speaker out, the judgmental listener tends to intrude his own personal values.

The probing listener asks a lot of questions in an effort to get to the heart of the matter. In the process this person attempts to satisfy his or her personal needs rather than those of the speaker. A probing listener will ask questions like, "What has this person done to you that prevents your getting along with him?" or "When did all of this start?" The probing listener tends to be inquisitive to the point of frustrating the speaker.

The smoothing listener adopts a strategy designed to reassure the speaker. The individual often says things such as, "Don't let that worry you because . . ." and "I understand exactly how you feel about . . . ." This individual believes that conflict is bad and should be avoided at all costs.

The active listener tries to encourage the speaker to express himself. This listener creates an environment in which the speaker feels free to develop his thoughts. The active listener commonly says things such as, "You sound upset about . . ." or "It seems that you are willing to go ahead and implement your ideas regarding . . . ." The active listener gives the speaker neutral summaries of what is being said. These summaries encourage the other party to continue speaking.

The most effective listener is the active listener because this person maintains the role of listener. The other four types of listeners are characterized by their attempts to influence or dominate the speaker. Work on avoiding the habits of these ineffective listeners and strive to become a more active listener.

portant part of their job as seen by the fact that managers are always writing memos, reports, evaluations, and so on.

How can you improve your own writing skills? There are a number of steps you can take. First, force yourself to write and rewrite material. If you do this long enough, your writing will become much more effective. Professional writers admit that writing is difficult work, but you can get better at it if you make yourself do it.

Second, make it a point to write at least three drafts of everything you do. The first draft is for gathering ideas. The second draft is for assuring that the material is accurate. The third draft is for polishing, making the material read smoothly and interestingly.

Third, see if you can get someone in your organization to review your written work and comment on it. There may be four or five problems that account for 90 percent of your inability to write effectively. Once you identify the problems you can correct them in your writing.

Finally, if possible, sign up for a course at a nearby college or university and force yourself to learn more effective writing skills. If this is either too time consuming or threatening, put together your own checklist of the most important things to look for in written communiqués and compare your written work with this checklist.[14]

■ ■ ■ ■ ■ ■ ■ ■ ■ ■ ■ ■ ■ ■ ■
THERE ARE A NUMBER OF USEFUL STEPS.

IMPROVING YOUR SPEAKING SKILLS

Speaking skills can also be improved. In fact, research among managers reveals that it is one of the basic shortcomings of many college graduates.[15] How can verbal skills be improved? One way is through what is called a PLAN approach.[16] The acronym, PLAN, stands for: purpose, logistics, audience, and nonverbal communication:

- Purpose—what is the reason for the presentation or speech?
- Logistics—when and where will the meeting be held?
- Audience—who will be present?
- Nonverbal communication—how can the room layout and the use of overhead transparencies and other audiovisual equipment be effectively used?

■ ■ ■ ■ ■ ■ ■

[14] For additional suggestions and practical guidelines for constructing this checklist see Gary Blake, "A Writing Report Card," *Training and Development Journal*, April 1986, pp. 49–51; Ronald E. Dulek and John S. Fielden, "How Well Do You Manage Writing?" *Business Horizons*, September–October 1986, pp. 38–42; and John S. Fielden and Ronald E. Dulek, "What Is Effective Business Writing?" *Business Horizons*, May–June 1987, pp. 62–66.

[15] Roger L. Jenkins, Richard C. Reizenstein, and F. G. Rodgers, "Report Cards on the MBA," *Harvard Business Review*, September–October 1984, pp. 20–30.

[16] Richard M. Hodgetts and Jane Whitney Gibson, "Building Effective Oral Presentations: The PLAN Approach," 1986 IEEE International Professional Communication Conference Proceedings, pp. 67–69.

FIGURE 12.9   **AN AUDIENCE ANALYSIS GRID**

| | **◄──── Friendliness Continuum ────►** | | | |
	Friendly	Neutral	Disinterested	Hostile
Resistant to Learning	(A) Show them personal profit from presentation	(B) Need a dramatic start to grab interest	(C) Stress benefit of this presentation given the fact they're there anyway	(D) Find and emphasize important benefit for them
Neutral to Learning	(E) Get them involved in the presentation	(F) Use icebreakers or humor to get their attention	(G) Get their interest fast!	(H) Concentrate on benefits of learning
Little Knowledge; Eager to Learn	(I) Pedagogy important for best results	(J) Quickly give them the facts they want	(K) Give them the facts; don't waste time trying to be friends	(L) Emphasis on education
Knowledgeable	(M) Straightforward presentation	(N) Warm them up by referring to their expertise	(O) Find a point to grab their interest	(P) Identify source of hostility and try to diffuse it

(Left axis: **Knowledge Continuum**)

Source: Richard M. Hodgetts and Jane Whitney Gibson, "Building Effective Oral Presentations: The PLAN Approach," 1986 IEEE International Professional Communication Conference Proceedings, p. 69.

These human relations considerations can greatly improve message delivery. So can a careful evaluation of the audience. Figure 12.9 provides a method for doing this. This audience analysis grid considers the friendliness of the audience and the group's knowledge and receptiveness to learning. By combining consideration of the two, an effective strategy can be formulated for delivering the message.[17]

· · · · · · ·

[17] For more on this general topic see Michael E. Cavanagh, "Making Effective Speeches," *Personnel Journal*, March 1988, pp. 51–55; and Steve Allen, *How to Make a Speech* (New York: McGraw-Hill Book Company, 1986).

SUMMARY

One of the best ways to achieve behavioral effectiveness in the work place is to communicate properly. In this chapter we review the ways in which effective communication can be attained. First we examine communication, which is the process of transmitting meanings from sender to receiver. In this process there are five essential elements: (1) the sender, (2) the message, (3) the medium, (4) the receiver, and (5) the interpretation given to the message. In conveying the message, three functions must be performed: encoding of the message, choice of a communication medium, and decoding of the message.

In an organization, communication has one of four basic directions: downward, upward, lateral, and diagonal. Each of these can play an important role in conveying messages throughout the hierarchy. However, many barriers can prevent effective communication, including perception, inference, language, and status. Perception is a person's view of reality. Since no two people have the same experiences and training, no two people see things exactly the same. For this reason there are degrees of perception, and what is crystal clear to the sender may be very vague to the receiver. Inference is an assumption made by the receiver of a message. Whenever messages are long, involved, or unspecific, there is a good chance that an inference will be made. Language is a barrier whenever two people have different meanings for the same word. Status is a problem whenever people modify messages according to who is receiving or sending them.

These barriers can lead to communication breakdown, but there are ways of overcoming them. Some of the most helpful are (1) knowing the steps in the communication process, (2) using simple, repetitive language, (3) using empathy, (4) understanding body language, (5) learning how to receive and give feedback, (6) developing effective listening habits, and (7) improving writing and speaking skills. Of these ways, the two that warrant most consideration are the first and the sixth. By knowing the steps in the communication process, it is possible for the manager to be aware of breakdowns and to work to overcome them. By being an effective listener, the manager ensures a closed loop in the communication process. The subordinate sends back a message to the manager, and the manager can use it to correct any problems that have occurred in the communication process.

KEY TERMS IN THE CHAPTER

communication process	perception
encoding	inference
decoding	attention

downward communication   **understanding**
upward communication   **acceptance**
lateral communication   **action**
diagonal communication   **empathy**
Fayol's gangplank theory   **proxemics**

REVIEW AND STUDY QUESTIONS

1. What are the five essential elements in the communication process? Explain each.

2. What is the purpose of downward communication? Upward communication? Lateral communication? Diagonal communication?

3. In what way can perception be a communication barrier?

4. What is an *inference*? In what way is it a communication barrier?

5. Is status a communication barrier? How? Explain.

6. What are the four steps in the communication process? Describe each.

7. How can empathy on the part of the manager help achieve effective communication?

8. In what way can simple, repetitive language lead to more effective communication? Explain.

9. What does a manager need to know about body language? Cite some specific examples.

10. What are some of the most effective ways of getting feedback? Giving feedback? Give some examples.

11. What are some of the important ways to develop effective listening habits? List at least six.

12. How can managers improve their writing skills? Speaking skills? Offer at least three useful suggestions for each.

SOLUTION TO THE NINE-DOT PROBLEM

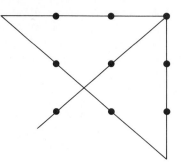

Note that you can solve the problem only by going outside the square formed by the dots.

TIME OUT ANSWERS: ANSWERS TO A MATTER OF INFERENCE

1. True—the first sentence of the story says so.
2. False—although we are never told exactly where the firm is located, we do know that it is in New England.
3. Inference—we are never told who gave Bart the order to engage in the crash R&D program.
4. Inference—we are never told the size of Bart's budget. The $250,000 he has allowed his top R&D people to spend might be coming from a special fund created for this purpose by the president of the firm and so may not be included in his regular budget.
5. Inference—we do not know what the five people are supposed to be doing with the money. They may be working to develop a new process or they may be trying to buy the process from someone else. The story is unclear on this point.
6. Inference—we do not know that the individual Mary Lou is talking to is a professor. The story refers to the person as a scientist, who may not hold a professorial rank.
7. False—the story says that Mary Lou is one of Bart's best people, so she is in the R&D department, not the plastics manufacturing department.
8. Inference—we do not know whether Mary Lou is one of the five people authorized to spend up to $250,000 or a sixth member of Bart's department.
9. Inference—we do not know that the company wants to buy the patent. Even if they do want it, they might be interested in giving the scientist stock in the firm and a position that pays about what the scientist is currently receiving but offers better fringe benefits. In short, they may want to trade for the patent, not to buy it.
10. Inference—Bart may believe this. However, he may also believe that the scientist is wavering and needs to be convinced by someone in higher authority who can spell out the terms of an agreement. Even this conclusion, however, is inferential.
11. Inference—we do not know why the scientist is coming with Mary Lou. Additionally, he or she may have decided not to accept any reimbursement of expenses so that there is no implied obligation to go along with the company's offer.
12. Inference—again, we do not know for sure why the scientist is coming to see Bart. Could it be that Mary Lou has told him or her that the firm will build a special research facility far better than that at the university and that this is motivating the scientist to fly in and talk to Bart?
13. Inference—we do not know in what area the scientist received the Nobel Prize. Nor do we know that the scientist is a man.
14. True—the story says that Bart and the president have lunch on a biweekly basis.
15. Inference—we do not know the basis for Bart's belief that he will have good news for the president. Can it be that the president assigned Bart to another project, which is coming along so well that Bart knows the president will be pleased?

ANSWER TO PHYSICAL LOCATION AND BODY LANGUAGE

You are seated in a correct chair. Individuals seated at an angle to each other are more likely to engage in cooperative interaction than are those seated either side by side or completely opposite each other. You and Person F can move closer to each other or farther away, making the corner position the ideal one for the two of you.

TIME OUT ANSWERS: INTERPRETATION OF ARE YOU A GOOD LISTENER?

Take your answer to each question and, using the scoring key below, determine the total number of points you earned.

QUESTION	**POINTS EARNED FOR ANSWER**							SCORE
	A	B	C	D	E	F	G	
1.	7	6	5	4	3	2	1	_____
2.	1	2	3	4	5	6	7	_____
3.	7	6	5	4	3	2	1	_____
4.	1	3	5	7	5	3	1	_____
5.	7	6	5	4	3	2	1	_____
6.	1	2	3	4	5	6	7	_____
7.	7	6	5	4	3	2	1	_____
8.	7	7	6	4	3	2	1	_____
9.	7	6	5	4	3	2	1	_____
10.	1	2	3	4	5	6	7	_____
11.	1	2	3	4	5	6	7	_____
12.	1	3	5	7	5	3	1	_____
13.	7	6	5	4	3	2	1	_____
14.	1	2	3	4	5	6	7	_____

Bonus point __+2__

Grand total _____

Scoring Interpretation

90–100	Excellent. You are an ideal listener.
80–89	Very good. You know a great deal about effective listening.
70–79	Good. You are an above average listener.
60–69	Average. You are typical of most listeners.
Less than 60	Below average. You need to work on developing more effective listening habits.

CASE: LOOKING TO MOVE UP

George Rather is a store manager for an eastern discount chain. When he took over the New Jersey unit a little over a year ago, the store's sales were down and employee turnover was high. However, George was not particularly concerned because he had faced situations similar to this before. He had taken a unit in Ohio and turned it into a winner, and before that he had turned around a company store in the Los Angeles area.

When George's boss asked him to take over the management of the New Jersey store, George was not pleased. "I've done more than my share of turning around unsuccessful stores," he said, "I want to move up from store manager to district manager. I've proven I can handle things at this level and I think I should be promoted." His boss agreed that George had done an excellent job at the store level. "I'm going to recommend you for the next opening that occurs at the district level. However, for the moment I need you in New Jersey."

A month ago there was an opening at the district level. Three people applied for the job. In addition to George, the manager of the largest store in the system and the manager of the store that had the greatest sales increase last year both applied. Two weeks ago top management announced its decision. The manager of the largest store was given the promotion. George was crushed. He had been certain he was going to get the job. On hearing the news, he called his boss. "I thought you said that I was going to get the next job opening at the district level. I had your word on it," he complained. His boss was embarrassed over the decision and did not hesitate to say so. However, he also pointed out that he had not guaranteed George the next promotion. "I don't have the authority to do that," he noted. "However, I did vote for you and did everything I could to help you secure the position. For what it's worth, you are a shoo-in for the next opening." George thanked him for his encouraging words and hung up.

Yesterday George announced that he would be leaving to join a competitive firm. He is to be their district manager. His boss called him up and wished him the best. "I know things didn't work out the way you and I wanted them to. I hope you find what you're looking for with your new firm."

Questions

1.   What communication barrier caused George to believe he was going to get the next promotion to district manager? Identify and describe this barrier.

2.   How could this problem have been overcome or minimized? What should George have done? What could the boss have done? Explain.

3.   What does this case illustrate about communication breakdown? Are there any lessons that can be drawn from this case? Identify and describe three. ■

CASE: GETTING PREPARED

Sandra Shelby is a training officer for a large metropolitan community. The community spends approximately $400 million a year on a variety of services including transportation, garbage collection, and police and fire protection. The training and development department has a budget of $7 million and is responsible for providing orientation to new community employees as well as on-going training to all public personnel.

Each year the board of commissioners of the community enacts a budget. Since there is a limited amount of funds, each department within the community must present and defend its budget requests. An effective presentation can result in a department getting all of the funds it requests, while a poor presentation can result in a department getting as little as 60 percent of its request.

Sandra has been chosen to make this year's presentation. The talk is to run 20 minutes followed by approximately 10 of questioning by the commissioners. In an effort to make the best possible presentation, Sandra plans on interviewing the manager and assistant manager of her department to find out which programs they feel are critical. She then intends to compare this year's proposed budget with last year's proposed budget in order to ensure that she has not left out any requests.

Sandra also knows that the six commissioners have very fixed views regarding the area of training and development. Two of the commissioners believe that the community is not spending enough money on training, two feel that too much is spent, and the remaining two tend to listen to the arguments that are made at the meeting and vote accordingly. Sandra believes that it would be wise to talk to the two commissioners who support training and development and get some information from them regarding what might be included in the report. She would also like to talk to the two who do not make up their minds until the meeting itself and see if she can find out from them some of the key facts that would influence their decision. The commissioners are easily approachable and Sandra knows she will have no trouble getting in to see the four of them.

Sandra intends to take all of this information and condense it into a 20-minute talk. She believes that the easiest way to present the information will be on a point-by-point basis. She intends to do this with the use of three overhead transparencies. "These will be easy to see and help the commissioners clearly focus on the points I want to make," she told her assistant. "In addition, I need to be prepared to answer their questions. So I am going to run through my talk with you as my only audience. When I am finished, we will critique the presentation and see how it can be strengthened. Then, after we finalize the talk, I want you to make up 20 questions that you believe they will ask me and we will discuss the proper responses."

Sandra believes that this approach will be effective in ensuring that her department gets its budget request. However, she is remaining flexible in her approach and if anyone in the department has constructive ideas, she intends to incorporate them into her presentation.

QUESTIONS

1.   In handling this assignment, how can the PLAN approach help Sandra? Explain.

2.   Could the use of Figure 12.9 be of value to Sandra? Be complete in your answer.

3.   What other things would you recommend she do in preparing for her presentation? ▪

EXPERIENCING NONVERBAL BEHAVIOR

PURPOSE

▪   To identify commonly understood gestures.

▪   To understand the importance of gestures in nonverbal communications.

PROCEDURE

1.   Students should form groups of three to five. Individuals should jot down five examples of commonly understood gestures, e.g., waving goodbye or signing "o.k."

2.   Group members take turns displaying one of their gestures for the group. Is it in fact commonly understood? For those that are not, what is the problem?

3.   When each group member has displayed his/her five gestures, make a list of all those which were considered commonly recognizable. List them from most easily recognized to least easily recognized. Make a second list of those which were confusing or unrecognizable. Share these lists with other groups.

4.   As a class, discuss these questions:
    a.   How rich a source of meaning are gestures?
    b.   How may gestures be used to complement verbal content? To contradict?
    c.   Are gestures culturally bound, i.e., would they be identically interpreted in other countries or cultures?

13

CHAPTER

THE MANAGEMENT OF CHANGE

GOALS OF THE CHAPTER

As discussed in Chapter 12, one of the most important duties of the manager for achieving behavioral effectiveness is to communicate well; however, this alone will not ensure overall effectiveness. Sometimes the manager may be able to communicate a message well but the workers will not accept it or they will resist it. One of the most common illustrations is that of change. Whenever change is introduced, for whatever reason, there is the possibility of resistance. Sometimes an organization has to introduce change if it is to remain effective. New machines may be needed in the production area, even though they will displace 20 percent of the workers, because the competition has installed similar equipment and will be able to offer better prices. In this case, there is a very strong likelihood that the workers will fight the change. Thus, sometimes what is good for the organization is not good for its members. As a result, the management of change continues to be a topic of great concern in the field of human relations. Before reading on, test yourself and see how much you know about the change process by taking the Time Out quiz on page 458.

The first goal of this chapter is to define *change* and examine how it takes place. The second goal is to answer the question, "Is resistance bad?" The third goal is to analyze human response to change, with specific consideration of rejection, resistance, tolerance, and acceptance. In particular, we study the main reasons why people choose to resist change. In the last part of the chapter we examine how to introduce and manage change properly. Our goal here is to study the dimensions of change, the steps in the change process, the importance of the time factor in introducing change, the value of participation and communication in this process, the usefulness of balance theory, and ways to remove anxiety brought about by the introduction of change. The last goal is to examine how organizational development interventions can be successfully used in the implementation of change. When you have finished reading this chapter, you should be able to:

1.   Discuss how change occurs.

2.   Explain the four most common responses to change: rejection, resistance, tolerance, and acceptance.

3.   Describe the five basic steps in the change process.

4.   Describe how balance theory can help the manager in introducing and implementing change.

5.   Tell why removal of anxieties is so important in the management of change.

6.   Explain how OD interventions can be effectively employed in dealing with change.

OPENING CASE

WORK, WORK, WORK

Hallbauer Insurance is a large dental insurer. Over the last five years dental insurance has become very popular, and Hallbauer is regarded as one of the leading firms in this field. The company insures 23 of the nation's largest 100 industrials and has been expanding at the rate of 21 percent a year for each of the last six years.

Three months ago Hallbauer landed a series of new contracts with four major conglomerates. The amount of work needed to get these contracts processed and on-line is very great. The company has announced that effective immediately everyone will be required to work two hours overtime every day plus all day Saturday. Those wishing to work on Sunday will be paid double time or in the case of managers, be given equivalent cash bonuses. This arrangement will stay in effect for two months, after which the new contracts should be on-line.

This news was not well received by the personnel. Most of them feel they are already being overworked, and they are now being pressured into working both longer hours and a longer work week. As a result, the error rate in claims processing has doubled and both tardiness and absenteeism are now at record levels throughout the firm.

In dealing with the problem, the company has brought in a group of consultants. After two days, they concluded that there were serious morale and other human relations problems and suggested that the company agree to letting them collect and analyze information related to the problem. The consultants would like to distribute a questionnaire to everyone in the firm to get feedback on those problems that are having the biggest negative impact. "We can then develop a plan of action for dealing with the situation," the head of the consulting team told Hallbauer's president. The president thinks that this might be a good idea, but he first wants to talk to some of the members of the board of directors as well as senior-level executives. He has promised to get back to the consultants with an answer by the end of next week.

1.   What response was made by the personnel to the announcement of the new work schedules?

2.   Why was this response made by the personnel?

3.   How can this situation be explained in terms of balance theory?

4.   What type of OD intervention are the consultants considering? Is this a wise choice? Explain.

Write down your answers to these questions and put them aside. We will return to them later. ∎

THE NATURE OF CHANGE

Any modification or alteration of the status quo is **change**. Sometimes change results in resistance from those who are encountering it. Before examining the importance of change in the field of human relations let us look at the nature of change by studying how it occurs and by answering the question, "Is resistance to change always a bad thing?"

CHANGE IS ANY MODIFICATION OF THE STATUS QUO.

HOW CHANGE OCCURS

When change takes place, three things happen: (1) there is a movement from one set of conditions to another; (2) some force(s) causes the change to come about; and (3) a consequence results from the change. The consequence is an alteration in the way things are now done. For example, in order to keep better track of inmates in prisons and to ensure that the wrong person is not accidentally released or transferred to another cell block, some prisons have introduced "eyedentity" technology. A high-technology machine takes a photo of an inmate's eye and since no two people have the same eye configuration, the machine can identify each prisoner individually. Befores someone is moved to another cell block or transferred out of the facilities, the individual is required to look into the machine, and have his "eyedentity" determined. The introduction of this new technology has dramatically improved the ability of prisons to keep

TIME OUT

HOW MUCH DO YOU KNOW ABOUT THE CHANGE PROCESS?

Before studying the management of change, take a minute to examine how well you understand the change process. Presented below are a dozen statements that relate to change. Read each carefully and then check whether it is basically true or basically false. Answers are given at the end of the chapter.

	BASICALLY TRUE	BASICALLY FALSE
1. Because change is so much a part of everyday life, most modern workers like new work procedures and policies.	_____	_____
2. Most work changes lead to an immediate increase in productivity.	_____	_____
3. Many employees like the status quo; change scares them.	_____	_____
4. If a computer designed to help them do their work were available, most employees would try to learn how to use the machine as quickly as possible.	_____	_____
5. Most organizational changes that are introduced are truly designed to increase efficiency.	_____	_____
6. If their friends at work are opposed to a change, most workers will also oppose the change.	_____	_____
7. Most people who resist change do so because they enjoy giving the organization a hard time.	_____	_____
8. People prefer to be told about new changes just before they are to be implemented.	_____	_____
9. People tend to be more supportive of changes they helped fashion than of those forced upon them.	_____	_____
10. Most managers tend to overrate the time needed to implement changes effectively.	_____	_____
11. Change always results, if only in the short run, in an increase in work output.	_____	_____
12. Unions tend to reject new work changes.	_____	_____

track of their inmates. This is an excellent example of change that is quickly accepted by the organizational personnel because it helps them do their jobs more efficiently. However, not all change is quickly accepted. Sometimes there is resistance.

A good example is provided by many forms of work-related technology. The introduction of microcomputers often frightens the personnel because they believe the machines will require them to do more work or will be used to replace them. The same is true for other types of machinery from production equipment to facsimile machines. Another major reason for resistance is that the personnel do not know how to use the technology or do not understand its value to them. Many people have found it difficult to learn computer operations, and each time they make a mistake they become more defeated. (Many students who now use the micro for writing term papers can remember their own early problems in using the computer. One of the most common "horror stories" typically involves a time when they accidentally erased material or failed to save their work and had to rewrite part of a paper.) As long as people do not know how to use the new technology, there is likely to be resistance.

IS RESISTANCE BAD?

Some people believe that resistance to change is inevitable. In many cases, this is true, for when organization employees weigh the benefits associated with the status quo against those they believe will result from the change, they opt for things the way they are. As a result, they resist alteration of the status quo.

Such resistance is not necessarily bad. There are several important functions served by it. First, resistance forces those supporting the change to build a case against the status quo, thereby providing management a chance to weigh the pros and cons. Here is an example.

■ ■ ■ ■ ■ ■ ■ ■ ■ ■ ■ ■ ■ ■
RESISTANCE IS NOT ALWAYS BAD.

> The Almuth Public Library is one of the largest in the city with over 700,000 volumes. Six months ago the city council voted the necessary funds to computerize the library. Many of the staff were delighted with the news but some opposed computerization, claiming that it would be very difficult to implement and would make exorbitant demands on their time. However, after a general meeting in which both sides had the opportunity to air their concerns, it was agreed that everyone would work together to implement the computerization. After the meeting, one of the employees, who initially had opposed the move, said, "After hearing the pros and cons, I realize that computerization would not increase our workload or threaten our jobs. So now I'm all for it."

A second benefit of resistance to change is that it encourages the organization to look before it leaps. This is particularly important when the change will be expensive to implement and, if wrong, could mean major problems for the enterprise.

In dealing with resistance and ensuring that change is properly implemented, the first place to begin is with careful planning. This involves consideration of three issues: (1) whether there should be a change; (2) if so, what type of change is needed; and (3) how the change should be implemented.

Technological advances recently brought computer conversions to Comerica Incorporated. The changes required that 75 percent of its work force be trained in new skills.

CHANGE AND THE EMPLOYEES

In many cases, change is good for the entire organization. For example, many technological innovations from computers to portable telephones to fax machines are making it easier and cheaper to communicate information. On the other hand, this does not mean that the personnel will go along with the change. There are many different responses to change. Some are a result of rational reasoning; others can be a result of unjustified concerns or biases that are brought about by fear, prejudice, or lack of trust. Whatever the reason, it is important to realize that the response to change can take numerous forms.

RESPONSES TO CHANGE

People's reactions to change will depend on the benefits they think will result from it. If they believe they will profit from the change, they will support it; if they feel they will lose status, prestige, earning power, or the job itself because of change, they will fight it. If we think of change as a stimulus, numerous responses can be made by the personnel, with varied outcomes and effects on the organization. For example, in Figure 13.1, eight workers are being subjected to the same change. As you can

■ ■ ■ ■ ■ ■ ■ ■ ■ ■ ■ ■ ■ ■
RESPONSE TO CHANGE IS OFTEN VARIED.

see, there are many responses: increase in absenteeism, resignation, working harder than ever, slowing down, arguing with boss, and so on. Overall, however, there is a negative effect on the organization. In this case, we may conclude that most of the workers do not like the change or that it was not properly introduced.

In examining the situation further, we need to take a closer look at the stimulus (change) and response (outcome) relationship. We can view the change or stimulus as a **causal variable**, and the response or outcome as an **end-result variable**. For human relations purposes, however, we need to investigate why different people respond in different ways to the same stimulus.

Some psychologists believe the answer can be found in the individual's attitude toward the stimulus. A person's attitude is a reflection of psychological factors, personal factors, and social factors. These factors will result in a particular evaluation of the change. In turn, the evaluation will lead to one of the four reactions: rejection, resistance, tolerance, or acceptance (Figure 13.2).

■ ■ ■ ■ ■ ■ ■ ■ ■ ■ ■ ■ ■ ■
REACTION TO STRESS IS A DETERMINANT.

One of the most important psychological factors affecting attitudes is the individual's reaction to stress, a topic discussed earlier in the text. Some workers are rather comfortable under stressful or high-anxiety-producing conditions, but other employees shun stress and seek a calm environment.

■ ■ ■ ■ ■ ■ ■ ■ ■ ■ ■ ■ ■ ■
SO IS PERSONAL EXPERIENCE.

One of the most important personal factors is experience; people who have encountered similar changes in the past draw on the results of

FIGURE 13.1   STIMULUS-RESPONSE-OUTCOME-EFFECT BROUGHT ON BY CHANGE

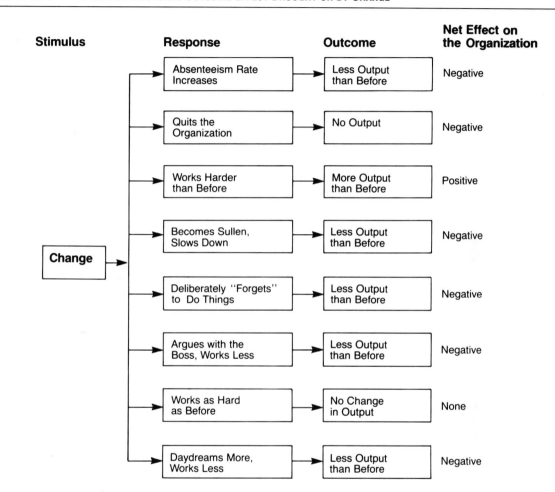

those changes to evaluate the current or pending change. For example, if the last time a company changed work procedures it tried to increase output requirements by 15 percent, the workers will probably fight the management's new attempt to change work procedures again. They are likely to believe that if they give in, the management will once more increase output requirements. Conversely, we can take the example of the organization that introduced a new hospitalization plan to save the employees money; the next time the company announces a change in the hospitalization plan, there is likely to be warm support for the move because the employees had a good experience with a similar change.

FIGURE 13.2   **ANALYSIS OF RESPONSE TO CHANGE**

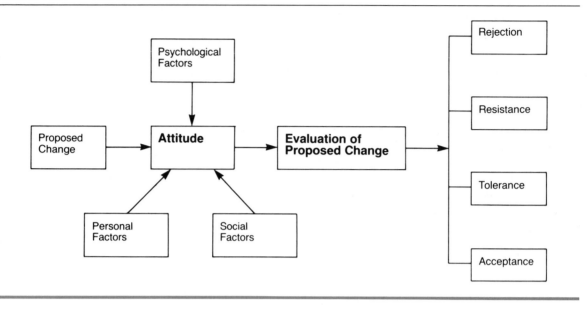

AND THE NORM OF THE WORK GROUP.

The social factors refer to the group in which the individual works. If there is a great deal of cohesion in the group, all the members will tend to stick together. If the proposed change conflicts with the norms and values of the informal group, it will not go along with management's attempt to introduce change. Conversely, if the change is supportive of its norms and values, the group will accept the change. Keep in mind that when we talk about group acceptance, one of the primary norms is always group unity. If the management makes any reorganizational changes that will break up the group, the members will oppose plans.

As a result of psychological, personal, and social factors, an employee will form an attitude regarding the change. This attitude will assist him or her in evaluating the impact of the change to determine whether it is acceptable. On the basis of this evaluation, the employee will reject, resist, tolerate, or accept the proposed change.

REJECTION CAN LEAD THE WORKERS TO QUIT.

REJECTION   When the change is perceived as potentially destructive **rejection** occurs. Those being subjected to the change view it as totally unacceptable. In this case, it is not uncommon to find workers resigning their jobs or going on strike. At best, management can expect to encounter increased turnover, alienation, and dramatic reductions in productivity and job satisfaction.

RESISTANCE   Whenever workers feel threatened by or extremely anxious about a particular change, they are likely to resist. The resistance can be either overt or covert. **Overt resistance** is observable; management can see it. Work slowdown, the setting of lower informal production norms, and outright sabotage are examples. **Covert resistance** is not readily observable because it is done under the guise of working as usual. For example, the management has brought in a group of consultants to study operations and make efficiency recommendations. The work force is concerned that some of them will lose their jobs or will be transferred to other departments. In an effort to thwart the consultants' efforts, the workers use veiled resistance. When the consultants ask for some data on a particular topic, a worker hands them a massive report containing the information. However, it will take two or three hours to find the material. In short, the workers are not refusing to go along; they are simply making it more difficult for the consultants to do their job.

WHEN WORKERS FEEL THREATENED, RESISTANCE IS LIKELY.

OVERT RESISTANCE IS OBSERVABLE.

COVERT RESISTANCE IS NOT READILY OBSERVABLE.

TOLERANCE   If the workers are neutral about the change or have equal positive and negative feelings, they will have **tolerance** for the change. For example, management decides that in the future all people who work in Section D must wear safety equipment when they are in the work area. Because of the particularly high noise factor created by the machinery there, management wants every worker to wear plastic earmuffs that will screen out the noise and prevent damage to hearing. Many of the workers admit that they are not particularly anxious to wear the earmuffs, but they can understand management's point of view, so they will go along with management's request. They have no particularly strong feelings either way.

IF WORKERS FEEL NEUTRAL, THEY WILL OFTEN TOLERATE CHANGE.

ACCEPTANCE   Sometimes the positive factors favoring the change are weighed much more heavily than the negative ones. In these cases the workers' **acceptance** of the change is likely. For example, instead of asking the workers to wear regular plastic earmuffs, the management has a set specially wired for each person. Through the set music can be piped so that workers can listen to music and do their jobs at the same time. Changes like this have been widely accepted in many industrial settings. Printing companies, especially large newspaper firms, often give this kind of earmuff to their pressmen, who, according to research, like the changed environment.

IF THE CHANGE IS VIEWED POSITIVELY, IT WILL BE ACCEPTED.

Muzak's studies indicate that worker productivity usually reaches its low point in midmorning and midafternoon and picks up just before people go to lunch or leave for the day. To boost productivity when the "blahs" set in, Muzak pipes in music. Is this approach really beneficial to productivity? "Bing" Muscio, president of Muzak, seems to think so. He claims that music has definite physiological and psychological effects on people. "It affects," he said, "the heartbeat and blood pressure, and moderates tenseness and anxiety." And an AT&T division manager agrees, pointing out that telephone operators report they are more relaxed with music by Muzak than they were prior to its installation. There are many other companies using Muzak's services, including Black & Decker and American Machine & Foundry Inc., who support these findings.[1]

STOP!

Review your answer to the first question and make any changes you would like. Then compare your answer to the one below.

1.   What response was made by the personnel to the announcement of the new work schedules?

The personnel resisted the efforts of management to make them work longer hours and work weeks. This is obvious from the increases in errors, tardiness, and absenteeism. ■

WHY IS THERE RESISTANCE TO CHANGE?

In most cases, workers do not reject change outright nor do they accept it. Rather they tend either to resist it or tolerate it. In our study of human relations, resistance is the reaction of greatest interest to us. After all, if the workers tolerate a particular change, there is really nothing for the manager to be concerned about. However, if they resist, the manager should find out why and then should determine how this resistance can be reduced or eliminated. Let us discuss in detail the most common causes of resistance to change.

MACHINERY MAY REPLACE PEOPLE.

OBSOLESCENCE OF JOB SKILLS   A bookkeeper who has worked for the same company for 20 years and learns that bookkeeping functions are going to be transferred to a computer will fight the change. An assembly-line welder who learns that the company has just bought automatic weld-

[1] Richard M. Hodgetts, *Management: Theory, Process, and Practice,* 2nd ed. (Philadelphia: W. B. Saunders, 1979), p. 18.

ing machinery that will weld things faster and more efficiently than can be done by hand will oppose the change. Additionally, while organizations will attempt to find these people other positions in the firm, the meaningful alternative jobs require special training that the displaced workers lack. These people have been on the job for so long doing the same thing day after day that their knowledge about other work is obsolete. Also, they do not qualify for the jobs being given to college-educated engineers and business specialists. In short, they have no real marketable skills, so they fight for the status quo.

FEAR OF ECONOMIC LOSS   Another reason for resistance to change is fear of economic loss. Sometimes workers are replaced or fired or find themselves in dead-end jobs. Technology often plays a key role here, turning rather demanding jobs into simple ones that can be done by anyone. When this occurs, the lower demands of the job are often reflected by a new pay rate, and the people now find that salary raises are much less than before. After all, who needs highly paid people if the job is automated so anyone can do it?

THE WORKERS MAY LOSE MONEY.

EGO DEFENSIVENESS   Sometimes a change will make a person look bad, so he or she will fight it. For example, Roberta has an idea for expanding the market effort out of the eastern part of the country and into the western states. If things go well there, the effort will then be expanded to the national market. However, her boss, Chuck, is reluctant to go along with her suggestion because it will make him look bad with his colleagues, who will all realize that Roberta was the one who thought up the new sales effort. Rather than allow this to happen, Chuck continually claims that he needs to develop the market in the east more fully before considering expansion.

OR THE CHANGE MAY BE EGO-DEFLATING.

THE COMFORT OF THE STATUS QUO   To put it simply, change is disturbing to many people. They feel more comfortable working in established routines and procedures than taking risks by entering into new ventures or undertakings. Any attempt to alter this status quo is met with resistance.

MANY PEOPLE LIKE ROUTINE.

SHORTSIGHTEDNESS   Many people know what is going to happen in the short run but not the long run. Therefore, they only look at the short-run effects of any change. We can illustrate this through an analysis of the impacts of autocratic and democratic-participative leadership. In the short run, if a manager changes from autocratic to participative

THE LONG RUN SCARES THEM.

FIGURE 13.3   **FROM AUTOCRATIC LEADERSHIP TO PARTICIPATIVE LEADERSHIP—AN ILLUSTRATION**

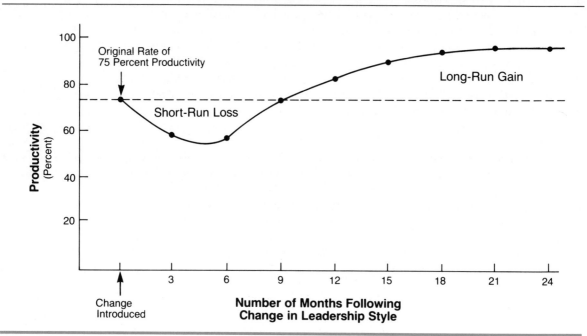

leadership, his or her department will often suffer short-term decreases in productivity (Figure 13.3). This will not last indefinitely, however; long-term increases will eventually follow. Research reveals that it takes time for such a change to bring about increased productivity. Unfortunately, many managers are not interested in riding out the short-run declines in order to reap long-run benefits and so are not interested in changing their leadership style.

■ ■ ■ ■ ■ ■ ■ ■ ■ ■ ■ ■ ■ ■   **PEER PRESSURE**   Many times people refuse to accept change because
THEIR PEERS OPPOSE THE CHANGE.   their peers are unwilling to go along with it. Remember, as noted in the discussion of group cohesiveness, if there is high cohesion, the group will stay together. If change is introduced, therefore, the group may collectively agree to resist it.

■ ■ ■ ■ ■ ■ ■ ■ ■ ■ ■ ■ ■ ■   **LACK OF INFORMATION**   Whenever people do not know what is going
THEY DO NOT FULLY UNDER-   to happen, they are likely to resist the change. The unknown scares
STAND IT.   them. Consider how you would feel if a doctor told you that you were very sick and had to have an immediate operation. Not knowing what is

wrong with you, what kind of operation you need, or what the effect of the operation will be, you would probably be very nervous, and unless you were convinced that the operation was indeed warranted, you would resist the doctor's advice.

SOCIAL DISPLACEMENT   Whenever changes are introduced, it is possible that work groups will be broken up and social relationships will be disturbed. People usually enjoy working with their fellow employees, and when these friendships are interrupted, a psychological letdown occurs. Research shows that in combat situations soldiers often fight the tendency to make friends among the other members of their platoon, because if one is killed or injured, the effect on the others can be disastrous. They would not be totally prepared to do their jobs and could be injured or killed themselves. When social relationships have been developed, people tend to want to maintain them and to fight social displacement.

> SOCIAL RELATIONSHIPS MAY BE DISTURBED.

STOP!

Review your answer to the second question and make any changes you would like. Then compare your answer to the one below.

2.   Why was this response made by the personnel?

There are a number of reasons for this response. One is that the workers are comfortable with the status quo. They feel they are already being worked hard enough and they do not want more work. A second is that they are shortsighted in that this work schedule will undoubtedly last only until the new contracts are on-line two months from now. ∎

INTRODUCING AND MANAGING CHANGE PROPERLY

Until now, we have been discussing how people respond to change and why they often resist it. Now we consider how the manager should introduce and manage change properly. Admittedly, change causes problems, but if the manager analyzes the situation properly, follows some basic steps, and remains aware of the important areas of implementation, he or she can effect many changes to the benefit of both the personnel and the organization. In particular, the manager needs to (1) understand the three dimensions of change, (2) know the basic steps in the change process, (3) consider the time factor, (4) be aware of the importance of par-

FIGURE 13.4   **DIMENSIONS OF CHANGE**

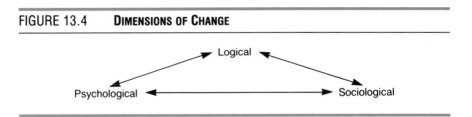

ticipation and communication, (5) know the impact of management attitudes on change response and the value of balance theory in this process, and (6) be aware of the need to remove anxieties both before and after the change is introduced.

THE DIMENSIONS OF CHANGE

The first things a manager must know are the three **dimensions of change**. (See Figure 13.4.)

IS THE CHANGE NEEDED?

First there is the *logical dimension*, which is based on technological and scientific reasons. Why is the change needed, from an organizational standpoint? The logical answer is found in responses such as increases in profit, productivity, or efficiency, and decreases in cost, worker fatigue, monotony, or machine down time.

IS IT IN ACCORD WITH WORKER VALUES?

Then there is the *psychological dimension*, the logic of the change in terms of the workers who would be affected. Do these people feel the change will be good for them? Is it in line with their values? If the answer is affirmative, the psychological dimension has been satisfied.

IS IT CONSISTENT WITH GROUP NORMS?

Finally there is the *sociological dimension*, which refers to the logic of the change in terms of the work group. Will the change be consistent with the norms of the group? Will it help maintain teamwork? Will the group members be able to live with it?

Unless the manager considers all three of these dimensions, implementation of the change will be less than ideal.

THE BASIC STEPS IN CHANGE

If the three dimensions of change have all been adequately considered, attention can then be focused on the basic steps in change. There are five basic steps in securing effective change, and each is vital to maximum effectiveness.

WEIGH THE BENEFITS AND COSTS.

First, the manager must answer the question, "Is this change *really* necessary?" The benefits and costs must be weighed. If the manager has examined the dimensions of change we have discussed, the answer to this question must be affirmative before further consideration of the change process is undertaken.

Second, the manager must consider whether the proposed change is the right one. In many cases there are alternative changes, any one of which might accomplish the desired result. The manager must choose the one that will provide the best results for both the organization and the personnel.

■ ■ ■ ■ ■ ■ ■ ■ ■ ■ ■ ■ ■
EXAMINE ALTERNATIVE CHANGES.

Third, and often most important, the impact of the change must be evaluated. What will be the effect of the change in the short run? In the long run? These may be difficult questions to answer, but the manager should attempt some investigation in order to compare the impact of various proposed changes.

■ ■ ■ ■ ■ ■ ■ ■ ■ ■ ■ ■ ■
EVALUATE THE FULL IMPACT.

Fourth, the manager must work to secure acceptance of the change. In this case, workers most directly affected by the change hold the key to success. Their anxieties and fears must be calmed if the company hopes to effect a successful change. Some of the steps for doing this are dealt with in the discussion of the importance of increasing the forces pushing for change, decreasing those pushing against the change, or both.

■ ■ ■ ■ ■ ■ ■ ■ ■ ■ ■ ■ ■
GET WORKER ACCEPTANCE.

Fifth, there must be some follow-up. After the change is implemented the manager has to obtain information on how well things are going. Has the change been accepted and implemented properly? More importantly, is it doing what was desired or was it a waste of time?

■ ■ ■ ■ ■ ■ ■ ■ ■ ■ ■ ■ ■
FOLLOW UP AND EVALUATE
THE OUTCOME.

CONSIDERING THE TIME FACTOR

Another crucial issue in the implementation of change is the time factor. There is a general rule of change: the greater the degree of change, the more advance notice the company must give. If the organization plans on building a new warehouse across the street and moving some of the warehouse personnel to this facility, a one-month notice may be appropriate. However, if the company plans on establishing a new branch office 500 miles away, it may be necessary to give at least six months' notice to the employees who will be transferred there. They have to sell their homes, find new ones, move their families, and locate schools and other services (doctor, accountant, lawyer) that they will need in order to settle into a comfortable life in the new location.

■ ■ ■ ■ ■ ■ ■ ■ ■ ■ ■ ■ ■
GIVE ADVANCE NOTICE OF CHANGE.

Research shows that most managers tend to underrate the time needed to implement change effectively. In many cases managers believe that they communicate change in advance, but subordinates report that this is not the case. Additionally, while the problem exists at the upper levels of the organization, it is also present at the lower levels of the hierarchy, and the lower the level of the organization, the more the problem is magnified. In Likert's survey, for example, as shown in Table 13.1, 100 percent of the top staff said that they always or nearly always told their

TABLE 13.1   EXTENT TO WHICH SUPERIORS AND SUBORDINATES AGREE
ABOUT WHETHER SUPERIORS TELL SUBORDINATES IN ADVANCE
ABOUT CHANGES

HOW OFTEN SUPERIORS TELL SUBORDINATES IN ADVANCE ABOUT CHANGES AFFECTING THEM OR THEIR WORK	TOP STAFF SAYS ABOUT ITS OWN BEHAVIOR (PERCENT)	FOREMEN SAY ABOUT TOP STAFF'S BEHAVIOR (PERCENT)	FOREMEN SAY ABOUT THEIR OWN BEHAVIOR (PERCENT)	WORKERS SAY ABOUT FOREMEN'S BEHAVIOR (PERCENT)
Always	70	27	40	22
Nearly always	30	36	52	25
Always or nearly always (total)	*100*	*63*	*92*	*47*
More often than not		18	2	13
Occasionally		15	5	28
Seldom		4	1	12

Source: Adapted from Rensis Likert, *New Patterns of Management* (New York: McGraw-Hill Book Company, 1961), p. 52. Reprinted with permission.

subordinates in advance about work changes, but only 63 percent of the foremen agreed. However, when asked the same question, 92 percent of the foremen said they always or nearly always told subordinates in advance about work changes, but only 47 percent of the workers agreed. Unless managers are aware of statistics such as these, they are likely to fall into the trap of believing that their workers are both aware of and in agreement with the impending change.

PARTICIPATION AND COMMUNICATION

ALLOW EMPLOYEE PARTICIPATION.

Participation is important in the change process because, as we know from research, people will be more supportive of changes that they helped bring about than of changes that were either assigned to them or forced upon them. Additionally, if some problem occurs with implementation of a change they have assisted with, the workers will help eliminate or work around the problem. However, if they have had no input regarding the change, they will sit on the sidelines and let management figure out how to solve the problem.

Research also reveals that although many managers believe they involve their people in the change process, workers do not think so. Table 13.2 supplies statistics gathered by Likert about whether or not superiors use their subordinates' ideas and opinions in solving job problems. As you can see, 70 percent of the top staff said that they always or almost always consult their subordinates, but only 52 percent of the foremen agreed. Likewise, although 73 percent of the foremen said that they practice a participative approach, only 16 percent of the workers agreed.

Much of the problem rests with the different ways managers and workers perceive the managers' actions. Sometimes the workers do not regard attempts by the manager to get them involved as inviting participation. At other times, the workers may give the manager a suggestion for a change that will increase productivity, and after thinking over the matter, the manager will decide to go ahead and implement it. Because the manager gives them no feedback, the workers are unaware that they generated the idea, and they tend to believe that the management is forcing the change on them.

We can make another rule of change on the basis of these statistics: never surprise the subordinates with a change; always give them plenty of notice of what you are doing and keep them informed as you go along. This is where communication comes into the picture.

Let us examine an example involving both participation and communication to see how things can get fouled up if the manager does not keep everyone informed about what is going on.

Allowing the work force to participate in planned changes increases acceptance. When Chrysler Corporation introduced robots to its assembly lines, its technicians were actively involved in the conversion.

> On Friday afternoon, the plant manager told Fred that he would be getting new machinery in his department. Fred had been after the top management to buy this machinery for almost a year. Now he was informed that the machines would be arriving the first thing Monday morning.
>
> In order to have room for the new equipment, however, the old machines would have to be dismantled, packaged, and moved off the floor. They were to be sold, the plant manager told Fred, to a firm in another part of the country.
>
> The good news was a big surprise to Fred and he was delighted. He hurried down to the plant floor and told his people to start dismantling the old machinery. However, he did *not* tell them why they were doing this. Fred decided to let them enjoy the surprise on Monday morning.

TABLE 13.2   **THE EXTENT TO WHICH SUPERIORS AND SUBORDINATES AGREE ABOUT WHETHER SUPERIORS USE SUBORDINATES' IDEAS AND OPINIONS IN SOLVING JOB PROBLEMS**

HOW OFTEN SUPERIORS USE SUBORDINATES' IDEAS AND OPINIONS IN SOLVING JOB PROBLEMS	TOP STAFF SAYS ABOUT ITS OWN BEHAVIOR (PERCENT)	FOREMEN SAY ABOUT TOP STAFF'S BEHAVIOR (PERCENT)	FOREMEN SAY ABOUT THEIR OWN BEHAVIOR (PERCENT)	WORKERS SAY ABOUT FOREMEN'S BEHAVIOR (PERCENT)
Always	70	52	73	16
Often	25	17	23	23
Sometimes or seldom	5	31	4	61

Source: Adapted from Rensis Likert, *New Patterns of Management* (New York: McGraw-Hill Book Company, 1961), p. 53. Reprinted with permission.

However, things did not go according to Fred's plan. As soon as he reached his desk on Monday, he received a call from the plant manager telling him that the Personnel Department had called and said that six of the fifteen workers in Fred's department had quit and three more had called in sick. Fred promised to get the matter straightened out.

He immediately called one of the workers who had resigned. "George, this is Fred. I was just talking to the plant manager and he tells me you're quitting. Why?"

"Listen, Fred," George answered. "I'm not going to sit around waiting to be fired. I spent all day yesterday looking through the want ads and there are plenty of jobs available for machinists. I have an interview in about an hour with another firm."

"But why do you want to quit?" Fred exclaimed. "What makes you think you'll be fired?"

"Are you kidding? Why were we dismantling those machines and packaging them, if the firm weren't getting ready to lay us off? There's nothing left for us to do. I know someone's getting ready to lower the ax on me."

"But that's not it at all, George! We have new machines coming in to replace those old ones. That's why we were packaging the old ones and shipping them out. We were making room for the new ones. I didn't tell you about the new machines because I wanted to surprise you," Fred explained.

"Well, you sure surprised me!" George promised to cancel his interview and come to work.

Fred spent the next hour calling the rest of the men and explaining the situation. By noon all of them were back in the plant helping assemble the new machinery.

Remember the discussion in Chapter 5 of the informal organization? People who work near each other tend to be on the same grapevine, and when there is incomplete information about something, they begin to construct rumors to explain the situation. They will give the matter their own interpretation rather than live with uncertainty or ambiguity. This is what happened in Fred's department. However, with participation and communication, the manager can overcome these dysfunctional results.

Another good example is provided in Human Relations in Action: The Japanese Way, which shows that one of the primary reasons for the success of Japanese firms in the United States is their ability to promote participation and communication in the change process.

HUMAN RELATIONS IN ACTION

THE JAPANESE WAY

Manufacturing plants opened by the Japanese in the United States have proven to be some of the most productive in the industry. Why? One of the primary answers is that the Japanese know how to use participative management and communication in introducing and managing change. Some of the basic principles that Japanese firms use are the following:

1.   Japanese managers identify closely with the workers and spend a great deal of time interacting with them. This allows the managers to understand the workers' concerns and needs better and when change is introduced, the managers have excellent insights regarding how the change will be perceived and what types of barriers will have to be overcome.

2.   Japanese firms get the workers actively involved in the change process. By getting employee ideas and opinions, management learns the concerns and fears of the personnel and can then develop an effective strategy for dealing with them.

3.   In dealing with change, Japanese managers carefully examine what needs to be done and what problems are likely to result. They spend much more time analyzing the situation than do their American counterparts. This has led some observers to note that Japanese managers follow the cliche "Don't do something . . . stand there!" which is the direct opposite of the way American managers do things. As a result, although formulation of a change may take a great deal of time, implementation often proceeds smoothly.

4.   If something does go wrong, management does not blame the workers. It blames the system. There must have been an error in the way the change was handled. Management did not do its job properly.

5.   Japanese firms use much flatter organizational structures than do American firms. This reduces bureaucratic red tape and encourages open communication on the part of the personnel.

Source: Robert R. Rehder, "Japanese Transplants: A New Model for Detroit," *Business Horizons*, January–February 1988, pp. 52–61; and Stephen C. Harper, "Now that the Dust Has Settled: Learning from Japanese Management," *Business Horizons*, July–August 1988, pp. 43–51.

MANAGEMENT ATTITUDES AND BALANCE THEORY

When it comes to change, very few things will get the manager in more trouble than having a negative personal attitude toward the change. If the manager does not agree with the proposed change ordered by the boss, he or she should voice opposition as soon as the order is issued. However, if the company is determined to implement the change, the

■ ■ ■ ■ ■ ■ ■ ■ ■ ■ ■ ■ ■ ■
HAVE MANAGEMENT SUPPORT FOR THE CHANGE.

manager's job is to help do so. If the proposed change conflicts with the manager's values or morals, he or she should transfer to another department or resign. In introducing the change to the workers, the manager cannot take the stance, "This is the proposed change. I personally disagree with it, and wouldn't blame you if you did, too. However, they told me to implement it, so I'm going to have to do just that." The manager should have a positive attitude toward the change at all times. Additionally, he or she should find out *why* the change can be beneficial to the workers and should use these positive features as selling points to obtain worker acceptance.

■ ■ ■ ■ ■ ■ ■ ■ ■ ■ ■ ■ ■ ■
IN BALANCE THEORY, THERE ARE THREE CRITICAL ELEMENTS.

One way of looking at management attitudes toward change and the strategy that can be used in bringing it about is through **balance theory**. In balance theory terms, change has three critical elements: (1) the manager, (2) the worker, and (3) the proposed change. A balance is needed among all three.

Let us examine Figure 13.5, a simple illustration of balance theory in action in which the relationship among the elements is positive. The manager has a positive attitude toward the change, the worker has a positive attitude toward the manager, and the worker has a positive attitude toward the change. We have a balanced triad.

The triad will be unbalanced whenever there are two pluses and a minus. Figure 13.6 provides an illustration. In this case the manager is positive toward the change, the worker is negative toward the change, and the worker is positive toward the manager. How can the balance be restored? There are only two ways: either the worker's attitude toward the change must become positive or the worker's attitude toward the manager must become negative. What should the manager do? Obviously, if the worker has a positive attitude toward the manager, the manager should try to get the worker to change his or her attitude toward the change. The manager should point out why he or she is person-

FIGURE 13.5   **A BALANCED TRIAD**

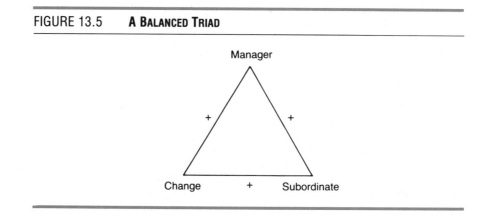

FIGURE 13.6   **AN UNBALANCED TRIAD**

ally in favor of the change. Now the worker has two options. He or she can say, "I like and respect you, and if the change is agreeable to you, it's okay with me." Then we have three pluses in the triad and balance is established. On the other hand, the worker may say, "I disagree with you. The change is a bad idea. I will not alter my attitude toward it." How can the worker have a positive attitude toward the manager and still disagree with the manager's point of view? The worker cannot do so, at least in the long run. So he or she will begin to reason, "The manager is not my friend. All he wants to do is manipulate me into accepting the change. I'm not going to do it, and I'm not going to trust him either." In this case we have two minuses and a plus. The manager has a positive attitude toward the change, and the worker has a negative attitude toward both the change and the manager. There is balance. However, it is the *wrong* kind. In short, the manager in this case must try to alter the worker's attitude toward the change. Otherwise we have a balanced triad that is anti-change. The only acceptable solution to this problem in balance theory terms is three pluses.

Let us take a last illustration, this time involving a manager who does *not* like the change. The situation is depicted in Figure 13.7. As you can see, the manager has a negative attitude toward the change, the worker has a positive attitude toward the manager, and the worker has a negative attitude toward the change. Here we have a balanced triad (two minuses and a plus), but it is a dangerous balance. The worker and manager like each other and both dislike the change. The only way to establish a different balance in the triad is for the manager's boss to convince him to be positive toward the change. If this does occur, of course, we will have (at least for the moment) an unbalanced triad. The manager will like the change, and the worker will like the manager and dislike the change. The situation can now be rectified if the manager shows the

FIGURE 13.7   **A BALANCED TRIAD**

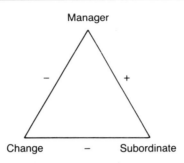

TABLE 13.3   **RELATIONSHIP BETWEEN MANAGEMENT'S APPRAISALS AND WORKERS' VIEWS OF SUPERIORS**

MANAGEMENT'S APPRAISAL OF SUPERVISOR	WORKERS' VIEW OF SUPERVISOR (PERCENTAGE OF WORKERS)			
	PULLS FOR THE COMPANY	PULLS FOR HIMSELF	PULLS FOR THE WORKERS	PULLS FOR THE COMPANY AND THE WORKERS
Immediately promotable	4	21	0	75
Promotable and/or Satisfactory-plus	23	11	9	57
Satisfactory	22	10	10	58
Questionable and/or Unsatisfactory	30	21	9	40

Source: Adapted from Rensis Likert, *New Patterns of Management* (New York: McGraw-Hill Book Company, 1961), p. 19. Reprinted with permission.

worker how the change can be good. If the manager is successful in this attempt, we will then have three pluses and a balanced triad.

In our recommended solution to this problem it is important to remember that the successful manager is interested in both the company *and* the workers, and he or she does not support either one over the other. This is clearly illustrated in Table 13.3, which summarizes the results of another study. Note that the supervisors whom the management considered immediately promotable were seen by the employees as pulling for *both* the company and the workers. This is in contrast to the supervisors who were rated as questionable or unsatisfactory by the management; they were seen by the employees as much more interested than the immediately promotable managers in pulling for the company alone (30 percent versus 4 percent) than for both the company and the workers (40 percent versus 75 percent). If you compare these two groups closely, you can see that the greatest difference between them was whether they were seen as pulling for the company alone or for both the company and the workers. This is the deciding factor in distinguishing the most successful from the least successful.

Balance theory is valuable because it shows how to manage change. If you construct your own examples and apply them to the triad, you can also work your own solutions. The only thing you must keep in mind is that the changes in attitudes must be logical. For example, it is unlikely to have a balanced triad in which the manager and the worker like the change but the worker dislikes the boss. People who dislike each other seldom have the same opinion about changes. The worker will think, "If the boss likes this change, and I don't like the boss, I'd better not like it. He's always out to get me, so this change must be something I should oppose." If you keep this concept of logic in mind, you can run through various examples of changes and determine how the manager should handle each situation.

■ ■ ■ ■ ■ ■ ■ ■ ■ ■ ■ ■ ■ ■
BALANCE THEORY SHOWS HOW TO MANAGE CHANGE.

STOP!

Review your answer to the third question and make any changes you would like. Then compare your answer to the one below.

3.　　How can this situation be explained in terms of balance theory?

In terms of balance theory, there are three elements: the company management, the personnel, and the change. The personnel do not like the change and, as a result, do not like the company management. The management, on the other hand, does like the change. There are two minuses and one plus which means that the triad is balanced, but it is incorrectly balanced. The company needs to persuade the personnel to change their feelings toward both the management and the new work schedules. Otherwise, the problems will persist. ■

REMOVING ANXIETIES

Consideration of the time factor, the importance of participation and communication, and the balance theory are all important tools by which the manager can reduce the anxieties that are so natural in the change process. Although these do not constitute all the things a manager needs to do in managing change properly, they are the most important for they help deal with anxiety, which is the major problem associated with change. In fact, this topic is so important that it warrants separate consideration.

Remember, as we stress throughout the chapter, that as people get ready to leave an environment in which they feel comfortable and familiar, they tend to become fearful and anxious. What will the new situation be like? This fear of the unknown can be a source of stress. As we noted earlier, it is often also a cause of resistance. The worker is concerned

■ ■ ■ ■ ■ ■ ■ ■ ■ ■ ■ ■ ■ ■
CHANGE OFTEN CREATES ANXIETY.

about how long it will take to learn the new skills and techniques being introduced, wondering what new criteria will be used to evaluate performance. The manager needs to pay close attention to these anxieties because they are the biggest factors in causing resistance to change. Herbert suggests ways to deal with such problems:

> Fears and anxieties may be allayed through removing penalties for failure in an experimental period. The change may be tried without measurement of individual failure or performance; those affected by the change may become familiar with what is involved in it and how they may adapt to it. Linking the goals of the change to the goals of the individuals and groups involved can also help to eliminate built-in conflict.[2]

■ ■ ■ ■ ■ ■ ■ ■ ■ ■ ■ ■ ■ ■

SEE THAT EVERYTHING IS
GOING WELL.

Also, although acceptance of the change is important, there must also be a follow-up program to see that everything is going well. (See Human Relations in Action: Some Do's and Don'ts for Managing Change.) If people accept change, they want to believe that they were right. An ideal example of this is the consumer who is persuaded by advertising to switch brand names and buy a different company's product. The consumer often begins to have second thoughts, so some of a company's budget has to be directed toward post-purchase advertising. In this way the consumer is assured that his or her decision was the right one and is encouraged to buy the product again. This process works for subordinates who have accepted some change. The company needs to reassure them that they made the right decision. Most commonly, the manager can do so by telling them what a good job they are doing because they have accepted the change.[3]

USING ORGANIZATIONAL DEVELOPMENT INTERVENTIONS

Sometimes change is created through the use of organizational development interventions which are typically conducted by an outside behavioral expert. **Organizational development (OD)** is an effort to improve an enterprise's effectiveness by dealing with individual, group, and overall organizational problems from both a technical and a human standpoint. The methods used in this process are called **OD interventions** and they take such forms as role playing, team building, and survey feedback. The individual who carries out or leads the intervention is called an **OD change agent**. This person's job is to introduce the intervention, get the

■ ■ ■ ■ ■ ■ ■

[2] Theodore T. Herbert, *Dimensions of Organizational Behavior*, 2nd ed. (New York: Macmillan Publishing Co., Inc., 1981), p. 360.

[3] For more on this subject see Joseph Stanislao and Bettie C. Stanislao, "Dealing with Resistance to Change," *Business Horizons*, July–August 1983, pp. 74–78.

HUMAN RELATIONS IN ACTION

SOME DO'S AND DON'TS FOR MANAGING CHANGE

In managing change, there are a number of things that the effective manager needs to keep in mind. These can be grouped into two categories: *do's* and *don'ts*. Here are some of the most important in each group.

Things To Do

- Keep in mind that most people like the status quo.
- Give advance notice about any changes you are going to make.
- Show the employees how the change will be beneficial to them.
- Be frank and honest about the changes that will take place and how they will affect the salary and job tenure of the people in the work unit.
- Realize that any change that affects group norms is likely to be opposed by members of the group.
- Weigh the costs and benefits of the change.
- Follow up and address any problems that still exist after the change is implemented.

Things Not To Do

- Don't assume that your employees will automatically accept any change simply because you explain why it is useful to them.
- Don't embarrass or ridicule those who question the change.
- Don't threaten to fire or punish those who resist the change.
- Don't underrate the impact of informal group pressures on the acceptance of change.
- Don't overlook the fact that most employees are more concerned with the short-run effects of a change than with the long-run effects.
- Don't be afraid to compromise if the situation warrants such action.
- Don't create lasting animosities over the change; remember, you have to work with these people on a day-to-day basis.

personnel involved, and show them how the particular intervention can help them deal with the problems they face.

ROLE PLAYING   One of the most common forms of training used in organizational development is **role playing**. It consists of the acting out of a realistic situation that involves two or more people. The purpose of the training is to acquaint one or more of the participants with the proper way of handling a given situation. For example, one person may be told that he or she is a plant supervisor and that absenteeism and tar-

ROLE PLAYING IS THE SPONTANEOUS ACTING OUT OF A REAL-LIFE SITUATION.

diness at the plant have been increasing dramatically. The supervisor's job is to reduce these irregularities by sending everyone home who arrives late, thereby penalizing the latecomer a day's pay. Another person is to play the role of a late worker who is trying to talk the supervisor out of sending him or her home. As the two people begin acting out their roles, the rest of the participants watch. When the scene is over, the trainer and the participants all have the opportunity to give their analysis of what each said and did. Then the trainer gives the participants and the other members of the group some *do*'s and *don't*s for handling similar situations.

The benefit of role playing is that it puts the participants in a situation that they are likely to face in the future, gives them a chance to react to the situation, and then provides feedback on performance. When these people return to the real work environment and face a similar situation, they experience less tension and anxiety regarding how to handle the matter because for all practical purposes, they have been in that situation before.

Managers of Southland Corporation participate in the "Team Building I," where they learn about their individual styles and personalities and how these interact in their work environments.

TEAM BUILDING   Currently, the most popular form of OD consists of approaches directed toward improving the effectiveness of regular work groups. The overall term given to these approaches is **team building**, and there are a number of different team-building interventions. Some of these focus on intact, permanent work teams and others are directed toward special teams or newly constituted work groups. Common objectives pursued by team-building interventions include:

1.   Increasing task accomplishment by improving the group's problem-solving ability, decision-making skills, and goal-setting approaches, and/or defining the roles and duties of the individual managers.

■ ■ ■ ■ ■ ■ ■ ■ ■ ■ ■ ■ ■ ■
COMMON OBJECTIVES OF TEAM BUILDING.

2.   Building and maintaining effective interpersonal relationships, including boss-subordinate relationships and peer relationships.

3.   Understanding and managing group processes and intergroup relations.

4.   Improving intergroup relations and resolving interpersonal and/or intergroup conflict.

5.   Developing more effective communication, decision-making, and task-allocation skills, both within and between groups.

One of the most popular methods of team building consists of having two work groups who are having trouble working with each other adjourn to separate rooms and draw up (1) a list of those things it dislikes about the other group and (2) a list of those things it believes the other group will say it dislikes about them. Then the two groups are brought together and each reads its first list. The only questions permitted are those that allow the person reading the list to clarify what the group means by a listed item. When both groups are finished, each then reads its second list (what it believed the other group would say about it).

Having now identified their real and imaginary problems, the two groups begin discussing the issues. Some issues are disposed of very quickly because they had been caused by lack of communication or simple misunderstandings. From here a list of the major problems that still exist between the two groups is constructed and ways of solving the problems are identified. Then the groups put together a timetable for solving the problems and list the specific steps that will have to be taken to deal with them. Having developed an action plan, the two groups then work together and follow the timetable to overcome their mutual problems. In most cases, the OD change agent checks back with the two groups to see whether they are making progress in resolving the problems or whether further meetings are needed to revitalize their efforts.

EVALUATION   Most OD practitioners have great faith in team building, which undoubtedly helps account for the approach's current popularity. However, there are some problems common to the intervention. The major difficulty is that one work group may fail to be honest with the other group, holding back feelings because it is afraid of being too forthright with people it has learned to distrust. However, this problem can be overcome early in the intervention if the change agent keeps everyone honest.

> The early stages of these interventions—making lists and sharing them and using the fishbowl technique—lead the participants to *experience feelings of success in dealing with the other group*. Feelings of anxiety, apprehension, and hostility start to give way to feelings of competence and success as the early stages of the interventions produce better communication and understanding than the participants had expected. Nothing succeeds like success, and the early stages are usually perceived as a success experience by both groups. This leads to the optimistic realization that "We *can* work together with those people." Participants are watching for subtle cues of defensiveness, resistance to the data, stubbornness, and the like, and the controlled nature of the process makes most of these unnecessary. This starts building momentum for feelings of competence and success.[4]

If carried out competently, team building can be very beneficial to both the personnel and the organization.

•••••••

[4]Wendell L. French and Cecil H. Bell, Jr., *Organizational Development*, 2nd ed. (Englewood Cliffs, N.J.: Prentice-Hall, Inc., 1978), p. 137.

SURVEY FEEDBACK　　　Another important and widely used intervention is that of **survey feedback**, a comprehensive OD intervention. The technique entails three distinct steps: (1) a systematic collection of data on the current state of the organization, usually obtained through questionnaires, interviews, or both, (2) a feedback of the findings to the organizational personnel, and (3) the development of an action plan for dealing with the problems that have been identified.

INFORMATION IS GATHERED.

GATHERING THE DATA　　　Data in the survey feedback intervention are often gathered by means of an objective-subjective questionnaire like the one illustrated in Figure 13.8. The survey is usually designed by a specialist in attitude measurement and is administered to the total organization, to a department, or to a representative sample of either.

FED BACK TO PARTICIPANTS.

FEEDING BACK THE INFORMATION　　　After the information is collected and analyzed, the results are revealed to the survey participants. In a nutshell, the OD change agent is saying, "Here's an overall view of what you told me about the organization. These are the things that everyone seems to like. These are the things that most people feel need to be corrected. Let us look at this information and decide what should be done about the situation."

AND AN ACTION PLAN IS
DEVELOPED.

DEVELOPING AN ACTION PLAN　　　The last phase of the survey feedback involves the development of an action plan. This plan is formulated by individuals at all levels of the group(s) that participated in the original survey. Often included in the action plan is a time limit for following up

---

FIGURE 13.8　　**SAMPLE SURVEY FEEDBACK QUESTIONS**

	STRONGLY AGREE	AGREE	UNDECIDED	DISAGREE	STRONGLY DISAGREE
There is a lot of teamwork in my work group.	_____	_____	_____	_____	_____
Very few people in this organization listen to each other.	_____	_____	_____	_____	_____
Management is as interested in the people as it is in the work.	_____	_____	_____	_____	_____
Most important decisions are made by management and then announced to the workers without any input from the latter.	_____	_____	_____	_____	_____
This organization is a good place in which to work.	_____	_____	_____	_____	_____

In your opinion, what are the three biggest problems currently facing the firm? Write your answers in the space below, and use the back of the page if necessary.

to see that the proposed plan is implemented. The follow-up prevents the OD effort from becoming only a short-lived, interesting experience.

> Several months after the OD survey is conducted, a check should be made to determine if the action plans developed in the earlier stages are being implemented. In one company an action plan was developed to realign the wage scale of first-line supervision. A three-month checkup revealed that nothing had been done. Prodding by the OD consultant and a representative from first-line supervision helped management begin some long-needed changes.[5]

EVALUATION   Survey feedback has proven to be an effective change technique. Bowers, for example, has reported that a study evaluating the effects of different change techniques in 23 organizations revealed that survey feedback was more effective than many other types of change strategies.[6] However, to keep these results in perspective, we should note that these survey feedback programs may have been better rated because they were more comprehensive than other programs. The positive results may reflect the superiority of more comprehensive programs to less comprehensive ones. On the other hand, some researchers have also noted that survey feedback is a cost-effective means of implementing a comprehensive program, making it a highly desirable change technique.[7]

STOP!

Review your answer to the fourth question and make any changes you would like. Then compare your answer to the one below.

4.   What type of OD intervention are the consultants considering? Is this a wise choice? Explain.

The consultants are considering survey feedback. This is a good choice because it will provide the company with information about how people throughout the firm feel about the new work changes. Additionally, if the consultants do their job correctly, an action plan will be developed for

·······
[5] Andrew J. DuBrin, *Human Relations: A Job-Oriented Approach*, 4th ed., (Englewood Cliffs, N.J.: Prentice-Hall, Inc., 1988), p. 428.

[6] David G. Bowers, "OD Techniques and Their Results in 23 Organizations: The Michigan ICL Study," *Journal of Applied Behavioral Science*, January/February 1973, pp. 21–43.

[7] For a complete account of the program see Alfred J. Marrow, David G. Bowers, and Stanley E. Seashore, *Management by Participation* (New York: Harper & Row, 1967).

dealing with the problem and evaluating the results. This intervention is the best choice. ∎

SUMMARY

Change is any modification or alteration of the status quo. When change takes place, three things occur: (1) there is a movement from one set of conditions to another, (2) some force(s) causes the change to come about, and (3) a consequence results from the change.

Some people believe that resistance to change is inevitable. While this may be true, there are some very good reasons for resistance. One is that it compels the pro-change forces to build a case against the status quo. Another is that it encourages the organization to look before it leaps.

How do most people react to change? There are many responses, but most can be put in one of four categories: rejection, resistance, tolerance, and acceptance. Of these, the most common is resistance to change. Why does a worker resist change? The most common reasons include: (1) obsolescence of job skills, (2) fear of economic loss, (3) ego defensiveness, (4) the comfort of the status quo, (5) shortsightedness, (6) peer pressure, (7) lack of information, and (8) social displacement.

Despite the various pressures and tendencies to resist change, it is possible to alter the status quo if the change is introduced and managed properly. One of the first things the manager must do is be aware of the three dimensions of change: logical, psychological, and sociological. Additionally, the manager should know the five basic steps in the change process: (1) make sure that the change is really necessary, (2) determine whether the proposed change is the right one, (3) evaluate the probable impact of the change, (4) secure acceptance of the change, and (5) follow up to be sure things are going according to plan. A third important consideration is the time factor. The greater the change, the longer in advance the notice must be given. Furthermore, participation by and communication with the workers to be affected by the change will help ensure acceptance. No one likes to be kept in the dark about a development that will change something important about his or her job. In addition, the manager needs to have a positive attitude toward the change and to know how to use balance theory to secure both acceptance and implementation of the change. Finally, the manager must discover any subordinate anxieties that have not yet been dealt with and work to overcome them. This can often be handled through a follow-up program that reassures the workers that the change was good for them and they were right in accepting it.

Organizational development (OD) is an effort to improve an enterprise's effectiveness by dealing with individual, group, and overall organizational problems from both a technical standpoint and a human standpoint. At the heart of OD is a concern for improving the relationships among the organization's personnel. This is often accomplished through OD interventions. The person who carries out or leads the intervention is called the OD change agent.

There are many kinds of OD interventions. Some relate exclusively to the individual and seek to improve behavioral skills. One of these is role playing. Other OD interventions, such as team building, are designed to improve intragroup and intergroup performance. Finally, there are overall or comprehensive interventions. One of the most popular is survey feedback.

KEY TERMS IN THE CHAPTER

change
causal variable
end-result variable
rejection
overt resistance
covert resistance
tolerance
acceptance

dimensions of change
balance theory
organizational development
OD intervention
OD change agent
role playing
team building
survey feedback

REVIEW AND STUDY QUESTIONS

1. How does change take place? Explain.

2. Is resistance to change bad? In your answer, be sure to make a case both for and against resistance.

3. One of the most common reactions to change is that of rejection. What happens when workers reject change?

4. Under what conditions will workers tend to tolerate change? Give an illustration.

5. One of the primary reasons for resistance to change is the fear of economic loss. What is meant by this statement?

6. What are the three dimensions of change? Why are they important to the manager in the change process?

7. What are the five basic steps in the change process? Describe each.

8. Is participation really of any importance in the introduction of change? How? Explain.

9. What is balance theory? Explain, incorporating in your answer

an explanation of how this theory can be useful to the manager in bringing about acceptance of change.

10.   The major problem associated with change is anxiety. What is meant by this statement?

11.   Role playing is one of the most common forms of training used in OD. How does role playing work?

12.   How does team-building intervention work? Why are these interventions so well liked by OD practitioners?

13.   What are the three distinct steps in survey feedback? How effective is this OD approach? Explain.

TIME OUT ANSWERS: ANSWERS TO HOW MUCH DO YOU KNOW ABOUT THE CHANGE PROCESS?

1. Basically false—most changes scare people and they, at least initially, tend to dislike them.
2. Basically false—most changes take time to be accepted so, if anything, there is an immediate decrease in productivity.
3. Basically true—as explained in number one above.
4. Basically false—they would regard it with fear or concern, wondering if the machine would have them do more work or even replace them.
5. Basically true—this is usually the objective of all organizational changes.
6. Basically true—workers tend to stick together, especially when change is involved.
7. Basically false—people resist because they are afraid of losing their jobs.
8. Basically false—advance notice is crucial, and the greater the change, the more the advance notice that should be given.
9. Basically true—participation in the change process is one of the most effective ways of ensuring successful implementation of the change.
10. Basically false—they tend to underrate the time needed to implement change effectively and end up pushing the change too quickly. The result is resistance from the workers.
11. Either answer can be right here so take one point regardless of your response—if the change is a positive one, it often results in a short decline in work output before things turn around and vice versa.
12. Basically true—unions usually fight change because they are afraid of the effect of the change on worker employment.

Add up your right answers. How well did you do? Use the following to measure your current knowledge of the change process:

11–12 right:	Excellent
9–10 right:	Above average
7–8 right:	Average
6 or less right:	Below average

Regardless of how well you did, you will find the answers to these questions in the chapter. So take heart and read on.

CASE: PARTICIPATION AND COMMUNICATION

Nine months ago Private Hospital was taken over by the county. The population in the local area had grown by approximately 125 percent in the last decade, and the hospital was unable to keep up with local needs. The people who owned the hospital felt that too great an investment was needed for additional emergency and patient rooms and their requisite equipment and inventory. They proposed that the county buy and run the hospital, and the county agreed.

Since the takeover, the hospital personnel has increased by almost 50 percent, while the budget has risen by 44 percent. As a consequence, a number of new cost controls have been implemented. The county management is particularly concerned about controlling expenses. A number of prominent citizens, as well as the local newspaper, have questioned the purchase of the hospital and are saying that it will cost millions of dollars more each year to run a county hospital than it would to have the hospital run by a private group. In response to these charges, the county wants to make sure that the hospital is run as efficiently as possible.

One of the changes introduced was a monthly cost control report. This report is specially designed to provide information to central accounting as well as feedback to the various departments.

Now that the reports have been in use for three months, it has become evident that some departments understand them, fill them out completely, and use them as a source of feedback in controlling their costs and expenditures. Other departments seem confused about the report, do not know what to put into it or leave out, and do not appear to be using the data to control their costs and expenditures.

Phil Albright, head of central accounting, decided to check out the situation for himself by visiting one of the departments that was filling out the form properly and one that was not. The first department is run by Pat Rogers, and after talking to both Pat and her personnel, Phil confirmed that Pat's people are familiar with the form, know the kinds of information that are supposed to go into it, and are aware of how to use the data for control purposes. Much of their understanding stems from a meeting that Pat had with them at which they discussed the report at length. By the end of the meeting, everyone in the department was familiar with the format of the report and was prepared to provide the necessary data.

Conversely, Paul Heckman's department is having all sorts of problems with the report. All three times it was submitted it was both incomplete and late. In addition, Paul's department is currently 21 percent over budget. In talking to the personnel, Phil learned that Paul had not discussed the report with his department. Rather, he had sent a photocopy of the form to each person announcing that the report was to be submitted monthly to accounting. He told his people that he wanted them to decide what they thought should go into the report and send this information to his secretary. He would then take the data and put it into the monthly cost control report. Phil realizes that this way of introducing the report undoubtedly accounts for most of the problems Paul's department is having with it, but he is unsure of how to begin discussing the matter with Paul.

QUESTIONS

1.   How important is participation and communication in effecting change?

2.   Has Pat's approach helped reduce the anxiety that often accompanies change? Has Paul's approach?

3.   What would you recommend that Phil say to Paul? Explain. ■

CASE: SATURDAY MEETINGS

Marcy Schuller works for a large retail chain. For the last three years Marcy has been a store manager and, given her performance, she is likely to be promoted to district manager within the next three years. A district manager coordinates the activities of 10 stores and can be expected to be a vice-president within five years.

A large degree of Marcy's success is a result of her ability to keep morale up, maintain high customer satisfaction, and reduce the infighting that sometimes occurs between the store's two major cliques. The previous store manager had been unable to control these two cliques and, as a result, had low sales and profits. That individual lasted only six months.

Last week the company's central office sent out a new policy statement. All store employees who are not working on weekends are expected to attend regional sales meetings every other week. These meetings take place on Saturday mornings and typically entail a question-and-answer period involving local employees and a representative of the central office. This is management's way of keeping track of what is going on around the country and getting feedback on the problems and concerns of the employees. The meetings have already been introduced in most areas of the country, so it was only a matter of time before they would come to Marcy's region.

Upon hearing the news, most of the employees expressed their displeasure to Marcy. "We work five days a week," one of them explained.

"Why do we have to come in for a half-day on Saturday as well. We all like you and know that you would not have supported this policy if they had asked your opinion. However, central management really doesn't care about us, and most of us don't care about them."

A majority of the employees agree with these sentiments. However, in an effort to accentuate their differences, members of one clique have announced that they fully support management's new policy. So now it is only members of the other clique who are in opposition.

Marcy has informed the district manager that there may be a problem getting the employees to go along with the Saturday morning meetings. However, the manager told Marcy that it is her job to ensure that everyone is present at the meetings. As a result, Marcy has decided that the best way to handle the situation is to sit down with the second clique and see if she can help them resolve their differences with the company so that they will agree to attend the meetings. The district manager is also trying to be helpful. He called back to say that the central office has an organizational development team which is part of the Training and Development Department. "If you would like them to come out and help you in any way, perhaps by conducting an organizational development intervention such as survey feedback, they'd be happy to do so. We've used them at other stores around the region, and they have worked out very well." Marcy thanked him for his assistance, and said that she would get back with him after she had given the idea more thought.

QUESTIONS

1.   Why is there resistance to change? What are the reasons?

2.   How could Marcy use balance theory to help persuade the members of the second clique to attend the Saturday morning meetings?

3.   If the organization were to use survey feedback with the store employees, how would this be done? Explain the process and the potential payoffs for the store and the firm. ■

EXPERIENCING TEAM BUILDING

PURPOSE

- To introduce the reader to the concepts of team building.
- To participate in an authentic team-building activity.

PROCEDURE

1. As a total class, generate as many responses as possible to the question, "How can this group (class) function more effectively to meet our goals, i.e., successfully completing the course objectives?" List as many ideas as possible. None should be evaluated or judged at this time although clarification may be sought.

2. Next, separate into four subgroups. Discuss each of the suggestions, group similar ones, discard those felt inappropriate by the entire group. List in order of importance the ones that are left.

3. As a total class, discuss each group's first priority. Why was it given top priority? Do other groups agree or disagree? Continue until all items are again listed and discussed.

4. As a class, choose the top five items. How can they be implemented to better meet class objectives?

5. Discuss what was learned and/or accomplished by this exercise.

PART 6

LOOKING TO THE FUTURE

In this book we have examined the areas that are of primary importance to the manager who wants to improve his or her human relations skills and abilities. We began by noting the significance of motivation, because the effective manager must be able to galvanize people so that they are willing to strive toward goal attainment. Then we studied the social system of organizations, which consists of individual behavior, group behavior, and the informal organization. The social system can be thought of as the people who work for (or in) the organization.

Next we studied the technical system, which is composed of formal organization design, technology, and job redesign and enrichment. The technical system represents the structure of the organization; it is the environment in which the people carry out their jobs.

Then we examined the organization's administrative system. To a large degree this consists of the way in which the management directs its day-to-day activities, with specific emphasis given to the human element. Of particular importance in this area were the fundamentals of leadership, the leader's role, and how the leader appraises and rewards performance of subordinates.

Finally, we turned our attention to behavioral effectiveness. There may be problems in the social system, the technical system, or the administrative system. How does the organization deal with these problems? By seeking to achieve behavioral effectiveness. This involves communicating for effectiveness, managing change properly, and using organizational development interventions where appropriate.

So far in this book, we have studied the entire field of human relations, which, as you will remember from Chapter 1, we defined as a process by which management brings workers into contact with the organization in such a way that the objectives of both groups are achieved.

Now we consider two important questions: What are the future challenges of human relations? And how can you use your human relations knowledge to help you obtain employment and move ahead in your chosen career? We answer these questions by first examining some of the developing trends that will have a major impact on human relations. These include the need for a greater focus on innovation, the growth of international business, changing social values, and the need to examine human relations practices in the best-managed firms. These areas are examined in Chapter 14. Attention is then focused on how a knowledge of human relations can be of value to you. We begin by investigating the area of career choice and noting the important questions which should be answered in an effective self-evaluation. We also offer human relations tips related to writing an effective resume and carrying out a successful job hunt. Guidelines for managing a career effectively are also suggested. The final part of the chapter describes the characteristics that successful executives must have in the future and discusses the challenges that face the human relations–oriented manager of the 1990s.

HUMAN RELATIONS CHALLENGES OF THE FUTURE

GOALS OF THE CHAPTER

Many human relations challenges will confront managers of the 1990s. The overriding goal of this chapter is to identify and examine four of the major ones. The first objective is to examine the area of innovation. One of management's challenges will be to use the full creativity of its work force. Much of this creativity currently is untapped, but it can be unleashed with the proper human relations approaches. Some of the ways of doing this will be examined.

The second objective is to study the need for effective international human relations. More and more firms are now "going international" or doing business with international firms here in the United States. The effectiveness of these relations can be increased through an understanding of cultural differences and the ways of dealing with them. Specific steps for doing so are provided in this chapter.

The third objective is to discuss the need for a greater awareness of changing social values. AIDS, the desire for greater privacy, and parental leave policies are used as examples.

The fourth objective is to review some of the human relations practices followed by the best-managed firms and to point out why other organizations should emulate these practices.

When you have finished studying all of the material in this chapter you should be able to:

1.   Describe the characteristics of creative people.

2.   Explain how creativity in an organizational setting can be both encouraged and nurtured.

3.   Define the term *culture* and explain some of the reasons for the differences that exist between cultural clusters.

4.   Relate steps that can be taken in dealing with international human relations challenges.

5.   Identify and describe two major social changes with which organizations will have to deal during the 1990s.

6.   Discuss some of the human relations practices used in the best-managed firms.

OPENING CASE

BIG FUTURE PLANS

The 1980s were very good for the Nerdquart Company. During this decade, sales increased by an average of 24 percent annually. In order to maintain this growth rate during the 1990s, the firm knows that it must expand operations into the international arena. At the same time, the company intends to develop new product lines at the rate of three per year. These new lines will be introduced and developed in the United States and then, once they have been proven winners, marketed overseas. To accomplish this objective, the company intends to work very hard to develop and maintain in-house creativity. The company also intends to start marketing some of its current products in the overseas market within the next 90 days.

The firm has placed four countries at the top of its overseas sales list: Ireland, Belgium, Venezuela, and Singapore. The marketing people will be examining each of these cultures to see which ones will be the easiest in which to market their products. These will be pursued first and then the company will move on to the others.

Two other areas in which the firm is developing new strategies are parental leave and stock ownership. The company firmly believes that these two areas will be extremely important in building and maintaining high employee morale. "If we're going to keep growing at such a rapid clip," the president recently noted, "we're going to have to maintain high motivation and loyalty. In accomplishing this objective, we will be continually looking for new techniques that will show the workers our interest and concern for their personal welfare." The parental leave program has not been finalized, but it seems likely that the company will give up to eight weeks of paid parental leave and another 18 weeks of unpaid parental leave. The stock ownership program is going to guarantee that employees will be able to purchase up to 25 percent of the firm through a payroll stock purchase program.

1.   What are some steps the firm could take in promoting creativity? Identify three.

2.   Which of the overseas markets identified in this case has a culture that is most similar to that of the United States? Which culture is least similar?

3.   Would parental leave be of interest to the personnel?

4.   Would a stock ownership plan be motivational? Why or why not?

Write down your answers to these questions and put them aside. We will return to them later. ■

GREATER FOCUS ON INNOVATION

The innovation and creativity process were discussed in Chapter 4. During the 1990s, however, organizations are going to do more than just try to understand how innovation works; they are going to focus their attention on using human relations ideas to help their people be more innovative.

CREATIVITY AND THE PERSONNEL

Most people are a great deal more creative than they believe. Additionally, most organizational jobs do not tap the full potential of the employee, so the latter does not use all of this creative potential. Figure 14.1 illustrates this idea. Notice that the ability of the employee is greater than that required by the job. The organization must learn to tap this asset. One way of doing this is to make employees aware of how creative they really are. Most people believe that only geniuses are creative. However, this ability is much more widespread than they believe, and individuals in the general population possess varying degrees of it. Some of the characteristics of **creative people** include:

1.   Creative people tend to be bright rather than brilliant.

2.   Creative people have a youthful curiosity throughout their lives.

3.   Creative people are open and responsive to feelings and emotions and the world around them.

4.   Creative people tend to have a positive self-image.

5.   Creative people have the ability to tolerate isolation.

6.   Creative people are frequently nonconformists.

FIGURE 14.1   **JOB REQUIREMENTS DISTRIBUTION SUPERIMPOSED ON ABILITY DISTRIBUTION**

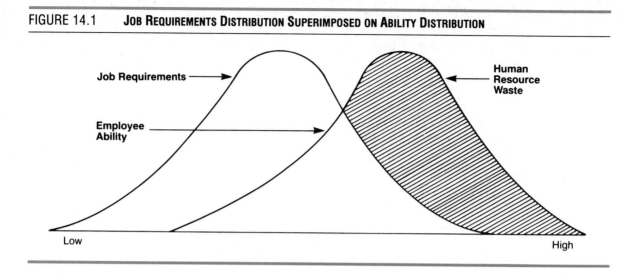

7.   Creative people enjoy finding imaginative solutions to problems.

8.   Creative people are persistent.[1]

ENCOURAGING CREATIVITY

One reason that people are not creative is that they go about it the wrong way. For example, many have erroneous, preconceived ideas about innovation that actually stifle their creativity. Here are some illustrations of these myths:

> Myth 1: *Innovation is planned and predictable.* In truth, innovation is highly unpredictable and can be introduced by anyone from a scientist in the research and development laboratory to a clerical worker who has discovered a better way to file invoices.
>
> Myth 2: *Innovation is the result of exaggerative daydreaming.* Actually, most accomplished innovators are practical people and base their ideas on realistic, down-to-earth developments such as piggybacking on someone else's invention and generating a smaller, cheaper, higher quality, or faster-working model.
>
> Myth 3: *Innovation is the result of carefully drawn up technical specifications.* In most cases this approach takes too long. Success-

■ ■ ■ ■ ■ ■ ■ ■ ■ ■ ■ ■ ■ ■
MYTHS ABOUT CREATIVITY.

■ ■ ■ ■ ■ ■ ■
[1]Andrew J. DuBrin, *Human Relations: A Job Oriented Approach*, 4th edition (Englewood Cliffs, N.J.: Prentice-Hall, 1988), p. 105.

ful innovators often rely on a try-test-review approach. Sometimes this is jokingly referred to as "ready, fire, aim." After they see how well they have done, the innovators make the necessary modifications.

Myth 4: *Large projects produce more innovative results than small ones*. This is untrue; research reveals that small project teams working with limited budgets typically produce better results because the participants have an opportunity to share their ideas, brainstorm, and quickly implement modifications and changes. There is no bureaucratic red tape such as exists in larger projects.

Myth 5: *Technology is the driving force behind innovation and success*. While technology is one source for innovation, the most important ingredient is people, who are able to modify new discoveries so that they are accepted by the market. In production work, for example, while American firms have spent billions of dollars annually to improve the quality of their output, they have been unable to close the gap with the Japanese. Why? Part of the answer is that the Americans have not focused enough attention on the human element.[2]

If individuals were aware of these myths, it would help improve their creativity. Organizations can also help by implementing time-proven principles. Eight of these are: (1) the personnel must be encouraged to actively search for new ideas, opportunities, and sources of innovation; (2) the ideas that are pursued should have practical application; (3) the project should be small and well-focused; (4) an initial schedule of events or milestones should be drawn up even if the project falls behind and does not meet all of these deadlines; (5) participants should be encouraged to learn from failures; (6) the personnel should remember that innovation requires hard work and persistence; (7) the participants should follow a try-test-review approach; and (8) innovative activity should be rewarded.

■ ■ ■ ■ ■ ■ ■ ■ ■ ■ ■ ■ ■ ■ ■
PRINCIPLES OF CREATIVITY.

Another way of improving creativity is to engage in mental games that require clever or imaginative solutions. Time Out: Improving Your Own Creativeness provides an example.

Quite often creativity and innovation are a result of improving on the ideas of others, outside the organization as well as inside. Many of the highly creative products that have been produced and sold by the Japanese, for example, are nothing more than modifications of goods that were initially produced by American firms. This practice is known as

■ ■ ■ ■ ■ ■ ■

[2] Karen Pennar, "The Productivity Paradox," *Business Week*, June 6, 1988, pp. 100–102.

TIME OUT

IMPROVING YOUR OWN CREATIVENESS

There are many ways of improving personal creativeness. One is by engaging in mental exercises that stir the imagination. This creativity test requires you to think of two rhyming words that describe a specific definition. Write your answer to the right of each definition.

EXAMPLES

	DEFINITION	ANSWERS	
1.	Highest ranking officer in the police department	Top	cop
2.	A fat porker	Big	pig
3.	The amount of difference between two very similar points of view	Fine	line

1.	An angry father	____	____
2.	A happy young boy	____	____
3.	A person who steals from a library	____	____
4.	A cloak worn by a gorilla	____	____
5.	An obese feline	____	____
6.	A beverage with very little alcohol	____	____
7.	A heavy crying spell	____	____
8.	A quick meal	____	____
9.	Food with very few calories	____	____
10.	A sickly escargot	____	____

"creative swiping" and is widely practiced by many organizations. One Japanese professor has explained the idea this way:

> When we want to do something, we just try to learn and absorb all the possible answers, alternatives and developments not only in Japan, but in Europe, in developing countries and in the U.S. Then, by combining and by evaluating the best of all this, we try to come up with the optimum combinations which are available. . . . we are very sophisticated copycats.[3]

· · · · · · ·

[3] Tom Peters, *Thriving on Chaos* (New York: Alfred A. Knopf, 1987), p. 229.

STOP!

Review your answer to the first question and make any changes you would like. Then compare your answer to the one below.

1.   What are some steps the firm could take in promoting creativity? Identify three.

Three of the steps the firm could take in promoting creativity include: (1) encourage the personnel to actively search for new ideas and opportunities; (2) ensure that these ideas have practical application; and (3) encourage the participants to learn from their failures. Others include: formulate initial deadlines or milestones, encourage the participants to follow a try-test-review approach, and reward innovative activity. ■

DEVELOPMENT OF INTRAPRENEURS

The development of intrapreneurs will be another significant step toward promoting employee innovation in the 1990s. It will also be a major human relations challenge.

Organizations are going to find that the development of intrapreneurs will require attention to two areas: creating the right culture and nurturing the entrepreneurial spirit of those who work there. The first is heavily influenced by the management's philosophy, beliefs, and attitudes. The second is most heavily affected by the reward structure that is in place. Ross and Unwalla have attempted to bring together these ideas through a consideration of intrapreneurial personality (IP) and intrapreneurial style (IS). The combination of the two is the individual's intrapreneurial performance quotient (IPQ). To determine your own IPQ, complete the tests in Tables 14.1 and 14.2 and combine your total scores for both tests. The interpretation of these scores follows.

MANAGEMENT PHILOSOPHY AND REWARDS WILL INFLUENCE ENTREPRENEURIAL SPIRIT.

SCORE	INTERPRETATION
60–80	You are an intrapreneur.
40–59	You are well suited to being an intrapreneur, but are not quite there yet.
Below 40	You will do better remaining in a bureaucratic organization.

Whether or not you have a high intrapreneurial performance quotient, it should be evident why organizations that are interested in de-

TABLE 14.1   DETERMINING YOUR INTRAPRENEURIAL STYLE

Each of the following items describes some aspect of intrapreneurial managerial behavior on the job. Circle the response that most nearly reflects your degree of agreement or disagreement with this type of behavior. Respond according to the way in which you would actually behave on the job. Add the numerical values for your responses and enter score on the intrapreneurial style (IS) profile.

IN THEIR BEHAVIOR ON THE JOB, SUPERVISORS AND MANAGERS SHOULD:	STRONGLY DISAGREE	DISAGREE	UNDECIDED	AGREE	STRONGLY AGREE
1. Try to avoid letting the systems and procedures of the organization get in the way of innovation.	0	1	2	3	4
2. Pursue innovation through administrative (managerial) as well as technical (scientific/mechanical) means.	0	1	2	3	4
3. Improve productivity and encourage innovation by delegation.	0	1	2	3	4
4. Encourage "idea champions" who are willing to risk failure to bring their idea to fruition.	0	1	2	3	4
5. Recognize that mistakes and false starts, kept within bounds, are the necessary byproducts of risk taking.	0	1	2	3	4
6. Orchestrate spirit and discipline within the organization's structure and among organization members.	0	1	2	3	4
7. Stay close to the customer, providing service and quality as the most important ingredients of company success.	0	1	2	3	4
8. Encourage creativity (thinking up new ideas) and innovation (making things happen) as well as independent thinking, if necessary.	0	1	2	3	4
9. Constantly seek new markets, new products, and new uses for old products.	0	1	2	3	4
10. Assist in institutionalizing and articulating a strategy of intrapreneurship, innovation, and productivity.	0	1	2	3	4

Source: Reprinted by permission of publisher from "Who Is an Intrapreneur?" Joel E. Ross and Darab Unwalla, *Personnel*, December 1986, p. 47. American Management Association, New York. All rights reserved.

veloping intrapreneurs will have to be concerned with both style and personality.

BETTER UNDERSTANDING OF INTERNATIONAL HUMAN RELATIONS

More and more business is being done on an international basis. During the 1980s as the U.S. dollar sank to new lows against foreign currencies, overseas customers began to buy more American-made products. This recent development has made the world a more lucrative target for U.S. manufacturers. At the same time, overseas firms continue to sell goods in

---

TABLE 14.2   DETERMINING YOUR INTRAPRENEURIAL PERSONALITY

Each of the following items describes some aspect of beliefs and/or behavior on the job that suggests an intrapreneurial personality. Circle the response that most nearly reflects your degree of agreement or disagreement with this type of behavior. Respond according to the way in which you would actually behave on the job. Add the numerical values for your responses and enter score on the intrapreneurial personality (IP) profile.

IN MY BEHAVIOR ON THE JOB, I SHOULD:	STRONGLY DISAGREE	DISAGREE	UNDECIDED	AGREE	STRONGLY AGREE
1. Focus on results (effectiveness), not on activity.	0	1	2	3	4
2. Question the status quo and have a desire to change things when the need is clear.	0	1	2	3	4
3. Be a Pygmalion—perceive employees as responsible people who want to get results.	0	1	2	3	4
4. Be motivated by problem solving and rational decision making.	0	1	2	3	4
5. Be ambitious and competitive.	0	1	2	3	4
6. Believe that the reward is in the work as much as in the pay.	0	1	2	3	4
7. Be frustrated by restrictive bureaucratic systems and develop a knack for operating within these constraints.	0	1	2	3	4
8. Develop an ability to resolve conflict and friction.	0	1	2	3	4
9. Understand that the organization is a system of interrelated technical subsystems and that my "niche" is a part of the whole.	0	1	2	3	4
10. Be motivated by effecting change and innovation, not only for myself but for employees as well.	0	1	2	3	4

Source: Reprinted by permission of publisher from "Who Is an Intrapreneur?" by Joel E. Ross and Darab Unwalla, *Personnel*, December 1986, p. 48. American Management Association, New York. All rights reserved.

the United States as clearly indicated by the billions of dollars spent on foreign goods each month by Americans. These developments point out the need for an understanding of international human relations.

GROWING INTERNATIONALISM

Many of the largest U.S. firms do a significant amount of business overseas. IBM, with its foreign headquarters in Paris, sells billions of dollars' worth of computers every year to customers from all over the world. Many other firms are continuing to expand their international focus, aware that these untapped markets may constitute the last "new" frontier for their goods and services. Examples include Boeing, Coca-Cola, McDonald's, Hilton, and the Walt Disney Company to name but five.

At the same time, many foreign firms are invading the U.S. market. In the automobile industry, for example, Toyota, Nissan, and Honda have extended their collective market share from 16.5 percent in 1980

Engelhard Corporation has recently expanded its joint venture with the West German firm Kali-Chemie, AG. Exhaust catalysts are now produced in Nienburg, West Germany. The company gains the benefit of producing products near the end market.

to 18.9 percent in 1987.[4] Quite clearly, business is a two-way street with many companies setting up operations in countries other than their own.

Still another interesting development is the increase in joint projects between American and overseas firms. The automakers are an excellent example. Notice from Table 14.3 that the Big Three auto manufacturers are contractually tied to Japanese firms in both producing and selling cars.

From a human relations standpoint, the international arena is important because American firms are going to be more and more affected by it. During the 1990s, an increasing number of U.S. companies will buy

· · · · · · ·
[4]*Business Week*, April 25, 1988, p. 92.

TABLE 14.3   **THE GLOBALIZATION OF THE AMERICAN CAR**

FORD

- Owns 25% of Mazda.
- Mazda plant in Flat Rock, Michigan, produces Ford Probe and Mazda MX-6.
- Assembles Mercury Tracer in a Ford plant in Hermosillo, Mexico, using Mazda components.
- Mazda supplies Ford affiliates in Australia, New Zealand, and Taiwan with sets of selected components for Laser model, to be combined with components from local sources and sold under Ford label in Pacific markets.
- Collaborating with Mazda on future models.
- Nissan and Ford studying possibilities for production of a new vehicle in North America, to be marketed by both companies.

GENERAL MOTORS

- Owns 41.6% of Isuzu.
- United Motor Manufacturing Inc. is a 50-50 joint venture with Toyota Motor Corp. Its plant in Fremont, California, produces the Chevrolet Nova and Toyota Corolla FX-16. Toyota manages the plant, with limited G.M. participation.
- Imports an Isuzu car, sold as the Chevrolet Spectrum.
- Isuzu and Fuji are building an assembly plant in Lafayette, Indiana, and G.M. is expected to be a supplier of major components for the Isuzu vehicle.
- Owns 5.3% of Suzuki, and imports a Suzuki car, sold as the Chevrolet Sprint.
- Building a joint venture plant with Suzuki in Ingersoll, Ontario, to produce small sports utility vehicles for sale by both Chevrolet and Suzuki.

CHRYSLER

- Owns 24% of Mitsubishi.
- Diamond-Star Motors Corp. is a 50-50 joint venture with Mitsubishi. An assembly plant in Normal, Illinois, is being built to produce one model for each company, starting late this summer. Management is joint, with Mitsubishi in the lead.
- Has imported Mitsubishi-made small cars and trucks for sale as Plymouths and Dodges since the early 1970s.
- Buys V-6 engines from Mitsubishi for various Chrysler models.

Source: *New York Times*, June 5, 1988, p. 8F. Copyright © 1988 by The New York Times Company. Reprinted by permission.

goods and services from foreign firms and/or sell these to them. Under-standing the cultures and norms of these countries will be very helpful to the companies.

THE IMPACT OF CULTURE

Learned behaviors such as norms, values, mores, habits, and customs are known as **culture**. Since culture often varies from one country to an-other, the way in which effective managers communicate, motivate, and lead people in these countries will also often vary. One way of illustrating this is through the use of cultural clusters as presented in Figure 14.2. A **cultural cluster** is a group of countries with similar values, customs, and beliefs. Notice from Figure 14.2 that there are a number of different

FIGURE 14.2　**COUNTRY CLUSTERS**

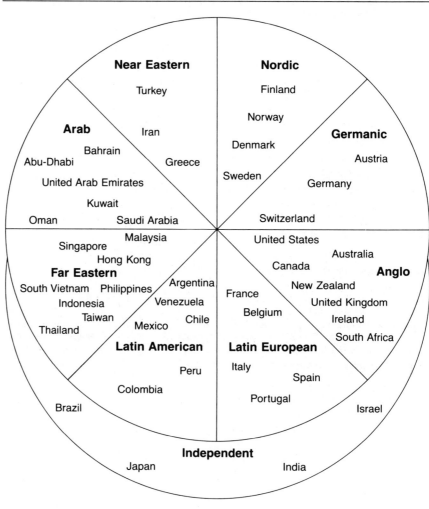

Source: S. Ronen and O. Shenkar, "Clustering Countries on Attitudinal Dimensions: A Review and Synthesis," *Academy of Management Review*, July 1985, p. 449.

■ ■ ■ ■ ■ ■ ■ ■ ■ ■ ■ ■ ■ ■ ■

CULTURE OFTEN VARIES FROM COUNTRY TO COUNTRY.

types of cultural clusters: Anglo, Germanic, Nordic, Near Eastern, Arab, Far Eastern, Latin American, and Latin European. Countries in the same cluster will conduct business operations in a similar way. For example, when doing business in the Anglo culture, effective managers would use similar leadership styles whether they were supervising Americans, Canadians, or New Zealanders. However, this style would not work well with Arabs because they come from a different culture. Moreover, there are some cultures that have been found to be sufficiently different so as to defy simple categorization. Brazil, Japan, India, and Israel (see Figure 14.2) are examples.

EXAMINING DIFFERENCES   There are a number of ways of examining the differences that exist between cultural clusters. One is by looking at the degree of individualism or collectivism that exists. For example, in the United States, people are taught to be individualistic and to look out for themselves. On the other hand, in countries like Japan and other Far Eastern nations, there is high collectivism. People have strong group loyalty and look to their bosses to give them orders and to direct them. Unless an overseas manager understands this cultural preference, he or she may be ineffective in motivating or leading these people.

A second difference is accounted for by people's view of time. Some societies are more oriented toward the past; others tend to focus more on the present; still others are futuristic. Americans and Canadians tend to be most interested in the present and near future. They make decisions that will carry them one or two years into the future. Europeans place more importance on the past then do North Americans. They believe in preserving history and continuing past traditions. They often are unwilling to break with the past in order to increase profits. Oriental countries are futuristic. The Japanese have very long-term, future-oriented time horizons. For example, when they hire someone, they often count on the individual staying with them for a long period of time and are willing to spend a great deal of money training and developing the individual. This is in contrast to many American firms that refuse to expend these amounts of funds because the individual may soon leave the organization.

■ ■ ■ ■ ■ ■ ■ ■ ■ ■ ■ ■ ■ ■ ■
VIEWS OF INDIVIDUALISM, TIME, SPACE, AND UNCERTAINTY OFTEN VARY BY CULTURE.

A third difference is in the use of private and public space. Among North Americans, there is a great preference for private space. Important managers have their own offices and the larger the office, the more important the manager. Anyone coming to see an important manager often has to go past a secretary (perhaps more than one) before being admitted to the manager's presence. In contrast, in cultures such as Japan the bosses sit together with their employees in the same large room. In the Middle East there are often many people present during important meetings.

A fourth difference is measured by the amount of uncertainty that managers will tolerate. In many western countries, the manager is not expected to have the answers to all subordinates' questions. The manager feels comfortable doing his or her job, while aware of the fact that there may be things going on that he or she does not understand or is not controlling. Many other societies prefer less uncertainty. The manager is expected to know what is going on at all times, and if a subordinate has a

FIGURE 14.3   **WILLINGNESS TO LIVE WITH UNCERTAINTY**

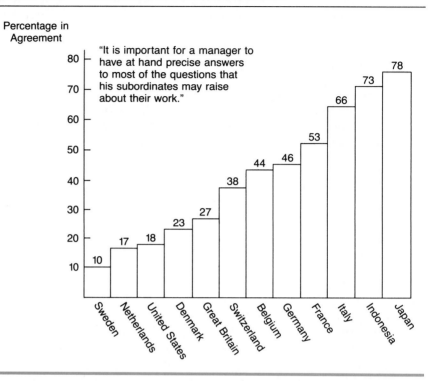

Source: Reprinted from Andre Laurent, "The Cultural Diversity of Western Conceptions of Management," *International Studies of Management and Organization*, Vol. XIII, No. 1–2, Spring–Summer 1983, p. 86 by permission of M. E. Sharpe, Inc., Armonk, N.Y.

question the manager should be able to answer it. Figure 14.3 provides an example of how managers in various countries feel about being able to live with uncertainty.

STOP!

Review your answer to the second question and make any changes you would like. Then compare your answer to the one below.

2.   Which of the overseas markets identified in this case has a culture that is most similar to that of the United States? Which culture is least similar?

The culture that is most similar to the United States is that of Ireland. The one that is least similar is that of Singapore. Of the other two, Belgian culture is more like that of the United States than is Venezuelan. ∎

DEALING WITH INTERNATIONAL HUMAN RELATIONS CHALLENGES

How can organizations deal with the myriad of human relations challenges faced in the international arena? The following four guidelines provide important answers.

BE AWARE OF PERCEPTUAL DIFFERENCES   How Americans see foreign businesspeople and vice versa will affect the relations between the two. There are many ways in which these differences play a role. For example, in most Latin countries it would be poor manners for an executive who was invited to dinner at a businessman's home to congratulate the host's wife on cooking a splendid meal. The remark might be interpreted to mean that the executive believed that his host was too poor to afford a cook. The best way of dealing with this type of problem is to become familiar with the customs of the country.

A second perceptual problem is stereotyping. Quite often cultural generalizations are both inaccurate and misleading. For example, Table 14.4 provides a list of some of the characteristics used by foreigners to

■ ■ ■ ■ ■ ■ ■ ■ ■ ■ ■ ■ ■
STEREOTYPING CAN CAUSE PERCEPTION PROBLEMS.

TABLE 14.4   HOW OTHERS SEE AMERICANS

CHARACTERISTICS MOST OFTEN ASSOCIATED WITH AMERICANS BY THE POPULATIONS OF:

FRANCE	JAPAN	WEST GERMANY	GREAT BRITAIN	BRAZIL	MEXICO
Industrious	Nationalistic	Energetic	Friendly	Intelligent	Industrious
Energetic	Friendly	Inventive	Self-indulgent	Inventive	Intelligent
Inventive	Decisive	Friendly	Energetic	Energetic	Inventive
Decisive	Rude	Sophisticated	Industrious	Industrious	Decisive
Friendly	Self-indulgent	Intelligent	Nationalistic	Greedy	Greedy

CHARACTERISTICS LEAST OFTEN ASSOCIATED WITH AMERICANS BY THE SAME POPULATIONS:

FRANCE	JAPAN	WEST GERMANY	GREAT BRITAIN	BRAZIL	MEXICO
Lazy	Industrious	Lazy	Lazy	Lazy	Lazy
Rude	Lazy	Sexy	Sophisticated	Self-indulgent	Honest
Honest	Honest	Greedy	Sexy	Sexy	Rude
Sophisticated	Sexy	Rude	Decisive	Sophisticated	Sexy

Source: *Newsweek*, July 11, 1983, p. 50.

describe Americans. Are these accurate descriptions of us? Or are they stereotypes? Moreover, although Table 14.4 does not include the Russians, the latter complain that Americans suffer from **ethnocentrism**, the belief that everything American is better than that of any other country. Unless Americans can overcome the tendency to believe that the way things are done in the States is superior, they will be unable to deal effectively with people in the international arena.

LEARN HOW INTERNATIONAL MANAGERS BEHAVE   International managers differ in their interpersonal behavioral approaches. Bass and Burger, for example, conducted a major study of managers in the United States, Belgium, Britain, France, Germany-Austria, Iberia, India, Japan, Latin America, and Scandinavia. They reported the following findings:

- Spanish and Portuguese managers were the most willing to be aware of others' feelings, to be concerned with their subordinates' welfare, and to accept feedback from others. The Germans, Austrians, and French were the least willing to do these things.

- Indian managers were the most concerned about rules while the Japanese were the least concerned.

- Indian managers saw themselves as the most dependent on higher authority, while German and Austrian managers viewed themselves as the least dependent.

- Dutch managers were the most willing to cooperate with others while French managers were the least willing.

- Japanese managers had a greater desire than any other group to be objective rather than intuitive.

- Japanese and Dutch managers were the least likely to deviate from positions that they took, while managers from the United States and Latin America were the most willing to compromise.

- U.S. and Latin American managers had much greater interpersonal competence than any of the other groups of managers.[5]

UNDERSTAND OTHERS' PHILOSOPHY OF WORK   Some people work very hard; others do not. Some people want to get everything done as quickly as possible; others do not feel these time constraints. Additionally, some people like to be rewarded for their individual efforts, while others prefer to be rewarded as members of a group. The Americans prefer individual rewards tied to personal performance; the Japanese prefer to be rewarded for group effort. The Dutch and the Israelis place high importance on work that is interesting and personally satisfy-

▪▪▪▪▪▪▪
INTERPERSONAL BEHAVIORAL APPROACHES.

PEOPLE'S VIEW OF WORK WILL DIFFER.

[5] B. M. Bass and P. C. Burger, *Assessment of Managers: An International Comparison* (New York: Free Press, 1979).

ing. For them, financial rewards are insufficient; they have to like what they are doing. When dealing with people from other countries, it is important to remember that their philosophy of work may be quite different from ours.

PREPARE PEOPLE FOR OVERSEAS WORK   One of the most effective ways of helping people deal with overseas customers and clients is by giving them training in the culture of those countries with which they will be doing business. This cross-cultural training can take many forms, as seen in Figure 14.4. If it is to last less than a week, the focus should be on "survival" training, which includes the basic things that someone visiting that country needs to know. These extend from the proper behavior when meeting a foreign business person (see Human Relations in Action: Understanding Japanese Business Practices on page 513) to learning how to say such basic things as, "Thank you," "It was a pleasure to meet you," and "May I have please have the check?" If time permits, many organizations provide their people with language training (again see Figure 14.4), role-playing situations in which they can learn how to behave correctly, and detailed instruction in the cultural values of the other country. In some cases, organizations provide in-depth training in the form of extensive language training, simulated experiences, field experiences, and evaluation by an assessment center.

■ ■ ■ ■ ■ ■ ■ ■ ■ ■ ■ ■ ■ ■
CROSS-CULTURAL TRAINING IS IMPORTANT.

Assessment centers are particularly useful in helping choose personnel best suited for overseas work. Many companies report that personnel sent overseas for two years often return after one year. Why? Because they do not like the environment. Had the firm done effective screening before sending them, personnel more suited to the assignment might have been sent. Careful screening is especially important in the case of female executives who, quite often, find it more difficult in the international arena than at home because few women overseas hold managerial positions.[6]

GREATER AWARENESS OF CHANGING SOCIAL VALUES

Many social changes are taking place in the United States. Some of them have a direct human relations impact and, during the upcoming decade, will constitute an ongoing challenge. Three of the major ones are AIDS,

■ ■ ■ ■ ■ ■ ■

[6] For more on this see William Q. Kirk and Robert C. Maddox, "International Management: The New Frontier for Women," *Personnel*, March 1988, pp. 46–49; and Nancy J. Adler, "Pacific Basin Managers: A *Gaijin*, Not a Woman," *Human Resource Management*, Summer 1987, pp. 169–191.

FIGURE 14.4   **CULTURAL TRAINING APPROACHES**

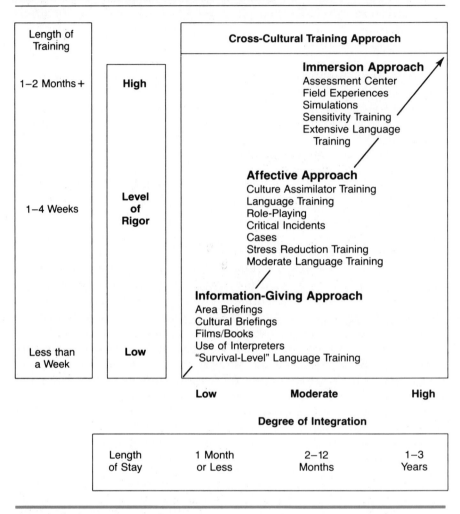

Source: Mark E. Mendenhall, Edward Dunbar, and Gary R. Oddou, "Expatriate Selection, Training and Career-Pathing: A Review and Critique," *Human Resource Management*, Fall 1987, p. 340. Reprinted by permission of John Wiley and Sons.

the desire for greater privacy, and the growing demand for parental leave.

AIDS

Acquired immune deficiency syndrome (AIDS) is one of the major health problems facing this country. Two important challenges it presents to or-

HUMAN RELATIONS IN ACTION

UNDERSTANDING JAPANESE BUSINESS PRACTICES

Japan is one of America's largest trading partners and many U.S. firms do business there. In preparing for such an overseas assignment, a manager must learn some common Japanese business practices. Here are four that are of particular importance.

■   *Business Cards.* Japanese business greetings almost always begin with the exchange of business cards. This is a ritual that Japanese businesspeople follow regardless of when or where they are introduced to someone: in a bar, a bus, or an airplane. Always have an abundance of business cards and be prepared to exchange them with the individuals to whom you are being introduced. This is true even if you know that they are not part of the business team with whom you will be working, or they are visitors from another part of the country and you will never see them again.

■   *Bowing.* Contrary to common belief, the Japanese greet their visitors by bowing only if the other person is also Japanese. Americans, Europeans, Chinese, Koreans, and other non-Japanese are not greeted with a bow. The Japanese businessman will typically extend his hand for a handshake and you should do the same.

■   *The Guest Room.* Company visitors typically are not invited to the office of the person whom they are to see. In fact, the higher the position of the Japanese manager, the less the likelihood that you will be invited into his office. This would be considered informal and sometimes even impolite. Instead, you will be shown into a guest room or drawing room. This is the place often used for business and serious negotiations.

■   *Gifts.* It is common, although not mandatory, for a Japanese to give a visitor a small gift when meeting the individual for the first time. The gift is often a conversation opener. It might be sake, whisky, canned goods, or a small product produced by the firm. You are not expected to reciprocate, but if you do, your gift should be of similar value. If you give a Japanese a gift that is very expensive, the recipient will be obligated to respond in kind or to return the gift by messenger. Many Japanese department stores set aside an area to display suggested gift items, and shopping consultants who can help you choose an appropriate gift are available.

If you receive a gift, it is acceptable to open it in front of your host. However, if you present a gift to a Japanese, do not expect to see it opened. It is customary for the person to wait and open it later.

---

ganizations include (1) how to educate employees about the disease and (2) how to provide assistance to personnel who have contracted AIDS.

EDUCATION   There is a great deal of misinformation about AIDS. In particular, people are unsure how the disease is transmitted. The result is a potential fear factor that can disrupt organizational activities when an

John Hancock Financial Services offers AIDS Case Management to its customers. Case managers assist in rendering services to AIDS patients. Hancock health benefits specialists believe it is a cost-effective approach to treating AIDS patients and doing it with a conscience.

employee is found to have the disease. Much of this fear can be addressed through a well-implemented educational program. As the U.S. Surgeon General put it, "The time for a company to educate employees about AIDS is before it has its first case. . . . I think employers have an obligation to convey information of how AIDS is spread and how AIDS is not spread."[7]

Firms are doing this in a number of ways. Some are bringing in an expert on the disease to talk to the personnel and answer their questions. Others are handling it through their training and development department which offers an "AIDS Understanding" program to the employees. Still others distribute literature to their people such as the pamphlet, "AIDS: Risk, Prevention, Understanding," which is provided by the National Leadership Coalition on AIDS. Organizations have a responsibility to address this issue with their people and to provide them the latest scientific findings on the subject regarding both prevention and transmission of the disease.[8]

■ ■ ■ ■ ■ ■ ■ ■ ■ ■ ■ ■ ■ ■

AIDS VICTIMS HAVE LEGAL RIGHTS.

LEGAL RIGHTS   If a person contracts the disease, what legal rights does he or she have? Most employees are protected from outright dismissal under the auspices of the Federal Rehabilitation Act of 1973 or various state laws that consider AIDS to be a physical handicap. The person can remain on the job and as the person becomes progressively weaker, the organization must take steps to accommodate him or her.[9] These rights must be spelled out to both the person and the person's superior.

Additionally, individuals with AIDS are entitled to protection of privacy. Managers, who are told by one of their personnel that the individual has contracted AIDS, are legally barred from passing on this information to the rest of the work group. Since there is no medical evidence to support the contention that other personnel are in any physical danger, there is no basis for violating privacy protection. Managers who have done so have been sued by AIDS victims who have won out-of-court

■ ■ ■ ■ ■ ■ ■

[7] Patti Watts, "AIDS Education in the Workplace," *Management Review*, April 1988, p. 38.

[8] For more on this topic see Frank E. Kuzmits and Lyle Sussman, "Twenty Questions about AIDS in the Workplace," *Business Horizons*, July–August 1986, pp. 36–42; Lorraine Lutgen, "AIDS in the Workplace: Fighting Fear with Facts and Policy," *Personnel*, November 1987, pp. 55–57; Margaret Magnus, "AIDS: Fear and Ignorance Still Plague the Workplace," *Personnel Journal*, February 1988, p. 28; and Terence Monmaney, "The AIDS Threat: Who's at Risk?" *Newsweek*, March 14, 1988, pp. 42–44.

[9] Robert H. Elliott and Thomas M. Wilson, "AIDS in the Workplace: Public Personnel Management and the Law," *Public Personnel Management*, Fall 1987, pp. 209–219; and Jose G. Fagot-Diaz, "Employment Discrimination against AIDS Victims: Rights and Remedies Available under the Federal Rehabilitation Act of 1973," *Labor Law Journal*, March 1988, pp. 148–166.

settlements. It is the organization's responsibility to familiarize its managers with the rights of AIDS victims and to ensure that these rights are protected. During the 1990s, this human relations challenge will continue to be of paramount importance.

DESIRE FOR GREATER PRIVACY

Currently there is a growing trend toward defending employee rights to privacy. These rights provide protection against organizations delving into the private lives of its personnel. A number of issues are under debate.

One, initially discussed in Chapter 10, is the right of organizations to require mandatory drug testing. Many employees argue that such testing is unconstitutional. In their view, unless there is reason to believe that a person is a drug abuser and that this is affecting the person's work, the organization should not be allowed to demand a drug test.

Another is the use of lie detectors. Research shows that these machines are invalid. In fact, there is a great deal of controversy regarding what polygraphs actually measure. This undoubtedly helps explain why recent federal legislation has severely limited the use of lie detectors in employment hiring. Many employees want these machines totally outlawed, and this may well occur during the next decade.[10]

A third issue is electronic surveillance including the monitoring of both computer information and telephone conversations.[11] For example, many companies have increasing access to electronic data bases that hold vast amounts of personal information on employees, and this is of major concern to these employees. Moreover, company snooping is not always limited to in-house data.

> Certain employers, such as banks and nuclear power plants, can get criminal histories of prospective employees from the Federal Bureau of Investigation's Identification Division data base on more than 20 million people. In some states, other employers can get FBI information, too. Now the Bureau is considering lifting a major restriction on its criminal history data base: It may delete a rule requiring that information on people who are arrested but not convicted can't be disseminated after one year.[12]

How can organizations meet the human relations challenge of employee privacy? Some of the steps that are proving to be most effective include the following:

∎∎∎∎∎∎∎

[10] Elaine Hobbs Fry and Nicholas Eugene Fry, "Information vs. Privacy: The Polygraph Debate," *Personnel*, February 1988, pp. 57–60.

[11] John Hoerr, *et al.*, "Privacy," *Business Week*, March 28, 1988, pp. 61–68.

[12] *Ibid.*, p. 64.

■ ■ ■ ■ ■ ■ ■ ■ ■ ■ ■ ■ ■ ■ ■ ■
WAYS TO DEAL WITH PRIVACY
PROTECTION.
1.   Identification of privacy issues that are of concern to the personnel.

2.   Formation of a management/worker privacy committee to review and deal with these issues.

3.   Formulation of a privacy procedure which spells out the protections afforded to every employee by the organization.

4.   Implementation of specific steps that ensure greater employee privacy, such as the writing of computer programs that limit access to personnel files and the restriction of polygraphs in investigations of in-house theft.

5.   Reprimand or dismissal by management of those employees who are found guilty of violating the right to privacy of any employee.

PARENTAL LEAVE

There is a growing movement toward a "family sensitive" work place. One of the best examples is the increasingly popular **parental leave policy**, which allows mothers, and in some cases fathers also, time off for the birth and early nurturing of a child. The conditions under which this can be done will vary by organization. The following are some examples of corporate parental leave policies.

.   *Avon Products:* Three months paid disability leave; three months unpaid maternal leave.

.   *Campbell Soup:* Six weeks paid maternal disability leave; up to three months unpaid parental leave for salaried employees.

.   *Eastman Kodak:* Average of eight weeks paid maternal disability, up to one year in some cases; up to four months paid parental leave.

.   *IBM:* Six to eight weeks paid maternal disability leave; up to one year unpaid parental leave with option to work part-time.

.   *Procter & Gamble:* Eight weeks paid maternal disability leave; up to six months unpaid parental leave.[13]

■ ■ ■ ■ ■ ■ ■ ■ ■ ■ ■ ■ ■ ■ ■ ■
PARENTAL LEAVE POLICIES ARE
GAINING IN POPULARITY.
A recent study of almost 4,000 employers found that 51 percent of firms with fewer than 20 employees and 72 percent of larger companies offered at least eight weeks maternal leave. Additionally, 17 states now have laws requiring employers to provide parental leave, and Congress is currently debating two bills designed to create a federally mandated parental leave policy. The Senate version, which is less comprehensive, would allow employees in companies with 50 or more workers to take up to 15 weeks of unpaid maternity leave and up to 10 weeks of unpaid family leave to care for newborn or newly adopted children. After three

■ ■ ■ ■ ■ ■ ■
[13] Ronald E. Roel, "Parental Leave Gaining Favor," *Newsday*, June 16, 1988, p. 61.

years these provisions would automatically broaden to cover employers with 35 or more workers.

These developments indicate that parental leave, both maternal and paternal, is going to gain in popularity during the 1990s. What can organizations do to meet this growing challenge? One is to become aware of the increasing desire for this benefit. A second is to realize that parental policies are cost effective. "These policies actually give companies a competitive edge in reduced turnover and increased productivity," notes David Balkenhorn, executive director of the Institute for American Values.[14] Others agree, including the executive vice-president of National Westminster Bank, who reports that the company, at any one point in time, has about 100 women out on maternity leave and 75 percent of them return to the job.[15] A third step that organizations can take is to familiarize themselves with similar benefits that are also growing in popularity. Child care services is a good example. A fourth step is to determine a parental policy that will satisfy employee desires while staying within the financial capabilities of the firm. Fifth, and most importantly, organizations must realize that social values will constantly change and that responding to these developments will be an ongoing challenge.

STOP!

Review your answer to the third question and make any changes you would like. Then compare your answer to the one below.

3.   Would parental leave be of interest to the personnel?

It certainly would. More and more firms are now beginning to offer parental leave policies. By the end of the 1990s it is likely that most large firms will have such a policy in effect. Parental leave policies are profitable in that firms offering this benefit have found that absenteeism often goes down while productivity rises. ■

KNOWLEDGE OF HUMAN RELATIONS PRACTICES IN THE BEST-MANAGED FIRMS

Research shows a growing need over the next 20 years for effective human relations. Guest, a human resources expert, has noted that in meet-

■■■■■■■

[14] *Ibid*.

[15] *Ibid*.

ing the challenges of the twenty-first century, a number of central human relations concerns must be addressed, including the following:

1.   From the top of the organization to the bottom, insufficient use is being made of the skills and motivational potential of organizational personnel.

2.   Organization structures and communications systems for managing human resources are becoming obsolete.

3.   There is inadequate coping with change, such as those in technology, the external environment, and the aspirations and value systems held by the personnel.[16]

How can organizations address these concerns? The most effective way is by creating an environment in which highly motivated, well-trained people are given the opportunity to pursue interesting, challenging work. This solution is heavily human relations in orientation and requires the organization to focus on a number of practices. The following sections examine these practices as they are used by the best-managed companies.

JOB SECURITY

Few firms are able to guarantee lifetime employment to their people. In Japan, for example, only about 30 percent of all employees have such a guarantee and these people all work for the large corporations. In the United States, IBM has long been touted as an example of a firm which offers lifetime employment. However, this is not totally true as seen by its recent efforts to trim its work force by offering attractive retirement packages. What is true is that many of the best-run firms offer their people "a fair measure" of job security. This takes a number of different forms.

One is the use of smaller work forces that are supplemented by part-time help that is let go when economic conditions become poor. In this case, the primary work force is virtually guaranteed continued employment. Another approach is to reduce the workweek of the regular staff so that no one has to be let go. A third is to trim the work force by not replacing individuals who leave or retire. A fourth, and complementary approach to some of the above, is to use a "feast and famine" strategy. When economic times are good, everyone is required to work overtime and on weekends. When times are poor, everyone's workweek is cut

■ ■ ■ ■ ■ ■ ■ ■ ■ ■ ■ ■ ■ ■
WAYS OF PROVIDING JOB
SECURITY.

■ ■ ■ ■ ■ ■ ■

[16] Robert H. Guest, "Management Imperatives for the Year 2000," *California Management Review*, Summer 1986, p. 62.

back. The psychological effect from providing job security is quite rewarding. When people know that their jobs are not at stake, they tend to be more productive.

CAREER-LONG TRAINING

Well-managed organizations realize the importance of career-long training, and in some cases the manager's performance evaluation is directly tied to this idea. For example, at Levi Strauss a significant portion of a manager's annual merit evaluation is determined by how well the individual trains his or her people. The typical manager is expected to cross-train at least two people a year and to take responsibility for mentoring one younger person. Other organizations spend millions of dollars sending their people off site for specific types of training. For example, Arco brings all of its upper-middle-level managers to its elegant training facility at Santa Barbara, California for a two-week training program. Wal-Mart, the giant discount retailer, has a two-part, multimillion dollar program which it conducts year-round. All personnel are provided technical and sales training at a corporate headquarters site. All district managers, store managers, and assistant store managers are given a one-week management training program (Phase One) at the Wal-Mart Institute headquartered at a nearby major university. Additionally, the company is now beginning to offer a Phase Two program at the Institute in order to provide more in-depth training of these managers.

■ ■ ■ ■ ■ ■ ■ ■ ■ ■ ■ ■
TRAINING IS BEING EMPHASIZED.

PARTICIPATION IN DECISION MAKING

Successful organizations provide their people greater decision-making autonomy and authority. In many cases this is done through the use of participative work-teams and quality circles. Another developing trend is that of getting the union involved in this process by making it a partner in some of the important decision making. For example, when Honeywell planned to conduct an employee attitude survey, the company first met with Teamsters officials to get their ideas about what items to include in the survey. The firm then voluntarily shared the results with the union. Moreover, some of the most recent labor contracts are a result of co-operative bargaining by both sides. Instead of labor negotiations becoming an "us against them issue," it is now becoming a joint effort. In some cases, management has even offered seats on the board of directors to the union so that it can more actively participate in company affairs. Organizations are realizing that shared authority often produces greater results than limited authority.

■ ■ ■ ■ ■ ■ ■ ■ ■ ■ ■ ■
SO IS PARTICIPATIVE DECISION MAKING.

FLEXIBLE BENEFITS

Flexible benefits can take many different forms. One is the cafeteria plans that were discussed in Chapter 2. These provide the employee with a wide variety of options including the following:

- supplementary group life insurance
- savings and investment plans
- retirement income plans
- medical assistance plans
- occupational death insurance
- basic health care plans
- dental assistance plans
- family protection plans
- long-term disability insurance
- group life and survivor insurance plans
- eye examinations
- holiday and vacation allowance plans

SABBATICALS ARE GAINING IN POPULARITY.

The future will see the addition of others, many of which are not financial in orientation. A good example is the **sabbatical**, which is a time period during which the individual receives full pay and benefits but does not come to work. Instead, during this period the individual is given time to unwind, refresh, and in some cases, do things that were not possible when working full-time. Some personnel will use this time to study. Others will formulate career plans. In any event, the individual often returns to work invigorated and does a better job than before. Sabbaticals are increasing in popularity. The Wells Fargo Bank in San Francisco gives three-month sabbaticals to employees who have been with the company for at least 15 years. Tandem Computers offers six-week sabbaticals to its people every four years. Rolm incorporates a financial incentive into its program by giving full-time employees the option of twelve weeks' leave at full pay or six weeks at double pay.

STOCK OWNERSHIP

Well-managed corporations have found that stock ownership is an excellent way of motivating people and getting them to do their best work. O'Toole, who has made an in-depth investigation of employee practices at the best-managed firms, puts it this way: "If you own a piece of the action, you are more likely to work harder than if you are a mere hired hand."[17] In recent years there have been many examples of companies

[17] James O'Toole, "Employee Practices at the Best Managed Companies," *California Management Review*, Fall 1985, p. 39.

sharing stock ownership with employees. In some cases the initial reason was survival; the company was in trouble and was looking to the employees to help it out. Yet, while the motivation may have been self-serving, the results were effective. Here are some examples:

> As part of the federal bailout of the Chrysler Corporation, employees assumed up to 20 percent ownership of the firm; to save Eastern Airlines, employees traded pay cuts for 25 percent of the carrier's stock; at the Weirton Steel Works, 6,000 employees purchased the plant from the National Steel Corporation for some $585 million; when the Great Atlantic & Pacific Tea Company announced it might have to shut down twenty Philadelphia A&P supermarkets, approximately 1,000 store clerks swapped pay cuts in exchange for a significant share of store ownership; and employee ownership has even come—indirectly—to General Motors. (In 1981, 1,200 workers bought a bearings plant from GM for some $53 million.) All told, between 1973 and 1983, some sixty corporations in deep financial trouble were purchased by employees. According to the Conference Board, only two of these employee-owned companies failed; and at least 50,000 jobs were saved during the decade.[18]

Other firms, not in deep financial difficulty, have found that promoting employee stock ownership is an effective human relations strategy. It makes the personnel realize that they are part of the overall team; and they know that every time they do something well, it can benefit them financially in the form of higher stock prices. Employee stock ownership plans help eliminate the perception that the organization is divided into two groups, managers and workers. These plans promote a team approach to viewing problems and formulating solutions. To the extent that they promote effective human relations, they serve two purposes: They are good for the company and they are good for the people.

STOCK OWNERSHIP IS MOTIVATIONAL.

STOP!

Review your answer to the fourth question and make any changes you would like. Then compare your answer to the one below.

4.   Would a stock ownership plan be motivational? Why or why not?

- - - - - - -

[18] *Ibid.*, pp. 39–40.

A stock ownership plan would be motivational for a number of reasons. One of the most important is because it allows the personnel to share in the success of the company. If the workers do a good job and profits go up, the company has a greater value. This value should be reflected in the price of the company's stock. If the employees own this stock, then they will also profit from the success of the company. ■

SUMMARY

The decade of the 1990s will see a number of important human relations challenges. One will be a greater focus on innovation. Most people are more creative than they believe, and creativity is widespread in the population. In encouraging creativity, organizations need to debunk some of the myths about innovation. They also need to implement innovation principles such as promoting the active search for new ideas, encouraging people to learn from their failures, and rewarding those who are most innovative. Another important step is the development of intrapreneurs.

A second major challenge of the 1990s will be the development of a better understanding of international human relations. When countries fall into different cultural clusters, their norms, values, mores, habits, and customs are different. These differences can often be accounted for by such causes as the degree of individualism or collectivism, people's view of time, the use of private and public space, and the amount of uncertainty that managers will tolerate. In dealing with this challenge, there are four things that can be done: Be aware of perceptual differences, learn how international managers behave, understand the other country's philosophy of work, and prepare personnel for overseas work.

A third major human relations challenge of the 1990s will be the need for greater awareness of changing social values. For example, organizations are going to have to learn both to educate the work force regarding AIDS and to protect the legal rights of those affected by the disease. Another social challenge will be to deal with the growing desire of employees for greater privacy. This will range from how to handle drug testing and the use of lie detectors to monitoring electronic surveillance of employees. A third social challenge will be to remain abreast of the movement toward a family-sensitive work place as reflected in the increasing popularity of parental leave policies.

A fourth major challenge will be the implementation of human relations practices that are being used by the best-managed firms. This will involve consideration of issues such as job security, career-long training, participation in decision making, flexible benefits, and stock ownership.

KEY TERMS IN THE CHAPTER

creative person   ethnocentrism
culture   parental leave policy
cultural cluster   sabbatical

REVIEW AND STUDY QUESTIONS

1.   Are most people more creative than their jobs require? Explain.

2.   What are some of the characteristics of creative people? List five.

3.   What are some of the myths about creativity? Identify and discuss three of them.

4.   How can an organization improve its innovation? Identify five useful principles.

5.   What is a cultural cluster? Give an example.

6.   How can one examine the differences that exist between cultural clusters? Discuss three areas that could be examined.

7.   In what way is ethnocentrism a problem in effective international human relations?

8.   How can firms prepare their people for overseas work? Explain.

9.   Do individuals with AIDS have any employment rights? What are they?

10.   What privacy issues are organizations likely to confront during the 1990s? Identify and describe two. How can organizations deal with this human relations challenge? Explain.

11.   How does a parental leave policy work? Why is it useful for organizations to be aware of the growing popularity of this type of policy?

12.   Is guaranteed job security a good idea?

13.   How would a sabbatical be of value to an employee? Are sabbaticals a good idea?

14.   Why are employee stock ownership plans useful motivational tools?

TIME OUT ANSWERS: ANSWERS TO
IMPROVING YOUR OWN CREATIVENESS

1.   mad dad

2.   glad lad

3.   book crook

4.   ape cape

5.   fat cat

6.   near beer

7.   deep weep

8.   fast repast

9.   lean cuisine

10.   frail snail

- 8–10   Excellent
- 6–7   Above average
- 4–5   Average
- 1–3   Below average

Regardless of how well you did, remember that creativity can be improved. Individuals who like crossword puzzles or enjoy puns tend to do best on these rhyme-type tests. Your creative interests may lie in other areas, so do not be disheartened. This test is only one of many that can give you insights to your own creativity.

CASE: *LOOK OUT WORLD, HERE WE COME*

Roxling Inc., a consumer appliance firm, plans on going international. The company designs and manufactures small, lightweight appliances. The organization has many patents on its products and is widely considered to be one of the foremost firms in this growing industry.

In the past, a number of companies from other countries have approached Roxling and asked for the right to manufacture or distribute its products overseas. Roxling has refused because it wants to maintain total control of both the production and the distribution of its products. Six months ago the firm concluded that it is now in a position to begin expanding internationally. The company would like to move into three countries within the next six months: England, Hong Kong, and Saudi Arabia.

Roxling's initial plan is to train salespeople for the overseas market. These people will operate out of small offices in these countries and will send their sales reports back to headquarters. These orders will then be shipped from the United States to the overseas customers. Over the next two years this approach will be modified with the company opening up manufacturing plants in both Europe and the Far East. This strategy will reduce both delivery time and transportation costs.

Some members of Roxling's board of directors have suggested that the company spend more time preparing for this overseas expansion. "You really don't know much about these overseas countries," one of them explained. "You are going to have to find out a lot more about the culture and methods of doing business there than we know currently. Doing business in Saudi Arabia, for example, is a lot different from doing business in Chicago. We can't assume that our methods are going to fit in overseas and that we can simply send people over and have them go out and get orders."

The company president agrees with these comments, but is unsure of what specific types of training to give his salespeople. "We are going to be selling products that have worldwide appeal," he explained. "This is going to help overcome a lot of the cultural barriers that most firms have to deal with. Also, there is no better way to learn the culture of a country than to go and live there, and this is exactly what we are going to have our salespeople doing. They are going to be within a day's drive of their customers, and if there are any problems they can quickly resolve them."

The firm intends to start its sales training program within the next three weeks. This will be followed by an initial scheduling of salespeople to overseas locations. Roxling intends to have a sales force in the field within six months.

QUESTIONS

1.   Could cultural analysis help the firm prepare for its overseas expansion? Explain.

2.   With which of the three overseas countries will Roxling have the greatest cultural problem? Why?

3.   What guidelines would you recommend to the company for dealing with the human relations challenges it will be facing overseas? Explain. ■

CASE: *IT'S ALL A MATTER OF TIME*

Over the past 50 years, Southern Bank has become one of the largest financial institutions in its geographic region. The bank offers a wide variety of services from regular checking and savings accounts to home mortgages, investment counseling, and estate planning. The bank has long been considered a good place to work, but in recent years its turnover has been fairly high and some of its competitors have put together better benefit packages for their own personnel.

For most of its history, Southern was run by members of the Shotte family who founded the bank. Five years ago Arthur Santini became president. Arthur had been a senior vice-president at another large bank which had a wide array of both personal and business services. Since this was the area into which Southern wanted to expand, Arthur was a prime candidate for the job. The bank gave Arthur a large salary and a free hand in planning long-range strategy. He accepted the job and began immediately to increase the bank's business services. This was followed, three years ago, by the introduction of extensive personal services. As a result of these strategies, Southern's assets have doubled over the last four years.

One of the keys to success in the banking business is the ability to maintain personnel. In particular, if managers move to other banks, they often take their customers with them. The loss of lower-level personnel is not as serious, but it does mean the bank will have to underwrite the expense of hiring and training replacements.

In an effort to deal with this employee turnover problem and to continue increasing its asset base, Arthur has decided to introduce some changes in bank operations. He intends to implement three initial programs within the next 90 days. The first is a job security program. Under this program, the bank will provide increased job security to its personnel. Anyone who has 10 years of service with the bank will be guaranteed employment until the minimum retirement time period is reached, which in most cases is 20 years of service.

Albert also intends to support an extensive career-long training program. This program will be handled by an in-house Training and Development Department which will be responsible for training personnel at all levels of the organization from tellers and clerks to branch managers and vice-presidents.

The third program will relate to flexible benefits. In addition to the regular financial benefits such as life and health insurance and retirement programs, Arthur wants to see the bank sponsor a sabbatical program that will be offered to managers every seven years and to other personnel every ten years. "If we introduce these programs," Arthur told his senior vice-president, "we will reduce employee turnover and develop one of the finest banking organizations in the country. And this is only the beginning. We will make additional changes over the next five years that will solidify our gains. It's all a matter of time and of incorporating the right human relations programs."

QUESTIONS

1.　Is Arthur's proposed plan a good one? Defend your answer.

2.　In addition to his current plan, what other programs might be introduced in the future? Identify and describe two.

3.　In what way will these programs help the bank? What human relations benefits do they offer? Cite and explain three. ∎

EXPERIENCING THE IMPACT OF INTERNATIONAL CULTURE

PURPOSE

- To understand the impact of culture on human relations.
- To learn the types of cultural barriers that must be overcome when "going international."
- To apply these concepts to on-the-job situations.

PROCEDURE

1. Divide the class into groups of three or four students each. With the exception of the Anglo cluster, each group is to choose one of the country clusters in Figure 14.2. If there are more than seven teams, the independent clusters (Brazil, Japan, India, Israel) may be used.

2. Each group should then choose one of the countries within their cluster and gather information on the cultural problems that the company described below (see Situation) would face. Interviews with foreign students and professors with specific knowledge of this country, as well as library research, should be employed.

3. After identifying the major cultural problems the company would face and the ways in which the firm should deal with these problems, present your findings to the rest of the class.

4. Note the similarities and differences faced by firms operating in the various cultures.

SITUATION

You are working for a firm that plans to open an overseas branch to sell its industrial machinery directly to customers in this foreign country. Your firm has never before sold its products outside of the United States directly. You are to present your boss with a list of the major cultural barriers which must be surmounted if this sales effort is to be successful.

15

HUMAN RELATIONS AND YOU

GOALS OF THE CHAPTER

Having studied what the field of modern human relations is, we now turn our attention to the ways in which you can use human relations to help you obtain employment and move ahead in your chosen career. Before reading on, test yourself in the accompanying Time Out to see how much you know about applying human relations to a job interview.

The first goal of this chapter is to discuss the ways of choosing a career including how to make a self-evaluation. This will provide you insights into your abilities and shortcomings.

The second goal is to study the ways of actually finding a job. In doing so, particular attention will be devoted to writing an effective resumé and carrying out a successful job hunt.

The third goal is to identify some of the most important steps in managing your career effectively. Consideration will also be given to the role and value of a mentor and the importance of dressing for success and organizing your office properly.

The final goal of this chapter is to examine the responsibilities and challenges for the modern manager. Here the focus is on the conditions you will face in carrying out your managerial tasks.

When you have finished reading this chapter you should be able to:

1. Set forth the key questions that should be asked in carrying out a self-evaluation.

2. Write an effective resumé and carry out a successful job hunt.

3.   Describe some of the major steps you should follow in managing your career effectively.

4.   Set forth some of the basic rules regarding both how to dress for success and organize your office properly.

5.   Discuss the challenges that face the human relations–oriented manager of the 1990s.

OPENING CASE

DEVELOPING A PLAN OF ACTION

Jed Miller will be receiving his undergraduate degree in accounting at the end of next semester. Jed would like to get an early start in looking for a job. He has signed up to interview with four firms that will be coming to campus within the next month. He will also be interviewing with six firms that are scheduled to be on campus at the beginning of next semester.

Jed has heard that it is a good idea to gather some information on the companies he will be interviewing. A friend told him, "They're really impressed when they find that you know something about them. It shows interest and initiative on your part."

Jed has also been getting some information on starting salaries. He asked the chairman of the Accounting Department and two friends who are graduating this semester. Between the three of them, Jed has determined a minimum and maximum salary range that should be offered to him.

Jed is beginning to think about questions that he might be asked during the interview and how he would respond. He knows that a favorite question is: Why do you want to work for us? Jed is also formulating questions that he would like to ask the interviewer. Jed realizes that most firms will offer him similar compensation packages and work assignments. However, he wants to get some information regarding his future with the firm. What type of work can he expect to be doing in five years? Ten years? How long will it take before he learns if he is going to be made a partner? What type of performance record would he have to achieve in order to be considered for such a position? Jed believes that these questions will help the recruiter understand how serious Jed is about the job. They should also be useful in helping him stand out from the other applicants and improve his chances of being made a job offer.

1.   In addition to the question presented in the case, what other questions might the recruiter ask Jed? List three.

2.   What should Jed say if the recruiter asks him: What were you looking for in terms of a starting salary?

3.   What are some useful guidelines that Jed should follow in managing his career? Discuss three.

Write down your answers to these questions and put them aside. We will return to them later. ■

CHOOSING A CAREER

The value of human relations is not confined to the management of others. It can also be used in choosing a career and succeeding in that choice. When applied this way, human relations concepts can be employed in making an accurate self-evaluation and a successful job hunt.

MAKE A SELF-EVALUATION

The most important initial step in applying human relations concepts to your career is that of evaluating yourself. What do you do well? What do you do poorly? In conducting this evaluation, some of the most important questions are the following:

1.   What do you do best?

2.   What do you like to do?

3.   What do you dislike doing?

4.   Do you work well with others or do you work best by yourself?

5.   Do you know your own talents and abilities? What are they?

6.   What do you think you would like to do for a living? Has your education prepared you for this career, or is further training necessary?

7.   How hard are you willing to work?

8.   What are your work habits? Do you work at a steady pace or in short bursts of intensive effort?

9.   Have you sought any information or professional advice regarding your career choice(s)? What have you learned?

10.   How will you go about beginning your career employment search?

These questions require you to apply many of the ideas you have studied in this book to your own career development. Included in this group are such concepts as: motivation, personality, values, group behavior, job design, leadership, communication, and your ability to deal with change. This type of self-analysis is helpful because it provides basic direction in assessing where you are and where you would like to go.

TIME OUT

INTERVIEWING EFFECTIVELY

One of the most important steps in getting the job you want is to impress the interviewer. Quite often, this individual will interview a dozen people and then recommend three or four for further consideration. If you cannot pass this initial screening, you will not get the job. Read and answer the following questions related to effective interviewing. Answers are provided at the end of the chapter.

		TRUE	FALSE
1.	Know something about the firm and make the interviewer aware that you have done this background research.	_____	_____
2.	Don't just answer questions; ask some. Interviewers like this feedback because it shows an interest on your part.	_____	_____
3.	If you are asked if you would be willing to relocate, say no because this indicates the willingness to take a position and stay with it.	_____	_____
4.	If you are unsure of how to dress for the interview, it is better to be too formal than too informal.	_____	_____
5.	It is important that you be on time for the interview, even if the interviewer is running late.	_____	_____
6.	If you are asked the starting salary you are looking for, give a figure that is about 20 percent higher than the going rate because you can always negotiate down.	_____	_____
7.	If you are asked about interviews you have had with other firms, make it a point to note that you were not very impressed with these other firms but are impressed with the current one.	_____	_____
8.	Be sure to ask detailed questions about the company's benefit and retirement program. This is one way of communicating a genuine interest in the job.	_____	_____
9.	If you smoke or chew gum, do so during the interview because this indicates a degree of individualism and most interviewers will be impressed by this.	_____	_____
10.	When the interview is over, make it a point to ask the individual when you can expect to hear from the firm.	_____	_____

This preparation also is important in helping you identify both the preparation and basic skills that will be needed for a successful career. For example, many companies require applicants for management jobs to have a college degree, and in some cases the degree must be in a particular area. Supervisors and first-line managers typically do not need to have majored in any specific area although many firms do like to hire business majors for these positions. Salespeople are often hired from all areas except when the product is highly technical and the firm knows that engineers make the best salespeople. Other jobs require specific training. Accountants must major in accounting; at advertising agencies, advertising majors have the inside track over other applicants; and most personnel departments will give the nod to those who have majored in personnel/human resource management.

An understanding of your basic skills is important because it helps direct both your educational and your career choice. If you are a highly analytical person, you should look for a career where this trait is a key factor for success. Examples include banking, market research, operations management, and stock brokering. If you have high social and personal/interactive skills, you should consider career choices such as advertising, personal services, sales, and training and development.

DO NOT UNDERRATE YOUR ABILITY   In your self-analysis, be sure not to underrate your ability. Otherwise you will be selling yourself short. One way of approaching this subject is to keep in mind that you not only possess ability, but you probably have more than enough to do most jobs. This idea is illustrated in Figure 14.1. People often have more ability than is required by the job.

If you do feel you are above average in ability, be sure to take this into consideration. What may be an interesting or challenging job for the average person could prove quite boring to you. Try to match your interests and abilities with the requirements of the job. At the same time, remember that you may not have the opportunity to use all of your abilities and talents immediately. Sometimes the first year or two entail a great deal of technical, boring work, and you will not find the job highly rewarding until you receive a promotion or two. You have to be willing to persevere if you want the chance to use your ability.

DEVELOP AN OVERALL PLAN OF ACTION

Once a self-assessment has been completed, the next major step is to formulate an overall plan of action. What jobs are available? What career choices have you identified? How should you go about writing your resumé? What steps need to be taken to ensure the most successful job in-

FIGURE 15.1   A CAREER PLANNING CHECKLIST

Below is a checklist to see how far along you are in your job search. Check off the areas you have completed.

ASSESS YOURSELF

SETTING

☐ I have chosen the setting in which I would like to work (i.e., large industrial, small business, government, non-profit).

☐ I have chosen one of the following locations: rural, urban, suburban.

SKILLS

☐ I have listed my three most useful job skills.

☐ I know what I am most successful doing.

☐ I have identified whether I want to work with people, data or things.

☐ I know whether I want to be supervised or be the supervisor.

☐ I know if I want to work with others or work alone.

INTERESTS

☐ I have listed some of the main career areas I might be interested in.

☐ I have decided whether I like "doing" or "thinking" activities at work.

☐ I have listed my favorite activities (hobbies, sports, etc.).

VALUES

☐ I have listed some of the most important values to me (i.e., prestige, security, variety).

☐ I know what kind of rewards are important to me in a job, i.e., social, monetary, job flexibility.

RESEARCH CAREER INFORMATION

☐ I am familiar with the career information in the placement office library so I am able to further explore my options.

☐ I have developed a list of career possibilities to research.

☐ I keep up with current trends in my field (salary, job requirements, growth).

☐ I have identified employers interested in interviewing people with my academic background and experience.

☐ I have compiled a list of potential employers who may not have immediate openings, but would be good prospects in the future.

☐ I have a list of three or more employers in the field I'm considering.

☐ I have made at least three contacts in my field.

☐ I have sought information and advice from people in my field.

TRY WORK OPTIONS

☐ I have narrowed down the career options I am considering.

☐ I have identified the needed additional educational or experiential background I need to better prepare for, or help test my choices, i.e., course work, part-time work, extracurricular activities.

☐ I have discovered ways my academic course work supports my career objective.

☐ I have participated in some work experience or internship program in my field of interest.

☐ I am aware of the daily realities of the occupational area I am approaching.

☐ I have visited several of the work sites being considered as my career choice.

☐ I have become an active member in at least one professional association to enhance my job awareness.

FIND YOUR JOB

☐ I have a clear job objective.

☐ I have written a resume which:
  ☐ shows how my skills and experience fit my objective
  ☐ speaks in terms of accomplishments and uses action verbs
  ☐ is one, or at the most, two pages
  ☐ has no spelling or grammatical errors
  ☐ has been typed and professionally duplicated

☐ I am ready to compose a specific cover letter to accompany each resume.

THE INTERVIEW

☐ I have thoroughly researched the employer with whom I am to interview.

☐ I have completed informational interviewing to gather information about employers.

☐ I have practiced my interviewing technique and am prepared to answer most interview questions.

☐ I have questions to ask employers during the interview.

☐ I will arrive at the interview on time and looking professional.

☐ I have written a thank-you letter after each interview.

Source: Courtesy of Florida International University.

terview? These questions should be put into the form of a checklist so that you do not forget to do something important. Figure 15.1 provides a sample checklist that can be used for this purpose.

FINDING A JOB

After your self-analysis, the next step is finding a job. This requires you to do two things. First, you have to write a resumé that attracts attention and points you out as someone whom the organization should pursue. Second, you have to conduct yourself properly during the job hunt, especially the interview.

THE EFFECTIVE RESUMÉ

Regardless of the job you are seeking, you should put together a **resumé** or summary of your education, work experience, training, and references. The resumé is typically the first step to the interview. After reviewing resumés of job applicants, an organization will choose those that look most promising and extend them an interview. Without an effective resumé, you will never get to the interview stage.

■ ■ ■ ■ ■ ■ ■ ■ ■ ■ ■ ■
A RESUMÉ IS A SUMMARY OF YOUR PAST EXPERIENCE AND TRAINING.

If you are just starting out in a career, your resumé should be simple, straightforward, and factual. A good general rule is to make it only one to two pages long, and, if you are looking at one organization only, gear it specifically to that enterprise. Otherwise, it can be more general. Some of the most important guidelines you should follow in putting together your resumé are the following:

1.   Group your information into four to six categories such as personal data, employment objective, education, work experience, special interests, and references.

2.   Start by listing your name, address, telephone number, and other personal information; then move on to your education and job experience, listing your most recent degree or job first and working backwards.

3.   If you do have a specific employment objective, state it, but avoid the use of generalities such as "wanting a challenging position" or a "desire to work with people." These do not really tell the reader a great deal.

4.   Use a format that is easy to read, has eye appeal, and provides a positive impression about you and your goals. If you feel it is necessary or useful, underline some words or capitalize them.

5.   Have duplicated copies of your resumé if you intend to interview with more than a handful of firms; these should be made up by a professional printer so that each copy looks identical to the original.

6.   If you want to send along a picture of yourself, do so. However, attach it to the resumé; do not have it printed as part of the resumé. In this way if the organization is prohibited by state law from requiring pictures or simply does not want them as part of the resumé, the picture can be removed.

7.   References are optional. If you are just starting out, it is useful to list them. If you have been working for a number of years, you may not want anyone to contact your references without your approval; in this case, simply state that these are available on request.

Notice that the seven suggestions all draw upon human relations concepts, and they help you present yourself in a positive light. Figures 15.2 and 15.3 provide illustrations of resumés that follow these suggestions.[1] The first example is known as a chronological resumé. A *chronological resumé* presents information in descending order with the most recent events listed first under each heading. The second example is known as a functional resumé. A *functional resumé* allows the individual to focus on skills, aptitudes, and qualities that can be applied to a number of situations. Skills are organized into categories that tell employers what the job applicant can do for them. The functional resumé is recommended for those who: (1) lack direct job-related experience; (2) want to work in fields not related to their academic background; or (3) have an education that is so general that they must find a way of bridging the gap between their education and the job requirements.

THE SUCCESSFUL JOB HUNT

If you have written an effective resumé, the next step is to get it into the right hands. One of the easiest ways, if you are about to graduate, is by signing up at the college placement office with prospective employers who will be recruiting on campus. Another way is to contact directly organizations that have job openings and send them your resumé. If things go your way, you will be interviewed and hired. From a human relations standpoint, however, there are six things you need to know.

■ ■ ■ ■ ■ ■ ■ ■ ■ ■ ■ ■ ■ ■ ■   **SILENCE CAN BE GOLDEN**   If you already have a job and are looking
SOMETIMES IT IS BEST TO SAY   for another, do not advertise this fact to everyone. Keep your search
NOTHING.   quiet, seeking help only from friends or business associates who can pro-

■ ■ ■ ■ ■ ■ ■

[1] For information on how to tailor your resume to each new stage of your career, see Hanna Rubin, "One Little Resume—And How It Grew," *Working Woman*, April 1987, pp. 100–104.

FIGURE 15.2   **A CHRONOLOGICAL RESUMÉ**

JUAN HERNANDEZ
1234 S.W. 123 Street
Miami, Florida 33199
(305) 123-4567

EDUCATION: FLORIDA INTERNATIONAL UNIVERSITY
The State University of Florida at Miami
Miami, Florida
Bachelor of Business Administration-Marketing
Anticipated date of graduation—April 1992
G.P.A.—3.6

MIAMI DADE COMMUNITY COLLEGE
Miami, Florida
Associate of Arts—June 1990
Graduated Cum Laude

EMPLOYMENT: Market Representative, Bigtime Enterprises
Miami, Florida—Summer 1989
Serviced area retail accounts. Maintained store displays and checked inventory. Introduced new products. Completed reports and supplied district office with statistics and marketing information.

Salesperson, American Services Incorporated
Miami, Florida—(1/88–1/89)
Assisted customers in clothing selections. Utilized effective communication skills in developing good customer relations. Identified quick selling items. Marked down merchandise and implemented promotional projects.

ACTIVITIES: American Marketing Association; Program Chairman, Student Government Association; Publicity Committee, International Week Festival.

HONORS: Dean's List; XYZ Scholarship Recipient 1989; Who's Who Among American College Students.

PERSONAL: Citizenship: USA
Languages: Spanish, working knowledge of French
Willing to relocate

REFERENCES: To be furnished upon request.

Source: Placement Office, Florida International University.

vide leads or introductions. If your boss will hit the ceiling or jeopardize your career should he or she find out you are looking for other employment, ask all potential employers to treat your application confidentially.

On the other hand, if this is your first career job, you should go out of your way to advertise it. Interview with all campus recruiters who have

FIGURE 15.3   A FUNCTIONAL RESUMÉ

JUAN HERNANDEZ
1234 S.W. 123 Street
Miami, Florida 33199
(305) 123-4567

EDUCATION

Bachelor of Business Administration-Marketing
FLORIDA INTERNATIONAL UNIVERSITY
The State University of Florida at Miami
Miami, Florida
Anticipated date of graduation—April 1992
G.P.A.—3.60

Associate of Arts
MIAMI DADE COMMUNITY COLLEGE—June 1990
Miami, Florida
Graduated Cum Laude

SKILLS

MARKETING: Maintained area accounts for large consumer goods manufacturer. Assisted customers in purchase selections, increasing department sales by 15%. Conducted survey of student enrollment to identify areas of interest for program development.

PUBLIC   Promoted positive company image while assisting customers and clients.
RELATIONS: Effectively resolved sales problems and complaints, reducing number of complaint files by 5%. Developed promotional material to advertise university programs. Worked in conjunction with local media to promote events. Developed student suggestion HOT LINE to improve working relationship between students and administration.

WORK HISTORY

5/91–8/91   Market Representative, Bigtime Incorporated
              Miami, Florida
5/90–5/91   Salesperson, American Services Incorporated
              Miami, Florida

ACTIVITIES

American Marketing Association; Program Chairman, Student Government Association; Publicity Committee, International Week Festival.

HONORS

Dean's List; XYZ Scholarship Recipient 1989; Who's Who Among American College Students.

REFERENCES

Available upon request.

Source: Placement Office, Florida International University.

job openings similar to your career objectives. Give all of your major professors a copy of your resumé for distribution to any employer they may meet who is looking for someone with your qualifications.

DON'T ANSWER EVERY EMPLOYMENT AD   Many firms place help-wanted ads in newspapers and trade journals. Most identify themselves and describe their job openings; some merely provide a brief explanation of the individual they are seeking and a coded box number to which one can send a resumé. The former ads, which seem to offer those opportunities you are seeking, are worth pursuing; the latter are not. In most cases, blind ads, as these are known, do not result in responses. The organization is usually trying to gauge the labor supply in the field or determine salary levels for certain types of jobs; so you may be wasting your time by applying.

KNOW HOW TO BE INTERVIEWED   When you get an interview, you are halfway toward your goal of a job offer. Now you want to be sure that you do not flub your chance. The first thing you should do is bone up on the company. What goods or services does it produce? How much did it gross last year? What is its reputation? If you know about the company, this is likely to impress the interviewer and improve your chances of a job offer. However, do not stop here. Develop some questions that demonstrate your knowledge of your field. Let the interviewer know that you know what you are talking about. Be prepared to go on the offensive.

The interview is a very important step in the successful job hunt. Being prepared will improve your chances of receiving a job offer.

Also keep in mind that the interviewer is checking to see if there could be personal chemistry between you and the organization. How you dress, act, and talk are all important. Keep things on a positive note. If you are asked about your ability to interact well with others, talk about your personality strengths. If you are asked why you are leaving your current job, discuss your desire for increased responsibility and challenge. Do not talk negatively either about yourself or your current employer. Such discussion casts a pall over the interview and can result in your losing the job.[2]

■ ■ ■ ■ ■ ■ ■ ■ ■ ■ ■ ■ ■ ■
BE POSITIVE IN YOUR APPROACH.

Other typical questions you should expect from the interviewer include: Aside from the information on your resumé, what else have you done that would prepare you for a job with this company? What are you looking for in an employer? Why did you apply with us? Where do you hope to be after ten years with this firm? What are your long-range objectives? If you are prepared with answers for the most likely questions, your interview is more likely to proceed smoothly.

■ ■ ■ ■ ■ ■ ■

[2] For additional tips see Shirley J. Shepherd, "How to Get That Job in 60 Minutes or Less," *Working Woman*, May 1986, pp. 118–120.

STOP!

Review your answer to the first question and make any changes you would like. Then compare your answer to the one below.

1.   In addition to the question presented in the case, what other questions might the recruiter ask Jed? List three.

Some of the questions that Jed is likely to be asked include: What are your biggest strengths? What are your major shortcomings? What do you think you could do for our firm? ∎

DOWNPLAY SALARY   How do you answer the question, "What salary do you want?" If possible, sidestep the question by explaining that salary is only one of your considerations and you would prefer to learn more about the job. If you are pushed into an answer, cite a range such as $18,000–$22,000 rather than a single figure, such as $20,700. If the employer is willing to pay $20,200 for the job, you are in the ballpark with a salary range answer but too high with a set number. Additionally, because they really do want the job, some people will drop their asking price to a lower level, such as $19,700. In this case, they have given up $500 since the employer is seldom inclined to pay more than is necessary.

TALK OPPORTUNITY NOT SALARY.

If you are just starting out, you really do not have to be concerned with knowing how much to request. Most employers have a specific salary range for positions and, if they do not, you can compare starting salaries and job requirements at interviews before deciding which job to take.[3]

STRIVE FOR ORIGINALITY   Most organizations will be interviewing more than one person for each job opening. If you are a typical candidate, you will do all of the usual things: write an interesting resumé, dress well, act properly. However, if possible, try to do something different. Look for a way to distinguish yourself from the others. While this requires some degree of creativity, it does not have to be truly unique. The following is an example:

TRY TO BE DIFFERENT.

> Career counselor John C. Crystal tells of one of his students, a high school teacher, who wanted to become a personal financial planner and counselor. He embarked on an ambitious

▪▪▪▪▪▪▪

[3] See also John Stickney, "Setting the Terms of Employment," *Money*, December 1984, pp. 127–132.

exploration of the field. "He visited 55 financial planners across the country," says Crystal. "When he called for interview appointments, he told each one what he was doing—surveying those in the field to learn about the business. After his first visits he could tell successive planners that he had just talked to so-and-so, and that opened doors for him. By the time he had completed his research, he had received eight unsolicited job offers."[4]

DO NOT LOSE HOPE   As you get into your job search, you may discover yourself sending out 30 resumés and getting 15 responses of which only 10 express any interest. You may also find yourself interviewing with seven of these firms and only two make you an offer, neither of which you feel is truly competitive. As a result, you may decide to start the process all over and send out resumés to new organizations. The important thing to remember is do not despair. Keep a positive attitude. You will eventually get something that will satisfy you.

■ ■ ■ ■ ■ ■ ■ ■ ■ ■ ■ ■ ■ ■
KEEP A POSITIVE ATTITUDE.

> To find a job you must sell your capabilities, and tired or unenthusiastic salespeople don't make sales. You can't let the stress of the job hunt lead you to undervalue your potential or restrict your options. There is no logical reason to despair. You know the kind of work you are capable of doing. The big catch is meeting the person who needs someone like you to do a job. Logic says that will happen sooner or later.[5]

When that job does arrive, be sure to ask the right questions before accepting it. Human Relations in Action: Asking the Right Questions notes what these are.

STOP!

Review your answer to the second question and make any changes you would like. Then compare your answer to the one below.

2.   What should Jed say if the recruiter asks him: What were you looking for in terms of a starting salary?

Jed should try to sidestep the question. Let the recruiter or the company set the salary and, if this is not acceptable, then negotiations can begin.

■ ■ ■ ■ ■ ■ ■

[4] "Eight Ways to Flub a Job Hunt," *Changing Times*, December 1981, p. 78.

[5] *Ibid.*, p. 79.

HUMAN RELATIONS IN ACTION

ASKING THE RIGHT QUESTIONS

No matter how much you want a particular job, there are some important questions you should ask before you agree to accept the position. In asking them, remember that you have to be direct while also being friendly. Six of the most important of these are:

1.   *What happened to the last person to hold this job?* If the person was promoted, ask why. Now you have an idea of what the firm is looking for from the person who holds this job. If the person was fired, find out why. This tells you what not to do.

2.   *Can I talk to someone who is doing the same basic type of job that I'll be doing?* This will help you find out what is good and bad about the department. No one knows better than the personnel, and they very often are willing to share this information with new people.

3.   *How, and by whom, will my performance be measured?* Find out what the organization expects from you and how they will determine if you are doing a good job. To head off confusion later on, keep the criteria as objective and measurable as possible.

4.   *What is the salary range for this job and what other compensation do you offer?* This may appear too direct, but most firms like to talk about their financial package. If you are moving from another job, this question is particularly important because you should not move for less than a 20 percent salary increase, unless you are very anxious to join the company. Additionally, you should find out about any bonuses, perks such as a company car or club membership, vacations, health insurance, pension, and profit-sharing plans. Get all of the financial data so you know exactly what you will be getting in terms of remuneration.

5.   *If relocation is involved, how much will the company help?* If you are commuting across town, the firm will not give you any assistance. However, if you must relocate, this will take time and money. In many major cities, you will end up paying a fee to secure an apartment. If you have to sell your house and buy another, there is a broker commission on the sale and there will be financial points on the new loan as well as, in all likelihood, a higher rate of interest. If the firm is unwilling to absorb any of these expenses, you have to add them into the cost of taking the job. Quite often a move to another location is financially unwise unless the firm helps with costs.

6.   *Would you mind putting all of this in writing?* It never hurts to ask for the agreement in writing. This is particularly true if your employment arrangement contains anything other than standard items such as salary, benefits, and vacation time. In this way, you do not have to worry about some manager later saying, "We never agreed to that. We don't pay those expenses for anyone." You will have it in writing.

Jed should focus on what the job will require and whether there is a right "fit" between himself and the company. ■

GETTING AHEAD

After you have secured a job, there are still ways in which human relations knowledge can help you. These include ways of managing your career effectively, getting a mentor, dressing the part, and organizing your office properly.

MANAGE YOUR CAREER EFFECTIVELY

After you have secured employment, your challenge becomes one of managing your career effectively. The most successful people do not allow their career paths to develop randomly. They take steps to ensure that things go their way; and when they do not, these people know how to adjust their career course. Falvey has offered the following ten career management guidelines:

1.   Don't wait for things to happen; manage your own career.

2.   You will have four to six career moves. Make the most of them.

3.   Mobility and maneuvering produce greater returns than misguided loyalty. Your first loyalty should be to yourself.

4.   Outside contacts are important to a career. These people can be of help to you, so build a good outside network of friends and associates.

5.   Work in line jobs not staff jobs. The more important your contribution to the firm, the more highly prized you will be.

6.   Don't be lured by long-run rewards that will not materialize for 20 years. Consider the shorter run.

7.   Always be prepared to leave so if things go badly in the organization, you will have a plan of action.

8.   There are millions of companies in the economy; do not limit yourself to just the largest 500 industrials.

9.   Submit a resumé after your employment interview and do not forget to send a thank-you note.

10.   Whom you know will always be more important than what you know. Effective career planning is often a matter of knowing the right people.[6]

Additional major steps are discussed below.[7]

■ ■ ■ ■ ■ ■ ■ ■ ■ ■ ■ ■ ■ ■
USEFUL CAREER MANAGEMENT GUIDELINES.

■ ■ ■ ■ ■ ■ ■

[6] Jack Falvey, "Career Navigation," *Training and Development Journal*, February 1988, p. 34.

[7] For still others, see Frank W. Archer, "Charting a Career Course," *Personnel Journal*, April 1984, pp. 60–64.

■ ■ ■ ■ ■ ■ ■ ■ ■ ■ ■ ■ ■ ■
MASTER YOUR WORK.

KNOW YOUR JOB   In every job there is a basic set of skills that need to be mastered. For engineers these skills are technical in nature; for personnel specialists they are behavioral in content; for managers they are a combination of technical and behavioral. Find out those skills that are most important to your job and learn and master them as quickly as possible.

■ ■ ■ ■ ■ ■ ■ ■ ■ ■ ■ ■ ■ ■
KNOW THE FORMAL EVALUATION
CRITERIA.

KNOW HOW YOU WILL BE JUDGED   Most people are judged on two types of criteria: formal and informal. Formal criteria tend to be measurable and often take such forms as volume of work output or productivity, sales increases, and/or profit. Those who do well in these areas receive greater raises or faster promotions than those who do not. Your performance on formal criteria is measured by some document or evaluation instrument. If you are determined to win the career promotion game, you must concentrate on doing well on these formal criteria and let other things go. On the other hand, if you find that formal criteria include the above-stated objectives as well as less quantitative criteria, such as personality, interpersonal skills, leadership styles, and work attitudes, you must broaden your attention and address these as well. Sometimes you will find that most people do quite well in pursuing the quantitative objectives, and it is the qualitative ones that separate the most promotable from the others. In this case, concentrate the bulk of your attention on the qualitative side. Here is where your current career progress will be decided.

■ ■ ■ ■ ■ ■ ■ ■ ■ ■ ■ ■ ■
AND THE INFORMAL EVALUATION
CRITERIA.

　　　Informal criteria are more difficult to describe. They are determined by your boss. Typical examples include the way you dress, whether you seem interested in your job, and whether you fit in as a member of the work group. The best way to meet these challenges is to watch the other successful members of your department or group and see how they do things.

KEEP A HERO FILE   The formal evaluation system is used by the organization to reward you for your contributions. However, at some point during your career you may decide to move to another enterprise. How will you be able to show your new prospective employer how good you are? One way, of course, is by pointing to your past promotions and current salary. A second way is by having your boss write a letter of recommendation for you (assuming he or she would comply). A third way, and best of all, is to keep a hero file which contains all of your accomplishments. Typical examples include memos congratulating you on your work, awards given to you by the organization, and samples of your work (a major report you wrote, an advertisement you designed, a financial analysis you conducted) that show the quality of your performance. Remember, modesty has its place, but sometimes it pays to blow your own horn!

DEVELOP ALLIANCES   Very few loners succeed in modern organizations. You have to be able to get along with others if you are going to advance. This requires the development of alliances. In doing so, begin with your subordinates by creating an effective work relationship with them. This will show others that you are qualified in your job and begin to open doors at the management level. Next you should begin developing peer-group relationships with others on the same level in the hierarchy as you. Finally, you should seek ways of developing work relationships with higher-level managers. If you violate this "from the bottom up approach," you may find it very difficult to develop meaningful alliances. Your peers will regard you as an apple polisher or someone who is trying to succeed at their expense; when possible, they will look for ways to undercut your performance and your reputation. Your subordinates will look on you as someone who is more interested in his or her own career than in helping them to get things done. They will retaliate by giving you minimum performance and helping create a reputation for you as someone who is not very effective in managing work teams. Since both of these groups can be just as harmful to you as they can be helpful, it is best to win their support and create an alliance with them as soon as possible.

■ ■ ■ ■ ■ ■ ■ ■ ■ ■ ■ ■ ■
CREATE EFFECTIVE WORK RELATIONSHIPS.

SHOW THAT YOU ARE A STAR   Strive to prove that you are a star on the rise. There are a number of ways that you can do this. One is by turning in top-notch performance. When your work is outstanding, this gets around. People begin to notice you.

A second way is by realizing the truth in the cliché that great performance is 99 percent perspiration and 1 percent inspiration. In modern organizations most people succeed because of hard work; it is still the key to great performance.

A third way is by making yourself a crucial part of the work team. The more your boss relies on you, the greater your chances for success. As your supervisor goes up the chain of command, he or she is likely to take you along. Of course, you may find that your boss is at a dead end. A classic example of the Peter Principle, he has risen to his level of incompetence. In this case—get out. Find another position in the organization or look elsewhere. Your mobility is limited. How do you know when your boss is no longer a fast-track manager? Simply compare the average time between promotions for other managers and for your boss. Typically, managers get promoted every three to five years. If your boss has been in the same position for seven years, he or she is probably not going anywhere. If you remain in the department, the same will be true for you.

■ ■ ■ ■ ■ ■ ■ ■ ■ ■ ■ ■ ■
LET THEM KNOW YOU ARE A WINNER.

A fourth way is by getting continuous feedback on how well you are doing. Stay alert to comments from your boss on what you are doing well and where you need improvement. Treat this feedback as a source for personal action. Sure it may hurt when the individual tells you, "Your report was incomplete," or, "Jones tells me that you were late for the meeting yesterday afternoon," or, "I want you to start paying closer attention to the cost data I'm sending you; your work group's efficiency is falling down." However, you are getting feedback on how to improve your performance. Accept it in a positive light and use it to help correct your shortcomings.

A fifth way is by standing out from the crowd. Do something that sets you apart. Take an assignment that provides you the opportunity to present your findings to the board of directors. Agree to serve on a committee that has representatives from all management levels and go out of your way to impress them. Volunteer for extra assignments that you feel you are qualified to handle and no one else wants. As you try to separate yourself from the crowd, remember that your strategy has its risks. If you fail, your career may be jeopardized. So be somewhat conservative and do not bite off more than you can comfortably chew.

TRAIN YOUR REPLACEMENT   If you are a rising star, you will leave a void when you are promoted, unless you have a replacement. In some cases your promotion may be delayed until there is someone to take your place. You can speed up your career progress by training your replacement early. If you are being promoted to another department or unit, your boss will be reluctant to let you go because he or she will be left without adequate assistance—hence, the need for a replacement.

HAVE SOMEONE READY TO STEP INTO YOUR SHOES.

PERIODICALLY REASSESS YOUR CAREER   As you begin to learn your job and show those around you that you are capable of higher tasks, continually reassess your career.[8] Sometimes there will be little chance for you to be promoted in your current organization. If your boss is five years younger than you are and it appears that he, in all likelihood, is content with the organization, you are not going to get promoted over him. You are either going to have to go around him by finding a job elsewhere in the organization, or seek employment in another enterprise. In deciding exactly what you should do, periodically reassess your career. Set some objectives for yourself, and if you do not attain them, consider moving. Typical objectives include: (1) if you do not receive two promotions in the first five years, you will leave; (2) if you do not receive an

SET GOALS AND ASSESS YOUR PERFORMANCE ANNUALLY.

·······
[8] David Squires, "Moving Out of a Dead End Job," *Black Enterprise*, August 1984, pp. 55–57.

average raise of 10 percent each year for the first three years, you will leave;[9] (3) if you are not in a middle-management position, with a group or unit of at least seven subordinates within five years, you will seek employment elsewhere; and (4) if you feel you are not going to be in top management by the time you are 45, you will leave. All of these are examples; none is meant to serve as a definitive guideline. However, they are representative of the types of goals high-achieving people set for themselves in reassessing their careers.

It is also helpful to examine where you are in your career and what lies ahead. For example, many people start out very fast but after getting a series of promotions, their careers plateau.[10] Can they get back on a fast track or is it time to move on? This requires careful analysis of where the company is heading and what role you will play. Quite often the best initial strategy is to sit down with your boss and discuss what your future looks like. If you like the scenario that is presented, you can stay. Otherwise, start looking around and see what other opportunities are available either within the organization or with another firm.[11] Perhaps your career field is no longer a growing one. Table 15.1 provides a list of the best careers at the present time.

STOP!

Review your answer to the third question and make any changes you would like. Then compare your answer to the one below.

3.   What are some useful guidelines that Jed should follow in managing his career? Discuss three.

First, Jed should plan on managing his career and not waiting for things to break his way. Second, he should also be prepared to leave if things do not go well for him in the firm. Third, he should maintain outside con-

....

[9] For an excellent discussion of this topic see Jeffrey Eisen and Pat Farley, "The Best Way to Ask for a Raise," *Working Woman*, November 1984, pp. 66–72; and Janice L. Greene, "Bargaining for What You're Worth," *Black Enterprise*, May 1983, pp. 47–49.

[10] John W. Slocum, Jr., William L. Cron, and Linda C. Yows, "Whose Career Is Likely to Plateau?" *Business Horizons*, March–April 1987, pp. 31–38; and Judith M. Bardwick, "The Plateau Trap, Part 1: Getting Caught," *Personnel*, October 1986, pp. 46–51.

[11] For more on this see Lorraine Dusky, "How Fast Is the Fast Track?" *Working Woman*, June 1986, pp. 91–99; Jane Ciabattari, "Seven Stages of a Woman's Career," *Working Woman*, December 1986, pp. 84–87, 121–127; Dennis C. Sweeney, Dean Haller, and Frederick Sale, Jr., "Individually Controlled Career Counseling," *Training and Development Journal*, August 1987, pp. 58–61; and Lester Korn, "Plotting Your Next Career Move," *Working Woman*, January 1988, pp. 66–68.

TABLE 15.1   **Eight of the Best Careers Today**

---

1.   *Corporate real estate manager.* This person helps the company effectively manage (sell, lease, leaseback, remortgage, etc.) its land holdings.

2.   *Service quality manager.* This individual helps ensure the high quality production of services by overseeing areas such as marketing research, customer surveys, and new product launches.

3.   *Industrial designer.* This person designs new products, packages, book covers, etc. that are eye-appealing and likely to attract sales.

4.   *Corporate identity specialist.* This individual works with top management to help determine what the company stands for, what its logo or trademark should be, and what corporate culture the enterprise wants to create.

5.   *Export manager.* This person, usually stationed abroad, helps the company to understand local customs and needs and to match its product offerings to this market.

6.   *Telecommunications manager.* This individual oversees computerized communications networks, telephone equipment, office automation, and maintenance and repair.

7.   *High-tech public relations manager.* This person is responsible for describing high-tech products in down-to-earth terms that can be understood by everyone.

8.   *Corporate trainer.* This individual provides a wide variety of training to company personnel on subjects ranging from general management to sales to technical specifications.

Source: *Working Woman*, July 1988.

tacts so that if he decides to move, there are people on whom he can call for advice and assistance. ■

One final note: if you do decide to leave, do so at your convenience and on a good note. Kleiner puts it this way:

> If your company lost an important government contract and you know there will be a lot of pink slips coming in the next few months (and you'll probably get one of them through no fault of your own), the time to find a job is now while you enjoy the status of being fully employed. It's amazing how much lower your market value can become once the other company knows you have been terminated by your last employer. It's not fair, because you have the same skills, but that's frequently the way it is. If the new company asks you why you are looking for another job while you are presently employed, just truthfully tell them that you are seeking to work for a company that will provide you with better prospects for advancement.[12]

■ ■ ■ ■ ■ ■ ■

[12]Brian H. Kleiner, "Managing Your Career," *Supervisory Management*, March 1980, pp. 20–21.

Furthermore, regardless of why you leave, stay on good terms with everyone. Bosses tend to remember your last days on the job more vividly than they do most other days. So if you need them to say something about you in the future, you want them to be positive and complimentary responses.

GET A MENTOR

Another important aspect of getting ahead is to get a mentor. A **mentor** is a person who coaches, counsels, teaches, and/or sponsors others. While it is possible to succeed in a large organization without having a mentor, it is easier to do so if you have one.[13] In fact, firms such as AT&T Bell Labs, Johnson & Johnson, NCR Corporation, and Merrill Lynch have all created formal mentoring programs.[14] One researcher, who has found that mentor and protégé relationships are quite common, has reported the following:

A MENTOR IS A COACH, COUNSELOR, AND SPONSOR OF OTHERS.

1.   Nearly two-thirds of the respondents had a mentor or sponsor and one-third of them had two or more mentors.

2.   Mentor relationships seem to have become more prevalent during the last twenty years.

3.   Executives who have had a mentor earn more money at a younger age, are better educated, are more likely to follow a career plan, and, in turn, sponsor more protégés than executives who have not had a mentor.

MENTORING IS POPULAR.

4.   Those who have had a mentor are happier with their career progress and derive somewhat greater pleasure from their work than do those who have not had a mentor.[15]

What, in particular, makes a mentor so useful? The primary answer is the individual's willingness to share knowledge and understanding with younger managers, helping them develop into effective leaders. The mentoring process is particularly important to individuals between the ages of 25–40. These people are still in the learning and growing period of their career.

MENTORS AND WOMEN EXECUTIVES   Hennig and Jardim, writing about the managerial woman, have reported that mentors are particu-

[13] Daniel Lea and Zandy Leibowitz, "A Mentor: Would You Know One If You Saw One?" *Supervisory Management*, April 1983, pp. 32–35.

[14] Michael G. Zey, "A Mentor for All Seasons," *Personnel Journal*, January 1988, p. 46.

[15] Gerald R. Roche, "Much Ado about Mentors," *Harvard Business Review*, January–February 1979, pp. 14–15.

larly important to the success of female executives.[16] Recent research continues to support these findings. Statistically speaking, women are more likely to have mentors than their male counterparts and tend to have more of them. For example, Reich has found that women place a higher value on the mentoring process than do men. Some of his other findings include:

1.   Political aid, such as career guidance and counseling on company politics, is considered more important by female than male protégés.

2.   A higher percentage of women feel that they gained greater self-confidence through the mentor relationship and that it enhanced the awareness of their strengths.

3.   More women than men report that mentors stimulate their thinking, give them feedback about their weaknesses, and allow them to set their own job goals.

4.   Women assign higher values than men to helping young people improve their managerial skills.[17]

TRENDS   Today the trend toward mentoring continues. Approximately 75 percent of all executives under the age of 40 have a mentor. As these people continue their climb up the ladder, they eventually lose their need for a mentor but begin taking on protégés of their own. So mentoring begets mentoring.

■ ■ ■ ■ ■ ■ ■ ■ ■ ■ ■ ■ ■ ■

THE MENTORING TREND WILL CONTINUE.

To a large degree this process is inevitable. Given today's complex and rapid-paced environment, increased demands are being put on managers. One of the best ways to meet these demands is by seeking out individuals from whose experience one can learn. Of course, you can succeed in any organization without a mentor, but it will help if you have one (or more) who can provide you assistance and advice along the way. A mentor cannot guarantee you will succeed, but he or she can give you that extra push that will help you move out from the pack. For example, Morrison and her associates at the Center for Creative Leadership have found that three major problems often derail successful women: (1) an inability to adapt; (2) wanting too much or being too ambitious; and (3) failure to perform up to expectations.[18] Figure 15.4 shows some of the strategies that a mentor can employ in helping a female manager avoid these problems.

■ ■ ■ ■ ■ ■ ■

[16] Margaret Hennig and Anne Jardim, *The Managerial Woman* (New York: Anaheim Press/ Doubleday, 1977).

[17] Murray H. Reich, "The Mentoring Connection," *Personnel*, February 1986, p. 52.

[18] Ann M. Morrison, Randall P. White, Ellen Van Velsor, and the Center for Creative Leadership, "Women with Promise: Who Succeeds, Who Fails," *Working Woman*, January 1987, pp. 79–82.

FIGURE 15.4   **FRAMEWORK FOR ANALYZING HELPING STRATEGIES**

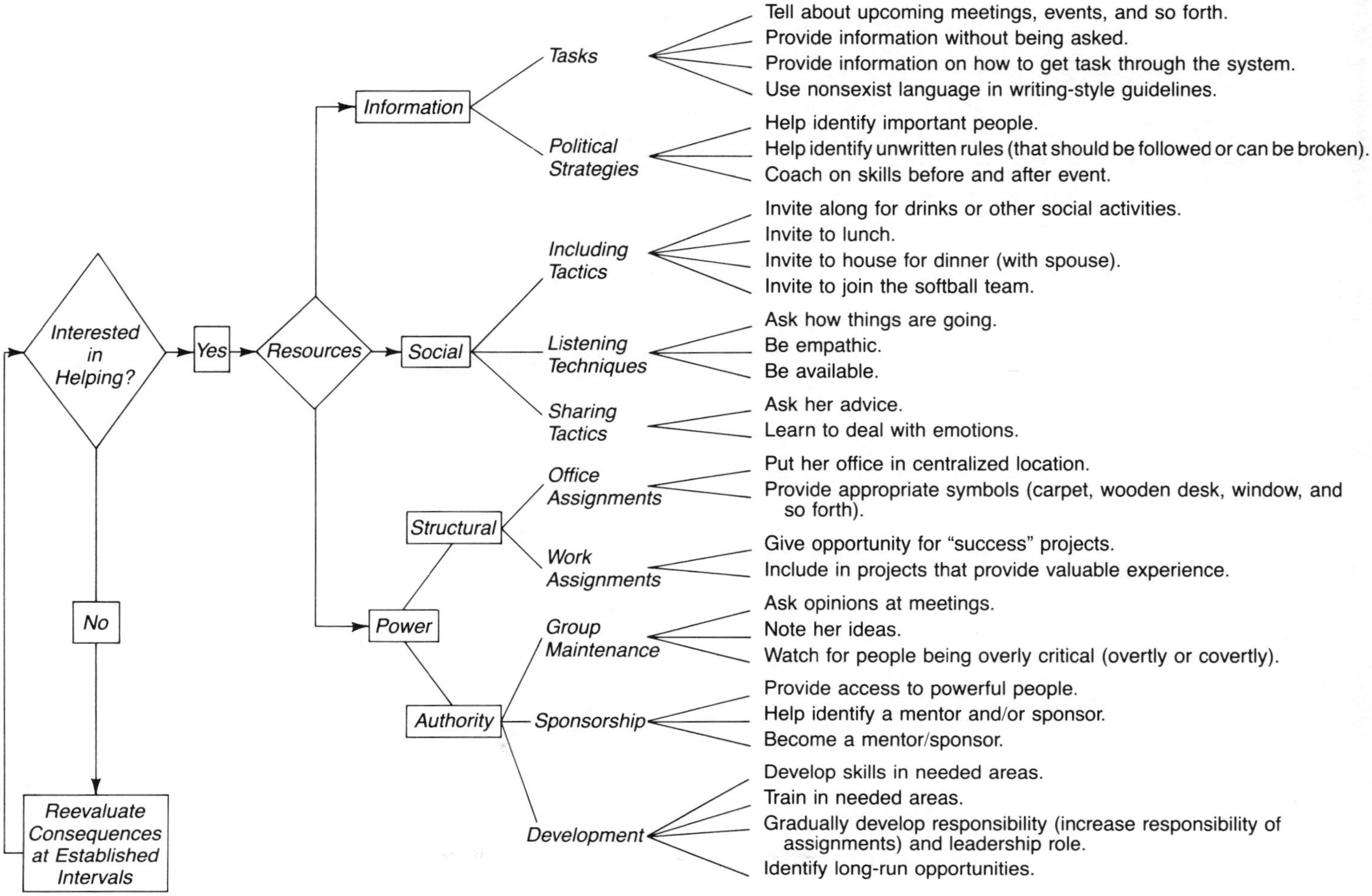

Interested in Helping?

Yes → Resources

No → Reevaluate Consequences at Established Intervals

Resources:

Information
- Tasks
  - Tell about upcoming meetings, events, and so forth.
  - Provide information without being asked.
- Political Strategies
  - Provide information on how to get task through the system.
  - Use nonsexist language in writing-style guidelines.
  - Help identify important people.
  - Help identify unwritten rules (that should be followed or can be broken).
  - Coach on skills before and after event.

Social
- Including Tactics
  - Invite along for drinks or other social activities.
  - Invite to lunch.
  - Invite to house for dinner (with spouse).
  - Invite to join the softball team.
- Listening Techniques
  - Ask how things are going.
  - Be empathic.
  - Be available.
- Sharing Tactics
  - Ask her advice.
  - Learn to deal with emotions.

Structural
- Office Assignments
  - Put her office in centralized location.
  - Provide appropriate symbols (carpet, wooden desk, window, and so forth).
- Work Assignments
  - Give opportunity for "success" projects.
  - Include in projects that provide valuable experience.

Power
- Group Maintenance
  - Ask opinions at meetings.
  - Note her ideas.
  - Watch for people being overly critical (overtly or covertly).
- Sponsorship
  - Provide access to powerful people.
  - Help identify a mentor and/or sponsor.
  - Become a mentor/sponsor.

Authority
- Development
  - Develop skills in needed areas.
  - Train in needed areas.
  - Gradually develop responsibility (increase responsibility of assignments) and leadership role.
  - Identify long-run opportunities.

Source: Reprinted with permission of the publisher from "Strategies for Helping Women Managers—or Anyone," by Marjorie A. Lyles, *Personnel*, January–February 1983, p. 73. © 1983 AMACOM Periodicals Division, American Management Association, New York. All rights reserved.

DRESS THE PART

■ ■ ■ ■ ■ ■ ■ ■ ■ ■ ■ ■ ■
DRESS FOR SUCCESS.
Successful managers dress the part.[19] Face it, if you are well groomed, your hair is properly cut and combed, your clothing is well pressed and neat, and your shoes are shined, you are going to make a much better impression than someone who is a casual, and basically sloppy, dresser. There are a number of ways of going about dressing correctly. One of the easiest is to buy your clothing from a quality store (and you should) where the salesperson can help you look your best. He or she is used to dressing people for success. A second, and complementary way, is to watch how people in your organization dress and emulate those who are known as "up and coming." A third is to pick up a good book on how to dress. Just remember that you want to look the part of a successful winner. Figure 15.5 provides some useful information for both men and women who wish to do so.

ORGANIZE YOUR OFFICE PROPERLY

Another important success variable is the way you organize your office. If you do have an office, you can employ psychological principles that will help you organize and arrange it most effectively. The first rule is: No matter how small it is, make your office look spacious and uncrowded by arranging the furniture appropriately. This should be done by giving initial priority to the desk. If the office is small, keep the desk fairly small or it will crowd the rest of the room. Conversely, if the office is spacious, get a fairly large desk that takes up more room. If at all possible, have a wooden desk or one that looks like wood. In contrast to metal desks, wood connotes power and authority and will help increase your status.

The size of the desk chair should be dictated by your own physical dimensions. If you are a tall or large person, a small chair will make you look like an ogre. If you are a short or slender person, a large chair will dwarf your appearance. Choose a chair proportional to your size and, if possible, one which has a back that comes up to the back of your head.

If you have your choice of chairs, get two that match your desk chair. Some of the most acceptable colors for these chairs are natural leather, rich brown, or deep maroon. Black, the most commonly manufactured color, is not as effective, because it lacks the richer look of these other colors.

Visitors' chairs should be placed in front of your desk. Do not put any of them on the side of your desk because this reduces your power and authority in relation to other people.

■ ■ ■ ■ ■ ■ ■

[19] Mark Beffart, "Image: The Visible Business Tool," *Working Woman*, November 1984, pp. 194–200; and Susan Bixler, *The Professional Image* (New York: G. P. Putnam's Sons, 1984).

FIGURE 15.5   **SELLING YOURSELF THROUGH CLOTHING**

Do clothes really make the person? Some individuals believe they do, including John T. Molloy, an acknowledged expert of how to dress for success. Some of the tips that he offers to men and women who want to look their best include the following:

FOR MEN

1. If you have the choice, dress affluently.
2. If you are unsure of how to dress, it is better to err on the side of conservatism.
3. Always dress as well as the people to whom you are selling.
4. Do not wear green.
5. Do not wear sunglasses or glasses that change tint as the light changes; people must see your eyes if they are to believe you.
6. Always carry a good pen and pencil.
7. If the choice is available, wear an expensive tie.
8. Do not take off your suit jacket unless you have to; it weakens your authority.
9. If it is part of your business equipment, always carry a good attaché case.
10. Never wear anything that might be considered feminine.

FOR WOMEN

1. Tailor your clothing to the demands of your job and your company.
2. Carry an executive gold pen.
3. Wear upper-middle class clothing.
4. Never be the first in your office to wear a fashion; fashion fades.
5. Do not carry a handbag when you can carry an attaché case.
6. Wear neutral-color pantyhose to the office.
7. Wear a coat that covers your skirt or dress.
8. Do not take off your jacket in the office.
9. Have a neuter rather than a masculine or feminine office.

Source: John T. Molloy, *Dress For Success* (New York: Warner Books, 1975), p. 147; John T. Molloy, *The Woman's Dress For Success Book* (New York: Warner Books, 1977), pp. 185–186.

If there is room, you can put a couch, coffee table, and/or easy chairs in this area. When this is done, the room is divided in two. The part with the desk is for business. The part with the couch and/or coffee table is for small group work or conferences.

Finally, for maximum psychological results, you must try to set up the office so that it draws attention to you. You have to "frame yourself" so that when people enter your office they are directed toward you—the central person there. There are two ways of accomplishing this. One way is by placing your desk in front of a window. The second, if you do not have a window, is by placing a picture on the wall directly behind your chair. In either case, the desk should be positioned symmetrically in front of the window or picture. Otherwise, visitors will feel that your desk is off center or the picture is askew.

■ ■ ■ ■ ■ ■ ■ ■ ■ ■ ■ ■ ■ ■
FRAME YOURSELF.

A final test of your office's effectiveness is to take a picture of it and take pictures of several friends' offices who are in the same line of work. Give these pictures to other managers (outside your organization) and ask them to rate the importance of the office holder based on the office arrangement. This will give you a good idea of how your office compares.

CONSIDER CAREER SWITCHING

Many people switch careers. In most cases this occurs because the individual has not been as successful as he or she would like and is looking for better opportunities. Common examples include people who (1) have been passed over for a promotion; (2) feel that their organization is falling behind the competition and want to work for an industry leader; and (3) are being moved onto a career track that will not get them to their long-range goals.

Most people who switch careers do so because there is no alternative. A sales analyst who has been laid off because of cutbacks in the industry may conclude that the only way to salvage a career is to change jobs and become a salesperson. A stockbroker who is laid off may look for a job in a bank or a real estate firm. Notice in both of these illustrations, the individual is seeking new employment in a related field. This is the easiest, and oftentimes wisest, approach because the person is going into something of which he or she has some knowledge or indirect experience. Businesspeople who decide to change careers often take jobs in business colleges teaching subjects that they know firsthand.

A second common career switch is to go into business for oneself. This has become quite common in recent years as middle- and upper-level managers have concluded that it is more profitable to break away from their large firms and set up their own operations. Many of them have been carrying out all of the important functions needed to run a competitive company, so breaking away to start a new venture is not a high-risk decision. Similarly, many salespeople have found that by leaving their firms they are able to take some of their customers with them and build successful businesses from this initial base.

A third common career switch is to take a job in an unrelated field. This can be a risky decision, but for many people it is the only available choice. A mechanic who dislikes his work may be willing to try a job as a salesperson for an insurance company. A social worker who dislikes the bureaucracy may be willing to start anew as a bank teller. Every year millions of people begin new careers.

The important thing to remember about career switching is that it typically requires additional training and education. This is particularly true when changing to an unrelated field. Not only is it necessary to learn new procedures and policies, but many jobs require the individual to know how to operate machinery and to learn how to interact effectively with customers and clients.

MEETING NEW CHALLENGES

In keeping your career on track, you must understand and meet new challenges. First, you will have to continually review your assumptions about the employees. Second, you will have to possess specific characteristics in order to be successful—and these characteristics are likely to change profoundly during the 1990s. Third, you will have to learn to live with ambiguity, as indicated by the rise of adhocracy, which is characterized by temporary organization structures that are created and then disbanded as needed. Finally, you will have to learn how to give career counseling to your personnel.

A NEW SET OF ASSUMPTIONS

As we noted earlier in the book, most managers are soft Theory X types. They do not adhere rigidly to Theory X tenets, but they have some faith in them.

If you hope to be effective, you will have to learn that high job satisfaction and high output occur most frequently in organizational climates in which there is a great deal of trust and mutual concern. When workers are nervous or afraid of the organization, they regard it with suspicion, and they do only what is required by organizational directive. Additionally, department and organization cliques make covert power plays, people try to manipulate each other for personal gain, and a great deal of an employee's energy is used to "cover tracks" so that if any error is found, he or she can claim to have followed the rules to the letter. These activities use up a lot of an organization's time and effort and accomplish very little in the way of attaining its goals.

On the other hand, if you can develop high trust and low defensiveness among the personnel, open and supportive behavior often emerges. For this to happen, of course, you must lead the way. Maslow has suggested managerial assumptions necessary to create the environment for such development:[20]

- Everyone can be trusted.
- People need to know as many facts and truths as possible regarding what is going on.
- People want to do a good job and they have a drive to achieve.

• • • • • • •

[20] Abraham H. Maslow, *Eupsychian Management* (Homewood, Ill.: Richard D. Irwin, Inc., and The Dorsey Press, 1964), pp. 17–33.

-    If given the chance, everyone in an organization can identify with the goals of the enterprise.
-    In a healthy organization there is good will among all the members, in contrast to enterprises where rivalry and jealousy abound.
-    Healthy people are able to admire the capacities and skills of themselves and others.
-    People need to be able to carry out their own ideas.
-    Everyone is capable of enjoying teamwork and friendship.
-    Most people can take the rigors of organizational life; they are a lot stronger than we give them credit for.

■ ■ ■ ■ ■ ■ ■ ■ ■ ■ ■ ■ ■ ■
MANAGERIAL ASSUMPTIONS FOR
EFFECTIVE LEADERSHIP.

-    People need to like their boss.
-    People have a tendency to improve things, to make them better.
-    People like to work rather than to sit back and loaf.
-    All people prefer meaningful work.
-    Most people make wise choices.
-    Everybody likes to be treated fairly and justly, especially in a public setting.
-    Most people would rather create than destroy.
-    People get more satisfaction out of loving than hating.
-    People would rather be interested than be bored.
-    People can become better than what they are; they are improvable.
-    Everyone wants to feel important, useful, needed, proud, and successful.

These 20 assumptions are reflected in Table 15.2, a description of the managers of today and tomorrow. They also embody the type of organizational behavior we have been discussing throughout this text. Most importantly, they point out the role of the manager in attaining the right organizational climate.

NEW DEMANDS FOR SUCCESS

You will also have to possess or develop characteristics in sharp contrast to those required of today's or yesterday's managers. Table 15.2 lists some of the differences. Note that some characteristics will increase in importance, others will diminish somewhat, and the need to be traditional will decline significantly.

From the data in this table it is obvious that the successful executive of the future must place a premium on creativity, futuristic thinking, and innovation. Also, he or she will have to be able to handle complexity and improve the environment. Feather has put it this way:

> Executives of the future will not toe the party line. They will speak their minds and scream for innovation. They'll spend long hours worrying about what's going on outside in the whole, wider world of political and social action. Why?

TABLE 15.2   **HOW MANAGERS OF THE FUTURE WILL DIFFER FROM THOSE OF TODAY**

CHARACTERISTICS OF SUCCESSFUL EXECUTIVES	Today			2000		
	NOT IMPORTANT	IMPORTANT	VERY IMPORTANT	NOT IMPORTANT	IMPORTANT	VERY IMPORTANT
Highly creative	X					XXX
Visionary/Futuristic	X					XXX
Able to handle complexity	X					XXX
Desires to improve the environment	X					XXX
Innovatively effective	X					XXX
Energetic		XX				XXX
Assertive		XX				XXX
Proven administrator		XX			XX	
Logical			XXX		XX	
Good contact personality			XXX		XX	
Good communicator			XXX		XX	
Traditionalist			XXX	X		

Source: Adapted from Frank Feather, "The Executive of the Future: A Creature of External Environment," *Business Tomorrow*, Spring 1978, p. 5. Published by the World Future Society, 4916 St. Elmo Avenue, Washington, D.C. 20014. Reprinted with permission.

Because the executive of the future who fails to heed the changing moods of the outside world will not be an executive for long.

Traditionally, executive thinking and professional habits were conditioned first by formal training and later by company policies and style. This was essentially an internal process.

In contrast, the executive of the future will be a creature of the external environment. The old internal influences will still exist, but their importance will fall considerably in favour of the new political and social pressures that are squeezing the business community on all sides.[21]

How will a concern with the external environment help the manager of the future cope with the human relations problems that arise in the organization? Without an understanding of the external environment and its influences on the workers, the manager will be unable to understand the workers' values, which they bring with them to the work place.

Workers will also be putting a premium on satisfaction of higher-level needs and so will managers. Workers will want "think" work, and managers must be able to handle this kind of work if they are to be suc-

▪▪▪▪▪▪▪

[21] Frank Feather, "The Executive of the Future: A Creature of the External Environment," *Business Tomorrow*, Spring 1978, p. 5.

Company career planning programs often focus on career development. Smith Kline & French offer career planning workshops and counseling sessions.

cessful. Workers will become more futuristic in terms of handling their own careers, and managers will have to echo this concern. Like other employees, managers will have to strive to be innovatively effective.

At the same time, however, the manager will have to be a good communicator, a good contact personality, and a logical thinker when dealing with the employees. These characteristics will not be as important in the future, however, because of the changing environment and the need of the executive to keep up with what is going on *both* inside and outside the organization.

ASSISTING WITH CAREER PLANNING

A final aspect of human relations that you will have to know about is how to assist the employees in planning their careers.[22] The assistance can be reduced to answering two simple questions: Where is the employee at this point of his or her career? Where does the employee want to be in the next 10 years (or 20 years, or by the end of his or her career)? The approach often used to answer these questions involves the employee and the manager doing the following things:

■ ■ ■ ■ ■ ■ ■ ■ ■ ■ ■ ■ ■ ■
EVALUATION OF AN EMPLOYEE'S CAREER.

1.   Making an assessment of life and career paths up to this point in time, noting the individual's highlights, particularly important events, strengths, and deficiencies.

2.   Formulating goals and objectives related to the individual's desired life style and career path. These are both future-oriented goals.

3.   Developing a realistic plan for achieving the goals and moving systematically toward accomplishing them. In this phase the goals are specified, action steps are outlined, a schedule of target dates is established for measuring progress, and control of the entire process is undertaken.

There are a number of ways this can be done. One of the most popular is for the employee to draw a horizontal line from left to right on a piece of paper representing his or her life span and indicating how long the employee expects to live. He or she then indicates present position on the line, the important things that have recently happened, and peak experiences that he or she hopes to have before ending the career. Finally, the employee is asked to write his or her own obituary.

■ ■ ■ ■ ■ ■ ■ ■ ■ ■ ■ ■ ■ ■
FOLLOWED BY SOUND ADVICE.

From this experiential assignment, you should be able to determine a number of things about the employee. Most important, you should be able to identify where the employee is currently and what he or she would like to have happen between now and the end of his or her career.

■ ■ ■ ■ ■ ■ ■

[22] Beverly L. Kaye, "How You Can Help Employees Formulate Their Career Goals," *Personnel Journal*, May 1980, pp. 368–372, 402.

You are now in a position to determine if the employee can attain these desired objectives. Will everything he or she is hoping for come true? If the answer is yes, you can help start planning the employee's career. If the answer is no, you have a responsibility to point this out, help the employee decide what success he or she might have by remaining with the firm, and what the chances for success are in another organization.

Some people believe that the manager's job should be one of keeping the organizational personnel. However, if the employee has a better chance for promotion or advancement with another organization, you have a responsibility to help him or her move in this direction. Remember, your job is to use people well by helping them attain satisfaction of upper-level needs. People strive for the chance to achieve, to be competent, and to self-actualize. Your job should be one of blending the needs of the individual and those of the organization. Career planning is an important step in this process.

■■■■■■■■■■■■■
HUMAN RELATIONS CHALLENGES
WILL REMAIN.

Let us make one final point: the demands on the manager of the future will change. However, the practice of human relations will remain a constant challenge. We defined human relations in Chapter 1 as a process by which management brings workers into contact with the organization in such a way that the objectives of both groups are achieved. This will be as true in 2000 as it is today.

SUMMARY

Our overriding objective in this chapter has been to illustrate how human relations concepts can be of value to you personally. The first part of the chapter discusses how to go about choosing a career; particular attention is given to self-evaluation and how to develop an overall plan of action.

The next part of the chapter addresses the issue of finding a job. Specific steps for writing an effective resumé are provided. Then a series of six steps designed to improve your chances of a successful job hunt are outlined.

This is followed by a discussion of how to manage your career effectively. At this point attention is directed at both succeeding in your current position and knowing when to move on. Associated topics such as mentors, the importance of dressing well, and the way to organize your office properly are addressed.

The last part of the chapter focuses on the new responsibilities and challenges that face the manager of the 1990s. Managers are going to have to change their assumptions about the workers. They must also develop different characteristics from those that were necessary to a successful manager of the 1980s. Finally, they will have to learn to provide career counseling for the personnel. Yet their overall objective, from a human relations standpoint, will remain the same: Future managers will have to bring the workers into contact with the organization in such a way that the objectives of both groups are achieved.

KEY TERMS IN THE CHAPTER

resumé   adhocracy
mentor

REVIEW AND STUDY QUESTIONS

1. What types of questions should a person ask when conducting a career-related self-evaluation?

2. In conducting a successful job hunt, what are six things the applicant should know? Identify and describe each.

3. A friend is preparing a resumé which she would like to be as effective as possible. What are some suggestions you would offer her? Be complete in your recommendations.

4. What are seven major steps that everyone who is interested in managing his or her career effectively should follow? Be specific in your descriptions.

5. What is a mentor? Of what value are mentors? Explain. Will their use increase or decline during the decade of the 1990s? Explain.

6. Your best friend has just been hired by a large corporation and wants to make a good impression. What recommendations would you give your friend regarding how to dress? What would you tell this person regarding how to organize his or her office? Be complete in your answer.

7. What are some of the career guidelines currently being recommended to young managers? Cite and explain six.

8. What assumptions will the manager of the 1990s have to make in order to lead successfully?

9. What characteristics will be needed by successful managers of the 1990s? Explain your answer.

10. How can the human relations manager help the personnel plan their careers? Explain.

TIME OUT ANSWERS: INTERVIEWING EFFECTIVELY

1. True. This often is regarded as a positive sign that you are interested in the job.

2. True. This indicates a genuine interest in the job.

3.   False. This may result in your being rejected. Many firms want to relocate their new people, so you should be flexible on this point.

4.   True. It is better to overdress than to underdress.

5.   True. Especially for a first meeting, promptness is imperative.

6.   False. In most cases the company will pay you a competitive rate regardless of who you are. If you ask for too high a starting salary, this may result in your being dropped from further consideration.

7.   False. Never say anything bad about the other firms because this reflects badly on you. Simply point out that you have interviewed with these other companies and let it go at that.

8.   False. Most interviewers are unimpressed by interest in the benefit and retirement program. After all, you are not going to be retiring for years, so why spend much time discussing these matters now.

9.   False. This will indicate that you lack social graces and is likely to count against you.

10.   True. You have a right to know and should not hesitate to ask.

CASE: *GIVING IT HIS BEST SHOT*

Within a day of the time that the placement service at his university listed the firms that would be interviewing on campus later that month, Jim Richardson had signed up to meet with five of the representatives. Jim's first choice was a nationally known consumer goods firm. The company typically hires six to eight graduates from Jim's university every year. He wants very much to be one of them.

Jim's interview took place three weeks ago. Unfortunately, Jim had been so busy preparing for a science exam that he overslept. When he arrived at the placement office, the head of the office was waiting outside. "Where have you been?" he asked. "I've been stalling the interviewer for almost 15 minutes. Go to Room 4 immediately. I'll get the man from my office and bring him down." After being introduced, Jim immediately told the interviewer that he was sorry for his tardiness, but that he had studied until after 2 a.m. and had overslept. The recruiter shrugged it off. "Don't be concerned. I've done it myself on occasion." Then, after some general pleasantries, the interview began.

The recruiter started to tell Jim about his company and then stopped. "Are you familiar with us?" he asked. Jim admitted that he did not know much about the consumer goods firm, although he did add, "but you are my first career choice." The recruiter then proceeded to give Jim some brochures that described the firm and its operations, and began to describe some of the company's major product lines and activities.

Later in the interview, the recruiter asked, "What starting salary would you be looking for?" Based on his discussions with the head of the placement office, Jim learned that the going rate was approximately $19,500. "I'd like to start around $22,500," he said, "with an opportunity to increase my salary by about 10 percent through overtime." The recruiter did not respond to this statement, but did write something on the piece of paper in front of him.

When the interview concluded 15 minutes later, Jim shook the man's hand and asked, "When can I expect to hear from you?" The recruiter told him that he would have a response within three weeks. Yesterday two of Jim's friends who had interviewed with the consumer goods firm received letters of acceptance. Today Jim received a letter. It said that because the company was able to hire only a limited number of applicants, it would be unable to offer him a position but wished him luck in his job search.

QUESTIONS

1.   Was showing up late a big mistake on Jim's part? Why or why not?

2.   Did Jim correctly handle the question about salary? Explain.

3.   Why might Jim not have gotten the job? Defend your answer. ▪

CASE: FORMULATING A CAREER PLAN

Pauline Caruthers has just graduated from State University. She currently is interviewing with several large organizations in Chicago. One in particular has impressed her. It is a finance firm, and its growth over the last five years has been phenomenal. The organization has offices in 84 locations throughout the United States and intends to double this number within 18 months. Its biggest location is the home office, and this is where the firm will want Pauline to work, if she gets the job. This is convenient for her because her family lives nearby and she would like to stay in the vicinity.

During her day-long visit at the firm, Pauline was introduced to a number of different managers. The one for whom she would be working is Charles Cooper, an up-and-coming young executive. Charles has been with the firm for three years and has been promoted every year. He currently is in charge of one of the largest offices in the firm's headquarters, and everyone has tagged him as top management timber. Charles and Pauline chatted for more than 45 minutes during her interview. Additionally, she had the opportunity to talk with some of the personnel in Charles's department. It is obvious from her conversation with them that when Charles moves up he intends to take some of these people with him. Charles appears to be a mentor for at least three of them. During her conversation with Charles, he made it clear to her that she too could expect to move along with him. "I need effective people on my team and I have a couple of them in the department right now," he told her. "You would be another. This job is too big for one person. However, with the right team of three to four people, it can be a stepping stone up the line. Along the way, my objective is to develop a cadre of management talent. Too many people try to get to the top by going it alone. In today's world, that person is rare. You need to use a team approach and the best way I know of putting together an effective team is through a well-thought-out mentoring program."

Pauline also likes the fact that the firm will put her in a position where she will be interacting with the public rather than just staying in the office all day handling paperwork assignments. The job promises to be not only challenging but also personally rewarding. Therefore, while Pauline is also considering three other offers from firms in the area and has two more interviews scheduled, she is convinced that she will be going to work with Charles's firm.

QUESTIONS

1.   If you were advising Pauline, what would you tell her about managing her career? In addition to what she knows already, what other things does she need to be aware of?

2.   Does Charles meet the requirements of a good boss in terms of helping Pauline with her career or should she turn to another company and look for a different kind of boss? Explain and defend your answer.

3.   Assuming that Charles is indeed a very successful manager, what assumptions do you think he has about the workers? What executive characteristics does he possess? If Pauline becomes disenchanted with her job after the first year, what recommendations would you give Charles regarding how to assist her in further career planning? Be complete in your answer. ■

Experiencing Interviews

Purpose

- To understand the dynamics of employment interviews.
- To experience interview questions and answers.

Procedure

1. The instructor will describe a job vacancy for which applicants are being interviewed.

2. One student will be chosen to act as the interviewee; the instructor will be the interviewer. They role play the interview for about 10–15 minutes.

3. After the role play, class discussion should center on assessing the performance of the interviewee. Were questions answered adequately? Confidently? What could have been done better?

4. Another student is chosen to take the part of the interviewee and #2 is repeated. Again, discuss the results.

5. In small groups, discuss ways in which you can prepare for job interviewing. Consider the following:
    a. What questions are almost sure to be asked?
    b. What questions should you ask?
    c. How should you dress?

GLOSSARY OF TERMS

The following glossary contains definitions of many of the concepts and terms used in this book. For the most part, the terms correspond to those given in the text and represent words that the reader is most likely to encounter in the business world. In addition, a few extra definitions not included in the book have been added in order to provide the most comprehensive and most useful glossary possible.

Acceptance The third step in the communication process, which involves getting the receiver to agree to comply or accept the directive. The term also refers to willingness to go along with a change because one sees more to be gained from the new conditions than will be lost by them.

Acceptance Theory of Authority Popularized through the writings of Chester I. Barnard, this theory holds that the ultimate source of authority is the subordinate, who chooses to either accept or reject orders given by the superior.

Achievement The desire to accomplish things. High achievers tend to want not only to get things done but also to receive concrete feedback on their performance so they can tell how well they have done (*see* High Achiever).

Action The last step in the communication process, which involves a duty on the part of both the receiver and the sender to follow up and do what was expected or see that it is done.

Ad Hoc Committee A committee that is appointed for a specific purpose and disbanded upon completion of the job.

Adhocracy The formation of temporary organization structures as found in the case of matrix designs used by project managers (*see* Matrix Structure).

Administrative Skills Abilities that help a manager understand how all parts of an organization or department fit together. These skills are very important for top managers, who must be able to operate the enterprise as an integrated unit.

Adult Ego State A psychological state in which a person deals objectively with reality. Problem solving and rational thinking are products of this state.

Aesthetic Value A principle characterized by interest in form and harmony. Artists have high aesthetic values.

Affective Component The emotional feeling attached to an attitude.

Assertiveness Training Human relations training designed to teach individuals how to determine their personal feelings, learn how to say what they want, and learn how to get what they want without being abusive or obnoxious.

Assessment Center An appraisal instrument used for evaluating the long-range potential of an employee.

Attention The first step in the communication process, which involves screening out all disturbances or other distractions that can interrupt one's concentration.

Attitude Questionnaire A survey instrument that measures a person's feelings, opinions, and other intervening variables that make up attitudes.

Attitudes A person's feelings about objects, activities, events, and other people.

Authoritarian Leadership A leadership style that tends to be heavily work-centered with major emphasis given to task accomplishment and little to the human element.

Authority   The right to command.

Automated Technology   Technology in which assembly-line machines are linked together and integrated in such a fashion that many functions are performed automatically without human intervention.

Autonomy   The degree to which a job provides freedom, independence, and discretion in scheduling the work and determining how to carry it out.

Balance Theory   A theory used to explain how people react to change. In essence, the theory places primary attention on the consideration of three relationships: (1) the attitude of the worker toward the change, (2) the attitude of the manager toward the change, and (3) the attitude of the worker toward the manager.

Behaviorally Anchored Rating Scales (BARS)   A performance evaluation method that consists of developing a series of critical incident behaviors, ranking them on a scale, and then using the scale to evaluate the personnel.

Behavioral Scientist   An individual highly skilled in one of the behavioral sciences (psychology, sociology, anthropology) who applies such training to the study of human behavior in organizations.

Behavior Modification   A system of motivation that tries to change an individual's responses by rewarding the individual for proper responses and failing to reinforce him or her for improper ones.

Boss-Imposed Time   Time that is used to accomplish the activities that one's superior wants done.

Brainstorming   Technique of calling out as many ideas as possible to stimulate creative thinking.

Bureaucracy   The hierarchical administration of an organization. It relies heavily on procedural rules, and, although not necessarily, it is often characterized by a distinct lack of concern for the personnel.

Burnout   A condition that often occurs among Type A people, it is the result of excessive mental and physical work and is manifested by exhaustion and/or withdrawal from the work situation.

Causal Variable   A factor that determines the results that will be achieved. Management decisions, business strategies, and leadership behavior are all illustrations (*see* Intervening Variable and End-Result Variable).

Central Tendency   A problem generated by the evaluator in which everyone receives an average rating, regardless of effectiveness.

Change   Any alteration of the status quo.

Child Ego State   A state in which the individual does things the way he or she did when a child. Common facial expressions, for example, include twinkling eyes, mischievous winks, and broad grins.

Cluster Chain   A grapevine network in which people selectively pass information to other members of the informal organization. In this process, some people are given information and others are deliberately bypassed. This is the most common grapevine network.

Coercive Power   Power held by those who can fire, demote, or dock a subordinate who does not comply with their directives.

Cognitive Component   The beliefs a person has about the object or event.

Cognitive Dissonance   A mental state that occurs when there is a lack of consistency or harmony between an individual's cognitions (attitudes, beliefs, perceptions) and the data he or she is receiving from the environment. The former is out of line with the latter. The individual must, therefore, change his or her cognitions or reject the environmental information being received.

Cohesiveness   The closeness or interpersonal attractions that exist among group members.

Collaboration   A conflict resolution approach in which all parties try to iron out their differences, realizing that without full cooperation all of them will fail.

Communication Process   The process of transmitting meanings from sender to receiver.

Competence   Control over environmental factors. This is often revealed in the form of a desire for job mastery and professional growth.

Complementary Transaction   An exchange between two people that progresses along expected lines. For example, the first person assumes the adult ego state when speaking and the second person answers as an adult (*see* Crossed Transaction).

Completed Staff Work   Staff work whose completed recommendation or solution can be either approved or disapproved by a line executive without the need for further investigation.

Compressed Workweek   A workweek arrangement that allows the individual to work a shorter workweek, such as four 10-hour days rather than five 8-hour days.

Compromise   A conflict resolution approach that involves each party giving something with no one of them being the clear winner.

Conative Component The behavior a person exhibits toward an attitude object.

Conflict The result when individuals or groups in the organization clash over some issue that, at least to them, is important. Sometimes this occurs on an interpersonal basis and at other times it takes place between groups.

Conformity Willingness to comply with the norms and/or sanctions of other individuals. Conformity, within bounds, is required if one hopes to remain a member of the informal organization.

Confrontation Problem solving on a face-to-face basis.

Contingency Organization Design A design enabling an organization to accommodate the specific needs of the situation.

Continuous Reinforcement Schedule A reinforcement schedule in which the individual is given a reward every time he or she performs a desired behavior.

Control Group A group that is not subjected to any change. Its purpose is to serve as a comparison to the test group (*see* Test Group).

Core Job Dimensions Characteristics that job-enrichment experts attempt to design into the work so as to increase worker motivation. The five most important are: skill variety, task identity, task significance, autonomy, and feedback.

Counseling The discussion of an emotional problem with an employee with the purpose of eliminating or reducing it.

Covert Resistance Resistance that is not readily observable because it is done under the guise of working as usual. Illustrations include "forgetting" to file reports or providing more information than is required in the hopes of swamping the reader and slowing up his or her progress.

Creative Person An individual who is bright (but not necessarily brilliant), has a positive self-image, is emotionally expressive, is interested in challenging problems, is often a nonconformist, and tends to be flexible and interested in solving problems in new and unique ways.

Crossed Transaction An exchange between two people that does not progress along expected lines, because the second person is not choosing the appropriate ego state. For example, the first person assumes the adult ego state when speaking and the second person answers as a parent to a child (*see* Complementary Transaction).

Culture Culture consists of learned behaviors such as norms, values, mores, habits, and customs.

Cultural Cluster A group of countries with similar values, customs, and beliefs.

Cultural Match The similarity of individual and organizational culture.

Cybernated Technology Technology in which machines run and control other machines.

Decentralization of Authority A system of management in which a great deal of decision making is done at the lower levels of the hierarchy.

Decoding Interpreting the message that one ha' received from a sender (*see* Encoding).

Delegation of Authority The process a man ager employs in distributing work to his or her subordinates.

Diagonal Communication Communication that occurs between people who are neither in the same department nor on the same level of the hierarchy.

Dimensions of Change Characteristics of a change in policy or procedure. They are (1) the logical dimension, based on technological and scientific reasons for the change, (2) the psychological dimension, the logic of the change in terms of the individuals affected, and (3) the sociological dimension, the logic of the change in terms of the work group.

Discharge The ultimate discipline penalty which calls for a separation of the individual from the organization.

Disciplinary Layoff A severe form of discipline that calls for the individual to leave the organization for a period of time and forfeit the pay for these days.

Division of Labor Work specialization that often brings about maximum efficiency.

Downward Communication Communication that takes place between superior and subordinate.

Economic Value A principle characterized by interest in what is useful. This value is important to the average American business person.

Elaboration Taking part of a message or story that is received through the informal organization and building it up to fit one's own point of view.

Empathy Putting oneself, figuratively speaking, into another person's shoes. In so doing, one begins to understand the other person's point of view.

Encoding Translating a message into a code (words, facial expressions, gestures) that will be intelligible to the receiver (*see* Decoding).

End-Result Variable A factor that reflects the result of a causal variable. Some common illustrations are profit, productivity, and output (*see* Causal Variable and Intervening Variable).

Equity   Fairness in the distribution of rewards for work. Equity plays a key role in expectancy theory. In particular, expectancy theorists like to point out that rewards must be commensurate with contribution, but also the individual must feel that what is given to him or her is fair or equitable.

Equity Theory   A theory holding that people will compare their work/reward ratio to those of others in determining if they are being properly rewarded.

Esteem Needs   The need to feel important and to have self-respect. These needs are often satisfied by attaining prestige or power.

Ethnocentrism   The belief that everything from one's own country is better than that of any other country.

Expectancy   A person's perception of the probability that a specific outcome will follow from a specific act.

Expectancy Theory   A motivation theory that holds that motivation is a force equal to the product of valence and expectancy (*see* Valence and Expectancy).

Experiential Assignment   An exercise that requires the participants to get involved or experience something to obtain a better understanding of it. For example, in teaching people how to be more effective communicators, the OD change agent may use an assignment that involves some of the participants and excludes the others. Then, concentrating on the latter, the individual asks, "How did you feel when you were left out?" After they say they did not like it, the individual tries to show them the relationship between how they feel and how subordinates feel when they are excluded from the communication process.

Expert Power   Power held by a leader because of knowledge and expertise. Leaders who have demonstrated competence acquire expert power.

Extinction   A learning strategy in which the individual is not reinforced for a specific behavior, thereby reducing the likelihood that he or she will perform the same act again in the future.

Extrinsic Rewards   Rewards that are external to the work itself. Common examples are money, increased fringe benefits, and a company car.

Fast-Track Manager   A manager who is aggressive, bright, self-confident, and capable of setting difficult but attainable objectives. These managers are often identified by the amount of decision-

making authority they have and the high salaries they command.

Fayol's Gangplank Theory   A theory of communication that holds that it is all right for the manager to use either lateral or diagonal communication as long as he or she obtains permission from his or her direct supervisor before undertaking the communication and informs the direct supervisor of any significant results of the cross-communication.

Feedback   The degree to which the work required by a job results in the individual receiving direct, clear information about his or her performance effectiveness.

Fiedler's Contingency Model   The best-known contingency model of leader effectiveness, which holds that the best leadership style will be the result of three situational variables: leader-member relations, the task structure, and the leader's position power.

5,5 Managerial Style   Often referred to as a middle-of-the-road management philosophy, which assumes that there is an inherent conflict between the concerns for production and people. This manager tries to compromise and balance these two dimensions.

Fixation   Behavior that is characterized by the use of the same behavioral pattern over and over again, even though experience has shown such behavior to be ineffective.

Flat Structure   An organization structure in which there is a wide span of control with only a small number of levels in the hierarchy (*see* Tall Structure).

Flextime   A flexible work arrangement that allows the worker some control over when he or she starts and finishes the workday.

Follower   An individual who goes along with whatever the opinion leader or the group at large wants done.

Force-Field Analysis   A technique for analyzing a change situation involving a determination of those forces pushing for the change and those pushing against it in order to choose the proper strategy for bringing about the change.

Fringe Group   Those who are seeking admission to the informal organization.

Frustration   The thwarting or blocking of an attempt at need satisfaction.

Functional Authority   Authority in a department other than one's own, as in the case of the comptroller who can order production personnel to provide him or her with cost-per-unit data.

Functional Departmentalization An organizational arrangement in which people are grouped on the basis of the jobs they perform. In a manufacturing firm, for example, it is common to find marketing, production, and finance departments reporting directly to the president.

Functional Group A group composed of workers all performing the same basic tasks. In a manufacturing firm, for example, it is common to find major functional groups or departments such as marketing, production, and finance.

Future Shock The effect of enduring too much change in too short a time.

Gatekeeper This person regulates the flow of information to other members of the group.

Geographic Departmentalization An organizational arrangement in which people are grouped on the basis of territory. An example is the company with four major operating divisions: Eastern division, Midwestern division, Western division, and Foreign division.

Goal Conflict Conflict that occurs whenever someone is asked to pursue two goals that are not in harmony. The term also refers to a power struggle that takes place between groups, in which one or more may win only at the expense of the others.

Gossip Chain A grapevine network in which one person passes information to all the others in the informal organization. This is one of the less frequently used grapevine networks.

Grapevine The name given to the communication network used to carry information among members of the informal organization.

Graphic Rating Scales The most widely used of all performance appraisal tools, it is a list of factors and degrees of each factor on which the individual will be rated. The evaluator reads every factor and then checks the degree of each that applies to the person being evaluated.

Group A social unit consisting of two or more interdependent, interactive individuals who are striving to attain common goals.

Group Think Social conformity to group ideas by members of the group.

Halo Effect A performance evaluation error caused by the rater's giving the ratee the same rating on all traits, regardless of actual performances.

Handicraft Era The first phase of technological development during which people made things by hand.

Hawthorne Effect The novelty or interest in a new situation that leads, at least initially, to positive results.

Hawthorne Studies Important behavioral studies that provided the impetus for the human relations movement.

High Achiever An individual who tends to like situations in which he or she can take personal responsibility for finding solutions to problems, is a moderate risk taker, and likes concrete feedback on performance to evaluate how well he or she is doing.

Human Relations A process by which management brings workers into contact with the organization in such a way that the objectives of both groups are achieved.

Human Resources Model A descriptive model that presents the worker as an ambitious individual who has self-direction, self-control, and creativity and who, if managed properly, will contribute to the extent of his or her talents.

Human Skills Abilities that help an individual interact with other people. These skills are very important for middle-level managers, who must lead other managers.

Hygiene Factors Identified by Frederick Herzberg in his two-factor theory of motivation, these are factors that will not motivate people by their presence but will cause dissatisfaction by their absence. Some he identified include money, security, and working conditions.

Illumination The third stage of creative thinking, it is characterized by the group realizing the best decision to make.

Immaturity–Maturity Theory Theory that compares the developments that occur as an individual matures and becomes more independent.

Incentive Payment Plans Wage incentive schemes designed to reward increased efficiency by individuals, groups, or the organization at large.

Incubation The second stage of creative thinking, it involves sitting back and letting the subconscious mind work on the problem.

Individual Culture The norms, attitudes, values, and beliefs that a person brings to the job.

Industrial Democracy A formal, usually legally sanctioned arrangement of worker representation in the form of committees, councils, and boards at various levels of decision making in the organization.

Inference An assumption made by the receiver of a message. Inferences are most commonly made about messages that are very long and involve a very large number of facts.

Instrumental Value A value that reflects the means for achieving desired goals.

Interest-Friendship Group A group formed on the basis of common beliefs, concerns, or activities. These groups are sometimes found within departments and in other instances cut across departmental lines.

Intermittent Reinforcement Schedule A reinforcement schedule in which the individual is given a reward on a variable or random basis for performing a desired behavior.

Intervening Variable A factor which reflects an individual's internal state. Loyalty, attitude, and motivation are all illustrations (*see* Causal Variable and End-Result Variable).

Intrapreneur An entrepreneur who works within the confines of an enterprise.

Intrinsic Rewards Rewards that are experienced internally by the worker. Common examples are a feeling of accomplishment, increased responsibility, and the opportunity to achieve.

Isolate A person who is generally ignored by the group and receives very little communication.

Isolation A psychological condition that results when individuals become detached from society. Technology is causing this state in some people, who are fleeing the big city and trying to raise their families in the relaxed, slower-paced life of rural areas.

Job Description A statement (or series of statements) that lists the duties and functions to be performed by the person holding the job.

Job Enlargement A job redesign technique that involves giving the worker more to do and, if possible, increasing his or her job motivation.

Job Enrichment A job redesign technique that attempts to build psychological motivators into the job. In particular, it is common to find the worker being given more authority in planning the work and in controlling the pace and procedures.

Job Profile Chart A device used to measure the degree of each core job dimension possessed by a particular job.

Job Redesign Any activities that involve work changes whose purpose is to increase the quality of the worker's job experience and/or improve his or her productivity.

Job Rotation Moving a worker from one job to another for the purpose of reducing boredom.

Laissez-Faire Leadership A leadership style characterized by a lack of concern for either the people or the work.

Lateral Communication Communication that takes place between people on the same level of the hierarchy. The most common reason for this communication flow is to promote coordination and teamwork.

Leader-Member Relations The relationships that exist between the leader and the subordinates.

Leader Position Power The authority vested in the leader's position.

Leadership The process of influencing people to direct their efforts toward the achievement of some particular goal(s).

Leadership Characteristics Characteristics possessed by effective leaders. The most commonly cited include drive, originality, persistence, and the tolerance of stress.

Leadership Dimensions Dimensions or concerns central to the process of influencing people to direct their efforts toward the achievement of some particular goal(s). There are two, concern for work and concern for people, and they are independent dimensions. Someone can be low on one without having to be high on the other.

Least-Preferred Co-Worker Scale A questionnaire that asks the leader to describe the person with whom he or she can work least well. The instrument is used by Fiedler in his contingency model.

Left-Brain People Individuals who are logical, rational, detailed, active, and objectives oriented.

Legitimate Power Power vested in the manager's position in the organizational hierarchy. For example, a vice-president has greater legitimate power than a district manager, who in turn has greater power than a unit manager.

Leisure Ethic A philosophy of work held by individuals who work as either an unfortunate obligation or as a totally undesirable or punishing experience.

Leniency A rater-generated problem in performance evaluation in which the manager gives all the people the highest possible rating.

Liaison The contact person who communicates with the other groups and gets information from them.

Life Positions Ways in which people go about relating to others. The most desirable one is, "I'm OK—You're OK."

Line Authority Direct authority, as that of a superior who can give orders directly to a subordinate.

Linking Pin Function Representing one's subordinates to one's superior and thereby serving as a link between them and higher management. If all groups in the organization are linked together, the entire enterprise will function effectively.

Management The process of achieving organizational objectives through the effective use of resources.

Management by Objectives (MBO) An overall performance appraisal system used at all levels of the employment hierarchy entailing six steps: (1) identifying the goals of the unit or department, (2) sketching out the duties and responsibilities of each individual, (3) meeting with the subordinate and mutually setting goals for him or her, (4) employing an annual goal-setting worksheet to push the subordinate toward the objective, (5) periodically reviewing the goals and revising them where necessary, and (6) at the end of the assigned period evaluating the results and starting the cycle again.

Managerial Grid A two-dimensional leadership model that permits simultaneous consideration of "concern for production" and "concern for people."

Matrix Structure A hybrid form of organization structure that contains characteristics of both the project and functional structures. It is typical to find both line and project authority in a matrix structure, the former employed by the functional department head and the latter used by the project manager.

Meaninglessness A condition occurring when employees are unable to determine what they are doing or why they are doing it.

Mechanistic Structure An organization structure that is often effective in a stable environment in which technology does not play a significant role.

Mechanistic Technology A phase of technological development during which interchangeable parts and job simplification were introduced on a wide scale.

Mechanization Era Technological era that was characterized by machine labor replacing man labor.

Mentor A person who coaches, counsels, teaches, and/or sponsors others.

Motivating Potential Score (MPS) An approach for identifying the motivating potential of a particular job that encompasses the five core job dimensions. The formula is:

$$\left[\frac{\text{Skill variety} + \text{Task identity} + \text{Task significance}}{3} \right] \times \text{Autonomy} \times \text{Feedback}$$

Motivation A psychological drive or force that directs someone toward an objective.

Motivational Force A mathematically computed motivational drive equal to the product of valence and expectancy (*see* Valence and Expectancy).

Motivators Identified by Frederick Herzberg in his two-factor theory of motivation, motivators are those factors that will build high levels of motivation and job satisfaction. Some he identified are recognition, advancement, and achievement.

Motive A "why" of behavior consisting of needs, drives, wants, and impulses within the individual.

Need Mix A term that refers to the fact that people tend to be partially satisfied and partially unsatisfied at all levels of the hierarchy simultaneously. It is never an all-or-nothing situation.

Negative Reinforcement Reinforcement that increases the frequency of a behavior while bringing about the termination of some condition.

9,9 Managerial Style A managerial style referred to as "team management," regarded by many as the ideal management style. The manager has high concern for work and high concern for people.

9,1 Managerial Style A managerial style in which the manager has a high concern for production and a low concern for people. The manager plans the work and pushes to get it out. Little interest is shown in the workers. If they cannot keep up, they are replaced by others who can.

Normative Reality Interpretive reality, in which there is no right answer. Matters of opinion related to personal taste, politics, religion, and other areas where there is no one correct answer are examples.

Norms Rules of conduct that are adopted by group members.

Nucleus Group Those who are full-fledged members of the informal organization.

OD Change Agent The individual who introduces the intervention, gets personnel involved, and leads the intervention.

OD Intervention A catchall term used to describe the behavioral science techniques used to intervene in a situation for the purpose of improving it.

1,9 Managerial Style A managerial style in which the manager tends to have a high concern for people's feelings, comfort, and needs and low concern for getting the work out.

1,1 Managerial Style A managerial style in which the manager tends to put people in jobs and then leave them alone. The manager does not check up on their work or try to interact with them by offering praise or encouraging them to keep up the good work. There is a low concern for both work and people.

Opinion Leader An individual who often is the informal leader of the group. This person receives more communiques than anyone else in the group and is most responsible for determining group goals and actions.

Oral Warning Usually the first step in the disciplinary process, which involves verbally pointing out that repetition of a particular act will result in discipline.

Organic Structure An organization structure that is often effective in a dynamic environment, where such things as technology play a significant role.

Organizational Climate The overall favorability of member attitudes and perceptions with reference to specific activities and features of an organization. The climate may be quite favorable for, say, good communication but relatively unfavorable for rapid change or tough-minded decision making.

Organizational Culture The environment in which a person works.

Organizational Development An effort to improve an organization's effectiveness by dealing with individual, group, and overall organizational problems from both a technical and human standpoint.

Organizational Iceberg The formal and informal aspects of the organization. The formal consist of structural considerations that can be readily observed, including job definitions, job descriptions, and forms of departmentalization. The informal are social-psychological processes and behavioral considerations that cannot be seen, including power, influence, interpersonal relations, and employee satisfaction.

Outer Group Those who have been rejected for membership in the informal organization.

Overt Resistance Resistance that is observable. Illustrations include worker slowdown, setting low informal production norms, and outright sabotage.

Paired Comparison Method A performance evaluation method, involving comparing each individual who is being rated against every other individual on a number of different bases, including work quality and work quantity.

Parent Ego State A psychological state in which the individual acts the way his or her parents acted. The parents serve as the role model for the individual's behavior.

Parental Leave Policy Personnel policy permitting mothers and sometimes fathers time off for the birth and early nurturing of a child.

Parity of Authority and Responsibility A principle of organizing that holds that the person who is given responsibility for a job must have the accompanying authority to get the work done.

Participative Leadership A leadership style characterized by high concerns for both people and work.

Participative Management An informal style of face-to-face leadership in which management and the workers share decision making in the work place. It is an example of shop floor democracy.

Paternalistic Leadership A leadership style that tends to be heavily work-centered but has some consideration for the personnel as well.

Path-Goal Theory of Leadership A leadership theory holding that (1) the leader can improve subordinate motivation by making the rewards for performance more attractive, (2) if work assignments are poorly defined, motivation can be increased by providing helpful supervision and goal clarification, and (3) if the work is already structured, the leader should concentrate on the personal needs of the individuals by giving them attention, praise, and support.

Perception A person's view of reality.

Performance Appraisal Cycle A four-step process used in appraising individuals, it consists of (1) establishing performance standards, (2) determining individual performance, (3) comparing performance against standards, and (4) evaluating individual performance.

Personal Characteristics Personal attributes often possessed by effective leaders. The most commonly cited include superior mental ability, emotional maturity, and problem-solving skills.

Personality A relatively stable set of characteristics and tendencies that determines similarities and differences between one person and another.

Physiological Needs Basic requirements such as food, clothing, and shelter.

Political Value A principle characterized by an interest in power. Politicians have high political values.

Positive Reinforcement Reinforcement that comes in the form of a reward and serves to strengthen the likelihood of the individual's performing the same act in the future.

Post-Industrial Society A society characterized by a service-oriented work force, dynamic growth of workers in professional and technical jobs, an increase in the importance of theoretical knowledge, and an interest in planning and controlling technological growth.

Power The ability to influence, persuade, or move another to one's own point of view.

Powerlessness A psychological condition that occurs when workers feel that they are at the mercy of technology. Workers on assembly lines, for example, report feelings of powerlessness because they are forced to keep up with the speed of the line. The technology controls them.

Preparation The first stage of creative thinking, it requires participants to get mentally prepared to make a decision.

Prestige The respect, status, and influence an individual has among other people.

Probability Chain A grapevine network in which people randomly pass information to other members of the informal organization.

Product Departmentalization An organizational arrangement in which people are grouped on the basis of product line. General Motors, Ford Motor, and RCA all use product departmentalization.

Productivity Output/input.

Profit-Maximizing Management A management era during which all decisions were directed toward making the greatest amount of money possible. Self-interest and the free market system were used in determining the most efficient allocation of resources. Although many businesses do not use this approach any longer, it is still typical to find these basic values and philosophies among small entrepreneurs.

Project Authority Authority exercised by the project manager over the personnel assigned to the project. In contrast to functional authority, project authority flows horizontally.

Project Group A group consisting of individuals from many different areas or backgrounds, the purpose of which is to attain its objective within predetermined time, cost, and quality limits. The group is disbanded when the goal is attained, and everyone goes back to his or her original department.

Project Manager An individual in charge of a project (*see* Adhocracy and Matrix Structure).

Proxemics The study of the way in which people use physical space to communicate.

Quality Circle A group of 5 to 10 well-trained employees and a team leader that study job-related problems and make recommendations for improvements.

Quality-of-Life Management The type of management characteristic of an emerging management era distinguished by emphasis on cooperation between management and personnel and the redesign of work so that it meets some of the demands workers bring to the work place.

Rationalization Behavior characterized by a search for excuses. For example, "The reason that Andy got a higher grade than I did in the human relations class was that the professor liked him a lot better than me."

"Red-Hot Stove Rule." A system of employing discipline that holds that all disciplinary practices should (1) be immediate, (2) offer advance warning, (3) be consistent from person to person, and (4) be impersonal.

Referent Power Power based on the followers' identification with the leader.

Regression Behavior characterized by a reversion to childlike behavior, as when a manager throws a temper tantrum when annoyed at a worker who asks too many questions.

Rejection Refusal to accommodate some condition or change because it is perceived as potentially destructive.

Reliability A measurement quality of a performance evaluation technique that refers to whether or not the instrument measures the same factor over and over.

Religious Value A principle characterized by an interest in unity. Members of the clergy have high religious values.

Resignation Behavior characterized by the decision, after frustration, to withdraw from the situation. For example, Mary has asked the boss for a promotion to the Eastern office on three different occasions and has been turned down each time, so she has decided not to ask again.

Resumé A summary of your education, work experience, training, and references. This form is used when applying for a job.

Reward Power Power held by leaders who can

give extrinsic satisfiers to subordinates who do their jobs well.

Right-Brain People   Individuals who are spontaneous, emotional, holistic, nonverbal, and visual in their approach to things.

Risky-Shift Phenomenon   The tendency to take greater risks in a group than when acting alone.

Role   An expected behavior.

Role Ambiguity   A role-related condition that occurs when job duties are unclear and the person is unsure of what to do.

Role Conflict   A condition that occurs when an individual faces a situation in which he or she must assume two roles and the performance of the first precludes the performance of the second.

Role Playing   A common form of training used in organizational development consisting of the spontaneous acting out of a realistic situation involving two or more people. The purpose of the training is to acquaint one or more of the participants with the proper way of handling a given situation.

Rumor   The unverified or untrue messages of the grapevine. Considered the most undesirable feature of the informal organization and often defined as "interest times ambiguity."

Sabbatical   Time period during which an employee receives full pay and benefits but does not go to work.

Safety Needs   Needs such as those of survival and security.

Satisficing Behavior   Behavior in which individuals accept results or payoffs that are adequate in contrast to choices that would maximize outcomes.

Scientific Management   A system of management, popularized by Frederick W. Taylor and others in the early twentieth century, that sought to develop (1) ways of increasing productivity by making work easier to perform, and (2) methods for motivating workers to take advantage of these labor-saving devices and techniques.

Scientific Method   An objective approach for identifying a problem, gathering information on it, analyzing the data, arriving at a tentative answer, and testing it.

Selective Filtering   The screening of rumors so that part of the story is maintained and the rest is discarded.

Self-Actualization Need   The urge to maximize one's potential, often satisfied through attainment of competence and a feeling of achievement.

Self-Estrangement   A condition that occurs when an individual can no longer find intrinsic satisfaction in what he or she is doing. The work becomes a mere means to earn a living, and if the individual could go elsewhere and make more money, he or she would do so.

Self-Imposed Time   Time used for doing the things that the manager originates or agrees to do personally.

Sensory Reality   Physical reality as characterized by objects such as an automobile, a house, or a car.

Shift Work   Work that is assigned based on time shifts, such as 8 a.m. to 5 p.m. or 5 p.m. to 1 a.m.

Single Strand   An informal grapevine network in which each person receives information from one individual and passes it to another. The flow of information moves down a line. This is the least frequently employed grapevine network.

Skill Variety   The degree to which a job requires the completion of different activities, all of which involve varying talents and capabilities.

Social Exchange Theory   A theory that holds that the organization consists of individuals who are exchanging supportive behaviors by doing things for others and expecting reciprocity.

Social Need   The urge for interaction with others for the purpose of meaningful relationships.

Social Network   Informal structures created by people in the work place and used for interaction and social exchange on the job.

Social Value   A value characterized by love of people. Social workers have high social values.

Sociogram   A schematic drawing that shows the social relationships existing among members of a group. It provides information regarding informal group behavior.

Sociotechnical Systems   The relationship of technology to the people at work.

Span of Control   A principle of organizing that holds that there is an optimum number of subordinates a superior can effectively manage. When not used as a principle, the term simply refers to the number of subordinates who report to a given superior.

Staff Authority   Auxiliary authority as held by individuals who advise, assist, recommend, or facilitate organizational activities. An example is the company lawyer who advises the president on the legality of contract matters.

Standard   The amount of work expected from each worker every day. This concept was popularized by the scientific managers.

Standing Committee A committee that exists for an indefinite period of time.

Status The relative ranking of an individual in an organization or group.

Status Discrepancy Conflict that occurs when people do things that do not fit with their status in the group. Union representatives can negatively affect their status by becoming too friendly with company supervisors, and so can managers who eat lunch with their subordinates.

Status Incongruency A discrepancy between a person's supposed status and the way he or she is treated.

Status Symbol Signs that help us understand where the individual ranks in the organization. Common status symbols include desks, big offices, rugs, and a key to the executive washroom.

Stereotyping Generalizing a particular trait or behavior to all members of a given group.

Stress A condition characterized by emotional strain and/or physical discomfort which, if it goes unrelieved, can impair one's ability to cope with the environment.

Stroking Any act implying recognition of another's presence.

Structured Interview An interview in which specific questions are asked in a predetermined manner.

Survey Feedback An overall or comprehensive OD intervention that entails three distinct steps: (1) a systematic collection of data on the current state of the organization, usually obtained through questionnaires and/or interviews, (2) a feedback of the findings to the organizational personnel, and (3) the development of an action plan for dealing with the problems that have been identified.

System-Imposed Time Time used to handle requests from other managers.

System 1 An exploitive-autocratic management style in which management has little confidence in the subordinates and makes wide use of threats and punishment in getting things done.

System 2 A benevolent-autocratic leadership style in which management acts in a condescending manner toward the subordinates and has little trust in them.

System 3 A consultative-democratic leadership style in which management has quite a bit of confidence and trust in the subordinates, decision making tends to be delegated to some degree, and there is some confidence and trust between superiors and subordinates.

System 4 A participative-democratic leadership style in which management has complete confidence and trust in the subordinates, decision making is highly decentralized, communication flows up and down the hierarchy, and the formal and informal organizations are often the same.

System Management A comprehensive OD intervention that consists of identifying the current state of management in the organization through determining which of the management systems is being used, System 1, 2, 3, or 4.

Tall Structure An organization structure in which there is a narrow span of control with a large number of levels in the hierarchy (*see* Flat Structure).

Task Concept Planning the work of every individual at least one day in advance so that the individual receives complete written instructions describing what he or she is to accomplish as well as how the work is to be done.

Task Identity The degree to which a job requires completion of a whole or identifiable piece of work.

Task Significance The degree to which a job has a substantial impact on the lives and work of other people.

Task Structure The degree to which the leader's job is programmed or specified in step-by-step fashion.

Team Building A popular OD intervention that consists of working with intact, permanent work teams in an effort to improve the relationships that exist among them.

Technical Skills Abilities that help an individual determine how things work. These are very important for lower-level managers such as foremen.

Terminal Value A value that is expressed in terms of a desired goal or end.

Test Group People who are subjected to some behavioral change and then studied to see the effect of this change (*see* Control Group).

T-Group Small-group interaction that takes place in an unstructured setting. In this setting, individuals meet in groups, focus on the "here and now" behavior taking place in their own group, and attempt to enhance their awareness of themselves and of the social processes.

Theoretical Value A principle characterized by interest in truth, system, and the ordering of knowledge.

Theory X A set of assumptions that holds that people (1) dislike work, (2) have little ambition, (3) want security above all else, and (4) must be coerced, controlled, and threatened with punishment in order to attain organizational objectives.

Theory Y A set of assumptions that holds that (1) if the conditions are favorable, people will not only accept responsibility, they will seek it, (2) if people are committed to organizational objectives, they will exercise self-direction and self-control, and (3) commitment is a function of the rewards associated with goal attainment.

Theory Z A management approach that blends Japanese and American management practices in arriving at a modified-American approach that uses consensual decision making, lifetime employment, slower evaluation and promotion, informal control, a moderately specialized career path, and holistic concern for the employee.

Tolerance Putting up with change. This usually occurs because the workers have no particular positive or negative feelings toward the change; they are basically neutral about it.

Traditional Model A descriptive model that presents the worker as an individual who is lazy, works only for money, and needs to be supervised and controlled, and that holds that if the work is simple enough and the people are closely controlled, they will produce up to standard.

Trait Theory The study of leadership characteristics.

Transactional Analysis The study of social exchanges between people.

Trusteeship Management The characteristic of a management era during which the owners are no longer the managers and the organization becomes much more interested in its interface with society at large. Most organizations today operate with this type of management philosophy.

Type A Person An individual aggressively involved in a chronic, incessant struggle to achieve more and more in less and less time.

Understanding The second step in the communication process, which involves getting the receiver to comprehend the meaning of the transmission.

Unity of Command A principle of organizing that holds that everyone should have one and only one boss.

Unity of Management A principle of organizing that holds that there should be one manager and one plan for all operations having the same objective.

Universal Design Theory Organization theory consisting of a series of principles that can be used in organizing any enterprise. Today this theory is regarded as only partially accurate.

Unstructured Interview An interview in which the interviewer may have a general direction or objective, but the questions are not predetermined and the interview is allowed to develop spontaneously.

Upward Communication Communication that takes place between subordinate and superior.

Valence A person's preference for a particular outcome.

Validity A measurement quality of a performance evaluation technique that refers to whether the instrument is measuring what it is intended to measure.

Value Something that has worth or importance to an individual.

Verification The fourth stage of creative thinking, it involves the group modifying or making final changes in the solution.

Vertical Dyad Linkage Theory A theory of leadership that investigates the formation of direct superior-subordinate relationships and the effect of these dyads on group performance.

Vertical Loading A job enrichment principle that involves closing the gap between the "doing" and "controlling" aspects of the job.

Work The use of physical and/or mental effort that is directed toward the production or accomplishment of something.

Workaholic An individual who obtains deep satisfaction from work but carries this interest to an extreme, which can be both physically and psychologically dangerous.

Work Ethic A philosophy of work held by individuals who believe that one should work hard, take pride in the job, and strive for advancement and promotion.

Worth Ethic A philosophy of work held by individuals who work because of the self-esteem or personal and intangible rewards they receive from doing the job.

Written Warning A form of discipline that involves placing a warning in the employee's file that can be cited as evidence if it is decided to terminate him or her in the future.

Photo Credits

Name Index

Rubin, Hanna, 536
Runcie, John J., 200, 201, 207

Sale, Frederick, Jr., 547
Salitore, Robert, 229
Salzman, Jeff, 357
Scandura, Janette, 364
Scanlan, Burt K., 242
Schaefer, Thomas E., 299
Schilit, Warren Keith, 353
Schneider, Benjamin, 168
Scholler, John, 351
Schoner, Bertram, 127
Schreier, James W., 348, 349
Schwab, Donald P., 381
Seashore, Stanley E., 15, 483
Shackleton, V. J., 211, 212
Shenkar, O., 506
Shepherd, Shirley J., 539
Sheridan, John E., 324
Shetty, Y. K., 223
Sims, H. P., Jr., 324
Skinner, B. F., 26
Slocum, John W., Jr., 324, 547
Smeltzer, Larry R., 229
Smith, Adam, 189
Smith, Howard R., 264
Smith, Terry L., 344
Smithin, Tim, 130
Snyder, Robert A., 168
Snyderman, Barbara Bloch, 51
Sproull, J. Ruth, 347, 391
Squires, David, 546
St. James, Diane, 29

Stanislao, Bettie C., 478
Stanislao, Joseph, 478
Steers, Richard M., 126
Stickney, John, 540
Stinson, John E., 324
Stogdill, Ralph, 296, 300
Strayer, Jacqueline F., 29
Struth, Michael R., 381
Sussman, Lyle, 514
Suters, Everett T., 357, 401
Suttle, J. Lloyd, 260, 261, 273, 274, 283
Swart, J. Carroll, 236
Sweeney, Dennis C., 547
Szilagyi, A. D., 324

Taber, Tom, 350
Taggart, William, 130
Tagiuri, Renato, 204
Tannenbaum, Arnold S., 352
Taylor, Hugh R., 350
Templeton, Mary Ellen, 55
Terkel, Studs, 23
Terpstra, David E., 29
Thacker, James W., 282
Tierlet, Bernhard, 209
Toffler, Alvin, 187, 193, 196

Unwalla, Darab, 502, 503

Van Velsor, Ellen, 550
Vernon, Philip E., 83
Vroom, Victor H., 57

Wallach, Ellen J., 103, 375
Walton, R. E., 282
Warihay, Philomena I., 374
Wartick, Steven L., 63
Wass, Donald L., 355
Waterman, Robert H., 13
Watts, Patti, 514
Weinel, Barbara M., 101
Whatley, Arthur A., 228
White, Randall P., 550
Whitsett, David A., 274
Wiener, Yoash, 106
Wild, Ray, 168
Wilkinson, Harry E., 351
Williams, J. Clifton, 297
Wilson, James A., 300
Wilson, Thomas M., 514
Witham, Donald C., 276, 277
Wolfe, Michael, 391
Worley, Larry, 348
Wren, Daniel A., 188
Wrich, James T., 348

Yager, Ed, 229
Yorks, Lyle, 274
Yows, Linda C., 547
Yukl, Gary, 61, 350

Zand, Dale E., 337
Zemke, Ron, 209, 381
Zey, Michael G., 549
Zorn, Theodore E., Jr., 374
Zuker, Elaina, 90

Subject Index

Acceptance
  of change, 463–464
  and communication, 434
Achievement need, 46–47
Administrative skills, 299
AIDS (Acquired immune deficiency syndrome)
  education regarding, 513–514
  legal rights, 514–515
Alcoholism, 344–347
Alienation, 200
Alternative work schedules
  compressed workweek, 235
  flextime, 235–237
  shift work, 237
Assertiveness training
  aggressive behavior, 99–103
  assertive behavior, 99–103
  goals of, 99
  passive behavior, 99–103
Assessment centers, 380–381
AT&T Shreveport, 281
Attitudes
  affective component, 90
  behavioral component, 90–91
  cognitive component, 90
  and intervening variables, 92
  measurement, 91–93
  questionnaire, 91
Audience analysis grid, 446

Authoritarian leadership, 306–308
Authority, 156
Automated technology, 189–190
Autonomy, 266–267

Balance theory, 473–477
Behaviorally anchored rating scales (BARS), 381–384
Behavioral management movement, 9–12
Behavioral scientists, 26
Benefit program, 396
Body language, 436–438
Burnout, 362, 363

Cafeteria plans, 66
Career
  career management guidelines, 543–548
  dressing the part, 552
  finding a job, 535–541
  getting ahead, 543–555
  helping others, 558–559
  interviewing effectively, 532–533, 542
  meeting new challenges, 555–558
  mentors, 549–551
  organizing the office, 552–554
  overall plan of action, 533–535
  resume, 535–536, 537, 538

  self-evaluation, 531–533
  switching, 554–555
  training, 519
  useful job hunting guidelines, 536–541
Central tendency, 390–391
Change
  acceptance, 463–464
  agent, 478–479
  and anxiety, 477–478
  balance theory, 473–477
  basic steps in, 468–469
  and communication, 470–473
  dimensions of, 468
  and employees, 460–467
  how it occurs, 457–459
  nature of, 457–459
  and organizational development, 478–483
  outcomes of, 461
  and participation, 470–473
  proper management of, 467–484
  rejection, 462
  and resistance, 459, 464–467
  responses to, 460–464
  and the time factor, 469–470
  tolerance, 463
Changing social values, 511–517
Cohesiveness, 123–124
Committees
  ad hoc, 139–140
  advantages, 140

580